Producing and Directing the Short Film and Video

Producing and Directing the Short Film and Video

Fourth Edition

Peter W. Rea
David K. Irving

AMSTERDAM • BOSTON • HEIDELBERG • LONDON • NEW YORK • OXFORD
PARIS • SAN DIEGO • SAN FRANCISCO • SINGAPORE • SYDNEY • TOKYO
Focal Press is an imprint of Elsevier

Focal Press is an imprint of Elsevier
30 Corporate Drive, Suite 400, Burlington, MA 01803, USA
The Boulevard, Langford Lane, Kidlington, Oxford, OX5 1GB, UK

Library of Congress Cataloging-in-Publication Data
Irving, David K.
   Producing and directing the short film and video / David K. Irving, Peter W. Rea. – 4th ed.
      p. cm.
   Includes bibliographical references and index.
   ISBN 978-0-240-81174-1 (alk. paper)
   1. Short films–Production and direction. 2. Video recordings–Production and direction. I. Rea, Peter W.
   II. Title.
   PN1995.9.P7I75 2010
   791.4302'32–dc22

                                                                                            2009046285

British Library Cataloguing-in-Publication Data
A catalogue record for this book is available from the British Library.

ISBN: 978-0-240-81174-1

For information on all Focal Press publications
visit our website at www.elsevierdirect.com

10   11   12   13   14   5   4   3   2   1

Printed in the United States of America

Contents

Part III
Postproduction

Chapter 16: Pix Postproduction 257

Chapter 17: Sound Postproduction . . 285

Chapter 18: Finishing/Online/ Laboratory 307

Chapter 19: Distribution/Exhibition . 319

Visit the companion site at http://booksite.focalpress.com/companion/IrvingRea/ and use passcode IRV2UT98SW69 to login; on the companion site, you will find:

Contents

FORMS to download, save, and print, including:

Since the third edition, the range of options available for the beginning filmmaker has multiplied tenfold. High definition (HD) has integrated itself firmly into production, distribution, and exhibition. A camera has been developed that is essentially a lens mounted on a computer (The RED). Professional postproduction software once linked to an editing system that filled a room can now be loaded onto a laptop. Essentially, anyone with a digital camera and a laptop is able to create a film that has the look and feel of a professional product.

Equally noteworthy, social networking channels such as YouTube, MySpace, FaceBook, and Twitter have altered the communication landscape. Broadband has helped usher in a true "Convergence of Media."

Insomuch as digital technology has transformed how films are made and distributed, "film" is very much alive as a professional capture format and still (for now) the primary exhibition format for feature films. Implementation of digital projection systems and satellite delivery are still on the horizon.

Very few of these changes affect the text in this book. Telling a story visually is juxtaposing one image with another and then next to another, the sum of which makes a narrative, documentary, animation, or experimental piece. However one captures the image, manipulates it editorially, or projects it for an audience, the basic steps of visual storytelling have been the same for the hundred plus years since film was invented. Technological advances can aid the process, but not sidestep any of the steps. The responsibilities of a producer and a director are directly tied to their hearts and minds, not their toys. No matter what the tools, art is created out of the heart.

In this age of multiple media sources competing for our attention, it is important to understand that "content" is still king. More and more festivals have been sprouting up yearly. Making your presence felt in the expanding market for shorts and a flooded Internet requires that you create a product that rises above the thousands of daily entries. Having something to say and saying it well never goes out of fashion.

To aid you in your quest, this edition boasts the addition of two new narrative films, one filmed in Super 16mm and one in 35mm. We have included a strategy for using a web site designed for your project as an effective tool for preproduction, production, and distribution that is woven in the text and expanded on our web site with several case studies.

Our web site at www.focalpress.com/companions will also include links for the short films, all the forms in this book, plus much important information for the beginning filmmaker. Besides updating the book to address new technologies, we have been fortunate to receive comments and suggestions from many of our readers since the book was originally published. We are happy to make changes to better explain a concept or illustrate a point.

EFFICIO COGNOSIO (LEARN BY DOING)

There is no substitute for experience. In this book, we want to emphasize the importance of the School of Hard Knocks. Whether you are in a film or media program or making a project on your own, this is an excellent time to be studying filmmaking.

There is no better way to learn how to make a film than by actually doing it. Books and manuals can serve as guides. Other films can act as inspiration, and talking about and critiquing films can trigger ideas. However, the two best teachers are failure and success. Experiencing the process of putting together a project, building work muscles, and understanding the craft and discipline of the process are ultimately the best ways to develop your skills.

THE POWER OF THE MEDIA

Finally, your short film has the potential to influence a great many people. Both media have gained great exposure in the past 20 years, and their potential is growing rapidly. All indications are that by the year 2010, products from the communications industry will be the United States' chief export commodity.

Coupled with the wide distribution of these media is the issue of the power of their content to influence. We are now grappling with crucial problems, from overpopulation to racial discrimination, from management of the earth's resources to the management of human resources. Film and video have a powerful voice in the dialogue about these challenges. Our hope is that in expressing yourself in this fashion, you will consider the world in which it will be viewed and will use your talents wisely.

Acknowledgments

FIRST EDITION

We would like to thank the following people who assisted us in the writing of this book—in particular, the faculty, staff, and students at New York University, Tisch School of the Arts, Undergraduate Film and Television: Arnold Baskin, John Canemaker, Pat Cooper, Carlos DeJesus, Tom Drysdale, Carol Dysinger, Dan Gaydos, Fritz Gerald, Chat Gunter, Ron Kalish, Julia Keydel, Marketa Kimbrall, Dan Kleinman, Lou La Volpe, Rosanne Limoncelli, Ian Maitland, Barbara Malmet, Rick McKinney, Lynne McVeigh, Lamar Sanders, Julie Sloane, George Stoney, Nick Tanis, Darryl Wilson, Brane Zivkovic, and especially Steven Sills. Also, New York University Professor Richard Schechner, who saw an early version of *Producing and Directing the Short Film and Video*.

We would also like to thank Mitchell Block, John Butman, Steve Hanks, the law firm of Rudolf & Beer, Doug Underdahl, Nancy Walzog, and a special thanks to Carol Chambers for her continued support throughout the writing process and Steve West for his editing skills.

We would also like to thank Ken Bowser, Hamilton Fish, Jr., David Gurfinkel, Tova Neeman, Priscilla Pointer, and Robert Wise, for inspiration and encouragement.

For the editorial and production skills they provided to Focal Press, we would especially like to thank Mary Ellen Oliver, Marilyn Rash, and Judith Riotto, who made the process of assembling these final pages a rewarding one.

SECOND EDITION

Special thanks to Mitchell Block, John Butman, John Canemaker, Michael Carmine, Gary Donatelli, Fritz Gerald, Fred Ginzberg, Chat Gunther, Milly Itzack, Suzie Korda, Dow McKeever, Stevin Michals, Marsha Moore, Mo Ogrodnik, Sam Pollard, Paul Thompson, Mike Thornburgh, Mika Salmi, Simon Lund, and Lamar Sanders.

Also, special thanks to Terri Jadick for her patience and support and Maura Kelly for her production skills.

THIRD EDITION

Special thanks to Norman Bebell, Mitchell Block, John Canemaker, Michael Carmine, Michelle Coe, Fritz Gerald, Joe Hobeck, Marsha Moore McKeever, Jamaal Parham, David Russell, David Spector, and Debra Zimmerman. Special thanks to Lou LaVolpe. We are also indebted to Etgar Keret for allowing us to reprint his short story. Adding a fourth film would not have been possible without the contributions made by filmmaker extraordinaire Tatia Rosenthal and the dean of the Savannah School of the Arts, Peter Weishar.

FOURTH EDITION

Special thanks to Geoffrey Erb, Marsha Moore McKeever, Dow McKeever, Jeff Stolow, Stevin Michels, Steve Elliot, Scott Bankert, Alex Raspa, Jessalyn Haefele, Gavin Keese, Camilla Toniolo and Amos Katz.

Special thanks to Howard Beaver and John Nymarky for their invaluable contributions.

Special thanks to Kevin Cooper, Kim Nelson, and Gary Goldsmith for their editorial advice.

And finally, special thanks to Jane Dashevsky for her incredible patience, Melinda Rankin for her production skills, and Elinor Actipis for her continued support.

Why make a short film? The idea of being in a darkened screening room and watching your film touch an audience is exciting. There is deep satisfaction in communicating on this basic level. The fantasy of creating something that has an emotional impact on others is what motivates many people to go into picture making in the first place. There is, also, the artistic satisfaction.

Most short works are created to give filmmakers an opportudnity to express themselves, display their talent, and develop filmmaking skills; to experiment with the medium; or to provide a stepping stone to a career in film and television. The key advantage to making a short is learning the filmmaking process on a project of manageable scale.

If the work turns out well, shorts can be entered into any of the hundreds of national and international festivals. They provide validation for your filmmaking skills and opportunities to meet people who can further your career. The producer and director can parlay awards and the fame of winning competitions into meetings, agents, and (ideally) employment.

The market for "shorts" has been traditionally limited. Rarely did shorts recoup their investments, let alone make money. For these reasons, the creation of a short work was usually motivated by considerations other than profit.

Over the years, however, opportunities for distribution and exhibition have grown substantially. Traditional distribution outlets still exist (see Chapter 19), but the short film can now be exhibited to a worldwide audience across myriad platforms. With this kind of exposure come expanding opportunities for beginners to profit from their work. From iTunes to iPods to webisodes, the short form finds itself a good fit with the new technologies of the twenty-first century.

INTERNET

What has made many of these opportunities for filmmaking possible is the growth of the Internet and its potential to create an integrated and consistent message across all media. As you develop your short film idea, the web can be used to promote awareness of your project, to raise funds, to reach out to cast and crew, and eventually to act as a distribution outlet. The Internet is a tool and, as such, can be employed to whatever extent you wish. We will outline many of the possibilities throughout the book. It is up to you, the filmmaker, to decide to what extent you wish to avail yourself of its possibilities.

CRAFT VERSUS ART AND COLLABORATION

Moving pictures are arguably the greatest art form of the twentieth century. After all, the medium combines elements of literature, art, theater, photography, dance, and music, but is in itself a unique form. For the sake of all beginning filmmakers who read this book, we take off the pressure by refusing to emphasize the creation of art. Instead, we stress the craft of storytelling, and telling a story well is not an easy task. Telling a short story well is even more difficult.

For us, it is difficult to think of filmmaking as an "art-making" endeavor. Orson Welles probably did not intend to make art when he conceived and produced *Citizen Kane*. Instead, he probably set out to make the best film he could from a particular script. The result was a well-crafted film, which was later deemed to be one of the finest feature films ever made and ultimately came to be considered "art." This label has more to do with the consensus of a critical audience long after the fact than it does with the intention of the filmmaker. Our advice to you is to set out to shoot the best short story you can and let the audience decide whether it is art.

Let's not give Welles all the credit for the success of *Citizen Kane*. Filmmaking is a collaborative enterprise in which many creative people lend their expertise to the director's vision. Too many ingredients affect the outcome of a film to allow any one person to take credit for its success. Welles himself said that "making a film is like painting a picture with an army." He thought so much of the contribution of his cinematographer, Greg Toland, to the film's success that he shared a card with him in the closing credits of *Citizen Kane*.

Above all, to make a successful short film, the entire creative team must share a passion for the material and the process. If there is no passion, the process will be no more than going through the motions of manufacturing a product. Lack of passion shows on the screen.

WHAT ARE THE STEPS?

How do you go about making a successful short film? Picture making is a complex and demanding activity, even for the experienced. A myriad of problems inevitably arises involving script, crew, budget, casting, lighting, and so on. Each project has its own unique set of challenges. For example, one film might need a difficult location such as Grand Central Station; another might call for a school gymnasium or an old-fashioned barbershop.

One script might require a talented young boy who must also be meek and scrawny; another might need a homeless person. One project might run out of money before postproduction; another budget might not allow for crucial special effects. Even before starting production, you must understand sophisticated technical crafts; resource management; political and social interaction; and personal, financial, and professional responsibility.

The process of producing a film, whether it is a half-hour or a five-minute piece, has been refined over the years and developed into an art. As you will discover, there is a straightforward logic behind these steps—a logic governed by the management of time, talent, and resources. Each step is informed by pragmatism and common sense:

- **Script development**. Your script must be well crafted before preproduction can begin.
- **Preproduction**. The production must be efficiently organized before the camera can roll.
- **Production**. The project must be shot before it can be edited.
- **Postproduction**. The project must be edited before it can be distributed.
- **Distribution/exhibition**. A film that is not seen or experienced by an audience serves only as an exercise.

This list is only a broad outline of what must happen during the production of a short work. It describes the general flow of activity, but it does not address what these steps mean or when and how they must be performed. Translating an idea into a film involves the execution of thousands of details over a long period of time. In fact, the success of any film project relies as much on management as it does on storytelling. Knowing where to put the camera to capture the right dramatic moment of a scene requires as much skill as marshaling the necessary people, equipment, and supplies to the location in the first place. One can't happen without the other.

THE ORGANIZATION OF THE BOOK

Producing and Directing the Short Film and Video is organized according to the general logic of how a short work is assembled. Each of the preceding stages of script development, preproduction, production, and postproduction is fleshed out in detail with concrete examples. Our goal is to impart to the beginner a fundamental understanding of what is required to organize and execute the production of a successful short picture. Bear in mind, though, that no two shows are alike and that there are no rules. This book is a guide, not a formula.

In addition, we have divided each chapter into two parts, reflecting the management, or "producing," skills and the storytelling, or "directing," skills. Presenting a clear picture of what the producer and director is doing at any given time gives the novice a detailed understanding of and respect for the processes of both producing and directing, one step at a time, from idea to final print. It can also serve as a practical guide to help navigate through creative and managerial straits.

PRODUCER AND DIRECTOR?

Unfortunately, students and beginners often find themselves taking on the dual role of the producer and director. Having to tackle two very different and complex responsibilities at the same time puts undue and unnecessary pressure on the novice. This problem exists for many reasons. Primarily, it is that the director, in most cases, financially supports the project and either can't find someone willing to do the job or is unable to trust someone the manage her money properly. The burden of having to direct and produce can have a deleterious impact on either important function. We discourage it.

If and when a producer does become involved with a student production, that individual often serves as either production manager or glorified "go-fer." Neither of these situations results in what could and should be a creative partnership, one that we believe best serves the needs of any production.

The Producer

The most misunderstood and mysterious role in the filmmaking process is that of the producer. We've been asked hundreds of times, "What does a producer actually do?" That his role is a mystery to most laypeople is not altogether surprising. The producer's position in the film and television industry is amorphous and has varying definitions. In addition, the producer never has the same job description from one project to another, and on many kinds of films, it is common to see from four to eight names with one of these producing titles:

- Executive in Charge of Production
- Executive Producer
- Producer
- Co-Producer
- Line Producer
- Assistant Producer
- Associate Producer

In this book, we use the term *producer* primarily to describe the driving force in the making of a short. We refer to this person as the "creative" producer. We also use *producer* to describe the person who engineers all the elements necessary for the creative and business aspects of production. This is the role of producer as *production manager*. In Chapter 6, this position is described in depth.

A movie begins with an adaptation from an existing short story, a script, an original idea, a true story, or simply an image that has dramatic and visual potential. The imagination and belief that such an idea or story can be transformed into a motion picture are what begin the process. What is not widely understood is that the producer can be, and often is, the creative instigator of most films: the one with the original inspiration who launches the project and then sails it home, with himself as the captain. This is the individual who is involved in all stages of production, from development to distribution.

In a general sense, we could say that without the producer, the picture would not be made. The Academy of Motion Picture Arts and Sciences gives the Best Picture Award to the producer of a film. This is the industry's acknowledgment that the producer is the person who is responsible for putting the pieces together, the person who creates the whole.

One of those previously named producers may have initiated the project but not have necessary skills or experience to "manage" it. One of the main elements—if not the most important—is the money. The producer is also responsible for raising it, budgeting it, and ultimately accounting for it to the investors. The producer as *production manager*, commonly called the *line producer*, is also in charge of coordinating the logistics of the production that are outlined throughout out the book (see Figure 1.1 for producer's responsibilities).

The Director

Because of the images of several contemporary superstar directors, including Spike Lee, Martin Scorsese, Jane Campion, Steven Spielberg, Wes Anderson, Kathryn Bigelow, etc., the role of the film director has taken on a romanticized image. The director shouts "Action," and the whole set swings into motion. The director chats with actors between takes and enjoys posh dinners after the day's wrap.

In reality, the director's work is never done. Because her job is to supply the creative vision for a one-of-a-kind and essentially handmade product, the choice and effect of thousands of decisions fall to her. Solving all creative problems on and off the set is the director's final responsibility, from how much light to what color blouse, from which location to how long a scream. The director alone has the "vision" of the whole film in her head, and she alone is obligated to make the sum of all her decisions throughout the process add up to its fulfillment. The director's goal is to deliver a finished film ready for an audience.

Although the producer strives to support the director's work and the director is the authority figure on the shoot, the director answers to the producer. However, the producer complements the director's work. When the director's decisions affect the budget or the schedule, she consults the producer. The responsibilities of the producer and director often overlap. Ideally, the director and producer should be able to work well together and understand the script in the same way. Picture making is, after all, a creative collaboration.

The director must be demanding but not dictatorial. She must do her best to draw out each cast and crew member by making him feel involved. The director is an active observer. She directs the actors by being part coach, part audience, and part performer. She will stand on her head if necessary to elicit a good performance. The director should have unlimited patience and be methodical, organized, articulate, and succinct. She should be broadly educated in the arts and have a working knowledge of the duties and responsibilities of each member of the team.

The director needs six things to execute a successful short: a good script, a talented cast, a devoted crew, adequate funds, good health, and luck (a major variable in any artist's work).

SIX SHORT FILMS

In this book's chapters, we try to illustrate that the potential of realizing magic on the screen is directly proportional to the quality of management in the production stages. To help you understand this critical relationship between organization and creative success, we use examples throughout the book from what we consider to be six successful shorts: four narratives, an animated film (also a narrative), and one documentary.

As teachers, we find it difficult to talk generically about production without using examples from specific films. Many basic concepts and terms are alien to the beginner, and relating them to an actual production creates a common reference and a strong context. Throughout each chapter, we quote from the filmmakers' personal narratives about that part of the production process. Citing their films, which you can see and whose scripts you can read, offers concrete evidence of the range of procedures and challenges encountered in producing and directing a short film. The rules of production planning for the short form can also be applied to any live-action (not animated) subject matter, whether it is narrative, documentary, experimental, industrial, or corporate in nature.

The case studies are *Citizen*, an 11-minute color narrative film written and directed by James Darling; *A Nick in Time*, a 10-minute narrative film written and directed by Be' Barrett; *The Lunch Date*, a 12-minute black-and-white narrative film written and directed by Adam Davidson;

Truman, a 12-minute color narrative film written and directed by Howard McCain; *Mirror Mirror*, a 17-minute documentary film produced and directed by Jan Krawitz; and *Crazy Glue*, a 5-minute animated short produced and directed by Tatia Rosenthal.

Each of these films has won competitions, and one, *The Lunch Date*, won an Academy Award. The four narratives were made as student films: *Truman, Crazy Glue*, and *Citizen* at New York University and *The Lunch Date* at Columbia University. *A Nick in Time* was made as an independent film. *Mirror Mirror* was made by a documentary filmmaker who teaches at Stanford University.

Truman is distributed by Direct Cinema Inc., *Mirror Mirror* is distributed by Woman Make Movies, *Crazy Glue* is self-distributed by Ms. Rosenthal, and *The Lunch Date* is distributed by The Lantz Office. More detailed information about these distributors is included below and in Appendix B. The script for *Citizen*, set in standard screenplay manuscript format, is printed in Appendix C.

Why did we choose these films? They are excellent examples of well-produced and well-directed short films. As stories, they are appropriate for the short form. We chose narratives that are similar in length but differ in storytelling styles, subject matter, and production organization. *Crazy Glue*,the animated film, affords us the opportunity to share the experiences and techniques required of this demanding form of film expression. It is also been adapted from another medium.

Mirror Mirror was included because the documentary is an important short form. Many young filmmakers explore the documentary as a means of self-expression. Although *Mirror Mirror* is different in nature and structure from most traditional documentaries, the form offered Jan Krawitz a unique arena in which to explore her views.

Contact information to rent or purchase a DVD copy of the short films follows:

Citizen
James Darling

A Nick in Time
Be' Garrett

Truman
Howard McCain

The Lunch Date
Adam Davidson

Crazy Glue
Tatia Rosenthal
Tel: 917-613-2667
rosenthal@yahoo.com

Mirror, Mirror
Jan Krawitz
Women Make Movies

462 Broadway
Suite 500
New York, NY 10013
Tel: 212-925-0606
Fax: 212-925-2052
Area of specialty: Films and videos by women about women
email: info@wmm.com

THE FILMMAKERS SPEAK

Culled from hours of interviews, relevant quotes from the six short filmmakers have been inserted to support the specific topic of each chapter. We hope that these pearls of wisdom will personalize their experience in producing and directing the short films we use as case studies in our book. All have gone on to do wonderful things with their careers. Check them out on imdb.com.

Adam Davidson is the writer and director of *The Lunch Date* (a live-action narrative); Adam made *The Lunch Date* as a graduate student at Columbia University School of the Arts.

Garth Stein is the producer of *The Lunch Date*.

James Darling is the writer and director of *Citizen*; he made it as an undergraduate student at NYU, Tisch School of the Arts, Undergraduate Film and Television.

Jessalyn Haefele is the producer of *Citizen*.

Be' Garrett is the cowriter and director of *A Nick in Time*.

Jan Krawitz is the director and producer of *Mirror Mirror* (a documentary); Jan is a professor at Stanford University.

Howard McCain is the writer and director of *Truman* (a live-action narrative); he made *Truman* as a student at NYU, Tisch School of the Arts, Graduate Film and Television.

Tatia Rosenthal is the writer and director of *Crazy Glue* (an animated narrative); she made *Crazy Glue* as a student at NYU, Tisch School of the Arts, Undergraduate Film and Television

CHAPTER BREAKDOWNS

Chapters 1 and 2 cover the development preliminaries that need to be dealt with prior to the preproduction phase of any project. Each chapter in Parts I and III that covers the preproduction and distribution processes begins with the producer's responsibilities. The production and postproduction chapters in Parts II and III begin with the director's duties. The typical timeline graphic shown in the introduction to Part I summarizes the activities of the producer and director during the process of making a short work. Although determining the specific amount of time needed for each phase is difficult, the following break-down may provide some insight:

- Financing might be immediately available or might take years to obtain.
- Scripts can come from many sources and may be ready to shoot or could take years to get into shape.

- Preproduction usually requires 2 to 8 weeks.
- Production usually takes somewhere between 1 day and 2 weeks.
- Postproduction details take anywhere from 2 to 10 weeks.
- Distribution can take as long as several months.

	PRODUCER	DIRECTOR
DEVELOPMENT **Script**	Developing the Script	Supervising or Performing Rewrites
	Ideas for scripts can be developed in many ways and come from many sources but there is one fact that cannot be disputed – without a well crafted script; you cannot have a good film.	
Finance	Raising the Capital	Pitching the Project
	Both the producer and the director can be engaged in the process of securing financing. Without funds, any preparation for a production is merely an exercise. The two documents required at this phase are a script and a financial planning package, or prospectus.	
PREPRODUCTION **Breakdowns**	Breaking Down the Script	Storyboards and Floor Plans
	Having achieved a tight screenplay, the producer and the director begin breaking down the script to prepare the company for production.	
Schedule	Building a Stripboard	Determining the Visual Plan
	The first document made from the breakdowns is the schedule. The producer creates the schedule from the script in conjunction with the director's visual plan for photography.	
Budget	Creating a Budget	Shooting for the Moon
	The second document made from the breakdowns is the budget. The budget defines the parameters of what can or cannot be achieved although the director will usually want to "shoot for the moon".	
Crewing	Hiring the Crew	Hiring the Crew
	The crew must be to the mutual liking of both the producer and the director. Once a crew member is chosen, the producer negotiates his or her deal.	
Casting	Auditions	Auditions
	The producer sets up the auditions and aids the director in making choices for the cast. Factors to be considered are talent, cost, and availability.	
Art Direction	Assembling the Team	Creating a Look
	The producer assembles the team, headed by the art director, which will help the director create "a look" for the picture. The look must be achieved within the parameters of the budget.	
Location	Securing Locations	Scouting Locations
	Working with the DP and art director, the director chooses the locations, and the producer secures them. If a site cannot be secured for the amount allotted in the budget, a new or backup location is explored.	
Rehearsals	Rehearsal Schedule	Working on Scenes
	The producer organizes and plans the rehearsal schedule. The director uses the rehearsal period to work with the actors to develop their roles and explore organic ways to block the action for the camera.	
Camera	Support	Collaborate
	Like the art department, the producer supports the requests and needs of the camera department. The director and camera department, led by the DP, must work like a hand in a glove.	

Sound	Control Environment	Record Clean Tracks
	The one ongoing battle on the set (unless you shoot on a sound stage) is the control of noises. The producer must do everything in his power to keep outside noises to a minimum. The director must try to get the best location sound. If the sounds being recorded are "dirty" because of noise, the director must advise the sound person on how she wants to deal with each recording.	
Art on Set	Construction	Guide
	Of all of the departments, art is the one that is most likely to expand unexpectedly during production. The producer must monitor this expansion while supporting the art director's needs. The director should guide the art department as much as possible to control any inflation of the budget.	
PRODUCTION **Set procedure**	Organize	Inspires
	The producer organizes a system for set procedures. It must function like a military operation with the AD as the chief lieutenant. The director sets the tone and mood of the set. Her energy (of lack thereof) defines how well the crew will perform.	
The Actor	Accommodate	Direct
	The producer organizes the cast schedule and is responsible for the cast's morale. The primary role of the director is to create a supportive and creative environment on set.	
POSTPRODUCTION **Picture**	Advise	Edit The "Final Draft"
	The director and editor cut the picture and sound to make the best film possible from what was captured on set. The producer acts as an objective viewer and advises the editing team accordingly.	
Sound	Supervise Postproduction	Sound Design
	Apart from the first day of principal photography, the most important target date is the mix date. The sounds in your film contribute to telling the story as much as a good shot or an outstanding performance.	
Finishing/ Laboratory/Online	Makes Prints	Time
	The producer oversees process of "finishing" the film. The director and director of photography oversee the final "look" of the film.	
Distribution/ Exhibition	Make a Deal	Publicity
	The producer is responsible for finding an outlet for the finished product. The director assists in publicizing the film.	

Chapter 1

Script

The script is everything. The importance of script is: it has to be on the page.

Be' Garrett

It all starts with an idea. For that idea to become a film; it must be fleshed out and developed into a **script** or **screenplay**. The script represents the vision of the filmmaker in practical form. It is also your guide through production. From it, you know the story, the characters, the locations, the approximate budget, the final length, and your target audience. With a script, you can finance the production and attract the creative team that will transform the script into a final product. The first member of that team is the director. Her job is to bring a personal vision to the material by either rewriting the script herself or collaborating with the writer until the script best suits a production based on her design.

This is the model we are following in this book. There are other scenarios as well. The director and producer can develop an idea with a writer, or a director/writer can develop the idea and bring on a producer (most film school situations). In the latter case, the producer serves as more of a production manager than a creative force. This scenario can lead to certain complications. For example, even if the director is a good writer, the process may reach a point when the producer feels that the script needs a fresh set of eyes. Negotiating this and other issues can be sticky unless the director is able to put her ego aside and focus on what is best for the project.

We believe that a productive synergy develops through checks and balances. The give-and-take over all creative and financial decisions from script to screen is not only healthy but essential in creating the best film from the material. Keep this in mind. However, whatever approach is taken, there is one fact that cannot be disputed—without a well-crafted script, you cannot have a good film.

This chapter introduces you to some necessary guidelines for writing a short film script. It does not, however, explore in depth the nuts and bolts of writing technique. We recommend that you consult books written specifically about screenwriting for the short form. You'll find suggestions in the Bibliography.

The guidelines in this chapter are not absolutes. Violating some of these narrative principles should not keep you from moving ahead if you feel strongly about the idea. You will be living with this project for quite a while, so it is important that you feel passionate about the material and its message. Remember, though, that film and video are art forms that communicate via visual images. If the script cannot convey a message visually, it might not engage an audience.

THE CREATIVE PRODUCER

Developing the Script

The first step in producing a short film is securing a script. There are many ways you can do this:

- You can write one yourself.
- You can develop an original idea with a writer or director.
- You can adapt a script from another genre (a play or short story) or true story.
- You can find a script that is already written.

The producer supervises the development of an idea until a director is brought on board to supervise the rewrites and prepare the script for production. What starts out as a simple notion might go through many evolutions before it is ready to go before the cameras. The goal is to end up with the best script possible from your original idea. No magic on the set will correct any unresolved story or structure problems. The old axiom holds true: if it isn't on the page, it won't be on the screen. Be prepared to work and rework the material.

When I sat down with each of my actors, I knew the characters inside and out. I had one actor in particular, the only woman in the film, who had come to trouble trying to figure out who her character was and how she fit into this whole story as the wife of the judge. But because I had spent so much time on the rewrites, she had an entire character bible that I had worked out so I was able to basically tell her who she was.

Be' Garrett

doi: 10.1016/B978-0-240-81174-1.00008-7

Producing a documentary script involves a different process than generating a narrative text. The specific nature of developing documentary idea is addressed later in this chapter. There may be those wishing to develop an experimental or avant-garde short. "Experimental" is not even considered a specific genre because the range of ideas for experimental projects is so enormous—from abstract images to installations to nontraditional narratives (see Appendix B for more information of genres).

The Academy of Motion Picture Arts and Sciences Student Academy Awards has a specific category named "Alternative." If you want to understand what "alternative" can represent, it's best to review past winners of this award. Compilations of student Academy Awards are now available on DVD. We will reference a number of filmmakers and films to view to sample a little of what can be done. (Appendix A on short films includes a list of important experimental films and filmmakers)

Whatever the genre, it is important to be able to create a written representation of your idea, the script. Writing a good short script is difficult. The most common mistake novices make is trying to explore complicated or grandiose ideas that are more suited for the feature film format. They want to say it all in 10 minutes. The short film idea doesn't have the time to explore more than one topic. It needs to be focused and specific. Simple is best. The six examples provided in this book are good scripts because they are simple stories told well. (See Appendix C and the web site for each film for the complete scripts.)

> Probably the biggest influence—besides all the films I'd ever seen in my life—was looking at student films, what was working and what wasn't. One thing that I thought wasn't working was that the stories went all over the place and that there was an emphasis on the technical rather than substance.
>
> Adam Davidson

Do Your Homework

Before embarking on a production, see and study as many shorts as possible to get a feel for the form and what can be accomplished in its time frame. The length for shorts varies from 2 minutes (*Bambi Meets Godzilla*, United States, 1969) to 34 minutes (*The Red Balloon*, France, 1956). Novices often struggle to develop stories for shorts because they are not familiar enough with the kinds of ideas that translate well into smaller packages. Shorts and features have dramatic principles in common, but in the same way that short stories are different from novels, there are specific limits to the dramatic scope and range of stories. A character can fall in and out of love, discover the meaning of life, or conquer a nation in two hours. In 10 minutes, a character may only be able to get up the courage to ask someone for a date.

Because television offers very little product in the short form other than half-hour sitcoms, commercials, or music videos, it doesn't come as a surprise that many ideas developed by first-time filmmakers are better suited for the big screen. It may seem that the short form is limiting in its creative and/or thematic possibilities, but after you study many short films and videos, it should become apparent that ideas expressed in this form are limited only by the imagination. All the short films selected for this book touch on serious issues and themes.

Finding and viewing short films is much easier than it ever has been. Students and beginners have access to YouTube, ITunes, Facebook, and the massive amount of product on the behemoth called the Internet. Anyone with an audience of one can post something on YouTube. The challenge is to sift through it all to separate the wheat from the chaff. Appendix B will be expanded to include links to web sites for shorts as well as excellent short film collections. It also contains recommendations for classic shorts of all genres and how to find them. In addition, the web site for this book will be updated to include recommendations for what we consider excellent examples.

> I think that I had seen a couple of films on eating disorders, and I had a feeling that I knew what was out there. I did seek out one film on beauty pageants, which was pretty irrelevant to this subject matter. But I do think that's important. I didn't want to make a film like this if there was a film that had just come out a year earlier. I did enough of a search to convince myself that there was really not one that took this particular perspective.
>
> Jan Krawitz

Make sure to explore the range of genres—comedy, farce, drama, tragedy, or melodrama—to learn what is best suited to the short film. Comedies, for example, lend themselves to the short form more comfortably than melodrama (film noir, Western, murder mysteries, sci-fi), which usually requires the development of a more complex plot.

Many of the great filmmakers were influenced by existing material. Orson Welles saw and studied John Ford's famous Western *Stagecoach* more than 50 times while preparing to shoot *Citizen Kane*.

> I made a list of the films that really affected me as a child. One of them was *An Occurrence at Owl Creek Bridge* (which most people have seen). Then, of course, so did *The Red Balloon*. In film school, I saw many other films, such as Truffaut's *Les Miston* (*The Brats*). This film didn't influence me in a conscious way but filled me up emotionally. It was so melancholy and beautiful that it made me want to run out and make films, even though I ended up making a film like *Truman*.
>
> Howard McCain

What Is a Script?

A script is to filmmaking as a blueprint is to shipbuilding or as a score is to a symphony performance. Imagine the ensuing difficulties of a shipbuilder who begins construction on a boat with only a few sketches to work from, or the cacophony of a full orchestra trying to play a concert from a sketchy musical score. Just as the drawings tell the shipbuilder exactly where to place the mast and the notes on the score tell the musicians what and when and how loudly to play, so a script dictates how each member of the production team is to go about fulfilling his or her job.

A script depicts the moment-to-moment progression of events by indicating what the audience will see and hear. Unlike a novel or a poem, the script is an unfinished work; it is only a part of the media-making process. It has no inherent literary value other than as a guide from which a film is wrought.

> I went to the Academy Award winning short screenings for a few years. Of those I saw, three caught my attention. The first, *Two Brothers or Two Soldiers*, is a film about an older brother going off to World War II and his 12 year [old] brother who runs away from home and falls into the recruitment center. That was a 40-minute short film, but it had great production values and an epic story.
>
> The second was a French film called *A Man Without a Head*, a fantasy about a society of underclass of people that live without heads. Incredible special effects.
>
> The third was [a] short told in a single shot with no dialogue. It is about these refugees who are trying to cross a border. It starts out on a vista and then all these people pop up from [the] grass and begin walking. Suddenly, helicopters and then soldiers appear and sweep around them, and take them away. The final image is of one guy who has managed to escape the clutches of the soldiers. And this is all in one shot.
>
> All those shorts created their own special universe in a very short time and were experimental—still great stories— but developed a world from a very unique perspective.
>
> James Darling

What Does a Script Look Like?

The scripts of *The Lunch Date* and *Citizen* in Appendix C are presented in Writers Guild of America (WGA) standard screenplay format. This format is an industry convention that has a direct relationship to how the script is photographed. (See Chapter 3 for more about screenplay format.) Writing a script in proper format has become simplified with the availability of software systems. Some of the current scriptwriting programs are Final Draft, Movie Magic Screenwriter, and Celtx Studios. (Both Movie

Magic and Celtx link to a scheduling and budgeting software). Most can format your script as you type it and include every genre, including TV. They can be found where computer programs are sold, and some companies will send you a free demo disk.

However, a story doesn't have to be presented originally in screenplay format to make dramatic sense. You can work from a **step outline** or a **treatment**. A step outline is, as the term implies, the story told in steps or **story beats** of one or two sentences describing the action and the dramatic tension in each scene. A treatment, similar to a **synopsis**, is the bare bones of a story told in narrative prose rather than in descriptions of individual scenes. A treatment reads like a short story and can be as straightforward as the way the case studies are described later in this chapter. A step outline also represents the bare bones of the story, but is not concerned with dialogue, details, set dressing, or minor characters, just the action of the scene, who does what to whom. Whatever method you use, it is imperative that the idea eventually conform to the standard script format.

A common format for documentary scriptwriting is a two-column page: one side lists the visuals, and the other side lists the audio. The reader will get an idea of the show by imagining these two elements together. However, unlike the script in a narrative production, this is a form that evolves after much of the footage has already been shot. Documentarians learn to be especially responsive to their material. By the time the documentary gels, the story might have changed, taking a direction very different from the original outline.

For example, in Errol Morris's Academy Award–winning documentary *The Thin Blue Line*, his original intent was to interview inmates on death row in Texas. In the course of conducting the interviews, he met and interviewed a man who was to become the sole subject of his film. Believing the man on death row to be innocent, Morris took his case to the film audience. The argument was so compelling the man was retried and eventually freed from prison. This example demonstrates not only the adjustments documentary filmmakers undergo in the discovery process of their topic, but also the power of cinema to make a change, to affect the world.

> During the interview with my first subject, I asked way too many questions. After shooting 800 feet on that single interview, I reduced the number of questions from eight to four and really simplified the content. Because, despite a "test" interview, I had overestimated how much information I could cover in a 400-foot (11-minute) roll of film.
>
> Jan Krawitz

Where Do Scripts Come From?

Scripts are developed from whatever might inspire you to express and communicate something in visual and dramatic terms. All the following sources can serve as the basis for a dramatic or documentary project:

Ideas	Dreams
Images	Real events
Characters	Fantasies
Concepts	Memories
Historical events	Real-life experiences
Places	Social issues
Adaptations from short stories	News stories
	Magazine articles

You might be inspired by a single event that occurred on a bus or train, an interaction between two people that strikes you as funny or poignant, an uncle who told you wonderful stories as a child, or a favorite teacher who was a memorable character. You might have a compelling need to express something about the social conditions in your neighborhood. The best scripts are written from the heart. They are based on subjects the writer knows on a first-hand basis.

Truman focuses on conquering feelings of inadequacy in public. Most of us can empathize with Truman's transcendental moment when his perception of himself in the world undergoes a major shift, a spurt of personal growth.

During the summer, I kept notebooks full of different ideas, random stuff. I kept drawing the picture of a little boy hanging from a rope. That image propelled me forward. I can't remember why. I also wanted to make a film that, if I were an eight-year-old boy, would amuse me. The sort of film teachers would roll out on rainy days in fifth grade. I wanted it to be fun to make. I wanted to enjoy it.

Howard McCain

The woman in *The Lunch Date* also has a personal revelation. She and a homeless man share an unusual moment together, and then she escapes back to the suburbs (see Figure 1.1). This moment probably does not have the same impact on her life as the events in *Truman* do on the boy because she is older. We see her experience the unexpected, which then affords her the ability to know the homeless in a new way. Both characters are changed in some way by the events of their stories.

I remember that several years before, I had heard a story similar to the one I used in the film, which was a story about a person misidentifying something of someone else's as belonging to themselves. And I thought this was a pretty human mistake that anybody could make and that I had probably made somewhere along the line—assuming something about somebody else. So I played with the idea of setting this story in New York and having the two most opposite people I could think of meet.

Adam Davidson

Citizen tells the story of a young man in the not-too-distant future who tries to escape from his homeland in the dead of winter (see Figure 1.2). As this teenage boy is chased by hunters through the harsh wilderness approaching the Canadian border, he is haunted by a fateful doctor's visit and the perilous choice he has made.

FIGURE 1.1 Two hungry diners, from *The Lunch Date*.

FIGURE 1.2   A scene from *Citizen*.

I read about these deserters from the U.S. Military that were seeking sanctuary in Canada. From my own family history—I am estranged from my father, but he did go to Vietnam, I was aware of the Vietnam era draft dodging community. I also spent my life crossing the U.S./Canada border visiting my extended family in Arkansas and Texas. Around those ideas I started thinking about what might happen if this trend continues, if the wars that America are waging are escalated just a little further so that people were calling for a military draft. Small advocacy groups—more on the anti-war side would not be fighting this war if everyone was at risk.

James Darling

A Nick in Time is the story of an old-school barber in Brooklyn, New York, who is confronted by a young man wanting a haircut but whose intentions do not seem to be that forthright (see Figure 1.3). To distract the young man from making a serious mistake, the barber digs into his past and tells a story of a key moment that changed his life in the hopes that he can save the kid's.

I had an idea to do a film. I began to kick around this idea of what kind of movie would I want to do that would be, particularly to me and my past and my history, that I would want to convey to others. I've always loved being in a barbershop. I remember going back home to Philadelphia and being in a barbershop my cousin owned at the time with my mom and my cousin, and I'd begin to tell them about the idea, the genesis of the idea which was this guy who comes into the store, and he's talking to the barber, but I need something to happen between the barber and the guy, and I'm thinking about maybe having some sort of twist where the barber tells him something.

Be' Garrett

FIGURE 1.3   Characters from *A Nick in Time*.

FIGURE 1.4   A masked woman surrounded by mannequins, from *Mirror Mirror*.

The film *Mirror Mirror* focuses on the topic of how women perceive their bodies. The filmmaker had a specific theme to explore and set about devising a situation that would allow women to express their innermost thoughts (see Figure 1.4).

> I believe that this self-deprecation and striving for an unattainable body type is a generalized experience among a lot of women. All you have to do is eavesdrop in department store dressing rooms or women's locker rooms to hear the laments that women have about their bodies.
>
> Jan Krawitz

Crazy Glue is an animated clay puppet short adapted from a story by Israeli author Etgar Keret. This **claymation** (see Glossary) film tells the story of one innovative attempt to patch up a disintegrating marriage—through the use of Crazy Glue!

Whereas *Truman, The Lunch Date, A Nick in Time, Citizen,* and *Mirror Mirror* are original ideas, *Crazy Glue* is an adaptation. Writer Etgar Keret is one of the leading voices in Israeli literature and cinema. Since the late 1990s, he has published three books of short stories and novellas, two comic books, two feature screenplays, and numerous teleplays. His stories have been published in 15 different languages and have gained both critical acclaim and success with the public. His book *Missing Kissinger* was named one of the 50 most important books written in Hebrew.

> As a going away gift when I left Israel I received a short book by Etgar Keret, the writer with whom I now work. I finished it on the plane. It was about 50 short stories of his. I thought every single one of them should have been a short film. In fact, I think since they do lend themselves so well, more than a hundred of his stories were adapted to short films at this point. I adapted quite a few of them through many different classes at NYU, and when it came time to have my senior thesis project made, that story "Crazy Glue" was just so beautiful. I thought it was the most beautiful short story I ever read. It also had a lot of magical realist sensibilities to it. I thought it was very appropriate for stop motion animation.
>
> Tatia Rosenthal

How Are Scripts Developed?

You should always be on the lookout for interesting material. Turn your eyes and ears outward to the world around you and write down the events that you observe in your quest for a good idea or story in a notebook or diary. If you use a computer, you can file incidents in a database under a variety of tags. Moments in life happen at breakneck speed. You might think at the time that you will remember them when you go home at night, but chances are you will have forgotten some significant detail that struck you as funny or compelling.

One result of typing and storing material is that you remember it better. Good ideas beget good ideas. The events you write down will stimulate your imagination further. Your writer's notebook could contain these categories:

Characters: Short films are mostly character based, so keep detailed notes of people who could be the basis of a story. We have all met people who in one way or another fascinate us. These could be ones you know very well or not at all. It could be what they do, how they do it, or what they know that interests you. Interesting people you see on a train or plane or meet at a party. Note how they look and dress and any unique behavior or mannerisms. Human actions form the core of drama, so people are the most obvious starting point for a writer.

Locations: Places create mood. Be on the lookout for visually interesting spaces that serve as compelling backdrops for dramatic encounters. Because certain behavior tends to occur in specific places, locations can serve as inspirations for story ideas.

Objects: Curious or evocative objects. They could be interesting pieces of clothing, objects found around the house, key chains. Objects in films can take on a significance based on the circumstance in which they are placed.

Situations: Revealing or telling situations that you witness or experience firsthand.

Unusual or Revealing Acts: Witnessing people act or behave in a way that reveals something powerful and unique about their character.

A News File: Save good stories in a folder that could serve as an inspiration for a documentary or narrative idea. Look at old magazines and newspapers that have items that are noncurrent material that no one else is using.

Picture File: Collect pictures from magazines, newspapers, and the Internet. Inspirations can come from dramatic pictures from war, crime situations, fashion images, or any images that stimulate your imagination. People say a "picture is worth a thousand words." Be on the lookout for those telling ones.

Dream/Fantasy Journal: Your dreams and fantasies are a sure indicator of your underlying concerns. Keep a notebook by your bed and write down each dream while you remember it. This part of your journal is for you to let your mind take off in any direction it wants, stimulated, we hope by the collection of material you collect.

Themes: Themes grow out of who you are and what you believe. They are the heart and soul of good stories. Write down themes that intrigue you or you feel deeply about. When you see a film or read a story that speaks to your own sensibilities, make note of it.

Workshop Your Idea

All the information you collect can be transformed into many different scenarios. Mix and match the various characters, evocative situations, and locations in your journal. Look for unlikely relationships. A constructive way to

deal with this accumulation of ideas and material is to "workshop them" with interested people. Ideas that are spoken out loud have a different impact than those that are read. They can either sound better than you thought or fall flat. Not only can you test an idea or concept on an ad hoc audience, but, more important, these verbalized ideas will be stimulating. A thought or image conjures up different impressions in each person's mind. If one of these ideas becomes the core of your final script, these brainstorming sessions will serve as a bond and the start of a long and fruitful collaboration that will, it is hoped, continue throughout the entire process.

> There was a phase in the middle of writing the script where I went off and tried to make it a little bit of a self-reflecting piece where the husband was going to go to work, and at work he's a three-dimensional animated character. So he goes to work, goes to the computer, and his job is to move inside a computer. It was quite amusing, but technically it would have made the script much much harder to produce. I ended up taking all of that out and going back to the original story as it was. The only one reference I left in there was when the woman is having an argument with her husband. She is doodling inside of a cookbook, and what she has done is made a flipbook inside the cookbook. That was the little leftover of that idea.
>
> Tatia Rosenthal

During the workshop phase of development, it might be necessary to develop many ideas before you discover one that reflects your own voice and that also suits the short form. There is no easy or quick path; there is only a process that if pursued on a regular basis will ultimately result in a story that you believe in and want to tell.

> The big thing I was struggling with is; how did I feel about the character? I was definitely putting myself in the character's shoes. What would I do in this situation? Ultimately, I decided that I did not want the film to necessarily take a point of view on the character. I wanted to inspire conversation afterwards. It was that idea that eventually got me to the concept: what if you really do not know what is going on until very near or close to the end of the film. That is when I had one of my early writing teachers at NYU give me one note. It is a *Twilight Zone* episode. It is perfect. I was like—okay.
>
> James Darling

Adaptation

The beginning filmmaker may also look for ideas for a short project from preexisting material. In our list of where scripts come from, we site short stories, real-life experiences, news stories, historical events, real events, and magazine articles.

The history of motion pictures has been dominated by adaptations, mostly from novels. At the height of the studio period in the 1930s, Hollywood was turning out more than 600 films a year. To supply this pipeline of production, studios looked to material that had already proven itself in the marketplace. Novels served this purpose. Although the studios in the United States produce nowhere near that number of films a year now, roughly half are adapted from another medium, usually from a novel or play.

The Academy of Motion Picture Arts and Sciences honors the craft of adaptation; a separate Oscar is given to best adaptation in addition to best original screenplay. Yet there are few books devoted to adaptation and only a handful that reserve a substantial section for this craft. Most how-to writing manuals focus on creating original stories. Although all the important lessons about dramatic writing apply, the ability to transpose a well-written short story (or even a real-life incident) into a film script requires a specific discipline.

Why Adapt?

One obvious reason to adapt is that you have already found a story that has inspired you to produce it as a motion picture. A short story comes with built-in characters, plot, setting, and a theme or central idea. You may have been moved by the words on the page; now you want to transfer those feelings to the screen.

There may be a short story that you always loved that you thought had dramatic or visual potential. It could have been written years ago and by someone not well known. It doesn't have to be an example of classic literature (because these stories may be out of your price range as well). Some successful adaptations have come from mediocre books or stories. What they did offer was a strong plot. There is a well-worn axiom that the best books make the worst movies (not always true). This has something to do with the expectations that come with adapting a classic. We have all experienced the reaction of "it wasn't as good as the book." At the same time, adapting a story by a well-known author can open doors to film financiers in a way original scripts or scripts adapted from obscure works cannot.

Another reason to adapt is that original ideas may be harder to come by. Developing an idea from scratch, alone or with a writer, may be more challenging than working with already-established material. But don't think that adapting a preexisting work is any easier. (This also goes for true stories that we will address at the end of this section.) Literature is another medium with its own set of rules. Capturing the spirit of the work but placing it in another package can be equally if not more challenging than developing an original idea for the screen. In this section, we will discuss some strategies to help you discover if the story you are considering is an appropriate candidate for a successful adaptation.

> Filmmaking today encourages the writer/director auteur and it is a bit of a shame because when you have the same person write and direct, you miss one generation of imagination. I think adapting from a book is having that one extra generation of imagination in both writer and person. I think it becomes more profound and valuable.
>
> Tatia Rosenthal

Rights

If you have found a story, comic book, magazine article, or video game that you want to adapt, the first step would be to find out if the underlying rights to the material are available. This step is a very important, and it is one that many beginning filmmakers fail to take. If the rights are available, you can take the next steps. If they are not, you will have saved yourself from a lot of effort for nothing (unless you were using the process as an exercise).

However, we suggest another step before approaching the author or the author's agent. Spend some time thoroughly scrutinizing the story's potential for the screen. Come up with ideas on how to adapt the work. If you are lucky to be able to contact the author personally, having a well-thought-out plan may be a key selling point in receiving the author's permission. If you are not offering a lot of money, you will have demonstrated that you have done your homework. You have nothing to lose and everything to gain. This step also should solidify your belief in the dramatic and visual potential of your story

Legalities

Rights and Adaptations (Preexisting Material)

For the privilege to profit from the commercial sale or rental of your short film or video, rights to original material must be purchased. This is also true if you intend to post your short project on the Internet. This gives you complete control of the story in that medium. For a well-known story, commercial rights can be expensive, if not prohibitive, for a producer on a limited budget.

It is essential for you to obtain permission to use existing material or even to dramatize someone's biography unless that person is within the public domain as a public figure (e.g., Madonna, Tom Cruise). If you read about some extraordinary man in the newspaper, get permission to write about him. You'll also need permission from the author of the article if she has exclusive information about the subject.

If you find a short story you like, make a legally binding arrangement with its author for the right to use it as the basis for your film. Contact the author's representative, perhaps an agent or an attorney, through the publisher. If the author is deceased, an agent or lawyer will represent the estate. If you have a personal relationship with the author, you might want to bypass the publisher, agent, or attorney and appeal directly to the author. This approach might also be worth trying in the case of well-known authors whose representatives categorically reject any request from unknown producers.

In any case, make no assumptions. You make think that a story is out of your reach, but you'll never know unless you ask. Nothing ventured, nothing gained. This philosophy applies to all aspects of filmmaking.

The work might be in the **public domain** and free to use if it has been 70 years since the author's death. A book is in the public domain when its copyright protection has expired. Examples are stories by Aesop, Dickens, or those from the Bible. If you have any doubt as to what is or isn't in the public domain, write to the copyright office: Reference and Bibliography Section, LM-451 Copyright Office, Library of Congress, Washington, DC 20559.

> Securing rights was a concern. With "Crazy Glue," Etgar Keret had an agreement with his publishers who owned the rights for his stories at the time that he can just grant students the right to use the material. It becomes an issue when money exchanges hands. I just had to ask his permission and I could do it. Maybe I should have had it in writing, but as soon as you know somebody—you know if you can trust—the reality they are presenting—he is a very trustworthy person.
>
> Tatia Rosenthal

Noncommercial/Festival Rights

Film students and beginners exhibit their work primarily at festivals, museums, or conferences (on the Internet as well, but these issues will be covered separately in Chapter 19). A basic use of a short work is as a springboard to future employment. Prizes at festivals are not considered profit, so it might be possible to strike a deal with the author's representative for a noncommercial or "festival license." These licenses are easier to obtain than commercial rights. They're also cheaper—sometimes even free. It is suggested, however, that you obtain a quote for full rights and mention this amount specifically in your festival license agreement. That way, you will know exactly what your licensing budget would be if a distributor is interested in your film. (This principle applies to music rights as well.)

Original Material

On the opposite end of the spectrum is an original story written directly for the screen. The producer has already discovered a screenplay that he wants to produce. If you decide to go this route, you should purchase the rights to the material from its author, even if only for a dollar.

A simple letter of agreement (see our web site, http://booksite.focalpress.com/companion/IrvingRea/) between you and the author will make the process legal. This letter is your protection against future disputes concerning ownership or division of any profits.

Copyright

The copyright law protects you from someone copying what you have written. A copyright certifies that the material existed on a certain date. If someone presents the same project later, you have grounds for a claim of copyright infringement. However, copyright law does not protect ideas. It protects only the "expression of an idea that is fixed in a tangible form." This means that an original treatment, outline, or screenplay is protected, but the ideas behind them are not. The more fully your ideas are realized, the more protection you have. A complete screenplay will be protected more than a short treatment. Register only the first draft unless the story changes dramatically from one draft to another.

Before applying for copyright, make sure to register your treatment or outline with the Writers Guild of America. Taking this step doesn't protect you legally, but it helps establish the history of the creation of your script—a paper trail so to speak. Make sure that the cover of your treatment or script contains the WGA registration number and the maximum amount of information about you: your name, address, phone number, email, agent (if applicable).

WGA registration is available for everyone, and the cost is very low (around $30). The WGA gives the treatment or script a number, puts it in a sealed envelope, and stores it in a vault for 5 years. No one can withdraw your script but you. The entire process can be handled online at www.wgawregistry.org.

To obtain a copyright from the Library of Congress, you can get a copy of FORM PA from the copyright office web site at www.copyright.gov/forms or by calling 202-707-9100. There are many registration forms, each for a different kind of work. These forms can be filled out and sent back or processed online. It may take months to hear back, so be patient.

A documentary producer must secure the rights to tell the story of a particular subject. Rights are not necessary when dealing with historical or public figures, however. Private subjects must sign a release (see our web site) providing the producer with all rights necessary. If you have any question about the process of securing rights to a non-public figure or subject, consult an entertainment lawyer.

Basic Guidelines for the Short Form

How do you evaluate an idea for a script? Short films can be developed from many different kinds of ideas. However, there are limits to what can be accomplished in the short form. Because most beginners are not familiar with its format, let's examine these common attributes and furnish a critical point of view. The following are general guidelines; there will always be exceptions.

Let's examine what *Truman, Mirror Mirror, The Lunch Date, Crazy Glue, A Nick in Time, Citizen,* and a few classic shorts have in common. This will give you a greater understanding of the dramatic parameters of the short form. Make sure to use these guidelines when you watch and critique other short works.

The screenwriting process is about research, discovery, and crystallization. Watching your story develop is an exciting experience. The final result should feel as if each scene is in the right place.

Achieving this feeling, however, comes from patience and hard work. You will soon understand the age-old rule: writing is rewriting. Subscribe to it. Be satisfied only with the best you can do.

Length

Is there an ideal length for a short? (The Academy of Motion Picture Arts and Sciences' length requirement for a short is up to 40 minutes.) The best length is the one that satisfies your particular story. Work from this point. If you are concerned about the ideal length for distribution markets, submit your proposal or script to several distributors for feedback. If you have already found a market for your picture, the ideal length might be predetermined.

Look at the length of films at well-known festivals. What is the average time? Films in the 10-minute range usually have a better chance of festival acceptance because festival organizers like to program as many as possible. YouTube shorts are even shorter. At the end of the day, your film is as long as it needs to be to tell the story.

STUDENTS

Eager to impress people with their talent, beginning filmmakers often want to say too much with their short film project. They tend to compress feature-length ideas into 10-minute pictures. Resist this temptation.

The Central Theme

The central theme is what the story is all about. It is the raison d'être, the cement that holds the story together. Themes are concerned with universal concepts—love, honor, identity, compromise, responsibility, ambition, greed, and guilt—that are experienced and shared worldwide. The universal quality of these ideas and emotions helps ensure that the audience will relate to the material on a deeper level than the plot. Without this unifying ingredient, there is no purpose or meaning to the work.

The theme represents the reason why you want to make the film in the first place: to say something about the human condition. In *Truman*, the theme is conquering a fear. *The Lunch Date* is about letting go of one's prejudice. *Crazy Glue* is an intimate story about a lonely wife's attempt to draw back her philandering husband. *Mirror Mirror* centers on how women see themselves juxtaposed with society's mirror. In *A Nick in Time*, success or failure in life can hinge on only one moment. One person can make a difference in your life. All the scenes in your film should be subordinate to the main theme. If a scene doesn't support your theme, eliminate it.

That is what it has always been about for me, the communication of ideas and stories: The desire to express oneself. What has really happened in the last few years with the web, with YouTube, with a lot of traditional media going onto the web, but also with amateur user generated content, filmmaking has become the new writing. There is writing that is published in a novel form, but there is the writing we do everyday between each other. Filmmaking, whether it is video conferencing, recording personal greetings; it has become ubiquitous in everything. So the big challenge that I and my peers seem to be facing is where does art begin? If everyone can do this—at different levels certainly—but what is culture vs. what is communication? It is a big question.

James Darling

Conflict

A basic element common to all visual drama is the need for a specific and identifiable conflict. Conflict creates tension. Tension engages the viewer's emotions, it keeps them engaged, until the conflict is resolved and the tension is relieved at the end of the piece.

What is conflict, and how is it created? Conflict is realized through characters. Someone wants something or is unhappy or unfulfilled in some way, takes action, and meets with conflict. Most narrative stories begin by establishing a problem, dilemma, or goal. The process of working out this issue defines the drama. Obstacles to solving the problem intensify the conflict. The necessity of overcoming obstacles to resolve the conflict places a greater value on the lesson learned.

The Law of Conflict: Nothing moves forward in a story except through conflict.... As long as conflict engages our thoughts and emotions we travel through the hours unaware of the voyage. Then suddenly the film's over. We glance at our watches, amazed. But when conflict disappears, so do we. The pictorial interest of eye pleasing photography or the aural pleasures of a beautiful score may hold us briefly, but if conflict is kept on hold for too long, our eyes leave the screen.

Robert McKee, *Story: Substance, Structure, Style and the Principles of Screenwriting*

The Basic Conflicts

Different kinds of conflict are possible in a story, regardless of whether it's fictional or nonfictional:

Individual versus self (internal)
Individual versus individual (personal)
Individual versus society (social environment)
Individual versus nature (physical environment)

Each one of these conflicts, alone or in combination, draws our attention to the plight of the main character, or protagonist, when confronted by personal or another individual's demons, or the forces of society, or nature. The filmmakers create a deep emotional connection between the audience and the protagonist by clearly identifying the protagonist's dilemma.

Citizen employs three levels of conflict: individual versus society (the state), individual versus nature (physical environment), and individual versus self (personal loss). The young man, fleeing from the draft, not only must overcome rough terrain, snow, a formidable wall, and the border patrol to make it to Canada, but also face never seeing his parents again.

The protagonist in *The Lunch Date* faces two levels of conflict: internal and personal. Her goal is to eat her salad. The obstacles are the homeless man (personal) and her prejudices (internal). This is the basis for conflict. How she deals with this unexpected situation creates a tension that will be resolved only when the woman either gets her salad or does not. The tension created by this expectation impels us to watch. We are eager to learn how she will handle this unique situation. Will she overcome her aversion to the homeless man? The transition from outrage to mutual respect is a satisfying leap for the character and the audience.

Crazy Glue shows a lonely wife's attempt to draw back her philandering husband through the use of common household glue. This individual versus individual story has a universal appeal.

Truman employs three levels of conflict: individual versus society, individual versus individual, and individual versus self. The class represents society and is punished because of Truman's weakness. By overcoming his fear and climbing the rope, Truman is accepted to the bosom of the group. The film also deals with the conflict of individual versus individual, with the coach as the antagonist. He tries to humiliate Truman into climbing the rope, thereby forcing the boy to make his final decision.

These two levels are, however, extensions of the primary conflict that is at the heart of the story: Truman's internal conflict with himself. His need to climb up the rope (and his fear of doing so) is the reason the story exists. As an audience, we strongly identify with that need and are emotionally involved in finding out if Truman can overcome his fear and climb the rope. Once he does, the conflict is resolved, the tension is diffused, and the story ends.

The conflict in *Mirror Mirror* is one of individual versus nature, society, and self. The goal is for the women to accept their physical appearance. Tension arises from the fact that their looks are at odds with society's standards of beauty. This tension is intensified by the emphasis and importance our culture places on how a woman's body looks.

In each of these stories, the filmmaker sets up an expectation by establishing a conflict. We are engaged by the main character's need to overcome the conflict and deal with the problem, and we will be satisfied only when the conflict is resolved. If the characters could get what they wanted easily, there would be no story.

Equally important, the basic conflict existed even before the story began. Truman was scared to climb the rope ladder, and the woman of *The Lunch Date* had her social prejudices well before the film began. The story setting presents a situation to reveal conflict that already exists. There is no time to develop conflict in a short piece, so conflict should be inevitable.

The Dramatic Arc or Spine

Every story should have a beginning, a middle, and an end—but, as Jean-Luc Godard once said, not necessarily in that order. In *Truman, Crazy Glue,* and *The Lunch Date, A Nick in Time,* and *Citizen,* each main character has a goal (the rope, the husband, the salad, the need to convince the young man, the border), and each has an obstacle (fear, her husband's indifference, the homeless man, the possibility of violence, the border patrol).

Most narrative stories can be reduced to this basic formula of goal-obstacle-resolution, creating this progression:

Beginning (setup)
Middle (development)
End (resolution)

This can also be stated in terms of character:

Someone wants something
Takes action
Meets with obstacles (conflict)
That leads to a climax
And a resolution.

This formula creates the natural arc or **spine** of all narrative and non-narrative drama. All stories follow this progression. The problem is introduced, developed, and then resolved. When the resolution has been achieved, the story is over.

> My whole script hinges upon the fantasy sequences. They are small and contained in the final film, but they are very important in showing who the main character is. What role they play in the film constantly changed. Originally, they were the entire film. But as the story developed, they became shorter and their importance changed. They became more an element of surprise and gave clues showing what Truman was feeling. But this weeding out and connecting occurred over 13 drafts; eventually, however, the fantasies found their proper place in the story.
>
> Howard McCain

The story should have some twists and turns along the way (complications) to add tension to its development. Either the characters or situations cause the events of a story. In the case of *Truman*, each time Truman attempts to climb the rope ladder, his fantasies distract him from achieving his goal. *The Lunch Date* has several unexpected twists along the way. First, the homeless man allows the woman to share his salad; then, he buys coffee for her; and finally, she discovers that it wasn't her salad after all. In *Crazy Glue*, the use of the key prop, a tube of glue introduced in the first scene, becomes the "bond" that reunites the married couple.

The additional twist of *A Nick in Time* is the reveal that the one getting the haircut is actually a cop who had his gun drawn under the cape the whole time. *Citizen*, on the other hand, plays with ambiguity of time. It is not clear if the young man had his "physical" for the army before deciding to flee or after.

Each of these events defies the dramatic expectation of the story setup. They give each story its originality. The director can map these emotional beats out on a graph so that no matter what scene is being shot, she can understand the dynamics of each moment and its relationship to the whole. This map allows the director to communicate with the creative team out of sequence. For example, knowing what transpires in scene 4 will inform her work with an actor in scene 3. If the actor plays scene 3 too forcefully, he may have nowhere to go emotionally for the climax in scene 4.

Most of these principles hold true for the documentary form. A documentary also needs a dramatic arc by which it can tell a true story.

One Primary Event

A short film should focus on a single event around which the action of the story revolves. *Crazy Glue, Truman, The Lunch Date*, and *A Nick in Time* are stories told in a contained time period: in *Crazy Glue*, prying his wife off the ceiling; in *Truman*, climbing the rope; in *The Lunch Date*, sharing a salad. In *A Nick in Time*, the story parallels between two haircuts in the same barbershop 25 years

apart, but the "realtime" or event of the film is the time it takes for one haircut. By experiencing the illusion of realtime, the audience is brought into the immediacy of the drama. The director's challenge then becomes to show what is outstanding about this bit of time.

Citizen focuses on creating a relationship between two events: the physical exam and the young man's run for the border. The time frame for the connection is clearly more ambiguous. The event in *Mirror Mirror* is the coming together of many women to express their feelings about their bodies. The single event is an important element in the success of each film. In a short of less than 30 minutes, it is difficult to balance any more.

By focusing on the playing out of just one event, the filmmaker can fully explore the event's dramatic potential. This simplicity of purpose frees her to give depth to the piece. The audience comes away satisfied because their expectations have been fulfilled.

> It was out of necessity that the structure had to be non-linear in order to keep the audience guessing. This allowed us to jump to this and then jump to that. My big influences were definitely the construction of *Memento* along with the Twilight Zone mystery aspect. Coming to terms with non-linear construction was a crystallizing moment as I started to write.
>
> James Darling

It's not always necessary to work within a confined time period to create a successful story. *Le Poulet (The Chicken)*, a 15-minute Academy Award–winning short film written and directed by Claude Berri (B&W, 1963), takes place over a period of days. *Le Poulet* is the story of a young French boy who becomes so fond of a rooster that his parents bought for Sunday dinner that he secretly decides to convince them that it's a hen. He steals an egg from the refrigerator and places it under the rooster. This ploy works until one morning when the rooster wakes up the father with its crowing. Frightened that his parents are now going to kill the bird, the boy pleads for its life. The parents, surprised and touched by the boy's attachment, decide to let him keep the bird as a pet.

The story focuses on a single conflict that arises out of the main character's goal to keep the rooster as a pet. That conflict takes place over a week, not hours. The film is told in small vignettes that underscore the young boy's dilemma and how he attempts to resolve it.

One Major Character

Truman, The Lunch Date, and *Citizen* are all approximately 11 minutes long. *Crazy Glue* is half that length. *A Nick in Time* runs about 15 minutes. This is time enough to focus on only one main character. A dilemma is introduced, expanded, and resolved for Truman, the wife in *Crazy Glue*, the woman in *The Lunch Date*, the young man in *Citizen* and the barber in *A Nick in Time*. It's true that the gym coach, the husband, the homeless man, and the young man in *A Nick in Time* go through some sort of change, but only in direct relationship to the main character. They serve as the *antagonist*. They force or initiate the conflict by serving as obstacles to the *protagonist*'s goal. Although there can be other characters, our emotions focus on one person's story in each film. We don't care for the other characters in the same way as we care for the main characters.

When a short film is expanded to 30 minutes, it is possible to deal fully with two characters, although their destinies should be interlocked in some way. An excellent example of a two-character piece is an award-winning short film titled *Minors*, written and directed by Alan Kingsberg (1984, New York University). This film is the story of a teenage girl who needs a subject for her science project and a minor league pitcher struggling to make it to the majors. The story brings these two people together. The girl, who is a baseball fanatic, convinces the pitcher that if she can teach him to throw a curve ball, he will be called up to play in the majors. She puts the pitcher through a training program, and he eventually develops a terrific curve ball. He is called up to the majors, but she is left without a project. He helps her present their pitching experiment as the science project, and it is a success. She passes her science class, and he pitches for the Yankees.

Even though there are two main characters in *Minors*, their goals intersect. Each wants something different, but the success of one is directly tied to the success of the other. The pitcher makes it to the majors because of the student, and she completes her science project because of him.

> What I knew from the script was the basic structure of the events that would happen. The important things to me were that the woman would get bumped, lose her wallet, miss her train, and that she'd enter this restaurant. She'd sit down, get up to get a fork, and come back, and the guy would be there. And they would share a salad, and he would get up and get coffee, and come back, and ta da. I had to figure out how I was going to reveal her mistake. That was the framework that I had. Then the lines, the bits of action, and the small details would come out of that.
>
> Adam Davidson

Follow-Through

Your main character must be capable of following through with the primary action or story purpose of the film. The conflict cannot be sustained if the character is not relentless in the pursuit of his goal.

The young man in *Citizen* is determined to cross the border. The barber in *A Nick in Time* works hard to convince the young man not to make the mistake of his life. Truman does not give up in his attempts to climb the rope ladder. Neither does the woman give up in her pursuit of "her salad" in *The Lunch Date*. Aristotle established this dramatic principle in his *Poetics* 2,000 years ago. It is this ability to follow through that keeps the audience engaged and the story alive.

Likewise, the antagonist must be a suitable adversary, up to the challenge of the main character. "Unity of opposites" is a common term in dramatic writing. The major characters must be at least evenly matched for conflict to exist. If the antagonist is even stronger than the protagonist is, the audience will question whether the main character will succeed, and when she does, the victory will be that much more satisfying. In *Citizen*, Mother Nature and the border patrol serve as worthy antagonists. The coach is also relentless in his attempts to make Truman climb the rope ladder before he will let the class have some fun. If he let Truman off the hook too easily, there would be no conflict and no story (or it would be much shorter).

Minimum Back Story

What is back story? It is the historical information, or exposition, about the characters that is necessary to understand their motivation during the course of the story. In a short, back story must be communicated quickly and efficiently. A feature film has 30–40 minutes of setup time, but a short has only a few minutes.

The character of the woman in *The Lunch Date* is well defined by her wardrobe, packages, and demeanor. She is a wealthy woman headed back to the suburbs. Her reaction to the street people in Grand Central Station sets up an expectation about how she will react to the man who has "stolen" her lunch. Truman is immediately presented as a young boy with a fear of climbing up a rope. We do not need to know any more about his history to relate to his present situation. A lonely wife in *Crazy Glue* fighting to revive her marriage is someone we can all relate to. The young man in *Citizen* is willing to risk his life to avoid being drafted. There is no need to know any more about these characters to understand the rest of the films.

A Nick in Time cleverly integrates the barber's back story into the fabric of the narrative. It serves two purposes. We learn important exposition about the barber, information that also serves as warning to the young man who may be considering making a big mistake in his life.

If understanding your main character requires the audience to grasp too much information before the story can start, find a clever way to integrate exposition into the body of the story or move on to another idea.

Internal Motives, External Action

Communicating internal problems is one of the challenges of writing for the screen. This is a visual medium. Dramatic events must be manifested through actions and sounds. Truman, the wife in *Crazy Glue*, and the woman from *The Lunch Date* expose their internal conflicts through their actions. Truman's outrageous fantasies are external representations of his fear. The wife in *Crazy Glue* sticks by her marriage, literally. In *The Lunch Date*, the woman's prejudice is revealed when she refuses help from a well-dressed black man. The barber in *A Nick in Time* warns the young man not to do anything that he would regret in an indirect way (because he knows he is cutting the hair of a cop) by telling him a story of his past. These stories throw their characters into unexpected situations. We *see* who they are by the way they *act*.

No Talking Heads

If your story contains a lot of dialogue and very little action or dramatic movement, it might be better as a radio drama or a play. Films are usually about action. The motives of the characters are exposed through their actions. Viewers should be able to watch a film with the sound off and still understand the story. The rule most often quoted is "show, don't tell." *Truman* and *Crazy Glue* have very little dialogue; *The Lunch Date* has little meaningful dialogue. The young man in *Citizen* barely speaks. His actions, willing to risk his life so that he can cross the border to Canada, tell the audience volumes regarding his dedication and commitment. Everything that the barber says to the young man in *A Nick in Time* is supported by a visual dramatization in the past.

The dialogue that exists supports the action, defines the characters, and enhances our appreciation of the images. If you are interested in adapting a play, you will need to "open up" the drama by devising actions and movement to replace many of the words and to create a visual component that doesn't exist on the stage. Documentaries should also seek visual action, rather than depending on one interview after another. Visuals should complement the aural narrative

Images Before Words

The dominant rule about visual storytelling is that if you can show it, don't say it. Many beginners mistakenly think you tell a story with dialogue. A director is aware that on the screen, the actor's face itself becomes part of the dialogue. A well-placed close-up could serve better than a word or phrase; an image usually speaks louder than any word. Dialogue supports the plot movement; it doesn't supersede that movement. Use the words to enhance, not replace, an image.

Movies SHOW…and then TELL. A true movie is likely to be 60 to 80 percent comprehensible if the dialogue is in a foreign language.

Alexander Mackendrick, director and screenwriter, *The Sweet Smell of Success*, *The Man in the White Suit*

Scripts are usually overwritten because writers feel the need to put it all in. It is the director's job to trim the "fat" (unnecessary words or actions). In *The Lunch Date*, the original screenplay called for the woman to be accosted by a homeless person on her way to the train after the salad incident. She was to tell the man, "Get a job!" The scene was shot because it was in the script, but it is not in the final film. In the film, the woman is approached by a homeless man on her way to the train, but she completely ignores him. Why? This physical slight seemed to the director far more potent a gesture than the words "Get a job!" Addressing the man acknowledges that he exists; ignoring him treats him as if he doesn't exist.

Collaboration

Working with a Writer

Some producers can write, and some can't. If writing is not your strength, develop your script with a writer who can effectively put your ideas on paper. You might become a cowriter or act in a supervisory role. Most producers follow the latter path unless they are confident writers themselves. The give-and-take between two creative individuals can energize the process, resulting in a union in which the sum is greater than the parts.

During the process of developing and producing a project, producers work with many different kinds of creative people. No two egos are alike. Learning how to maximize people's varied talents is essential to becoming a good producer. The writer is the first of these individuals.

> We wrote the idea, my writing partner and I with whom I went to school, Tina Landsmark. We got together and wrote the short story. We put it together and we went through several, several drafts of it to get it to the point where we actually submitted it to a couple of contests. We ended up winning one for the Organization of Black Screen Writers. We won for Best Short Film. It proved we could tell a story.
>
> Be' Garrett

Any agreement with a writer to develop an idea, whether it is the writer's idea or yours, should be formalized on paper in a deal memo (see our web site). Once a director is brought on board, it will then be the responsibility of the producer to supervise the collaboration between the director and the writer (if the director is not going to personally rewrite the script herself).

Rewriting

The axiom "writing is rewriting" is true. Stories go through evolutionary stages. They are like puzzles, worked at until all the pieces fit together. The goal is to find the right balance among the elements. Each draft reveals something that was hidden in the previous version.

Professionals know that creating a well-crafted script takes time, patience, and devotion. The key is to get it right before walking on the set. Don't hope to work out script problems during the heat of production. During preproduction, you have the time. Take it.

> I counted 13 drafts altogether, but I don't think that is a lot of drafts for a 10-minute film. Part of it is due to the fact that the short film form is not necessarily a very natural writing form; it's sort of a sonnet. It's very tough. Thirteen drafts is pretty much the average. Looking back through my files, it's clear that in each draft the story became shorter and clearer and also moved closer to becoming a shooting script.
>
> Howard McCain

What Is the Story About?

You have found a short story that you love and want to adapt; there is a screenplay that you are interested in producing; you have been developing several ideas with a writer and have a draft that you are in the process of reworking. Knowing and understanding the basics of the short form, you and your writer are ready to test the dramatic and visual potential of any of these projects. Equally important to scrutinize: is it an idea best suited for the short form? Many beginners try to squeeze a feature film concept into a short film script. These projects do not turn out very well.

This next step involves picking apart the story to discover the relationship between the characters, plot, and theme. Read the story or script over two or three times so it is firmly in your head.

Ask these questions:

- What do you feel after you have read the story? Why does the story move you?
- What does it say about the human condition? Do you identify with the theme?
- Are you able to tell what happens in the story in one sentence?
- Whose story is it? What does the main character want?
- How much of the story is developed through internal thoughts and feelings?
- Does the main character change? If so, is that change demonstrated externally through action?

Find Your Plot and Characters

To find the plot (what actually happens), strip the story of its dialogue and internal monologues (what the characters are thinking and feeling). This will reveal the dramatic through line of your story. Once you have eliminated what you can't see or hear, what do you have? Is there a single action that unites the incidents of the story? Do you have a character who wants something? Is there conflict? Is there a beginning, middle, and end?

The well-to-do women in *The Lunch Date*, the boy in *Truman*, the wife in *Crazy Glue*, the barber in *A Nick in Time*, and the young man in *Citizen* are defined by what they do and say. Their actions represent their internal life. Among the three films, only *Truman* attempts to get inside the head of the main character. Truman's fears are illustrated by his colorful, dramatic, and funny fantasies. We know Truman is scared, but these fantasies bring us closer to what he is experiencing

In Tatia Rosenthal's adaptation of Keret's story *Crazy Glue*, a frustrated wife takes a creative approach to livening up her sexual connection with her husband who has been playing around with another woman. She glues herself to the ceiling. This is the action that defines the story and the main character. However, there is a subtle difference between the structure of the story and the film. The short story is told through the husband's point of view. Tatia shifted the focus and presented the action through the wife's point of view in the film. It is now her story.

Crazy Glue
By Etgar Keret

She said, "Don't touch that."

"What is it?" I asked.

"It's glue," she said. "Special glue. The best kind."

"What did you buy it for?"

"Because I need it," she said. "A lot of things around here need gluing."

"Nothing around here needs gluing," I said. "I wish I understood why you buy all this stuff."

"For the same reason I married you," she murmured. "To help pass the time."

I didn't want to fight, so I kept quiet, and so did she.

Continued

Crazy Glue—cont'd

"Is it any good, this glue?" I asked. She showed me the picture on the box, with this guy hanging upside-down from the ceiling.

"No glue can really make a person stick like that," I said. "They just took the picture upside-down. They must have put a lamp on the floor." I took the box from her and peered at it. "And there, look at the window. They didn't even bother to hang the blinds the other way. They're upside-down, if he's really standing on the ceiling. Look," I said again, pointing to the window. She didn't look.

"It's eight already," I said. "I've got to run." I picked up my briefcase and kissed her on the cheek. "I'll be back pretty late. I'm working—"

"Overtime," she said. "Yes, I know."

I called Abby from the office.

"I can't make it today," I said. "I've got to get home early."

"Why?" Abby asked. "Something happen?"

"No... I mean, maybe. I think she suspects something."

There was a long silence. I could hear Abby's breathing on the other end.

"I don't see why you stay with her," she whispered. "You never do anything together. You don't even fight. I'll never understand it." There was a pause, and then she repeated, "I wish I understood." She was crying.

"I'm sorry. I'm sorry, Abby. Listen, someone just came in," I lied. "I've got to hang up. I'll come over tomorrow. I promise. We'll talk about everything then."

I got home early. I said "Hi" as I walked in, but there was no reply. I went through all the rooms in the house. She wasn't in any of them. On the kitchen table I found the tube of glue, completely empty. I tried to move one of the chairs, to sit down. It didn't budge. I tried again. Not an inch. She'd glued

it to the floor. The fridge wouldn't open. She'd glued it shut. I didn't understand what was happening, what would make her do such a thing. I didn't know where she was. I went into the living-room to call her mother's. I couldn't lift the receiver; she'd glued that too. I kicked the table and almost broke my toe. It didn't even budge.

And then I heard her laughing. It was coming from somewhere above me. I looked up, and there she was, standing barefoot on the living room ceiling.

I stared openmouthed. When I found my voice I could only ask, "What the hell...are you out of your mind?"

She didn't answer, just smiled. Her smile seemed so natural, with her hanging upside-down like that, as if her lips were just stretching on their own by the sheer force of gravity.

"Don't worry, I'll get you down," I said, hurrying to the shelf and grabbing the largest books. I made a tower of encyclopedia volumes and clambered on top of the pile.

"This may hurt a little," I said, trying to keep my balance. She went on smiling. I pulled as hard as I could, but nothing happened. Carefully, I climbed down.

"Don't worry," I said. "I'll get the neighbors or something. I'll go next door and call for help."

"Fine," she laughed. "I'm not going anywhere."

I laughed too. She was so pretty, and so incongruous, hanging upside-down from the ceiling that way. With her long hair dangling downwards, and her breasts molded like two perfect teardrops under her white T-shirt. So pretty. I climbed back up onto the pile of books and kissed her. I felt her tongue on mine. The books tumbled out from under my feet, but I stayed floating in midair, hanging just from her lips.

Translated by Miriam Shlesinger

The story you are interested in adapting may include several characters but no leading contender for the main one. In the Raymond Carver story "Are These Actual Miles," a man in desperate financial straits spends a day in his house, while his wife is out trying to sell their car and his kids are with their grandparents. Nothing actually happens inside his home. The man sits around and drinks and mulls over how he and his family got into the fix they are in. The action or plot of the story (selling the car) takes place somewhere else, and his and our only contact with its progress is through the telephone. The bulk of the story, however, is internal and communicated through the man's thoughts and feelings while he waits for his wife to come back. Although, as written, it is the husband's story because the world is seen through his eyes, the wife is the only active character.

Make the Internal External

The Carver story underscores one of the ways literature differs in its capacity to explore internal conflict and the human condition. In "Are These Actual Miles," the narrative unfolds inside the main character's mind as he thinks about the events leading up to that day. The richness and descriptive nature of the language and original writing style keep us engaged and involved, but nothing really happens. Our primary information in a filmed story should be communicated through the characters' actions, not their thoughts. If we filmed Carver's story as is, we would spend 15 minutes in a room watching a passive, unsympathetic man drink and mull over his fate while his wife desperately tries to sell their car for much needed funds.

The types of stories to look for that externalize the drama and translate more effectively to the screen are in the vein of those written by the great American short story writer O. Henry, the pen name of William Sydney Porter (1862–1910). O. Henry stories are known for their wit and colorful characterizations but mostly for their surprise twist endings, to the point that such an ending is often referred to as an "O. Henry ending." Many of his stories take place in New York City, and deal for the most part with ordinary people: clerks, policemen, and waitresses.

You can pick up a selection of his stories or rent *O. Henry's Full House*, the 1952 feature film featuring the dramatization of five of his stories. The following are short synopses of two stories that are included in the film.

"The Gift of the Magi" is about a young married couple who are short of money but desperately want to buy each other Christmas gifts. Unbeknownst to Jim, Della sells her most valuable possession, her beautiful hair, in order to buy a platinum fob chain for Jim's watch; while unbeknownst to Della, Jim sells his own most valuable possession, his watch, to buy jeweled combs for Della's hair. "The Ransom of Red Chief" is about two men who kidnap a boy of 10 for ransom. The boy turns out to be so bratty and obnoxious that the desperate men ultimately pay the boy's father $250 to take him back.

Dramatic Expectations

Question the dramatic expectations of the material. Do they exceed the short form? In 6–30 minutes, can you expect us to believe that your character could arrive at a major life decision? Will the young man in *A Nick in Time* take the barber's advice? Will Truman climb the rope ladder? Will the woman be able to eat her salad? Will the wife fight for her husband? Will the young man in *Citizen* make it across the border? These are attainable goals within 12 minutes. Could we expect the woman to change her attitude toward the homeless in 12 minutes of screen time? Certainly not. In fact, as she leaves the cafeteria, she completely ignores a homeless man asking for spare change, and as she enters the train, she collapses in relief. That is not to say change can't happen, but it must be small in scope. We must believe it could happen in the short "screen time" we have with these characters

What Do You Do Now?

You have dissected your story or screenplay completely. If your screenplay meets the requirements we have outlined in this chapter, you can look to bring a director on board. If you have been examining a short story for dramatic potential, you must ask these questions: Do you have a story that will translate to the screen? Does this wonderful literary property you have fallen in love with fulfill the dramatic requirements of a film story?

If so, now comes the specific craft of adaptation. How creative you and your writer will have to be will be based on the nature of the story. Tatia Rosenthal had little to do other than shift the point of view. In Rosenthal's short film *Crazy Glue*, the wife is now the active character who, faced with a marriage problem, decides to do something about it. In Carver's story, we suspect a great deal would have to be done. The following section provides some general guidelines to follow.

General Guidelines for Adaptation

Film and literature are separate media; they shouldn't have to compete with one another. Neither film nor theater can surpass the power of literature to explore the internal life of the characters, but what a film can offer that a book cannot is powerful images (as well as a creative use of sounds). The idea that a picture is worth a thousand words rings true. The camera has the ability to see into the soul of the character and read her true intentions. With film dialogue, what is not said, the subtext, is often far more meaningful than the words themselves.

These are some general guidelines to follow as you or your writer tackles the adaptation of your story:

- Find the dramatic spine of your story.
- Be aware of the economy of time, place, and action.
- Be true to the essence or spirit of the story.
- Be willing to reinvent.
- Keep it simple.
- Make it your story.

Short stories can be episodic and take place over decades. There may be many characters with many goals. Keep the action focused in time (a short as possible), in place (as few locations as possible), and in action (one plot line). *Truman* and *The Lunch Date* take place over an hour at best; *Crazy Glue*, over two days. *A Nick in Time* takes place over the span of one haircut. In each of these stories, there is one main character with one goal in one to two locations. The time frame of *Citizen* is centered on two actions: the physical examination, which takes only a few minutes, and the character's quest to cross the border, which takes approximately a day and a night.

Probably the biggest hurdle to overcome is the feeling that you are obligated to the author of the story (or in case of a true story, the facts) to retain as much as possible of the structure and dialogue of the story. This is a normal reaction, but one that will not result in the best adaptation.

The goal is to create an organic piece, not one that has been constructed piecemeal from another medium. You are out to make the best motion picture possible and one that will retain all the emotions of the story, it is hoped, but presented in a different package. Achieving this is the goal of adaptation. The enormity of the task will depend entirely on the nature of the story you have chosen. The lesson from this section: look for material with active characters.

True Stories and Events

Follow the lessons of literary adaptation if you have the rights to a true story or something that happened to you, a friend, or a member of your family that you thought would be the foundation of a screenplay.

Don't be seduced by the notion of "this is really what happened." Mark Twain once said, "Why shouldn't truth be stranger than fiction? Fiction, after all, has to stick to possibilities." The events of life are arbitrary, strange, and unpredictable. It is the artist's job to manipulate those facts to satisfy the dramatic need of the story.

Use an event as a springboard to develop a character. Just like Howard McCain used the rope ladder to express an event that could have happened to anyone of us and to explore a child's fear, look inside the event that you would like to express in a film. What does it mean to you? What truth does it reveal about life, and what do you have to do to manipulate the event to make that truth self-evident?

DIRECTOR

Supervising or Performing Rewrites

When the screenplay is well into development, the producer brings in the next important member of the creative team: the director (unless she is also the writer). The producer seeks an individual who is aware of the material's dramatic potential and shares or complements the producer's vision. The director will shepherd the script through the final stages of development, supervising the rewrites or completing them herself and freeing the producer to focus on fundraising and preproduction.

The director puts her personal stamp on all projects through the creative decisions she makes along the way, such as guiding the actors, approving the choice of crew and locations, and determining the visual style. She provides the creative glue that holds the project together. However, the foundation on which all else is built is the script. A director who writes or rewrites the script or collaborates with the writer contributes her personalized vision to the project. In so doing, she should ensure that the final draft is the best it can be. After all, any story worth telling is worth telling well.

Working with the Writer

If the producer has developed the script with a writer, several important decisions are made at this point. If the writer has been paid to turn in several versions of the script, the producer has the right to terminate the relationship and bring in the director to take on the responsibilities of rewriting the script. However, if all parties are pleased with the progress of the script, the writer will now work with the director to complete whatever work has yet to be done. It makes sense to keep a writer whose work has been good, but a writer can become creatively dry and be unable to further enhance a project. Also,

the director and the writer may not be able to see eye to eye on how to solve the creative challenges of the script. At this point, the director can either take over the writing responsibilities or request that another writer be brought on.

Up to this point, the writer has supplied the creative direction for the project. His vision, coupled with the producer's, has governed the direction of the screenplay. With a director on board, it will be her vision that guides the project. Depending on how much work has to be done (from polish to complete rewrite), the progress made will depend on the creative relationship between the writer and the director. The success of this collaboration is key, and it is the producer's job ultimately to see that the project is best served by this union.

STUDENTS

It is our experience that most students want to write their own scripts. They feel that it is not "their story" if they don't. However, the failure of many student projects is most often the result of script, not directorial, problems. There are writers, there are directors, and there are some who can do both. Recognizing where your talent lies is a part of the learning experience. Developing a relationship with a writer in a film school setting will more accurately mirror what will happen in the professional world, where directors usually don't write their own scripts but sometimes must work with many writers on a single project.

Director as Storyteller

The director must evaluate whether the story is being told properly. Is the present draft the best realization of the central theme or concept behind the story? If the script needs work, the director must work with the writer or apply her own storytelling skills to reshape the screenplay.

The work to be done might vary from a slight "polish" (minor dialogue changes) to a complete rewrite (restructuring the story). If the script is in relatively good shape, the director need only prepare it to be photographed by creating a **shooting script**. This process requires numbering the scenes to reflect the (See figure 4.2 in Chapter 4) locations. Each scene is given a number to make the breakdown of the screenplay precise. When this stage has been completed, the real work of preproduction can begin—that is, the stripboard, budget, and schedule.

Elements other than story content and structure can influence the development of the screenplay. The director might be inspired by a location, a particular actor, or the work being done during rehearsals. While scouting locations, she might come upon a unique setting that inspires a rewrite of a particular scene or even the whole story. After hearing a strong performer read a part, the director might decide to shape the character to better fit the talents of that actor. Some directors use the rehearsal period to clarify and sharpen character development or to find dialogue that feels more natural to each character's voice.

> It's always, I think, about discovering the story. You write it on paper. You rewrite it. Then you start shooting it. You shoot a lot. You start editing the film together and then— where's the story? So you've got to find it all over again. You start editing things out, changing things around slightly.
>
> Adam Davidson

Story Questions

When you analyze your story/script, these are questions to keep in mind:

Who is the main character? For a short film, it is best to focus on no more than one character's story.

What does he/she want? **Is it clear what the character's goal is?** Is it tangible and specific? Love, respect, and honor are worthy goals, but can they be accomplished in 20 minutes?

What are the stakes? How important is it for characters to get what they want? What does it mean to them?

Is the main character's goal achievable (and believable) within 15–30 minutes?

Is your main character actively pursuing his goal in every scene? Are the characters active versus passive?

What is the conflict? What are the obstacles preventing the main character from getting what he wants? Have you identified an antagonist?

Can we ultimately believe that the character can achieve the goal at the end of the film? Is the climax satisfying and believable?

Scene Analysis

How does each scene:

Advance the story and expand our awareness of the characters and the conflict?

Follow from the previous scene?

Lead to the next scene (the importance of transitions)?

Advance the arc of the character(s)—what do we know that we didn't before?

Feel rhythmically?

Change the relationship between the characters?

Give information to characters?

Give information to the audience?

Resolve the dramatic need of the main character?

> I was amazed at how hard it is to have a cohesive story come across and be moving, or even clear. I think I was so terrified by my live action film experiences in the early years of film school that I went into animation in order to hone my story-telling skills in a more contained environment.
>
> Tatia Rosenthal

Readings

Once the script is close to being finalized, the director should conduct readings to audition the material. It is one thing to write a line on paper, but quite another to hear that line read aloud or see it performed by an actor under a director's guidance. What the director and actor want to discover is whether the lines ring true. How do the words flow off the tongue? Are there too many words or too few? Is the space between the words (pauses) more poignant than the words themselves?

After you live with a project for such a long time, it becomes difficult to analyze what comes off the page because you know too much. You have all this back story swimming in your brain and expect that we know the characters as well as you do. You know how to read between the lines. We don't. You must be able to take a step back and be critical about what each scene tells us, not what you hope it tells us.

> We had a good script in the beginning, and by the time we had gotten to the point of actual principal photography, we had figured out the arc of each person's story.
>
> Be' Garrett

The Shooting Script

Having supervised the rewrite or having rewritten the screenplay herself, the director must now develop the shooting script, which is a visual plan for the project. This draft is written in the standard format of the Writers Guild of America and has markings and numbers that communicate the director's vision to the producer and the camera and art departments. Up to this point, it has not been important for the script to reflect shots or visual references. The emphasis has been on structure, character, and dialogue.

The first step is to number each scene, enabling the production team to identify each scene by its numbered code. The director then previsualizes the script; that is, she creates a shooting plan for each scene. The plan should reflect how the director will "cover" each scene in the project. The term **coverage** refers to the amount and type of shots the director will need to tell the story adequately in each scene. Developing a shot plan requires that the director break down the script and create floor plans, storyboards, or both. (See Chapter 3 for more information.)

The director then marks the script with her shot plan. It will include abbreviations such as *CU* (close-up, a very tight shot on an object or a character's face), *LS* (long shot, in which the camera takes in a lot of visual information), *2S* (two-shot, in which two characters are in the frame at the same time), and *OTS* (over-the-shoulder shot, which is like a two-shot except that the camera favors the face of one of the two characters).

The shooting script gives the producer information from which to construct an accurate schedule. The rest of the production team obtains from the shooting script a point of view from which to design the project.

How Do Scripts Affect Budgets?

To begin fundraising, the producer needs to have an accurate budget that reflects the complete cost of producing the script. Changes in the script that affect the budget must be examined at this stage. Suppose, for example, the writer describes a character's interaction with another in a crowded restaurant. The extras become one of the many items that must be delivered to the set on the day when the particular scene is to be shot. The producer looks at the script and says to himself, "Where do I get the 50 extras? Won't it require extra makeup personnel? Where am I going to get the costumes? Where am I going to hold them? How much food will be required? How much will it add to the budget?"

Aware of budget constraints and responsible for the schedule, the producer might ask that a more manageable and less expensive solution be found. If the story is not compromised, an outdoor table, which is a smaller, well lit, and a less expensive production item, could replace a crowded restaurant. The producer should request this substitution during preproduction rather than on the day before the scene is to be shot.

Sometimes, compromises cannot be made without adversely affecting the project. In *The Lunch Date*, for example, one location could not be compromised. Grand Central Station is a very expensive location, but it had to be secured for two days of shooting. The film would not have had the same impact if it had been shot in the train station at Stamford, Connecticut.

> From its inception I wrote the script knowing that I did not have a lot of money. So, I would say for young filmmakers the thing to do and what I learned when I came out of film school, was write a script that is doable. Write a script that you know I can use x amount of dollars if I can get my hands on it to shoot this.
>
> Be' Garrett

Animation

Live action usually starts with a script and then a breakdown, which is often followed by storyboarding. An animator will often start with concept sketches and a short treatment followed by an elaborate storyboarding process. Live action boards often block out the basic shots in a scene. Animation boards frequently show every "beat" of the scene. There can be a new beat with every change in emotion or significant character movement. For animation, specific production notes often accompany the boards. Animators often use the boards and sketches as guides to build a rough animation known as an animatic. The animatic can have crude details and unrefined movement. It is meant to resolve issues of blocking, composition, and, most important, timing. Because CG character modeling and setup take such a long time, studios often produce the animatic while primary modeling is still under way.

> A crucial question I always ask myself before setting out to make any film is, is this subject eminently "filmable" and uniquely appropriate to be treated in film? While I'm making a film, I try to foreground that issue to ensure that I am exploiting (in a good way) the unique properties of film—the interface of sound and image, and an opportunity to frame things differently from how one normally processes the world.
>
> Jan Krawitz

Documentaries

Because the development and execution of a documentary (nonfiction narrative) might take months or even years, be sure to choose subject matter about which you feel strongly and have a great desire to learn more. You might need to do extensive research to determine whether the subject matter warrants making a short film. You might have to view films or videos on the same or similar subjects, research newspaper and magazine articles, or conduct pre-interviews. (An excellent collection of documentary shorts is distributed by the Full Frame Documentary Film Festival.)

There are a few basic questions to consider when you have found a subject that you believe is worth pursuing:

- What is the subject's underlying significance to me?
- What is unusual and interesting about it?
- Are there compelling characters?
- Where is the specialness really visible?
- Do the characters or the story move the heart?
- Is there food for thought and or inspiration?
- Is there a story?
- What can I show?
- Why do it (at all)?
- Why do it now?

The subject matter should contain inherent dramatic value that engages the viewer in the same way a narrative story does, but with real, not imagined, events. This could be an examination of an individual's or a group's struggle to overcome adversities. There also must be filmic possibilities to support the interviews, a corresponding visual story that complements the aural.

> I thought I was interested in this whole notion of the "ideal" and how women in our culture are tyrannized by the belief that there exists an ideal body type and that it is ultimately unattainable. I wanted to present the ideal as something not fixed in stone, but as a representation of something separate and different from all of us. I was interested in the vagaries of the ideal. So I began to read a lot of books about concepts of beauty during different decades, trying to identify the prescriptions for this ideal type. I read about how the White Rock girl, who adorned bottles of White Rock, was redesigned every decade so that her dimensions would reflect the changing concepts of the perfect physical type.
>
> Jan Krawitz

From research notes, an outline for the documentary can be created. This outline serves as the genesis of a script during preproduction. From the outline, a series of questions is prepared for each interview. The combination of on-camera interviews, stock footage, and cinema verité (in some cases, staged events) constitutes the visual components of the piece.

It is acceptable to write out the script in its entirety. This includes creating the answers you anticipate recording. By writing out the script, you can prepare questions that will help your subject respond according to your design. This gives the director a target during the interviews. The questions might be answered very differently than you expected, but together with the subject, you can explore fully the issues at hand.

> A lot of documentarists, and particularly women, have moved into fiction films after 5 or 10 years. They say, I got tired of sitting around waiting for people to say what I wanted them to say. I always find that so interesting because for me, that's why I will stay in documentary—because you never know what people are going to say, and I really like the unpredictability of it.
>
> Jan Krawitz

Depending on the subject, the questions you compose can be easy or provocative. If the subject is forthcoming with the information required, the questions can be probing but cordial. If the subject needs to be drawn out, a more provocative approach might be required.

> I asked my 13 subjects the same set of four questions, changing the composition for each question. I knew that I would intercut their responses, relying on a jump-cut technique. One question was, "Describe your body from head to foot, discussing different parts as you go." Some women would start with their hair, and were very diligent about hitting every body part, and some people would start with their neck and jump to their knees, and that was okay. If they did that, I didn't ask them to talk about their breasts, waist, or hips.
>
> It was quite revealing to observe what they chose to talk about or ignore. Some parts were complimented, and some parts were totally derided. A second question was, "If you could redesign your body to conform to the concept of your ideal, what would it look like?" I didn't realize it at the time, but the two questions are essentially the same. Because while they were redesigning, they might say, "I really hate my shoulders," for example, and that was an answer to the earlier question.
>
> Jan Krawitz

The final script for a documentary can be fully developed only in postproduction. With all the visual and audio materials in hand, the director begins to grasp the shape that the film will eventually take. The audio portion of the show will be the voices from the on- and off-camera interviews, the track of the verité footage, any audiotape recorded, and possibly a narration. The assemblage of these audio elements, especially the narration (if applicable), becomes the final script.

Developing a Web Presence

In the same way that you are developing your short film idea, you can simultaneously be researching the possibilities of actively using the Internet to promote awareness of your project, raise funds, reach out to cast and crew, and eventually serve as a distribution outlet. The Internet can be used as a tool to whatever extent you wish to use it. We will be outlining all the possibilities throughout the book (Our web site will contain a link to how a web presence can be developed and utilized). It is up to you, the filmmaker, to decide to what extent you wish to avail yourself of its possibilities.

As you develop your short film idea, you can

- Create a plan for your site.
- Explore different designs.
- Create a site flow chart.
- Develop a trailer for the project.

This is a team project and, of course, you will require someone to serve as web designer. Given the technical know-how of most young people today, this should not be a problem. It is, however, one more key individual to be a part of the production team.

KEY POINTS

- Without a good script, you cannot have a good final product.

- Proper format has a direct bearing on the production breakdowns.
- Good scripts are not written; they are rewritten.
- Understand the short form. As the feature is to the epic poem, the short is to the haiku.

Chapter 2

Finance

We basically put a lot of things on credit cards—my credit cards.

Adam Davidson

PRODUCER

Raising the Capital

If there is one role with which the producer is traditionally associated, it is the role of fundraiser. The producer finds the money to fund the film. This role is paramount because money is the lifeblood of any project. In fact, without adequate financing, there is no project. However simple the production demands might seem, it is impossible to produce something for nothing.

Most beginners get turned on by romantic notions and the tantalizing creative possibilities of the visual media, but they soon find out that much of their time and energy are focused on raising funds. Independent filmmakers spend much of their time filling out grant applications, writing to investors, and organizing fundraisers. Howard McCain, Tatia Rosenthal, Adam Davidson, and Jan Krawitz struggled to secure financing for their projects. James Darling used a trust fund, and Be' Garrett relied on family and favors from people he had worked with. For Jan, it was a process that lasted years.

> I wrote a lot of grants over the years, and I finally got the first grant in the spring of '87. Initial money came from the Paul Robeson Fund for Film and Video. I only had two grants when I began shooting, and the subsequent three came during postproduction. I think that's significant, because I find it's always a little easier to get funding once you have something to show from the project.
>
> Jan Krawitz

Basic Fundraising Problems

You can expect to encounter two basic problems in funding your projects. The first is the potential of either a sizable return on an investment or no return at all. Overwhelming odds support the latter. Suffice it to say that the market for short films is financially anemic. (This problem is discussed at length in Chapter 19.)

The second problem you will face is lack of experience. How do you persuade an investor to finance a first-time producer or director, someone who has yet to complete a project or, at best, has only a minimal track record? To look at it another way, would you hire a contractor who had never built a house?

All novices confront these two major obstacles as they start out to create their first films. The problem of inexperience is no less real or daunting than the problem of a limited market, but the producer and director definitely have more control over it. Although it might seem like a catch-22—the "Can't get a job without experience, can't get experience without a job" syndrome—there are specific ways to overcome this seemingly insurmountable obstacle. Each year, many young filmmakers with little experience but with lots of ingenuity, energy, and verve are able to persuade investors to believe in their talent and trust them to manage their dollars responsibly.

There is no secret formula for raising money successfully. In the pursuit of funding, you are almost guaranteed to come up against tremendous odds and constant rejection. Many potential investors will say no before one says yes. Some may even say yes at first and then change their minds. To sustain excitement for your beloved project after weeks, months, and sometimes years of effort demands a strong belief in yourself, the utmost patience and perseverance, and an unbridled passion for the medium and your message.

> We were doing *Lunch Date* cheaper than you would generally do a student film. Generally, I would estimate $1,000 a minute. This project was definitely budgeted for less. Adam didn't have a lot of money, and he didn't want to spend a lot of money. I think originally he wanted to spend $5,000 because it was going to be a fun project to do. He had a little extra money, and he wanted to make this film. It ended up costing more because in postproduction he wanted to spend that money. He wanted to get a good sound editor and get good music and do a good mix. But he always had the option to not do that, to just finish it cheaply, do his own sound editing and mix.
>
> Garth Stein, Producer of *The Lunch Date*

doi: 10.1016/B978-0-240-81174-1.00009-9

How Much Money Will You Need?

A short narrative film can cost somewhere between $500 and $100,000. The variables that impact your budget are the nature and complexity of the screenplay, the resources of the filmmaker (what you can get for free), what is provided by a student filmmaker's school (equipment, stages, personal, post facilities, etc.), the availability of professional and affordable digital tools, whether originating on film or video, and finally, the intended workflow. It can be tricky to determine how much a film really costs if in-kind services have been provided (see below). Professional shoots, especially those using several unions, will certainly come in on the high budget range. (For more on these topics, see Chapter 5.)

The cost of originating on film (stock and processing) is normally more expensive than shooting video, but rental houses, eager to keep young filmmakers shooting film, are offering deals on super 16 and 35mm equipment and Kodak has been known to donate film stock. Digital media, on the other hand, although cheaper on the front end, can have hidden costs along the way, depending on what format the filmmaker is intending to finish on.

> So, I wrote letters and made calls to both Fugi and Kodak. We were going to shoot on whoever would give us more. Kodak donated 8,000 feet of film on 35.
>
> James Darling

The tools in this book will give you a measure of control to understand the costs of producing a short film. Every project is unique and handmade. You start with an idea, how much you can spend, and you work from there.

> Total funding for *Mirror Mirror* was $12,000, and the final budget through release prints and a one-inch, but not including festival entry fees, was $14,300. The film stock, processing, location travel expenses, and the cinematographer's salary were the major production expenses. A lot of money went to research and acquisition of the archival footage. And all the postproduction costs, sound mix and all of that, probably ate up $4,000 or $5,000. Easy.
>
> Jan Krawitz

Funding Options

Both students and independent filmmakers can employ similar methods for raising funds. However, some opportunities available to students are not open to independents and vice versa. For example, some students can take advantage of their university's tax-exempt status without having to create a not-for-profit business entity. In certain urban centers like New York, Boston, or Los Angeles, there are arts organizations that will serve as fiscal sponsors offering investors tax exemptions for contributions to your project. In addition, students work in a supportive environment with resources such as equipment and a sizable pool of free and willing labor. Independents must put their production teams together from scratch. On the other hand, student filmmakers are almost completely shut out of the grant world.

There are no rules when it comes to finding money. If you win the lottery, use it to finance your project. Putting the lottery windfall aside, the following sections describe possible sources of money for short films and videos.

> It was a struggle to stay at NYU financially and then I was awarded the Universal Studios Fellowship my senior year. That took care of tuition so the money my family and I had been saving to pay for that last year could now be put towards my thesis film. That was my starting capital.
>
> I then did a variety of fund-raising screenings in NY and Toronto, but those were not terribly successful. Most of the money I did get came after I had a cut of my film. I didn't have to pay for any post production costs. The money came from post grants from NYU and from the The Television Producers, Writers and Directors Caucus Foundation in LA.
>
> I was also able to get donations from friends who had attended the fund-raising screenings but who had not been able to give me anything at the time. Some had since gotten banking jobs and could now help me out. The most important advice from all this: stay in touch with friends and family. You will discover that a lot of your friends from high school are following more stable and lucrative careers, while your film school college friends are just as desperate and broke as you are.
>
> James Darling

Private Investors

Private investors include any individuals who are interested in investing in your project. They might be friends, family members, or associates—even complete strangers. Some people might invest because they want to see you succeed even though they understand they might not see a return on their investment. Others might be looking for a tax shelter, and still others might be shrewd business people who believe in the investment opportunities and market potential of your project.

Fiscal Sponsorship

Fiscal sponsorship status allows the filmmaker to receive charitable deductible contributions from individuals—a major incentive for those considering making a donation to your project. For a donor to receive a tax credit, that donation must be given to a bona fide nonprofit organization, known by the IRS classification as a 501(c)(3). The filmmaker can either create her own 501(c)(3) organization (which is very time consuming and expensive) or find a fiscal sponsor that already has 501(c)(3) status.

A fiscal sponsor can be any organization that already has nonprofit status, including media arts centers, hospitals, schools, or associations. The sponsor acts like a non-profit tax-exempt umbrella that accepts and administers contributions and provides limited financial and legal oversight for your project. Once sponsored in this way, the filmmaker is eligible to solicit and receive grants and tax-deductible contributions that are normally available only to 501(c)(3) organizations. The sponsor is legally responsible for the funds received on behalf of the fiscally sponsored project. However, this does not mean that the sponsor is connected to the content or actual production. All artistic and proprietary rights, title, and interest in and to the completed project will belong to the filmmaker.

Simply put, the sponsor will accept a check for your project. The check is made out to the fiscal sponsor with your project as the beneficiary in the note section at the bottom of the check. Then the sponsor deposits that check and returns most of the money back to the filmmaker. The sponsor and the filmmaker negotiate the fee that will be kept by the umbrella organization. An average range is between 5 percent and 10 percent. Some well-known fiscal sponsors for filmmakers include

Bay Area Video Coalition and San Francisco Film Society (San Francisco)
Center for Independent Documentary, Filmmakers Collaborative and Documentary Educational Resources (Boston)
Chicago Filmmakers (Chicago)
From the Heart Productions, International Documentary Association (Los Angeles)
New York Foundation for the Arts, Arts Engine, Fractured Atlas, Make Movies (New York)
Southern Documentary Fund (North Carolina)

To help you locate more sponsors, the San Francisco Study Center, in conjunction with the Tides Center and the National Network of Fiscal Sponsors (NNFS), has created a *Fiscal Sponsor Directory*. You can search by state, service category, or keyword for information on nonprofit fiscal sponsors. Profiles include eligibility requirements, fees, services, and types of projects supported. The directory also provides statistics and resources on fiscal sponsorship.

You can also use the Foundation Center's *Foundation Grants to Individuals*, available in print or as a searchable web-based database, to identify organizations that offer fiscal sponsorships to individuals and non-501(c)(3) non-profit groups.

Most of the listed fiscal sponsors have excellent web sites with detailed information regarding eligibility requirements, fees, past histories, downloadable application forms, etc.

> The big thing I would emphasize is anywhere you can get money is still money. We set the project up with Arts Engine, a non-for-profit organization, so personal donations could be tax deductible. They like to support projects that have "messages". They run a film festival that I was rejected from, even though they helped finance the film.
>
> James Darling

Private Foundation Grants

There are hundreds of private foundations in the United States, but only a few support film and video projects. Finding the ones that might be interested in your particular project requires exploration. The Foundation Center Libraries contain many books that list foundations, their areas of interest, application procedures and grants that have been given in the past, as well as basic books on how to write grants. The Foundation Center maintains cooperating center branches in every major city in the United States. For the one closest to you, call 1-800-424-9836 or visit the web site at www.fdcenter.org. The main branches are in New York City, San Francisco, Washington D.C., Cleveland, and Atlanta.

> The seed money for my film came from a trust fund from my grandmother but the bank misquoted us as to what it was. We learned this about five weeks from our originally scheduled start of principal photography in March 2005. We anticipated shooting a 25 page script for $25,000, following the old thousand-dollars-per-minute rule but learned that the trust was closer to $10,000. I was faced with the choice of doing everything at half of the production level or cutting the script in half and producing it in five weeks.
>
> James Darling

Public Foundation Grants

Some public foundations financed by federal, state, and local governments offer grants and other forms of financial aid to filmmakers. The National Endowment for the Arts (NEA), the National Endowment for the Humanities (NEH), and the American Film Institute (AFI) are three examples.

> I started with \$5,000, and then when I was in the editing stage, I received three more grants of \$3,000, \$2,000, and \$2,000—three grants totaling \$7,000. That was my total outside funding.
>
> Jan Krawitz

It might be easier to secure financing from your home state, city, or town, rather than from national organizations. By tailoring your short project to a particular local issue (especially for documentaries), you have a greater chance of finding financial backing.

Corporate Sponsorship

Private and public corporations sometimes fund films; for example, Mobil and Sony have traditionally backed public television shows. The public relations people at these corporations will guide you through the application process for various proposals. Contact as many companies as you can. To avoid wasting your time, research the types of projects each company has funded in the past.

Bank Loans

Banks will loan almost anyone money if the borrower provides sufficient collateral. Taking out a loan against a car, boat, or house can provide adequate funding for a short film project. The money is not a gift or an investment, and it will have to be paid back with interest.

Personal Savings

If the cost of a short work is not exorbitant, your personal savings might be sufficient. Saving money gradually in an account earmarked for your project might take less time than you think. Although a financial adviser might try to convince you that your savings are for the future or for hard times, investing in yourself is also protecting your future.

> I took money from my savings, I sold my motorcycle, and I borrowed money from my parents. I raised enough to get me through the first stage, which was shooting and developing the rushes.
>
> Adam Davidson

In-Kind Services and Donations

Anything that is given or donated is called **in-kind**. In-kind donations are the equivalent of hard cash. If 70 percent of your total costs are raised as currency and the remainder comes in the form of goods or services, it still equals 100 percent of your budget. Examples of in-kind donations are food from a local restaurant, deferred laboratory fees, reduced car or van rental, and a free location.

These donations are usually given in exchange for a screen credit and for the goodwill. One possible way to acquire in-kind donations is to shoot your project in your hometown. This might prompt newspaper articles with a "hometown boy/girl makes good" slant, inspiring favorable public relations with businesses that could translate into money or in-kind donations.

There is also a practice in the business called **product placement**. This practice involves a producer convincing a manufacturer to donate goods to the production in exchange for featuring its product in a film or video. For example, Ford might loan cars to a production for use both on and off camera with the agreement that Ford cars and trucks be used prominently in the film. Should the producer interest a clothing manufacturer, a similar arrangement might work for costuming.

Other in-kind opportunities exist for independent media artists. Here are some examples:

- Low-cost or free access to production or postproduction equipment and facilities
- Financial support for artists facing work-related personal emergencies
- Information on or assistance with taxes, record keeping, accounting, or financial management
- Free legal advice or referrals (*Volunteer Lawyers for the Arts*)

> I have always been told not to answer and never tell how much it costs. So I am going to stick to that. What I did was, I went to my family. My family has been probably my biggest supporter ever since I decided to have dreams of shooting films. I came to them much like a filmmaker comes and says, "I have a script, I have a budget and I need you all to help me." So, my family basically came in and they gave me money. Not all of it, but I would say about \$20,000 of it. I then went into my own personal savings and pulled up money, and I got close to the budget. After that it was a matter of doing what you do with credit cards and you kind of finance the rest of it.
>
> Be' Garrett

Do Your Research

Organizations all over the world encourage and support short films and videos, but these opportunities come and go. Go to Google and enter "short film funding." The playing field will keep evolving, so make a habit of checking the Internet on a regular basis. If you think that thousands of other filmmakers are hitting the same sites, that's all the more reason to prepare the most professional presentation. You can also find a plethora of short film and video contests. Your reason to make a short may not satisfy the requirements of any of these, but per our advice with film funding sites, keep searching.

The Prospectus

To attract private or corporate support, the producer should create a proposal called a **prospectus**.

The prospectus should excite potential investors by communicating on paper a strong sense of the project in a professional manner. The information gathered for the prospectus can easily be rewritten to fulfill a grant application or tailored to the needs of a specific investor.

The prospectus could contain any of the following elements:

- Cover letter
- Title page
- One-liner
- Table of contents
- Director's statement
- Synopsis of story
- History of project
- Research
- Top sheet of budget
- Production schedule
- Cast list
- Brief résumés of creative team
- Press clippings
- Description of market for project
- Letter from fiscal sponsor (if applicable)
- Letters of support
- Financial statement
- Means of transferring funds

Cover Letter. Use the cover letter to introduce the project to the investor. It can be targeted to all potential investors or slanted to a specific individual. The impression you make with this letter sets the tone for everything that follows. Be clear about what you want. Are you asking for many small investments or donations? What is the total amount of capital you are trying to raise?

The key to a good cover letter when soliciting funds is to tailor each letter to the specific investor/contributor. As the market for short films is limited, an investment will rarely see a return, so the investor must be putting up funds for some other reason. What does the investor want? What is in his best interest?

A wonderful enticement to invest is as a tax deduction. If an investor is in a tax bracket such that he has the option of contributing money to your project through a not-for-profit fiscal sponsor, then the investor

gains something, a tax write-off, as do the filmmakers, production capital.

Following is an example of a cover letter geared toward an investor who wants to both support the filmmaker and be eligible for a tax deduction.

Dear Investor,

This letter will serve as an introduction to my short film titled *Everyman*. Planned for around 15 minutes, this 16mm film is a comedy about a romance between a bum and a princess. Through a series of comical events, we discover that the bum was once a prince and the princess is a phony. But love triumphs, and the film ends on a very happy note.

Everyman is my thesis film here at Citizen's University, and I am seeking funds with which to make the film. The university provides each thesis student with equipment and postproduction facilities. The remainder of the budget, approximately $12,000, is raised by the individual filmmaker—me.

Therefore, I humbly seek your support to make this film a reality. Each dollar contributed to the project is eligible for a tax deduction through the university's Film Production Fund. Simply make out a check to Citizen's University, and specify in the "transferal of funds" document enclosed in this prospectus that you would like the funds to go to my project, *Everyman*.

I am a dedicated filmmaker with a 3.76 GPA. I have made four very short films, a documentary on dog walkers, and an animated short shot on 35mm film. As you can see by the letters of support from my professors, my chances to complete this project successfully are extremely high.

I hope you will take this opportunity to help a budding artist.

Sincerely,

Title Page. A good title conveys the essence of the project. Keep it short; a short title has more punch. Include artwork on the title page that catches the eye and makes an immediate impression. The right image can capture the feel and tone of your piece. Any artwork here or anywhere else in the prospectus must look professional.

One-Liner. A one-liner is a brief and succinct description of your project. It is also known in the industry as a **log line**.

Truman: An 11-year-old boy confronts his imaginary fears while attempting to climb a rope ladder during gym class. (See Figure 2.1.)

The Lunch Date: A well-to-do woman has an unusual encounter with a homeless man while waiting at a train station to return to the suburbs. (See Figure 2.6.)

Mirror Mirror: A documentary featuring women speaking about how they and others perceive their own bodies, intercut with historical footage of how the media emphasizes woman's bodies. (See Figure 2.3.)

FIGURE 2.1   Scene from *Truman*.

FIGURE 2.2   Scene from *Citizen*.

Crazy Glue: An animated clay puppet tells the story of one innovative attempt to patch up a disintegrating marriage—through the use of crazy glue! (See Figure 2.4.)

A Nick in Time: An old school barber recounts an incident from his past to a troubled young man who is on the verge of making a major life-altering decision. But can the barber get through to him before things spiral out of control? (See Figure 2.5.)

Citizen: In an eerie not-too-distant future, a young man tries to escape from his homeland in the dead of winter. As this teenage boy is chased by hunters through the harsh wilderness approaching the border, he recalls the perilous steps of his journey and the fateful doctor's visit that motivated his departure. (See Figure 2.2.)

Table of Contents. This list is necessary if the prospectus is lengthy. It helps potential funders find sections easily.

Director's Statement. Student filmmakers often include a statement about who they are and why they want

FIGURE 2.3 Scene from *Mirror Mirror*.

FIGURE 2.4 Scene from *Crazy Glue*.

to make films. This part speaks to the passion they feel about expressing themselves as visual storytellers and why this project fulfills a dream they have had for years.

Synopsis of Story. The synopsis is a brief narrative of the story's action that moves the plot forward with minimal details. The synopsis is difficult to write because you must capture the flavor of the piece and tell the story at the same time. It is, however, a more effective selling tool than a copy of the script. Most people are distracted by the technical details of the script format. All they require is a story told simply. Following is the synopsis of *The Lunch Date*. You will find the synopses of the rest of our short films in Appendix C and/or on our web site for each film.

FIGURE 2.5   Scene from *A Nick in Time*.

FIGURE 2.6   Scene from *The Lunch Date*.

Synopsis of *The Lunch Date*

A well-attired and seemingly elegant white matron arrives at Grand Central Station after shopping in New York City. Hurrying through the concourse, she bumps into a well-dressed black man knocking her purse out of her arms, her possessions spilling out all over the floor. Refusing his attempt to help, she quickly picks up her personal effects and runs to her track, only to just miss the train. She checks her purse and finds that her wallet is missing. She seems lost and close to tears.

With time before her next train, she buys a salad with her remaining small change at a nearby cafeteria. She places the salad and her packages at a booth and goes back to the counter for a fork. She returns to discover a homeless black man eating her salad. Indignant, the woman plants herself in the booth and grabs for her salad, but the man refuses to let

go. Gathering her courage, she spears a piece of lettuce with her fork and glares at him. When he ignores her, she keeps picking at it, and they share the salad. He walks away, and she prepares to leave, but he reappears, carrying two cups of coffee. He offers her sugar. She smiles and drinks. This is their "lunch date."

The woman hears her train being called and gets up to leave. On her way to the platform, she realizes that she has forgotten her packages and rushes back, only to find the homeless man and her packages gone. Pacing back and forth, the woman finally sees that her untouched salad and packages were at the next booth the whole time. Realizing what's happened, she grabs the packages and heads for the train, hurrying by a black panhandler. This time she makes the train.

History of Project. Briefly describe how the project evolved. Elaborate on the subject matter and what inspired you to want to make this film. This section of the prospectus helps personalize the prospectus and answers any question the potential funder might have about the filmmaker's connection to the topic. This section is especially applicable if the idea comes from another medium (stage play, short story, etc.).

Research. Research is imperative for a documentary project. Potential investors will need to understand the materials on which your story is based. Is this a true story of a living person? Is it based on a real event? Has the story been done before? What slant will the director take? Have the rights to tell this story been secured?

Top Sheet of Budget. The top sheet summarizes the budget (look ahead to Figure 5.1). This summary should represent the broad categories; it is not a detailed or itemized breakdown. Too much information might prompt an investor to question why you need $400 for a special wig. You don't want to end up justifying this and every cost of the project. Investors need to trust that you are the expert. It is your business, not theirs. Only after you have prepared an accurate budget for the script can you begin to finance the project realistically. However, you might have begun to raise money long before this by approaching investors with an early draft of the script or a "treatment" and a projected estimate of production costs. Experienced producers and production managers have the skill to examine a script and estimate the cost of the project. If you have been involved in other productions of similar size and scope, you might get a sense of how much money you need before you actually work out the budget.

At the prospectus stage, the budget is likely to be an overall guesstimate. Later, it will be modified to include input from all department heads, including the director. At the prospectus stage, the director can help the producer by confirming that the bottom-line figure in the budget adequately covers her needs.

You might be able to complete the project for less than your projection, but ask for more than you anticipate needing. Who knows? You might get it and you might need it. (See Chapter 5 for more information.)

Production Schedule. Give the approximate dates when the production will begin and end should financing become available.

Cast List. Draw up a list of the prominent cast members and give a succinct résumé of their credits. The quality and ability (and in some cases recognizability) of the cast are part of the insurance that investors require to feel confident that their money is being spent wisely.

Brief Résumés of Creative Team. Present the pool of talent associated with the production at the time the prospectus is written. The personnel can be introduced in simple paragraphs or in complete résumés.

Writing a résumé is an art in itself. A résumé can be anywhere from a single paragraph to a full page in length. Try to find a balance between giving too much information and too little. Clearly identify each person's strengths, relevant experiences, and job description. A résumé for a producer that indicates that he can write, direct, produce, shoot, and act might overwhelm investors.

Press Clippings. Generate as much press coverage as possible both about the project itself and the production team, even if the source is a hometown newspaper. These clippings could also include reviews from previous films.

Description of Market for Project. Devise a distribution plan to include in the prospectus that should include all conceivable ways this film will reach its audience. (See Chapter 19 for further details.) Talk about the rise in interest in the short film. This section would include a partial list of well-known film and video festivals you plan to enter and make note of a few of the successful short films that have performed well at these festivals.

Financial Statement. In the financial statement, you should estimate the income you expect to receive, based on your distribution plan. In addition, explain your business identity.

Letter from Fiscal Sponsor (if applicable). Potential investors will need to see a copy of the fiscal sponsor's official 501(c)(3) letter provided by the Internal Revenue Service. In addition, ask the fiscal sponsor to write an enthusiastic "to whom it may concern" cover letter that explains why the group or organization decided to sponsor the project. Make sure to keep brochures and promotional materials about the fiscal sponsor available if the investor is not familiar with the sponsor.

Letters of support. Keeping an ongoing file of letters of support should be standard procedure for all filmmakers. A letter is a written validation of one's achievement. These letters could come from a variety of sources—from professionals you have worked for to professors (for students).

Means of Transferring Funds. At the end of the prospectus, include a letter addressed to the company from the investor, committing the investor to a specific figure. The letter should show how money can be transferred to the production account.

People respond to visuals. The prospectus should be peppered with graphics that support the project's concept and lend excitement to the presentation. If you can create images that connect potential investors to the idea of your piece, it will enhance their appreciation of the supporting data.

We remind you that there are no rules. Although not all potential investors will know how to judge the subtleties of a varied background, an eclectic résumé might indeed catch an investor's eye. Work experiences as a camp counselor, location scout, or editor of a student film all point to leadership skills.

Presentation Is Everything

A well-written prospectus makes a professional impression. When writing the prospectus, use easy-to-understand and grammatically precise language. Stick with simple declarative sentences and clear, unpretentious words. Arrange your thoughts logically, avoid jargon, and make the ideas flow.

Don't give potential investors an obvious reason to turn down your proposal. "No" is the easiest decision to make because nothing is risked by making it. In fact, most people look for reasons to say no. Imagine yourself on the other side of the table. Would you support someone whose business plan wasn't thought out carefully or who didn't take the time to proofread her work? Would you trust this person with your money? Here are the benefits of creating a prospectus:

- **It forces the filmmaker to think objectively about the project as a whole.** The challenge becomes how to communicate an idea's potential to a complete stranger who might not be interested in the project. Beginners think that enthusiasm is enough to sell an idea. This energy can be contagious, but it must also be followed by hard information about the exact nature of the project, the talent, and the investment structure.
- **It is an important tool for galvanizing interest without having to pitch verbally to hundreds of people.** It also identifies the sincerely interested parties whose concerns can then be addressed specifically and personally. Some producers are naturally facile and relaxed communicators. You might be one. Even if you have an innate ability to sell in person, the written presentation must be well designed. Good interpersonal skills will come in time. The byproduct of a thoroughly prepared prospectus is twofold:
- **It trains you to think logically and sequentially about your idea.** When you do have the opportunity to speak face to face with potential investors, you will be well prepared.
- **It is an important step in the preproduction process.** Now you have your first budget!

I started writing proposals. The first one was to the American Film Institute, which resulted in a rejection. I actually applied to them three years in a row and got rejected three years in a row for a historical legacy idea. But when I started refining the idea, I abandoned the whole thing, and the reason was because I felt this was too hard to do on film. It was really more like a slide show because it was all inanimate, and it worried me that I would have to rely on still material and a disembodied voice.

Jan Krawitz

Spending the Money Responsibly

As a producer, you have the responsibility of handling and managing the money after it has been raised. You will need to create some type of corporate identity to receive funds.

Creating this entity might involve something as simple as setting up a bank account into which checks can be deposited, or it can be as complex as choosing a corporate structure. Consult an entertainment attorney for details.

The business and legal skills required to handle money responsibly are based on the needs of the production. Throughout the production process, the producer supervises the allocation of cash, or the **cash flow**, through the production pipeline. This ensures that he will be able to deliver a thorough financial statement to the investors at the end of production.

The Digital Prospectus

Much of what can be placed in a beautifully bound pamphlet that can represent what the project is all about can be reformatted and designed for a web site. A web site is ubiquitous and fluid; it can be kept fresh on a regular basis with updates on the status of your production planning. This clearly has many benefits, none the least expense, because it eliminates the combined cost of production, duplication, and distribution.

I created a web prospectus, but I didn't duplicate the complete book version on the site. The reality of my creative process is that while I was fund-raising, I was still figuring out what the movie was all about and was relying more on people's faith in me as opposed to the project . . . But I had a web site which included a pitch with photos of locations and links to my previous work. These included films going back to high school because these were some of the people I was appealing to. The pitch played up the timeliness of the story and the relevance of what was going on now.

General Fundraising Suggestions

Be Positive and Be Patient

Project supreme confidence in the picture and in your ability to execute it successfully. People are investing not only in the picture, but in you. In addition, you must be able to sustain a positive attitude over the long haul. If you are the kind of person who requires short-term rewards, this business is not for you. Perseverance and patience are the watchwords. Looking for money requires a dogged determination. You'll need the energy of the hare but the patience of the tortoise.

I thought I'd really like to make a film and figured I could probably raise enough money somehow to shoot it. I didn't think it would be very expensive. It basically came down to the fact that I was just dying to get near a camera and shoot something. What was the worst that could happen? I'd lose some money.

Adam Davidson

Act Professionally

Professionalism is a theme that we stress in all aspects of the production process, and it is also vital when you approach potential investors. You will be respected if you appear to be organized, efficient, well prepared, and articulate. You might see yourself in the role of the artist, but fundraising is a business proposition. You are asking people to trust you with their money. If you can give the impression of knowing what you are doing, you will most likely get your foot in the door. Once in, assuming that there are quality and substance in your project idea, a coherent presentation will be critical to your success.

Be sure to allocate enough time to raise the money you need. It won't happen overnight. If you are planning to shoot in several months and have not yet begun fundraising, you'd better hope that you win the lottery.

Be Informed

Do your homework. When you are looking for funding sources, knowing what information to seek is as important as knowing where to find it and what to do with it. The goal is to know how things work and how to work them to your advantage. Read as much as you can. Surf the Net. The Internet is an indispensable tool for research. Examine the budgets of pictures of a similar length.

Be dogged in the pursuit of the facts. Examine all sides of a problem; there could be more than one solution. Go to conferences. Talk to professionals and amateurs who have been successful at fundraising, particularly with genres similar to yours. Become adept at asking the right questions. Don't be shy. Believe it or not, people like to share their knowledge with beginners as long as doing so doesn't cost them anything. With this information in hand, evaluate the potential investor pool.

The key is to consider everything. Focus your energies on multiple strategies. Don't pin your hopes on getting that one investor or grant. If it doesn't work out, you will be left stranded. Learn to keep many balls in the air and learn to live with rejection. You may hear "no" 100 times before you finally hear one "yes."

Thank You!

Don't minimize the importance of saying thanks. Saying it costs nothing and reaps great rewards. Even rejections should be followed up with a letter or email that acknowledges the individual's careful consideration of your project.

FUNDRAISING TIP

Financing can be secured in two tiers. First, there's the money you need to get the project shot and "in the can." This money is raised on a script and a pitch. When the principal photography has been completed, you will require "finishing," or postproduction, money. This second phase of fundraising can be done while the project is being edited. Use the footage to show potential investors just how fabulous the picture will eventually be. As opposed to the first funds, which were raised on the ephemeral qualities of a pitch and a prayer, the second phase of fundraising is enhanced by having footage to show, which makes a more solid presentation.

Sources for Students

What help is available to students? The following brief list summarizes resources you should explore:

- **Other Students.** Other students are invaluable resources of solid advice and information. Who better to ask about fundraising strategies than fellow students who are in the same position? Surprisingly, many students overlook their peers as resources. It is up to you to brainstorm with others who are seeking production support.
- **Internships.** If your film or television program is located in a media center such as New York, Los Angeles, Chicago, or San Francisco, it behooves you to take advantage of internship opportunities to learn about not only the raising, but also the management, of money.
- **Facilities.** Students at media programs have access to free equipment. They also have the use of production and postproduction facilities, such as stages, locations, editing rooms, mixing facilities, and screening rooms.
- **Learning Opportunities.** Keep your eyes open for ways to develop yourself. Listen to guest speakers from the industry. Take courses in a business school. Tackle writing, acting, and public speaking classes. In a pitch meeting, the topic of conversation could easily switch from your project to current events to acting techniques to writing styles. Students with varied interests and a broad background will be best equipped to converse on a number of topics and will make a favorable impression. Your ultimate goal is to know both how to communicate and what to communicate.

As a recent alumnae, I was eligible to apply for the $100,000 Richard Vague Award from the Kanbar Film Department at New York University. Based on the work I did on *Crazy Glue*, I received the award to expand my short claymation film into a feature. It was an amazing, amazing gift. I plan to use that money to make the first five minutes of the film.

Tatia Rosenthal

Student Fundraising Strategies

Find creative ways to earn money. Entrepreneurial students capitalize on their skills by creating a product to sell. Hard cash is made each week by those who know how to bake, garden, arrange flowers, do accounting, type, troubleshoot computers, and videotape weddings.

Generate interest and create energy around your project. Set up fundraisers, have parties, and hold screenings of your unfinished work. Use the newspapers. Create publicity by sending a press packet to newspapers and magazines.

You need not look only for big-dollar investments. It is common and understandable for people to flinch when asked for thousands, even hundreds of dollars. Make a list of everyone you know and everyone your parents, relatives, and friends know, and ask them for a modest amount (from $25 up). They will be surprised when you ask for a small amount and will gladly donate a few dollars to the cause. If 25 friends each give $25, you'll collect $625! This is enough to buy and process three rolls of 16mm film or 60 rolls of tape stock.

This $625 can now represent your seed money. With this money in the bank, you can approach other potential investors and impress them with how much you have already raised. Money has a habit of generating money. If these potential high rollers hear that others have believed in your project enough to give money, it gives them more confidence in the value of your project.

> I'm in debt, but I got lucky in several ways. I was no longer paying for film school because I had become a graduate assistant. My parents didn't pay for my undergraduate education, so they were ready to pay for graduate school. Since I didn't have to pay for tuition, the money went into production. My high school friends who had done well financially helped me. So between my friends, my parents, and student loans, I paid for the film.
>
> Howard McCain

DIRECTOR

Pitching the Project

Next to the film's concept, the director and her abilities are the key elements that the producer touts when raising funds. The director must infect investors with her enthusiasm for the project. If she has a track record or other career support, such as an award for a previous work or glowing reviews, investors will treat the venture more favorably. As we stated earlier, investors often know very little about how to read a script or how to respond to production problems. What they do understand is good storytelling ability. The director who can "pitch" her film idea well is more apt to impress investors with her vision than someone who becomes tongue-tied or is shy. Verbal agility is crucial at the moment of "closing."

The Elevator Challenge

Imagine that you are entering an elevator with someone who is a potential investor. You are both traveling to the 20th floor. Knowing you have this person's undivided attention for those few minutes, now is the time to "pitch" the idea for your short film. You may never have this opportunity to be in the same space with this person again. It is now or never. You will need to capture this person's attention with your confidence and enthusiasm for the project, and just enough story information to hook him. If he is intrigued and wants to learn more, follow up with your professional-looking prospectus or the link to the web site for the project. A moment like this can happen at any place and at any time and maybe only once. Are you prepared for this potential opportunity?

Whether you like it or not, you are now into sales. Smart investors look at the bottom line, but they are greatly influenced by the presenter. Everyone appreciates a performer and an entrepreneur. Keep in mind, however, that there is a fine line between showing some razzle-dazzle and being obnoxious. The former is a turn-on, the latter a turnoff. Learn to observe, by the reaction of those to whom you are pitching, which approaches seem to work and which don't. There is nothing like asking for money; this task trains the producer and director to deal with a naturally uncomfortable situation gracefully. Through the process of defining your project and shaping your pitch, you will learn how best to sell your idea.

> I get really unhappy when I hear of people, not just students but independent filmmakers, who pitch an idea, start developing a particular idea, because they feel like that's what's "fundable" these days. I think the thing people fail to understand is that originality is what gets attention, not derivative filmmaking.
>
> Jan Krawitz

Steps to a Successful Pitch

In the verbal and written pitches, present a tone that grabs the target investor's attention. Use active and colorful words. Some people have a talent for this type of promotional presentation. A director's raw enthusiasm, coupled with a clear interpretation of the material, makes an effective presentation. In a verbal presentation, be enthusiastic, but speak clearly and slowly. When pitching material with a partner, know when to be silent and when to assist. If you seem to be a cohesive team, your target will be impressed. There are six questions you will need to address when pitching your story: Who? What? Where? How? Why? When?

Who is the movie about? This is usually the first question most people want to know. Who is the main character and what does he want?

What is the genre of your film: comedy, drama, coming of age, etc.? This lets the listeners know what kind of story to expect.

Where and when does the story take place? Locate your story in time and space. It sometimes helps to start your pitch by bringing the listeners into the world of your story first and then establishing the main character. ("In a time long ago in a galaxy...")

Why should we care about the main character? This is probably the most important part of your pitch because an audience becomes engaged only if they care about the fate of your protagonist. Will your hero overcome great odds to achieve his goal? Will he find happiness? In your answer, they will see how much you care and believe in your story.

The how is what happens in the story. The log line is your starting point. If the listeners want more, give them a beat-by-beat breakdown of what happens in each scene. This is the tricky part: knowing how much information is needed to convey the basic narrative without getting bogged down in unnecessary details. This could take the listeners out of the spell you are weaving. If they start asking too many questions, you know you have lost them. Having a synopsis to work from will help you prepare for this situation.

The order in which you present these points is not set in stone. You will discover the proper sequence based on the genre and the particular story. We do recommend, however, that if you are pitching a comedy, let the listeners know up front. Comedies have one basic rule: it has to be funny. Many of the dramatic principles get thrown out in the service of a laugh. Practice your pitch alone and with friends. Being comfortable with your presentation will give you the confidence to respond to the unexpected. The listeners may distract you from your prepared pitch or ask questions you had never thought of. If you have done your homework, you should be able to respond to these situations with ease.

KEY POINTS

- Allow ample time to generate the funds you will need to shoot the entire picture.
- Present your project and yourself in a professional manner. Use a prospectus—a professional business plan with which investors are familiar.
- Research your targets for funds. If you know as much about them as they do, they will be impressed.
- Generate enough enthusiasm to pitch the project and sustain yourself for the year or two it might take to make your film.

Part I

Preproduction

I have learned to be on time, be honest, stay honest, and be very prepared. Which means being prepared for the things you can't prepare for, but at the same time having a certain level of preparation to handle the things that were unforeseen a little bit better if you never thought about them at all.

Be' Garrett

You have a script you feel strongly about and are eager to get out into the field and begin production. Assuming that you have secured the appropriate funds (or are well on your way to doing so), you are now ready to start *preproduction*. During this phase, you will prepare virtually every element for the filming process. Decisions made during this time are the foundation on which everything else is built. The producer and director share many of these responsibilities. The next 11 chapters of this book indicate the specific responsibilities of each. These responsibilities are outlined in Figures I.1 and I.2.

THE STUDENT PRODUCER—DIRECTOR CONUNDRUM

Although the producer and director share many of the responsibilities, they each have their own sphere of focus. Our timeline in the beginning of the book (see page xxiii) articulates the director's and producer's flow of activity from script to screen. They intersect on creative decisions but veer off on organization and management. They both are involved with choosing a location; however, the location manager scouts these locations and the producer negotiates the deal. The producer works hard to execute the creative plan within the budget.

If the producer and director are one and the same, not only is the important give-and-take lost between the creative desires and the realities of what is possible and affordable, but the director must now do double duty. She must not only choose the right locations for the story, but must also spend hours scouting, negotiating with the tenants, and securing the permits (if necessary). Swamped with "producing or managerial" duties, the novice inevitably puts little time in her role as director. The directorial plan (visual style, floor plans, story boards, etc.) is often devised at the last minute.

We also acknowledge that "student producers" do not follow the industry model. The director usually brings the money to the table. A student producer's role is more that of a production manager or line producer but, if he does the job right, he can be an indispensable asset and aid to the director. Jessalyn Haefele, the student producer of *Citizen*, says this about producing:

> When James emailed me the original draft of "Citizen" and asked if I would be interested in producing it, I was blown away. The script was very, very good (it was tight and gripped me), but almost more importantly, the entire time I was reading it, I was thinking to myself, "How the heck can I pull this off?" The challenge of actually getting this film made is one of the main reasons I was attracted to this project.
>
> There are a lot of great things about producing films, especially student thesis films, but here are a few reasons why, if you ultimately want to be a producer, you can learn more from them than anything else:
>
> 1. Most student thesis films are self-financed, or the money is already in place. This means that you don't have the pressure of fund-raising on your shoulders, or not having money at the last minute—the money is already there. And even better, it's not your money! It's someone else's, and you get to figure out how to make the best use of it. It's a real, practical learning experience.

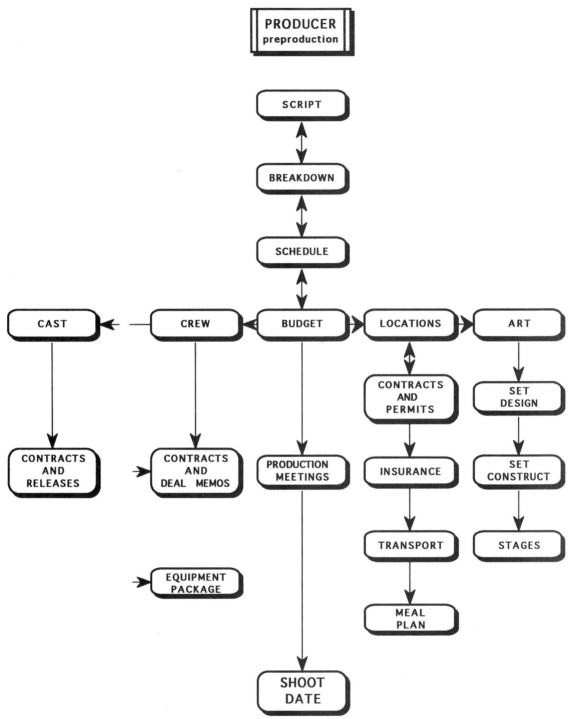

FIGURE I.1　Producer's preproduction responsibilities.

2. Most (if not all) student films are already provided with production insurance through the school. This means you don't have to blow your budget buying production insurance, and it's really a convenient thing to have.

3. You easily have more access to crew members, and there is a good chance that many of them are your classmates and you already have a working relationship with them.

4. Mistakes are more easily tolerated, and as a learning environment, there is less pressure. It's a good environment in which to hone your skills and discover what works and what does not

Jessalyn Haefele, Producer of *Citizen*.

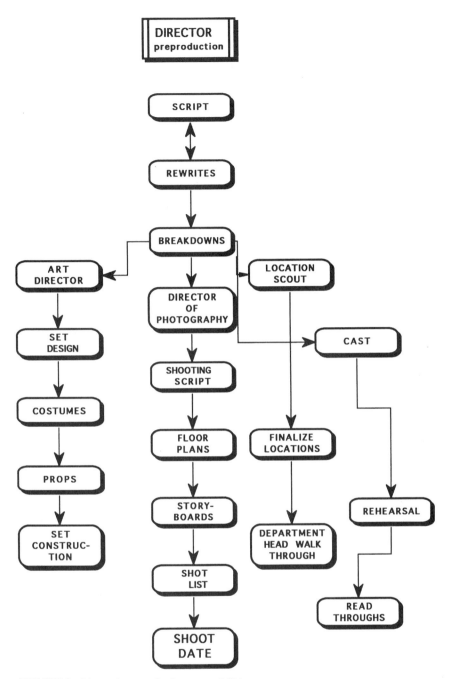

FIGURE I.2   Director's preproduction responsibilities.

PREPARE THOROUGHLY FOR THE SHOOT DATE

Preproduction is the time to research and develop your idea, to design what it should look like, and to explore all the variables such as cast, crew, and locations needed to create a successful production. The more thoroughly a project is planned, the smoother the production will be. **The general rule is: You can't do too much preproduction work**. For some reason, this is a difficult concept for many novices to understand. They often return from their first major shoot dejected, having experienced just how ill

prepared they really were. They realize too late that mistakes or disasters during production could have been averted if they had been more organized before they started to shoot. All the talent in the world won't help if your schedule isn't realistic, the meals aren't served on time, you lose the use of your location, or you don't have enough film stock on hand. These are only a few of the contingencies that require forethought.

One of the major goals of preproduction is to try to anticipate anything and everything that can go wrong during a shoot. This gives you time to react sensibly to things that could not have been anticipated and are entirely beyond your control (and invariably occur, such as unusual weather, acts of God, etc). These things happen because all film shoots are ruled by Murphy's Law: Anything that can go wrong inevitably will. When you plan a production and work with this assumption, always plan for the worst-case scenario.

> The best advice I can give is to have a sense of humor about film production. Embrace the Murphy's Law of it all—for everything that can go wrong surely will. But if you expect it, and are prepared for it, you will greet these obstacles with a smile rather than a scream.
>
> Jessalyn Haefele, Producer of *Citizen*

> After two days of shooting, New York got hit with the worst blizzard in 50 years.
>
> James Darling

PREPRODUCTION IS QUALITY TIME

During preproduction, you have an abundance of something you won't have when you start shooting: time—time to consider various ways to shoot a scene, pick the right actor, settle on the right location, or spend on the subtleties of the script. Never lose sight of the fact that this is cost-effective time. All the effort you expend on preparation now will pay off during production. When you're actually shooting, spending time is spending money. Settling on an efficient game plan and solving potential production problems during preproduction will save precious dollars later.

> I spent a lot of hours in Grand Central, almost an entire day, getting a sense of the building. That was when I first noticed how the light streams through the windows.
>
> Adam Davidson

WITHOUT A GOOD SCRIPT, YOU CANNOT MAKE A GOOD FILM

Even after developing a good script, as discussed in Chapter 1, there is no guarantee of producing a good film. However, a poorly thought out script has little chance of yielding a successful finished product. You would be ill advised to go out into the field with a story that doesn't live up to its full potential. The investment of time, money, talent, and effort will be wasted unless the original blueprint is solid.

To ensure that you have the best script possible, be prepared to rewrite many times. Don't expect to solve lingering script problems magically during production. Rewriting the script on the set is usually too demanding for beginning filmmakers. The pressures of filming the original script will keep you more than occupied.

It is true that many serendipitous events can occur during shooting and editing that will add evocative imagery, inspired characters, and atmospheric locations to your project. Unexpected surprises in action or dialogue will add measurably to the texture of a scene, but don't count on them. The script will come to full-color life, but the progression of events—your story—will not change. Script problems will then become editing challenges. What is on the page will end up on the screen. Get it right before your start.

PREPRODUCTION GUIDELINES—PLEASE READ!

Intangible managerial skills are as important as technical know-how in preparing successfully for production. The following are some general guidelines to help with the intangibles of preproduction. It all starts with confidence and a positive attitude.

Keep a Positive Attitude. Lack of experience makes it difficult for beginning filmmakers to assess their day-to-day preproduction progress. There are so many elements (cast, crew, locations) that have to fall into place that you might sometimes doubt that so many tasks could possibly be accomplished by the shoot date; perhaps you have one part still uncast, there is no sound mixer, and the key location has not yet been secured. Don't panic.

Living with uncertainty is part of the process. Professionals understand that things can come together at the last moment. A positive attitude is as important as efficiency and organization. The producer situates himself at the middle of all the activity and keeps the production team focused. He must inspire confidence that all the elements will come together in time, no matter what the obstacles.

Allow Enough Time for Preproduction. How long should it take to prepare a short script for production? Answering this question is difficult because much depends on the experience of the creative team and the complexity of the script. A story set in one room with two characters is easier to preproduce than one demanding 10 different and unique locations. However, any short project can seem overwhelming to the first-time filmmaker.

Aside from the time spent securing the financing, a workable formula is to allow one week of preproduction for each day of principal photography. This step might take less time or more, based on script complexity and the director's experience. In the end, you will do it in the time that is available.

Set a Preproduction Schedule. Use your shoot date as the final target. Create deadlines for securing cast, crew, and locations, and strive to follow them. (See the sample at end of this section.)

Hold Regular Production Meetings. Schedule regular production meetings and stick to them. Don't rely on ad hoc gatherings to keep everyone informed. Events happen too fast and plans change too often for everyone to be kept abreast via casual chats. Keep in constant touch with the key creative staff. Learn to work in a nonlinear fashion. It is a juggling game. The production team needs to work on many things at the same time.

Delegate Responsibility. Preproduction responsibilities fall on many shoulders. The producer must assign tasks to the whole creative team (art director, director, director of photography) and then keep track of each person's progress.

Never Assume Anything. Double- and triple-check everything. If the producer assumes that the location manager has checked the electric supply of an apartment location, chances are only 50–50 that he did. Do you want to take that chance?

Break Some Rules. This book is meant as a guide to a complex process. Picture making is built on ingenuity, creativity, improvisation, and instinct. The entrepreneurial spirit is alive in the film and video business. Often, it is the breaking of a rule (unless, of course, if safety issues are involved) that leads to an exciting opportunity.

Remember That All Things Change. The process of preproduction is an evolution. The script, schedule, and budget will go through many changes before they are finalized, sometimes right up to the shooting date. The essential caveat is that once shooting begins, changes cease and you must concentrate on fulfilling the script, schedule, and budget.

Stay Healthy. Putting together all the ingredients needed to create a film or video can be exciting but stressful, especially if you're doing this for the first time. The daily stress makes demands on the body. You want to be healthy when you are in production. This means taking care of yourself during preproduction and staying at your peak. You cannot slow down production because of a cold or postpone it because of the flu.

PRODUCTION MEETING SUGGESTIONS

Production meetings are opportunities to brainstorm ideas and to solve problems. The key to running an effective production meeting is to be organized and to stick to the agenda.

Maximize the time you spend with the crew. Respect all points of view, but don't linger too long on one issue with the whole crew present. Deal with a particularly thorny issue later with only the appropriate crew members. You might have to set up smaller meetings with individual department heads—art, camera, sound, wardrobe, props, hair, and makeup—to deal with specific issues in their respective areas.

Here are some additional suggestions:

- Hold the production meeting at the same time and place each week.
- Have refreshments available.
- Before the meeting, make sure everyone has a copy of the script.
- Set a time limit for the meeting.
- Publish and hand out a written agenda if possible.
- Moderate the meeting, keeping everyone focused on one topic at a time.
- Deal with one department at a time.
- At the end of the meeting, summarize the points of agreement.
- Assign tasks to appropriate crew members.
- Set an agenda for the next meeting.
- Distribute follow-up notes of decisions made (via email).

Email and text messaging are efficient ways of communicating with cast and crew. Alerting them about a change of time or venue of your next production meeting can be handled in seconds.

INTERNET ACCESS

If you have established a website for the project, it can be used to communicate with the crew about upcoming production meetings. Preproduction blogs can keep everyone abreast of the progress report of the film. It can be tempting to use these tools instead of meeting in person, but there is still nothing more effective that brainstorming ideas around a table.

SAMPLE PREPRODUCTION SCHEDULE

To give you an idea of what the flow of activity looks like from week to week, this section includes a sample preproduction timeline for a 12-page script. It is difficult to predict how your project will fit into this model because each project has its own set of challenges. Your project might require devoting more effort to cast, location, or crew. The challenge of *Truman*, for example, was to find a 10-year-old boy to play the lead, children for the supporting characters, and a gym that was available for a whole week. *Crazy Glue* required months of building the puppets and sets. The producer of *The Lunch Date* needed to secure Grand Central Station and a luncheonette. Jan Krawitz had to find suitable women to interview for *Mirror Mirror* to bring the issue alive. Be' Garrett needed to find a barbershop for *A Nick in Time* that would be able to look old in one particular time period and new in another. Finally, James Darling needed to find a gated U.S./Canada border crossing for *Citizen* that would look believable.

The sample schedule assumes six shooting days. At two pages a day, this is a reasonable schedule for a student or beginning filmmaker. Our formula for a beginner allows one week of preproduction for each day of principal photography. This gives you six weeks to prepare for the shoot. Depending on the experience of you and your crew and on the complexity of the script, the preproduction period might be longer or shorter. This prototype will at least give you an idea of what must happen before the cameras can roll. The order and the time during which each task occurs will vary from production to production.

The following schedule assumes you have the following:

- A finished script
- A director
- Adequate financing
- A preliminary budget
- A shoot date

Week 1

Producer
Sets up office/furniture
Buys supplies
Sets up phone/answering machine

Leases photocopier
Buys or leases computer
Creates filing system to keep copies of all
   agreements
Establishes company name (DBA, "doing
   business as")
Buys cards/stationery
Opens bank account
Advertises for actors
Advertises for crew
Breaks down script
Creates stripboard and schedule
Submits script to insurance company for
   estimate
Crew
Production manager
Location manager

Director
Finalizes shooting script
Scouts locations
Discusses script with art
   director

Art director
Casting director
Production coordinator
Production Meeting 1—Key Points
   Introduce all crew members.
   Set up preproduction schedule.
   Set goals for next meeting.

Week 2

Producer
Reviews budget
Reviews shooting schedule

Collects, organizes head plans,
   idea shots
Signs SAG waiver or guild
   contract
Sets up auditions

Reviews proposed insurance
   package
Orders all necessary forms
   (location agreements,
release forms, call sheets, petty
   cash envelopes, etc.)
Crew
Director of photography
Office production assistants
Production Meeting 2—Key
   Points
   Discuss art director's plans.
   Request art budget.
   Go over preliminary schedule
      and budget.

Director
Scouts locations
Art director presents her ideas
   for the project
Reviews head shots for actors

Analyzes script

Discusses script with director of
   photography (DP)

Week 3

Producer
Sets up auditions
Looks for postproduction facilities
Advertises for editor
Settles on insurance package
Negotiates with laboratory for
   overall package
Researches equipment houses,
   vendors
Crew
DP (starts lighting designs)
Wardrobe
Props
Special effects (if needed)
Production Meeting 3—Key
   Points
   Approve art department budget.
   Narrow down location choices.
   Approve construction schedule
      (if appropriate).

Director
Reviews location pictures
Visits locations with DP
Holds auditions

Week 4

Producer
Sets up more auditions
Finalizes locations
Forms crew

Director
Holds callbacks
Finalizes locations
Develops visual plan

Reviews shooting schedule,
    budget
Sets up dailies, projection
    schedule
Negotiates agreement with
    caterer (meal plan)
Makes transportation plans
Rents vans, recreational vehicles
Sets up account with lab, sound
    transfers
Crew
Assistant director
Makeup/hair
Transportation coordinator
Production Meeting 4—Key
    Points
    Discuss casting alternatives.
    Settle on final crew needs.
    Finalize transportation plan.

Reviews wardrobe, props with
    art department
Reviews lighting plan with DP

Production sound mixer
2nd assistant director
Production Meeting 5—Key
    Points
    Discuss wardrobe, props, hair,
        and makeup issues.
    Discuss budget considerations.
    Have script timed.

Week 5

Producer
Finalizes cast
Negotiates cast contracts
Secures location contracts
Finalizes crew, crew deal memos

Publishes cast, crew contact
    sheet
Secures parking permits
Secures shooting permits
Makes security arrangements
Approves expendables request for
    all departments
Orders complete equipment
    package
(camera, grip, electric, sound,
    dolly,
generator, walkie-talkies, etc.)
Orders first-aid kit for set
Sets up tentative postproduction
    schedule
Crew
Key grip

Director
Begins rehearsals
Finalizes shot list
Reviews script
Reviews makeup, hair designs
    with art department
Finalizes lighting plan with DP

Week 6

Producer
Checks weather report
Finalizes budget
Distributes contact sheet
Finalizes schedule
Reconfirms locations
Confirms crew

Distributes one-liner schedule to
    cast, crew
Distributes call sheets for first-day
    cast, crew
Distributes maps of locations
Purchases film, tape stock
Orders expendables
Obtains certificates of insurance for
    locations, equipment, vehicles
Crew
Gaffer
Boom
2nd assistant director
    Production Meeting 6—Key Points
    Go over shooting schedule, day
        by day, with all department
        heads.
    Give general pep talk.

Director
Holds rehearsals
Supervises script changes
Visits set construction
Finalizes shooting script
Does final location scout
Performs walkthrough with
    department heads

Week 7

Producer
Picks up equipment,
transportation
SHOOT DATE

Director

Chapter 3

Breakdowns

We would have a nightly meeting for an hour. We would go over the schedule, which matched the lined script, which matched the storyboard, which matched the breakdowns.

Howard McCain

PRODUCER

Breaking Down the Script

Before a shooting schedule can be devised, the producer in his role as **production manager** or line producer examines the script from all practical angles. Up to now, the emphasis has been on making the structure and the dialogue of the story work. Although it might be dramatically effective for the main characters to have an intimate conversation in a park during a rainstorm on a bridge at night, from a practical and safety point of view, accomplishing this shot might be difficult. The producer must think about the difficulty of obtaining permission to shoot in the park, the problems of making rain, the safety issues of shooting on and lighting a bridge at night, and the need to record dialogue with the sounds of rain and traffic in the background.

The producer is trained to see the logistical repercussions of every aspect of the script. A scene in Grand Central Station (such as the one in *The Lunch Date*) might be stylistically or thematically correct, but such a location may have a significant impact on the schedule and the budget. To evaluate the feasibility of this or any scene in the context of the whole picture, the producer must first extract, or break down, all relevant production information from the script. The longstanding film industry term **breakdown** is the process of logging each significant element needed for production of a scene (such as cast, costumes, special effects, cars, and stunts) onto a breakdown sheet to create a means of communication and documentation between the production team and the various departments. If a prop, vehicle, light, costume, or camera isn't on location when you need it, you can't shoot that scene. The combined breakdowns of all the scenes give the producer an overview of the practical challenges of the project and allow him to create a shooting or production schedule.

A producer can't begin to raise money for the project until he has an idea of how much it is going to cost. He can't know how much the project will cost unless he knows how long it will take to shoot and what equipment the film requires. Finally, the producer can't begin to create a schedule until the script is broken down to reveal the important and relevant production information.

In essence, the producer cannot begin preproduction until the script has been completed. Although the script might change, the producer works at the breakdowns and incorporates the changes as they arise. To assist the producer, the director prepares her shot list, which will provide information for the schedule.

> **STUDENTS**
>
> If the producer and director are the same person (which we discourage with extreme prejudice), often the budget will dictate the aesthetics. Money will define how ambitious the idea can be.

Production Book

Organization is the key to a successful production. To stay organized, the producer needs easy access to the production information that he will gather during preproduction (the director will have her own production book). An effective way of doing this is to buy a large loose-leaf binder and a set of tabbed dividers so that each section can be easily identified. The first document in this book should be the script. As the preproduction period progresses, more and more will be added to this book. It will become the producer's "bible," containing the following elements:

- Script (with each updated draft)
- Lined script (broken down)
- Breakdown pages
- Budget (current and future drafts)
- Schedule
- Art direction breakdown (props, wardrobe, costumes, etc.)
- Cast and crew list (with phone numbers and email addresses)

doi: 10.1016/B978-0-240-81174-1.00010-5

- Casting schedule and casting notes
- Glossies (of actors chosen)
- All signed release forms
- Transportation and meal plan
- Location breakdown (addresses, contacts, permits, agreements)
- Insurance forms
- Itemized breakdown of all expenses (with receipt package)

Proper Script Format

Before you can begin breaking down the script, it must be in proper screenplay format, which refers to how to organize the script information on a page. Professional scripts are written in a standard format to enable the producer and/or the production manager to evaluate the production value of each page correctly and translate it into the schedule and budget.

A properly formatted screen page should equal approximately one minute of screen time. For this formula to work, the script must be typed to include a specific amount of information on each page. If you have crammed too many words of description or dialogue on one page, a 10-page script might, in fact, turn out to be a 15-minute project. Conversely, a loosely typed script will also give you an inaccurate assessment of the length of the project. Time equals money, and an accurate estimation of time is imperative for you to know how to schedule and budget a project.

Keep in mind that this "one page equals one minute" rule is only a guess. A five-page dialogue scene might run up to six or seven minutes in length, whereas five pages of action, say a chase sequence, will most likely play quicker on the screen. This rule is merely an average of the action and dialogue elements in the script.

The format size relates to the size of the type (12-point Courier), the spacing between dialogue and action (two lines), the width of the margins, and the length of the page. (See the sample script page for *Citizen* and *The Lunch Date* in Appendix C.) The standard settings are as follows:

- Left margin: $1\frac{1}{2}$ inches
- Right margin: $1\frac{1}{2}$ inches
- Tab for left dialogue margin: $2\frac{1}{2}$ inches
- Tab for right dialogue margin: $2\frac{1}{2}$ inches
- Tab for speaker's name: $4\frac{1}{2}$ inches

These elements should be capitalized in the script:

- All camera instructions (use sparingly until writing the shooting script draft)
- All sounds, including music ("The log SNAPS")
- All characters the first time they appear
- Every word in the header ("INT. GRAND CENTRAL STATION"—DAY)
- The speaker's name, above each line of dialogue

There are many computer software programs on the market (examples are given in the Bibliography) that automatically conform your screenplay to proper screenplay format. Final Draft is the most commonly used one.

Breaking Down the Script

Following are the first steps in organizing a production:

1. Breakdowns
   - Line the script.
   - Fill in breakdown sheets.
   - Prepare strips for the stripboard.
2. Schedule
   - Place strips on the stripboard.
   - Arrange strips to create schedule.
3. Budget
   - Price each line item.

These steps are discussed in more detail in this chapter.

> After reading the script, I prepped for my very first meeting with James [Darling]. For each project I produce or work on, I buy a notebook specifically for that production. I keep all of my notes, questions, and information there. I carry this with me on tech scouts, and scribble ideas or foreshadow problems that may come up. It's extremely useful and helps me keep a handle on things.
>
> So I printed out the script and began to mark it up. I knew it might not be the final version of the script, but lining the script gave me tons of information I would need to think about over the next few days. I learned about the locations James wanted to use—the woods, a school, a doctor's office, a border checkpoint, and a minivan driving down the road. I learned of the special effects James wanted, and the various things we would need in order to bring his story to life: cast, props, clothing, snow, etc.
>
> Jessalyn Haefele, Producer of *Citizen*

Step 1: Breakdowns

Prepare Breakdown Sheets

Breaking down the script requires that all the production elements that affect the schedule and the budget (cast, locations, props, wardrobe, etc.) be lifted from the script and placed in their respective categories on breakdown sheets (see Figure 3.1). Each scene from the script is given its own breakdown sheet. The breakdown sheets inform the budgeting process because they single out the production requirements of each scene that will likely cost money (see step 3).

Once the relevant production information has been separated from the script, the producer need not refer back

SCRIPT BREAKDOWN SHEET

(DATE) _____

CODE – BREAKDOWN SHEET
Day Ext – Yellow
Night Ext – Green
Day Int – White
Night Int – Blue

production company	production title/no.	breakdown page no.
scene no.	scene name	int/ext
description		day/night
		page count

CAST RED	STUNTS ORANGE	EXTRAS GREEN
	EXTRAS/SILENT BITS YELLOW	
SPECIAL EFFECTS BLUE	PROPS VIOLET	VEHICLES/ANIMALS PINK
WARDROBE CIRCLE	MAKE-UP/HAIR ASTERISK	SOUND EFFECTS/MUSIC BROWN
SPECIAL EQUIPMENT Box	PRODUCTION NOTES	

FIGURE 3.1 Script breakdown sheet. Visit the companion web site to download and print a copy of this form.

to it unless changes are made in casting, locations, or props. Dialogue changes do not affect the breakdowns unless they alter the length of a scene. This is a concept that students and beginners have difficulty understanding because it is common for scripts to be tweaked right up to production.

The breakdown sheets are color-coded to indicate day/exterior, night/exterior, day/interior, and night/interior scenes. If the project takes place outside during the day, you need only use day/exterior-colored breakdown sheets. The color code is a helpful scheduling tool.

The first step in the process of breaking down a script is to number the first scene (if it isn't numbered already) and draw a line in black pencil across the page at the scene's end. This line visually isolates the scene you are about to break down (see Figure 3.2).

Breakdown Sheet Header

Before adding the important information, fill in the following items at the top of the breakdown sheet:

- **Date.** The date that you are preparing the breakdown page is important when revisions are made.
- **Title of script.** Breakdown page number. This will most likely correspond to the script page, but not always.
- **Name of production company.** Give your production unit an identity. This information can come in handy when identifying yourself on the phone, on letterheads, on cards, and, most important, on the production bank account.
- **Scene number.**
- **Scene location.**
- **Interior or exterior** (indoors or outdoors).
- **Description.** This should be a brief and concise description, or "one-liner," of what happens in the scene. The

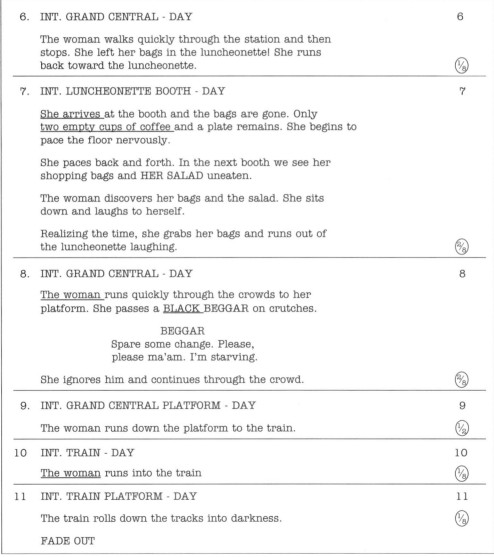

6. INT. GRAND CENTRAL - DAY   6

The woman walks quickly through the station and then stops. She left her bags in the luncheonette! She runs back toward the luncheonette.   (1/8)

7. INT. LUNCHEONETTE BOOTH - DAY   7

She arrives at the booth and the bags are gone. Only two empty cups of coffee and a plate remains. She begins to pace the floor nervously.

She paces back and forth. In the next booth we see her shopping bags and HER SALAD uneaten.

The woman discovers her bags and the salad. She sits down and laughs to herself.

Realizing the time, she grabs her bags and runs out of the luncheonette laughing.   (2/8)

8. INT. GRAND CENTRAL - DAY   8

The woman runs quickly through the crowds to her platform. She passes a BLACK BEGGAR on crutches.

         BEGGAR
    Spare some change. Please,
    please ma'am. I'm starving.

She ignores him and continues through the crowd.   (2/8)

9. INT. GRAND CENTRAL PLATFORM - DAY   9

The woman runs down the platform to the train.   (1/8)

10 INT. TRAIN - DAY   10

The woman runs into the train   (1/8)

11 INT. TRAIN PLATFORM - DAY   11

The train rolls down the tracks into darkness.   (1/8)

FADE OUT

FIGURE 3.2 A script page from *The Lunch Date* that has been broken down.

description plays an important part in quickly and efficiently identifying the scene.

- **Day or night.** You can also indicate dawn or dusk if appropriate.
- **Page count.** Proper page count is an important factor in scheduling. Pages are broken down into eight sections, with one-eighth approximately equal to 1 inch. If a scene is smaller than 1 inch, it is still considered to be one-eighth of a page. Use a ruler and mark the page horizontally into inches. This will serve as a guide. Put the total page count, in eighths (for example, a scene might be 33/8 pages), at the end of the scene on the right side, and circle it. This will indicate the page count for that particular scene. (See Figure 3.2.)

Lining the Script

Now that you have filled in the breakdown sheet header, the next step is to mark up the rest of the scene and transpose the relevant information to the breakdown page. You will need the following:

- Several pencils and a pen
- Transparent ruler
- Colored pencils or crayons
- Three-hole punch
- Blank breakdown sheets (use the sample breakdown sheet in Figure 3.1 as a model or design your own)

The colored pencils are used to "line" the script, which is printed on white pages. This color-coding of the script enables the reader to identify specific breakdowns at a glance.

Begin with the first scene in the script. As you line, or mark, each sequence in the script, transpose the information onto a corresponding breakdown page. Don't mark the whole script and then go back to fill in the breakdown pages. You might change the configuration of scene numbers. For example, what the writer has indicated as scene 4 you might actually mark to be a continuation of scene 3.

Make sure to underline, not highlight, the script. The important elements will not show through if you photocopy the script. Use colored pencils to make the following distinctions:

Cast (red). This refers to anyone with at least one word of dialogue. The name of each speaking character should be underlined the first time she appears in the scene and once on each succeeding page of the same scene. The first time a character appears in the script, her name should be typed in capital letters.

If the script calls for a minor (under 18) in a role, this fact should be flagged and referenced in the production notes. Depending on the age of the child, a teacher/welfare worker may have to be hired. Each state has its own child labor laws. Children, by law, are able to work only specified hours and must have specific rest and recreation periods. The younger the children, the less time they can work.

Extras and Silent Bits (yellow). This refers to a "silent bit" of action (no dialogue), performed by an extra, that has an effect on the plot. For example, the homeless man who wanders around Grand Central Station in *The Lunch Date* interacts with the main character and is a physical presence in the film, yet he has no specific dialogue.

Extras and Atmosphere (green). Extras fill out the frame and create atmosphere around which the central action takes place. Extras are used in crowd scenes and background activity. The choice of extras is important in setting the right tone for each scene. Note that working with extras might require additional crew. Holding extras for many days can become expensive. If possible, schedule crowd scenes together.

Stunts (orange). Any physically hazardous activity that a character performs, such as a fistfight or a fall, is a stunt. These activities should be performed by a trained stunt coordinator. If you have many stunts in your project, it is wise to hire a stunt coordinator. A stunt need not be more than a character pushing someone against a wall in a scene.

Wardrobe (circled). Any reference to specific wardrobe to be worn by anyone should be circled in the script. If the script indicates that food or blood must stain costumes, have doubles for these wardrobe items.

Makeup and Hair (indicated by an asterisk,*). This highlights any situation requiring special makeup or hair in the course of a scene or for the run of the show. Examples are wigs, facial hair, bruises, or special aging requirements. Projects set in different time periods have special hair requirements that have to be researched for accuracy. This should be noted on the breakdown page.

Props (violet). Any object indicated in the script that is handled by a character in the course of a scene, such as a knife or gun, a key, or a glass, is considered a prop. It is imperative to have backups for disposable props, such as breakaway glass and food. Props (lamps, pictures, knick-knacks) should not be confused with set dressing, which is a fixed item on the set that is not handled by the characters in the course of a scene. Weapons have to be certified and rented from a prop house and require permits.

Special Effects (blue). This can refer to explosions and fireworks, but it also relates to any physical or mechanical activity that must happen on-screen. Examples include a special lighting effect, blood packs (squibs), and firearms. When a scene calls for special effects, ample time should be allocated for setup and rehearsal, and a special effects person should discharge the special effects.

Special Equipment (boxed in ink). Using a pen, draw a box around any activity in the script that requires special equipment to execute a scene, such as a dolly, crane, zoom, or Steadicam. Special equipment needs might be specifically indicated or implicit in the way the action is described ("We move through the train station" or "Truman's moving POV up the rope ladder").

Vehicles (light pink). This refers to "picture cars" (vehicles used by the actors in the course of the scene) as well as vehicles used as background for atmosphere.

Animals (dark pink). This flags the need for an animal to perform an action in a scene. A special trainer, or wrangler, is necessary because waiting for animals to perform specific stunts can be time consuming and frustrating. The wrangler will train the animal to perform the specific task before the shooting so the scene will go smoothly.

Sound Effects and Music (brown). This refers to sound or music that must be prerecorded and played back on the set during production. This could refer to music that the actors will mouth, or lip-sync, or to particular sounds that you want an actor to respond to on the set, such as a door slamming or a gunshot.

Production Notes. This space on the breakdown sheet is provided for additional thoughts or questions about production issues reflected in the script that raise safety concerns but are not covered in the preceding categories such as shooting in these areas: rooftops, tunnels, balconies, railroad exposure, train stations, subways, bridges, abandoned buildings, and shooting in and around water. Appendix E contains a full list of safety issues)

Also make note of how many scenes take place at night. We have mentioned that shooting at night, even with the most seasoned crew, is not only less efficient, but plays havoc with a schedule. The breakdown could contain questions for the director as to how she plans to cover the scene. Your job as producer is to evaluate the exact production needs of a scene to create a realistic schedule and budget. Leave no stone unturned.

Prepare Strips for the Stripboard

After you have marked each scene and transferred the information to a corresponding breakdown sheet, you are ready to begin preparing a stripboard. A portion of the information you have culled from each scene can now be transposed to a production strip—a thin, 15-inch-long strip of cardboard. One strip represents each sequence in the script (see Figure 3.4). Each strip should contain the following information about the particular scene:

- Breakdown page number
- Day or night
- Interior or exterior
- Location or studio
- Scene number
- Number of pages
- Where the scene takes place
- Who is in the scene
- What happens in the scene

- Special effects/stunts
- Extras/atmosphere
- Animals and vehicles
- Any special requirement unique to the script

Create the header first; the header serves as a key to the strips. All the characters, extras, animals, and so on are given a corresponding code number, which serves as shorthand so that all the information will fit on each individual strip.

Color-Coding

Color-coding the strips allows you to see your project in groups of shots with a common designation. It gives the department heads an immediate visual reference of how the shoot will unfold. Indicate day or night, interior or exterior, location or studio, and anything out of the ordinary by a colored strip. At once you can see the passage of days into nights, moving from interiors to exteriors, stunts, "magic hour" shots, and major special effects, all of which have an impact on the schedule.

The production board is laid out with any color combination the producer chooses. A typical use of color is as follows:

- All day exterior scenes on powder-blue strips
- All day interior scenes on white strips
- All night exterior scenes on blue strips
- All night interior scenes on yellow strips
- All **magic hour** (see Glossary) scenes on purple strips
- All special effects and stunt shots on red strips

Step 2: Schedule

Place Strips on the Stripboard

A production stripboard is the producer's shorthand, or "show-at-a glance" (see Figure 3.3). When lined up on a stripboard, each strip becomes a building block of the production schedule. A stripboard is a series of cardboard panels into which strips can be inserted and removed with ease. From these strips, grouping scenes together can create shooting days.

The schedule is determined by arranging the strips in the order that makes the most "production sense"—that is, that requires the least amount of time to shoot. There are many variables that affect what makes good production sense. The next chapter discusses in detail all the variables that you must consider when creating the schedule for your project.

Step 3: Budget

Price Each Line Item

From the breakdown pages, the producer can accumulate vital information from which to make an accurate budget. Every item that will cost money should be pulled from the

	Scene # 1	2	3	4	5	6	7	8	9	10	11
Shooting Day											
DAY/NIGHT	N	D	N	D	N	D	N	D	N	D	N
Scene #	1	2	3	4	5	6	7	8	9	10	11
EXT/INT	I	I	I	I	I	I	I	I	I	I	I
Description	Barbershop - Bob begins to cut Ted's hair. Evan enters the shop. Bob starts the story.	Barbershop (Flashback) - Judge Rivers and Bessie enter. Mr. Lee rec. Young Bob to cut Judges hair.	Barbershop - Evan asks for bathroom. His friend waits outside. Bob continues story.	Barbershop (Flashback) - Young Bob is nervous as he starts on Judge hair. Bessie watches.	Barbershop - Bob tells story and watches Evan.	Barbershop (Flashback) - Young Bob makes a mistake. Bessie sees it.	Barbershop - Bob finishes shaving Ted. Evan takes a seat.	Barbershop (Flashback) - Judge questions young Bob's pace. Bob & Bessie make eye contact.	Barbershop - Evan is nervous. Bob asks if he plays chess.	Barbershop (Flashback) - Young Bob finishes the Judge's hair- fixing his mistake. Judge & Bessie are happy.	Barbershop - Bob finishes Ted's hair. Evan leaves shop. Ted's police uniform is revealed. Bob closes the shop.
No. of Pages	1 7/8	3 5/8	1	4/8	1 1/8	4/8	3/8	3/8	6/8	1 1/8	1 7/8
EXPORT (X)											
Bob Delagard	X		X		X		X		X		X
Ted Dupree	X		X		X		X		X		X
Evan Wiley	X		X		X		X		X		X
Young Bob Delagard		X		X		X		X		X	
Mr. Lee		X		X		X		X		X	
Judge Rivers		X		X		X		X		X	
Bessie		X		X		X		X		X	
Mr. Stanley		X		X		X		X		X	
Customers		X		X		X		X		X	
Teen Boy			X								

Interface panel (left): dusk | dawn — goto — E/I — **A Nick In Time** | Script Days — strip | DAY/EXT. | element — new | DAY/INT. | new — edit | NIGHT/EXT. | goto — fwd | NIGHT/INT. — bkwd | keys on — divider | clear | keys off — export scene info | export elements — sort | unsort | filter — C St B A Ef S Pr V — W M Eq Lo No

FIGURE 3.3 Header and stripboard. Visit the companion web site to download and print a copy of this form.

breakdown pages and assigned an estimated price. This includes props, costumes, locations, special effects, special makeup, picture vehicles, and animals.

These lists will become important when you prepare the preliminary budget. You won't have to refer to the script again unless it goes through changes during the rewriting process. If there are changes, everything, including the breakdown pages, the strips on the stripboard, and the budget, will need to be adjusted to reflect these changes.

The Digital Producer

This chapter provides the student or beginner with the basics of how a schedule has been prepared for 60+ years. Although the producer must still extract the necessary information from the script and fill out the breakdown pages, the traditional stripboard has been replaced by computer software. Although these programs don't replace hard work and diligence, they make organizing the information faster and more efficient.

Production management applications offer easy-to-use scheduling and breakdown software that provide a depth of features for the film producer, production manager, or assistant director. The most commonly used professional program is EP Scheduling (formerly Movie Magic Scheduling) from Entertainment Partners. It can break down your script into dozens of predefined or custom categories (for props, vehicles, stunts, costumes, audio, lighting, and talent). You can sort and print a variety of reports and lists such as shooting days, shooting schedules, shot lists, breakdown sheets, calls sheets, cast lists, prop and costumes lists, and general production forms. You can even bring storyboard images into your breakdown sheets and create schedules that are linked directly to your script.

Over the years popular spreadsheet programs have been utilized to prepare budgets for both large and small productions. These programs allow users to break down and define every phase of production and the associated costs. Because every item of the production process is listed on the budget form, it acts like a checklist ensuring that no budget consideration, however small, is neglected. The better programs are designed for the feature film industry but are easily adapted for the short form. EP Budgeting (formerly Movie Magic Budgeting) from Entertainment Partners is flexible and easy to use; plus, it offers libraries of databases for rates, crews, and talent charges and subgroups for handling multiple versions of a budget and is the companion software to EP Scheduling.

DIRECTOR

Storyboards and Floor Plans

To create a fully realized schedule and budget, the producer needs to know not only how the director plans to visualize the words on the page, but what actors and locations she

```
┌─────────┐
│    D    │
├─────────┤
│    2    │
├─────────┤
│    I    │
├─────────┤
│         │
├─────────┤
│         │
│  Barbershop (Flashback) - Judge Rivers and Bessie enter.  Mr. Lee rec. Young Bob to cut Judge's hair.  │
│         │
├─────────┤
│  3 5/8  │
├─────────┤
│         │
├─────────┤
│         │
├─────────┤
│         │
├─────────┤
│    X    │
├─────────┤
│    X    │
├─────────┤
│    X    │
├─────────┤
│    X    │
├─────────┤
│    X    │
├─────────┤
│    X    │
├─────────┤
│         │
└─────────┘
```

FIGURE 3.4 A Strip.

intends to choose to fulfill her vision for the material. The director will also add other information not reflected in the script, such as complicated camera movements, special lighting requests, and the number of extras needed.

Important decisions like these spring from a deep understanding and interpretation of the material. Understanding, memorizing, absorbing, and living the script are all part of the director's homework. Keeping a director's journal of your impressions about how a scene should look or feel helps in this respect. This is an ongoing process. As more elements of the project become solidified, like cast and locations, things will change.

You should have a specific vision for the script and firm ideas about how you want to realize that vision. At the same time, however, you should remain flexible.

Why does the director have to be so prepared? Organization in preproduction leads to flexibility on the set. In the heat of production, changes, additions, alterations, and compromises are made. Perhaps a location falls through, requiring the company to move to a backup location. A cast member leaves the production, or the sun won't cooperate. Only a director who knows her material cold will be able to guide the production through troubled waters and come out the other side with a well-told story.

Flexibility also means the ability to alter the plan to accommodate the creativity of the moment if an actor or crew member has a good idea. A well-prepared director should be open to the creative ideas of her crew as long as they fit within her overall interpretation of the script.

> I had done my homework and done my time line. I was always very conscious of where my energies should be going at what time. I was allocating my time in terms of getting things done as they were supposed to be. It all goes back to being a production assistant on the feature, where I really saw that if you didn't have your act together you were going to sink and you were going to be pretty miserable while it happened.
>
> Howard McCain

Developing a Shooting Plan

The director is responsible for every element in front of the camera. She must be clear as to why each element, each character, each speech, and each detail is in the film. Every element should have a function and make an impression that will affect the telling of the story. A story takes place in time and space, and the director defines that time and space. In addition, she determines the pace at which the story is told.

Every creative decision flows from her vision of the script. The director defines this vision by developing a profound understanding of the script and a clear sense of its theme or central idea. It is from that point that she begins to break down each scene to discover how it will serve that central idea. There are many decisions to be made as to what the camera and actors will reveal at any given moment.

The director's preparation for principal photography centers on breaking down the script into shots. This shooting plan, or shot list, is an important factor in finalizing the shooting schedule.

How does the director convert the script to a visual plan? The process, called previsualization, can be done with simple drawings, an extremely detailed shot-by-shot storyboard (See Figure 3.8) or with a more general summary coupled with floor plans (see Figures 3.5 – 3.7).

The director, having a good idea of the resources available to her, translates the script into shots by previsualizing it on paper. She confers with the director of photography, the art director, and the production manager to confirm the feasibility of her choices. Each of the director's choices will affect each department in a different way. If a **dolly shot** (see Glossary) is called for, the director of photography prepares the appropriate equipment and crew. A low-angle shot might require the art director to prepare a ceiling piece. The addition of a key actor in a scene can cause the production manager to reexamine the schedule. (For specifics on hiring these personnel, see Chapter 6.)

The director follows these 11 basic steps to arrive at a shooting plan:

- Know the script.
- Know the theme.
- Develop a history for the main characters.

- Know what each character wants in the story.
- Break down each scene for dramatic beats.
- Determine a visual style for the story.
- Study the locations and sets.
- Rehearse the actors.
- Settle on pacing and tone.
- Create floor plans and storyboards.
- Make a shot list.

Know the Script

The director must know the script inside and out. At any given moment during production, she must be able to focus her actors and crew on a specific dramatic moment and be aware of how it fits into the whole. Because films are rarely shot in continuity, having a comprehensive knowledge of the script is a vitally important skill. If the director gives a direction that makes the moment of too great or too little importance, it will affect the entire piece. A director dreams of a good script. The beats, the build, and the pacing in a good script are easy to determine. A poorly written script usually causes a director problems and can get her into trouble. She should discover the answer to these questions when analyzing each scene of the script:

- Why is this scene here? How is it crucial to the telling of the story?
- What would happen if the scene were removed?
- What do I need to achieve with this scene to ensure that it supports my story?

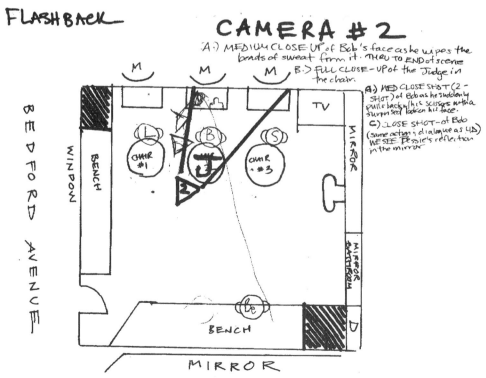

FIGURE 3.5 Floor plan from *A Nick in Time*.

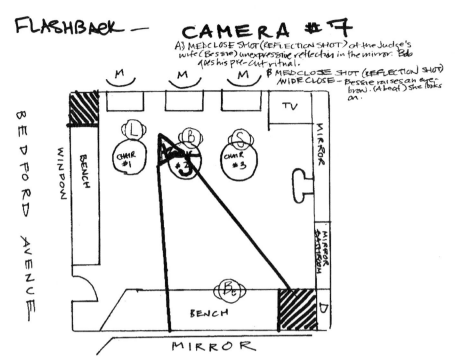

FIGURE 3.6   Floor plan from *A Nick in Time*.

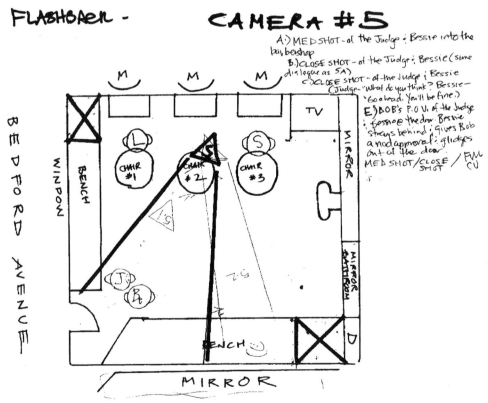

FIGURE 3.7   Floor plan from *A Nick In Time*.

- How does this scene advance the arc of the character(s)? What do we know now that we didn't know before?
- How does it follow from the previous scene?
- How does it connect to the next scene?

These questions are at the core of your script breakdown. If you are not clear on the importance and necessity of each scene in your project, you are not ready to direct those scenes. Before you can begin creating a dramatic and visual plan, you must clearly understand the objective of each and every scene in your script.

Know the Theme

It is not enough merely to know the story line; the director must also understand the central theme—what the story is really all about. The theme represents your desire to communicate something specific about the human condition. It may be one of the reasons that attracted you to the story in the first place.

The message of *Truman* is the importance of confronting one's fears early in life. This message is embodied in the coach's last line, "Today it was only a rope, but when it's your big turn in life…." By climbing the rope ladder, the boy gained a small victory that one hopes will give him confidence to face challenges in the future. Your theme and how you present it will influence all your creative decisions for the project, such as cast, crew, and locations.

Develop a History of the Main Characters

To gain a deeper understanding of each character's objectives, it is important to know not only what the characters say and do in the script, but also what they might have said and done before and even after the story ends. This is called the characters' **back story**. It can be as detailed (in-depth life history from birth) as it needs to be to help the actors really "know" the characters they are playing. Depending on the actors and their training, the director can use this history to help the actors shape their parts during rehearsals and in production.

For example, is the character an eccentric? What elements in the script bring out this quality, and how is the eccentricity revealed? How can a director use the camera to illustrate this trait? The director of *The Lunch Date* fleshed out the well-to-do woman's character by filming her compulsively cleaning her fork and the table

In the theater, the director and actors of a play are given a tremendous amount of rehearsal time to explore the script and the characters that inhabit the story. In a film, the director might have very little or even no rehearsal time. To get an actor up to speed and "in character" requires that the director know the character intimately. She needs to develop a verbal skill for communicating her ideas about the character quickly to the actor.

However, we encourage beginning filmmakers to rehearse as much as possible. This will allow them time to develop a rapport with the actors, explore creative ways to interpret the material, fine-tune the script, work out blocking for cast and camera, and work with the actors to develop their roles. The rehearsal period is an opportunity to tap the creativity of the actors without the pressure of having to perform on the set.

Know What Each Character Wants in the Story

The director needs to understand each character's objective during the course of the story or during the time that character appears in the story. The nature of that objective can be conscious or unconscious. The woman in *The Lunch Date* wants to eat her salad and get back to the suburbs, but the homeless man's motivation is less clear. Why does he not only allow the woman to share his salad, but also buy her coffee? In reacting to the unusual turn of events, the man decides to treat the woman to an experience she will most likely never have again. Unlike the woman's objective, his objective is ambiguous and more unconscious in nature. For an actor, however, it is difficult to play "ambiguous." He must be given an action that, when seen by the audience, is interpreted as ambiguous.

The primary action of the barber in *A Nick in Time* is to prevent the young kid from making a mistake that could adversely affect the rest of his life. The kid doesn't know that the barber is cutting the hair of a policeman (hidden by the barber's drape). The barber must convince the kid to come back another time without creating any suspicion on the kid's part. This is the basic conflict of the piece.

The young man in *Citizen* has a clear-cut goal: to leave the country. The reasons and the time line for doing so are not so clear-cut as the time frame in which the story is told. The wife in *Crazy Glue* wants to revive the affections of her philandering husband.

Truman's objective is to climb the rope ladder; the coach forces him to. The kids support Truman because if he climbs, the coach will let them play kickball. At first, it seems as though the coach is just being mean, but later he reveals that his motivation is to teach Truman a life lesson. By gaining a clear understanding of each character's objective in the story, the director can make sure that each scene, and each dramatic beat within each scene, reflects that objective.

Break Down Each Scene into Dramatic Beats

The director controls what the audience should be seeing and hearing at all times within the shot. Storytelling is all about understanding how each dramatic moment or beat connects to the next. **A beat is a moment of change, a shift in the narrative flow.** The primary beats of a story are its beginning, middle, and end. Within these major beats are the scenes, and within each scene are smaller beats that represent the subtler dramatic shifts from moment to moment.

Beats are motivated by the characters' objectives. When the action or objective changes, so do the beats. They are the internal signposts that guide us along the emotional road that the story or scene is following.

In analyzing and breaking down each scene in the script, the director must determine the following:

- What are the beats?
- How will they be built?
- How will they be staged?
- What is the pace of each beat?
- How will the characters move from one beat to the next?
- How do all the beats together make up the scene?

Every scene has one major objective, and the characters define that objective. In the following scene from *The Lunch Date*, the woman's objective is to eat her salad. She thinks that the homeless man has taken hers, and because she has no more money (having lost her wallet), she can't buy another. The obstacle to her objective is the homeless man; this causes the conflict. We have broken down the scene into the beats that chart the progression the character is making toward or away from her goal.

```
INT. LUNCHEONETTE BOOTH-DAY
The woman sits down across from the home-
less man in the booth.
                  WOMAN
          That's my salad.
         HOMELESS BLACK MAN
          Get out of here.
                  WOMAN
          That's my salad.
(This is the end of beat 1. We wait for her
next move.)
(Woman: Stake her claim)
She reaches for the plate. He pulls it
back.
         HOMELESS BLACK MAN
               Hey!
(Beat 2. There is a pause.)
(Woman: Checking him out)
The woman watches him chomping away at
the bits of lettuce. He ignores her.
Moments pass.
(Beat 3. We wonder, "What will she do?")
(Woman: Test the water)
She reaches over with her fork and swipes
a piece of food off the plate. She looks
to the man to see if he objects. He con-
tinues eating. She takes another bite.
Then another. And another.
Still, the man does not respond. Suddenly
he stands and walks down the aisle.
(Beat 4. Left alone, she continues to
eat.)
(Turning point)
```

```
She continues munching away at what
remains. He returns with two cups of cof-
fee with saucers. He places the cup on
the table and sits.
(Beat 5. She finishes.) (Man: Makes a
peace offering)
He offers her sugar.
                  WOMAN
No, thank you.
He offers her a packet of Sweet & Low from
his coat. She accepts.
                  WOMAN
Thank you.
(Beat 6. The scene has reached its climax.)
(Woman: To accept his offering)
Checking her watch, she stands with her
purse and leaves. He watches her exit,
somewhat disappointed.
(Beat 7. The scene winds down on a sad
note.)
```

Each beat in this scene is a moment when the direction of the story could shift; instead of letting her share his salad, the man could simply refuse. At each beat, each character reassesses the situation and then decides to act or not. All beats, however, are not created equal. Certainly, an important beat in the scene is beat 4 when the man walks away. This is arguably the turning point of the scene. Turning points are the major beats on which the action of the scene hinges. If he doesn't allow her to share, the scene will most likely end here. In this regard, the most dramatic turning point is the climax, when he brings her some coffee and they have their "lunch date."

Within the primary objectives or actions of the scene are smaller but equally important ones that motivate the actor's intentions, beat by beat. Her overall intention is to eat her salad, but faced with how the man responds to her objective, she must shift gears and try different means to achieve her goal.

The woman's first attempt to retrieve her salad is verbal. Rebuffed by this, she reaches out for the salad, only to be snubbed again. This is beat 1. Her action with this beat is to stake her claim. Moments pass as she considers the situation. This is beat 2, to check him out. At beat 3, her action is to test the water. This results in her quickly reaching out to snatch a piece of salad. She stops for a reaction, and when there is none, she takes another bite and then another. Without responding, the man suddenly stands and walks away. This is beat 4, the turning point. By his action, he has tacitly allowed her to share his salad with him. When he returns with her coffee, his action is to make a peace offering, which is beat 5. Beat 6, the climax, is when she accepts the coffee and sugar. Her action is to accept his peace offering. The tension between the characters shifts to camaraderie. There is a deflation of energy in the scene upon her exit as he watches her, somewhat disappointed. This is beat 7.

These directions are conjectures on our part, but they seem to work with the action of the scene. You may come up with others that would work equally well. The bottom line is, will they help the actor? During rehearsals, the actor and director discover and shape each of these beats. Shaping the beats together is also called phrasing a scene.

Another example of an important beat in your story is the introduction of the main character. What is the character doing when we first see him? The introduction of *Truman* is a good example. All eyes are focused on Truman, the last to climb up the rope ladder. Introducing or revealing a character can be an exciting visual moment. The character can suddenly appear on a cut, you can cut to an empty frame and have the character step out of the darkness into the light, or the character can be revealed at the end of a long pan. The character's behavior and the way it is photographed will give the audience a world of information. Take full advantage of this golden opportunity.

Determine a Visual Style for the Story

Now that you understand the important moments or beats of each scene, you need to develop an appropriate way to capture those moments on film. The director looks for visual motifs that best complement the material. An excellent way to begin this process is to pore over paintings, photographs, and even magazine advertisements to look for images that express a visual style similar to the one you want to capture. (See Chapter 8 for ideas on how to define a look.) One key image could serve as a visual motif for the entire project. Sharing your visual ideas with the director of photography will begin the collaborative relationship that will ultimately and ideally lead to a mutual approach. In preparing for *The Lunch Date*, the director shared his love of Alfred Stieglitz's photographs as an inspiration for style.

Just as I had written every version of the script, I visualized every version of the movie. In my first draft, I was imagining it as a fake documentary, so it was going to be handheld, dirty and grimy. But a crystallizing moment happened after I watched the show *Lost*. I wanted my short to look like that. It is easily the most cinematic show on television. They are shooting in such an epic location—Hawaii, as this island—but they do a really good mix of standard, very traditional film-making like slow push-ins and beautiful epic crane shots, but then they'll mix it up with a lot of handheld stuff.. They use the perfect shot for every moment. I was also inspired by Christopher Nolan's aesthetic and Stanley Kubrick.

James Darling

You can begin to think visually when you understand the story, the characters, and the theme. What is the nature or genre of your script? Are there conventions that should be followed or broken?

The style in which a horror film is shot is very different from the style for a comedy. Horror films are usually dark and moody, and the camera work is often shaky or canted. Comedies are generally brightly lit, and the camera is often static or fluid, allowing the actors to perform their comedic action without camera distractions. Or you can think about playing against the expectation of the genre.

The overall visual plan for a sequence, or mise-en-scène, requires that the director decide whether the camera will be static or moving and whether the shots will be long or short. The beauty of the art of filmmaking is that the director's style, combined with the nature of the script, will always make for a unique approach to the text.

There's no such thing as a compelling subject; there's only a compelling filmmaker. You can give the greatest subject in the world to a mediocre filmmaker and they'll make it boring and nonfilmic.

Jan Krawitz

Study the Locations and Rehearse the Actors

As soon as a location is set, the director should absorb the confines of the space, imagine how it can be transformed into the world of her story and how she might choreograph the drama. It is ideal if the director can actually rehearse the actors in the location they will be shooting in. If not, she can put tape down in the rehearsal space to duplicate the parameters of the actual location.

Settle on Pacing and Tone

Rhythm and pace drive the audience to the emotional response that a scene demands. This is one of the director's primary responsibilities. A well-written script has a built-in style and pace. The author clearly presents the time and space of the story. The director merely translates the written word into pictures. This is why it is said that obtaining a good script is half the director's battle. Does the script indicate that the pace of a scene should be slow or fast, frantic or constrained?

Workshop Ideas on Video

It is understandably challenging for a beginner to be able to project how the script will play rhythmically, how the actors will move around in the locations, and where to put the camera to capture those key dramatic moments. The rehearsal period is an opportune time to develop the pace of the story. The director is able to explore performance and staging options and make whatever adjustments are needed to represent the best that the script has to offer. By shooting these sessions on video and studying them afterward, the director can begin to discover what blocking works best for each scene and where to place the camera to capture what is important.

> Once we arrived at a shot list I hired a storyboard artist. He had a program that allows you to storyboard on the computer. We sat down in his apartment over the course of several days and boarded out the whole film. Everything had been worked out. The only thing left to chance was what the actors were going to bring to the table.
>
> Be' Garrett

Create Floor Plans and Storyboards

With a thorough understanding of the script, the characters, and the visual style for the show, the director can be specific about the shots she plans to use to tell the story.

At this point, the director can work out the kind of coverage she will want for each scene. Coverage refers to the number and kinds of shots needed to tell the story through each scene. To record a scene, you might use a series of rapidly edited images or a single, long, choreographed shot. To facilitate this process, it is recommended that the director work with floor plans and storyboards.

> After I made the shot list, I prioritized which ones were our most important shots. There were always a few little shots, or a few other angles at the end of each day, that I would have liked to have covered, but I never got the opportunity.
>
> Adam Davidson

Floor Plans

A floor plan is a ceiling viewpoint of the space in which you will be shooting your scene. On it, show the character's movements and the camera angles necessary to cover the scene properly. The camera angles are indicated by small v's, and the direction they are pointing (with indicated camera moves) allows the director and all department heads to know where the camera will be positioned (see Figures 3.5 to 3.7 from *A Nick in Time*). Furniture pieces, walls, and set dressing can be indicated and shifted to allow the director to visualize her best angles.

A floor plan will help you consolidate your intentions for blocking and indicate how to use the fewest and most effective camera angles. This diagram, growing out of the blocking developed during rehearsals and adjusted by the realities of the location, can help in working out editing ideas in advance and can enable the director of photography (DP) to devise a complementary lighting plan. The art department will know from the floor plans which part

of the set or location will be in the frame and which part will be out of the frame. The location department will see from the floor plans where the cars and trucks can be parked so that they will not appear in any of the shots.

From this floor plan, the director can prioritize her shot list, leaving extra shots, sometimes called beauty or "gravy shots," until the end. If she goes over schedule, she can sacrifice a gravy shot, but she will still have the meat of the scene in the can.

> At this point, we brought out our little overhead maps of the gym, which was basically just a basketball court with lines drawn on it. We started laying out camera positions, determining who would be seen and what would be needed in each shot, and then we tried to group the shots in terms of efficiency: you know, those facing the same direction, so you're using the same lighting setup or the same number of kids in the shot.
>
> Howard McCain

Storyboards

Storyboarding is one of the ways in which directors prepare for a production. The detailed use of storyboards, or continuity sketches as they were originally called, began at Walt Disney Studios as early as 1927, in the creation of animated films. This technique consists of making a series of sketches in which every basic scene and every camera setup within the scene is illustrated like a black-and-white comic book. Storyboards give the director and all department heads a visual record of the film before it is shot (see Figure 3.8).

> The class at NYU where I made the film is a yearlong class. The first six months I was very, very, very lax. I only did storyboards, which were very helpful. John Canemaker, my teacher, was giving the course. He is a major advocate of storyboarding. He thinks it is one of the most important tools in the animated short.
>
> Tatia Rosenthal

Having a storyboard is not essential for a dialogue sequence of two people in a room. Floor plans are just as effective because they give the filmmaker the sense of depth, something that is difficult to re-create in a two-dimensional drawing. Storyboards are critical, however, for an action sequence or montage (see Chapter 11 for a *Truman* montage).

A director's stick figures are usually adequate to suggest image size and spatial relationships, but if the budget can afford the expense, a storyboard artist can flesh out the director's visual ideas. The director can also use computer software programs that are now available such as Story-Board Quick or StoryBoard Artist, both created by

FIGURE 3.8   Storyboards from *Truman*.

Power Production Software (www.powerproduction.com) or FrameForge 3D Studio by Innovative Software, LLC (www.frameforge3d.com).

What can be equally useful is a digital storyboard—digital photos of visual ideas, taken during rehearsal or on location, input into the computer and sequenced. These photos can be viewed with the DP.

I had a pretty complete shot list. As the script was getting closer and closer to a final draft, I started to storyboard. The storyboard really just mirrored the shot list, but again, it also informed the shots and changed the shots slightly. You begin to realize you don't quite need as many shots as you thought.

Howard McCain

Make a Shot List

The list of the shots required for a particular sequence is termed a **shot list**. The shots indicated on the storyboards and floor plans are prioritized so that a shooting schedule can be ascertained from this list. The assistant director and production manager need to know the number of shots planned to be able to schedule each day correctly. Once the storyboards, floor plans, and shot list all have been approved, the director can turn to principal photography confident that she has an effective shooting plan.

> I did a combination of storyboarding and floor plans, but mainly I relied on a floor plan. In terms of storyboarding, I knew I wanted to have a closeup of her hands getting the ticket, and the stuff with the wallet falling out, and her entrance. I designed it to have the camera here for this shot, here for that shot, here for that one there. We numbered the shots and then made a shot list.
>
> Adam Davidson

A shot list is not a list of setups. The term **setup** refers to every time you move the camera. A shot list details every shot. From one camera position, you might change lenses and therefore have two or more shots from one setup. Your choices when making a shot list range the entire width and breadth of camera language. Here is a partial list of elements you can explore before you decide what shots you will employ in your piece. For a more detailed exploration of visual grammar, refer to Chapter 11.

- **ECU**: Extreme close-up (eyes and nose)
- **CU**: Close-up (complete face)
- **MS**: Medium shot (torso)
- **WS**: Wide shot (full body)
- **LS**: Long shot (full body in landscape)
- **XLS**: Extreme long shot (small body in vista)

The following is a sample of the order in which the scenes of *The Lunch Date* could have been shot: Scotty is the actress playing the well-to-do woman and Bernard plays the black businessman.

Monday

1. Scotty gets on train
2. Train leaves, Scotty in frame
3. Train leaves, nobody in frame
4. CU shot of Scotty after train missed
5. Medium shot Scotty straightening up

Lunch

6. Master of accident action
6A. Post train master

7. Super dolly of entire action
8. Dolly on face
9. Dolly on purse
10. Tight 2-shot collision
11. After all pickup, Bernard hands Scotty last stuff; she rushes off
12. Medium shot Bernard pickup
13. CU Bernard pickup
14. Medium shot pickup
15. CU shot pickup

Tuesday

1. Scotty enters, dolly (with bags)
2. Scotty enters, again, dolly (without bags)
3. Scotty enters, last time, dolly (different speed)
4. Scotty takes out ticket
5. Panhandler approaches—wide
6. Panhandler talks—2-shot
7. Ladies room sign (shot not used in film)
8. Ladies room door (shot not used in film)
9. Scotty decides not to go in (shot not used in film)

In the world of animation, much of the work is shot like a test on video, so you can actually see the film as it unfolds in the computer or on the animation stand.

> I shot *Crazy Glue* with no video assist. People use lunchboxes to see how their animation is going. They don't take the next frame unless they know it works well with the animation. We didn't have that, so I didn't use that. You shoot it on a lunchbox first. You test your animation as you go along. For stop motion we didn't have a lunch box. Today there are solutions that are computer based for such things, but at that time there was no computer software that would do the same thing. The lunchbox was a device hooked up to a video camera—a little hard drive that takes one frame at a time and it's hooked up to a TV monitor and plays it in reel time for you. Then it looks at the next frame that you are about to film but you haven't committed to yet and plays that with the sequence you already have committed to film, and you get to choose if it's a good idea or not to have the frame exactly there.
>
> Tatia Rosenthal

The Final Word

It is not easy to transfer the script onto storyboards or floor plan sketches. Both aesthetic and practical factors must be considered. The director must ask, "How can I best cover this scene?" and, at the same time, "Do I have the resources to realize my vision for the camera choices I have made?" Aesthetic and practical considerations are often so inextricably bound together that the director will often make decisions about shots purely by instinct. The final word rests with the director. It is part of her job.

KEY POINTS

- Breakdowns are the link between the script and the budget.
- The shot list, storyboards, and floor plans inform the schedule.
- The director breaks down the script beat by beat.
- Be familiar with visual language.

Chapter 4

Schedule

I remember thinking there were four major components to building the shooting schedule. One was location restraints. Two was actor availability. Three was scene order. Four was the individual shots within the scenes, particularly with regard to how difficult they were as camera movements or how tough they were going to be for the actors.

Howard McCain

PRODUCER (AS PRODUCTION MANAGER)

Building a Stripboard

Once the producer has dissected the script and stripped it of the essential production elements, he can create a shooting schedule. The shooting or production schedule shows the order in which scenes are to be shot during production. The schedule is the primary road map of the production and an essential factor in discovering how much the picture will actually cost. The reason is that there is a direct link between the number of days required to shoot the project and the budget. We will focus on budget in the next chapter, but it is important here to understand the logic of how these steps relate to one another. Don't tackle a detailed budget before you have made a schedule. These are the steps:

1. Script
2. Script Breakdowns
3. Schedule
4. Budget

This chapter focuses on the variables that you will need to consider when making your schedule. Films are rarely shot in continuity—that is, in the exact order in which they appear in the script. Shooting out of continuity is a common practice in the industry because production considerations such as actors' schedules, locations, and crew availability usually make it impossible to follow the script's chronology when filming. The shooting schedule is designed so that scenes are grouped together in an order that allows for the most efficient use of time, personnel, and resources. Production efficiency is paramount to getting the most from each dollar

If you have correctly broken down the script into breakdown sheets and have transferred the key information onto production strips, you are ready to create a schedule. The scene strips are the tools, and the stripboard is the mechanism on which the order of the scenes can be easily manipulated. The stripboard serves as a visual representation or overview of the production schedule. The beauty of this time-tested system is the ease in which strips can be maneuvered in and out of the board (whether manually or by computer) and the ability to access the entire schedule at a glance (see Figure 4.1).

Don't think that this first pass at a schedule will be the final one. You are creating what might be considered a first draft. It is a launching point, not something written in stone. This initial schedule will go through many transformations during the preproduction period. Many factors influence the ideal shooting order of scenes for any particular project, and these factors invariably change as the shoot date approaches.

General Guidelines

There is no mystery to working out a schedule. It is a process that is governed by logic and common sense. For example, it makes good sense to group together all shots from one location, all night exteriors, or all crowd scenes. Remember, with color-coded strips, the schedule can be laid out and grouped by color, which will afford the department heads an overview of the schedule at a glance. The strips will be moved around until your schedule falls into place.

Each film is unique and is designed with its own set of assumptions. No schedule is set in stone until the camera rolls, and even then, adjustments can be made. Consider the following general guidelines as you arrange the strips on the stripboard—that is, as you put the scenes in the order in which they are to be shot.

> I wanted to shoot in September but I was working as a producer in commercial advertising, so I was overseas at that time. That bugged me out. So I picked a date and said January 22. We are going to shoot on that date, hell or high water, we are going to shoot. So, that began the process of pre-production that began with everything from breaking down the script, figuring out the shot list, the cast, etc.
>
> Be' Garrett

doi: 10.1016/B978-0-240-81174-1.00011-7

Shooting Schedule

Day One: Friday, February 10, 2006

2	INT. MINIVAN: Jonathan sits in back	4/8 pp
4	EXT. FOREST ROAD: Jonathan leaves family	6/8 pp
26	INT. PRISONER TRANSPORT: Jonathan thrown in vehicle	2/8 pp
27	EXT. BORDER STATION: Jonathan driven back to U.S.	3/8 pp

******* END OF DAY 1 FRIDAY FEBRUARY 10, 2006   TOTAL PAGE COUNT 2

Day Two: Saturday, February 11, 2006

22	EXT. FOREST: Jonathan eats sandwich	2/8 pp
23	EXT. FOREST: Jonathan runs	4/8 pp
24	EXT. FOREST: Hunters catch Jonathan	1 1/8 pp

*************************MINI MOVE*************************************

6	EXT. FOREST: Jonathan sees shimmer of wall	4/8 pp

******** END OF DAY 2 SATURDAY FEBRUARY 11, 2006 TOTAL PAGES 2 3/8

Day Three: Sunday, February 12, 2006

3	INT. DOCTORS OFFICE: Doctor intro	3/8 pp
5	INT. DOCTORS OFFICE: Allergies	4/8 pp
7	INT. DOCTORS OFFICE: Exercise	1/8 pp
9	INT. DOCTORS OFFICE: "Multitasking"	2/8 pp
11	INT. DOCTORS OFFICE: Weight	1/8 pp
13	INT. DOCTORS OFFICE: Fully undressed	1/8 pp
19	INT. DOCTORS OFFICE: Drawing Blood	1/8 pp
21	INT. DOCTORS OFFICE: Just relax	1/8 pp
23	INT. DOCTORS OFFICE: Blood Pressure Cross Cut	4/8 pp
25	INT. PUBLIC SCHOOL HALLWAY: Jonathan sees lineup	3/8 pp

*****END OF DAY 3 SUNDAY FEBRUARY 12, 2006 TOTAL PAGE COUNT 2 5/8

Day Four: Monday, February 13, 2006

8	EXT. FOREST: Jonathan runs into wall	3/8 pp
10	EXT. FOREST WALL: Jonathan uses phone to find passage	3/8 pp
12	EXT. FOREST WALL: Jonathan contemplates small hole	2/8 pp
14	EXT. FOREST WALL: Jonathan throws clothes over wall	2/8 pp
16	EXT. FOREST WALL: Jonathan enters Canada	2/8 pp
18	EXT. FOREST: Jonathan hits head on wall	4/8 pp
20	EXT. FOREST WALL: Jonathan leaves trail of blood	2/8 pp

*************************COMPANY MOVE******************************

15	INT. UNDERGROUND TUNNEL: Jonathan crawls	5/8 pp
17	INT. UNDERGROUND TUNNEL: Jonathan's leg caught	1/8 pp

********END OF DAY 4 MONDAY FEBRUARY 13, 2006 TOTAL PAGE COUNT 3

FIGURE 4.1   Shooting schedule for *Citizen*.

Fixed Dates

You might encounter situations beyond your control involving actors or locations that will set fixed parameters before you've even begun to formulate a schedule. Perhaps an actor has a prior commitment to start another project on a specific date before or after your picture begins, or perhaps a particular location is available only on specific dates or during certain hours. Barbershops are usually closed on Sundays and Mondays, so the crew of *A Nick in Time* had only two days to shoot the film because the entire film takes place in a barbershop. Otherwise, they would have had to compensate the barbershop monetarily for time lost. The crew of *The Lunch Date* was not permitted to shoot in Grand Central Station during rush hours. This restriction limited shooting time to four hours in the middle of the day.

Working with fixed parameters such as these can be difficult. Normally, you would prefer the schedule to be totally flexible. However, if there are givens, you must adhere to them. A note pinned to the stripboard will remind everyone of fixed dates as the strips are shuffled.

Scotty was just starting a play, so she was in rehearsals and had to be out every day by five. That wasn't a problem at Grand Central because we had to be out of there by two. The last day at the restaurant we got her out in time as well. Scotty was basically in every shot. I had Clebert come down just one of the shooting days because he was just in the one scene there. I tried to stick as close as possible to continuity, where things like locations became important.

For example, as I mentioned before, we were only allowed to shoot on the train platforms when the supervisor came down. So suddenly in the middle of the day, we would have to stop and go to the platform. That was day one. On the second day, the supervisor didn't show up. So we went down on the platform and started shooting and then got kicked out.... They just didn't want us near the platform because of the danger of the electrical rails.

Adam Davidson

Locations

Group all your locations. The goal is to complete photography of all the scenes in any given location before going on to the next one. In the industry, this is referred to as **shooting out** a location. It doesn't make sense to travel back and forth to a location because every move the production company makes takes time and must be factored into the schedule This was not an issue in the case of *Truman, Crazy Glue, A Nick in Time*, and *Mirror Mirror* because each film took place in one location. However, in *The Lunch Date*, it made sense to shoot out the cafeteria before moving to Grand Central Station or vice versa. *Citizen* grouped each day of the four-day shoot around a specific location (see Figure 4.1).

The doctor stuff was shot in the same location as the hallway scene at Xavier Heights High School, a couple of blocks away from Union Square. It was a very easy location for all of our extras to get to, despite the blizzard, which was the day we shot there. Had we been in a more remote location, I doubt we would have had the turnout we ended up getting.

We had a location at a state park in Long Island which we used for the Canadian border and for the parents dropping him off. The big thing we had to negotiate for this location was actually flying a Canadian flag instead of the parks flag. I do not know what my producer (Jessalyn Haefele) said to them but she got them to change their mind.

James Darling

If your story requires multiple locations (as did *Citizen*), it is advisable to locate them as close as possible to one another. This will reduce travel time and permit the establishment of a home base close to all the locations that will serve as a production center.

If the script requires shooting at a distant location, travel days must be factored into the schedule. (See Chapter 9 for variables to consider when making this decision.)

Organizing and executing a quick and efficient move of the entire production company, a **company move**, is an art unto itself. A move is considered to be a company move if it is across the street, across the city, or across the county. Making a move once or twice in a day is not uncommon, but adequate time must be allocated in your schedule for such moves. For example, if you were to schedule two company moves across town in a day, it might take 2 hours to break down all the equipment, or **wrap out** of the location, and move it across town. Two moves would take up 4 hours, or a third of a 12-hour day.

Beginning filmmakers often underestimate how long it really takes to move the production unit, no matter how small a crew. On the other hand, a skilled **location manager** (see Glossary) can save a production company time and money by executing an organized company move quickly and efficiently.

Cast

Along with locations, the availability of actors is a major factor that influences the formation of the schedule. There are many variables you should consider when scheduling cast members. If you are working with members of the Screen Actors Guild (SAG), you must honor SAG contract rules and regulations regarding the length of a workday, travel time, meal guarantees, and turnaround time. Actors usually work a 10-hour day. The crew needs setup time at the beginning of the day and wrap-out time at the end of the day. Therefore, if an actor's schedule is pushed, so are the hours of the crew.

When planning the schedule, make the most economical use of your talent. Actors work for a daily, a weekly, or a picture rate. If there are fewer than 10 days between shooting for an actor, he becomes eligible for a weekly rate; that is, if an actor works as a day player and then is called back to work 4 days later, the actor's contract is adjusted to a weekly player salary. You can hire an actor on a daily rate and then upgrade him to a weekly player, but it doesn't work the other way around. The actor on a weekly rate gets paid by the week, so if the picture schedule carries the actor over even 1 day, he must receive the full week's rate.

Picture actors are paid a flat rate for the whole project and are available for the entire schedule, so their availability is not a factor. However, it doesn't make sense to pay an actor for two weeks if you only need her for the first and last day. It would be best to adjust the schedule and move the actor's scenes to the beginning or end of the schedule to "shoot out" the actor. This approach can benefit the production, even if it means going into overtime with the crew to keep the actor from having to return to the set for another day. If, however, the actor's salary is less than the cost of the overtime, it would be wiser to wrap and return to the location the next day.

> We knew that we could only get the kids at certain hours each day. We promised the parents that we would be working from eight to six every day, with an hour off for lunch. We really had to maintain that schedule with all the kids, so then that went for the rest of the crew, too.
>
> Howard McCain

STUDENTS

Actors who work for free or whose salaries are deferred under an agreement with SAG might have full- or part-time jobs that limit their availability to your production. You might need to adapt your schedule to these constraints. If this is not possible, you may need to replace them. It is always good to have backups.

Exteriors

It is recommended that you begin the shoot with any exterior scenes. This general industry rule should be adhered to if possible. If you complete all the exterior scenes first, then when the company moves indoors, bad weather can no longer force you to change the planned schedule. If, on the other hand, you shoot all the interiors first, when the production moves outdoors, you will be at the mercy of the weather.

In this case, it would be advisable to keep at least one interior location, or **cover set** (see Glossary), available to move to in case of bad weather. Without a cover set, the production company has to shut down until the weather improves. A delay like this can be expensive as well as disruptive to your carefully organized schedule.

Night Shooting

It's best to consolidate all the night exteriors of each location. (Most night interiors can be shot during the day by blacking out the windows.) There are two schools of thought on how to schedule night exteriors. You can either shift the entire schedule over to nights and, instead of shooting from 6 a.m. to 6 p.m., shoot from 6 p.m. to 6 a.m., or you can organize the schedule to work on **splits**, meaning noon to midnight. This requires the company to shoot sunlight or exterior/day scenes the first half of the day and devote the second half of the shooting day to exterior/night shots. The nature of the material might dictate only one of these alternatives.

When scheduling night shooting, you must remember that the actors require 12 hours (per the SAG contract)

between the end of one day and the beginning of the next. This period is referred to as **turnaround time**. This regulation means that you can't end a day shoot and immediately begin a night one and vice versa. Weekends are often used to make the transition from a day schedule to a night schedule or vice versa. Otherwise, the required turnaround time must be absorbed into the daily schedule.

SCHEDULING

Be aware that night shoots are hard on the body, even if the crew requests a night routine. Don't expect the crew to work as efficiently at night as they would during the day. Reduce your expectations of how many scenes you'd like to accomplish in an hour and factor this into the schedule.

Night exterior shoots are expensive and logistically challenging. Arranging for the amount of equipment needed to illuminate a night exterior is complicated. The smaller the shot, the better your chances to accomplish the scene.

Continuity of Sequences

Although you might not be able to shoot the entire project in its order in the script, it is recommended that you shoot sequences in continuity as much as possible. This allows the actors and the director to work through the dramatic arc of a scene naturally. It would be awkward and emotionally difficult to start the day's work with the end of an argument and then end with the beginning.

Shooting Out

In filming interior scenes, try to complete as many shots as you can from each lighting setup. This is done by "shooting out" one side of the room before turning around and shooting with a new lighting setup. This approach might interfere with the continuity of the sequence, but it is standard procedure. It is also common sense. Having to keep changing lighting setups between each shot wastes time and energy.

Child Actors

There are strict rules governing the use of child actors. Generally, they can't work as many hours as adults can, and their parents or a teacher or social worker must be present during shooting if the children are missing school to be in the picture. Consult the SAG guidelines and child labor laws in your own state for more details.

A child's short attention span and limited energy can also be a major factor in shooting a scene. It might take longer to shoot a scene with a child, especially if the child is not a professional actor. Factor this into the schedule.

I remember one of our first ideas was to shoot in script order to make it easier for the kids. It's such a short script, I figured we could have the luxury to do that. I was afraid that if the kids got disoriented, they would get bored, confused, and tired. We did decide to do all the fantasy scenes on the first day. We thought that was a good way to get the kids really involved in the process. They got to do three costume changes, dress up as Robin Hood, wear the Civil War costumes, do the little fire engine thing....We believed that if the first day seemed exciting and appealing, we could hold their interest and make the whole shoot seem like an adventure.

It also worked out well for the costume person who had to come up from New York to fit the kids and iron all the costumes; she had to leave after two days to go back to New York for another job, so that was a good piece of planning.
Howard McCain

Time of Year

The time of year when you are planning your production is an important consideration when scheduling exteriors. The amount of available daylight varies from summer to winter, the winter months having less available daylight, particularly in the north. To catch as much available light as possible for exteriors in winter, begin each day early.

Weather

The biggest variable in a production that features outdoor locations is the weather. Weather conditions such as extreme heat, cold, snow, rain, and strong winds always have an impact on exterior photography, slowing down the company's usual pace. Cold weather will naturally slow down the movement of people and equipment, and even more so at night. Extreme cold can affect the camera's mechanism, shorten the life of a battery, and damage sensitive video equipment. You can shoot in a moderate rain, but not at a normal pace.

Research natural weather conditions (rain, snow, hurricanes, tornadoes, etc.) for the time of year that you plan to shoot. The weather bureau puts out breakdowns for annual precipitation, and farmer's almanacs are amazingly accurate when it comes to weather prediction. As you get closer to your shoot date, see Weather.com for up to 10-day forecasts. You should keep a permanent bookmark at this site. In addition, check the date when daylight saving time begins and ends.

There are three types of weather situations for which you should be prepared:

- **Light.** Light rain, light snow, light fog, and so on are weather conditions that should not affect your shoot. Light rain stops and starts, and it is invisible to the camera lens as long as it is not backlit. Light snow melts quickly. Keep the equipment and actors dry and continue shooting.

- **Medium.** It rarely rains all day. Show up at your location and wait. The rain might stop.
- **Heavy.** It is impossible to shoot in heavy weather, such as a storm. This is a good opportunity to move to a cover set.

Special Effects, Stunts, and Animals

Whenever the script requires a special effect, even something as simple as an active fireplace, special preparation and execution time must be added to the schedule. This guideline also applies to stunts and the use of animals. The availability of specialists required to be on the set such as fire marshals, animal wranglers, weapons masters, or stunt coordinators also needs to be factored into the schedule.

Any physical action requiring an actor to fight, fall, jump, run, and/or perform in an athletic manner and any other potentially hazardous situation are considered stunts. Depending on the type of stunt being performed, a trained stunt coordinator may be required to supervise.

For any stunt work, use of prop weapons or pyrotechnics and any other potentially hazardous scenes conducted on public property or within view of the public (i.e., a storefront) must also be cleared by the local mayor's office and police department. The American Humane Association publishes a series of safety regulations called Guidelines for the Safe Use of Animals in Filmed Media, which is designed to ensure the comfort and well-being of all animal actors. The Guidelines are periodically updated to address new issues. You can download a copy of the Guidelines from the AHA web site at http://www.americanhumane.org/protecting-animals/programs/no-animals-were-harmed/.

As a general rule, it always takes three to four times longer to prepare and shoot anything that is considered out of the ordinary. Special effects, stunts, and animals' parts should all be rehearsed long before the shoot. This preparation will give you a chance to meet the production schedule.

Crowd Sequences

It is advisable to consolidate crowd sequences. The organization, feeding, and wardrobing of large crowds of extras (also referred to as **background**) is a logistical challenge and a large expense. Additional personnel must often be hired to support the assistant directors (ADs), the costumers, and the hair and makeup artists. Police might even be required for traffic control. Proper communication often involves the use of bull horns and walkie-talkies. Always schedule more time than you think you'll need when working with crowds.

A background PA—designated solely to wrangle actors, make them sign releases, and keep them happy and from wandering around the set—is a great asset for any days you are shooting and require a large crowd. This person definitely has to have a loud voice and know how to control a group of people. Because we had such a small cast, Selom, our amazing first team PA (who wrangled the lead actors during the shoot) was able to do double duty and handle background as well. This was beneficial for the actors, as they were more relaxed knowing there was someone with them to keep them in the loop about the shoot and answer their questions. It also kept production in control.

Jessalyn Haefele, Producer of *Citizen*

Special Equipment

You might need to rent additional equipment for a specific sequence, such as a Steadicam, or dolly. Steadicams require the hiring of an operator in addition to the rig. Scenes requiring any special equipment should be consolidated to save money.

Turnaround, Setup Time, and Swing Crews

Transportation to and from the set, prelighting, set dressing, and construction are all factors that you should take into consideration when setting up the stripboard. For example, it can be frustrating if the production department settles on a schedule only to discover later that it will not coincide with the construction timetable. In this case, the art director should inform the production manager of the amount of time required to get the sets ready so that art department turnaround time becomes part of the equation.

Money can easily solve this sort of problem by allowing you to hire additional construction personnel. If money is tight, however, the production staff will need to go back to the drawing board to rearrange the schedule to accommodate this new information.

Much time can be saved if the production can afford to have a swing crew of electricians prerig the lights at an interior location. While the primary crew sleeps, the B team can set up the lights and "rough in" the lighting plan dictated by the director of photography (DP). Then, when the A team arrives on the set, the crew merely has to tweak the lights, and the cameras can roll.

Novice producers usually have problems estimating how long it will take to move and set up grip and electrical equipment. Consult with as many experienced people as possible when scheduling your project. An experienced director of photography, gaffer, or key grip can be of enormous help in this area.

Animation

Animation requires its own set of scheduling parameters. Preproduction considerations include writing the screenplay, storyboarding, creating the soundtrack, using animatics, and then creating a rough animation. Production issues include lip-synch, textures, and lighting. Postproduction is all about rendering and compositing.

One takes the storyboards and makes a story real with the soundtrack. So you record both actors, you would read for your own use for animating later the soundtrack frame by frame, so you know exactly which syllable, which letter is sitting on which point in time, frame by frame. Alongside with that you would have a story reel. So you make a video of all your storyboards set to their corresponding time on the soundtrack, and you just watch your film without motion but just with the images of the storyboard and see if it makes sense. I do believe I did that a long time ago. After that you have your soundtrack broken down to frames. You decide exactly how long each shot would be. I think when I came to shoot *Crazy Glue*, it was nearly edited in camera. I would just pick up the 16-mm Bolex, put it down, animate the shot, move it to the next cut and shoot from there, which is not how it's usually done, but that's how *Crazy Glue* was 80 percent done. Just shot in order.

Tatia

In animation, a first recording of the dialogue is done for timing because the artist must match his creations with the actors' voices. This is referred to as a *predub* and is executed in a standard automatic dialogue replacement (ADR) facility. When the animation is completed, the actors may be brought back to rematch their voices.

Other Considerations

Examine your script for any special circumstances unique to your project that will have an impact on the schedule. Each script poses its own particular set of problems. Keep an eye out for any unusual scheduling challenges.

Beginning the Schedule

Must you keep all these factors in mind at all times when creating a schedule? The answer is no. Each script has a unique set of organizational challenges. The right schedule for your project evolves over time. Begin with a rough draft that takes into account the major considerations and then gradually factor in the issues that are relevant to your particular project. Don't expect to solve all of them in the first pass. The shooting schedule might not be finalized until the week or even the day before actual shooting begins.

In fact, it is not uncommon for the schedule to continue to change during principal photography. A lost location, a sick actor, or an unexpected weather condition could force the production unit to shift around scenes and even shooting days. Beginners might have to keep adjusting their schedules because they have overestimated how much they can shoot in a day.

> It was really just kind of like having that fortitude to say, pick a date and you have to shoot. Once you go down that road you realize that, as, Rudyard Kipling, one of his famous poems, always said, once you start something, providence will move and things that you could never believe that will come and happen in your favor begin to happen. That's sort of what happened in my case. The things I needed; camera equipment, people, actors, crew; it just started to happen because I believed in the process.
>
> Be' Garrett

Creating the Schedule

Don't start scheduling actual shooting days until you have grouped all the scenes in a logic that is governed by the important guidelines described in the preceding sections. This will enable you to conceptualize the "big picture" before deciding how to structure each shooting day. Follow these general priorities for scheduling:

- Start with any fixed dates of which you are aware. These dates will become the anchors around which you must work.
- Group your locations together, but try to place the exteriors first.
- Factor in the actors' schedules.
- Factor in the day and night schedule if appropriate. Remember that 12 hours of turnaround time is required between days and nights. Use the weekend to make this transition.
- Identify any other special adjustments your project demands, such as special effects or crowd sequences.

Begin to form the strips into days to get a rough idea of how long it is going to take to shoot the picture. Start off with an easy day if you can. Don't schedule the climactic love scene before the actors have had a chance to work together.

> Everything went smoothly for me, I thought, in terms of getting what I wanted in the shots, feeling they were working okay—until we got to the restaurant and I did the shot of her entrance, I just couldn't get it to work. I wanted to cover it all in one shot, but it felt like it was taking forever.
>
> This was the first shot of the day. I began to panic. I felt that the time I was spending on the shot was eating into my already tight schedule. I was getting bogged down, and it

> threatened to put me behind, but I didn't want to settle for anything that wasn't right. It started off as a two-minute shot, so little by little, I eliminated business. Scotty started by asking for the salad, picking out the salad, speaking with the cook, etc. My problem was that I was looking at the scene in realtime, not film time, which is death. Also, in a long take, one time the actors may work well, but the dolly is off. Another time the dolly hits the marks perfectly, but the focus puller misses his mark. We did eight takes, and during that time, the shot dropped from 2 minutes to 30 seconds.
>
> Adam Davidson

The First Day

The first day of principal photography is very important because it sets the tone for the entire shooting period. On the first day, the cast and crew are galvanized behind the director's leadership. A director who can instill confidence and make the first day's pages quickly earns the respect and cooperation of the crew. The director can approve a schedule with one of three approaches:

- **Day 1 is very light.** An easy first day gives the cast and crew time to build up a momentum and allows for the kind of first-day mistakes that are inevitable.
- **Day 1 is an average day.** Every day is important, so a day that has an average number of pages to shoot is a fair day. This choice does not treat the first day as anything special.
- **Day 1 is heavy.** A deliberately heavy day in which the cast and crew have to hit the ground running is an opportunity to galvanize the company. Dead weight becomes obvious very quickly.

Making the Day

How is a *day* defined? How do you know how many pages a day your unit will be able to complete? The phrase **make the day** is an industry term that refers to successfully completing photography on the scenes scheduled for a particular day. The production unit should get off to a good start by making the first couple of days and keeping on schedule. Remember that many members of the cast and crew might not have worked together before. Considering all the variables, going over schedule is easy to do. Successfully completing the first few days provides a psychological lift that bonds the unit and gives everyone confidence to complete the rest of the shoot.

Most feature films complete an average of between 2 and 3 script pages a day. Many low-budget features and television movies, on the other hand, average from 5 to 10 pages a day. Student projects usually come in at around 2 pages a day. Remember that these are

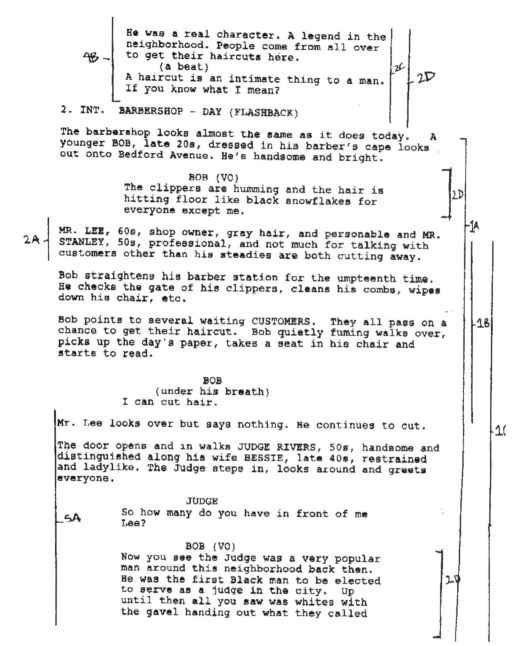

He was a real character. A legend in the
neighborhood. People come from all over
4B - to get their haircuts here.
(a beat)
A haircut is an intimate thing to a man. 2C - 2D
If you know what I mean?

2. INT. BARBERSHOP - DAY (FLASHBACK)

The barbershop looks almost the same as it does today. A younger BOB, late 20s, dressed in his barber's cape looks out onto Bedford Avenue. He's handsome and bright.

BOB (VO)
The clippers are humming and the hair is hitting floor like black snowflakes for everyone except me. 2D

1A

2A - MR. LEE, 60s, shop owner, gray hair, and personable and MR. STANLEY, 50s, professional, and not much for talking with customers other than his steadies are both cutting away.

Bob straightens his barber station for the umpteenth time. He checks the gate of his clippers, cleans his combs, wipes down his chair, etc.

Bob points to several waiting CUSTOMERS. They all pass on a chance to get their haircut. Bob quietly fuming walks over, picks up the day's paper, takes a seat in his chair and starts to read. 1B

BOB
(under his breath)
I can cut hair.

Mr. Lee looks over but says nothing. He continues to cut. 1C

The door opens and in walks JUDGE RIVERS, 50s, handsome and distinguished along his wife BESSIE, late 40s, restrained and ladylike. The Judge steps in, looks around and greets everyone.

JUDGE
5A So how many do you have in front of me Lee?

BOB (VO)
Now you see the Judge was a very popular man around this neighborhood back then. He was the first Black man to be elected to serve as a judge in the city. Up until then all you saw was whites with the gavel handing out what they called 2D

FIGURE 4.2 Shooting script from *A Nick in Time.*

averages. The industry is governed by what it can afford. Television budgets are small, so the tight schedules reflect that fact.

If your budget will allow, set your sights on averaging 2 pages a day. This does not mean that you always end up with exactly 2 pages completed each day. There might be days when you can accomplish only 2/8 of a page of difficult action (see Figure 4.2). There might also be days when you will be able to make 5 to 10 pages. This is usually the case with dialogue scenes. Dialogue tends to take less time to shoot because it involves fewer lighting setups. Once the lights are in place, you can achieve a variety of shots quickly and efficiently.

At NYU, though it is probably true of any place, the first thing that occurred after settling on an idea was choosing a shooting date. The shooting date is so important because it gives you something definite, a tangible thing from which to work. From there I could create a timeline, a calendar which told me by November I should have a draft, by December I should be casting, by January I should have the locations lined up. Without that, you can lose your way and postpone endlessly.

I often saw students who were not set with their dates who'd write and write, and at the end of the semester they'd say, "I need to shoot now." They left themselves three weeks for preproduction and, consequently, were doing preproduction while shooting.

> I think choosing a date and sticking to it is very important because it forces you to create a funnel where everything is marching toward that moment in time. It keeps you structured, keeps you organized, and really makes you focus in on something. It keeps you from letting anything slip.
>
> Howard McCain

> on Saturday night and brought in much of the stuff that we used to prop the set. But part of the great thing about this location was that a lot of it was already there. What we brought in was a lot of the additives to establish the time period.
>
> Be' Garrett

Shooting During Preproduction

It is sometimes necessary to be in production during pre-production. If an actor needs to appear on television during a scene, the video portion of the show must be recorded in advance of the shooting day. If you are shooting a scene that requires playback of an original song, the song must be recorded before the shoot. Playback, which is music piped onto the set for the actors and musicians to lip-sync to and mime, eliminates the need for a live recording. With a live recording, mistakes might slow down the production. With playback, the director knows that the song will be perfect each time.

Keep the Day Under 12 Hours!

The two-page daily average should be accomplished in no longer than 12 hours. The day begins at crew call and ends at wrap time. The crew must also be given proper turnaround time before reporting to the set the following day. *Do not schedule days longer than 12 hours.* A tired company works less effectively than one that's well rested. Too many long days will force the law of diminishing returns. As the day drags on, the crew's performance diminishes as crew members execute difficult lighting setups and complicated camera moves.

Student productions start out with the best intentions of working within the 12-hour limit, but something usually happens during the shoot that slows down the day. An inexperienced crew will take longer than expected to execute lighting and camera setups. As a result, the director will need to simplify her shot list to make the day.

The following is a true story about the dangers involved when cast and crew are subjected to extremely long shoot days (excerpt taken from the IA Local 600 web site at http://www.cameraguild.com):

Animation Lip-Sync

Lip-syncing is the process of making a character's mouth move so it looks as though it is speaking. In computer graphics (CG), the animator will create multiple versions of a character's head with the mouth positioned in different phonemes. A phoneme is the shape a mouth makes when it is forming different sounds (e.g., a circular shape for an "oh" or closed lips for an "em"). Usually, the animator will make expressions as well (happy, sad, etc.). The animator will then load the soundtrack into the 3D software and match the phonemes to the sound along the time line. The software will use a process known a morphing, or blend shape, to make the transition smooth between phonemes.

On March 5th, 1997, Brent Hershman, the second assistant camera person on the movie *Pleasantville* drove an hour from home to work in Long Beach for a 6:30 AM call. He worked for nineteen hours. After helping to wrap three cameras and a Power Pod, he reminded his co-workers on the camera truck to drive carefully and left for home. Midway through his trip, the exhaustion overcame him. He drove his car off the road and was killed. He leaves behind a daughter, Hannah, who is three and a half, and his wife, Deborah.

> So I recorded the voices during preproduction so I could lay out my storyboards and get a proper timing for the shoot.
>
> Tatia Rosenthal

Locking the Schedule

This incident sparked an industrywide campaign for more humane working conditions, which generated a petition with the names of over 10,000 industry professionals, calling for a limit on the number of hours worked in a single shoot day. As a result, all local labor unions and performers guilds have joined forces to promote the limiting of hours worked on motion picture sets.

All the department heads should be consulted before you lock down the board. As the shoot date approaches, the producer arranges a meeting with the director, the DP, the location manager, the assistant director, the art director, and the production manager (if you have one) to thoroughly review the schedule. If you have sound mixer already on board, he should be here as well. The goal of the meeting is to have all departments sign off on the shooting schedule, especially the director, who has to shoot it, and the AD, who responsible for keeping everyone on it.

> The shoot took two twelve-hour days. We shut the barbershop down. Most barbershops are generally closed on Sundays and Mondays, so as not to mess with their ability to make money as barbers, we took the Sunday and the Monday. We loaded it

The AD "walks" everyone through each location and each day, including the scenes to be shot and the director's visual plan. The number of scenes you can comfortably schedule in a day is influenced by the speed of the director and the director of photography. You might be lucky enough to work with a director who can knock off 30 setups in a day. Because lighting setups and camera moves require the most prep time, the DP must be confident that he can accommodate the director's shot list. The art director and location manger must be confident that all the sets and/or locations can be prepped to meet each deadline. This is the final opportunity to recommend changes. Any reservations the director or any of the department heads have should be addressed at this meeting.

For example, if a department head doesn't believe he can accommodate the schedule, the producer will need to intervene. The director may have recently added a new dolly shot to one sequence. The DP doesn't believe that he can execute the shot in the present schedule. The shot adds time (to set up and execute the shot) and money (to extend the dolly rental). If money is not a major consideration, the producer is able to approve the shot. If the budget cannot accommodate the cost, a discussion takes place. If the director firmly believes that this new shot will be an important addition to her visual plan, she may have to sacrifice a dolly shot in another scene. The DP might suggest alternate approaches to visualizing the scene.

This is an example of the give-and-take that can happen when the creative ambition of the director needs to be balanced with the limitations of the budget. Sometimes, these discussions lead to more creative solutions that don't tax the budget. The producer plays an important role in moderating this process. He needs to respect the director's aspirations and, at the same time, honor the realities of the budget.

Once all parties sign off on a schedule that is realistic and can be accommodated by the budget, it is finalized, published, and distributed to the cast and crew as the working shooting schedule.

The producer of *Citizen*, Jessalyn Haefele provides a breakdown of what influenced her schedule:

When James Darling, Jon Gardner (our AD) and I sat down to schedule the movie, we had chosen certain dates for a few specific reasons:

1. With most film rental houses, they only bill you Monday through Friday for rentals. Since we were shooting over the weekend, checking out the equipment on a Thursday and returning it on Tuesday (as was the original plan), we were saving a bundle of money.
2. We knew that most people who were coming to crew with us were either working professionals who had M–F jobs, or film students who usually had classes during this time. By shooting over the weekend, and on that particular Monday (which was President's Day, so most people had off from work and school) we were able to maximize everyone's availability.
3. Because Monday was a holiday and the rental houses were closed, we were also saving an extra day's rental charge on all of our equipment!
4. (Our most important reason!) It was supposed to snow during the week we were prepping to shoot, which meant that fresh snow would be on the ground upstate when we were ready to film. Snow was initially called for in James' script—the hunters are able to track the deserter by the trail of blood he leaves in the snow when he cuts his leg climbing under the wall. We were sincerely hoping the Weather Channel was right and that we would have the perfect natural set decoration for our shoot. In case it did not snow, James had come up with an alternate way to show the hunters discovering the deserter.

Call Sheet

The call sheet is the distillation of the schedule. This single sheet of paper is handed to all cast and crew members the night before each day of shooting. If the shoot is only a few days, a call sheet might reflect the entire shooting period. The call sheet is a distillation of all pertinent information regarding the next shooting day, including call times, locations, actors' call times, special equipment, crew call times, and scene shot list. Figure 4.3 shows the call sheet for *The Compatriot* (aka *Citizen*). It includes everything from the location of the local hospital to when the first meal was to be served. It is a very good model.

The director supplies the shot list segment of the call sheet. All the other information on the sheet is culled from the stripboard or production schedule and breakdown sheets. The shot list is the list of scenes to be recorded during the next day's production period. It is customary for the director to review the call sheet just before it is printed for distribution. Should the director want to change the order of the scenes to be shot, she has this last opportunity to do so.

If the order is to be changed, the director should do so before the day of the shoot. If it is changed on the day of the shoot, there is no time to change the calls for actors, the crew, and the equipment. The director might want to change a shot list for several reasons:

- A scene needs to be completed from the previous day.
- An actor will play a scene better at a certain time of the day.
- A light or sound problem might influence the schedule.

the compatriot

Director: James Darling	**Saturday, February 11, 2006**	**SHOOT DAY**
Producer: Jessalyn Haefele		**2 of 4**
1st AD: Jon Gardner	CREW CALL	
2nd AD: Aaron Jackson		**SUNRISE/SUNSET**
watching a movie is sexy,	**8:00A**	**6:55A / 5:26P**
making a movie is sexier	Grip/Electric PreCall **N/A**	**WEATHER**
	SHOOTING CALL	Hi 40° Lo 26°
SET PHONE: 267-254-4489	**9:00A**	PM Snow Showers 40%
JON'S PHONE: 978-985-0794		
NO VISITORS WITHOUT PRIOR APPROVAL OF UPM		***NO FORCED CALLS WITHOUT PRIOR APPROVAL OF UPM***

SCENE	SET	D/N	CAST	PGS	LOCATION
	CREW VAN LEAVES UNION SQUARE (CORNER 14th and Broadway) @ 6:30 AM sharp *breakfast served @ crew van*				
6	EXT. FOREST Jonathan sees shimmer of wall	D1	1	4/8	Russek Property 217 Eastwoods Road Pound Ridge, NY
22	EXT. FOREST Jonathan eats sandwich	D1	1	2/8	
23	EXT. FOREST Jonathan runs	D1	1,3	1 1/8	
24	EXT. FOREST Hunters catch Jonathan	D1	1,3,4	4/8	
	CATERED LUNCH @ 2P		**TOTAL PAGES 2 3/8**		

#	CAST	CHARACTER	STAT	REPORT	MU/HAIR	SET	NOTES
1	Jonathan Everman	Justin Fair	W	8:00A	8:15A	9:00A	Self Report
2	Doctor	John Grady	H				
3	Older Hunter	Chance Muehleck	W	8:00A	8:30A	9:00A	P/U Union Square @ 6:30A
4	Younger Hunter	Tim Meyer	W	8:00A	8:45A	9:00A	P/U Union Square @ 6:30A
9	Soldier School	Sean Simms	H				

ATMOSPHERE, STAND-INS, BITS:	SPECIAL INSTRUCTIONS
	PROPS: Guns PBJ Sandwich in Foil- Strawberry Jelly! SET DRESS: Shimmer

EQUIPMENT TRUCKS: Per Pound Ridge CATERING: 1st Meal Ready @ 1:30 pm, serve at 2pm	HOSPITAL: Four Winds Hospital 750 Route 35 Cross River, NY 914-763-8151

Key Crew

DP	Ryan Webb	**Production Designer**	EricaTorres
Gaffer	Jamison Grella	**Key MakeUp Artist**	Amy Spiegel
Key Grip	Keith McNicholas	**Art Director**	Matt Henderson
Best Boy Grip	TJ Alston	**1st AC**	Olivia Kuan
Best Boy Electric	Mark Beattie	**2nd AC**	Andrew White
Sound Mixer	Cory Choy	**Boom Op**	Nick Feitel
Script Supervisor	Keir Morano	**Wardrobe Supervisor**	Rebecca Myatt
Craft Service	Rebecca Darling	**Transportation**	Jon Darling

PA DUTIES

Marcus	Walkie PA
Selom	First Team PA
Johnny	Breakfast PA
David	Unit PA
Justine	Key PA
Dave. B	Jon G./PA
Brennan	BG Pass PA
Jacob	Set PA

UPM: ALEX DORMAN	1ST A.D.: JON GARDNER	2ND AD: AARON JACKSON

FIGURE 4.3 Call sheet for *The Compatriot* (aka *Citizen*).

Each day, a schedule for the following day was printed up and distributed before we wrapped. It started out with a wakeup time, then loading vehicles, call time on the set, lunchtime, wrap, and finally home. We handed out one of those to every crew member. Additionally, any revisions we realized we had to make were included in that schedule. Every night after we went home, the director of photography, the assistant director, and the production manager (those being the key people) would go over the next day's schedule. We would talk about what we had initially intended to do and whether that was what we were still going to do. Could we foresee any new problems we hadn't anticipated? That's how we set up the schedule on a daily basis.

Howard McCain

Scheduling Documentaries

Unlike the narrative form, documentaries are scheduled on a piecemeal basis. The scheduling of shoots is based on the availability of a subject or an event. For the most part, a documentary can be scheduled on weekends or on a day-to-day basis.

Some aspects of scheduling a documentary can be easy: book the subject and the equipment for a particular day and then shoot. Plan a full shooting day so as not to waste the equipment rental. If you own your equipment (which many documentarians do), the scheduling is even easier. In contrast, if your subject is tied to specific dates and times of day, it behooves you to be there by her side. This might require a more rigorous schedule than a narrative shoot.

I had to work around the schedules of my subjects. They were busy during weekdays, so I filmed them exclusively on weeknights and weekends. I tried not to schedule more than three interviews a day for our sake. Obviously, it didn't matter to them as they came in one at a time. I usually took about two hours with each person. They arrived, I explained the process to them, and I tried to make them comfortable while we adjusted the lights, and so on. I didn't want to feel rushed or to adopt an assembly-line approach.

Jan Krawitz

Student Scheduling Tips

Break Up the Shooting Schedule. It may be advisable to schedule your first production, if possible, not consecutively but over several weekends or smaller periods of time. Scheduling this way will enable you to gauge how well you are able to "make" the planned schedule and, if not, make the necessary adjustments for the next sequence. It also will enable you to see your rushes before the next shoot date. If you are not happy with what you are getting either from the performances or from the camera

and sound, this approach will allow you the time to make adjustments. For beginning filmmakers, this type of schedule can sometimes prevent the crew from making the same mistakes throughout the entire shoot.

The downside of planning this way is that this schedule makes it difficult to create momentum with your crew. It may take a couple of days for the production unit to gain a rhythm and feel comfortable with one another. Student productions may, in fact, have little choice in this matter. If actors are not being paid and have day jobs during the week, weekends may be the only time available to them to work.

Schedule Reshoots Ahead of Time. Assume that you will need to reshoot some of your project either because it didn't come out the way you expected or because you weren't able to get it the first time around due to unexpected problems or an unrealistic schedule. Warn everyone that reshooting might be required to ensure that your crew and actors will be available. Make sure to determine the schedules of cast and crew members after the shoot. Finally, schedule reshoots far enough in advance that you are able to view all the rushes before you return to production.

In all my films, I've never had the possibility to go back to any of the subjects because they've been location shoots all over the country. I am used to working that way. The whole notion of pickups in documentary has been completely moot for me in my work. We have never done it. The only kind of subsequent material would be stills or archival footage, but no more live shooting after the shooting period. Period.

Jan Krawitz

Make Use of Available Resources. Review the schedule with your production instructor or other experienced personnel as many times as possible during this process. Most students and beginners start off with unrealistic expectations of what they can achieve in a day. They are usually too ambitious. This enthusiasm must be constantly tempered with doses of realism, common sense, and experience.

Consolidate Locations. Your schedule, limited by money and available resources, might not accommodate all the locations the script dictates, forcing you to consolidate existing locations. By combining several locations into one, you can simplify your production needs without necessarily compromising the requirements of the story.

Schedule MOS Days. If a sequence does not absolutely require location sound, you might be able to save valuable time by shooting without recording sound on the set. In the industry, this is called **MOS**. Not having to wait for planes to pass or annoying neighbors to quiet down will shave minutes from each take and allow the production company to schedule more scenes in a day.

Don't Be Afraid to Postpone the Shoot Date. You might sense that the preproduction period is being unnecessarily rushed. Perhaps you are having problems finding the right cast, crew, or locations as the shoot date approaches. Perhaps it is your first production, and you want everything to be right. By pushing back the shoot date, you might lose a specific location or actor, but what you will gain is a smoother shoot (and a little peace of mind).

Before you think about postponing the shoot date, however, make sure that you don't have any fixed dates that are necessary for your production, such as a parade (which obviously can't be rescheduled) or a special event that plays prominently in your story.

Web Presence for the Project

If you have already established a web site for the project, it can be used on a regular basis to communicate with the crew, posting updates on schedules and production meetings.

DIRECTOR

Determining the Visual Plan

The director should be very involved in setting up the production schedule, as described in the first half of this chapter. She must be the one to finally say, "I can shoot this script on this schedule." Just as the producer factors into the schedule actor availability, prerigging, and a desire to shoot out locations, so, too, he must consider the director's needs within the parameters of the budget.

A director's main responsibility is to make the best film possible based on the script. Her secondary charge is to shoot the pages scheduled for each day. Making the pages means ending a day of production having reached the goal, set during preproduction, of that portion of the script.

The director sets the pace. If you are slow, the shoot will be slow. Your energy impels the cast and crew. It is as if the energy of the director is translated through the cast and crew and onto the screen. Therefore, an understanding of the schedule involves an acknowledgment of one's capacities. Take care of your body with ample sleep and nutritious foods so that you will have the stamina necessary for the grueling pace of a shoot.

Coverage = Time = Schedule = Budget

The director determines how a sequence is to be staged and shot. **Coverage** is the number and types of shots used to record a sequence. The director might base her plan on conversations with the screenwriter, art director, director of photography, storyboard artist, editor, or indeed anyone who has a good idea about an approach to a sequence. The final decisions, however, rest with the director.

A scene can be photographed or covered with a combination of master shot, minimasters, over-the-shoulder shots, and one or two close-ups, or the director can light and rehearse one or two complicated dolly moves and shoot the entire scene toward the end of the day after exhaustive technical rehearsals. Each shot can be communicated to the department heads through storyboards, floor plans, photos, paintings, etc. Although the plan for shooting is determined during preproduction, on set, as the scene takes on a life of its own, the director may alter or enhance the planned coverage.

A producer might assume that a dialogue sequence of five pages can be executed in a single day. However, if the director plans several complicated dolly moves to cover the scene, one day might not be adequate. Conversely, a seven-page dialogue scene can be shot in one day if the photography is kept simple or is planned as one or two long takes. Remember, complicated dolly moves for every shot invite overtime. Therefore, it behooves the director to indicate to the producer where she plans anything out of the ordinary, including crane shots, dolly moves, and extreme high angle shots so that they are factored into the schedule and budget.

If the scene is excessively storyboarded (too many shots per sequence), and especially if any one thing goes wrong (an actor arrives late, fuses are blown, etc.), the potential to go over schedule increases. This is not to suggest that you compromise your shot list; instead, make certain that it reflects a practical schedule.

A scene that reads on paper like an easy sequence might take on an entirely different character when envisioned by the director. For example, one director might shoot a scene in which a woman is stabbed to death in a shower in one take. After the scene is lit, she might need only 10 minutes for that one shot. On the other hand, a director such as Alfred Hitchcock might design a more stylized scene that involves 88 setups and requires three days to shoot. (You'll find more on coverage in Chapter 11.)

Each scene was numbered, as well as the shots within the scene. We then started putting the shots in the order of how we would shoot them. As it went along, there were constant little changes, based on things like the availability of the fire net or putting in a variable-speed motor and what day could we get these items for the cheapest rate. We made several revisions on the schedule as we moved closer toward the shoot.

When most of our unknowns were resolved, we gave each shot a time value—how long we estimated the setup and execution of the shot would take—and we broke that down into 15-minute intervals. You could say something took two hours and 15 minutes, or 45 minutes, or a half an hour. So hopefully, we knew within 15 or 20 minutes where we should be each day.

> I was very, very concerned about keeping my promise to the parents that the filming be only between 8 a.m. and 6 p.m.
>
> We were fairly tight on the time, so we tried to be honest with ourselves about how long each scene would take. Based on this kind of macro to micro approach of when events had to happen and when we wanted them to happen, we could finally print up a schedule about which we felt very, very confident.
>
> Howard McCain

Contingency Plans for Overages

If the director falls behind on day 1, she will be playing catch-up throughout the shoot. Going over sometimes means returning to a location, another company move, additional days of principal photography, and more money.

Although the director is shooting a movie and not a schedule, there is psychological strength in meeting the day's pages. Playing catch-up is a drain on the director. Often, to get back on schedule, she will condense a scene or make judicious cuts in the script.

Things Change

The schedule might constantly change during preproduction and production. The director needs to be flexible. She should memorize the schedule as well as the script so that she can make quick adjustments to her plan.

KEY POINTS

- The efficient use of time is directly related to production value.
- Memorize the schedule so that you can adjust easily to alterations.
- Settle on the priorities and coverage that will determine the basic approach to the schedule.
- If possible, shoot exteriors first because of weather variables.
- Shoot out interior locations if possible. It is not cost efficient to have to come back to an interior location and relight it.

Chapter 5

Budget

Don't let money hinder your process. If you feel like you don't have enough, don't let that be a reason not to shoot your film. If you have enough to at least get started, I suggest doing it. And if you have a lot of money, I suggest being careful of how that money is being spent. Just because you have a lot of money doesn't necessarily mean you're going to come out with a good film.

Adam Davidson

PRODUCER

Creating a Budget

Now that you have some idea of how long it will take to shoot your project and what elements will cost you money, creating a budget will be that much easier. If you have only so much money available or have set a limit on the amount of money you feel comfortable spending, put these figures aside for the moment and concentrate on creating a realistic budget for the script you want to produce. After the ink dries, see how your original figures compare to your financial limitations.

Even if you have all the money in the world, it doesn't make sense to spend it all on one picture. Throwing money at a project will teach you nothing about proper fiscal management, and it will leave you less money for your next endeavor. The goal is to get the most bang for your buck. Spend only what you need to spend.

The budget defines the parameters of what can and cannot be accomplished. It contains a complete and detailed breakdown of what it will cost to finish the entire project. This breakdown includes all projected expenses for preproduction, production, postproduction; distribution expenses such as making posters, DVDs, festival fees; etc. Each and every line item, whether it is photocopying scripts or securing a location, has a price and must be itemized, categorized, and ultimately accounted for.

Production Value

Production value is the quality of your production efforts in relation to the money you have spent. It is dictated by how many pages are to be shot per day on average, coupled with the amount of money allotted for each day: The budget (minus postproduction costs) divided by the total number of script pages equals the cost per shooting day.

You can get a feel for what kind of quality you're likely to end up with by comparing how much money you have to spend per day with your production demands. A high-budget picture burdened with expensive sets, many special effects, and high fees might have to be shot quickly for a large amount per day. Conversely, a low-budget show with few production needs might shoot over a longer period.

It's true that money can solve most production problems. However, money is often at a premium, especially in a low-budget arena, so ingenuity must take the place of unlimited funds. No matter how large or small your budget, its total is based on the production items needed to fulfill the script.

Many film producers get through the shooting stage by moving money from the postproduction categories to the production categories ("robbing Peter to pay Paul"), and ultimately, they cannot complete the picture because of lack of funds. When budgeting, err on the side of too much because it is better to come in under the budget than over the budget.

When I produced *Citizen*, I had already graduated from NYU and was working as a production assistant on a feature film called *Michael Clayton* in NYC. My experiences working on professional film sets and production offices offered me a great array of knowledge on how to run a production. I decided that the best way to approach James' film was to mimic everything that would happen on a professional film. This included using almost all the same paperwork and forms, and following all the same protocol regarding locations and turnaround times for crews and actors. My reasoning was that even though this was a student film, if we treated it as a professional shoot, everyone would take us more seriously and we could avoid many of the setbacks I had come across on other student films I had crewed on. I also hoped to become more familiar with the overall flow of production paperwork during the shoot, which would help me later in more of my professional experiences.

Jessalyn Haefele, Producer of *Citizen*

Script and Budget

The script and the budget are the two cornerstones of the production: the script is the creative bible, and the budget is the financial bible. They are inextricably tied to one another: script decisions become budget decisions.

Say the director wants to add a car chase. Before the decision can be made as to whether to include the sequence, a budget must be prepared that itemizes all the expenses associated with the chase, such as the cost of the vehicles, stunt drivers, extra camera crews and cameras, water and fire trucks, police, standby physician and ambulance, traffic monitors, and, of course, feeding and possibly housing all these people for the days it will take to execute the sequence. The artistic value of the chase can then be weighed against its cost:

- Is the creative impact of the sequence worth the price?
- Can the present budget absorb the extra cost?
- If not, can the producer raise the additional money?

Money management performs an important role in picture making and can play havoc with one's idea of "artistic freedom." Sooner or later, it dawns on every filmmaker that artistic freedom comes with a price: you must pay for every decision, every choice. This is an ironclad and immutable fact of life in the media arts. Even the lone videomaker shooting on the run with a camcorder has to eat, purchase tape stock, and pay for travel and housing.

Who Creates the Budget?

The producer or production manager is responsible for drafting the budget. If you cannot afford to hire a production manager or an experienced producer, you will have to put together a budget yourself, even though the word *budget* may make you nervous.

> I planned to spend about $6,500, and I came in at $6,000. This covered production.
>
> Howard McCain

However, accomplishing this seemingly onerous task will enable you truly to understand the nuts and bolts of how a production actually runs because, like it or not, it runs on money. Putting together the financial foundation of your project can be an exciting challenge. Through the mastery of learning what things cost and why comes the satisfaction of knowing that you have gotten the best deals without skimping on the needs of the script.

STUDENTS

Because this book is written for independents (who lack the resources of a film program) as well as film students, we approach the budget from a perspective that is valid for all short projects. Although as a student, you might not pay for labor or equipment (other than through your tuition), knowing their commercial worth fosters a healthy respect for these resources and prepares you for the realities of the professional world after school. If your school provides some of the line items for your project, such as stock and equipment, it is a good exercise to budget these items as deferred figures. That way, you will be aware of the full cost of a production.

Budgeting Software

If you have used EP Scheduling to break down and create a schedule of your script, all this information can be fed into EP Budgeting. Linking these two programs will guarantee that any changes to the script will be reflected in the schedule and ultimately the budget. EP Scheduling and Budgeting software is the gold standard in the professional world. These programs can serve as invaluable tools for your film. The two of them can be bought separately, but bundling them together is less expensive. Students can get a discount although many institutions already license the software.

The Budget Form

The standardized budget form simplifies working up a budget and demystifies the process somewhat by outlining all potential expenses. The budget form is separated into two parts. The first part is the top sheet (see Figure 5.1). This "budget-at-a-glance" offers a financial overview or summary of all costs related to manufacturing the picture. These costs are placed into major budget categories, which are also called **accounts**, and each budget category is given its own account number for easy reference.

The following information can be gleaned from the top sheet:

- Subtotals of all categories
- Above-the-line and below-the-line costs
- Contingency
- Grand total

Film budgets are typically divided into two sections: above-the-line and below-the-line. This "line" separates two fundamentally different kinds of costs associated with a production. Above-the-line costs include fees negotiated for the producer, director, script, and actors. Below-the-line costs are all expenses related to the rest of the personnel and resources required to manufacture the picture—essentially, what it costs to actually make the film.

SHORT BUDGET TOP SHEET

Production: Date:
Length: Shooting Days:

ACCOUNT#	CATEGORY	BUDGET	ACTUAL COST
001	Script and Rights		
002	Producer		
003	Director		
004	Cast		

ABOVE THE LINE TOTAL _____

005	Production		
006	Crew		
007	Equipment		
008	Art		
009	Location		
010	Film and Lab		
	PRODUCTION TOTAL		

011	Editing		
012	Sound		
013	Lab		
	POSTPROD TOTAL		

014	Office Expenses		
015	Insurance		
016	Contingency		
	OVERHEAD TOTAL		

BELOW THE LINE TOTAL _____

GRAND TOTAL _____

FIGURE 5.1 The top sheet of a short budget. Visit the companion web site at http://booksite. focalpress.com/companion/IrvingRea/ to download and print a copy of the "Short Budget Top Sheet."

The second part of the budget form, called a **detailed budget**, is a complete breakdown of each category (see Figure 5.3). The detailed budget is completed first, and the total for each category is then entered under the appropriate budget column on the top sheet. For example, the total for the category "Equipment" on the top sheet reflects the cost of all the camera, sound, lighting, grip, and special equipment required for the production of the picture. (The other pages of the detailed budget can be downloaded from our web site.)

If you are creating a budget for the first time, you will need a thorough understanding of each department and how to evaluate its needs. Computing an accurate figure for each category requires an investigation into the process, as well as prices and resources available at the time and place of your shoot.

Above-the-Line Costs

Consider above-the-line costs to be flat fees, or amounts that are negotiated for the run of the picture. For example, the director might receive $2,000 for her services, the writer will sell the script for $1,000, and an actor can be hired for the duration of the show for $3,000. These fees are normally paid out in installments

THE COMPATRIOT

Finalized? Budget
2/2006

ACCNT	CATEGORY	AMOUNT	UNITS	X	RATE	SUB-TOTAL	TOTAL
BELOW THE LINE							
13-00	**CAMERA**						
13-03	Camera Package						
	Arri MovieCam	3	Days	1	$542	$1,625	$1,625
13-04	Additional Camera Equipment						
	Lens Package	3	Days	5	$65	$975	$975
13-05	Film Stock (w/ discount)						
	(Kodak 5218)	10	Rolls	1	$100	$1,000	$1,000
13-06	Expendables						
	Misc	1	Allow	1	$250	$250	$250
					Total for 13-00		**$3,850**
15-00	**SOUND**						
15-03	Sound Package						
	Rental	1	Week	1	$0	$0	$0
15-04	Walkies						
	Rental	1	Week	20	$10	$195	$195
15-05	Expendables						
	Misc	1	Allow	1	$150	$150	$150
					Total for 15-00		**$345**
16-00	**ELECTRIC AND GRIP**						
16-01	Pckg. Rental (w/ dolly)	3	Days	1	$892	$2,675	$2,675
16-05	Expendables						
	Misc	1	Allow	1	$525	$525	$525
					Total for 16-00		**$3,200**
18-00	**PROPS**						
18-03	Prop Rental						
	Weapons	2	Days	2	$50	$200	
18-04	Misc. Purchases	1	Allow	1	$200	$200	$400
					Total for 18-00		**$400**
19-00	**SET DRESSING**						
19-03	Purchases						
	Misc	1	Allow	1	$400	$400	$400
19-04	"The Wall" Construction	1	Allow	1	$1,000	$1,000	$1,000
					Total for 19-00		**$1,400**
20-00	**WARDROBE**						
20-02	Purchases						
	Clothes	1	Allow	1	$200	$200	$200
					Total for 20-00		**$200**
21-00	**HAIR & MAKE-UP**						
21-01	Key Make-Up Artist Kit						
	Shoot	5	Days	1	$50	$250	$250
21-02	Additional Make-Up Kit						
	Shoot	1	Day	1	$40	$40	$40
					Total for 21-00		**$290**

FIGURE 5.2 Budget for *The Compatriot* aka *Citizen.*

Continued

THE COMPATRIOT

Finalized? Budget
2/2006

22-00	**CATERING**					
22-01	Catering	5 Days	20	$10	$1,000	$1,000
22-02	Craft Service	5 Days	1	$75	$375	$375
				Total for 22-00		**$1,375**
23-00	**LOCATIONS**					
23-02	Locations Fees					
	Heckscher Park	1 Day	1	$500	$500	
	Pound Ridge	1 Day	1	$250	$250	
	Xavier High	1 Day	1	$300	$300	$1,050
				Total for 23-00		**$1,050**
24-00	**TRANSPORTATION**					
24-01	Passenger Van	1 Week	1	$632	$632	$632
24-02	14 Ft. Cube Truck	1 Week	1	$726	$726	$726
24-03	Additional 15 Pass	1 Day	2	$155	$310	$310
24-04	Additonal Cube Truck	1 Day	1	$164	$164	$164
24-05	Overnight Parking	1 Allow	1	$300	$300	$300
24-06	Gas	1 Allow	1	$400	$400	$400
				Total for 24-00		**$2,532**
25-00	**FILM AND LAB POST-PRODUCTION**					
25-01	Lab Negative Process	5000 Feet	1	$0.13	$650	$650
25-02	Telecine (to DV Cam)	5000 Feet	1	$0.14	$700	$700
25-03	Sound Sync	2 Hours	1	$75	$150	$150
25-04	Color Correction	2 Hours	1	$300	$600	$600
25-05	Negative Cutter	1 Allow	1	$500	$500	$500.00
25-06	Final 35mm Print	1 Allow	1	$750	$750	$750.00
				Total for 25-00		**$3,350**
26-00	**EDITORIAL**					
26-01	Editor	6 Weeks	1	$0	$0	$0
26-02	Sound Editor	2 Weeks	1	$200	$400	$400
				Total for 26-00		**$400**
27-00	**MUSIC**					
27-01	Composer	3 Weeks	1	$0	$0	$0
27-02	Expenses	1 Allow	1	$100	$100	$100
				Total for 27-00		**$100**
29-00	**CONTINGENCY**	1 Allow	1	$1,000	$1,000	$1,000
				Total for 29-00		**$1,000**
			TOTAL ABOVE THE LINE			**$0**
			TOTAL BELOW THE LINE			**$19,492**
			GRAND TOTAL			**$19,492**

FIGURE 5.2—cont'd

rather than at a weekly or daily rate—for example, 25 percent of the negotiated salary on signing the contract, 25 percent on the first day of principal photography, 25 percent on the last day of principal photography, and the final installment of 25 percent on completion of the work.

001 Script and Rights

As mentioned in Chapter 2, securing rights means negotiating with an author, the author's agent, the author's estate, or the author's publisher for permission to use her material as the basis for your short work. It is imperative that you secure the story rights if your short film is based on a copyrighted work. If you profit in any way from the sale or distribution of your film, you need to own the rights to the underlying material. There are three exceptions to this rule:

1. **You Are the Author of the Work.** If you have written an original piece, you own the rights to it. To register your copyright, access the copyright web site www.copyright.gov/forms for information and to download forms. The fee is approximately $20.

2. **The Material Is in the Public Domain.** An author's work sometimes becomes public property 70 years after her death. The Bible and the works of Shakespeare, Dickens, and Twain are all available at no cost. Be aware, however, that the author's heirs can extend the copyright of her work. An entertainment lawyer can perform a title search to check on the material's copyright status. This can be also done on the Internet.

3. **You Do Not Intend to Market the Final Product.** A film made for a class or screened in a noncommercial venue does not violate existing copyright laws. However, legal action can be taken against you if you use copyrighted material without securing the rights under these situations:
   - The project is sold to a distributor.
   - You sell DVDs of your film on the Internet.
   - You post your film on the Internet (YouTube, etc.).
   - The film is entered in a festival.

Whether you profit or not from exposing your work on the Internet, you still must secure the rights as well. Festivals are treated somewhat differently because prize money is not considered profit. You must still receive permission to use the material (if you win a prize or not) but have another option: **festival rights**. These rights may be negotiated separately and could either be secured free or for far less than commercial rights.

Consider the marketing plans for your piece and keep in mind that securing rights after you have completed the project might be difficult, expensive, or even impossible. Copyright laws apply to music as well (see Appendix F for complete information on music rights). If you are making a television commercial and want to give the client an idea of how it might sound, you can use any music you like for the promotional reel. However, when the commercial is approved, before entering it into the marketplace, you must purchase the music or replace it with original music.

002 Producer/003 Director

If the producer or director is paid a salary, whether it is cash up front or a deferred sum, the amount should be entered in the budget. If no salary is involved, write in either "N/A" (not applicable) or "0.00."

004 Cast

The cast category refers to everyone who performs in your project, including principals, bits, and extras. Payment for these actors ranges from nothing to union wages and more. During casting, you might find that the actor best suited for an important part is a union member. In this case, you might decide to pay for the security of knowing that the role is well cast. Whether or not you pay for your cast, it is advisable to be familiar with the cost of union labor. You might not have to work with Screen Actors Guild (SAG) or American Federation of Television and Radio Artists (AFTRA) actors on this picture, but these unions will no doubt play a large role in most of your future projects.

The Screen Actors Guild. When you use union talent, you must sign a contract with the union or guild. Becoming a signatory with the Screen Actors Guild—which also covers the American Guild of Variety Artists (AGVA), the American Federation of Television and Radio Artists (AFTRA), and Actor's Equity stage performers—is easy. Call SAG and speak to a representative. The guild will send the appropriate forms, and as long as you abide by the SAG Codified Agreement, you will be allowed to hire union talent.

Read the agreement carefully. The Screen Actors Guild rules governing rates, penalties, per diems, overtime, and so on are spelled out in detail. Play by the rules, or you might have to pay penalties later. On occasion, actors tell the producer that they are willing to "fudge" their time cards without informing the union but then turn around and report the inequities.

Nonunion Talent. The only way around union rules is to hire nonunion talent. With nonunion talent, you can negotiate any deal you like with the actors. If you are working under a SAG agreement, you can hire only union talent. If you can obtain a waiver to hire nonunion actors, they will not be eligible to join the guild after working on your production if this is their first film job. The Taft–Hartley Act stipulates that after their second professional acting stint, these performers will be eligible to join the union.

There is a good reason why SAG is such a strong union. Its members are familiar with a difficult craft. They understand their duties and act like professionals. They are skilled in developing characters, listening to other actors, hitting marks, memorizing lines, and pacing themselves for long hours. Nonunion talent might not possess these skills.

STUDENTS

Some film schools have made special arrangements with the union for salary deferment. If your picture sells, you must compensate the actors before you repay yourself for the cost of making the film. For example, if you employ an actor for one day, you "owe" him one day of scale (minimum salary), which is approximately $700 ($2,500 a week). If the film never sells, you need not pay the actor anything. If you do sell the film, though, your SAG bill will be $700 for that one actor. Keep this fact in mind as you schedule talent because there is no need to run up a big bill and have actors wait around the set if they are not needed. The Taft–Hartley Act, which allows an actor to join the guild after a second professional gig, does not apply to the student-SAG agreement.

Below-the-Line Costs

Whereas above-the-line personnel are usually paid a flat fee, below-the-line personnel are paid a weekly or daily rate. In a short film, there might very well be no fees, except possibly deferred fees, payable from profit. All other direct and deferred costs are reflected in the below-the-line section of the budget.

Profit, Negative Cost, and Deferred Fees. Profit is defined as the money the production company receives after it recoups the negative cost. The **negative cost** is the cost of making a film project from preproduction through a final print. If individuals are promised money for their services to be paid from the profit generated by the project, these fees are termed deferred. **Deferred** fees are not guaranteed. Individuals or service companies can work for no upfront money, opting to take their pay from the profits. If there are no profits, they will never see any money.

Film-developing laboratories often offer another option for payment. They sometimes agree to develop and process the negative film for no upfront money. If a laboratory has faith in your project, it might be willing to wait until you can generate enough funds to pay the bill. This type of deferment is simply a postponement of the bill.

I had edited the script down to 10 pages and with $10,000, I was ready to shoot the film. I also had a bit of reserve funding. It is important to emphasize that you should budget for half of what you have so you will have an extra 50 percent for those post production costs that will come up down the road and because in production, you start hemorrhaging money like you would not believe. I was proud of what we did for the money we had.

James Darling

Basic Decisions

Before you can begin to put down numbers, you must make some basic decisions about the nature of your production. Every decision, whether it involves cast, crew, equipment, location, etc., has a financial repercussion and will affect the hard costs of your project. Your decisions may change for a variety of reasons. For example, you might have to scale down your project to accommodate what you can raise, or you might find you have more money to spend than you had anticipated. Ultimately, your final budget will reflect what you can afford.

What is your workflow? It is important to determine what format you will be using for each of the following stages before you go into production:

- Acquisition
- Edit format
- Master format
- Deliverable
- Distribution

16mm, Super 16, 35mm, super35mm, standard def, high def, HDV, DV, XDCAM, Pro Res, DVC Pro, etc. With so many cameras and formats to choose from, it is a world that can easily be called a technological Wild West. In this case, before starting any project, whether it is standard definition, HD, or film, we highly recommend starting at the end and working backward. This approach requires looking at all the technical steps and then talking to key technical people, from the end to the beginning. Start with the format you will be delivering on; then move backward step by step to postproduction and then to production. The question to ask each technical person along the way is: what do I have to do to get from here to there, and how much will it cost? The goal is to have a technical road map from your first shot to the final delivery and a cost estimate of each step. (There are sample postproduction flow charts in Chapter 16.)

Discover the format needs of the market you are interested in targeting: theatrical, nontheatrical, network, cable, festivals, QuickTime movie, streaming video, YouTube, etc. (See Chapter 19 for more information.). This may be your most important step: discovering the end game. Knowing what format you require will allow you to take the right steps in *advance* to be sure the movie is suitable for these outlets. Research the primary festivals you are planning to enter and talk to distribution companies.

I did not submit *Citizen* to any film festivals unless they could screen 35mm. If you can't screen a film print, you're not a film festival in my opinion. I've been to many small festivals where they're screening DVDs and everything is the wrong aspect ratio, things are squished or stretched. I wanted to give them something that could last for a hundred years.

James Darling

Will you shoot your picture on film or video? This fundamental decision will have an impact on cost, equipment, choice of crew, and the "look" of the final product. Kodak and Fuji offer a range of superb 16- and 35mm fine-grained film stocks with wide exposure latitudes, enabling them to be shot in low light (Kodak's Vision line of stocks is superb). The latitude of film is much greater than that of video, even if you use the new Red Camera and it is still the best archival format.

Shooting film costs more than shooting video due to the expense of film stock and processing. However, film rental houses are willing to make great deals on camera, super 16 and 35mm equipment.

If you choose to shoot on film, what format should you select? The three basic film formats are 16mm, super 16mm, and 35mm. Some people still work in super 8mm even though fewer labs process it and the equipment is harder to rent.

The cost of shooting in 35mm is prohibitive for most beginners. It has a wonderful look, but to get 10 minutes of film, you have to shoot more than double the footage of 16mm (1,000 feet of 35mm equals approximately 400 feet of 16mm), and 35mm production equipment is expensive to rent.

If you need a 35mm print for distribution but can't afford to shoot 35mm, super 16mm is an option. It can be enlarged, or blown up, to 35mm. (Super 16 is discussed in Chapter 11.) Super 16mm has also become the preferred film format because its native aspect ratio of 1.66:1 is a perfect fit for the HDTV aspect ration of 1.77:1, commonly referred to as 16×9.

Another decision that can have a financial impact on your budget is whether to shoot in color or black and white; 16mm black-and-white raw stock is less expensive than color, but there are fewer labs that regularly process it. One lab known to excel in black-and-white processing is Alpha Cine in Seattle (http://www.alphacine.com)

If you decide to shoot on video, what format should you select? The video market is changing at such a rapid rate that whatever this book recommends could quickly become obsolete. HD Tapeless formats like Panasonic's HVX 200 and the Sony EX1 are two of them. The Red Camera has now entered the scene (see Chapter 11). These new cameras pose problems in workflow if you don't do your homework.

How are you planning to edit your project? Avid Media Composer, Final Cut Pro, and Adobe Premier are the three editing software systems available at the higher end. We will discuss some of the pros and cons of all three in Chapter 16.

005 Production Department Staff

A good production manager and assistant director are worth their weight in gold, especially if the director is a novice. These people keep the production running smoothly and on budget. Experienced production and crew members can be hired for an upfront salary, a deferred salary, or a combination of the two. Inexperienced crew members might work free merely to gain experience.

> The actors were paid the minimum for a short film. I paid my crew as well. Often times people say, you don't have to pay your crew, get a bunch of friends to do it. What I found over the years is if you pay people, you get better performance out of them, even if it is a meager amount. There is an old African saying that goes "he who pays remains free."
>
> Be' Garrett

006 Crew

The size of your crew will determine a large part of your daily production costs—that is, how many people you need to pay, feed, transport, or house (if it is a distant location) while the picture is in production. It is therefore extremely important that you decide how many crew members are essential to support the demands of the script. (Refer to Chapter 6 for the 3–30 rule.) There are several factors to consider when making this basic decision:

The Director's Style. The director might have certain specific requests regarding the size of the crew. She might prefer to work as light as possible, or perhaps she feels secure only with more bodies around her. Documentary crews are by nature small, but some fiction directors prefer this approach as well.

Elaborateness of the Production. It is logical that a two-character piece shot in a small apartment will make fewer technical demands than one shot during a high school basketball game. You can double and triple up on many positions, but don't think that you can get away with less than you need for something so "seemingly easy" as the two-character piece. The success of a single shot, whether in an apartment or at a high school basketball game, requires that many technical chores be performed perfectly on every take. *The Lunch Date* had a crew of 5, *Truman* was shot with a crew of 10, *Crazy Glue* had a crew of 1 to 8, depending on art direction, and *Mirror Mirror* had a crew of 2. *Citizen* had a crew of 25

In the next chapter, we list many of the important positions that are necessary for executing a well-run production. These positions represent the actual duties that must be performed on a set. Of course, not all productions are alike, but particular functions are essential to ensure a smoothly run shoot, no matter how modest the scale.

Stage versus Location. The decision to shoot your film on a sound stage, in a practical location (an existing site), or both will have a specific impact on your crew requirements. Having to design, construct, and dress a set on a sound stage requires crew members whom you will not need if the entire production is shot in a practical location. (See Chapter 8 for details.)

Visual Effects. If you are planning to use compositing effects, green screen, or motion capture, these effects need to be planned and budgeted for specialty crew.

Animation Crew. The first and most important thing a producer should know about animation is that it takes time—lots of time. Animation can add beautiful and compelling visuals to your piece, but it will require a different, more deliberate, way of working than live action.

Note that the time to experiment or make changes is during the boarding or animatic phase. After this point, hundreds of hours may go into the creation of even a relatively short scene. If you are paying the animators by the hour, changes after this point will be extremely expensive. If there is a flat fee on the job, multiple large changes to fully animated scenes will deteriorate a working relationship. On the other hand, an experienced animator will expect the storyboarding process to be rather fluid and subject to hours of discussion, so don't worry about expressing all your concerns and ideas at that time.

> In total I spent around $2,000 from start to finish. Of course, my shooting ratio was one to one.
>
> Tatia Rosenthal

Documentary Crew. Documentary crews are usually small and mobile. They require a highly skilled director of photography (DP) and production mixer (who can also serve as a boom operator) who can move quickly and efficiently. Assistants can be employed to help set up lights and sound equipment and to control traffic.

> I did sound on the shoots, and we always went out as a two-person crew, including on *Mirror Mirror*. We never had more than two people on location.
>
> Jan Krawitz

Union versus Nonunion Crew. If you can hire a union crew, you are usually guaranteed to get your money's worth. These highly skilled and trained individuals are prepared to perform under the stressful time constraints of large and small projects. Nonunion crew workers range in experience from recent film school graduates to seasoned professionals. The pay scale for nonunion labor is usually based on what the market will bear and on the crew member's experience.

Union minimum rates are available in *The Producer's Masterguide* or *Brooks Standard Rate Book* (see the Bibliography for details). It might surprise you how much even "scale" (minimum salary) is for most of the crew positions on a set. To help you keep these rates in perspective, Local 600 (camera guild) rates are as follows:

	Daily	Weekly
Director of photography	$653	$2,787
Camera operator	$509	$2,043
First assistant	$333	$1,348
Second AC	$262	$1,244
Film loader	$220	N/A

But keep in mind that although these are decent minimum rates, anyone on a production team might work only six months out of the year. Here is a formula for calculating the salary or rental cost for the picture:

$$\text{Days at} \times \text{rate} + \text{prep and wrap} = \text{fee.}$$

The fee for prep (preparation) and wrap is customarily less than the rate for the shoot. Different crew positions require different amounts of prep (see the flow chart in Chapter 3). The DP should come on as early as possible. The camera operator may need just a few days.

What you can expect is a flat rate per day, per week, or for the run of the show. The rate should be based on an agreed "day" of so many hours (usually 12). Because there are no nonunion regulations defining overtime pay, there should be some agreement about compensation for extra-long days. Everything is negotiable. Many directors of photography and production mixers work with their own equipment, so the price they quote includes labor and equipment (or, as it is sometimes called, their *kit*).

Learn about union work regulations. Such items as meal penalties, overtime, double overtime, and golden time can greatly inflate the budget. The union code of regulations and ethics should serve as a model for your production behavior, even if you do not use union labor. These regulations were developed to protect workers from exploitation and to guarantee extra payment if they are required to work additional hours.

The 12-hour cap should be strictly adhered to and, if abused, can have dangerous repercussions (see the rules in Chapter 4). Pushing the crew too hard without giving something back is considered exploitation. In addition, if the crew is too exhausted to work effectively, you will reach the point of diminishing returns.

Credit and Experience in Lieu of Compensation (CELC). If you can find experienced crew members who want to make the jump from their current position to a more advanced position, such as a 2nd assistant director who wants to work as a 1st assistant director or a location manager who wants to try her hand as a production manager, you might obtain their services free. The production benefits from their general experience, and they benefit by gaining specific experience in a new position.

When Do You Need Them? The "Producer" section of Chapter 3 contains a detailed week-by-week preproduction schedule that indicates when particular crew members should begin work. There are no absolutes in this area, but this schedule can serve as a guide. The DP and art director are two key crew members that should be brought on as early as possible in preproduction.

007 Equipment

Before approaching a rental house, you need to have some idea of the size of your equipment package. Following are some of the primary factors that will influence this decision.

Director's Visual Plan for the Picture. The director's ideas for the project might include the use of a dolly or some other elaborate equipment such as a Steadicam, jib arm, or crane. Eventually, you might discover that you cannot afford these items, but it is still wise to get an idea of their cost. It might be possible to negotiate a few days' rental of a dolly as part of a larger equipment package. Steadicam operators usually come with their own rig.

Special Equipment Requirements. Identify and budget the specialty rigs and camera equipment that the script demands, such as a car mount (if there are many driving scenes) and zoom lens motors. Now is the time to explore different equipment options and their cost. There are imaginative ways to shoot people talking in cars without elaborate rigs and slow motor zooms.

Size of Interiors That Must Be Lit. Your equipment package should accommodate all lighting requirements dictated by the script. You might need to scale down some of the lighting packages or else change the script to find a balance. Often, when the cost of a lighting package is examined, the all-important night scene easily can be shifted to an all-important day scene. In any case, it is a good idea to pad this area because you don't want to get caught with too little money for grip and electric.

An alternative approach to reducing the amount of required lighting units is to shoot with more sensitive film stock and/or use **super speed** lenses (see Glossary).

Ability to Work with Small Lighting Packages. The ability of the director of photography to work with small lighting packages can't be judged until you begin hiring, but it is good to know what you can afford so you can approach potential DPs with realistic expectations of the kind of equipment with which they will be working. If your DP is comfortable with the limitations of your budget and doesn't demand more lights, it is a good sign that you have hired the right person.

Deals You Will Be Able to Negotiate. Once you have determined the equipment required for the shoot, shop for a rental house. You can negotiate a deal at a special rate if you rent all your equipment from one source. Besides the big items like the camera, dolly, lights, and dolly track, you must allocate money for expendable items such as construction materials, bounce cards, gels, and diffusion material. (See the "Producer" section in Chapter 11 for more about rental houses.)

It is best to price a number of equipment packages. Think of them as A, B, and C lists. The A list is the wish list, and the C list is the make-do list. The B list stands as a compromise between what you would like to have and what you can realistically afford.

008 Art Department

The art director supervises the team that is responsible for the total look of the picture. Props, wardrobe, set dressing, set construction, hair, and makeup all fall under the auspices of the art department. This catchall category also includes many items customized for your show, such as animals, special effects, and picture cars. A small-scale project might need or be able to afford only one to three people to handle this important area. Much depends on the requirements of the script and what you can make do with, given your limited budget.

A number of factors will affect how you approach the budget for this department. They include the following.

The Art Director. How experienced and frugal your art director is will have an impact on how much you get for your money. Inexpensive building materials and frequent trips to thrift shops can save money for the production.

Although the art department category is budgeted before the shoot, it should be well padded. Many unanticipated changes or necessities can arise, resulting in petty cash flowing like water from a leaky bucket. There is high risk of going over budget in the art department.

Script Requirements. The breakdown sheets provide you with a list of the props, wardrobe, and special hair and makeup required for the picture. From this starting point, you can begin pricing these items. The script of *The Lunch Date* called for the protagonist to wear a mink stole. This means renting or borrowing one, unless you are lucky enough to hire an actor who has one of her own and is willing to wear it for the show.

> I said to the wardrobe designers, "Here's $1,200. You can take out of it what you want, and pay yourself what's left over." Basically that worked. They paid themselves $400, and used $800 for the costumes.
>
> Howard McCain

Sets That Must Be Built. Set construction—renting a stage, building sets, and dressing them—is a big ticket item. Set construction is labor-intensive work and requires building supplies such as lumber, canvas, nails, and paint. There are ways to economize in this area, such as redressing already built sets, but there is no getting around the extra costs compared to working with practical locations. Because of the costs involved, the producer traditionally oversees set construction directly.

Amount of Set Dressing Required. How a location is to be dressed doesn't usually show up in the script. The writer might describe the general look or feel of a room without going into much detail. Set dressing comprises the objects that make up the world your characters inhabit. It is different from props, which are described in the script, but is no less important. Set dressing can come from many sources, including the actors themselves. A found location might already have personal items that are suitable for your picture, or it might have to be stripped down and dressed from scratch.

> I paid for the location and we paid for quite a bit of the equipment as well. Some things we got for free, some things we didn't, or we got at a discount. The meals were catered, and we had vehicles. At a certain point it was "here are my credit cards; I have got to go direct now" and I figured I'd deal with the bills when it's over.
>
> Be' Garrett

009 Location

The breakdown pages will furnish you with a list of all the location demands for the production. It's possible that one location can serve for many in your story. Perhaps one apartment can be dressed to feel like two. Although you might hope to secure most locations free, it is best to budget as if you were going to pay for them (even if it's just $50). An exchange of money, however minimum, signifies a business transaction. It changes the relationship between you and the individual who is renting the location.

Near or Distant? Your script might indicate a location that is not available locally. Without having to scout different areas, the producer can contact local film bureaus, which have on file pictures or descriptions of available locations that suit the needs of the script. Shooting at a location more than 50 miles from your home base (in some cites, this distance changes, so do your research) obliges you to transport, house, and feed the cast and crew for the duration of the shoot. This decision puts a strain on the budget but might be unavoidable given the requirements of the script. For example, if the production base is in a city and the script is set in the woods, the company might have to travel to the countryside (the exception to this example occurs if a big city park can be manipulated to look like the woods).

This budget category can become inflated with little or no warning. Locations fall through or become more expensive on the day of the shoot. A neighbor can decide that he is disturbed and needs to be paid off to remain quiet. Vehicles break down, gas prices rise, it rains, there's an earthquake!

Transportation. The movement of people and supplies to and from the shooting location is an important part of a successful production. Transportation requires proper vehicles and responsible drivers. This budget category also includes funds for gas, tolls, and parking. Rental companies often make good deals, so it pays to shop around.

Your transportation budget should reflect three basic items:

- **Size of Equipment Package.** The size of the equipment package will define the kinds and numbers of cars, trucks, or vans you will need to rent. Several cargo vans might be sufficient to handle a small grip and electric package.
- **Size of Cast and Crew.** If you are shooting at a convenient location in and around your home town, you will not need to transport cast and crew to the set. However, if you are moving the production unit to a distant location, you will need to rent enough passenger vans for the run of the show.
- **Requirements of Location.** If you are shooting at an exterior location without an available green room nearby for the actors (see Chapter 9), you might need to rent a large van or recreational vehicle for the actors to dress, make up, and relax in when they are not required on the set. This is especially true for cold-weather shoots.

Food. Cast and crew members run on their stomachs, and they like their food to be prepared well and tasty. You can estimate your food budget by using the following formula:

No.of days × no.of personnel × dollar amount per head
= food budget

Caterers will quote how much they charge per person per meal. It might be $3.50 for lunch and $4.50 for dinner. Ask about specific menus for each meal, and have the caterer come to your office with samples.

You will usually be required to serve two meals a day: breakfast and lunch, or dinner and a late snack if shooting nights.

Craft services. Budget for a standing table of water, juices, fruit (warm drinks if it is winter and you are shooting exteriors), but keep away from junk food, donuts, chips, candy, etc.

STUDENTS

Feeding a cast and crew can be expensive. If you wait until the last minute and have to send out for pizza or sandwiches, the price per head will be high. Plan out in advance each meal of each shooting day, decide who is going to make the food, and determine how it will arrive on the set. Heating up a big pot of stew or cooking pasta for lunch can result in big savings. Keep a large coffeemaker on the set. Keeping coffee brewing will be less expensive in the long run than sending out for individual cups of coffee. Finally, always try to buy what you can in bulk from discount warehouses.

Do not neglect the creature comforts. If you travel out of town, sleeping and traveling accommodations do not have to be first class (unless you are so obligated contractually), but if eight crew members sleeping in one hotel room means no sleep for anyone, the next day's work will reflect their dissatisfaction and fatigue.

Howard McCain

Housing. I had a friend of my mother's cater, and I paid her $100 for the week and the rest went into food. You better be prepared to spend a great deal. It is important to keep your crew happy and make sure your meals are served on time and are good. A problem people often run into is they serve good meals but not on time. With kids, especially, you have to be very regular; otherwise they are going to get upset. No matter where we were in the day, we would stop at noon and have lunch. That time was for everybody to do what they wanted until we started again.

Meals are very important. They should be adequate and nutritious. For that part of the budget, you have to plan how many paper plates you're going to buy, napkins, etc. Caterers take care of that for you, but it costs money.

If you are offering to fill a number of rooms for a set period of time, hotels often make deals with production units. Remember, they're in business to rent their accommodations. They would rather have their rooms occupied than empty.

010 Film and Laboratory

Laboratories will make overall discount deals with filmmakers for processing and printing. You can calculate the lab bill based on the amount of stock you are planning to shoot. The price of stock, however, is a fixed figure (students are able to get up to a 20 percent discount from Kodak). Film from Kodak or Fuji should be all from one batch; that is, the serial numbers for the film stock should be consecutive. Videotape should come from the same batch as well. This guarantees that the quality of the entire batch will be consistent from roll to roll. Shooting in a

tapeless format eliminates the cost of film, processing, and tape stock because P2 cards can be used over and over again.

Buying old stock or short ends (film leftovers from another production) can be risky but is an excellent way to trim costs. With old stock and short ends, you need to weigh the savings against the risk that the stock might be outdated and therefore unusable. Video stock should always be new.

The laboratory's price for film developing the negative and making a work print is based on a price per foot. You can easily calculate this figure to place in the budget. Check this figure again as you get closer to production because laboratories change their prices often.

If you plan to shoot on film and edit digitally, you will receive *video dailies* that can be synced up at the lab or by the editor. Contact the lab and pick up a brochure. Learn about its recommendations for the proper technical steps of matching back to film and the potential cost. This will enable you, for example, to weigh the difference in price of having the lab or your editor sync up the dailies. Even with a brochure, we recommend that you visit the lab personally, especially if you are doing this for the first time.

STUDENTS

Many laboratories offer a student rate. Kodak offers a discount for raw stock to registered film students.

You can determine the amount of stock you will need for your show once the director and the director of photography become involved. It is possible, however, to estimate how many rolls of raw film stock to order based on a projected shooting ratio (the ratio of film shot to film developed). If you are preparing a 10-minute film and anticipate a 4:1 shooting ratio, you need to buy 40 minutes of stock (four rolls of 16mm at approximately 11 minutes per roll). This particular shooting ratio is considered lean even by professional standards and requires that the director be well prepared and economical with her shots. A more realistic shooting ratio for beginners would be somewhere between 6:1 and 10:1. It is best to budget for the larger figure, as it can always be pared down with input from the director when the budget is revised.

Adam Davidson

Amount of Stock to Order. We underestimated slightly the amount of film stock we needed. During the production, the last day, we had to run out and get some more. I went through a film broker. I asked a DP who I knew for short ends, but he didn't have any 16mm short ends, so he gave me 35mm short ends instead. I traded those in for 16mm black-and-white stock.

> I budgeted myself 14 rolls of film, and that's exactly what I shot.
>
> Howard McCain

Video stock is inexpensive and rarely a budgetary consideration. This is an advantage if you are producing a documentary where the shooting ratio is usually very high.

Postproduction

Postproduction overwhelms many beginners. They focus so much energy on mastering the complexities of production planning that they neglect postproduction. You are sure to encounter hidden costs and unknowns that can't be clearly understood at this stage. How long a film will take to edit and complete depends on many variables. (See Chapters 16 through 18 for more details.) As we have stated, it is important to know what format you want to end up with. This decision will influence many of the steps in between. This applies particularly to those wishing to shoot film, edit digitally, and finish on film.

Strike a balance between allowing ample time to make the correct artistic choices and the amount of time that the budget can support. It is a reasonable estimate that your postproduction budget will equal your production budget. This equation is a good starting point when evaluating your numbers.

011 Editing

The main items in the editing category are the cost of the editor and the rental of the editing room. The cost may also be influenced by the editing software. (There is also the purchase of a hard drive.) The final cost to complete your project will depend largely on how much time it will take to **lock picture** (complete editing) and complete all the sound work leading up to the final mix.

The postproduction schedule depends on the following factors.

Who Edits? A professional editor will speed the editing process along. A professional editor may also be fluent in the two software systems that are being used predominantly, Final Cut Pro and Avid. A beginner might take months to do a job that an experienced editor can do in several weeks. If you are editing a short film for the first time, allow for a slow startup as the editor feels her way around the editing room. Beginners have been known to spend an inordinate amount of time working on a 15- to 30-minute short.

Access to Editing Room. This applies mostly to students and independents on a budget. Students with full-time class schedules or jobs might be able to work for only sporadic stretches at a time. It is difficult to sustain creative momentum with this limitation. Independents with limited budgets might have to rely on low-cost facilities from local media groups that don't allow full access to the equipment. Some expensive video facilities give customers a special price if they come in on a will-bump basis or during the graveyard shift.

Shooting Ratio. Even for professional editors, the more footage they must wade through and cut, the longer it will take to shape the film into a final product. Documentaries traditionally use a very high shooting ratio, especially if they are using tape or tapeless format. It is only during the editing process that the true shape of the documentary emerges, so it is best to budget for a long postproduction period.

Rental or Purchase Deal. Many students and beginners edit on a Mac loaded with Final Cut Pro or another software system.

012 Postproduction Sound

The area of postproduction sound encompasses sound effects, Foley, automated dialogue replacement (ADR), mixing, and the music track. There are a multitude of details related to these steps that involve the expenditure of money.

Postproduction houses may offer the student or beginner a set price for the sound design/editing/ADR and the mix based on a flat rate per minute. Bargains may be available if you are not in a rush and the post house can work on your project in the off hours.

The dimension and complexity of the job will ultimately define the final price. Projects requiring elaborate sound effects and a great deal of ADR will be more costly. Research this area well. Talk to several postproduction houses and bring your script with you. However, don't confine your search to the larger sound houses. Because computers and digital technology have reduced the size and scope of the equipment needed to complete this kind of work, many sound designers have turned their houses/apartments into mini-sound studios.

Music. The music for your project, if needed, either will come from prerecorded sources or will have to be composed especially for the picture. One method is not inherently less expensive than the other. The right to use a few bars of a very popular song could cost far more than original music for the score of a short film. Film composers in the early stages of their career will often complete a score for very little money for the chance to get valuable experience and expand their reel.

It is difficult to know at this stage what role music will play in your final product. Sometimes a piece of music indicated in the script has an important relationship to character, mood, or plot. If it is a popular song or recording, research the rights to the music now before it becomes a permanent fixture in the cut. Securing the rights to well-known songs can cost hundreds and even thousands of dollars, depending on when the song was released and the popularity of the recording artist. (See Appendix F for more information about music rights.)

Mix. During the film mix, the entire soundtrack for the project comes together. Call around to various mixing facilities and ask for prices. Most offer student or night rates for independents on a budget. This usually means having a trainee mix your film. If you have finished your soundtrack on a digital audio workstation (DAW), you will still require a final mix. Sound needs to be adjusted and balanced for viewing in a theater (unless, of course, YouTube is your only destination); this balance is important if you plan to enter festivals. The dynamics shift dramatically from the headphones to the screen.

STUDENTS

If your institution has an ADR, Foley, or mixing facility, it is best to work with it as much as you can. Mixing a 10- to 15-minute project professionally can add $2,000 to your budget. Make the first pass at your institution. Spend the time learning the intricacies of the mixing board without the financial pressure of the clock (at $150 to $250 an hour). If you are not happy with the result and decide to opt for a professional mixing stage, what you will have gained in experience and confidence will far make up for what you might have lost in time.

---

013 Laboratory Postproduction (Film)

If you plan to finish on film, obtain a price list from the lab you plan to use. If your script is 15 pages long, figure that the film will be 12 minutes, or 425 feet. For postproduction lab expenses, such as the answer and release print, use the budget breakdown and simply multiply 425 times the price per foot. Make sure you include money for opticals, negative cutting, reprints, tax, and so on. This budget category should be **padded**. You will encounter unanticipated expenses later, so it's wise to have enough money in the budget to cover them.

If you're shooting on film, cutting on a nonlinear system, and matching back to film, make sure you spend time working through the details with the lab before beginning to budget. The **negative cutter** (refer to Chapter 18) is a key player; make sure you contact her in advance as well. **Animation and Computer Graphics**. In a live action film, integrating animated or computer graphics (CG) images needs to be coordinated from preproduction (storyboards) through production and married to the print in post. It is a good idea to have an experienced CG artist or visual effects (visfx) supervisor on set. It is best to consider the workflow backward. The creation of a character model can take a great deal of time depending on the complexity, the amount of movement, and screen time. In a CG feature, the lead characters usually take from three to four months to model, texture, and rig. Rigging is the process of creating an internal skeleton for the model that helps the character bend, deform, and move in a believable manner. A background character may take just a few days. Preplanning is crucial with characters because a good CG animator will do only what is necessary. For example, if the character is an extra and you decide to give it a speaking part, the animator may not have rigged the mouth to open or modeled any teeth.

As the costs have dropped dramatically, independent filmmakers have been drawn toward CG for relatively low budget films. For a CG effect to be effective in a live action film, it must be photorealistic with believable lighting, texture, proportions, and scale. A CG character must be equally convincing with lifelike movement and behavior to blend seamlessly with shot footage. Photoreal effects and animation require a great deal of skill, knowledge, planning, and hard long hours to achieve, so a filmmaker should use them only when necessary and with the proper resources.

014 Office Expenses

A good formula is to budget 5 percent of the below the-line budget for your production office expenses.

015 Insurance

Do not neglect insurance. Many companies insure film and video shoots. Equipment and personal liability are the minimum insurance packages. You can purchase additional insurance for such items as stunt work, foreign or hazardous locations, and the negative; the last coverage protects the film once it reaches the laboratory. (See Appendix F for a complete breakdown of insurance options.)

STUDENTS

Some film and video programs automatically supply basic liability and equipment coverage.

016 Contingency

A contingency is a buffer between the budget and insolvency. The normal contingency figure is 10 percent of the below-the-line total. Although this number might seem high, contingency money is a key protection against cost overruns. Think of this as a slush fund for costs you cannot anticipate like transportation costs for crew that live in totally different areas, the cost of cleaning up the house you used as a location, dry cleaning for the tuxedos you borrowed but must be returned and pressed, one-time setup fee the lab charges on certain services, the late charge you had to pay because you returned the equipment late, or the $70 replacement cost for the 200-watt bulb that blew during the shoot.

Petty Cash

Petty cash is all the loose cash spent during production (not checks or prearranged expenses) on a variety of expenses. During principal photography, money seems to fly out of the producer's pocket. One of the easiest ways to drain a budget and incur overages is to lose track of your petty cash. Buy or make up petty cash envelopes. Then give each department head a fixed amount, say $100. This person then puts all receipts in the envelope and writes the expenses on the outside. These figures can be transferred to a breakdown sheet and itemized by department (See Our web site for this form).

When this allowance is spent, the department head turns the envelope over to the production coordinator, who advances another $100. When possible, pay bills by check. Checks provide good record keeping for production expenses and for the government.

> **STUDENTS**
>
> Don't neglect petty cash! Make sure you keep at least $50 on hand each day to take care of unexpected expenses. At the end of the day, make sure that you document where it has gone (keep all receipts).

Beginning the Budget

Armed with your shooting schedule and a set of basic assumptions, you can now enter some numbers. Remember that you have stripped out from the script the items that will cost money, so refer to your breakdown pages. They will tell you to which items you will need to assign a cost. Once you have decided on the size of the crew, estimating crew costs is just a matter of multiplying the number of people by the number of days you will be shooting, including prep and wrap time.

The Budget Process

Consider this first pass at the budget as one of many drafts. The budget might go through many incarnations as more production information is funneled into the process. It will also be affected by changes to the script. Your estimates will become more realistic as you hammer out deals on locations, equipment packages, caterers, cast, and crew.

Put the numbers in their appropriate categories and add up the total. It is always good to overestimate at this point. If the numbers add up to less than you expected, you have room to pad specific areas. If the total is greater than you anticipated, look at the bigger budget items and begin to trim.

Information Is Power

The more choices you have, the better prepared you are to make the most sensible decisions. As you look around for the right deals, it is important to understand that the telephone and the Internet are your tools. Be ready to use them a lot. When seeking out the best deal for a van rental or production equipment, secure a local production guide (see the Bibliography) or a phone book and begin calling. Search engines can locate companies in a nanosecond. Here are several important tips for phone work.

Be Aggressive. Don't wait days for your call to be returned. If vendors don't call you back within a reasonable period of time, call them again. You are competing with others who want the vendors' attention. Keep plugging away until you get it. Remember that the squeaky wheel gets the grease.

Get the Name of the Person with Whom You Speak. Write down the complete name of whoever gives you information about a price or deal. Later, you can verify the figures by quoting the individual who gave them to you on the first call. Otherwise, another party can deny that anyone in the company ever gave you such a quote.

Take Notes of What You Are Quoted on the Phone. Get as much information as possible about what the vendor is offering and the price. Write it down neatly and carefully, and organize the notes in your production book so you can refer to the information. If, after you hang up, you realize you forgot to ask a specific question, call back.

Beware of the Really Cheap Deal. If you find a price that is suspiciously lower than everyone else's quote, be wary. Examine and test all goods. A *good* deal does not necessarily mean faulty equipment, but an incredible deal might spell disaster.

Meet the People with Whom You Will Be Working. This tip especially applies to film or video equipment rental houses, postproduction facilities, and film laboratories. You are creating a relationship not just for the duration of this particular project, but, it is hoped, for many to come. Vendors receive hundreds of phone calls a day, so be sure to help them connect your face with your voice. The personal connection will make an impression and might allow you to negotiate a better deal.

Don't Rush Through This Process. Take your time. Beat as many bushes as you can to find the best deals. Don't be satisfied until you have checked out every available rental company. Your legwork in preproduction might save enough money to enable you to purchase more stock or to rent the perfect location. The heat of production affords you little or no time to negotiate; production is not the time to strike deals.

Everything Is Negotiable. Don't be afraid to ask for what you want. Always start with your lowest bid for services, talent, and materials. All people can do is say "No." Enter a negotiation with a figure culled from the budget in mind, but try to get it for less. If you can secure a location or make a deal with a caterer for less, you can use the difference for a line item that costs more than you budgeted.

> As far as equipment goes, develop a relationship with the vendors you are interested in renting from. If it is a student film, tell them! (Student filmmakers can get huge discounts on everything! Milk it for all it's worth.) Never be afraid to negotiate or ask for a deal. Make sure you get quotes from a few different places, so you have options and can see where you might be getting a bad deal. Take yourself seriously, and vendors will too.
>
> Jessalyn Haefele, Producer of *Citizen*

Get It on Paper. Get all agreements confirmed in a Letter of Commitment. Verbal agreements can be forgotten.

Above All, Be Friendly. Personal relationships are the foundation on which all business is conducted in the industry. This is a given. People generally want to work with individuals they know and with whom they are comfortable.

Learn by Doing

To gain an idea of what things cost, work on as many productions as possible in whatever capacity you can, ideally in some job that allows you access to the set. This entry-level job will most likely be as a production assistant, a catchall title for the person who does the grunt or "gofer" work (go for this, go for that) that isn't handled by any defined crew position. A production assistant might get coffee for the director, run errands for the producer, or help with traffic or crowd control, among other duties.

A set is a living laboratory. Soak in as much of the atmosphere as possible. Learn to identify all the people on the crew, what they do, and how they handle themselves. Get to know as many people as you can. You can't afford to be shy in these situations, although you should learn when it is acceptable to ask questions and when you should be silent. After a job is over, keep in contact with the key people you've met.

> I got a job as a production assistant and just hung around with the grips for a while and started doing grip work. There was a shot with the fence swinging open in the wind, and I was there behind the tree with a fishing line pulling the thing back and forth.
>
> Adam Davidson

The set is the ideal place to learn; however, working in the production office can also be educational. Aiding the production coordinator and production manager, even if it is by photocopying contact sheets, is an invaluable opportunity to experience the ebb and flow of daily production activity. Be enthusiastic about every job you are asked to do, no matter how menial it might seem. Prove yourself first on the basic tasks before bucking for the more demanding ones.

STUDENTS

Get as much experience as you can on "professional" shoots as well as your own student productions. Exposure to professional standards will invariably help your own work. You can never have too much experience. Each production has its own set of unique problems, and learning how others work through the process of solving them is an important part of your education. Through this process, you will surely learn valuable lessons that you can file away for use in similar situations on your own productions.

Student Budgets

Certainly in the film school scenario, one individual may be the writer, the director, the producer, and the editor (and, let's hope not, the cinematographer as well). But if the student or beginner is lucky to have a producer, that person may be simply performing the duties of a production manager.

Following are the key **production budget** items for a student film. They will be the bulk of the hard costs required to get a picture into the editing room. (See Figure 5.2, Budget for *The Compatriot* aka *Citizen*).

- Stock (film, video, flash cards)
- Processing (film only)
- Food (meals and craft service)
- Location expenses
- Art department (props, costumes, set design/dressing, etc.)
- Transportation (van rental)
- Expendables (gels, DAT tape, batteries, etc.)
- In-kind donations (food, locations, film stock, etc.)
- Petty cash ($50 a day minimum)
- Equipment rentals

Students might also spend extra for special equipment that is not included in the equipment package they receive from their program, such as 35mm cameras, special lenses,

SHORT BUDGET – 3		Detail	Budget	Actual Cost
006	CREW			
	Director of Photography			
	Camera Operator			
	Assistant Camera			
	Second Assistant Camera			
	Sound Recordist			
	Sound Boom			
	Gaffer			
	Best Boy			
	Key Grip			
	Grip(s)			
	Driver			
	Overtime			
	Fringes			
	Other			
	TOTAL			
007	EQUIPMENT			
	Camera Package			
	Sound Equipment			
	Lighting Package			
	Grip Equipment			
	Dolly/Crane Rental			
	Generator Rental			
	Special Equipment			
	Expendables			
	Truck Rental			
	Gas, Oil			
	TOTAL			
008	ART			
	Air Director			
	Prop Person			
	Wardrobe Person			
	Hair/Makeup Person			
	Set Dresser			
	Prop Expenses			
	Wardrobe			
	Set Dressing			
	Hair/Makeup Expenses			
	Stage Rental			
	Set Construction			
	Construction Supplies			
	Petty Cash			
	TOTAL			

FIGURE 5.3 Another sample budget.

dollies, and car mounts. If funds are tight, be sure that you will have enough money to get the film out of the lab (this is not an issue with video). You can use the time during postproduction to raise money to complete the project. See the sample expendable list from *Citizen* on our web site.

Marketing /Distribution/Web Site. Developing a promotional web site (more about this on the web site for the book), creating press releases, developing distribution strategies, and entering festivals all cost money. It is best to look at ahead and anticipate these costs at the front end.

DIRECTOR

Shooting for the Moon

The director is not usually involved in calculating the budget. This is the domain of the producer. When asked, the director will most likely want to "shoot for the moon" and surround herself with as much time, equipment, and personnel as she can to achieve her goal. However, the director needs to know what went into preparing the budget. In the professional world, the director "signs off" on the budget. This means that she agrees to shoot within the means of what has been agreed upon.

A seasoned director can serve as a welcome consultant to the novice producer during the budgeting process by bringing her experience to play in several key areas, such as her shooting plan and her crew, equipment, and cast needs.

The budgeting process is a team effort. An experienced director can serve as a guide while the producer does the roadwork, making the calls and negotiating the deals. There can be a healthy dialogue between the two as the producer fleshes out the figures that represent the script's needs.

The director can also advise the producer about her minimal needs to do the picture. There can be a "wish" version of the budget, as well as a "bottom-line" version of the budget. Ultimately, the director strives to make the best picture possible with the available resources, but it is also her duty to fight for her vision. If she feels that she needs additional time or equipment, she should request it. Her goal is to shoot for the moon while understanding the constraints of the budget.

Adam Davidson

Garth (the producer of *The Lunch Date*) was terrific. I couldn't have made the film without him. Basically, what happened was I had all the locations locked, and then as the film got closer, I started having to worry about how I would shoot it, so I loaded all the production concerns on him, and he was great.

KEY POINTS

- Estimate the size of the production. Will you need a big cast, lots of crew, or many locations?
- Examine your resources and potential funding. Do not try to make an epic on a shoestring.
- Balancing the budget and the script is a constant struggle. If money becomes too tight, the script itself can be altered to reestablish a balance.
- Establish a system of petty cash vouchers to keep track of the cash flow. The art department can be an unexpected drain on the budget.

Chapter 6

Crewing

The most important rule of filmmaking is to always feed your crew well.

Howard McCain

PRODUCER

Hiring the Crew

The **crew** is defined as all the personnel, besides the actors, who are employed in the making of a film during principal photography. Just as important as finding the right actors to flesh out the story in front of the camera is the search for the right support group behind the camera. The crew represents the nuts and bolts of the production machine. The success of the project lies in their ability to collectively carry out the director's vision of the script. The sum of their energies and creative input is responsible for the project being produced.

The best-laid plans are only as good as the talented people who carry them out. The production hours are long and hard. Crew members who can be creative and inventive under pressure while maintaining a sense of humor are worth the search. These positions might not be romantic or showy, but they are all essential to the making of the film. If a production assistant doesn't control the flow of traffic, the director can't get the shot. If the assistant camera operator doesn't clean the film gate properly, a whole roll of film could be scratched. If the lens is not properly set or the lighting is inadequate, even the most brilliant performance will be out of focus or impossible to see.

Who Hires the Crew?

The producer's responsibility is to surround the director with the best creative team the project can afford. The director participates closely in the selection of the key crew members (DP, Art, Sound, AD), but it is the producer (in his role as production manager) who negotiates, makes the deals, and, if necessary, does the firing. This is to ensure that the director's relationship with the crew is on a purely creative level and that any tension over business issues does not interfere with what should be a positive and supportive relationship. Once key crew members are in place, they will select and hire their support crew.

When Do You Need a Crew?

"Prep Time Is Quality Time"

Crew members not only need to be present for the duration of the shoot, but they also need time to prepare. This period is termed **prep time**. After the shoot, the crew requires a cleanup, or **wrap**, period to complete any work that has to be done after principal photography. The only exception to this is if a crew member is hired to perform a specialty job, such as prosthetic makeup, an explosion, or the operation of a second unit camera.

The amount of prep time needed depends on many factors. For short films on tight budgets, it depends on the availability of key people to give as much time as possible without being paid. As with all things in preproduction, ***the more prep time, the better***, especially for the director of photography and the art director. These two key crew members and the director form a triangle that is the creative backbone of the project.

(*The Introduction to Preproduction* outlines a sample preproduction schedule, which indicates when particular crew members should ideally come on board. Each project has its own set of requirements, but this schedule should serve as a model.)

> The director of photography did have a meeting with the assistant camera, the grip, and the gaffers, his whole crew, for an hour or so the week before the shoot. They went over what he was trying to do, how he wanted to do it, and how he was going to run his department.
>
> Howard McCain

How Big a Crew Do You Need?

Only by recognizing the script's technical needs and understanding the director's design for translating the story into images can the producer adequately crew the project. If the director's shooting plan calls for several dolly moves, as did those of *Truman, The Lunch Date, A Nick in Time,* and *Citizen,* there will have to be experienced crew on the set, at least on certain days, who can handle this technical responsibility. Tatia's crew for *Crazy*

doi: 10.1016/B978-0-240-81174-1.00013-0

Glue fluctuated each day between one (herself on camera) and eight, depending on art direction requirements.

It is important for you to be familiar with the many positions that exist on a film crew and to understand the primary responsibility of each. Crew size is also a budget issue. The crew members have to be fed, transported, and, if they are lucky, paid.

Documentary crews are small and compact by nature. They must be able to move quickly in and out of confined spaces. At the other end of the spectrum, a full union crew will have a size and complexity that most beginning film-makers do not need and cannot afford.

The 3–30 Rule

Short film projects employ a crew of from 3 to 30 members. If you are filming a small non sync (MOS) film with available light in a few locations, it could be accomplished with a

- Writer/director/producer
- DP/AC
- Art department/AD/grip

Add multiple locations, sync sound shooting, set design, the decision to rent a dolly, and you may be up to 15–20 crew members. The size of the crew expands to fulfill the needs of the production. The budget, however, may restrict how many crew members can be hired. Your challenge, should you have fewer than this number, is to determine how the positions will be filled by the number of personnel employed on your shoot. For example, if the script requires 30 crew positions, but you can afford a crew of only 10, each person will have to perform an average of three jobs (see Figure 6.1).

Producers may have to double as assistant directors, editors as script supervisors, and so on. This requires, however, that every member of the crew knows exactly what jobs he is responsible for. Set operations must function like clockwork. If a piece of furniture needs to be moved, you can't have three people grabbing at it at the same time.

STUDENTS

Directors often want to do everything. This is in part because they most likely have raised all the financing. The director needs to delegate authority if she wants to spend her time directing and not producing. That's what the producer is for.

Selecting the Crew

You are looking for crew members who are hard working, talented, and enthusiastic. If you are asking people to work for free, for small wages, or even if you have all the money in the world, you want a crew that is creatively stimulated by the script and the challenges of bringing it to life. Crew members must also be available on the dates you are scheduled to shoot. And because your schedule may change, make sure you know their work schedule in and around your production dates. Good people get busy, so for this reason, make sure you have backups.

It is also important to find crew members whose personalities complement one another. Crewing is similar to the casting process for actors. The chemistry of the group is important because these people will be working closely under the stress of production. It is also valuable to know the kinds of egos with which you will be working. Are these team players or prima donnas?

FIGURE 6.1 Crew flow chart.

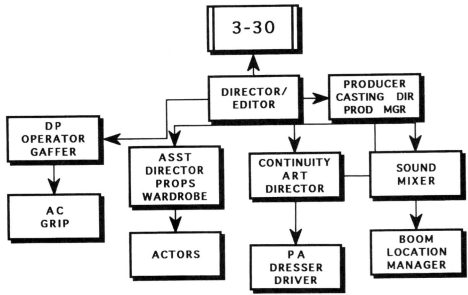

Talk to producers, directors, or anyone who has worked with these individuals in the past. Find out as much as you can before you decide to hire. If this is not possible, you must go with your intuition and instinct. There is no need to feel pressured to hire a supposedly "great" director of photography (DP) if you are uncomfortable with his attitude or arrogance. Beginners are bound to make mistakes in this area, but the more experience you acquire, the more astute a judge of character you will become.

If your choices prove to be wise ones, this project could signal the beginning of professional and creative relationships that last a long time. As a producer or director, you have to rely on dependable and talented crew members to execute your ideas. Finding people you can trust, you enjoy working with, and who are good at what they do is a promising start of a solid creative network from which you can draw in the future. Remember that this business is built on relationships.

> The worst and best choices you will make are your people choices—in other words, the crew and the actors. Everybody you choose to work on the project is going to influence the outcome, so you really have to be very careful about whom you're choosing: Are these people going to get along? Are they going to help me? Am I choosing this guy simply because I heard he was the best director of photography around? But if he has an ego problem, you're really going to regret that decision later....
>
> You want people who like you, who like the project, and who want to be there, for obvious reasons, not somebody who's just doing you a favor. Students often throw people together just to get somebody there, and they get a person who doesn't want to be there or with whom they have a problem. The project gets made, but it becomes a very unpleasant experience, and people end up enemies. I've seen it many times.
>
> Howard McCain

Attracting the Right People

How you present your project to others will have an impact on the quality of the people who are interested in working with you. If you appear to be an organized and professional person, you will attract more of the same. Create a professional-looking flier to post at film programs, media organizations, and high schools or on web sites (e.g., *Mandy.com, ShootingPeople.org* and *craigslist.org*). Place advertisements in media journals, magazines, and newspapers. Nothing can replace the tried-and-true method of word of mouth, a very powerful agent. Make sure you don't minimize the requirements of the job to convince a crew member to work on the project. You will just be setting yourself up for problems down the line.

STUDENTS

You have the benefit of being able to draw personnel from your class and your program. Because a great deal of work is being done at film and media programs around the country, you'll find many young and old professionals alike eager to work on student projects. Professionals who agree to work on student projects know that there isn't much in it for them financially. They are attracted by the opportunity to work and, most important, by the material itself. A good script attracts good people, no matter what its source. Most people would rather invest their time and energy on a project with some inherent value, something they can be proud to put on their reel as a sample of their work.

INDEPENDENTS

You can advertise in all the places students do. There are many eager students, hungry for experience, who are willing to put in long hours on a semiprofessional shoot. The good ones can be of great help in understanding the low-budget world because that's where they work and live.

Evaluating Credits

How do you know who did what? Hiring people that you either don't know, haven't worked with before, or both can be risky. Scrutinizing their reels and talking to producers, directors, and other crew members about them will definitely help. However, these solutions are not foolproof. Making a film is a collaborative endeavor. So many people can have an influence on the final product that it is often difficult to discover who really did what. Consider these examples:

- The director of photography's reel might look great, yet he may have worked with a director with a good eye or he might have had an excellent gaffer who was responsible for much of the lighting.
- A film might be well edited, but the editor may have been slow, and you might not have the budget to accommodate her lack of speed.

You are on the right track if you find consistency from show to show. The fact that most of someone's work is mediocre except for one piece will tell you that someone else might have been responsible for that one piece's success. You hope to get honest answers from the people who worked on these films but this is not always the case. Who really did what might change depending on the person to whom you speak.

If you do your research well, you will reduce the risk of making a serious mistake. If things don't end up well, you always have the option to fire that individual and find another.

Negotiating the Deal

The producer negotiates a fee with each crew member. This is generally a flat daily or weekly rate, with some proviso for extra-long days. It is a good business practice to draw up a simple deal memo for each crew member. A **deal memo** is a letter of agreement between two parties that defines what services are to be rendered and the compensation for those services. The deal memo also either details the crew member's screen credit or contains a clause giving the producer the right to assign credit at his discretion.

If you negotiate a flat fee with the crew, the crew members will give you the hours you need as long as you do not abuse their time and energy. If crew members are on a daily or even an hourly rate, you need to pay special attention to their schedule. For example, if you need an extra hairdresser for a short period, make an effort to allow that crew member to perform her task and then leave the set, rather than linger and accrue additional compensation.

Key Crew Members

The first step in assembling a crew is to choose the key people who will form the creative and technical nucleus of the production. Once you have chosen the key personnel, you can assemble the support crew based on their recommendations. These pivotal crew members work with their own smaller teams on a regular basis.

The following are the key people on a production crew:

- Production manager
- Director of photography (DP)
- Art director
- Assistant director (AD)
- Production sound mixer

> A big thing that ended up happening is because I shot after we'd all graduated; every one of my key crew members had professional experience. They had been on real sets, independent and studio sets, and knew the routine. We weren't winging that. We were a well-oiled machine when all cylinders were firing.
>
> James Darling

Production Manager

When the producer has a lot of money at his disposal, he hires an individual who is known in the industry as a **production manager**. This individual breaks down the script and creates a schedule and a budget. Once the budget is agreed to, the production manager (with the producer's approval) begins to organize the production. After the approval by the producer and the director, the production manager hires the department heads, who, in turn, suggest personnel to make up the support teams for their departments. Unfortunately, a production manager is a luxury that most beginners can't afford. The producer usually assumes this important position on low-budget productions.

The production manager plays a pivotal role in the production process. The production manager performs these tasks:

- Coordinates, facilitates, and oversees all preproduction
- Prepares the script breakdown and preliminary shooting schedule
- Establishes and controls the budget
- Makes deals with the crew
- Makes deals for equipment
- Oversees daily cash flow
- Supervises the selection of locations
- Oversees day-to-day production decisions
- Facilitates schedule changes
- Manages all off-set logistics
- Arranges for housing and meals
- Sets up necessary insurance
- Ensures that permits are obtained
- Secures releases
- Keeps on top of all production activity to keep ahead of the director in production planning
- Completes a daily production report reflecting the status of the picture's cost

The production manager is the engine that drives the project. The importance of this position cannot be emphasized enough. It is also the least glamorous key position. It must be occupied by a well-organized person who wields power efficiently. The production manager answers to the producer.

> The first person I chose after the director of photography was the production manager. Production managers take on such an enormous role, particularly on student films. I was fortunate that I had someone who was not only my friend and a good filmmaker but who really liked the idea. Not only did he fulfill the production manager role by lining up caterers and the like, but he was involved in the story process as well. He was one of the people who sat down with me, went over the story, and got excited by it. When people get excited, they put more of themselves into it at all levels.
>
> Howard McCain

Support Crew

The production manager's support crew consists of the following personnel.

Production Coordinator. The production coordinator is the liaison between the producer or production manager and the cast and crew. She is a key player at the hub of the production office. Some of her responsibilities are the following:

- Facilitates communication
- Disseminates information to cast and crew
- Coordinates transportation in the absence of a transportation coordinator
- Completes paperwork, cast and crew lists, call sheets, and so on

The production coordinator should be a highly organized, efficient, and even-tempered individual who is accustomed to remaining calm in the middle of a storm. She is the producer's or production manager's right hand.

Location Manager. This crew member is the primary scout for the production company. He secures locations and serves as liaison between the production company and the location. He is the face of the production to the community and responsible for addressing the issues that may arise due to the production's impact on the community, which may involve negotiating arrangements with neighbors and nearby businesses.

The location manager sets up each location so that the production unit can shoot properly, and then he arranges for the cleanup. His other duties include arranging for parking and catering and obtaining permits, location contracts, and certificates of insurance.

STUDENT FOOD

Most students are unable to afford a caterer, so the job of creating a meal plan for the shoot falls on the shoulders of the student producer. Engineering a daily meal schedule on a budget with ample craft service requires ingenuity, common sense, and forward planning. Don't expect to put meals together on a daily basis. And stay away from pizza unless served with a salad. The saying goes, "Serve too much pizza and you get a pizza movie."

Caterer. All crew members and actors like to eat. Shooting a film burns up calories that must be replenished. Having someone manage the food affairs of the shoot can make for a smooth ride. The craft services people set up a table with food near the set for snacks throughout the day, and they arrange for midday meals in a comfortable setting.

My craft service department was my mother and my brother. Having a mother in charge of feeding the crew was great. She was always looking after people and making sure that everyone was well fed.

I've been around a lot of really bad on-set mothers, but my mom has an artistic background and understands what I was going through. This was helpful when I had to re-write the whole movie mid-way through the shoot and could vent to her. My family doesn't have a lot of money but they have a lot of love. It was a resource I knew I could take advantage of.

James Darling

Transportation Captain. If a project requires many vehicles, a key driver called the *transportation captain* is responsible for transporting the production from location to location. Being able to wrap out of a location and move to the next shot with efficiency saves time and money. It takes an ever-watchful eye to keep tanks filled with gasoline and maintain the vehicles. The captain hires a team of drivers to shuttle actors and equipment to and from the set, and she makes deals for picture vehicles. This position is often filled by a grip or a production assistant.

I sent the script out to a DP who I had met through another friend. His name is Barry Markowitz. Barry is a dynamite DP who had shot several notable films for a couple of directors of Hollywood caliber. So, when I sent it to Barry I had no idea that he would actually read it, let alone sign up to do it. Sure enough he called me back two days later and said I want to shoot this. If you can raise the money, I'm in. That was yet another sign that I had a good cast, a good script, and now a great DP. Everything else just started falling into place in terms of finding the crew and finding all the other elements that you needed.

Be' Garrett

Director of Photography

The producer's and director's concern is to hire the best director of photography they can afford. This is an important decision. The DP's job is to fulfill the director's visual design for the project and to participate in building the camera team. This means that before bringing on any of the camera crew, you must decide on a DP. On most small projects with a limited budget, the DP also operates the camera. So you are, in fact, looking for a DP and a camera operator in one.

The director of photography must be resourceful and able to make use of simple lighting situations or none, depending on the situation. He must be flexible and able to light and shoot on the run. If yours is a project like *Mirror Mirror*, the technical demands might be less rigorous. With only one setup in a studio situation, there was ample time to set up lights.

STUDENTS

On student productions, the DP might serve not only as the camera operator, but also as the gaffer and the grip! Try to avoid this situation.

Evaluating Potential Directors of Photography

When deciding among potential DPs, consider the following criteria.

Previous Work. Look at the professional reel. However, you are not always looking for the quality of the work, but for the different kinds of lighting situations with which the director of photography has worked. A DP may be able to function with the flexibility of a set, but not be experienced or comfortable with limited lights in practical locations. (If the DP has professional experiences, make sure to check IMDb.com for credits).

Is there something identifiable about the DP's style that is compatible with your story? If his work is excellent but his lighting style(s) is very different from what you envisioned for your project, you may want to talk with him anyway. He may have been typecast to do a certain kind of work and may be eager to branch out and try something different.

> The first person who was on board from the beginning was my Director of Photography. He was the same Director of Photography from my intermediate film. I have just a great working relationship with him.
>
> James Darling

The Formats, Cameras, and Stocks He Has Worked With. It might be an obvious point, but if you are looking for a DP to shoot video, he should be fluent with the specific format of video you wish to shoot. These days, there are many to choose from. (You might lock into a specific video format because of a lucrative deal you have negotiated.) The DP must also know how to shoot and light for video. The lighting requirements for video differ from those for film.

If you're looking for a DP for film, ask about the experience candidates have had with different equipment and, more important, their experience with different film stocks in your chosen format. If a DP is shooting in 35mm or 16mm for the first time, it is appropriate to ask for tests with the equipment and stocks until you are confident that the DP is comfortable with the new format.

Speed. How long does it take the DP to set up the camera and lights? His sample material might look terrific, but if a candidate takes a long time to set up for each shot and you are working on a tight schedule, he might not be the best person for you. You want someone who can create stunning images, but you want it fast unless, of course, you have a luxuriously long schedule.

You can research a DP's speed by talking with the producers or directors who have worked with him in the past. Often, a DP will spend the morning lighting and breeze through the afternoon. If you want to sacrifice speed for a particular look, you can offset the longer setups by planning a smaller shooting ratio of 2:1 or 4:1. Use the extra setup time to accommodate the actors' needs to either run their lines, rehearse, or just rest.

> One of the great things about the cinematographer was that he was able to work very quickly and improvise as well. He could work under tough situations, with no light. That was important for me, having someone I could trust doing the camera. There were a few times when I didn't even look through the camera other than to maybe say, when we were first setting up the shot, "This is perfect," or "Maybe a little tighter."
>
> Adam Davidson

Whether He Has His Own Equipment. Many DPs come with their own cameras and sometimes their own lights as well. The fee they quote includes their services and their equipment package. This can be an asset because not only does it simplify things, but if anything happens to the equipment, the DP is responsible. He might even have his own insurance policy. Don't assume that because a DP has his own equipment he is automatically good; the equipment is just a bonus.

Compatibility with Director and Art Director. The director, the DP, and the art director must get along and share a mutual vision of the piece. These three should have a tight creative bond. It is the producer's job to support the director within the boundaries of the budget by providing her with a DP who satisfies her creative needs.

Schedule. Is the DP available and can he work on your scheduled dates? Is he booked so tightly that if your schedule fluctuates, he will not be able to accommodate you? Finally, can the DP work within your (probably tight) schedule?

> The crew. There was my DP, whom I met at NYU sophomore year. He is an incredibly gifted cinematographer and director in his own right. He was my second brain. He didn't have to be there every day at all. He was with me during the second round of storyboards. He would set up every shot, angles, and lights, and then I would be there for a couple of days by myself animating it. So he was there every other day—every three days.
>
> Tatia Rosenthal

Troubleshooting

The following warning signs could have an impact on your production planning and budget:

- An inexperienced DP asks for too much high-end equipment. Watch for these items in particular:

HMI lights, expensive dolly, large equipment package, Steadicam, Luma crane, or camera car. This might occur because the DP wants the opportunity to work with the fancy equipment or because he is not able to evaluate properly the technical needs of the show. Insecurity might lead the DP to order as much equipment as possible and then decide what he needs during the shoot. After doing a detailed location scout and discussing the director's visual ideas for the project, an experienced and resourceful DP should be able to give an accurate breakdown of the project's equipment needs for the entire show and know how to maximize the equipment package that you can afford. You might have room in the budget for some or all of these items, but you might not actually need them to fulfill the director's visual plan for the script. The money you save could be better spent on props, costumes, or an interesting location.

- You have hired a seasoned DP on a student or inexperienced crew, and the DP is trying to take over the creative aspects of the shoot. This can happen when an insecure crew doesn't stand up to someone who appears to know what he is doing. The DP might have strong ideas about how scenes should be photographed or staged that might not be in sync with the director's vision. If the DP's work is terrific, you don't want to antagonize him, but if he gets his way, the result won't be the piece that the director envisioned. This is a tough situation for beginners. As soon as this problem appears, it is best that the producer confront the DP. Remember that it is your film or video you are making, not his. However, if the director is insecure and doesn't provide leadership on the set, this will create a power vacuum, and it is usually the DP who will fill it.

If you are working with an inexperienced or student DP, an experienced gaffer or camera operator can be very helpful.

> The next important search was to find a DP; I wanted someone to go over the storyboards; I wanted someone to be involved. I found an older student, and every week we'd have a story meeting where we'd talk about the story as well as the storyboards. In those sessions, other problems became apparent. We realized we'd need a 5.9, a very wide lens. We'd need to rent a variable-speed motor. But if you need a variable-speed motor, where are you going to rent it? The production manager was there and I'd say, "Ian, can you call a few equipment houses in Rochester and find out what their rates are for the day?" which then impinges on your budget. So when you start talking to each other, you realize how interconnected the process is.
>
> Howard McCain

Support Crew

Now that the DP is aboard, you can hire the support crew—camera, grip, and electric. The size of your particular crew will depend on the budget (what you can afford in the way of salary, transportation, lodging, and food), the demands of the script, the size and difficulty of lighting and filming the locations, and the director's visual plans for the material.

Does the director want a fairly static camera, long dolly moves, or both? Does she want high-key or low-key lighting? She might even be thinking of using a Steadicam for several scenes. After the director and DP finalize their overall visual plan, you will have a better idea of the crew needed to match the creative requirements of the production.

The DP will want to have around people he has worked with before. In most cases, a DP's speed and effectiveness result from his support team. The support crew for this department consists of 10 positions with specific responsibilities for operating the camera, lighting for the camera, and moving the camera.

Operating the Camera

Camera Operator. Often, the director of photography is also the camera operator. If he decides to concentrate on the lighting, he has the option (budget permitting) to hire an operator whose job will be primarily to operate the camera. This is the optimal situation because it frees the DP to spend more time with the director.

Assistant Camera (AC). The AC's duties include changing lenses, following focus, and assisting in setting up the camera. He is the protector of camera equipment and very knowledgeable about all cameras—a very important position on student shoots!

2nd Assistant Camera. The 2nd AC, also called the *loader*, threads the film into the magazine. The 2nd AC slates each take and is therefore in communication with the script supervisor as to the numbering of the shots. The 2nd Ac fills out the camera reports for the lab and for the editor.

Stills. A stills person takes photographs of key sequences on the set for publicity. He usually takes still photographs during rehearsals. A professional stills photographer can shoot the actual take, but only with a silent camera housing.

Lighting for the Camera

Gaffer. The gaffer serves as the DP's left hand. He is responsible for setting the lights and securing the power to illuminate them.

Grip. The grip will shape the lights.

Best Boy/Electrician. The best boy is the gaffer's assistant. He runs cables to the set from a generator.

2nd Electrician. He rounds out the electrical team if the DP needs more than two assistants.

Moving the Camera

Key Grip. The key grip serves as the DP's right hand and supervises the physical movement of the camera. He coordinates the rigging of light stands, dolly, silks, and so on. He is the safety coordinator for the set and is capable of creating all kinds of rigging for the camera.

Dolly Grip. The dolly grip is the key grip's assistant and the person responsible for pushing the dolly.

Swings. These are crew members who can do both grip and electric work.

The director of photography may be able to recommend a sound mixer with whom he has worked on other shoots. All hired crew can recommend other technicians for you to interview.

Art Director (Production Designer)

The art director is a very important position and one that beginners often slight. It is also complicated by the fact that there are two positions, **the art director** and the **production designer**. The production designer works closely with the director and the DP to design the total look and feel of the film, and the art director executes it. The production designer is primarily concerned with creative decisions, whereas the art director typically deals with budgeting materials and labor, scheduling construction crews, and dealing with the prep and restoration of all the sets and locations.

In a well-budgeted production, there will be not only a production designer and art director, but an entire art department team (see Chapter 8 for more details). In low-budget and student productions, the position may be collapsed into one. The production designer will also serve as the art director. She will supply the artistic vision and supervise the execution. James Darling, the director of *Citizen*, had a production designer and an art director, but they both were involved with all aspects. For the purposes of this book, we will call this individual the art director and refer to the specific functions.

You will most likely find promising candidates among those trained in designing for the stage. However, there are fundamental differences between designing for the stage and designing for film or video. The stage requires designing for an entire proscenium, whereas film or video requires designing only for what the camera will see. The camera might only see a wide shot of an entire room for several seconds and concentrate on a corner of the room for most of a scene.

Evaluating Potential Art Directors

Use the following criteria to select an art director.

Experience in Films and Videos. Your first choice should be an art director who has experience with cameras, not just theater, and who understands what the camera sees and how to control the visual environment. If your candidate is eager to get into motion pictures but has little experience, she should be prepared to spend time analyzing films as well as different architectural styles, well-known photographers, and traditional artists like John Singer Sergeant, Winslow Homer, Rembrandt, Norman Rockwell, Magritte, etc.

Ability to Work Within a Low Budget. The art director must be inspired to use imagination instead of money. This might mean scrounging around thrift shops for bargains or creatively rearranging an existing environment. On the other hand, directors and producers must realize that an art director is not a miracle worker. Often the difference between a good and a bad film is determined by the art direction, but the art director can do only so much with limited funds

Compatibility with the Director and the DP. The art director must share the director's creative vision of the story and be able to work effectively with the DP. A creative bond should develop among these three individuals. This bond is essential to ensure the director's vision is executed properly.

Support Crew

The art director is responsible for putting together her support team, which might consist of the following positions:

- Art department coordinator
- Construction coordinator
- Scenic artist
- Set decorator
- Set dresser
- Property master

Depending on your budget for the project, the art director might be asked to handle many of these responsibilities, including set dressing, props, and even wardrobe.

> I knew art direction in the fantasy sequences would play a big, big role. I started calling older students, which is always a great idea when you've got production problems, and I found out who had made films with heavy costume designs or heavy makeup effects. I got names, and I started calling. That's how I met Jan Fennel, a costume designer in New York who does off-Broadway, commercials, and small production stuff. For costumes and salary, I had a total budget of $1,200.
>
> Howard McCain

Art Department Coordinator. This person keeps track of the art budget, assists the art director, and runs the art department while the rest of the art team are shopping, overseeing the construction of the set, or being on set.

Construction Coordinator. The construction coordinator plans, budgets, and oversees the work of building the set. He must estimate labor and material costs and determine how many carpenters and construction grips will be needed to build the set and how many scenic artists will be required to paint and wallpaper it.

Scenic Artist. The scenic artist is responsible for plastering, painting, and aging the set as well as the furniture and key props. This key member of the art team plays a substantial role in creating the illusion of reality. Scenic artists can make a cheap plywood floor look like marble or manufacture rusty-looking pipes in a basement.

Set Decorator. The set decorator is in charge of the entire set dressing department: furnishing the sets, whether existing locations or built sets; shopping for all the artifacts; and also restoring the locations back to their original condition. The set decorator may need to supply everything from furniture to chandeliers, carpet and tile, artwork and draperies. The set decorator's right-hand person is the **leadman**, who runs his team of set dressers.

The set decoration department is also responsible for providing **greenery** by either adding plants or trees to a set or location or making a summer scene look like it is autumn by adding fall trees. This undertaking can be large and expensive depending on the scope of the shots, and if necessary, the set decorator will hire a **greens department** to handle this responsibility.

Set Dresser. The set dressers are responsible for wrapping, moving, and storing existing furniture in a location set. They are also responsible for protecting the set, laying down cardboard, and protecting wood floors from the rest of the crew. They may be required to apply tile, carpet, or linoleum to a set in addition to replacing chandeliers or other light fixtures.

During the shoot, the set dresser is on standby in case any of the set pieces must be adjusted or painted. The set dresser also works ahead of the company, if possible, to dress the set for the next day's photography.

Property Master. This crew member gathers all necessary hand and set props for the project and doles them out as needed. For example, if the actors are eating a meal on camera, it is the prop master's responsibility to keep the glasses filled and steam on the food from take to take and from angle to angle.

Depending on the size of the crew and the budget, the property master often represents the art department on set once shooting begins. Although the property master deals specifically with objects that the actor handles, he is also required to pay close attention to continuity from take to take and should have a good relationship with the director and the actors.

Related Crew

The following positions are not considered part of the art department but should coordinate their efforts with the art director and the DP. For example, it must be decided whether wardrobe, makeup, and hair colors are to blend in or contrast with the overall color palette of the film.

Costume Designer. Everything the actors wear in the show is designed or chosen by the costume designer. Her goal is to enhance a character's persona, through the visual design of garments and other means of dressing within the framework of the director's vision. The designer must work in consultation with not only the director, but also with the art director and DP to ensure that the overall design of the production works together. She might also collaborate with hair and makeup.

The designer needs to possess strong artistic capabilities as well as a thorough knowledge of pattern development, draping, drafting, textiles, and costume/fashion history. She also must have awareness of poise when in period dress and be sensitive to the creative direction that the performers want to take their characters. Even if the actors supply their own wardrobe, the choices must reflect the overall design of the film.

Costumer or Wardrobe Supervisor. On set, a costumer assists the actors in and out of their wardrobe. One costumer is employed for the men and another for the women. If there are many actors and extras, additional costumers might be hired for big sequences.

Makeup Artist. The makeup artist designs and applies the actors' makeup and facial hairpieces. The makeup artist's responsibilities include the maintenance of continuity and script days.

Hairstylist. This crew member designs and styles the actors' hair and manages any wigs used in the production. The hairstylist also maintains the continuity of hairstyle. On a windy day, he stands by and recombs hair that has become mussed.

Storyboard Artist. The storyboard artist translates the director's vision of each sequence of the script into drawings or panels that represent what each shot will contain. Quick pencil drawings and marker renderings are two of the most common traditional techniques, although nowadays Flash, Photoshop, and other storyboard applications are gradually taking over. The digital camera is one of the latest techniques in creating storyboards.

Storyboard artists report directly to the director, not the art director. Storyboards are most effective for sequencing action shots or incorporating extreme camera angles or special effects.

Assistant Director

The assistant director (AD) works closely with the producer or production manager to create a shooting schedule. He also has the responsibility on set of making sure that the production sticks to that schedule and must be prepared to make recommendations about adjustments should the need arise. Most importantly, he must be in total sync with the director.

The assistant director communicates with all the actors and crew members; he is the company sergeant, the ship's pilot, the traffic cop. He has the onerous task of making sure that everyone is in the right place at the right time. He must constantly remind the cast and crew members of the schedule and must perform this task with grace and tact. The assistant director watches the clock while the director of photography sets up and fine-tunes the lights, the production sound mixer places microphones, the set decorator or set dressers "dress" the set, and the director rehearses the actors.

> I don't know, it was a miracle. We were never more than 25 minutes off our schedule. The AD did a great job. He was always looking at his watch, without making me nervous. He always knew where we should be and where we could make up time, which is the job of a good AD. Everything stayed fairly constant, it was like a vacuum-sealed environment—the same crew, the same people, the same location every day.
>
> Howard McCain

Support Crew

The assistant director's support crew (if hired; if not, the 1st AD will assume the following responsibilities) consists of the following personnel.

2nd Assistant Director. The 2nd assistant director's duties include preparing the call sheets, arranging call times, and coordinating all cast and crew arrivals to the set. The assistant director is also responsible for directing the background action. The 2nd AD is the off-set person responsible for having the actors prepared for their calls.

2nd 2nd Assistant Director. The 2nd 2nd AD telephones the actors in coordination with the production coordinator to set up the next day's shoot. If traffic or crowd control is needed, all the AD's are involved in securing the set.

Continuity (Script Supervisor). The script supervisor works closely with the director to determine what coverage has been shot and what shots remain. He marks the script with a description of each shot of each scene. He takes detailed notes after each take regarding action, dialogue, gestures, lens used, costumes, makeup, and so on to ensure continuity of all these elements from shot to shot and scene to scene. This script is then sent to the editing room so the editor has a written reference to the shoot. The script supervisor's other responsibilities include matching each actor's actions from take to take and from angle to angle. Neglecting this attention to detail can create major continuity problems in the editing room (see more about Script Supervision in Chapter 14).

The Digital Assistant

The **digital assistant** (DA) is a relatively new job on film sets that has grown in prominence with the emergence of tapeless digital formats and powerful laptops capable of running high-end editing software. The DA is primarily responsible for downloading, managing, and backing up the raw digital media as it is being shot. When working with tapeless formats like **P2** or **RED**, the DA is essentially handling the equivalent of your master tapes or film negative, so you need to hire someone who will take great care with this job! However, digital assistants can also be a valuable addition to any crew, regardless of shooting format. When working with film or tape, a DA can still capture a digital dub of all the footage from the director's monitor and sound mixer, allowing rapid nonlinear video playback and on-set editing.

When used effectively, the digital assistant can be an invaluable aid to the director, DP, script supervisor, and art departments, helping to ensure continuity and coverage of scenes. Indeed, the ability to literally assemble your footage into sequences as it is being shot opens up a whole new window of creative exploration on the film set, but it can be double-edged sword. Having all the footage at your fingertips can easily become a distraction for cast and crew, and it is important to establish a clear set etiquette around the digital assistant. For example, some actors may insist on reviewing their footage, which can sometimes be a hindrance to performance. On a low-budget or student production, every extra crew member is an extra cost, and the digital assistant can seem like an unaffordable luxury.

If you are shooting on a tapeless format, however, you should really consider whether you want your only copy of the footage handled by someone who likely has a half dozen other jobs on set. Additionally, digital assistants can bring their own unique skills and experience to set, especially if they have experience with editing and continuity. If called upon, the digital assistant may be willing to share shot ideas to help ensure the editor has everything he needs in postproduction, thus avoiding costly reshoots and pickups. Working as a digital assistant involves learning a great deal about production and postproduction, procuring a laptop that can run editing software, and putting together a rig that can handle a variety of shooting formats.

Production Sound Mixer

What separates many student productions with professional ones is in the area of production sound. Although production sound has improved considerably over the years, it is still an uphill struggle for many student filmmakers to consistently capture good "clean" dialogue on the set.

Beginners and students are usually more focused on getting the best DP they can than the best production sound mixer. Recording sound is not as glamorous as recording images. This priority for camera is usually continued on the set as well. Time will be spent making sure the lighting is right, but many crews are hard-pressed to repeat a take because of a sound problem. This attitude can result in acting that is beautifully seen but not properly heard.

This situation happens, in part, because it is technically possible to rerecord all the dialogue and add in other sounds in postproduction without going back to the original locations. It is far more expensive to have to reshoot a scene as a result of camera or lighting problems because the entire cast and crew have to be reassembled at the original locations. The issues student productions face are

- Securing a good sound team (mixer and boom)
- Securing a good sound team for the duration of the shoot
- Successfully dealing with sound problems on a location

It is common for students to find sound crews for only part of their production schedule. This means that at least two if not more crews will end up recording sound for your project, making consistency almost impossible.

Make all efforts to record clean dialogue, or **production sound**, on the set. Capture the "magic" that can happen between actors during a scene. Dialogue can be rerecorded during the postproduction period (using ADR), but this kind of sound work can be time consuming and expensive (see Chapter 17). In addition, some actors, especially nonprofessionals, are not adept at re-creating in a dark recording studio months after principal photography the dramatic chemistry they worked hard to convey on the set.

> There was one guy doing sound. He was operating the Nagra and the boom, and then eventually he enlisted one of the homeless guys to help us, which turned into a disaster.
>
> Adam Davidson

Evaluating Potential Production Sound Mixers

One of the inherent problems of evaluating a production sound mixer is not knowing if the dialogue in the final print was recorded on the set or in a recording studio. If it was recorded in a studio, was the reason that unavoidable problems with the location made it impossible to record clean production dialogue or because the production sound mixer did a poor job? These questions can be answered only by the producer, director, or editor of the project.

When selecting a production sound mixer, consider the following criteria.

Knowledge of Equipment. The production sound mixer should know the timecode DAT recorder, DVD Ram system, analogue Nagra, or whatever recording device you will be using. This point might seem obvious, but it is helpful for you to explore the candidate's technical sophistication. Most important, is the candidate experienced with a wide assortment of microphones, such as radio microphones and lavalieres?

Own Equipment? The production sound mixer who comes with his own recording equipment and microphones is very common in the industry. She is comfortable with her own rig and can rely on it. For the producer, it means that she can quote you a price that includes her services and her equipment. This figure is usually less than if you hired the production sound mixer and had to rent the equipment separately. However, do not hire a mixer just because she has her own rig. Always go for the best you can find. The rig should be a bonus.

Experience. Does the candidate have a wide range of experience working in challenging practical locations? It is less demanding to record *clean dialogue* (free of unnecessary sounds or noises) in a soundproof environment like a sound stage. You need to question how the sound mixer has performed on locations that were not "sound friendly"—that is, those with distracting or loud ambient noises that interfered with the dialogue.

Temperament. The ideal production sound mixer is easygoing but assertive on the set. She is adept at asserting herself if she feels that things are not right for sound. She might have to fight to be heard because the needs of the production sound mixer are many times subjugated to those of the camera. The production sound mixer must be sensitive to actors' needs and be able to discreetly but accurately tape a radio mike or lavaliere to an actor or to request volume adjustments. The production sound mixer can be a sea of calm in the midst of chaos.

> My sound recordist is also my sound designer and mixer. He was in the midst of opening his own sound studio while we were in production. This was a great project for him, because he got to sort of test everything out. It is definitely a rare thing to have your sound recorder also be your sound designer.
>
> James Darling

Support Crew

The **boom operator** and if necessary the **utility sound technician** comprise the support crew for the sound department (see more details in Chapter 12). The boom operator is an important position and should not be filled by just anybody. The best production sound mixer in the world can't record proper sound if the microphone is not pointed in the right direction. The production sound mixer you hire will most likely insist on a boom operator with whom he likes to work. The boom operator's duties include collaborating on the placement of the microphones and positioning the boom pole during takes to best record the dialogue or ambient sounds.

Hiring an Animator

Animation takes time—lots of time. Animation can add beautiful and compelling visuals to your piece, but it will require a different, more deliberate, way of working than live action. The creation of a character model can take a great deal of time depending on the complexity, the amount of movement, and screen time. In a CG feature, the lead characters usually take from three to four months to model, texture, and rig.

About 15 years ago, the software and hardware necessary to produce computer-generated images (CGI) was prohibitively expensive. It was therefore rare to find independent artists working as CGI animators. The cost of powerful computers and their components has dropped dramatically. The software has become more feature rich, inexpensive, and user friendly, leading to the rise of many small one- and two-person shops. With that said, there is still a steep learning curve and price tag for a CGI studio. The most common professional animation software is Autodesk Maya. Many other excellent packages are available. 3D Studio Max, Soft Image XSI, Lightwave, and Cinema 4D all have their followings as well.

Digital compositing and editing packages have also become more ubiquitous and inexpensive. The most popular are Apple's Shake, Adobe After Effects, the AVID line of composing products, Apple Final Cut Pro, and Combustion (and the higher-end versions Flame and Inferno). The list goes on. You will find that each software package tends to have its own niche market and loyal following. For example, 3D Studio Max (or just Max as it is known in the trade) is favored by game artists because of its extensive modeling capabilities, plug-ins, and software development kit. Many broadcast designers will use Cinema 4D with After Effects because they are straightforward on the Mac platform. Maya and Shake are favored by the makers of feature films because of the extensive features and node-based compositing. The popularity and capabilities change with each software upgrade. So the preceding combinations of tools will vary a bit from year to year.

When you are hiring a CG artist, it is a good idea to see the studio if you can. A professional should have more than one computer, a high-speed network, a high-speed Internet connection, backup drives, a means of video out (a DVD burner can suffice), as well as legal copies of the software. You won't be able to tell too much about what is under the hood of the computers, but if the primary workstation is over four years old, the artist may have trouble running the latest applications. Of course, the right hardware and software are not a substitute for talent, but they might indicate whether or not the person can get the job done without amateurish equipment problems. If the job is more than just a few frames, it is not unreasonable to ask for an equipment list.

Production Assistant

Production assistants (PAs) can be placed in any and all departments, depending on the needs of the company; the neediest department gets help first. If the company requires another driver, another camera assistant, a grip, or a dresser, the producer can place a PA in that position.

> Students never plan for enough crew, and more importantly, they don't plan for enough PAs. You should have one or two PAs just to run around, pick up stuff, drop stuff off, and help the production manager. It's always the last person assembled in a student crew, and it's always a big mistake because then the energy starts draining away from the set; people are leaving to go buy extra quarter-inch tape, batteries, or whatever is missing at the moment. All of a sudden the crew is being cannibalized to become runners and PAs, and the set starts to fall apart. You lose a lot of time. Getting PAs for student films is always a difficult task. I was fortunate: My father was my PA. He took a week off work and ran around for me. Because he had no ego problems about doing that, it worked out really well.
>
> Howard McCain

Interns

Salaries on short films often hover around nonexistent. The distinction between a PA and an intern is that the PA is assigned to perform a specific task or to assist a particular department. Interns often float between departments (so they can learn the ropes) and lend a hand where one is needed.

> There were about 12 people that we found on Animation World Network who volunteered. They each gave us a day or two a week and that was the crew. They were there mainly for preproduction of the set. Most of them built the set with the art director, so anything from cutting wood to detailing, dusting, painting, building trees, building little models.
>
> Tatia Rosenthal

Specialty Crew

There are many other crew members who cover specialty areas. They include special effects, choreography, standby painters, Steadicam operators, greens people, animal wranglers, tutors, and stunt coordinators.

Video Shoots

All the positions just discussed apply to video. In single-camera video shoots, there are some differences in the way jobs are performed. The most significant difference is that narrative video shoots require slightly different lighting plans.

Digital video is a constantly evolving technology. Larger video formats such as HDTV require special camera crews to service the camera on set to maintain consistent color and contrast. On a professional crew, for example, a producer is advised to hire a digital imaging technician (DIT). A designation of Local 600, IATSE, the cinematographer's guild, this crew member oversees and maintains advanced coloring (controller duties), setup, operation, troubleshooting, and maintenance of digital cameras (oversight of camera utilities), waveform monitors, down converters (high-def to other formats), monitors, cables, digital recording devices, terminal equipment, driver software, and other related equipment. He has a complete understanding of digital audio acquisition and timecode processes and how they are integrated into digital acquisition format and postproduction environments. He is also responsible for in-camera recording. His is a supervisor responsibility for the technical acceptability of the image.

Documentarians work with a light crew so they can move freely in the field. Video cameras have microphones mounted on the camera; so technically, a video shoot can consist of one person.

> In terms of roles, I wore many hats in *Mirror Mirror*. I was the production manager, I handled the budget, I decided on stocks and ordered fill, and I spent a lot of time trying to track down appropriate and affordable mannequins to use in the set.
>
> Jan Krawitz

Documentary Crews

What factors play an important role in hiring the crew for a documentary shoot? Documentary crews are usually composed of the director/producer, DP, and production sound mixer who will also serve as boom operator. These crews need to be small and mobile. This has to do with budgetary concerns as well as aesthetic ones. Documentaries might be shot over long periods of time, and their budgets can't support a high overhead. Crews must keep a low profile and not get in the way of the people they are photographing. They should be able to move quickly and follow the action if necessary.

The requirements for the DP may differ for documentaries than for staged drama. Whereas lighting is the main responsibility for the fiction DP, operating is paramount in documentaries. In an interview, the DP must be able to listen and be responsive to the intensity of the moment.

"Cinema Verite" filming demands that the DP be able to see through the camera lens and keep the other eye open and ready to respond to the action around him.

It is not unusual for the documentary filmmaker to serve as the producer, director, writer, and DP or production sound mixer. For example, Jan Krawitz has recorded the sound on all her projects (see the following quote). The documentary filmmaker conceives, develops, finances, and creates the project. Producing a documentary can demand an intensive devotion over many months or possibly years of work.

> This was now my sixth film in which I worked with a two-person crew—myself on sound and a cinematographer. What's important to me as both the director and the sound person is to get the best sound possible by wearing the headphones at all times so that I can monitor what is coming off the tape. In the case of *Mirror Mirror*, it wasn't too hard because I set up a boom, so I didn't have to worry about handling the mike. Those women were in a static position—I knew they weren't going anywhere. For each interview, I would just set up the boom to an optimal position, check levels, and then I sat just to the left of the camera. The mike was far away from the camera, so we didn't have to worry about camera noise. I was just there with the Nagra, and I would ask my questions and be attentive to their responses while checking the modulometer periodically.
>
> Jan Krawitz

Developing the Right Chemistry

Preproduction is the time to shake out any potential crew problems before principal photography begins. If you hire key people early enough in the preproduction process, you will have time to get a sense of how well they will work with the director, producer, and other crew members. If you sense that potential problems are brewing, confront them immediately. Try not to wait until you are so close to production that replacing a key player would create a serious dilemma. If there is tension during preproduction, you can be sure it will only escalate during production.

If you discover you have a serious problem with a crew member, air it out reasonably. If the problem cannot be resolved amicably, it is time to look for a replacement. It is up to the producer to be the heavy and do the firing. Try to break off working relations as amicably as possible. Just because a crew member is not the right choice for your current project doesn't mean she won't work out another time. Don't burn your bridges with anyone if you can avoid it.

Always be prepared for the eventuality that someone you hire might not work out because of schedule conflicts, health problems, creative or personal differences, or for some other reason. You must be able to get on the phone and find a replacement immediately. This is possible only if you have a list of backups—that is, people you didn't choose for the position initially but who were good candidates. Backups are essential for the crew as well as for the cast and locations. An efficient producer will hold onto the names and phone numbers of the rejected candidates for all positions. Approaching people you have already rejected is usually not a problem as long as you were reasonable and fair the first time around. This is an established part of the business. If your backups have been working for a while, they should be used to this situation.

PRODUCTION

If you are in the heat of production and have to fire a key player, try not to fire that individual until you have found a replacement.

Web Presence

Selecting a Creative Director

While the producer is hiring crew for the film's production, the Internet project manager is selecting important personnel for the project's web site. The key individual is the creative/art director. **Creative director** is a position traditionally found in advertising and media industries and is now prominent in web and software development. The creative director oversees the design of **branding** (see Glossary) and advertising for a client and ensures that it fits in with the client's requirements and the image the client wishes to promote for its company or product. This person interprets the client's communications strategy and develops creative approaches that align with that strategy. The creative director is ultimately responsible for the quality of the final creative work.

The creative director supervises a team (see the following list), but budget restraints may require overlapping and collaborative tasks to be performed by fewer individuals (similar to the 3–30 rule). It is not uncommon to split up important tasks among a few specialists. The creative director may not only come up with the concept for the site, but also do the graphic design, production, animation, and even some coding. Additional positions may include the following:

- **Graphic Designer**. This person is responsible for the design and production of the graphical user interface (GUI; pronounced *Goo- ee*).
- **Information Architect**. This person designs and organizes the site structure and content. She also creates site maps, wire frames, and case uses.
- **Writer**. This person crafts the written content.
- **Digital Editor/Compressionist**. This person reedits and/or compresses digital video.

- **Flash Animator**. This position is available if there is a need to incorporate Flash-based content. There is a good chance that your video content will be served up in a Flash format (an embedded .swf/.flv).
- **Developer/Programmer/Coder**. This person creates any code and back-end development, including database programming.
- **Web Master**. This person is in charge of updating and maintaining the web site once it is launched.

This team will interface with many members of the film production crew as needed, to gather content or understand context. It has become increasingly common for a new specialized position, the digital assistant from the film production team, to be the main point of contact.

DIRECTOR

Hiring the Crew

The director is intimately involved in choosing the key people around whom the crew will form. She must trust these crew members to execute her vision for the script. She looks for creative partners as well as people with whom she can work and communicate. The production hours are long and hard, and the director must feel confident that those around her will come through for her when needed.

During the process of choosing the crew, the producer and director have the opportunity to develop a complementary working relationship. They need to bond as a team and to develop a strategy for dealing with all sorts of production-related issues. It is difficult to make important decisions in a vacuum. The producer represents another set of eyes and ears as the director homes in on the right people for the project.

Together, the director and producer should develop a strategy for interviewing prospective crew members. After each interview, the director and producer can discuss how they felt about the candidate. Differences of opinion can be important not only in making the right choice, but also in learning about how each other views people. The ultimate choice must rest with the director (as far as the budget will allow), but by sharing impressions in an open forum, the director and producer develop a rapport and have a productive dialogue, the goal of which is to secure the best crew for the project.

Choices about the crew are only the first of many that will include decisions about the cast, locations, sets, props, costumes, hair, makeup, and so forth. The entire preproduction process involves a long string of decisions that will have a direct impact on the resulting film or video. As more of these decisions are made, the producer and director must develop into a tight-knit team, both moving to the beat of the same creative drum.

Director's Disease

There is a phenomenon in the business known as *director's disease*. It is a rash, a cold, or a headache that is directly related to the pressure under which the director puts herself.

> I was by myself in the room and it was so beautiful and the film actually moved along, and I couldn't believe it. It was worth all the hard work. I had some tragic, tragic health hazards happening with *Crazy Glue*. I was so tense that I had a vein burst in my eye, so during a good portion of the shoot my eye was full of blood. And I inhaled a pin one day! 'Cause you use pins to move the eyeballs of the puppets. I inhaled it and had to exhale it somehow. The entire thing was very tiring and grueling. But when the dailies came back, the three weeks of torture were worth it.
>
> Tatia Rosenthal

While shooting *Beauty and the Beast*, Jean Cocteau developed horrid boils that had to be lanced each evening. Miraculously, when the picture wrapped, the boils disappeared. Good health is a key factor in maintaining the rigorous pace of a shoot.

> We started shooting on a Monday—it was the Martin Luther King holiday—and that weekend, out of nowhere, I suddenly came down with a 102° temperature. It was totally psychosomatic. I didn't even think I was going to make it to Monday. But then you just start working, and you go and you do it.
>
> Adam Davidson

The following guidelines should help a new director through those first projects.

Make It Clear Who Is in Charge. There must be a leader and a decision maker on the set. The director should know what she wants and be able to communicate her desires to others. The best way to ensure this is to be prepared. Do your homework before you walk on the set.

Treat all Crew Members with Respect. In most cases, the crew (and cast) is working for little or no pay. Remember that they are all part of a team and that everyone on the team is important.

Know What Everyone Does. If you understand the value of every position, you can evaluate what you really need for a particular production. Know also what every piece of equipment does.

Clarify Job Requirements. If crew members hold more than one position apiece, be sure that job requirements don't conflict and clearly establish who will do what. There shouldn't be any assumptions on the set; you don't want to hear, "I thought *he* was taking care of that." An effective crew should be able to accommodate any demands asked of it.

> **STUDENTS**
>
> We have identified several problems that are specific to student shoots. Understanding at an early stage what it means to be a professional takes time and experience. Let the crew members do their jobs. If you have more experience at a particular position, hold back from telling your crew member how to do the job. Tell the effect you want, not how to get it. If you want a warmer feel in the lighting setup, let your DP know; don't tell the gaffer where to put the light.

KEY POINTS

- The department heads are responsible for hiring their own crews.
- Make sure that the crew members you hire are people you want to be around for long days.
- If a certain crew member is not pulling her load, do not hesitate to terminate that person's employment. No one is irreplaceable.
- Crew members often have more than one job. Define all crew responsibilities.
- Maintain good health. The stamina needed for a shoot can be taxing.
- Qualified people are often interested in working on a short project to build their reel or to jump into another crew position for the experience.

Chapter 7

Casting

Casting was everything. I felt that with a good script and a good cast, everything else would fall into place. Casting took a really long time. I got a lot of help from a lot of friends who I've made over the years in the advertising business. The person who took the longest to cast was the lead actor Isaiah Whitlock, who played Bob, the older barber, because I was very particular on how I wanted him to look and how I wanted him to sound. I didn't want to go with the typical stereotypical old Southern black man who lived up north telling wives' tales. I wanted him to be urban yet still with wisdom and a mother wit that he could impart upon the kid who walks into his barbershop.

Be' Garrett

PRODUCER

Auditions

The credibility of the project rests on proper casting. We cannot stress enough how important it is to find the right actors for characters in your story. The actors are the words with which you will tell your story. They allow the audience to enter the world of your drama by bringing to life the scripted characters. No matter how slick the camera work or how beautiful the locations, it will be difficult for viewers to empathize with your story if they don't believe in your characters. It is equally important to search for the right interviewees for a documentary. Finding the most willing and articulate subjects can be a substantial challenge. (See the extended quote from Jan Krawitz on how she found the women for *Mirror Mirror* at the end of this chapter.)

All the characters in our short films—*The Lunch Date, Truman, Citizen,* and *A Nick in Time*—seem to inhabit their roles effortlessly. As viewers, we experience the characters, not actors playing parts. This is also true with the anthropomorphic attributes of the claymation characters in *Crazy Glue*. This illusion is due partly to their performances and partly to their being physically right for the characters. Had the actors' physical and vocal types not suited the characters they were supposed to play, no degree of performance could have overcome this false impression.

I think the most important thing is to pick someone who you trust and whose work you respect. I don't think someone can create what you want if it's not their sensibility. I think the casting process is the most important one. You have to pick somebody you absolutely think is right and are profound and have subtext in their performances and then let them bring it out while giving them some direction in what it is you are looking for.

Tatia Rosenthal

No matter how many people participate in the casting process, the final decisions should rest with the director. Not only must the actors fit her vision for the project, but she must feel comfortable with their working relationship. The producer's job is to ensure that the director has the widest choices of talent to review. The producer also lends support by serving as a creative sounding board when the director requires an objective opinion.

RESPECT FOR ACTORS

We want to suggest a simple but effective credo: treat all actors with respect and courtesy. Make each experience pleasant and professional no matter how wrong for the part an actor may be. The actor has made the effort to come in and put himself on the line. Respecting that effort, you create goodwill with that individual and at the same time show respect for the whole acting profession. You never know; they might be right for your next project. For those who are eventually cast, this first encounter represents a positive and congenial foundation on which to build.

The Casting Director

An important addition to the creative team is the casting director. After gaining an understanding of the director's requirements, the casting director sifts through many of the submissions so the director sees only those actors who are genuine possibilities. The casting director looks at a script and, based on her experience in the field, establishes a viable list of actors for each part.

doi: 10.1016/B978-0-240-81174-1.00014-2

The following are some of the elements a casting director brings to a production:

- Valuable creative input
- A solid resource bank (file of actors)
- Awareness of new talent
- Good working relationship with agents and managers
- Ability to make deals with actors (understanding of Screen Actors Guild [SAG] rules)

A good casting director does all the setup work so the director and producer need only make the decisions. If you can afford the expense, this is a valuable and worthwhile person to have on the production team. If you cannot afford to hire a casting director, the producer and director assume these duties.

To find a casting director, inquire of other producers and directors who work in the low-budget arena. Breakdown Services publishes a useful guide, the *Casting Director Directory for New York and Los Angeles.*

I had a dedicated casting director who coordinated the entire casting process. He was a student in the drama department and a year younger than me when we made the film but had worked for some casting directors and knew the ropes so our auditions were professionally run. He had the headshots from Backstage mailed to his place. When you put out these casting notices, you get hundreds of them. It's an incredible amount to sort through but he handled it all.

James Darling

The Basic Casting Steps

Although the exact method used to cast a production varies from project to project, the following steps provide a useful overview of the basic process:

- Advertise specific roles.
- Scout local theater companies.
- Scout acting schools.
- Contact state film commissions.
- Organize submitted head shots and résumés.
- Arrange casting calls.
- Arrange callbacks.
- Negotiate with selected actors.
- Deal with rejected actors.

Advertise Specific Roles

Use advertising to let the creative community—actors, agents, and managers—know about your project and the specific parts available. It is easiest to locate a variety of talented performers in major metropolitan areas. Actors are attracted to these areas because of the opportunities they offer for professional work. Before submitting your

request, you will need to create a **breakdown**, which is a detailed description of your casting requirements and any applicable information about your project. It should include the following:

- Character description (age range, gender, ethnicity, etc.)
- One-sentence synopsis of the film
- Film format (16/35mm film, video, HD)
- Shoot schedule and location
- Compensation (fee, or food, travel, credit and DVD copy)
- Audition schedule
- Production contact information for auditions and headshot submissions
- Note that it is a student film (if applicable)

Here are some suggestions for advertising your project:

1. For a small fee, you can submit an advertisement in the trade publication called *Backstage* (it covers the New York City and Los Angeles market at www.backstage.com). The ad should be succinct yet clearly represent your casting requirements as presented by our suggested breakdown.

2. Create a professional-looking flier that clearly represents your project and available parts. Post it at acting schools, schools for the performing arts, community theaters, local college theater programs, high school drama societies, and community and acting guild bulletin boards.

3. Submit your project to Breakdown Services (www.breakdownexpress.com). This company is an excellent casting resource. It distributes vital information about what films and videos are in the casting process and what roles are available throughout the United States. Agents and personal managers pay a weekly subscription fee for this information. You pay a small fee to submit a synopsis of your project and descriptions of your principal parts. This information is submitted to all the agents and personal managers in your area who subscribe to this service. Represent the nature of your project accurately. That is, is it a non-SAG production? Does it include violence, nudity, or sex? Interviewing actors under false pretenses wastes everyone's time and will blemish your reputation as an ethical producer.

4. Locate a copy of the *Academy Players Directory*. This huge and expensive two-volume set is put out by the Academy of Motion Picture Arts and Sciences and contains a photographic listing of practically every actor in the motion picture business, along with each actor's agency representation and guild affiliation. You can usually find this directory in a library. You can also purchase it directly at a media bookstore or online at www.playersdirectory.com. The directory has recently been converted to e-book form.

These are also web sites where you can post casting notices. Some of these are only in New York or Los Angeles, and some are ubiquitous:

- mandy.com
- nycastings.com
- shootingpeople.org
- actingzone.com
- thebuzznyc.com
- nowcasting.com
- craigslist.org (under the "TV film radio jobs" bulletin)

> I started out with *Backstage*. I put my ad in for $27 and got a whole stack of head shots. Next I wrote to Breakdown Services, which sent me people more in line for the gym teacher. Then I contacted talent agencies, which now is a very accepted thing, but it was not at that time in New York. I just said, "I'm doing this great film. It would be a wonderful reel piece . . . will pay expenses . . . Do you have anybody?" At the time, there was something called *Manhattan Kids on Stage*. I saw some performances and had a few more kids audition for me.
>
> Howard McCain

Scout Local Theater Companies

If you live in a major metropolitan area that has small theater companies, such as New York, Chicago, Los Angeles, Boston, or San Francisco, it can be useful for you and the director to scout out the currently running shows for new talent. These cities have many small and interesting theater groups, but don't discount the many community theaters all over the country. Don't ignore summer stock and dinner theaters either.

Check the cast lists for the specific types for which you are looking and plan to see these actors in action. If you are impressed by an actor's performance and feel that he might be right for your project, go backstage after the show and introduce yourself. The actor will be flattered by the attention.

> I was affiliated with Blue Man Group doing some video work for them at the time and also working in the lobby. One of the Blue Men, Andrew Miller, had a beautiful, beautiful voice. We spoke one day and I realized that not only did he have a beautiful voice, there was something about his demeanor that was just right for the character of the husband in *Crazy Glue*. So I asked him to do the voice and he said yes.
>
> Tatia Rosenthal

Scout Acting Schools

Many acting programs in metropolitan areas run their own theater groups, and they can be a good source of talent. Posting a flier may work, but contacting the teachers personally might be more effective. Ask them about the best ways to approach their students. They might allow you to sit in on a class. If you live outside a metropolitan area but close to a university, look into whether it has a theater program. Drama students should be eager to have experience in front of a camera.

Contact State Film Commissions

Each state has its own film commission (see Appendix G) that exists to promote the growth of film and television projects within its borders. Many provide access to talent through links to the local acting communities in that state. We can't generalize that all these commissions offer the same service, but this is a good place to start. We discuss the role film commissions play in expediting your search for suitable locations in Chapter 9.

Organize Submitted Head Shots and Résumés

When interested actors or their representatives hear that you are casting, they will submit a photograph, or glossy, with a résumé attached to the back. Most of these will now be sent via email. From the résumé, you can cull the following information: experience, height, weight, age, union affiliation, and the actor's contact number. A single advertisement in *Backstage* has been known to attract hundreds of 8 × 10 glossies. Organize and file the glossies according to the part.

From these head shots, look for actors you are interested in auditioning. This is a tough call because you will most likely be flooded with applicants. When choosing actors to audition, base your decision on their "look," their experience, and your gut instinct. However, be aware that a glossy may be an idealized version of what the actor really looks like (Photoshop can do wonders). You may be in for a surprise when the actor appears in person for the first interview.

Arrange Casting Calls

Find a space in which to hold the auditions. It should have some kind of waiting area where the actors can study the pages they will read for the audition. The audition space should be large enough to allow the director, producer, camera operator, and reader to sit comfortably and to allow the actors to move around with ease. The space you choose should also have adequate light for video.

Set up a working schedule for the day or days you plan to audition. Find out how many actors the director wants to see each day and for how long. Start with a plan for 15-minute intervals and work from there. Call the actors or their agents to schedule appointments. If you can't reach an actor, leave a phone number or email address where he can reach you or leave a message.

Casting is an exhausting process for the director, especially for a beginner, so it may be appropriate to begin with a "light day." Once she has gotten into the casting rhythm, you can then pick up the pace.

On the day of the audition, be sure to do the following:

- Arrange for a digital camera and operator.
- Have a production or casting assistant log the actors in at the door.
- Be sure you have plenty of copies (at least one per actor) of the sides to be read.
- Arrange to have someone read opposite the actors. (The director should not read with the candidates because it will hinder her objectivity.)
- Have a pitcher of water and paper cups available for the actors.
- Keep the auditions as close to schedule as possible. It is impolite and unprofessional to keep actors waiting for long.

There's more information on holding auditions in the "Director" section of this chapter.

My background in advertising made me fortunate enough to have friends who were able to put together casting sessions for me. So we were able to put out a big call for SAG actors, some non-SAG, but mostly all SAG actors came in. I looked at a lot of people in the course of two eight-hour days. You also have to see how they all pair together when you put them on film. Do they feel like they belong in the same stage? You can't have someone who looks like they belong in 1980s and someone who looks like they belong in 2008. It's just not going to work. So it has to be a level of authenticity not only in their look but their demeanor.

Be' Garrett

Arrange Callbacks

It is now that the casting process begins in earnest. The goal is not only to look for the best actors for the parts, but also to find the right chemistry or balance among the players. This chemistry is especially critical when casting a love story. Your two lovers must seem to be attracted to one another. To achieve the right chemistry, read actors opposite each other in different combinations. The best combinations can then be put on video. (See also the "Director" section in this chapter.)

The Screen Actors Guild allows its members to attend three callbacks without a charge to the producer. After three callbacks, the producer must pay actors to attend additional casting sessions.

Negotiate with Selected Actors

By the time you sit down with the actor you want to hire or with the actor's agent, everyone involved should already have an understanding about your budget constraints. Be honest and upfront at the beginning about how much money you have to spend.

If you have no budget for talent, your only hope to attract good actors is a well-written script with good parts that can showcase performers' talent. A DVD of the project might prove to be payment enough.

If you are working primarily with "struggling actors" who do not earn a living from their craft, you might have to work around their schedules. They usually have day jobs to pay the rent.

It is not uncommon for non-SAG talent to receive little or no compensation for work with beginning or student filmmakers. Generally, their entire compensation consists of the following:

- A screen credit
- A DVD of the completed film
- Transportation to and from the set
- Meals during the shoot
- Dry cleaning of the actor's personal wardrobe

If you are obligated to pay one of your principal actors, however, you should pay all of them (at least all the speaking parts) to avoid resentment on the set.

You can hire a nonunion player with a simple deal memo or letter of agreement that indicates the compensation (if any) and the performance dates (see our web site).

If you hire SAG actors for your project (this applies to student projects as well), you must deal with a SAG contract, which involves minimum payments for daily or weekly rates, or what is called **scale**. What SAG actors receive even for scale can put undue financial stress on a small budget. If you hire a union player, you must become a signatory to the SAG contract and agree to all its provisions. When negotiating with a union member, remember that unions require payments to pension and welfare funds. In addition, if you have one SAG actor in a show, the union requires that all the actors be on a union contract. There are some exceptions to this ruling. Check with your local SAG representative.

STUDENTS

In some situations, scale payment for SAG talent is deferred. Film and media programs in the United States have worked out an agreement with the Screen Actors Guild that enables the actors' salaries to be deferred until the film is distributed. Then, the first dollars from the distribution royalties (excluding film festival prizes) go directly to pay the actors' salaries.

In effect, these salaries are tacked onto the negative cost of the picture at the end of the production process. This arrangement enables first-time directors to work with professional union actors without having to pay them if the project does not make money. Note, however, that if you use SAG, Equity (stage), AGVA (variety), or AFTRA (TV) actors under this waiver and book them for your shooting dates, they are under no obligation to stay with your project if they get a paying job. This often happens, so you are advised to have backup actors.

Deal with Rejected Actors

The producer should be the "heavy" when it comes to breaking the bad news to actors who have not been cast. It is emotionally difficult to call an actor who has come in for several callbacks to tell him that he has not been cast. The life of an actor is not easy. Actors constantly audition for parts they don't get. Most work at acting intermittently. Many work at other jobs to pay their bills. When an actor auditions, he usually competes with dozens of other actors for a single part.

The actor will appreciate a courteous phone call thanking him for his time and enthusiasm during the casting session. Always strive to build good relationships with good actors. What if you rudely reject the next Dustin Hoffman? Equally important, you may need backup actors if your first choices have to drop out. Actors understand that there are many variables in the casting process. If they are treated with respect, they will usually be more than willing accept the role even though they were not your first choice.

Added Benefits of Casting

The casting process offers many benefits besides finding the best talent for your project. The producer can get a sense of how the director works with actors. Is she comfortable? Does she put the actors at ease? The ability to find a rapport with her actors is a necessary part of the director's craft.

Casting offers an excellent opportunity to audition the script as well. Hearing the lines spoken will give the director and writer a sense of what works and what doesn't. Scenes are often overwritten, and readings can expose fat that might be eliminated.

Finally, the casting process offers the producer and director an opportunity to meet and build relationships with talented performers. Once you have worked with an actor, if you feel that the results and relationship were successful, you might want to work with that actor again. The bond that results from the actor–director relationship is very special. It might last only for the duration of the shoot or for a lifetime.

From a selfish point of view, my documentary work has been a passport to experiences and people that otherwise would be completely off limits. For example, when I made *Cotton Candy and Elephant Stuff*, I literally ran away with the circus for a month because I was making a film about them. Otherwise, I never would have lived with the circus for a month. And with *Little People*, I came to know a lot of dwarfs and midgets who are still in my life 12 years later.

Jan Krawitz

Web Presence

If your web site is being used as an internal (intranet) communication hub or base camp, you can set up special links for crew members to keep track of the casting process. Audition schedules can be posted not only for key crew members, but for actors as well.

As actors become set, their pictures and bios can now be placed in the public-facing or promotional part of the web site. Posting their information becomes important for a variety of reasons, none more important than for potential investors. If you are still looking for funds, having actors committed is a comforting sign, and it places real faces for the characters in the story. Potential investors can keep track of your progress quickly and efficiently.

DIRECTOR

Auditions

The director's relationship to the actor is extremely important. The producer is involved in casting and is ultimately responsible for hiring the cast, but it is the director–actor dynamic that breathes life into the characters that propel the story.

The director, cinematographer, and art director exercise their craft behind the camera. It doesn't matter how they look or how they feel when they work because they are not exposed to the camera's eye. The actor, though, is the very instrument through which the drama is played.

Actors must sometimes call on deep, personal feelings. Helping an actor discover the emotional life of a character is a trying, exciting, and sometimes painful process. When casting, you want to find the actors who have the craft to make truthful discoveries about the characters and the talent to reveal these discoveries to others.

To help you understand something of the actors' work process and language, we strongly recommend attending acting classes. This will allow you to viscerally experience the process and develop a true awareness of the degree of difficulty with which actors pursue their craft. It will also give you the necessary vocabulary to communicate with terms that the actors will understand and lead to drawing out the best in performers.

I took acting classes while I was a student at Columbia University. We had a course in directing actors, but it wasn't enough, so I took some acting classes with Stella Adler. I learned you must respect actors and their process.

Adam Davidson

It also is important to note that finding the right actor is only the beginning. What the audience experiences in the final work is the result of many creative steps, each shaping how an audience connects emotionally to the story and the characters.

How does the audience identify with the characters in your film? These are the basic steps to how performance is created:

- Develop and refine the script (a good script attracts good actors).
- Break down the director's script and analyze characters.
- Cast the leads (cast right and you are 80 percent there).
- Cast the ensemble (develop the right chemistry).
- Rehearse (explore possibilities of the script).
- Develop activity or actions (**business**) that define the characters.
- Create the physical attributes of the characters (costume, makeup, props, etc.).
- Develop the world of the characters (locations and/or sets).
- Photograph the script with enough footage to properly shape the performances in each scene.
- Edit the shots and scenes into a cohesive story.
- Mix in sound effects and music.

Casting

The audience attends a film to witness a story told through actors. If viewers do not care about the characters, they will not care about the story. The case studies used in this book present characters in situations we care about. Will the woman in *The Lunch Date* stand up for herself and get the food she believes is hers? Will the couple reunite in *Crazy Glue*? Will Truman climb the rope? Will the women in *Mirror Mirror* tell the truth about their bodies? Will the young man in *A Nick in Time* make the mistake of his life? Will the young man in *Citizen* make it over the border to Canada?

The important creative relationship between actor and director begins during the casting process. If the filmmaker makes an error at this juncture, this mistake will affect the whole production. Choose wisely. Take your time. Remember that the casting process is not perfect. Some actors, for example, audition better than others. This does not necessarily mean that the actors who audition well are the better actors.

Casting Children

Finding talented child actors can be particularly challenging. There are far fewer child actors than adult actors, and even trained child actors can be difficult to control. There are acting programs specifically run for children. Each age presents a different set of circumstances and demands. Many children are born performers. An untrained child can often give a more spontaneous and engaging performance than a professional child actor (see Figure 7.1). When casting, assess a child's energy and attention span as well as her talent. With all the variables to consider

FIGURE 7.1 Finding your lead actor is an exciting moment. An important moment in *Truman*.

while casting children, an important one to remember is this: *cast the parents*. Beware the backstage mom or dad who hovers around and wants to be a part of the action. This is a warning sign. You want the parent who drops off the kid and asks for a pickup time or is content to wait in another room during the audition.

> I had three casting sessions and didn't find anybody. Finding the little boy for *Truman* came out of sheer persistence. I told my acting teacher I was desperate and asked if he knew any-one (even his second cousin) who looked like the person I needed. He said, "Well, I met this playwright, and she had this kid with her, and he kind of looked like what you were talking about. I'll give you the number, and you can call and make your pitch." That's what I did. Once the kid walked through the door, I said, "That's Truman!"
>
> Howard McCain

Audition Guidelines

For a successful audition and to make the most of the search for the best actors, we recommend following the guidelines in the next sections.

Before the Audition

The audition can be held in any quiet room; a rented rehearsal hall is an ideal place. The space should contain at least three chairs: one for the actor, one for the director, and one for the person who will read opposite the actor. Some additional personnel might be present at the audition, including the producer, the casting director, and a camera operator if the audition is recorded on videotape. Keep in mind that auditions are stressful situations both for the actor and the director.

Beginning the Audition

Introductions. The production assistant ushers each actor into the audition space. The director should greet the actor, introduce the people in the room, and make small talk before beginning the audition. You will find that actors are usually nervous. The director should create an open and pleasant atmosphere to relax the actor and put him at ease. This will encourage the actor to feel confi-dent, and the audition will go smoother. The actor will perform at his best, and the director will be able to make an informed decision.

The actor will bring to the audition a recent photo-graph, called a **head shot** or **glossy**. Attached to the back of the photo will be the actor's résumé, which contains information about the parts the applicant has played. It also describes the actor's talents and interests and lists the teachers with whom he has studied.

This material can be used as a good place to begin small talk. For example, you might say, "I see you studied with Mira Rostova" or "Do you enjoy doing Mamet?" or "When you say here you speak French, are you fluent?"

Depending then on how much of the script the actor has read, you might briefly tell the story you plan to shoot. This will put the audition scene in context, which will be helpful to the actor. Only when the director feels the actor is ready should she begin the audition.

Types of Auditions

Sides. The most common method used to audition actors for a film or video project is to have them read a scene or part of a scene from the script. These pages are called **sides**. When an actor reads the sides for the first time at an audition, it is called a **cold reading**. With a short script, there is no reason why each actor should not be able to read the entire script in advance. This allows him to get a better feel for the arc of the story and eliminates the need for the director to set up the character and the scene before the actor reads.

Auditions for the first call usually run at 5- to 15-minute intervals. This allows for some time after the actor leaves to share your impressions of each audition. The scene you ask the actor to read should be short. This will allow you to make the most of the meeting. The actor will need to act with a partner the production provides. The reader can be the producer, a production assistant, or another actor, but not the director. She needs to observe and assess the perfor-mance. There is no way that the director can fully concen-trate on the reading when she is participating herself.

The reader should make eye contact with the actor. This gives the actor someone to whom he can relate. Because the audition is for the actor, not the reader, the reader should not "act" nor read in a monotone, which would be equally distracting.

When the actor begins reading, allow him to read through the scene with no direction, but encourage him to move around if he so desires. This might reveal how comfortable the actor is with movement or how he feels about his body. Be sensitive to the actor's creative inter-pretation of the material. Does he bring a unique slant to the character, one you had not considered before? How does he listen to the other actor reading with him?

If you like the actor, ask him to read the scene again but give him a simple direction, or what is called an **adjustment**. This direction can be as basic as he has to go to the bathroom badly but doesn't want the other char-acter to know. You are looking for a difference between the first reading and the second. How well and how quickly the actor receives and incorporates direction is more important than whether he understands the character. This second reading is key because it gives you an idea of the actor's range and flexibility.

Take notes on your assessment of each actor. Your notes will help you decide at the end of the day which actors you would like to use or which you would like to call back.

Monologue. In addition to or instead of the cold reading, you can ask the actor to prepare a monologue for the audition or the callback. A monologue is a speech for one person from a play or film. It gives you the opportunity to witness a prepared performance. The combination of the cold reading and a prepared monologue offers that much more information on which to make casting decisions.

Improvisation. Another useful technique is to have the actor improvise a scene from the script—that is, to act like his character, spontaneously, in a situation you create. Improvisation is a specialized acting form. Some actors, especially comedians, are very adept at this type of performance. Other actors do not have this facility. It is, however, an acceptable request to make of an actor. Improvisation can also be a useful tool when auditioning children as long as the atmosphere is fun and challenging. (Directors who have studied acting themselves will be more adept at this technique.)

> I like to bring in the script and a particular set of sides. I allow the actors to read generally without much instruction other than setting the scene. After they've read, I'll begin to tweak, to have them pay particular attention or play with a certain kind of motivation. So, in doing so, I'm looking for certain things from an actor. I am looking for an ability to have stretch room. Can this actor not play a stereotype? Can he come out of character and not be himself? Can he become this person?
>
> Be' Garrett

Evaluating the Audition

The primary goal of the audition process is to discover the actor's range of talent and his ability to take direction. If the actor reading for the part is absolutely perfect, indicate this in your notes, but never offer an actor a part during the audition. You never know who might come in later and cause you to change your mind. If the actor is not ideal but has interesting qualities, this, too, should be noted. After all, the ideal actor for the part might never audition. You will have to cast the role based on the talent available. If you are absolutely certain that the actor will not be called back, it is polite and respectful to let him know after the audition. There is no reason to string him along. A simple "thank you very much. I am sorry we can't offer you anything at this time. Perhaps there will be something that we can work on together in the future" is sufficient.

Keeping an Open Mind. The readings are an excellent opportunity to explore many different casting possibilities, and these possibilities are as varied as the actors who walk through the door. Remain flexible and open-minded as to the many ways a part can be cast.

Too often, directors have a set image of a character in mind during the audition. If an actor matching that image doesn't appear, the audition is merely an exercise. Casting against type often makes the script even more vital. Can the part be played by an African American, an Asian, or a physically disabled actor? It might be interesting to cast as the villain of your piece an actor who has the appearance of a nice guy. This will create a doubt in the viewers' minds and add a tension that wouldn't otherwise exist.

Use your imagination when casting. If a talented blond actor auditions, but you see the character as a redhead, consider using a wig or asking the actor to dye his hair. The director must be aware of how the various departments can help shape an actor's look.

The audition process requires stamina and concentration. Reading actors all day with only a short lunch break can be exhausting. Be sure to give adequate consideration to the last few actors who audition. Among them could be the actor who is just right for the part. Remember, casting can make or break your project.

Notes. If you write pertinent observations on the actor's résumé or on a separate log sheet during the reading, you can later review the day's many auditions. It is also important to note the actor's schedule and availability. (See Figure 7.2.)

Casting Evaluation Form

Actor's name: _____
Address: _____
Phone: _____
E-mail: _____

Role: _____

Availability:	Full	Partial	NG

Notes on availability:

SAG Member: Yes   No

Audition Evaluation:

	Excellent	Acceptable	Not Appropriate
Appearance:			
Interview:			
Monolog:			
Sides: (script pages:)			

Comments:

Call Back: Yes   No

FIGURE 7.2 Casting evaluation form.

I videotaped all of the callbacks. I think that's important, because it helps to make a decision. You see so many people over the course of a day coming in and out; there is no way to recall them from a headshot. Once the casting session is over I will look back or I'll have pulled aside cards of people I particularly liked, and I'll view their casting tapes, to kind of solidify whether I want to bring them back for a callback. From there, I get down to my wish list of my first choice and second choice. Then I do a callback and I bring those people back, we'll do it again, and then from there the call goes out and we'll see whoever gets the part.

Be' Garrett

Videotaping. Videotaping is an excellent way to review auditions and helps in making a casting decision. Recording the audition on video gives the creative team an opportunity to review the different combinations of actors at a later time. It also allows you to see how an actor relates to the camera. Certain actors have an affinity for the lens, and some don't. Some very talented people freeze under the scrutiny of the lights and the camera. The choice of whether to tape the first round of auditions or wait until the second or the callbacks is up to you. With so many actors appearing for the first round, videotape may be a useful tool to recall them all at the end of the day. It will certainly become more important as you narrow your choices.

Using video during auditions is most effective with actors who have little or no exposure on film or tape. It is vital that you see them on tape before making any final decisions. A film test is ideal but is more expensive than shooting on video.

If you use a video camera during the audition, set up the equipment unobtrusively. For example, the camera might be placed in a corner, with a long lens at an angle, out of the actor's eye line.

VIDEO OPERATORS

Plan for enough light for the video camera. Shoot with lenses of several sizes. Start wide to see how the actor moves and communicates with his body. Make sure to follow if he moves around the room. Then move in to a medium shot and finally a close-up to see the actor's face, particularly his eyes.

Callbacks

When the general auditions have been completed, the producer arranges for callbacks. A callback is another audition, but with actors who have already read for the director once and are being considered seriously for the part.

The callback can be conducted in the same fashion as the first audition, but with some modifications. The time periods are generally longer, say 15 to 30 minutes, which permits the director to work on specific details in the scene. Actors are asked to read opposite other actors who are being considered to determine whether there is the right kind of chemistry between them.

If the lead has been cast, you can ask that she read with all the candidates who might play opposite her in the film or video. This process, referred to as **mix and match**, is useful in casting family members.

If you can't find the actors you want, you might have to look beyond the normal casting arena. Leave no stone unturned.

Happy Accidents

The journey to discover the right talent for your script can take unusual twists and turns. James Darling had secured an actor to play the doctor in *Citizen* but needed an expert to ensure that the procedure the doctor followed was believable. Within days of shooting, the actor had to back out because he got a paying job. He was replaced by a fourth-year med student (see Figure 7.3). The following quote explains what can happen when you are open and flexible.

FIGURE 7.3 Still from *Citizen*.

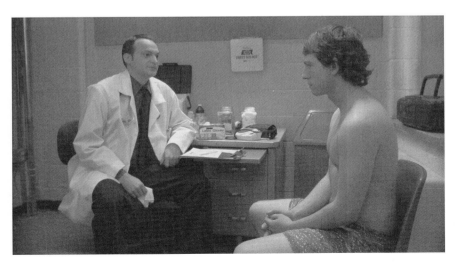

Through the rehearsal phase I wanted a medical expert involved so the procedures on screen were believable and accurate. Thankfully, the make-up artist had a boyfriend who was a fourth year med student and very familiar with the procedures for a military physical. He even found an actual military check list.

He worked with the actor we had cast with such things as how to handle a stethoscope properly. Then that actor dropped out the day before we had scheduled to shoot his scene to do a commercial in Miami that was going to get him into SAG. I understand the choice he had to make so we scheduled an emergency casting session that night at the Starbucks in Union Square. We saw some actors who were good but then my assistant director suggested, "Why don't you see how well the actual doctor reads for it?" We had him read and his behavior was genuine and real. He looked great; I do not want to say creepy, but he definitely had an imposing face. He got cast and everyone loves him. So you never know.

James Darling

FIGURE 7.4   Jerry Klein, who played the coach in *Truman*, was the Midas Muffler Man.

Points to Keep in Mind

Benefits of the Casting Session. The casting session is a learning process for the director. How lines are read, how a character is interpreted, and how a scene is performed all add to the director's excitement and enthusiasm during preproduction. Although the casting session is not foolproof, it is a time-tested process that generally provides successful results.

My experience was if someone's not busy and they're professional and they like you and they like your script, they'll do it. So I just started picking people out of the *Academy Players Directory* because there I could see their faces and head shots. And I hadn't really got anything I was satisfied with in Backstage. So I found this guy, Jerry Klein, and he came in, and he was terrific. He looked right. And even though the role is fairly one-dimensional, he brought something to it that made it kind of fun. . ... He's a professional actor—the Midas Muffler Man. He does all sorts of things.

Howard McCain

The "Nonaudition." If you're interested in using a recognized actor of some note, her body of work should be enough on which to base your decision (see Figure 7.4). Actors like to work. They especially like to work on projects with good scripts. A short film may only take up three to five days of the actor's time. The saying goes: "It doesn't hurt to ask."

I had advertised in Backstage and met a lot of people, but I didn't find anybody right. I went to a talent director, and she gave me Scotty's name, but she told me I couldn't

audition her because she's doing it as a favor and she is beyond auditioning. All I could do was an interview. So I met her, we talked, and it was great.

Adam Davidson

Casting the Documentary

A great deal of research goes into finding the right subjects for your documentary project. Documentaries are only as good as the relationships that permit them to be made, and few relationships of trust are achieved quickly. They must be cultivated thoughtfully and carefully. You may spend days, weeks, or even months getting to know your subjects and allowing them to trust you. In the following quote, Jan Krawitz, discusses how she found the subjects for her documentary, *Mirror Mirror*.

Casting *Mirror Mirror* was an interesting process. I put a little survey out and said I'm a filmmaker. I didn't say I'm interested in meeting women who want to be in a film because I think that can be pretty threatening and off-putting. I just said I was doing research for a film about women and body image and I was interested in talking to as large a group of women as possible about their experiences with this. They had to fill in their name, height, weight, age, and phone number. I got about . . .65 responses that way. I wrote them all a letter and thanked them for the responses and said I'd be back in touch with them.

I invited 60 women who had filled out questionnaires at a local film festival to attend one of several discussion group meetings that I had. My intent was to set up informal groups where the women would feel comfortable talking about issues related to body image and I could observe how articulate they were, what stories they had, and so on. The original questionnaire didn't ask for women willing to be in a film but only to participate in discussions as part of my information gathering. I gave them a choice of six different dates and some evenings.

Two women might show up, and other nights, there would be a group of eight. None of the women knew each other or me. I decided not to prerecord at these sessions as I wanted the conversation to be as uninhibited as possible. However, after the session, I would make notes about what stories each of the women shared so I could use those as aids in casting the film. I made mental notes of what they each looked like. At the end of these informational pre-interviews, I asked them all if they might be interested in appearing in the film. Every single person I pre-interviewed was interested in being in the film, although the initial call was just for information gathering and discussion. Not one person said no at the end of those sessions, which I found pretty extraordinary.

There were a lot of great women among those initial 50, but there was a preponderance of women between the ages of 25 and 40, and they were mostly white. I knew from the outset that I wanted the film to be multicultural and, of course, to transcend any particular ethnic or racial delineation. So I had to cast the net a little farther, and I found out about a women's spirituality group at the Unitarian Church that was specifically for older women. I got permission from the organization to pitch the idea to them. From that group I was able to cast three women who wanted to be in the film.

Jan Krawitz

KEY POINTS

- Leave no stone unturned in your search for actors. Once you have cast a part, there is no turning back.
- Watch for chemistry between actors who play opposite one another.
- Understand the life and process of the actor. This will enable you to get the most out of an audition.
- Be prepared to cast a backup actor in case your actor of choice must leave the production.

Chapter 8

Art Direction

The director chooses the subject of the painting.
The production designer sketches the image on the canvas.
The DP paints the colors on the canvas.

Geoffrey Erb, ASC

PRODUCER

Assembling the Team

The producer has two major concerns with regard to the art department: hiring the best creative people for the project and creating a special "look" within the parameters of the budget. **Production value** is the delicate balance between fiscal responsibility and respect for the artistic aspirations of the script and the vision of the director. A good producer takes pride in stretching money as far as possible to support the artistic goals of the project. The measure of success lies in seeing those dollars up "on the screen."

The producer's role in terms of art direction involves these five steps:

1. Hire an art director (production design).
2. Enable the team to establish a visual style.
3. Approve the budget and the schedule.
4. Approve the hiring of key support people.
5. Supervise the preproduction/construction schedule.

Production Design

Some History

If there is one person who did more than any other to demonstrate the importance of art direction in filmmaking, it was William Cameron Menzies (check IMDb.com for his credits). For *Gone with the Wind*, producer David O. Selznick wanted Menzies to be heavily involved in the preparatory stages so he could plan the whole film on paper. He also wanted Menzies to prepare continuity sketches, showing lighting and camera angles and to handle the montage sequences. For undertaking these tasks, Menzies was given the title "production designer," while Lyle Wheeler, who handled the more traditional aspects of set and costume design, was called "art director."

Menzies also directed about 10 percent of *Gone with the Wind*, including the Atlanta fire scene, and thus was one of four directors who ultimately directed parts of the film. That the film was a success despite having had so many directors must be attributed in large part to the visual unity provided by Menzies's design program.

Ironically, Menzies was not eligible for an Oscar nomination because the Academy of Motion Picture Arts and Sciences did not recognize the production design credit. Historically, the head of the art department was the art director, so the Academy Award in 1939 for art direction went to Lyle Wheeler. Realizing the inequity of bypassing Menzies, the Academy created a special award and presented Menzies with a plaque "For outstanding achievement in the use of color for the enhancement of dramatic mood in the production of *Gone with the Wind*."

After the production design credit was introduced, everyone in the art department moved up a position: all art directors became production designers and assistant art directors became art directors. However, the job responsibility also expanded. Because filming outside the studio back lots became more common in the 1950s and 1960s, one of the production designer's essential roles now became scouting and selecting locations, something an art director rarely had to consider when the sets were built on the studio lot.

Today, the production designer oversees the set decoration and prop department and works closely with the director and the director of photography (DP) to design and shape the overall look and feel of the film. The production designer works closely with the art director, whose job is to manage the entire art department and whose duties include drafting and constructing sets outlined by the production designer, budgeting materials and labor, scheduling construction crews, as well as handling the prep and restoration of all the sets and locations. Although the production designer sits on top of the art pyramid (see Figure 8.11 illustrating the art department flow chart), the Oscar is still awarded for "art direction," but the award is given to the production designer and the set decorator, not the art director.

doi: 10.1016/B978-0-240-81174-1.00015-4

Although there is a distinction between the role of the "production designer" and the "art director," we will use the title "art director" to refer to the crew member who, in conjunction with the director and DP, is responsible for the visual "design of the production." She might also be responsible for managing and implementing that design, the traditional role of the art director. This is often the case in low-budget and independent films and certainly in most student projects.

Anyone selling herself as a "production designer" for these kinds of films must be able to fulfill the traditional roles of both the production designer and the art director. In fact, she may even have to handle all the duties of a full art team.

The Art Department

The art director is the person ultimately responsible for the overall look of the picture. She must be able to collaborate with the director and the director of photography and work effectively within the parameters of the budget. She creates the world of the picture, and the DP is responsible for lighting that world. She strives to fulfill the director's vision of the piece but must do so economically. The art director scrutinizes the script carefully and, in conjunction with the director, arrives at a visual plan for the picture. Whatever the plan, the art director must come up with a comprehensive budget and a schedule to accomplish her task.

Most beginning filmmakers work with small budgets, forcing them to look for an art director who has experience working with limited resources. In hiring for this position, compare the candidates' flexibility, experience, and fee. Keep in mind that one art director might cost more than another but might be more inventive or a better negotiator and thus will actually save you money. (The topic of hiring the art director is discussed in more detail in Chapter 6.)

In many ways, money definitely makes the producer's job easier. With enough money, you can hire a comprehensive art department. If you can afford the expense, you can hire a hair and makeup person for the entire shoot, ensuring day-to-day consistency. An alternative is to rely on the actors to do their own hair and makeup. If you can afford standby painters, they can quickly take care of sets that need to be touched up or recolored. An alternative is to anticipate such changes and schedule around them.

No matter what the budget, someone has to make sure the crew is accountable for its work. The producer is the guardian of the budget and the schedule. He approves the budgets and production schedules devised by the key crew members and sees to it that everyone adheres to these figures and dates.

We had a production designer who had a fair amount of experience on NYU projects and on extremely low-budget feature films. She had worked professionally as a set dresser in an entry level position and had learned where to find things like weapons and such. For *Citizen*, she had a design budget of over $2000 which was the most she had ever worked with on this kind of film.

She also had an art director helping her who she met on set. He was great and ended up having a cameo as one of the guys being driven across the border. The production designer is in charge, but in terms of how involved they are with the actual fabrication of things is up to their discretion and skill set. The sense I get is that the art director is more of a coordinator – the one finding the props, etc. My production designer and art director were both doing that, and so was I. Having an art department of two people was quite a luxury. It really sells your world.

James Darling

Images Can Tell a Story

As the producer, you are responsible for supporting the creative team and realizing the potential of the script. The audience must believe that the actors are the film's characters, that the rooms they live and work in and the clothes they wear are true to the world of your story. Nothing in any frame of your picture should disrupt the illusion you are striving to create.

Think about the seedy hotel room Travis Bickle inhabited in the film *Taxi Driver* or the interior of the *Millennium Falcon* (the spaceship Han Solo pilots in the original *Star Wars* trilogy) or the complex futuristic world of *Blade Runner*. Each of these decorated sets gives the audience a wealth of information about the identity and idiosyncrasies of the characters and the world they live in. The producer's job is to spend as little as possible and still achieve these effects.

Adam Davidson secured Grand Central Station free for *The Lunch Date*. Using this authentic location lent great credibility to the project, and getting it free was probably the only way he could afford it. Howard McCain was able to shoot in a gymnasium for *Truman*, thus ensuring the realism of his script. Be' Garrett found a true-to-life barbershop for *A Nick in Time* that could be dressed equally well for the present and the past. James Darling was able to create the illusion of a Canadian border crossing in Westchester, New York, for *Citizen*. Jan Krawitz surrounded her masked women with an array of mannequins for *Mirror Mirror*. This imaginative set inexpensively symbolized and reinforced the theme of stereotypical female physical perfection.

Responsibilities of the Art Department

Stages and Locations

During preproduction, you must decide whether to shoot your story on a sound stage, in practical locations, or both. There could be practical, artistic, or financial reasons influencing this decision.

If you face this dilemma, compare the costs of constructing and dressing a set on a stage against the location fees. (Chapter 9 addresses the pros and cons of working on a stage or in a practical location.)

In a practical location, the art director is confined to the space at hand. Her involvement in the search for locations, therefore, is crucial. She will have to transform these spaces into the world as defined by the director's vision of the script. She can alter and redress them, but only within the limits of the existing dimensions and only with the permission of the owner.

On a sound stage, the world must be created from scratch. A **sound stage** is a soundproof, hangar-like structure that is used for the production of theatrical motion picture and television shows. It is a self-contained filming environment with its own lighting grid. A set built on a stage can be designed for flexibility, ease of manipulation, and good camera angles, and it imposes none of the constraints of a "real" location. Having a soundproof environment ensures that all the dialogue recorded will be "clean" and unaffected by the natural sounds of a practical location.

What Does the Script Require?

The script might define specific kinds of locations, or it might describe locations so vaguely that it allows for leeway. "EXT. FIELD—DAY" gives little indication of what kind of field, how large, what kind of foliage, what time of year, and so on. "INT. OFFICE—DAY" leaves the kind of office open-ended. Is it a high-tech, ultramodern, antiseptic office or a wood-paneled, warm, cluttered room? The general nature of these descriptions can allow the director a great degree of flexibility and artistic license when it comes to picking a suitable location.

Chapter 9 outlines in detail the steps to finding and securing locations. It may come to that point when the creative team has exhausted all hope in finding a practical location to house the characters in your story that you have to turn to building one from scratch. Whatever the case, if you plan to shoot some or all of the interior scenes on a stage, these are the basic steps:

- The art director analyzes and breaks down the script.
- She engages in conceptual and practical discussions with the director who has a vision for the piece as well as practical requests regarding the kind of coverage she plans.
- The art director furnishes the director with ideas through sketches of set renderings and pictures. These sketches might later be modified or altered. The process of previsualization can also be achieved through the use of software.
- On approval of the basic design, a drafter executes blueprints. If necessary, a model of the set is constructed.
- The art director presents budget and building schedules to the producer. These should contain construction and strike time. Design changes might be made to reduce costs. The department heads give final approval.
- The construction coordinator supervises the construction of the set according to the approved design.

The completion of a set must fit into the production schedule. If multiple sets have to be built, the construction schedule of each set must be timed so that the set is available when needed.

Probably the most important consideration when constructing a set on a stage is determining precisely what the camera will see. Finalizing the design of the set requires that the director have a thought-out visual plan. The art director must find a balance between (1) how the director envisions the scene and (2) the budget, allowing some leeway for adjustments. If the director only needs to see a bed in a corner of a room, the art director should not build a fully dressed four-walled room. Similarly, the director should not order a fully dressed four-walled room and then shoot only the bed in the corner. The entire art direction budget will be stretched during the shoot, so waste should be avoided. (See Figure 8.1.)

However, during the course of the preproduction period, the director and DP could decide to widen the frame to see more than originally planned, so the art department needs to be prepared for this eventuality.

I was thinking about painting the floor in front of the mural. I knew I wanted it to be fairly monochromatic. I didn't want color in these sets, but I don't really know why. I suppose I wanted the women to stand out from the backgrounds and for the backgrounds not to be too assertive. I had a bunch of black-and-white linoleum tiles in my garage. You know, it is funny how ideas emerge. I was really wrestling with this floor dilemma, and suddenly I thought about those tiles and how I could make an interesting design with them. So I brought them into the studio and laid them out on the floor and thought that it looked pretty striking. Audiences commented on the floor—really noticed the black-and-white floor that the women are standing on.

Jan Krawitz

WALL

94.3 Poly,sheet metal
557.44 Plastic, etc
Tools (camera stands)
3.6 Sample paint
43.13 Paint
216 Matt (wood, barbed wire)
47.62 Paint
30 Delivery
111.36 stingers, nails, tarp, etc.
14.9 Crew food
15.65 Crew food
10.97 Drill & saw
79.8 wood

1224.77

WARDROBE

150 Rebekah
20.83 BP Patch
53.21 Army patches
27.9 BP Jacket
39.26 BP Uniform
35.15 Vests
93.75 BDU

420.1

TUNNEL

12.32 wood burner
12.11 Foam
1.82 sand
48.3 Foam
11.03 Smpl foam
4.47 Spray paint
28.51 Boxes
24.92 Spray paint, lights, paper

143.48

Other Props

39.99 BP Monitor
190 Gun Rental
-190 PAID BY JAMES
22.65 camp food n shovel
58.34 etc from home depot
8.43 Batteries
77.67 tape etc

207.08

SIGNS

53.68 ink
290 PrintFacility
51.66 paints, paper,etc
8.29 laminate

403.63

TRAVEL

4.5 Toll to BK to build
4.5 ""
4.5 ""
4.5 ""
4.5 ""
4.5 ""
6 Toll to LI
6 ""
14.5 Train Ticket 1/7/06 production mtg
7.25 Train Ticket 1/16/06 BK Home Depot Scout
14.5 Train Ticket 1/24/06 art/wardrobe mtg
14.5 Train Ticket 1/29/06 production mtg
12.92 Gas 1/20/06 BK to Build
14 Gas 1/27/06 BK to Build
18.92 Gas 2/06/06 NJ for Signs
17.32 Gas 2/10/06 SHOOT
23.73 Gas 2/11/06 SHOOT

181.14

TOTAL
1224.77
420.1
143.48
207.08
403.63
181.14

2580.2

2500 $ Received
-2580.2 $ Spent

=80.2 To reimburse

FIGURE 8.1 Art budget for *Citizen*.

Communication with the DP

There should be an ongoing creative dialogue between the director, the art director, and the DP during the preproduction period. It is customary in the professional world for the art director as production designer to be hired early in preproduction, well before a DP is brought on board. However, if crew members are not being paid (as in most student shoots), there is no reason other than availability why the art director and DP should not be involved as early as possible in planning the overall look and design of the project.

To adequately previsualize the director's vision for the script, both the art director and DP must work closely together to avert potential problems during the shoot. Whatever sets are designed and built and whatever locations are chosen, the DP is in charge of developing a lighting design that enhances the dramatic mood of every space. A set is only half a set until it is properly lit. Director of Photography Geoffrey Erb describes the working relationship that must develop between the director, the DP and the production designer in the following quote.

When beginning a movie, one of the first tasks I do is sit down with the director and the art director to discuss the palette and style of the movie. The three of us need to be working toward the same concept. The director will have a sense of how he wants the movie to look and will express this in terms of artwork and other movies. You never want to duplicate the look of other movies, just use them for references.

I spend hours going over the production designer's drawings. He is limited by the budget and by time, so his designs change constantly. A dark warehouse scene may become an alley scene due to budget reasons. I want to be there each time a change is made to approve or disapprove. This is the time when changes can be made. When shooting principal photography it is very difficult and costly to change.

The visual concept is a process of evolution. A month or two before the movie there are generalities. These generalities become specifics as the weeks go on. It depends upon the locations, affordable equipment, actors, realities of the script, and budget. You always shoot high and do the best you can.

Geoffry Erb, ASC

Set Dressing

The **set decorator** is responsible for "dressing" the location according to the director's wishes. The locations and their details set a tone for the film. They help tell the story by conveying valuable information about the world in which the characters live. A successfully dressed set or location should become as much a part of the actor's persona as the clothes on his back.

Set dressing includes rugs, lamps, furniture, paintings, windows, chandeliers, and cabinets, as well as all the extraneous details, such as plates in the cabinets and bulbs in the chandelier. Set dressing does not include smaller items, such as guns, canes, lighters, or rings that the actors use specifically. These are props.

Dressing a location might be as simple as spreading a few leaves near a park bench to make it look like fall

or as complex as furnishing an entire set from scratch. If a director walks into a living room and decides it will work for the film, this might mean that the room can remain as it is, or it might mean that the room must be stripped down to the bare walls and everything, including the stains on the rug, must be "imported" from another location.

The set decoration department is one of the largest subcomponents of the art department (see Figure II.1 in the Part II intro). In fact, since 1955, separate statuettes are given to the art director and set decorator for the film winning the Academy Award for best art direction.

James Darling needed to construct an exterior wall that represented the border between the United States and Canada for *Citizen*. Because he didn't have the funds to build a real fence, he had to manufacture a facsimile and stage and photograph the scene to create the illusion that it extended much further than it did in reality. (See Figure 8.2 and Figure 8.3.)

Be' Garrett included rich details on the walls of the barbershop that lent an air of believability to the space (see Figure 8.4).

The question became, how big does the wall need to be? This was a conversation that I had with the DP and the production designer in preproduction. I went on shopping trips with the production designer to look at different materials we could make it out of, and we ended up making it out of plastic painted with very shiny paint. This was the most cost effective and futuristic solution we found.

However, it wasn't very long. I was originally thinking I might do some CG to extend it but was concerned about

---

FIGURE 8.2 Painting of the plastic wall from *Citizen*.

FIGURE 8.3 The wall from *Citizen* on location.

FIGURE 8.4 Shots from the walls of the barbershop from *A Nick in Time*.

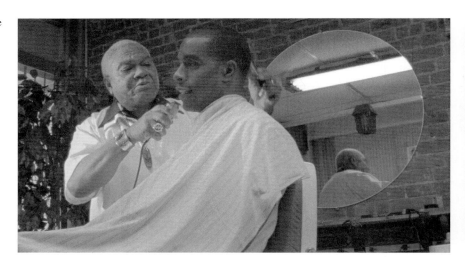

the cost. When we got to the location and framed the shot, we came up with a more practical and less expensive solution. We used the deer fence we built it on and cheated the shot to extend the perspective so the thin deer fence and the plastic one we had made looked indistinguishable from one another.

James Darling

Duplicate Set Items

Each department is responsible for the manufacture or purchase of duplicates—that is, items that are to be destroyed, distressed, or consumed during the course of

shooting a sequence. If a table is broken during a scene, it will need to be fixed or replaced for each take. It is also helpful to provide duplicates for items that are small or fragile, such as sunglasses that could be either lost or accidentally damaged in the course of shooting.

Props

The **property master** is responsible for all the props identified in the script. A prop is a movable object used by an actor that is integral to the story. Props include jewelry, glasses, books, and weapons. Although technically not a

FIGURE 8.5 Weapons of any kind can be dangerous. Scene from *Truman*.

part of the art department team, the property master must integrate his ideas seamlessly with those of the art director and the set decorator.

The property master provides an assortment of props based on the needs of the script. He rents, buys, or makes the props. Most property masters own their own kit or box of common props. This is called a **box** or **kit rental**. Instead of shopping outside for some props, the producer can rent them directly from the prop master. He might also use personal props provided by the actor. Like the costumer and the set dresser, the prop master should consult with the actors concerning their preferences. If there is little or no time for prior consultation, a good prop master will have several props available from which the actors can choose.

The beauty of film is that something doesn't have to be real to look real to the camera. Costume jewelry, for example, looks as real to the camera as do true gems. A person cannot deceive the camera, but a thing can.

Duplicate Props

Often props are eaten, damaged, or distressed during the shoot. The property master and director should discuss how many backups will be needed, and the property master should provide extras, just in case. When disposable props are involved, have an idea of how many takes and retakes might be involved. Err on the side of having too many props rather than too few.

Weapons

All weapons (guns and knives) fall into the prop category. The use and handling of weapons is a serious issue. It is the property master's duty to ensure safety with regard to these props (see Figures 8.5 and Figure 8.6). Permits must be arranged with the local police and the weapons' firing pins must be removed. There is never a need to have live rounds on a set. (The effect of a gunshot can be manufactured in post).

> Working with guns is a serious business. NYU's insurance policy would not cover any film production that uses real firearms and blanks, so we had to rent prop guns. The prop house we used issued a certificate for the insurance company stating that the weapons had been rendered non-functioning. On set the guns were the exclusive responsibility of the art department when they weren't in the hands of the actors. Despite my inability to have an on-camera "shot," I really wanted to strive for realism with our gunplay. I consulted with an experienced marksman who came to our rehearsals and trained the actors on proper handling of the weapons. I learned that a proper warning shot is fired into the ground and NOT into the air as is the usual Hollywood convention. But to sell the actual gunshot in the film was ultimately about sound design.
>
> James Darling

Food

The property master handles all on-screen food. If a scene requires that food be consumed, it is his job to make sure that it is purchased in advance, it is stored in an appropriate place, and someone can prepare it. Buy all food items in bulk if possible and try to use wholesale clubs or discount warehouses to get the best buys. The property master is also required to pay close attention to continuity from take to take. This task can be especially tricky with keeping track of how much food has been consumed in various takes shot out of "continuity." (See *The Lunch Date* for a good example.)

FIGURE 8.6 James Darling directing a guard holding a weapon. Scene from *Citizen*.

Wardrobe

The **costumer**, or **wardrobe designer**, works hand in glove with the art director; this department's contributions on a feature film are also acknowledged with an Academy Award. Together with the director, the costumer develops the look for the show's wardrobe. What each actor wears provides worlds of information about the character he portrays. Even though we are taught not to judge a book by its cover, most people form a strong first impression based on how a person is dressed.

The script will often give specific clues as to how characters are dressed, or the director might decide to dress the lead actor in bright colors and the secondary characters in grays. Or the director and costumer might choose pastels or specific materials—whatever they feel contributes to the overall statement of the story, the characters, and the style of the production.

> The idea of the mask (see Figure 8.10) was there from the very beginning, although I don't remember what prompted it. I look back at my first proposal and see that it's in there. Two years before I shot the film, I was interested in homogenizing the faces so that the viewer's attention would be deflected away from the face toward the body. People look at bodies in this culture, but they are also judgmental about a woman's face. I wanted the audience to focus their attention on the bodies of the women and not have access to their faces.
>
> Jan Krawitz

In *The Lunch Date*, the contrast of wardrobe between the woman and the man having lunch together says a great deal about their stations in life (see Figure 8.7). The woman is dressed in a fur coat and fur cap with elegant jewelry. The homeless man wears a hat with the manufacturer's tag still attached. This is a wonderful, subtle touch, which helps inform the audience of the type of character under the cap. Can you imagine the scene if the wardrobe were reversed, if the woman were dressed in rags and the homeless man were in a coat and tie? In *Citizen*, the border guards are identified by the insignias' on their cloths. These had to be designed and attached to their clothing (see Figure 8.8).

Make sure the wardrobe doesn't look as though it just came off the rack (unless this is your intention). The clothes should be aged, tattered, and stained with grease. The process of attaining this look is referred to as **distressing** the wardrobe. A garage mechanic should look like a garage mechanic, and the audience should believe he is a mechanic before he utters a line.

Consulting the Actors

Who better understands the character than the actor who must portray him? Soliciting the actor's suggestions about style, color, and specific choices will increase his involvement in the show. If the costumer gives him an outfit that the actor feels is inappropriate, "creative differences" could result. It is best that the costumer consult with all actors or at least have several choices from which the actors and director can choose.

> I went over the wardrobe with the actors. I had them bring down a few things, and my art director, Claudia, was there, and we discussed it together. This coat would be better than that. What was in the purse? The contents had to be identified.
>
> Adam Davidson

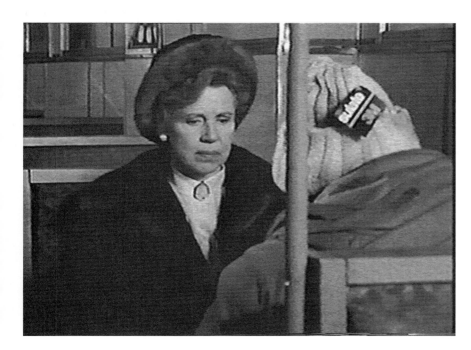

FIGURE 8.7 A well attired woman and homeless man from *The Lunch Date*.

Using an actor's own wardrobe is an inexpensive way to obtain clothes that fit. If your actors offer to supply their own clothes, ask them for a number of different items from which to choose. The company should see that the clothes are not damaged and that you pay for the cleaning of all wardrobe pieces that are worn.

Thrift shops are another source of some very interesting costumes at reasonable prices. Remember that clothes can be altered, dyed, and borrowed.

Specialty Garb

Period pieces, of course, require period clothes. Paying attention to history is critical. Each period of dress must be carefully researched and represented accurately. The barbershop in *A Nick in Time* flashes back to the 1980s. Be' Garrett wanted to capture clothes characteristic of that time to contrast with the present-day part of the story. Certain genres, such as film noir or science fiction, require a special look that must remain consistent throughout the picture to maintain a specific style.

> Research was done in the library of how people dressed back in the mid-eighties and what styles they were wearing and the things that were popular. I did a lot of research to make sure that when you brought people back to 1986 you felt authentic and could believe the time period.
>
> Be' Garrett

Duplicate Costumes

If a scene calls for damage to the costume, the costumer will need to have doubles and triples of the same clothes. Suppose, for example, that a character is supposed to be

FIGURE 8.8 Drawing of wardrobe for guard in *Citizen*.

stabbed in the chest. A blood pack under the shirt is rigged to ooze red liquid, giving the illusion that the character has been wounded. When the director calls for a second take, the dresser replaces the stained shirt with a new one.

If an actor gets wet in a scene or spills ketchup on a costume, the wardrobe department will need to have another standing by for each additional take. Stunt people who double for an actor need to have a costume that is identical to the actor's. For some shoots, having stunt doubles might require three or more of the same suit.

Consulting the Director of Photography

The director of photography should be consulted for wardrobe and makeup. The costumer consults with the DP regarding colors and materials. Most DPs, for instance, are adamant about not allowing actors to wear bright white clothes. White can make lighting difficult because it reflects the light. He should also preview the style of makeup, and if any special effects makeup is planned, he will insist on a camera test to preview what it will look like, especially if the project is be shot on film.

Continuity and Script Time

The costumer is responsible for maintaining the continuity of the costumes. Using the stabbing example again, some scenes involving the bloodied victim might be shot before the actual stabbing scene itself is recorded. In this case, the costumer needs to distress one of the duplicate shirts to represent a stab wound as exactly as possible. Matching the bloodied stain can get very complicated. Ideally, the assistant director will schedule the shoot with this problem in mind.

Script time is the logical progression of the days in the script. Wardrobe and script supervision are the departments most responsible for script time. If a story takes place over three days and there is a different wardrobe for each day (most people change clothes every day), the wardrobe department keeps a chart of what clothes are worn in each scene. Then if the script is shot out of continuity, the character will be wearing the correct clothes throughout the filming.

Makeup

The glamour of Hollywood is exemplified by the bright, clean, unblemished look of movie stars. In the old days, audiences did not seem to mind that their heroes on the screen could be kicked and beaten yet still look like a million bucks. Audiences today are more sophisticated and prefer greater realism.

Men wear less makeup than women. Sometimes, actors wear no makeup at all, or a director might demand that they wear none. Usually, though, they wear at least a base, a skin-toned makeup called **pancake**, which is spread evenly over the face and hands. With a base, the makeup artist can help the actors maintain a consistent skin tone throughout the picture. In addition to a base, women generally wear lipstick, eyeliner, mascara, and powder.

There is specialty makeup for creating cuts, wounds (fresh, oozing, and recently healed), moles, bruises, and so on. Anything more elaborate than these specialty items falls under the domain of the special effects makeup department.

Special Effects Makeup

The special effects makeup department might work in conjunction with the makeup artists or as a separate unit, depending on the nature of the project. These artists work on large-scale specialty makeup jobs, such as monsters, which require major prosthetics. They might also be called on to perform more subtle tasks, such as making an actor look older or younger. Special effects makeup techniques generally employ large latex pieces to reshape the actor's face or body. Special makeup sometimes requires camera tests. Hire a stylist to design makeup for each actor and ask the actor to be responsible for sustaining it.

Hair

Hairdressers often use hairpieces, wigs, beards, and toupees. Many balding actors have maintained a full head of hair for years with the aid of a hairpiece. Some women prefer to wear a wig when performing because they don't have to sit in a chair for hours while the hairdresser creates an elaborate hairdo. They can slip the wig on and off without worrying about destroying the style. Another advantage to hairpieces of all types is that they can be maintained at a constant length and color. Actors need to have their own hair trimmed frequently to maintain continuity.

Men can use facial hair to achieve a different type of look. Beards and mustaches have to be made and fit well in advance of principal photography to ensure enough time for alterations. In addition, several pieces must be made as backups because facial hairpieces disintegrate after several wearings.

A typical production problem involves a character who has a "change of look" in the story. Say a female character goes from long hair to short hair. This can most easily be accomplished with a short haircut and a wig. If no wig is used, the schedule must reflect this choice; any scenes that require long hair must be shot before the performer's hair is cut.

Actors might be required to change their hairstyle or hair color or even add facial hair for a role. Experiment before committing to a particular look.

Animation

In traditional cel animation and with computer-generated images (CGI), the art direction is part and parcel of each frame drawn. Creating a color palette for the world of your film is a critical detail in animation art direction. In live action animation, as in claymation or any form of **pixillation** (see Glossary), the design of the characters and the settings is manufactured on a small scale (see Figure 8.9). The principles are similar to any live action shoot; the technique is specific to the scale and materials of the animation project.

> The class at NYU where I made the film is a yearlong class. The first six months I was very, very, very lax. I only did storyboards, one of the most important tools in the animated short. So I did that and recorded the voices. That was first semester. Then second semester hit and I went into a frenzy. My art director was in town. A woman I knew from childhood who was very talented and had a degree in industrial design. She knew how to use power tools. There is an expectation when you're a student animator that you can do all yourself. You will build a set yourself, you will do the puppets yourself, write the story yourself; the entire thing is usually a one-person effort. My biggest decision was to give the set design to someone else. I gave it to her and that decision probably made the film possible. First of all she came up with two beautiful sets for the office and for the apartment, and it freed me up to make the puppets and concentrate on that and the animation.
>
> Tatia Rosenthal

FIGURE 8.9   *Crazy Glue* office sequence.

FIGURE 8.10 Each of the women in *Mirror Mirror* wears a mask.

The Producer's Role

Review Budgets Carefully. Always expect that the art department's first pass at a budget will be "padded" and higher than you expected. Don't be afraid to play the heavy and challenge a production request. There is always a customary back-and-forth, or "haggling," that goes on during all films. The director needs to be cozy with her creative team, but the producer doesn't. His job is to be cozy with the budget.

Question All Requests (Within Reason). During the creative discussions between the director and her art director, the producer should, within reason, question every request.

The creative process involves a series of discussions in which many ideas are bandied about. The solutions to a problem can run the gamut from very expensive to inexpensive. For example, should you wish to fly a character through the air, there are several ways to accomplish this stunt, including a wire-flying rig, blue-screen photography, and imaginative framing. The difference in cost among these three choices is enormous. The director considers each idea and, with deference to the budget, makes a suggestion that will be cinematographically satisfactory. When there is a choice, it behooves the producer to opt for the less-expensive solution, of course.

I originally thought I would have the women wear different masks, and I spent a lot of money buying a variety of masks. After trying on the masks at home, I realized they were quite grotesque and not what I wanted. Finally, I found an inexpensive white kabuki-type mask in a costume store, and the minute I saw it, I knew this was the one. So I bought six of them, and I cut out the lips so the sound wouldn't be muffled.

Jan Krawitz

Keep Tabs on Weekly Spending. Money flows very quickly through the art department. Don't give the department the entire budget amount at once. Keep on top of the cash flow. Have each member of the department turn in receipts each week for everything bought or rented. (See the section titled "Petty Cash" in Chapter 5.)

Keep an Eye on the Construction Schedule. If the construction personnel promise that a set will be completed by a particular date, follow their progress. When you're scheduling, it is prudent to allow extra time in the construction timetable. If the construction coordinator swears that the turnaround time for the next set is three days, schedule four.

Web Presence

Designing the Interface

It is at this point that the **communication strategy** for the web site is brought to life through graphic design. The web team seeks to integrate the visual style of the film into the web interface. Success relies on a productive collaboration between the project manager, the creative director, the art director, and DP of the film and also the result of the research and organization that has preceded it. The more source material that has been organized and collected, the more data the creative team will have to work with.

The creative director must create a consistent look across the entire site that will complement the film's visual style. Navigation needs to be simple and easy. The creative director develops page layouts for primary or secondary pages using software such as Adobe Photoshop or Illustrator. Drawings or even collage work of primary elements might even suffice. The web site could be infused with images and style treatments from the film. There are many ways to go. The web style could serve as an understated backdrop for the content of your project. Your main goal is to provide a conceptual and visual framework for the next step in the design process: the implementation and organization of the web site's interface.

DIRECTOR

Creating a Look

The "look" of any film project has its origins in the script. The screenwriter's descriptive stage directions and dialogue instill in the reader's imagination the environment, mood, and tone of the piece. As she embraces the story as her own (unless she also is the writer), the director supplies her interpretation to what the words on the page inspire. This will define her vision. Every creative decision flows from how the director pictures the film in her mind. Give the script to five different directors, and you will get five different interpretations.

After the director and the director of photography plan how they will photograph the script, the art department details the elements within the frame and realizes them. Once the major location decisions have been made with the producer, such as construction, distant locations, or stages, the director works with the art director to shape the sets and locations.

The director must be familiar with the capabilities of all the production departments, especially her art direction team. Knowing how clever the team can be in stretching the budget is instrumental to her creative decisions. It is unfair to the production to request an item that might enhance the show but would overtax the art department's time, talents, and money.

> The rental of the mannequins was too costly, so I had to be resourceful, and figure out how to get them for free. A friend of mine knew someone who worked in a large department store and he dressed the mannequins. He thought he might be able to loan me some damaged ones. So that's what I did. I went and borrowed five mannequins from this huge department store—unbeknownst to them, I think. He gave me a bunch of damaged mannequins from a back room and I was able to use them for the two-week shoot and then I returned them.
>
> Jan Krawitz

Architect of Illusion

The director in consultation with the producer chooses the actors who will portray the characters, the location or production manager secures the locations, and the cinematographer lights and frames the set. The art director is responsible for everything else. It is a key position and one that beginners frequently misunderstand, undervalue, and fail to appreciate. The reason is that the ability to create an illusion through art direction is like a magic trick: everyone admires the end result, but no one realizes that it took hard work and special talent to achieve what is only an illusion.

The art director supervises a creative team (that includes the set dresser, property master, and costumer; see Figure 8.11, which shows a diagram of the art team) that designs, builds, and dresses the sets and helps choose and dress the locations. Anything that communicates information to the audience involves a decision of some kind. Every piece of clothing, hairstyle, prop, or article within the frame tells us something about the character and the world of a story. Many aspects of art direction are also story points, such as the salad in *The Lunch Date*, the photo in *Crazy Glue*, the scissors in *A Nick in Time*, or the rope in *Truman*.

The art director is responsible for interpreting the director's ideas and transforming them into a visual plan. Working from the script, photographs, paintings, and other films, these two department heads create a "look" for the film or video. The art director and her team are also responsible for overseeing the continuity and consistency from scene to scene.

The art director's duties vary from project to project. The script might require designing sets or simply altering existing locations. The screenwriter strives to craft a story in which every scene and character support the theme. The art director's job is to ensure that every article within the frame complements the story, illuminates the characters, supports the theme, and serves the director's vision.

For example, a cheap cardboard column is painted à la trompe l'oeil to look like marble, and voilà, the audience sees a stone pillar. A small off-screen wind machine blows small white polystyrene pellets at the actors, who pretend to struggle to stay afoot, and a "blizzard" is created. Knowing how materials react to light and how they "read" on film and video helps the art director avoid buying unnecessarily expensive materials. A good art director knows that rayon chiffon looks exactly the same as silk chiffon on film.

> We hired an art director and I took him through my references. I am a director who references a lot of things. I read a lot of magazines and I actually clip out, I call them tear sheets or clip art, and I keep a lot of files around. So I was able to share the research with the art director, not tell him what to get, but to inspire him and give him a direction on how to proceed. I believe a director hires a crew to be artists themselves. That is why we all do this, because in some ways we are all artists and what the art director brought back to me was my vision.
>
> Be' Garrett

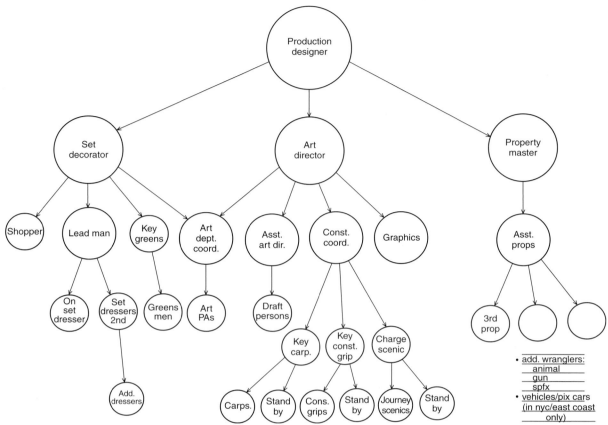

FIGURE 8.11 Typical Union Art Department Hierarchy.

How to Define the "Look"

The director has spent weeks, possibly months forming a mental image of how she sees her story unfolding on the screen, one scene at a time. She also has a deep understanding of the dramatic theme. The effective art director needs to embrace the director's ideas and translate them into what will become the visual narrative, or "look," of the film. An important aspect of this "look" includes establishing a unifying color palette that serves the story.

For this to happen, the director and art director must discover a common artistic ground. Words are usually inadequate when it comes to explaining mood and style. For example, each of us has our own sense of a particular lighting style; "mood lighting" may have a different connotation for different people. To bridge this artistic gap, communication may begin with references to traditional artists and photographers like John Singer Sergeant, Winslow Homer, Rembrandt, Norman Rockwell, Magritte, etc. Using established art and a variety of images can help create a common visual vocabulary.

The director can also gather concrete examples that represent what "mood lighting" means to her. Searching the Internet, poring through magazines, looking through photography and art books, the director searches for the images that represent the mood, color, or look she wants. She may also use scenes from films that best evoke the kind of "mood lighting" she sees for her project.

Discovering the look, visual design, and color palette is a process of discovery. However, once the art director shares the director's vision, the two are able to, with cooperation from the DP, design a unifying visual and lighting plan that supports the story and theme.

The art director and I were able to pare it down to get the exact look and feel of what we wanted to be the art on the wall, the pictures on the back of the barber's stand, the kind of clippers that we wanted. Every little thing, every little detail we had worked out in nuance and stuff like that. We wanted the barber shop to look old in one particular time period and look new in another particular time period so we bought a certain kind of vinyl seat covers so that that way it would was clean so then when you cut back to the present day of 2006 it had the vinyl torn up and stuff like that. So all of those kinds of things we really worked through, we looked at, we tried to make sure that we nailed it because we knew that authenticity would read if you got it right. You take nothing for granted in that sense.

Be' Garrett

Basic Decisions

The art director will want to know whether the project is to be shot on film or video. Chapter 11 discusses the many formats. This choice will very likely have an influence on the art director's creative decisions, but it must be discussed before she starts prepping for the production.

Black and White versus Color

A good art director must have a comprehensive knowledge of color, color combinations, and the dramatic effect of color on an audience. She must also understand, if you plan to shoot with black-and-white film, as did Adam Davidson with *The Lunch Date*, the challenges of creating a world in shades of gray. Both color and black and white can subtly influence an audience's response to the visual story, but they do it in different ways. A red ball in a white room pops out in color film. In black and white, the ball reads simply as a gray object. The art director will consequently use different stylistic choices when she works with these two media to create the world of the story.

Breakdowns: Listen to the Script

The look of the project has its origins in the script and in the director's visual ideas for it. An in-depth analysis of the script affords the art director an understanding of the story, character, and theme evolving through the plot, all of which can and should be reflected by the art direction.

Sitting down and reviewing the script with the art director can be an enlightening experience for the director. The art director will delve into the minutia of every scene. Unless stage descriptions are very detailed, there are usually many questions that have to be answered. What does a room look like? How messy is messy? What statement do you want to make about the main character?

Sometimes the descriptions in the script are so general that it is wise to review each scene carefully with the art department before making any decisions. If the script calls

for a EXT. FOREST – DAY (as it did in *Citizen*), there will be extensive discussions as to what kind of forest the director had in mind. This kind of discussion occurred when Be' Garrett looked for the right barbershop for *A Nick in Time* and Howard McCain searched for his perfect gym for *Truman*.

The next important question is this: what is the audience seeing at any given time? This is why having a visual shot plan for your project is so important. If the director wants to establish a room with a wide master shot, the art director must be able to dress an entire room.

Consider an example of an art director's breakdown for one scene in *The Lunch Date*:

```
INT. LUNCHEONETTE–AFTERNOON
The woman walks into a station luncheonette.
  It is a simple place—a grill, some booths,
and rows of refrigerated cabinets filled with
salads and sandwiches. She reaches into a
glass case and removes a salad.
  A COOK stands behind a white linoleum
counter. He fiddles with his white paper hat
and white apron.
```

Art department personnel break down this scene from *The Lunch Date* by creating lists of what they have to rent, buy, or make:

- **Location**. The scene takes place in a luncheonette. The location needs to look as if it belongs in a train station. To find the appropriate location, the art director scouts for a real train station luncheonette. The location manager attempts to secure an actual luncheonette. If a real location cannot be found, the art director either builds a set on a soundstage or redresses an existing location to give the illusion of a working luncheonette. For this scene from *The Lunch Date*, the director decided to redress an abandoned lunch counter to look like a functioning establishment.
- **Set Dressing**. Once the decision was made to use the defunct restaurant, the art department created a plan to bring the location to life. That meant cleaning, putting up signs and posters, and adding elements such as ashtrays, salt and pepper shakers, napkins, and extra salads.
- **Props**. The key props for this scene included the salad, silverware, the woman's personal effects, her handbag, Bloomingdale's bags, and change.
- **Wardrobe**. The woman's wardrobe is the same throughout the piece. For this scene, the costumer needed to find a chef's hat and apron for the actor playing the cook.
- **Makeup and Hair**. No special concerns.
- **Effects**. No special effects.

Defining the Space with Visual Ideas

For adequate preparations, the director needs to give the art director the dramatic intention, mood, and visual elements of each scene as well as how she plans to use the camera as a storytelling device. Will scenes be "covered" traditionally, or will the camera be constantly moving? Is the director planning to use depth (wide-angle lenses) or shallow focus?

These ideas can be communicated through rough sketches, floor plans, storyboards, or even verbal instructions. Analyzing the script, scene by scene, the director and art director look for common ground from which to create a frame. How much does the camera need to see? What should the character's habitat look like? How much of the space needs to be art "directed"?

Communication is the key to a successful shoot. If you have a set with no ceiling piece and in your storyboards you indicate a low-angle shot that will include the ceiling, the art director must make appropriate arrangements beforehand. If the director decides on the day of the shoot that she now wants a low-angle shot, the budget probably won't cover the cost of constructing a ceiling that quickly.

Camera Tests

Depending on the nature and design of your project, it is highly recommended that you shoot tests with the actors in full makeup and wardrobe. Taking these test shots is an added expense, but it will clarify what you will be shooting during principal photography. Camera tests also inform the director and producer of the dynamics between the cast and crew in a work environment.

KEY POINTS

- Duplicates must be purchased, made, or rented for many items, such as food and wardrobe.
- Unless you shoot a scene only once, the art department will need to match each take with the previous one in terms of wardrobe, makeup, and hair.
- Much of art direction is an illusion. A piece of costume jewelry looks like the real thing to the camera.

Location

I brought my key people on a tech scout. My DP, art director, and line producer. My art director went into the location and saw what had to be done. We talked about choices and its relationship to the budget we had to work with.

Be' Garrett

PRODUCER

Securing Locations

In his task of securing locations for the shoot, the producer should communicate trust and confidence. People who might grant permission to use their home, restaurant, facility, loft, office, or building must feel that the production crew will take proper care of it. **This means the crew should leave the location in as good a condition as when they found it (if not better). This is a cardinal rule.** No matter how much or how little you pay for the location, this is proper professional behavior. The producer wants to establish a good reputation in the film community. It also might be necessary for the company to return to the location for reshoots.

Price, proximity, schedule—the producer sees all locations with these elements in mind. He negotiates for the location once members of the key creative team have made their choice.

If the director requests a particular location that is priced out of reach of the budget, the producer should suggest an alternate or backup location. Should the director insist on a particularly expensive location, the two will have to strike a compromise.

> **STUDENTS**
>
> If you are filming in your hometown, avenues can open up because friends and family usually want to help aspiring young filmmakers. Expensive locations such as cafeterias and office space can often be secured for little or nothing.

Where to Look for Locations

Following are some suggestions to pursue to find locations:

- See whether your city has a film commissioner at city hall.
- See whether your state has a statewide film commission (see Appendix G).
- Put up fliers on community bulletin boards, at schools, and at local media organizations.
- Look in the paper for apartments for rent and inquire at local realtors.
- Advertise in the local paper.

Sometimes, a house that is for sale can be rented for a short period of time. Ask friends, painters, and interior designers for leads. These methods are especially useful for finding locations and housing when shooting at a distant location.

Beginners are usually hesitant to contact city or state film commissions because they don't believe they will be taken seriously. This is not true. Film commissions believe in nurturing the next generation of filmmakers who will continue to shoot in their state. The commissions have already done the work of accumulating thousands of photographs of every sort of location available for filmmakers. This saves hours of legwork, and there is no charge for this service!

It's best to find locations as close to the production office as possible. When locations are 50 or more miles from the production office, the union rules governing professional actors and crew change. So, too, do the logistics, which will have an impact on the budget.

Take pictures of interesting locations with a digital camera so that photos can be stitched together for panoramic or 360° views of an area. A video camera also can be handy when scouting locations (see Figure 9.1a–f for a series of location stills from *Citizen*).

> I went looking for a restaurant, and it was difficult. I spent a few weeks going everywhere in New York, Queens, the Bronx, and Brooklyn looking for one that had a row of booths. By accident, I was walking down 43rd Street, and there was this burnt-out space, and next to it was a bar. I looked through the smoked-up windows, and I could see that it used to be an old diner. I went into the bar next door, and the guy said he would let me take a look around. The place was a disaster. There had been some sort of fire, probably an insurance fire. It was cold, water was on the floor, and

FIGURE 9.1 (a-f) Six location stills from *Citizen*.

the ceiling was caving in. It was also being used as a storage space for pretzel carts! But there were these booths, and it was the right style. I told him I was a student. He charged me $500 for the day, including electricity.

Adam Davidson

Scouting the Locations

A location scout is begun by the location manager (or location scout) although all key crew members can keep their eyes open for the best site. Once the number of potential locations has been narrowed down, the director,

director of photography, art director, and sound mixer (if he has been hired already) visit the prime candidate sites. When the final decision has been made, all department heads do a walk-through of the location called a **tech scout** as the director talks the crew through possible shooting plans.

To evaluate a location properly, consider lighting, power, sound, and other variables, in addition to the script breakdowns. Use the following location checklist—lighting, power, sound, green room, safety and security, proximity, and backups, the points that apply to your project—as a guide. Once a decision has been made, detail floor plans with exact dimensions (power outlets, windows, closets, etc.) should be created of each location.

> I knew I wanted the recruitment center to be at a school. My producer and I went to the various commission offices, looked at photos, and made appointments with various custodians at public and private schools. I was looking for something that said "high school" to me—a long hallway with lockers. I wanted it to look like a public school, but we ended up shooting at a private school, which had a very public school looking hallway annex. The hallways on the floors look more like Oxford. It was a fun little artifact, location wise. From there, we knew we were looking for a spare room we could art direct to look the way we wanted, and that was literally the boiler room. It was designed to look like a doctor or nurse's office.
>
> James Darling

Lighting

If you plan to shoot in one location for an entire day (either exterior or interior), create a chart of how the light moves across the space during the day.

- How will the scene be lit?
- Where is the light source?
- Where will your source light come from?
- If the location has windows, how long will the set receive direct sunlight?
- Is there ample space to place the lights in the location?
- Can you prerig or rough in any lights before the day of the shoot?
- Can you put spreaders on the ceiling without damaging the walls?
- Will you need to provide a fan to cool the room?
- For an exterior, will the sun provide adequate light for proper exposure, or will you have to supplement the sunlight? Will you need silks to even out the light?

Power

- Where is the power source?
- Does the power source have enough amperage to accommodate the lighting instruments you plan to use?

- Have you checked the amperage available at each outlet? The gaffer will calculate whether the lighting instruments can function with the power available. If there is not enough power, you will need to rent a generator.
- If you will need to rent a generator, do you have ample cable to run from a generator to the lamps?
- Is using a generator within the fire codes?

Sound

Locations are usually scouted long before the sound team is hired and often selected without any regard for noise or acoustic conditions. Unlike the camera lens, which can frame out items the director does not wish the audience to see, the microphone cannot be as selective in what it hears. A sound mixer cannot "frame out" unwarranted sound; background noise (traffic, air conditioners, planes, etc.) will permeate a set regardless of camera framing.

To prevent this intrusion of background noise from happening, the producer needs to alert the scout to find locations suitable for the story and those that will also be "sound friendly." Location scouts need to learn how to scout "with their ears," to examine a potential site with their eyes literally closed for 15 minutes. This is long enough to hear what is happening in the space. When visiting a site, the scout also needs to consider the issues described next.

Scout the location on the day of the week and at the time of day that you will be shooting. Visiting an apartment in an urban setting on Sunday when all is quiet will not indicate how the exterior will sound on a Monday with busy morning traffic.

- Is the location quiet?
- Is there an abnormal amount of traffic outside?
- Can you use sound blankets to dull the traffic noise?
- Is the outside noise the same all day long?
- Do the neighbors have a noisy dog or child that must be quieted?
- Can existing sounds, such as refrigerators or air conditioning units, be silenced during shooting?
- Can the shots be planned so that the microphones point away from the windows?
- Are there plans for construction nearby during the shooting period?

Also, be sure to research well in advance for any planned civic activities.

Green Room and Other Special Areas

- Is the green room (a holding area for the actors) far enough away from the set?
- Are there toilet facilities for the cast and crew? Is there someplace they can go to relax?
- Is there a quiet area away from the set where you can leave food out all day for the company?

- On an exterior shoot, is there a place where the company can retreat from the elements if necessary (preferably someplace inside, such as a coffee shop)?
- Can a dressing room be rigged for the actors? Will you need partitions?
- Where will the actors apply their makeup?
- Is there an area off the set to store equipment?

Safety and Security

- How will you load equipment into the building? If shooting in an apartment building, check whether there is a freight elevator. If not, ask whether the building superintendent will allow heavy equipment in the passenger elevator.
- Does the location require any security?
- Have you made arrangements to lock up any valuables?
- If the equipment is stored in a van and parked in a lot, is the lot bonded (insured)?
- Can the equipment be left in the location overnight?
- Do you need police from the city for traffic control?
- Are you performing any stunts or tricks that would require additional safety precautions?
- Do you have additional personnel to direct traffic or hold parking spaces?
- Do you have a fire sequence that requires a standby water truck?
- Are there stunts that require a standby nurse or ambulance?

Proximity

When deciding among several different locations, keep in mind that the crew will have to travel between them. Unless you are shooting your project a few days at a time, try to pick locations that are close in proximity to one another. This cuts down unnecessary travel time.

Backups

One final word about locations: it is highly advisable to secure a backup location in case the location you have chosen suddenly becomes unavailable. A standing set, one that is always at the ready, is called a **cover set**. This is the place where you might run on a rainy day.

One thing I have learned is that if you want something, you have to ask for it. There is nothing to be lost from simply asking—the worst someone can say is "no." This is especially true when thinking of locations. If there is a location you are interested in shooting in, do not be too intimidated to ask. Prepare your pitch beforehand. Explain to the owners that the property will be fully insured (this is usually a big concern for them) and make sure to let them know you are responsible and trustworthy. Keep your promises to them. If you tell a location that you will only be shooting there specific hours, adhere to your schedule. Put down cardboard to avoid damage to floors or carpets. If you are not paying them a location fee, offer to pay their electric bill for the month in which you shoot there (especially if you are going to take over their outlets and fuse box). Keeping the owners of your locations happy is essential to your shoot.

Jessalyn Haefele, Producer of *Citizen*

Securing the Location

You have now decided on the appropriate locations(s) for your project and need to contact the proper representatives. You must communicate clearly why you want the location and for how much time. (See our web site for a sample location contract.) The following sections describe the next steps.

Location Contract

- Have you signed an agreement between the company and the location owner?
- Is the person signing the contract indeed the owner of the location?
- Have you been honest about the time you require (here it is best to overestimate)?
- Have you promised in writing to return the location to "as good if not better" condition?
- Have you offered the location owner a credit in the end crawl?
- Do you have permission to use the restrooms?
- Do you have the option to return for reshoots written into the contract?

I had to find out if I could shoot in Grand Central Station. I found out that Grand Central is privately owned by Metro-North. I spoke to the public relations person there, and she said, "Yes, we love to help students." I asked about the cost, and she said it was free, as long as I didn't plug in any lights. Once I used their electricity, I would have had to pay some guy $15 an hour to sit there and watch the plug.

One of the stipulations for shooting in Grand Central was that I could only shoot between rush hours, 10 a.m. to 2 p.m. each day.

Then we ran into the usual hassles. Every morning when we got to Grand Central and started unloading the equipment, the stationmaster would come and kick us out. Because of the bureaucracy, the messages weren't coming through that we were allowed to shoot there. So we would run and find the woman in the publicity department—and get permission again!

Adam Davidson

Location Fee

- Have you negotiated a fair price for the use of the location?
- Does the fee include the use of power at the location?

STUDENTS

Even though someone may be willing to offer a location for free, some sort of compensation is recommended (however small). This payment elevates the exchange from a favor to a business relationship.

Permits

Every locality has its own requirements for securing permits. Make sure to research carefully.

- Have the appropriate permits been obtained for the time and place of the shoot?
- Are the permits on the set, ready to be shown to authorities?
- Sometimes you need to secure additional permits, i.e., stunts, special effects, weapons. Do you have all the permits you need?

Insurance

- Have you obtained adequate insurance for the location?
- Does the insurance cover all the types of shooting that you are planning?
- Does the owner of the location require any special insurance?
- Have you allotted adequate time to process the insurance forms?

Communication

- Double-check all location arrangements. Have you alerted tenants of the production's impending arrival?
- Have a phone list of people to contact if there are problems but limit this list to a select few (1st AD, locations manager).
- Make sure to confirm who will let you in and who closes up after you leave.
- Have you prepared maps and directions to the location for the cast and crew?
- Have the appropriate city officials been notified of your presence?
- Have you rented walkie-talkies for the crew? Locate a place at the location to charge them.

Transportation

Shooting sites, whether near or far, require that all departments, equipment, and actors be transported to and from the set. Transportation logistics must be planned in advance to maximize the time allotted for production. On feature films, a transportation captain is responsible for coordinating all this activity. On a short, the producer or the production coordinator must assume this responsibility:

- Rent vans, trucks, and cars.
- Arrange for drivers.
- Coordinate company moves to and from each location.
- Calculate the time required for each move. Allow extra time for problems.
- Make travel plans for distant locations.
- Find and secure all on-camera picture vehicles.
- Make parking plans for all production vehicles.
- Rent the proper car mounts for moving vehicles. Hire an experienced grip to set the camera. You might need to secure special insurance and permits for towing picture cars.
- Create proper signage to direct the cast and crew to the location.
- Calculate all contingency plans, including weather, gasoline rationing, disaster, and personnel problems.

During the production period, drivers are constantly out in the field picking up actors, special equipment, and supplies. Pickup times are designated on the call sheet, and adequate time should be allowed for traffic and trips to the gas pump. Drivers are responsible for the vehicles to which they are assigned.

At the end of the day, during the *wrap*, the drivers return to the production office to drop off actors, run to the laboratory to drop off film, or take the principals to screen the dailies.

Parking

- Have arrangements been made ahead of time for parking?
- Have the appropriate permits been obtained and posted?
- Will the vehicles ever be in the way of a shot?
- Do you need parking spaces for picture vehicles?
- Will the equipment be safe in a parked car, van, or truck? Is the lot bonded?
- Does a street need to be blocked off the night before a shoot?

Company Moves

If your project calls for several locations, you might need to move the production unit during the production day. The time it takes to wrap out of one location, travel to another, and then unload and set up the equipment can monopolize a big chunk of a production day. This type of move should be avoided if possible. If it cannot be avoided, factor the time into your production schedule and remember the following:

- Create a detailed daily transportation plan.
- Assume that each move will take longer than anticipated.
- Do not leave equipment unattended in a vehicle.
- Keep the gas tanks full at all times.
- Travel time is time taken away from principal photography.

Catering

Like an army, a production cast and crew run on their stomachs. However, providing food need not cost a fortune. Planning ahead will always save money.

- Calculate a meal plan schedule for the entire shoot.
- Audition caterers by having them prepare a meal.
- Check with the cast and crew for any particular dietary needs.
- Have coffee and healthy munchies available all day (craft services).
- Provide hot food for the midday meal if possible.
- Arrange a place where cast and crew can sit down for the midday meal and a short rest.
- Make provisions for a second dinner should the day's shooting run longer than anticipated.
- Assemble a list of local restaurants around the location of the shoot.

DIRECTOR

Scouting Locations

As important as it is to choose the right actors for the piece, it is equally important to choose the right world, or at least the illusion of that world, for those actors to inhabit. The credibility of the story depends on it. By seeing where and how the characters live, we learn about who they are even before being introduced to them.

The texture and feel of an environment can quickly and efficiently bring us into the province of a story as well as communicate exposition about the characters. Locations have symbolic meanings. What does a particular environment do for the story? How can a specific locale enhance or detract from the script? Will the setting lend itself to an interesting visual background? This is subtle information that must be communicated. Your choices should not be arbitrary.

It was crucial for the audience to feel that they were in a metropolitan train station for *The Lunch Date*, in a real gymnasium for *Truman*, and in a real barbershop for *A Nick in Time*. The mannequins used as backdrops in *Mirror Mirror* served to visually

represent society's ideal form. Every aspect of the sets in *Crazy Glue* made us feel we were in a real clay location.

> I take location scouting seriously so I hired a location scout. I had someone go out and take pictures of places that I thought might work and then we scheduled a date to go out and look at them, myself, my line producer and my location scout. We went out and looked at them and we came back with some places that we liked and once I went there I really kind of fell in love with one particular barber shop because it had the authenticity of being in two different time periods. It's in Brooklyn.
>
> Be' Garrett

Aesthetic Concerns versus Practical Limitations

Location scouting is an exciting and inspiring time for the director. The goal is to find places that represent the words on the page. You must find a balance between your aesthetic concerns and your practical limitations. The aesthetics of the location are based on the dictates of the script. A "dingy bar" does not mean the Oyster Bar at the Plaza Hotel, a "suburban house" does not mean an apartment building, and a "small park" does not mean a forest. The search for the appropriate location means ensuring that what the viewer sees on the screen is what was indicated on the page.

The practical considerations for choosing a specific site are based on what the budget can afford and the schedule will allow. A specific apartment might excite the director visually, but it might also involve inherent problems for one or more of the production departments. There may not be adequate power for the lights, it may be in a noisy neighborhood, or it may be too small or cramped. Balance is the key to a final decision about where to shoot a sequence.

> The location became important to me early on. I saw getting a gym for a week for free and getting it near where these kids come from as a big problem. So I spent a great deal of time nailing down the gym. Then I could dream about it and mentally place my characters there. It wasn't just something I was hoping or wishing for. I knew it was there and that it was mine.
>
> Howard McCain

Be Flexible

Learn to be open and flexible. Don't look at locations (as with actors) with fixed ideas. Often a director will find a location that she never considered but that exceeds her expectations. Visually dramatic locations have been known to inspire directors. The director will then either alter the script or envision a completely new scene to incorporate the location into the script. If you are in a real bind, you can always alter the script to accommodate locations that are available. This may sound like a compromise, but it could end up having a positive impact on the production.

The Power of Illusion

As in so many aspects of production, you can employ tricks with the location to create illusions the script requires. For example, you can create movie magic by transforming a less than exciting site into a glamorous one described in the screenplay. The art department can work miracles to redress a location to look like the required setting. If the shots are specified, the redressing need only be done for the angles the camera will see. If you avoid shooting telephone wires and cars, your local park can look like a forest. By carefully choosing your camera angles and lenses, you can make a large loft space look like a tiny apartment.

In addition, you don't have to find your ideal location all in one place. A home can be pieced together out of many rooms in various houses that seem to fit together. Suppose, for example, that an actor walks out a door and the camera picks him up in the corridor. He walks to an elevator and gets in. We are inside the elevator with the actor. He alights into the building lobby and crosses to the front door. From outside, we see the actor come out onto the sidewalk. This could all be done at four different locations: a corridor, an elevator, a lobby, and a building exterior. The audience assumes the locations are all part of one building.

The cafeteria in *The Lunch Date* was not actually adjacent to Grand Central Station (it was several blocks away), but the audience connected the two because the filmmaker did. Adam Davidson did this with the sound. In both the station and in the cafeteria, we hear intermittently a train station announcer calling out track numbers and destinations over the public address system. Hearing the announcer in the station and in the restaurant binds the two locations together. What is amusing is that there is no public address system in Grand Central Station. The filmmakers went to Penn Station to record the announcements! Finding everything in one place is convenient but is not essential.

James Darling's art director made the audience believe that the young man in *Citizen* was crossing the border back to the United States by designing and building a simple "Welcome to the Unites States of America" sign (see Figure 9.2).

Many concerns about location are applicable to both narrative and documentary forms. With documentary subjects, however, you may not have any choice of where you film. Characters live and work where they live and work. The challenge is to work within the confines of each location and do it as unobtrusively as possible.

Each of the short films explored in this book is defined by the space in which it was shot. *The Lunch Date* employed New York's Grand Central Station; *Truman* was shot in a gymnasium (see Figure 9.3); *Crazy Glue* had its two sets, an office and a living room; and *Mirror Mirror* was photographed on a soundstage (see Figure 9.4). *A Nick in Time* was filmed entirely in one barbershop, and *Citizen* was shot in a high school and at several exterior locations within 50 miles of the home base.

FIGURE 9.2 Sign: "Welcome to the United States of America" from *Citizen*.

FIGURE 9.3   The gymnasium in *Truman*.

FIGURE 9.4   A set built on a soundstage.

Identifying the Location

Each location is broken down into four categories for identification: interior or exterior, day or night, stage or practical location, and near or distant. These are the major factors you must consider when scouting your shooting environments.

Interior or Exterior

The location you are identifying will either be interior (INT.) or exterior (EXT.): inside or outside. Both of these location settings carry with them a variety of factors to be weighed when determining a suitable background. Interiors are easier to control, but exteriors are less confining. Interiors can be blacked out, or tented, and shot at any time of the day, whereas the shooting schedules for exterior locations are dictated by the sun and the weather.

Day or Night

The script will indicate whether the scene is a day scene or a night scene (or dawn or dusk). Exterior day scenes mean that the source of light will be the sun. Remember that the sun has an arc, the sun may go in and out of the clouds, and daylight saving time reduces the number of daylight hours. Interior night sequences can be shot during the day if the windows are blacked out.

Stage or Practical Location

A scene will be shot either on a shooting soundstage or in a practical location. The stage is an ideal environment for controlling both light and sound, but the facility rental fee can be expensive. Practical locations look real but come with problems relating to space and control.

Stage

There are three main factors in determining whether you should use a stage.

Cost. Soundstages can be expensive. Check out prices. An unused stage might be rented to a film crew for a limited period at a reasonable rate to make a short. Empty warehouses and empty floors of buildings can be used as a stage. However, they are not soundproof.

Control. Soundstages exist for the sole purpose of providing the director with a soundproof, controlled environment in which to shoot. Stages provide a grid for hanging lights, which can be a major problem on a practical location. Stages come with unlimited power, heating and air conditioning, offices, dressing rooms, parking, telephones, bathrooms, and other conveniences that make the shooting process more convenient and comfortable than in a practical location.

A stage gives you the freedom to build any set and any backdrop (see Figure 9.4). There is adequate room for the placement of lights, camera, and sound (unless it is an insert stage). This undisturbed freedom can translate into a focus on the job at hand that might not be available in a practical location. If the production team on location has to stop and start constantly due to noisy neighbors or cramped quarters, it drains the energy on the set.

> I knew from the outset that I was interested in shooting it in a studio. Although I have done only location shoots in the past, with *Mirror Mirror*, I wanted to use the studio sets to make a visual statement and thereby enhance the themes of the film. I felt that to have a woman talking about her body while seated in front of bookshelves in her living room or at her kitchen table would make a boring talking-head film.
>
> Jan Krawitz

Sets. If sets are required, they must be constructed. A stage is an empty shell that can be outfitted with walls, rooms, facades, and backdrops. The art department will rent or build walls, ceiling pieces, furniture, rugs, ashtrays, lamps—the works. Transforming an empty space to a lit set takes time. Constructing, furnishing, and striking the sets are additional costs that need to be factored into the stage rental.

Practical Location

Practical locations have two bright sides. The first is the cost. If your budget is tight, a soundstage will most likely be out of the question. Practical locations might be expensive, or they might be free. If the cost of a location is high, most likely the cost to reproduce the location on a soundstage will be higher. The second advantage of a practical location is "the look." A practical location will always appear real to the camera, whereas it is a challenge to make a set look like an actual location.

One of the main drawbacks to a practical location is the "boxed-in" feeling. Walls cannot be moved; ceilings cannot be raised. Lights must be set off camera in limited space. When the camera, lights, boom, actors, and crew are all assembled, the quarters are cramped, hot, and confining. Keep several fans on set for air circulation. In a cramped set, even the choice of lenses will be limited by the space allotted. An additional drawback is that often power is limited, which may require renting a generator.

Near or Distant

Your location, whether it is a practical location or a stage, day or night, interior or exterior, will either be near to the production office or distant from it. Having to transport cast and crew to and from the location is a major budgetary concern. If you employ union actors (SAG), the definitions of *near* and *distant* are very clear. On a map of the area of your production, circle everything within a 50-mile radius (because zones differ in each city, do your research). Any location within the circle is considered "near," and any location outside the circle is "distant." For a distant location, actors' travel time is factored into their hourly rate as if it were part of their workday. Also, a near location does not require the production company to transport the actors to and from the set.

Even if your company is a small unit with a van and several cars, traveling to and from the location uses up valuable time that might be better put into production. If a suitable location is found closer to the production office, precious time can be shaved off the production schedule.

> It had to be something, first, that I could get for a week and, second, was located near the kids. I made *Truman* in Rochester, New York, where I grew up. This helped because I was able to draw from all of my connections. I got free scaffolding from a high school friend whose father was in the construction business.
>
> Howard McCain

If the location is so distant that plane or train tickets as well as hotel accommodations become necessary, your budget will need to reflect these costs. Employ a local contact person to smooth over rough edges with locals and to receive any goods or communiqués the company needs to send. There are some distinct advantages to working on a distant location. The cast and crew will bond quickly. The locals at most distant locations see a film or video shoot as a novelty. This may translate into *cooperation* and possibly free goods and services.

The following is a narrative from Jessalyn Haefele, producer, of the steps that were taken in scouting the locations for the film *Citizen*.

James Darling, his mother, and his brother John went on an initial tech scout over the holidays to some state parks out on Long Island, including one called Hecksher Park. In addition, they drove upstate to Ward Pound Ridge Reservation, a heavily wooded area that James was familiar with, having shot another friend's NYU thesis there. James also was in contact with a friend at NYU, Alex Russek, whose family owned property near Pound Ridge. This property included a very long deer fence cutting through thick woods. James felt that we could possibly build our wall onto the existing fence. James sent Ryan (our DP), Erica (our production designer), and me pictures from the tech scout and then we all got together to discuss.

After the holidays, James, Ryan, Erica, her art director, Matt, and I drove out to Heckscher State Park to take measurements and do a more thorough tech scout. We met with the park ranger and photographed our location. Ryan and James walked through the scenes that would take place in those areas and James showed Erica what he wanted in terms of production design. While Ryan and Erica measured, I did my own location assessment. It's very important to know where things are while you are shooting on location. I surveyed the area. My initial questions are always the same:

Where are the nearest bathrooms? (This will ALWAYS be important to know on any production!)

Is there an area we can use for equipment holding?

Where can we park our trucks and cars?

Is there an area that can become a dressing room/hair and makeup for actors?

Is there an area that can serve to hold crew and cast?

How will we generate power at this location? Are there outlets? Where is the nearest fuse box? (And if you are shooting outside and will be using a generator, is there an area you can move the genny to away from the shooting area?)

Is the location residential? Will the neighbors complain of noise from a genny and bright lights outside at night?

Is there an area we can use to hold craft service and serve meals? Where do we dispose of trash?

Our group then went to visit the Russek property, the location where we would build our giant "wall" and shoot some scenes in the woods. The path leading from the house down into the woods was steeper than any of us had imagined, and Ryan (DP) began to worry about how the heavy film equipment would be dragged to the bottom of the hill where we were shooting. It was very possible for someone to fall on the rocks everywhere. We noticed a cleaner path leading directly into the woods near where we stood, but it turned out that the path in question belonged to a dour neighbor of Alex's. Alex wasn't sure that she would allow us onto her property, but I knew we had to ask. So James and I went to her house. We explained to her what we wanted to do, and the magic words, "We have insurance and would insure your property." She agreed to let us shoot there as long as we did a small favor for her: there was a dead mouse in her garage, and she wanted us to remove it. (I let James handle that one!)

Jessalyn Haefele

Walk-throughs

Once you have secured the locations, it is advisable to call for a walk-through with the key personnel (DP, art director, 1st AD, and sound mixer). During this floating production meeting, indicate how you will place the camera for the scenes in that particular location. The DP can sketch out a lighting plan so that on the day of the shoot, the gaffers will know where to place instruments and how to locate power. The production sound mixer can identify problems that might conflict with the track. All the department heads can ask questions during the walk-through. It is, in essence, a dry run of the production.

KEY POINTS

- Scout your locations with the full crew before the shoot.
- Try to centralize your locations.
- Arrange for locations with written contracts.
- Make sure you have backup locations.
- If possible, prerig an interior location by dressing it in advance and roughing in the lights.

Chapter 10

Rehearsals

We had one day of rehearsals. I had one day with the cast that was in the past and one day with the cast that was in the present. So, my two casts never met each other until we actually had a screening of the film because it was two different stories that were tied together.

Be' Garrett

DIRECTOR

Working on Scenes

One of the director's primary responsibilities is to assist the actor in discovering and playing his role. The director accomplishes this through script and character analysis and staging. Once casting has been completed, the character development process begins with rehearsals.

During the rehearsal period, the following takes place:

- The director gets to know the actors.
- The actors bond with each other.
- The director and the actors develop a mutual trust.
- A character research method is devised.
- Fresh approaches to scenes are explored.
- Scenes are shaped, beats are discovered, and business is created.
- Blocking is worked out.
- The director and actors develop a shorthand for communicating on set.

Do not wait until the cast is assembled on the set during principal photography to rehearse. This puts unnecessary pressure on the director, especially a beginner. Although the scene can be rehearsed on the set, time will not allow for long rehearsals with the entire crew standing by at full pay. The crew's presence can be distracting, and their salary is a drain on the budget. The set can be cleared for rehearsal, or you can move the cast to a separate space while the crew completes their preproduction work on the set. This might cause some delay in the day's schedule, but it is better than rushing a scene.

> The first goal in rehearsal was getting Truman's confidence and trust.
>
> Howard McCain

Before Rehearsals

Getting to Know the Actors

Before rehearsals, the director can meet with the actor in a casual, nonworking setting. This is an opportunity to begin developing a rapport. There is little pressure in a meeting of two artists simply talking about their work. You might ask the actor questions like these:

- What are your work methods?
- How were you trained?
- How do you like to approach the development of a character?
- What does this character want (in the short and long term)?
- How do you see this character in relation to the other characters and to the plot?

You might discuss the following with the actor:

- Your working method
- Your feeling about the material
- Your interpretation of the character
- Your plan for a shooting style
- Any difficulties you foresee in the production

In *The Moviemakers' Master Class: Private Lessons from the World's Foremost Directors* by Laurent Tirard, film director Sidney Pollack talks about his experience of working with actors:

> My principal interest is in relationships. For instance *Three Days of the Condor* is about trust. You start with a spine. Even the set must reflect the central idea. I never give an actor directions in front of the other actors. The first thing I do is keep the actors from acting. I say: no acting, no performance, just read the lines. That relaxes them a lot. What I am trying to do, really, is hold the acting until it happens by itself. Because it will. Pretty soon they'll start moving around as they say their lines, and you'll get a sense of what they want to do. The actor needs only to understand what he needs to live truthfully in an imaginary set of circumstances. Because all acting comes from wanting something. It's want you want that makes you do something, not what you think.
>
> Sidney Pollack

doi: 10.1016/B978-0-240-81174-1.00017-8

Developing Mutual Trust

Discussing the actor's character casually over coffee starts the process of discovery and trust in the director–actor relationship. Discovery is the process of finding things to help build the character, of seeing the character grow. Trust allows the director to be an integral part of that growth. Trust developed now will carry over through the rehearsal period and then onto the set. Without trust, unfortunately, there is usually friction and miscommunication.

> The first aspect of rehearsal is actually no rehearsal at all. . . . I took Truman out for ice cream; we played video games and did "kid things." It was a way to gain his trust and make him feel comfortable.
>
> Howard McCain

Researching the Character

An actor starts to build a life for his character based on the text. All the information that the actor and director need to develop a character should be found in the script. The author will have indicated important physical characteristics, emotional motivation, and pertinent surroundings. The story itself is the key to the arc of the character. For example, in *Moby Dick*, Captain Ahab begins as a rational and collected character. During his journey, as revenge comes near his grasp, he starts to lose his sanity. He will do anything to kill Moby Dick, no matter what the cost. The journey of that character, which spans the course of the novel, is referred to as **the arc** of the character. We say that a character has an arc when there is a discernible and significant change in that character. The range of change in a short film is significantly smaller than in a feature, but change is still possible as evidenced by the characters in *A Nick in Time, Truman,* and *Crazy Glue.* The woman in *The Lunch Date*, however, does not. Leaving the cafeteria, she rushes past a homeless man begging for change and then almost lunges into the train with a sigh of relief. Whatever shift of consciousness she might have experienced in her "lunch date" was only temporary.

Most importantly, the director and the actor should be in agreement throughout the shoot on the arc of the character. Filmmakers rarely record the scenes in screenplay order. If you must shoot the last scene first, it is imperative that you know how the characters arrive emotionally at that point in the story. Knowing the emotional arc of the piece allows you to shape each moment so that there is an appropriate dramatic build. If the final scene is played too low key, you will have nothing toward which to build. Conversely, if the final scene is played at a fever pitch, the actors might never be able to build truthfully to that pitch over the course of the shoot.

Back Story

The actor develops his own character under the director's guidance. Many actors will, after studying the script, do their own homework and develop a detailed biography or back story of their character. Everything the character does in the story is rooted in the patterns of the past. Knowing what that character experienced growing up, the relationships with family and friends, and the ups and downs of life furnish depth and credibility to the performance and allow the actor to be able to justify everything his character does in the story.

On the other hand, there are some actors who simply rely on the script for inspiration. You need to respect all approaches. For the actors who need some guidance, you can share some of your ideas. You may need to mention only a few key elements of the character's history. Then allow the actor the time and space for his own discovery. The more inexperienced the actor, the more help he might need from you. You can also suggest that he develop his character by observing and studying similar characters. If his character is based on a real person, the actor can research material written about that individual and can seek out audio or visual records of the person's life, not with the goal of literal imitation, but to discover some essential characteristics. Ultimately, your job is to stimulate the imagination of the performer while still respecting his own methods of character development.

> So, I had one day with my actors of the past and we sat down and we brought in clippers and we talked about the script and part of what I usually do in my rehearsals is we just talk at first. We talk about what is it they want out of the film, what are they looking to do, who are they, what are their experiences. I am learning about them the same way they are learning about me. They don't know me at all, but they have to trust me at some point. Then from there we kind of warm up into talking about the script and I get their feelings about the script. What are the things they like about the script and what are the things they don't like about the script.
>
> Be' Garrett

Rehearsals

Benefit of Rehearsal

The rehearsal period is a good time for the director to meet alone with each actor to explore ideas, to encourage, develop, or make adjustments. This period may also reveal problems with a particular actor, his working methods, or his chemistry with another actor. These kinds of problems can lead to a part having to be recast. Without a rehearsal period, these problems could surface on the set when it is too late. Unless you are able to shut down production, your only choice is to shoot around the actor until you get a replacement.

As the formal rehearsal period starts, it is important to keep an open mind. This should be a process of discovery. You may already have very specific ideas about blocking or how characters should play their parts. Keep them to yourself. Don't steer the rehearsals in the direction you think they should go. There are many ways to play a scene. Follow the creative energy of the actors and the spirit of collaboration. Explore the possibilities of the material. This process may open doors you never thought existed.

Read-Through

The first step of rehearsal is to assemble the entire cast for a read-through of the script (before they have memorized their lines). This will give you and the cast an idea of how the whole piece flows and let everyone become familiar with the dramatic arc of the piece. It is an exciting experience and the first opportunity to address where potential problems may exist, such as in a particular scene, an actor, or even both. The read-through provides an opportunity to see how the actors interpret their roles and how they all work together.

Actors should be encouraged to use natural movement if they feel it is appropriate, although the primary purpose is to focus on the meaning of the words. Give little or no direction; you want to see what they spontaneously bring to their role and to the piece. Encourage the performers to work together. Although you have strong ideas about how the piece should be played, be receptive to your actors' input. This approach will send a message that you respect them as intelligent and creative people, that they are partners with you as you mutually explore the dramatic possibilities of the script.

The first read-through might reveal problems with the script itself. Is a scene too long? A scene or part of a scene that feels totally extraneous should be eliminated.

> We do a dry read. From the dry read eventually we go into acting it out a little bit. Then from there we might give them a couple props to play with. As a result of this everyone starts to warm up to one another. We videotape all of this as well, because I look at it later to refine my script as well as learn about the actors, looking for nuances.
>
> Be' Garrett

Develop the Theme

The read-through is the appropriate time to discuss the theme of the story. It is not about critiquing the script but how each actor experiences the material and his role in it. Ask your actors to discuss the purpose of the story. This discussion might reveal a wide variety of opinions. Encourage all points of view, but impose none of your own at this time. Try to avoid lecturing; rather, adopt a way of directing the actors' attention to the meaning of the piece with probing questions. Even if you have written the script, you may discover new approaches or possibilities that you hadn't considered. Use the actors' intelligence and sensitivity to explore the outer reaches of the story, remembering that as director, you always make the final choices. Allowing the actors to participate at this juncture will involve them even further as creative collaborators. The goal is to have everyone on the same page, but if it is jointly arrived at, the actors' commitment to the film is strengthened.

Keep Notes

Remembering all your impressions during the rehearsal period can be tough. Because you will need to always stay on top of what is going on, early impressions may be taken over by later ones. Avoid this situation by carrying a large scratch pad on which you can occasionally write brief notes.

Scene by Scene

After you have explored the arc of the story and its theme, you can now begin work on each individual scene. Try to rehearse the scenes in their order in the script; this way, you can create some continuity. Don't worry about the memorization of lines (so you can avoid the actors getting locked into a specific reading). It is more important for the actors to understand the meaning of a scene than to know all its words. Work with defining conflict, character objectives, and, ultimately, the development of subtext.

Start off by not giving the actors too much instruction. Have a clear idea of what you want to achieve in a scene, but remember that the director should be flexible. An actor, following the flow and inclinations of the character, might discover a completely new approach to the material. Learn to guide actors in the direction you want to explore, but do not hinder their creativity.

The British director Ronald Neame (*The Odessa File, Hopscotch*) told this story during an interview with the American Film Institute:

I first learned this lesson from Alec Guinness of being completely fluid when I go on the set.... As a director the first film that I made with him was *The Promoter*. It was only the third film I had directed. I had got it all beautifully worked out. I had done my homework. We came on the set one morning and I said, "Alec, I thought that maybe you should do this, that, and the other thing."

He said, "Well, Ronnie, I've been thinking. I'd rather like to play this scene lying on my back underneath the table."

I said, "Lying on your back, underneath the table?"

He said, "Yes."

I said, "Well, you're out of your mind, Alec. What's that got to do with the scene?"

He said, "Now wait a minute. Don't get impatient. Just bear with me a minute." Of course he suggested something in relation to the scene and it was absolutely marvelous played on his back underneath the table. That was the way that we shot it.

If an actor can bring you something and wants to do it his way, provided that he is following the character accurately and he's not being absolutely stupid, then he should be encouraged to do it this way.

Ronald Neame

The goal of every actor is to have the camera capture every moment as if it were happening for the first time. There is no such a thing as rehearsing too much as long as you are exploring deeper layers of meaning within a scene. The director needs to be sensitive to her actors and should strive to find a balance that will allow the actors to be "fresh" during principal photography. If the actors perform for the camera as if they have been drilled, the performance will lack spontaneity; therefore, some directors do very little rehearsing. They want to save it for the camera. You will develop your own style, based on what you find works successfully for you.

Tape the Rehearsals

Once the actors have memorized their lines and are moving freely around, it is useful to shoot the rehearsals with a video camera. This can be done with a continuous take or documentary approach so the flow of each scene won't be interrupted. The camera operator can move or zoom in for closer shots when appropriate. A few of the benefits of taping the rehearsals are as follows:

- Taping provides an opportunity to judge the work on the screen from seeing what works on the screen.
- The cast becomes comfortable with a camera present.
- The director may catch subtle mannerisms in an actor that may need to be addressed.
- The director can begin to see where best to put the camera and from what angle.

These videotapes become part of the director's homework for shaping performances and for planning her visual approach for the project.

Special Situations

The director is often faced with a great diversity of acting styles from the talent she employs within a scene. Some actors are trained to improvise; others are trained in a Method school of acting. The director will need to use all her wiles to meld these acting styles and special situations together so that the scene looks as though everyone on-screen is part of a whole.

Shape the Scene

Blocking Action

When *blocking* or choreographing a scene, don't "show and tell" the actors what to do. Instead, allow the scene to grow organically. Start the actors with no movement, perhaps seated. When it is indicated in the script or when the actors feel compelled to make a move, they should do so. Little by little, as the scene is repeated, various actions, known as *business*, will evolve, and the scene will begin to take shape. The idea of business is to integrate authentic behavior into an actor's performance. Examples of business are the lighting of a cigarette at a key moment in the scene or the jiggling of a set of keys to break a tense moment of silence.

It would be ideal to rehearse each scene in its "real" location, allowing the actors to interact specifically with their surroundings. If this is not possible, try to simulate the location. Use masking tape to mark out the floor plan of the location, including the walls, windows, and prominent set pieces. Then when the actors arrive on the set or location, they will already be familiar with it.

> We actually took the lead actor up to the location where the fence was in the midst of being built. In terms of physicality, he actually ended up digging the hole that he ended up going into. We all helped, but he got really into it. He was like, well, if I'm going into this hole I want to be sure I could fit in it.
>
> James Darling

Discovering Beats

Just as the director breaks down the scene into shots and angles, she must also help the actors break down the action into dramatic beats. This process enables the actors to develop the arc of their character moment to moment. Each scene has many small beats that together make up the major objective of the scene. As we established in the breakdown chapter, beats are influenced directly by character objectives. Each character has his objective for the whole story, each scene, and the beats within each scene:

- The woman in *The Lunch Date* wants her salad.
- The young man in *Citizen* wants to leave the country.
- The barber in *A Nick of Time* wants to avoid a confrontation with the young man.
- The boy in *Truman* wants to climb the rope ladder.
- The wife in *Crazy Glue* wants her husband's attention.

The script gives each actor a situation. The actor explores with action and with dialogue how he might respond. With each change of the situation, a new beat begins. The director and the actor explore the beats of each scene together.

When the young man in *A Nick in Time* wants to go to the bathroom, the barber knows that he must stop him (he knows the cop has his gun drawn under the barber's cloak, but we don't). The barber's objective at that point is to stop the kid from going to the back of his barbershop and possibly save his life without letting the kid know that he is "on to him." This is the major beat and the turning point in the story.

This is all apparent in the text and in how the director has broken it down into beats in preproduction. Occasionally, the director finds that what read well on paper does not play well in action. Often, action can replace dialogue or might render words unnecessary. The luncheonette scene in *The Lunch Date* is a good example of a scene in which a few lines of dialogue and a wealth of silent business and reactions create a full conversation. The rehearsal process is an excellent opportunity to trim any fat from the script or to revise the dialogue to accommodate blocking, props, or set pieces.

> Part of my rehearsal process is to improvise. If you are in the moment and you are playing the moment, the words generally take over and you feel what needs to be said. Sometimes it is better than what you have written.
>
> Be' Garrett

Improvisation

During the rehearsals, directors and actors often like to improvise a scene to help clarify the meaning of the scene, the subtext, or the dramatic beats. Improvisation is a spontaneous use of invention in which the actor keeps the character and the situation but is not tied to the text. Knowing which actors are comfortable with this form of work should be addressed early in the process.

For example, suppose a scene from the script is set at a park bench. A man is attempting to break off his relationship with a woman. The director can ask the performers to improvise the scene many ways, with each performance exploring different and subtle emotional nuances within that particular situation:

- The man can't go through with his speech.
- The park is empty.
- The park is crowded.

In the middle of the improvised scene, the director might add information to the situation; for example, it begins to rain, the woman begins to cry, or a nearby musician plays "their song." During the scene, the director might whisper a direction to the actor that will further adjust the direction of the scene. For example, she might tell him, "You suddenly realize you love her" or "Try to get the ring back." Each of these whispered directions will allow the actress to react without prior knowledge of what the director desires. An interesting discovery made during an improvisation can then be used in the scene.

The use of improvisation is an effective way to loosen up the actors. It can help the director discover new meaning in a scene as well as learn how well the actors play off each other in unscripted situations. Improvs can also lead to discovering interesting staging ideas and novel bits of business.

> Because there wasn't much dialogue for Truman's first rehearsal, we played some games. He pantomimed climbing up a rope with his eyes closed as well as various other little physical actions. Then I asked him to draw me some pictures—pictures of what he thought his character looked like and what he felt.
>
> At the third session, we brought in the gym teacher so they could get comfortable with each other. They just talked and had a hamburger. From there, we actually did some minor improvs between the two of them. I had Jerry pretend to be his father. From that I could gauge how the little boy would react to him as a figure of authority.
>
> Howard McCain

Pace and Rhythm

Pace is defined as the rate of movement or progress. It is the amount of time required to bring the audience to the height of the emotions the scene requires. This is a primary responsibility of the director. During rehearsals, the director and actor determine the pace of each moment, each scene, and ultimately the entire show. The director can then instill the project with a pace, which can make or break it. If the actors peak emotionally too early or too late, the delicate fabric of the story can be torn. The director memorizes her feeling of the pace during rehearsal so that she can be objective during the shooting period and remind the actor both of the pace itself and of how the pace fits into the arc of the story. Once the performances are recorded on film or tape, any further adjustments to the pace can take place only in the editing room.

Four key directorial phrases are often employed during rehearsals and when photographing a scene: louder, softer, faster, and slower.

However, rather than imposing these words arbitrarily on a performer, encourage him to "use urgency" or "take your time" at a certain point of the scene, thereby allowing the pace to come out of the character.

An equally effective means of controlling pace is to give the actor a new objective or action. If a scene seems to be dragging, tell the actor, for example, that he has just learned that his friend's house is on fire and he needs to call the fire department. This action or directive will inject a more organic urgency to the scene.

Communicating on the Set

The director and the actors constantly refine a scene by honing beats, restructuring dialogue, and inventing business. With each adjustment, they come closer to developing a shorthand for communicating what they want to do. The director's notebook will include important details based on her observations during rehearsals and her private conversations with each actor. She will discover that certain kinds of directions work better than others. The director relies on these notes so she can say the right thing on the set to trigger the performance she seeks. The next time the director and the actors will work together is on the set, where time will be a critical factor. If they can work efficiently together, problems relating to script and performance can be solved quickly.

> We spent a long time going over the script, page by page, examining each thing that would happen—where Scotty would be, what was going through the character's head, etc.—which paid off in the end because I could do things on the set like say, "This is just after you lost your wallet, and this is going to happen next," and Scotty would know where she was, in terms of the character's emotions. We didn't actually rehearse until the day we arrived on the set.
>
> Adam Davidson

Comedy

Comic acting is based on talent, skill, and timing. Many comedians excel at improvisation; spontaneity is an integral facet of the comic actor's skill. Because timing is so critical in comedy, it often takes considerable time to work out a routine or even a moment within a scene. Chaplin was famous for rehearsing on camera. He sometimes shot a sequence a hundred times, constantly refining the routine until the only business left was his exit through a revolving door.

Comedy is serious business. Just because the crew laughs doesn't mean that the scene will play in a screening room. The director is the only audience on the set who matters. If she thinks the scene is working, she can shoot it and then move on.

Understatement

Whether the scene is dramatic or comic, understatement will always work better than overstatement. It is easy for actors to play big, broad, and loud. For one thing, it feels good to use their instrument with full broad strokes. The line or moment that is understated, though, has twice the meaning. The camera picks up the most subtle details. The director needs to carefully watch actors who were trained for the stage. Their tendency is to play a scene to a large audience. In film, less is more.

Untrained Actors

Working with untrained actors can be both rewarding and frustrating. An untrained actor might be a natural for the part, but he will not be familiar or comfortable with the technical aspects of the actor's craft. Working to find a character, sustaining a performance, shooting out of continuity, and even hitting marks will be a mystery to him.

> In this situation, the director must be especially patient. She should explain the process at each step, coaxing a performance out of the actor. With an untrained actor, it is permissible to give a line reading, which means asking the actor to repeat a line just as the director delivers it. Ask the performer to think the line before saying it. One of the things I did in terms of casting the film was I worked on food lines at Grand Central every night before filming, and I saw this guy Willie the night before. He had this harmonica and this great face, and I asked him to show up.
>
> Adam Davidson

Interviews

Documentaries are based on spontaneity. The subject of a documentary is not an actor, so there is no rehearsing for a scene. Often, the director is in the field with a camera, capturing the subjects as they go about their lives. This doesn't mean the subject is totally "cold." A documentary director might inform the subject before the interview what topics and questions she might introduce. This gives the subject an opportunity to think about the shoot and how she might phrase her answers. Most importantly, the interviewer must be prepared and have a clear expectation of what each interviewee will contribute. There may even be pre-interviews conducted in person or on the phone.

In *Mirror Mirror*, the director interviewed her subjects using a set of questions she felt would reveal interesting material on the topic of women's bodies. (These questions are listed in Chapter 15.) From the hours of responses to her questions, she pieced together a story that captures the spirit of her subjects.

> I met these women a month before the shoot. I did not want to give them the questions in advance because I knew that if they thought too long about an answer, the responses would lose spontaneity. So when they arrived at the set, I said to them, "You're going to be seated there, and I will ask two questions. Then we'll move over here and do two more questions." I told them that any time they wanted to stop between the questions, they should let me know because I knew that the mask got hot. So I let them know that they were somewhat in control of the process.
>
> Jan Krawitz

Sometimes the director must probe for the kinds of answers she feels will best match the script she has previsualized. This approach might require asking provocative questions designed to stimulate the subject.

PRODUCER

Rehearsal Schedule

The producer is in charge of the logistics and planning of the rehearsal schedule. As soon as the parts are cast, make a list of everyone's availability and work out rehearsal times. Most people find it easier to work to a predetermined schedule, and it communicates an aura of professionalism. Make rehearsals brief and frequent rather than long, comprehensive, and potentially exhausting. You want to keep your cast fresh and lively; too long and there could be the issue of diminishing returns. Schedule the rehearsals in a quiet room or a setting similar to your location and make sure refreshments are available. There should be no crew, no equipment, and no time pressure—just the work.

> We had a soundstage for a day. We read a few times. They were on books while reading it, so they didn't need to memorize it. I just had to find a good performance and to direct them a bit, and that was it. It was very easy and fast.
>
> Tatia Rosenthal

During this time, the producer is finalizing the main cast's contracts and keeping abreast of how the rehearsals are progressing. It's during rehearsals when the first signs of a needy actor may become apparent, so a producer needs to have his finger on that pulse!

KEY POINTS

- The goal of the rehearsal period is to work out the beats and the business. There will be little time to do this during production.
- The process of discovery is everything. Once you know how the piece should work, it will inform all aspects of principal photography.
- Use the rehearsals to develop a mutual trust with the actors and a shorthand for communicating with them.
- There is a fine line between rehearsing too much and rehearsing too little.

Chapter 11

Camera

Once we arrived at a shot list I hired a storyboard artist. He had a program that allows you to storyboard on the computer. We sat down in his apartment over the course of several days and boarded out the whole film. Everything had been worked out.

Be' Garrett

DIRECTOR

Collaborate

All the planning, storyboarding, and previsualization that occur during preproduction are translated into a finished product during production by the camera. The camera is the tool through which the director realizes the script. The use of this tool is limited only by the imagination of the filmmaker.

Cinematography is an illusion—a magic trick. It is 24 still frames projected each second to create the illusion of a moving image. Video is captured at 29.97 frames per second (fps) although many HD cameras offer multiple frame rates of 24p, 25p, 30p, 29.97p, 23.98p, or interlace formats (60i, 59.94i).

The illusions the director can create through cinema are boundless. Almost every aspect of film can employ a cinematic trick, perhaps a computer-generated optical effect, a miniature set, or the use of paste jewels in place of real gems.

Keeping Up with Technology

Technology moves quickly. It is an extremely complex area, and this is a book about the process. There are many excellent technical books and an array of web sites that do an excellent job of reviewing and explaining the dense and complex digital world of production and postproduction. For more detailed information about the current line of Panasonic and Sony equipment (the major suppliers of standard-definition and high-definition cameras and equipment), log on to their web sites at www.panasonic.com and www.sony.com. For more independent evaluations of the current market, and, ultimately, what's best for you, there are web sites put up by professionals and teachers. We have listed other such sites on the book's web page.

At the upper end of the digital video revolution is the RED Camera. It is capable of filming high definition at an amazing 4,520 lines of horizontal resolution. Known as "4k" technology because the scan lines exceed 4,000, it WILL POSSIBLY be the future industry standard (more about this camera later in the chapter.)

> Whether to shoot digital or film; I believe that film still has certain things over HD. HD is closing the gap in leaps and bounds. A lot of the films I watch and then I go back and research them, I find out many of them have been shot in HD and I could not tell the difference. So, I think it depends on the project itself whether to shoot HD or not.
>
> Be' Garrett

Style

What is a filmic style? It is the particular way each filmmaker uses the language of sight and sound to tell the story. The style can reflect the personality and sensibility of the director. Style presents itself with

- How a director chooses to stage the action of the script
- Whether she prefers to stage the action in fluid shots or break down the action into "traditional" coverage
- What lens she prefers to use (how much of the world is presented)
- Whether she loves to move the camera or rarely moves the camera
- How she approaches lighting as an aesthetic (high key, low key, etc.)

When choosing a style for a project or when developing a personal style of her own, the director should look first to the history of the medium. She needs to know what has come before so that she can help originate what will come after. The language of film is a relatively new vernacular (it's about a hundred years old), but it is rich in tradition and ripe for innovation.

A personal style comes only after acquiring knowledge of the craft and by much experience. By thoroughly understanding her craft, the director can respond to and meet each situation in production with confidence. Why a director makes a decision, alters a shot, or adjusts a

doi: 10.1016/B978-0-240-81174-1.00018-X

performance is based as much on her intuition as on her knowledge. In the heat of principal photography, it is often an improvised moment, a jury-rigged set, or an accident that makes for exciting dramatic moments. The director may find it important to experiment with various styles, even imitating those of directors she admires, until she settles on a style that fits her own particular way of seeing the world and expressing herself artistically.

Listen to the Material

When choosing an appropriate visual style for your project, work inside out, not the other way around. Don't shoehorn your idea into a style; discover the visual style that best suits your story. An inappropriate style will just call attention to itself and possibly throw your audience out of the story. If your idea is best represented by a static camera, resist the impulse to move it.

Personal identity with the form and the subject is what makes for a strong visual style. Jean-Luc Godard said, "Style is just the outside of content, and content the inside of style, like the outside and inside of the human body—both go together, they can't be separated." This is excellent advice.

Just as I had to write every version of the movie, I visualized every version of the movie as well. In my first draft, I was imagining it as a fake documentary, so it was going to be handheld, dirty, and grimy. But a crystallizing moment came after my roommate suggested I watch the TV show *Lost*. I watched that show and I wanted my short to look like that. It is the most cinematic show on television, easily. They are shooting in such an epic location—Hawaii, as this island— but they do a really good mix of standard, very traditional filmmaking like slow push-ins and beautiful epic crane shots, but then they'll mix it up with a lot of handheld stuff, too. They just use the perfect shot for every moment. That's the kind of work I want to be making in my career, so I need to make my calling card live up to that. I was also inspired by Christopher Nolan's aesthetic and Stanley Kubrick. I tried to do some Kubrician shots too, definitely, but those three influences were what I was trying to go for.

James Darling

Documentary

One cannot categorize a particular documentary style. Subject matter and the director's point of view are the starting points. The raw material can come in the form of footage of people and places, people talking, interviews, reenactments, library or archival footage, graphics, still photos, etc. The range of possible subjects includes social commentaries, poetics (such as *Baraka*), nature subjects, historical subjects, educational subjects, experimental subjects, traditional subjects ("talking heads"),

voice-overs with visuals to illustrate the text, or cinema vérité/direct cinema.

One of the keys to developing a documentary style that is appropriate to your subject is being flexible and open. As you delve into the world of your subject (research), an appropriate style or stylistic approach will take shape. Immerse yourself in the classic examples of the many and varied documentary forms. Only by being exposed to the possibilities of what can be done can you begin to know how your idea will take shape.

Do Your Homework

The success of principal photography depends on proper preparation. During preproduction, the director creates a plan on paper in the form of storyboards and floor plans. She might tape some scenes to evaluate their cinematic qualities. She balances her shot list with the planned schedule and determines at this point that, barring catastrophe, she will be able to realize her vision successfully. The director's "homework" gives her a thorough understanding of what she wants to see at each moment of the story, how she wants to manipulate the audience with sights and sounds, and how she plans to effect her vision (see Figure 11.2. One page of the director's homework from *A Nick in Time*. Our web site contains more examples).

The director brings weeks of work and preparation to the set. The seriousness with which she has approached the project will not only prepare her for the shoot, but will rub off on the cast and crew. People will follow an organized visionary anywhere. Her vision and the way she communicates it will evoke respect in the entire team.

Introduce the Camera During Preproduction

It is highly recommended that you work with a video camera during your preproduction rehearsals to experiment with different ways to photograph each scene. The frame is as much a part of the scene as are the actors. What is included in the frame, what happens there, and how it moves are all part of visual storytelling. Some of the benefits are

- The mobile camera does not inhibit the actor's freedom of movement.
- The cast soon ignores the camera and you can expect natural and unrestrained performances.
- The camera is choreographed into the process, allowing for more organic ideas to emerge.
- The director can explore different cinematic options to photograph each scene.
- The director judges what works on-screen from *seeing* what works on-screen.

FIGURE 11.1 For *The Lunch Date*, studying the light at the location meant scheduling a shot for a particular time of day.

Consult with the Director of Photography

A successful director taps the creative resources around her. The camera crew executes the director's visual ideas for each scene. The director of photography (DP) heads the camera team and is responsible for translating those ideas and creating the look and feel of the story. A good working relationship between the DP and the director is key to a successful shoot. Along with the art director or production designer, the DP realizes the dreams of the director. Their relationship is like a marriage; there has to be a productive synergy between them. Following are some of the key functions of the director of photography.

In Preproduction:

- Study and analyze the script, characters, and world of the story.
- Collaborate with the director and production designer on the style and visual approach to the picture.
- Consult on choices for colors and textures for sets and locations as well as makeup and hair.
- Scout and collaborate on choice of locations.
- Consult with director and producer on the type of film or digital camera.
- Choose and approve the camera crew, film stock, lab, and equipment.
- Generate an equipment list for the camera, electric, and grip.
- Estimate and order film stock (if shooting film).

- Estimate the type/amount of digital storage needed for shooting (if digital).
- Consult with the production manager on the shooting schedule.
- Walk through locations with the director and devise a shooting plan.
- Visit cast run-throughs and rehearsals.
- Shoot tests for stock, style, lab, camera and lens, or any special effects.
- Participate in planning visual effects such as greenscreen.
- Devise a shot list with the director if requested.
- Design a lighting plan and rigging for stages and locations with the gaffer and key grip.
- Walk through locations and stages with all departments to discuss requirements.

In Production

- Watch rehearsal of scenes to be shot.
- Collaborate with the director with on lens choice and composition.
- Design lighting to support the story, style, and dramatic content of the film.
- Make sure the mood and tone help tell the story.
- Match the light value for each setup (exposure).
- Design lighting for minimum setup time between setups.
- Work out any technical problems with the camera operator, assistant camera, dolly, and crane grips.
- Work out any sound problems.
- Manage the photography of each scene.
- View dailies with the director, producer, and editor.

Bob's movements show a purpose & resoluteness that is genuine not cocky like earlier before the mistake (He felt like he had to prove himself) 10.

IDEAL:

8   INT.   BARBERSHOP - DAY   (FLASHBACK)   8

I think whom-ever I cast as the Bob character young :ola I will need to send them to barber ing school or tutorial w/ Ty or Ade in Philadelphia. They must look like a real barber confident w/ a razor or barber's clippers.

Bob quickly grabs a pair of clippers and begins to fix the
Judge's hair. Bob eyes the clock, Bessie sitting across from
him and then back at the Judge's hairline.

Note: All of the eye shots and facial expressions must imply a tension that has the audience uncertain of what is going to happen

                    JUDGE *(peeks at the clock)*
          What's taking so long?

                    MR. LEE
          How's it going?

Bob doesn't answer immediately. He looks at Bessie, who
looks at Mr. Lee and then back to Bob. A moment of silence
is shared between the two.

Bob demonstrate a subtle confid-ence that helps ease Bessie's anxiety enough for her to ex-tend him the chance to correct his mistake.

                    BOB
                (hesistantly)
          Everything is fine.
                (to the Judge)
          Not much longer sir.

Bob commences to fix the Judge's hair.

9   INT.   BARBERSHOP - NIGHT   9

Evan nervously taps his foot on the floor.

Ted looks Evan over from head to toe. Evan leans over,
studies the chess board.

                    BOB
          Do you play?

                    EVAN
          I wish.

Bob walks to the sink and washes out the shaving bowl. ~~Bob
looks out the window and sees the FIGURE across the street
walk out of view.~~ He motions Ted with his eyes to look out
the window.

                    BOB
                (to Evan)
          Come by and I'll teach you some time.
          Chess is a lot like life. Every move you
          make has a consequence.

Bob, turns off the water and walks back over to Ted. Evan is
surprised by Bob's offer.

                                                     (CONTINUED)

FIGURE 11.2   One page of the director's notebook for *A Nick in Time* (for complete notebook, visit the companion website).

Postproduction

- Photograph additional scenes or reshoot existing scenes if necessary.
- Color time the picture.
- Supervise and approve film or digital transfers to electronic or film media.

The DP should be thoroughly versed with the storyboards and the floor plans developed during preproduction. These tools will help him translate the director's ideas efficiently into shots and enable him to create lighting designs for the floor plans and ultimately realize the director's vision for the script.

Until the film is processed, there is no sure way of knowing whether all the ideas created in preproduction and during the shoot were executed properly. This is one advantage of working with tape or tapeless formats, where, for better or for worse, you see the results immediately.

> **STUDENTS**
>
> The DP should be allowed to choose some, but not all, of the shots. He should be able to express his creativity on the set, but not be allowed to take over the show. This situation can occur if a director is tentative and indecisive. In this scenario, a creative vacuum can develop, and it is usually the DP who, by default, fills it. On the other hand, a dominating director will reduce the DP to a mere technician. This scenario might cause resentment and affect his overall performance on the picture. The best solution is a healthy creative partnership in which both the director and the DP "own" the visual design of the film.

Camera Team

The DP must be able to accurately assess the crew demands of the shoot and work within the parameters of the budget. The camera department consists of the director of photography (DP), camera operator, 1st assistant camera operator, loader/clapper, and stills photographer (keep in mind the 3–30 rule for student shoots). The gaffing department lights the scene (see Chapter 6). Under the direction of the director of photography, electricians move lighting instruments that will illuminate the set or location. The DP and the key grip are in charge of moving the camera. If the director calls for a complicated shot, the DP and grip will find a way to maneuver the camera to best advantage. Given enough time, they will find a solution to almost any problem.

> We chose to shoot on super-sixteen millimeter film. It is less expensive than thirty-five, but more expensive than video. And, more importantly, I thought super-sixteen would give us the look that felt very cinematic. And at super-sixteen if

> I ever decided to blow it up to thirty-five it would still hold its integrity. What you get with film is a richness and a scale in terms of the look of the film that appears bigger than what it is.
>
> Be' Garrett

Basic Decisions

The format (either film or digital video) to use may have been decided early in the preproduction and budgeting process. This decision may hinge on getting a good deal from a rental company or for a film student; it may be dictated by what equipment the program offers. It also may be influenced by what the DP recommends and has had success with in the past.

Film still offers the greatest latitude, but it comes with built-in expenses (film stock and processing). However, as of the writing of this edition, rental houses in larger urban areas are offering competitive prices on Super 16 and 35mm film cameras, and because more and more production is migrating toward digital, film labs are offering great deals on the cost of film processing.

The expanding digital market, the advent of 24p digital video, and multiple HD formats have expanded the choices available to beginning filmmakers. DV, HDV, HD, and now Digital SLR cameras like the Canon 5D Mark II and Nikon D90 have entered the arena. Then there is The RED at the higher end of this spectrum. Following are some of the considerations:

- Will your choice of a format hold up on the big screen?
- Is your format sufficient if your film is going straight to the Internet or an iPod?
- Are looking for a more "film-like" look without shooting film?
- Are you interested in images that look great out of the camera, or do you plan to do a lot of compositing or color correction in post?
- Will you shoot tapeless or with tape? Documentary shooters may opt out of tapeless formats because that will require having a laptop to download the P2 cards.
- Is flexibility important? Do you need to be able to "run and gun"?
- Are you planning to shoot greenscreen?
- Does your DP have the skills to work with the format you choose?
- What can your budget afford for camera rental?
- What are the production and location challenges of your project? Are you shooting primarily interiors, exteriors, or a blend of both?
- What kind of lighting package can you afford? Don't think that digital needs less light than film. In fact, it may need more. Film's stocks are rated at 500 ASA!
- Are you shooting color or black-and-white?

These new toys have appeal, but as we like to stress, a good story well told can be shot on whatever you can afford. Instead of putting your money on a high-end camera, it might be better served spent on a good cast, crew, art direction, locations, food plan, and above all, a great script. Audiences are only wowed by compelling stories and interesting characters.

Use of Color or Black-and-White

The choice of filming in either color or black-and-white will have a defining impact on aesthetic and practical considerations. Visual ideas have to be geared to the palette you are working with. Black-and-white film renders images as tones of the grayscale, whereas color duplicates the colors of the visible light spectrum. Your choice, whether it is black-and-white, color, or even a combination of the two, will have a significant impact on the audience's emotional response to the story. It will influence not only how locations, props, and costumes are chosen, but the budget as well. As was discussed in Chapter 8, the sets, costumes, and locations read differently in black-and-white than in color.

Imagine a wide shot of a playground on a gray day. A boy in the background bounces a ball. To keep the viewer's eye on the boy, the director has him dressed in a red shirt and makes sure that he is the only element in the frame that is moving. If the same scene were filmed in black-and-white, the boy's red clothes would translate as a shade of gray, hardly an eye-popping item. To attract our eyes in a black-and-white world, they boy would have to be dressed in a white shirt.

What must also be thought out and planned carefully is the *meaning* of color in your story. There is no one set formula. Red doesn't have to always signify "danger"; it can imply a range of emotions or feelings. It can signify whatever you want it to, as long it is used consistently as a motif in your story. It is up to you and your creative team to form your own set of color rules throughout the film.

Black-and-White

In *The Lunch Date*, the black-and-white photography contributes a timeless feel to the film and a storybook quality (see Figure 11.1 from *The Lunch Date*). One of the film's greatest attributes is that the story can be appreciated the world over. Black-and-white, when used properly, can be beautiful. One only has to look to the history of film to find endless displays of cinematic beauty crafted in black-and-white by the great Hollywood and European cinematographers.

The inspiration to shoot in black-and-white begins at the script stage. You may feel that your story idea feels better suited to this palette. For the beginning filmmaker, shooting in black-and-white can be a more "forgiving"

format. Color film is balanced for either daylight or incandescent light. Both DOUBLE-X and PLUS-X (Kodak's black-and-white negative stocks) can be shot with a variety of lights balanced for different color temperatures, interior or exterior, without requiring any special filters.

> I had thought a lot about shooting in black-and-white, but I wasn't sure. I started talking to the director of photography about the possibility of shooting in black-and-white. It turned out that it was going to be to our advantage because without lights, black-and-white is a little more forgiving.
>
> Adam Davidson

Color Palette

The color scheme, or **color palette**, refers to the actual color of the objects (sets, props, and wardrobe) in the picture. Designing and executing a color palette that best serves your story is a complex challenge, even for a professional. It starts with the problem of communication and color identification. Let's say you want to use red as a motif in your film. Your DP or art director will ask what kind of red you are thinking of. The problem is that everyone has a different idea for even the basic primary colors of red, blue, or yellow. Just go to a paint store to see swatches of all the "red" colors that are available.

Learning color basics will help bridge this gap. Three terms can be used to describe any color: **hue, brightness**, and **saturation**. *Hues* are the basic colors: red, green, blue, cyan, magenta, orange, yellow, and violet. *Brightness* refers to how much "white" is mixed with the color, and *saturation* (also referred to as *chroma*) refers to the purity or intensity of the hue. A fully saturated red is extremely vivid; it has no other colors mixed with it. The opposite of saturation is *desaturation*. A color becomes desaturated or less vibrant when it is mixed with its complementary color.

How Can Color Be Controlled?

The best way to control color is to limit the color palette itself. Remove the colors that clash with the general motif you plan to use for your film. If you want your film to be red and saturated, place only red and saturated objects in the frame. An experienced art director knows how to balance and mix the right colors to achieve the "look" you seek for your film. However, as we stated a number of time in Chapter 8, the art director's ideas must be coordinated with the DP.

Color can also be controlled during production in a number of ways. Any of these techniques should be tested in advance.

- **Lens Filters.** Filters can be used on the camera lens to alter the color of the image. For example, adding a yellow filter on the lens will make objects in the shot look more yellow. The filter doesn't add yellow; it removes the complementary color (blue), which makes yellow appear more dominant. A wide range of filters can be used in this way.

- **Lighting Gels.** Placing colored gels on lighting units will alter the color of the light falling on the subject. Standard gels are usually calibrated in degrees Kelvin and can accurately warm up (with an orange gel) or cool down (with a blue gel) the color of the lighting.
- **Time and Location.** Color can be affected by the time of day when you shoot, the color of your location, and the specific weather conditions. The color temperature of daylight (measured in degrees Kelvin) changes as the sun moves across the sky. A sunrise appears more lavender, noon daylight is bluer, and sunset is redder in tone. Filming during what is referred to as the "magic hour," a short period of time (actually much less than an hour) when the sun is already below the horizon, produces a special quality of soft blue daylight. To see this effect beautifully rendered on film, watch the Terrence Malick film *Days of Heaven*. Weather conditions, such as an overcast sky, will make the daylight bluer and cast an even glow to the images.

The color of light can also take on the dominant tone of a particular location. For example, the light that filters through the leaves of a forest is greener than that coming directly from the sky.

> We definitely had some conversations with both the DP and the art director about colors. We wanted all the winter stuff to be really cool color wise and the doctor stuff to have kind of a fluorescent green and yellow kind of feel, both to sort of ground things in. We needed to establish that these were different places and different times. That was how I thought of the look.
>
> James Darling

Film Stock

Color can also be controlled by your choice of film stock and how it is exposed. Different film stocks have different color characteristics depending on the manufacturer (Kodak or Fuji) and the ASA (the sensitivity to light) rating of the particular stock. Generally, the lower the film's ASA number, the more saturated the colors will appear. Some stocks look warmer or cooler or more or less saturated. Lower-speed stocks (less sensitive to light) have traditionally had finer grain and sharper images, and faster-speed film stocks (more sensitive to light) have had more noticeable grain structure.

Film stocks are balanced for either indoor or tungsten light (3,200° Kelvin) or daylight (around 5,400° Kelvin). (To put this in perspective, a normal incandescent light is rated around 2,700K; and a candle, 1,800K.) Most films are shot with **negative film** stock rather than **reversal**. (Reversal film is processed to a positive print. There is no "negative." It is the equivalent of shooting 35mm slides.) Negative stock can handle a greater range of lighting conditions and is more forgiving of exposure errors. It is easier to make a good quality print with a good negative than in reversal. Labs offer more options and services; some don't handle reversal at all. There are also far more negative stocks on the market than reversal.

There are only 2 black-and-white negative film stocks available for 16 and 35mm, but there are approximately 10 different negative color stocks available from Kodak and 7 from Fuji. Kodak's Vision 2 and Fuji's Eterna stocks offer a range of speeds from 50 ASR to 500. For more information, it is best to go to the Kodak and Fuji web sites.

The questions most beginners struggle with have to do with mixing stocks with different speeds, as well as indoor and outdoor ones. They become concerned with the artistic consistency of style. Many of these decisions come down to price, availability, and flexibility. Your DP should be your guide in the selection of a stock. If you are in any way unsure, make sure to shoot multiple tests of different stocks.

The ascendancy of color in the film industry makes it difficult to find laboratories that do high-quality black-and-white processing (see Alfa Cine in the Bibliography). Good contrast is the key to this beauty. When the blacks turn muddy or there are no clear whites, the image looks dull. On the other hand, a print with too much contrast has a short tonal range and looks harsh. Films that mix black-and-white and color are printed on color film stock. Balancing color print stock to achieve a pleasing black-and-white look can be difficult, however.

Digital Video Format

For the videomaker, videotape stock or tapeless formats (P2 cards) have no inherent visual qualities. It is the camera's pickup tube or its charge-coupled device (CCD) that determines the sensitivity to light and color.

Because of the use of high-end postproduction software in the marketplace, directors and producers should be aware that doing "too much" in camera (experimenting with visual effects) when shooting on a digital format is often not advisable. The hue, brightness, saturation, contrast, resolution, sharpness, and exposure latitude can be programmed into the camera.

Most film editors will tell you to "shoot it clean" and create your stylistic effects in postproduction. Filmmakers have more options in the editing room if the unprocessed "raw" image a short has been shot in contrasts to locking into an effect or style that the director may want to change later.

Tests

Many elements (film stock, digital format, lens size, filters, lighting effects, etc.), combined with the director's aesthetic design for a shot, are calibrated to cause a specific result. If the result the director wants is complicated or out of the ordinary in any way, it is recommended that tests be made in preproduction to determine how the desired results can be achieved.

We recommend shooting tests (as we have stated a number of times in this chapter) in any circumstances, and if possible, with the exact equipment you will be using on the shoot. Doing so is especially important if you are deciding on which film stocks to use. Kodak and Fuji offer a wide range of choices, so there may subtle differences that can be confirmed only after doing a test under circumstances that resemble your visual style.

> My DP was really big on using floor plans. I drew some rough storyboards of the character when he was moving through obstacles and the tall grass on his way to the wall, but most of the shots were determined by the locations which we were securing at the last moment.
>
> I had story boarded a sequence for the location we had secured for the U.S/Canadian border but then we lost that location and I had to restage my whole visual plan. At that point, I stopped storyboarding.
>
> James Darling

The Camera as Storyteller

No one on the set, from the DP to the set dresser, can begin to work until the director makes two decisions: first, where the camera will be placed, and second, how the actors will move in front of the camera.

The writer uses words and sentences to convey thoughts and ideas. The camera is the director's storytelling device, and shots are the basic element of the director's visual vocabulary. In placing the camera, the director or DP will ask, "Is the camera in the right place to tell the story properly? Are we seeing what we want to see?"

All other camera decisions, including size and composition of the frame, derive from this basic judgment. To determine where the camera is placed, ask yourself, "From whose point of view is the scene experienced? Who is doing the seeing here?" Is it a main character's point of view, or that of an unknown bystander or the omniscient storyteller? The point of view can shift from objective to subjective within a scene, but you should always know from whose vantage point the scene is unfolding.

The director decides how to present the action to the audience. She uses the camera to direct the audience's eye to what she feels is dramatically or visually important.

These are some of the important decisions that have to be made:

- Where to put the camera (the motivation for the shot)
- What to put in front of the camera (how to choreograph the action)
- How much of the action and/or information is contained in each shot
- How much of the world to reveal in each shot (size of shot: wide to telephoto)
- Whether that action should be broken up into several shots or one unbroken take
- Whether it is a static or moving shot
- Whose point of view the shot is from
- How the shot will cut to the next one
- What the rhythm and pacing of action are from shot to shot

The camera is normally placed at eye level. This is the position at which an audience sees the world. In the shot of Truman shown in Figure 11.3, even though he is eight feet off the ground, the camera has been placed at eye level, affording the audience the opportunity to share Truman's difficulty holding onto the rope. Altering this perspective by either moving the camera higher or lower or to the side can affect the audience's response to a scene. They will instinctively feel that something has changed.

It is commonly expressed that a camera placed low, looking up at a character (see Figure 11.4), makes that character seem powerful. This perspective can be used to create this impression, but there are no rules that state it has to. Orson Welles shot with this perspective throughout much of *Citizen Kane*; it was integral to the visual "style" of the film. The other commonly held truism that if the camera is positioned to look down slightly on one character, it makes the other characters seem superior is another film cliché. Hitchcock often placed the camera high above a character for a variety of filmic purposes.

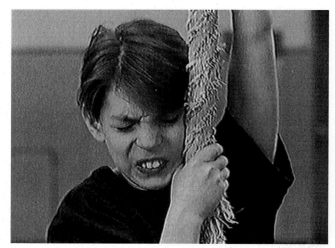

FIGURE 11.3 Camera placed at eye level from *Truman*.

FIGURE 11.4 Low angle of the barber from *A Nick in Time*.

The point is that your narrative should define how the camera functions; it is the context for a shot that gives it its meaning. A low-angle shot in your story may signify something very different than presenting the character as "powerful." You may want to show the character dwarfed by his surroundings. Each shot should fit into the overall visual plan of the film. To suddenly change the visual rules of what has been established to try a "cool shot" will most likely disrupt the audience's connection to the story.

Another important decision is whether the shot is objective or subjective. Distant shots tend to be objective. They are inherently neutral and well suited for the storyteller's point of view. The closer the shot, the more subjective it becomes. Point-of-view shots, the most subjective, place us completely in the character's personal experience of the scene. We are literally seeing what the character is seeing (and hearing), intensifying the audience's identification with the character. Both *Citizen* and *A Nick in Time* start

with point-of-view shots. The opening frames of *Citizen* contain a few shaky seconds of what we will eventually come to discover is the young man's point of view as he is trying to run from the border guards. The opening sequence in *A Nick in Time* establishes the barbershop through the eyes of the policeman who is the first customer.

Characters speaking to one another with the camera directly over one character's shoulder (over-the-shoulder shots or OTS shots) also create a subjective point of view. Techniques for playing a scene along this axis, or eye-line, are discussed later in this chapter (refer to Figure 11.29).

Directors often use low- or high-angle or pull-back shots to signal the finale of a story. In the final shot of *The Lunch Date* (see Figure 11.5), like many closing shots, the director has chosen to put the camera on the ground to show the train speeding away from the station for dramatic effect. (See also the high-angle shot from *Truman* shown in Figure 11.6.)

Coverage = Shot List

The ideas developed with the DP during preproduction are transformed into floor plans, storyboards, and finally a shot list. This is typically called **coverage**, the director's plan for photographing the film. The shot list represents the sum of all the shots that go into the making of a sequence and eventually the whole film. There might be 20 different shots that make up, or "cover," a one-minute scene, or one shot that covers a five-minute scene.

A traditional approach to coverage is to shoot the important elements of a scene from a variety of angles or points of view. When pieced together in the editing room, they provide the director with a variety of choices

FIGURE 11.5 Low-angle final frame from *The Lunch Date*.

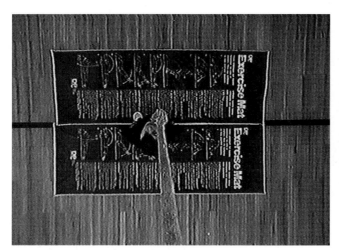

FIGURE 11.6 High-angle from *Truman*.

by which to control rhythm and pacing as well as the performances of each scene. The scene with multiple shots—perhaps a combination of a master shot, two-shots, close-ups, and dollies—is picked apart in the editing room, taking 10 frames from one angle, 20 feet from another, and so on, until the scene has the desired pace and rhythm.

Although you will carry the script and all these breakdowns with you onto the set, it's a good idea to write down the shots that you plan for each day on a three-by-five-inch index card, perhaps putting a bright-colored asterisk on those of highest priority. Keep these cards in your pocket, and as the shots are completed, tick them off one by one. At the end of the day, all the shots listed on the card should have a check next to them (see the sample shot list in Chapter 3).

> We got most of the shots I needed. I would have loved to have had more cutaways. I wanted things like a comb going into the barber's side and it just drops in. Little small little nuance things. Before I shot I consulted an editor and said to him could you take a look at my script and read it and tell me what you think I should get. He said to get a lot of texture. Shoot everything. Get a lot of cutaways. He said make sure you get your sound recordist to get the sound of the actual barbershop, what is happening there and then tell him to go outside and walk around the neighborhood and get a bunch of sounds and get all kinds of things that you don't even think about, but later on you might need. I would have loved to have had a third day.
>
> Be' Garrett

Type of Shot (Traditional Coverage)

Staging for the Camera

Staging, or blocking, is at the center of the director's craft. Blocking is the physical manifestation of the drama through the actions of the actors. The director can block the camera,

the actors, or both. Everyone needs to know where the actors will be moving and then how they will be filmed. It is the point of contact for acting, cinematography, and editing. Following are the ways in which the director organizes her staging ideas for the camera:

Master. Generally, the master is a wide establishing shot of the scene. (An establishing shot and a master shot can be the same.) Often, an entire scene is first shot in one complete master. The actors can be staged to the camera (static master), or the camera can be staged to the actors (moving master).

Shooting a master allows the actors to feel the organic flow of the scene from beginning to end, before the director breaks down the scene into individual shots. It establishes everyone's spatial relationship to one another and the specific actions that have to be duplicated each time the director shoots the scene from a different angle (it's the job of the continuity person to keep track of this information). By establishing the geography of the setting early on, the master shot also prevents the audience from possibly becoming confused. (see Figures 2.5 and 11.41 from *A Nick in Time*).

Minimaster. In a long scene, coverage can be broken up into several short, or minimaster, shots. Whereas a master shot for *Truman* might take in the entire gymnasium, watching the action in that large setting would soon prove boring. Moving the camera to the action, but still keeping the angle wide, affords the director an opportunity to stage a good deal of the scene as a minimaster (see Figure 11.39).

Four-Shot. Any scene with four actors in the frame at the same time is a four-shot (see Figure 11.14 from *Truman*).

Three-Shot. Any scene with three actors in the frame at the same time is a three-shot.

Two-Shot. Any scene with two actors in the frame at the same time is a two-shot (see Figure 11.8 from *Crazy Glue* and 7.3 from *Citizen*).

It is worth noting in the example from *Truman* shown in Figure 11.9 that height becomes a factor when staging a two-shot. Having the coach squat down puts the two characters at a similar eye level, thus making the two-shot and over-the-shoulder shot easier to execute. Had the

FIGURE 11.7 Extreme close up from Citizen.

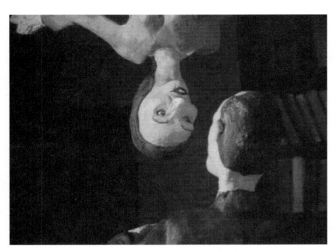

FIGURE 11.8 Unique two-shot from *Crazy Glue*.

director kept the two characters standing, both the two-shot and the over-the-shoulder shot would have been awkward.

If the director chooses to have the two characters stand, the two-shot would have to be very wide to accommodate both characters' bodies. An over-the-shoulder shot would have required a tall ladder behind the coach and a low-angle high-hat shot for the complementary angle behind Truman. Sometimes this is unavoidable. Even when it is unavoidable, it is permissible to cheat slightly the true distance between the characters' heads. An apple box could be used to bring Truman closer to the coach's size (see Figure 15.2).

Over-the-Shoulder Shot. A shot of one actor speaking to another when a portion of the second actor's shoulder appears in the foreground of the frame is an over-the-shoulder,

or OTS, shot (see Figure 11.10). This shot allows the audience to get closer to each character while keeping the other one still in the frame.

Single. A single is a shot of one actor. This can be done as a close, medium, or wide shot. In shooting a dialogue scene with single shots, film the reverse angle with the matching camera position and frame size so the eye-lines connect with each other. This will maintain the integrity of the 180° line (look ahead to Figure 11.29) and create a smooth editing pattern when you cut back and forth between the two shots. In the two shots of the main characters in *The Lunch Date* shown in Figures 11.11 and 11.12, the woman is looking left to right and the man right to left.

Close-up. A close-up is a tight shot of a portion of a frame, an object, or one actor's face and shoulders. In shooting a close-up of an actor, know that when the character is looking toward the camera (see Figure 11.32), we are placed in a closer relationship with that subject than if she were framed in profile. The profile shot places us in a more neutral relationship; the character is more distant.

> When they were sitting at the table, I covered the scene in a standard way. I did a medium wide shot, both of them in frame, and then came in for close-ups. Then I got insert coverage of the plates.
>
> Adam Davidson

The Frame

Think of the frame as a picture frame surrounding a painting. But different from a canvas that an artist works with, your frame has fixed parameters. A painter

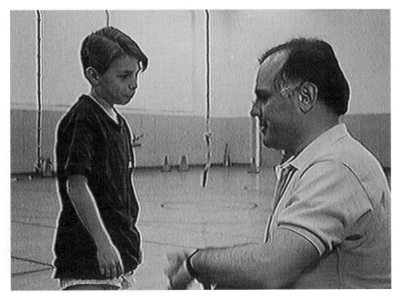

FIGURE 11.9 By staging the coach in a crouch, the director can get a tight two-shot from *Truman*.

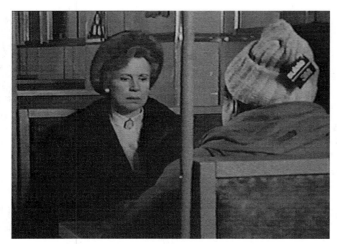

FIGURE 11.10   Over-the-shoulder shot from *The Lunch Date*.

FIGURE 11.11   Left to right from *The Lunch Date*.

FIGURE 11.12   Right to left from *The Lunch Date*.

has the freedom to work on a canvas size that best represents his artistic vision. The filmmaker is limited by the frame defined by the aspect ratio (see examples of different aspect ratios in Figure 11.47) of the format of her choice.

Both the painter and filmmaker, however, work with a two-dimensional picture frame; both face the challenge of formulating a three-dimensional world out of a two-dimensional space.

The frame can utilize a "flat" perspective or composed for depth. It can be empty, full, askew, off-balance, or in motion. Shots tilted sideways are called *Dutch angle* or *canted* and can be used to create tension to a static frame. The placement of characters and objects inside the frame can be balanced or unbalanced. A dramatic tension can be established, depending on how the director uses the frame, including foreground and background.

Composition

The director arranges the objects in the frame for dramatic, pictorial, and narrative considerations. How a shot is "composed" is the visual glue that delivers these elements to the audience. Superior composition not only makes the subject accessible, but also heightens the viewer's perceptions and stimulates the viewer's imaginative involvement. Each frame should contribute to the telling of the story and to the tone and mood of the scene; it should also reveal something about the relationship of the characters.

In the extreme high-angle shot of Truman studying his nemesis, the rope (refer to Figure 11.6), the composition of the shot speaks volumes about the character. Here, he is small, in the dead center of the frame, looking up. The rope comes from the top of the frame, thick and ominous. The complementary rectangular mat further frames the rectangular floor. The omniscient view of the character demonstrates how insignificant Truman is in comparison to his challenge to climb the rope.

Composition can be very personal. It represents how the director views the world pictorially. (You can recognize many of Stanley Kubrick's movies, for example, by the way he frames his subjects.)

Composing a shot also takes into account the confinement of the set or location, the limitations of the equipment, the time allotted for setup of the shot, the outcome of the rehearsal, and the ability of the production team to solve problems successfully and quickly.

However, the visual nature of a shot shouldn't be judged simply on whether it is pleasing to the eye. Because each image will be juxtaposed with another, the director must be conscious of how each shot will cut with the next. (Refer to the sections on editing later in this chapter.) There should be a stylistic consistency that connects the different images within a scene and the whole piece.

Depth

Although the frame is two-dimensional, the audience can experience the illusion that there is great depth within the frame. One way to accomplish this is with a wide-angle lens. For example, in *The Lunch Date*, Adam Davidson placed a woman by herself in the distance of a huge train station platform, giving the audience a feeling of isolation (see Figure 11.13). This effect can be accomplished by placing objects in the foreground of a shot, giving the audience what are called *depth cues*. Finally, exploring the space with a moving camera is another effective device for creating and emphasizing depth. When we see Truman in a close-up with his peers in the background sneering at him, a feeling of tension and compassion is created.

In *A Nick in Time*, Be' Garrett uses the mirrors in the barbershop to expand the space of the shop, create depth in frame, and accomplish shots that include characters in the foreground and background (refer to Figure 11.4 and 8.4 from *A Nick in Time*).

Drawing the Viewer's Eye

Framing draws the audience's attention to what the director wants them to sees. In the shot from *Truman* in Figure 11.14, the director uses the kids and the coach as a frame within a frame, an effect that focuses our attention to the plight of Truman. In motion pictures, sounds, as well as images, are used to direct the eye. A blacksmith hammering a horseshoe in the upper-right background of a frame becomes more prominent if the only sound heard is the clanging of hammer on metal. The director can further encourage the audience to focus on the blacksmith's work if a portion of the foreground frame is obscured by something, such as the hanging branch of a tree. The partially obscured frame forces viewers to look at the blacksmith.

Extending the Frame

The director can even design (and control) the space beyond the frame. Incorporating off-screen elements with sound through the audience's imagination is called *extending the frame*. For example, a beautifully composed landscape devoid of characters holds the audience's attention for several beats. A voice and a bell heard off-screen pique the audience's interest. The voice and bell get closer and closer, and finally a man and a cow enter the frame.

Focus

With focus, the director both literally and figuratively informs the audience what it should be witnessing at any given moment. A telephoto lens is able to minimize the depth of field and isolate a character in space. If a face in the foreground is out of focus and the background is in focus, the director wants us to look at the background. An excellent example of the use of sharp and soft focus is the shot from *The Lunch Date* shown in Figure 11.15. The director chose a camera position (close to the subjects) and lens (25mm) so that the main character is in focus, while the homeless man who represents the confusing city life is soft.

Racking focus is a device used to shift the audience's point of view or focus from one plane to another in one shot. In *Citizen*, this device is used several times; noticeably after the young man has dug his way under the fence.

FIGURE 11.13 A solitary figure in a wide frame of isolation from *The Lunch Date*.

FIGURE 11.14   Four-shot from *Truman*.

FIGURE 11.15   Focus creates depth in the frame from *The Lunch Date*.

There is a shot of the woods which shifts or *racks focus* to reveal the barb wire fence in the foreground.

Size of Shot

The director needs to have a thorough understanding of lenses and what they can do. Understanding lenses is the equivalent of knowing proper grammar. The size of the lens is a factor in determining how much information can be placed in a frame. The choice of lens plays an integral part in achieving the director's vision. If a scene looks too empty, use a tighter lens or move the camera closer to the subjects. Conversely, if a frame is too tightly packed

with people or objects, move the camera back or switch to a wider lens.

The composition of the frame is directly related to the size of the shot. The frame size is dictated by the size of the lens placed on the camera body and/or how close the camera is to the subject. Lenses come in a variety of sizes. Long lenses compress the image, whereas wide-angle lenses distort the image. A long lens (250mm) can shoot a close-up of a lion at 100 yards. A wide-angle lens (10mm) can shoot the entire British royal family on the steps of Buckingham Palace from 10 yards (these are 16mm lens sizes).

Shot size can enhance or distance our identification with a character. A close-up brings us into an intimate relationship with the subject. The further the character is from us in the frame, the more abstract he becomes. Adam Davidson chose a 10mm lens for an extremely wide establishing shot of Grand Central Station (see Figure 11.16). The people are small and insignificant. From this image, we begin a story about the lives of two of these people—in other words, about any one of us.

Lens

The size of a shot determines how much or how little of an image the director allows the audience to see (see Figure 11.17). The following abbreviations are added when the script is completed. Their use distinguishes a screenplay from a shooting script. Most shots will be from this group:

FIGURE 11.16 Wide establishing shot from *The Lunch Date*.

- ECU—Extreme close-up (eyes and nose)
- CU—Close-up (complete face)
- MS—Medium shot (torso)
- WS—Wide shot (full body)
- LS—Long shot (full body in landscape)
- XLS—Extreme long shot (small body in vista)

Shot Perspectives

A shot can be taken from several different perspectives. The director informs the audience of the point of view, whether it be that of the character, the director, or a "god's-eye" view.

Point-of-View Shot

An effective way of using the fourth wall and taking full advantage of the "voyeur" aspects of cinema is to use the point-of-view shot. It gives the audience an insight into what the character is thinking in cinematic terms by allowing the audience to participate in the character's decision-making process. This type of shot is especially useful in an action sequence.

For example, a man being pursued runs down an ally. He stops. We hear dogs in the background. The man has a choice. He either runs down one alley or another. He looks; we see one choice (a POV shot). He turns his head and looks; we see the other choice (another POV shot). We cut back toward his face. He pauses. What to do? He looks back to the sound of the dogs, and we see the other fateful choice.

As we have stated both *Citizen* and *A Nick in Time* use the point of view shot effectively. In *Truman*, Figure 11.30 establishes that Truman is looking up and 11.31 tells us

where he is looking. This technique firmly establishes our connection with the character's point of view.

The Reveal

The *reveal* is a rich piece of film language usually requiring moving the camera. In this technique, the scene starts with a pan, dolly, or zoom shot that stops on a character, prop, or location that reveals something about the story. *The Lunch Date* utilizes this technique twice. The first occurs when the woman walks back to her booth carrying her fork; the camera trucks in front of her and, as it comes to a stop, she looks down with a stunned expression. The next cut is a point-of-view (POV) shot of her salad and, as the camera tilts up, the reveal is that it is being eaten by a homeless Black man.

The second use occurs after the man and woman's "lunch date." Having forgotten her bags in the cafeteria, the woman rushes back to discover that the homeless man and her bags are gone. The camera pans back and forth with the frantic woman, revealing to the audience that her bags and her salad had actually been in the next booth all along. The woman then stops and notices herself with these four shots (Figures 11.18 through 11.21). With a short laugh, she grabs the bags and leaves.

The Fourth Wall

In the theater, the audience often looks at a proscenium stage. The two side walls and the rear of the stage make up the set. The wall on which the curtain is drawn is called the *fourth wall*. This is the invisible window through which the audience witnesses the events of the play.

In a film, the camera lens is the fourth wall. If a character speaks directly to the audience—that is, if he speaks

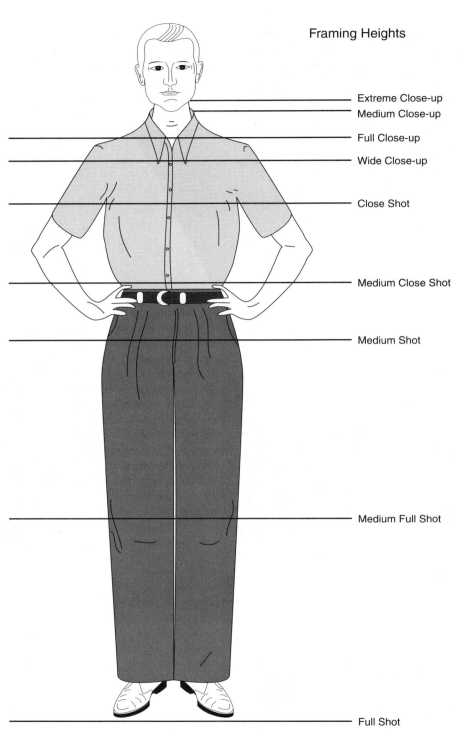

Framing Heights

Extreme Close-up
Medium Close-up
Full Close-up
Wide Close-up
Close Shot
Medium Close Shot
Medium Shot
Medium Full Shot
Full Shot

FIGURE 11.17   Full body.

directly to the camera—he "breaks" the fourth wall (see Figure 11.22). Because this can be disturbing to the audience, it is done for dramatic or comic effect only. If the character looks just to the right or left of the lens or over or under it, the result does not betray the drama.

In the cafeteria, I knew there would be a couple of dolly shots to have her walk down the aisle, to have him revealed. And then I figured out, I would like to do a pan to reveal that she sat down at the wrong place.

Adam Davidson

FIGURE 11.18 Panning is a contrast reveal from *The Lunch Date*.

FIGURE 11.19

FIGURE 11.20

FIGURE 11.21 The camera reveals that there are no bags.

FIGURE 11.22 Looking right down the barrel of the lens "breaks" the fourth wall from *Citizen*.

Camera Movement

When choosing a cinematographic style for your piece, you should consider whether the camera will be static or moving and why. In the classic Hollywood style, camera movement was always motivated. For example, to dolly to a scene, the director usually used the movement of an actor or an extra to either start the movement of the dolly or as a tool to carry the audience to the main action of the scene.

Today's animated use of the camera developed out of the cinema vérité style of documentary filming and has been universally integrated into all realms of films, music videos, televisions shows, commercials, and certainly a mainstay of reality TV. Just compare *The Bourne Identity* with its two sequels to experience the difference between using a static camera and an animated camera.

We believe there needs to be a rationale to move the camera from a story perspective. *The Lunch Date, Citizen, A Nick in Time*, and *Truman* all employ a few moving shots that are seamlessly integrated into the narrative. These shots are used to reveal exposition. Camera movement is one of the devices (as well as art direction and lighting) in *A Nick in Time* that contrasts the past and present. The flashback is designed with slow dollies and pans; the present-day scenes are mostly presented in static shots of the barber and a few pans to connect the characters in space. *Citizen* uses a mixture of tracking shots and pans to follow the young man on his trek toward freedom. This technique intensifies the movement.

Movement can come from within the frame, the motion of the frame itself, or a combination of the two. The camera can be stationary, with the action in front of the lens choreographed, or staged, to its angle. Actors then move toward the camera into a close-up or away from the camera into a long shot.

To give her film an interesting pace, the director can use the camera to bring energy into a scene by moving the frame. A pan, tilt, dolly, zoom, or crane shot adds tremendous vitality to the images. For example, suppose that two characters are eating dinner in a restaurant. A waiter walks through the kitchen door and places the couple's order on the table. You can use the waiter to motivate the pan or dolly through the restaurant to the table. In a dialogue sequence that is photographed with a slow, constantly moving dolly, the movement is not motivated by any action but will add mystery and tension.

Camera moves can liven up a static dialogue scene. Allow the actors to explore the natural movement that either of the two characters might make (the rehearsal period is the time for this). The question you want to ask is: Do people in this situation actually stand in one place and talk to one another, or do they move in the space, sit down, open a window, and so on? If there is movement, plan small but effective camera moves. Here are some other motivations for moving the camera:

- To follow the movement of a character(s) alone or in a dialogue scene
- To establish a landscape or scene geography
- To move in to a character to intensify our relationship with a character or object
- To move away from someone or something to see it more objectively
- To move the camera to reveal important information
- To reframe or accommodate a rearrangement of characters
- To move the camera up or down for dramatic purposes (crane or jib up)

Moving the camera can energize a scene but will take up time in the production day not only for executing the shot, but for rehearsing it as well. The less experienced the crew, the more rehearsal is required.

Balance

Excessive camera movement may distract the audience from the flow of the story. The director must find a way to motivate the camera and to keep the movements subtle enough so that there is a balance between the storytelling and the energy from the camera. Also, the director shouldn't move the camera dramatically if it clashes with the established style of the film. She should be guided by what the scene calls for. Sometimes, traditional coverage—a master, over-the-shoulder shots, and close-ups—is all that is needed, as in *The Lunch Date* or the doctor scene in *Citizen*.

One Long Take

Choreographing the camera, lights, and actors in a single shot, called a **planned sequence** or **fluid master**, is an ideal way to maintain the energy within a scene. Should you then use a dolly or trucking shot?

Using one long take allows the actors to develop the beats within the scene organically. Using the dynamics of these elements of photography in one shot is the height of cinema aesthetics. However, staging a single-shot scene is time-consuming. It requires a great deal of rehearsal for the actors and for the crew. If you find that the shot becomes too difficult to execute, you can resort to covering the scene in several different shots. Always have a backup plan.

A single-shot scene photographed in a single take is unusable unless it has the correct pace and rhythm. Therefore, when you design a sequence to be taken all in one shot, film some insert shots to give yourself an "out" in the editing room. Often, to save a single-take scene, the editor can use the beginning of a scene, cut to a matching insert or close-up, and then return to the single-take scene, using a different but better take.

Creating Camera Movement

There are several ways to move the camera:

- Pan
- Tilt
- Pan/tilt combination
- Zoom (cheap dolly)
- Dolly (with or without tracks)
- Trucking shot
- Handheld camera work
- Crane
- Steadicam
- Car, helicopter, boat (traveling shots)

These methods can be used in different combinations.

Pan/Tilt. In a pan, the camera moves horizontally to the left or right, and in a tilt, the camera moves up or down. The pan/tilt combination is a useful tool. The pan shot is not only versatile, but is one of the easiest moves to execute. It also doesn't offer the dramatic shift in perspective that tracking or handheld shots do. A pan can be used to

- Follow the action as it moves
- Connect two or more points of interest graphically
- Connect or imply a connection between two more subjects
- Reveal space greater than can be viewed through a fixed frame

When drawing storyboards, you indicate pans or tilts by drawing several frames with arrows pointing from one frame to the next. This signifies camera movement. The most difficult pans are those across landscapes or still objects because any unevenness in the movement becomes evident. They must be slow enough to avoid strobing unless you are planning a **swish pan**. Tilts are prone to the same issues.

Zoom. The zoom lens is able to change focal lengths optically without the camera moving or the background changing. You can zoom in to a telephoto shot and zoom out to a wide angle. In this way, this technique can serve as a "poor man's" dolly (in contrast to the dolly shot, which allows the background to change). The zoom lens comes with all video cameras.

Dolly. With this technique, the camera moves back and forth. The dolly (see Figure 11.23) moves on tracks or independently. The example in Figures 11.24 through 11.26 is a dolly back from *Citizen*. Note how the main character's relationship to the frame stays the same.

> We had a fisher dolly. That was the toy we decided to spend our money on so we could do all sorts of different camera moves. I did the shot list with the DP because he knew all the equipment and what it could do. I would say, I want the camera to do this, and he would say, well, it can't do this, but it can do this. Again, it was just working within your means.
>
> James Darling

Trucking Shot. With this technique, the camera moves sideways with the action (see Figure 11.45).

Handheld Camera Work. Handheld camera work brings a special dynamism to a scene. A slight movement in the camera, especially if the angle is from a character's point of view, adds both realism and tension to a shot.

Be advised, however, that too much movement in a shot disorients viewers. Wide-angle lenses are more appropriate choices for handheld work because they stabilize the image. Handheld camera work is most often used to give a documentary, realistic, or cinema vérité feeling to a shot. This shot can substitute for a dolly shot because, if you are pressed for time, shooting handheld saves considerable setup time.

Crane. In a crane shot, the camera is placed on a moving support that can be lifted off the ground.

Jib Arm. A jib arm is a mechanical extension supported on a dolly, tripod or other device which is counterweighted to hold a camera for an increased range of motion.

Steadicam and Traveling Shots (car, helicopter, and boat). These shots are discussed later in the chapter.

Editing

Think ahead to the editing room and consider editorial techniques when choreographing camera movements. Learn to think like an editor. Ask yourself these questions:

FIGURE 11.23 Setting up a dolly shot in the woods for *Citizen*. A full motion version of this can be viewed on our Web Site.

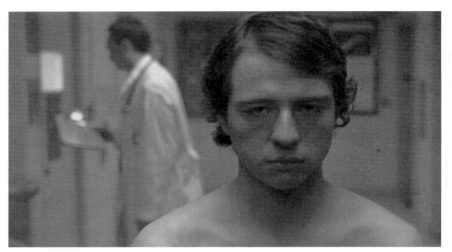

FIGURE 11.24   Figures 11.24 - 11.26, Dolly back from *Citizen*.

FIGURE 11.25

FIGURE 11.26

FIGURE 11.27   Medium reaction shot from *The Lunch Date*.

- What will the shot about to be taken cut from?
- What will the shot about to be taken cut to?

Answering these questions will lead you to discover the transitions either between beats or between scenes. It will force you to think how you want to begin and end a shot. Will the scenes dissolve into one another, fade out and then fade in, or **wipe** (see Glossary). How would the story be affected if every scene ended or started with a close-up of the main characters?

Create a visual flow that disguises any editorial technique unless used for dramatic effect, such as a smash cut, a wipe, or a flip. (See Figures 11.27 and 11.28 reaction shot to insert shot.)

Some of the best directors have years of editing room experience. Editors quickly develop a sense of what works well cut together and what does not. All directors, DPs, and script supervisors should be aware of how a scene that is being shot will ultimately cut together.

FIGURE 11.28   Insert shot from *The Lunch Date*.

Ahead are 10 shots (see Figures 11.30 through 11.39, page 179) from the "hanging scene" in *Truman* that indicate roughly the coverage needed to tell a story of this scene:

1. First, we see Truman looking up at his adversary.
2. Then we see his point of view of the humongous distance he has to make.
3. The third shot is his reaction to the task.
4. The next shot is him on the rope hanging on for dear life.
5. The wide pull back shows how high he is and who is egging him on.
6. Next is a reaction shot from the other schoolchildren.
7. Another reaction shot from some other kids follows.
8. Truman looks up as the rope is pulling apart.
9. We see a close-up of the frayed rope ready to dump him.
10. Finally, we see a wide shot of the coach and kids experiencing rejection and failure.

> **STUDENTS**
>
> Many students plan too many shots. Experience will show you how to plan a day. A good rule is to aim for 5 well-executed shots rather than 10 sloppy ones. Be prepared to either cut or collapse several shots into one.

Continuity

Continuity in visual storytelling means creating the illusion of continuous action as we cut from shot to shot. Creating this illusion requires keeping track of screen direction, eye-line matches, and the 180° axis. It also requires that the actors match their action on each take. The script supervisor (and/or the digital assist) is instrumental in helping the director keep track of these important continuity issues on the set.

Overlapping Action

Actors are required to match their actions from angle to angle. Cutting on an action produces a smooth transition from one shot to the next. Suppose a character sits down in a wide shot. The next camera position is a medium shot of the character in the chair. On "Action," the director should have the actor "sit into" the shot. Having the action of sitting from both angles will give the editor different choices to find a perfect place in the action to make the cut.

The 180° Rule

One of the more confusing areas of coverage has to do with the 180° rule (see Figure 11.29). The 180° rule is a basic film editing guideline that states that two characters (or other elements) in the same scene should always have

FIGURE 11.29   A demonstration of the 180° rule.

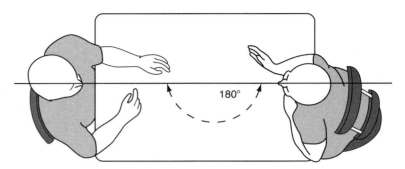

the same left/right relationship to each other. Although it is not inviolable (many directors have disregarded this rule), cutting from one character who is speaking to another character can look odd if the rule is not followed.

The eye-line, or where a character is looking, relates to screen direction. Viewers must be able to follow the eye-line from the character's eyes (see Figure 11.30) to what the character sees (see Figure 11.31). The camera operator needs to be sure of the match so that the cut will work in the editing room.

Refer back to Figure 11.29. If the director never crosses the 180° line, a character will always appear to be looking at the person to whom he is speaking. If the director crosses the line, it might appear as though the character is looking away from the person to whom he is speaking.

If character A looks at character B from screen left to screen right, character B must look at character A from screen right to screen left if the audience is to believe that they are speaking face to face (Please refer to Figures 11.11 and 11.12). For an over-the-shoulder shot, the camera should be placed over character A's right shoulder. The complementary, or reverse, angle would have the camera placed over character B's left shoulder. With this setup, the characters will appear on-screen to have eye contact with one another.

For a close-up of character A, the camera is placed where character B was sitting, or even a little closer, and the actor is asked to look to camera right. The off-camera actor can put his face right next to the lens. This gives the on-camera actor the correct eye-line. If the confines of the set do not allow the character B actor to stand next to the camera, he must deliver his lines from elsewhere. To ensure correct eye-line, the camera operator can place a piece of white tape on the right side of the lens and ask the actor to speak to the tape.

Another important aspect of the 180° axis is that the closer to the axis the camera is, the more the viewer's point of view resembles the characters, and thus he feels WITH the character. This technique encourages the important identification with the characters that viewers should feel.

When shooting a dialogue scene in which the camera swings around to shoot the reverse angle, the director and script supervisor can easily become confused as to which direction the character should look. Should he look screen left or screen right? (This is not an issue if shooting video or if you are recording the video tap and can review the previous take.) Rather than take a chance, shoot it both ways. Having two shots gives the editor an opportunity to choose the correct position in the editing room.

Crossing the Line

You can cross the 180° line with a dolly move or **cutaway**. A cutaway is a shot that has no reference to the continuity of the scene but can be used to direct the audience's attention away from the principal action. When you cut back to the scene, a new axis can be established. The dolly can accomplish this by moving the camera position across the line from one axis to the other (refer to Figure 11.45). By changing the audience's viewpoint, you can then establish a new 180° line.

Make it clear to the audience where the scene is taking place. If, in a master shot, the director has clearly indicated where the characters are positioned and what the set pieces look like, it is easier to move the characters and the camera in this space to maintain clarity.

Screen Direction in Movement

Suppose that a character walks from screen right to screen left. If the next shot is a continuation of the walking shot, the character should maintain the same screen direction. If another character walks in the opposite direction and is intercut with the first character for parallel action, the audience will assume that the two characters are walking toward each other and might eventually meet.

A moving vehicle traveling screen left to right should always maintain that direction unless the director wants to change the direction of the vehicle. She can execute this change by having the vehicle move directly toward or away from the camera. The director can then change the screen direction on the next shot (see Figure 11.40).

Second Unit

An inexpensive method of recording material that doesn't require sound (in film these are called *MOS shots*) is to

FIGURE 11.30
Character's head indicates camera direction.

FIGURE 11.31
Point-of-view shot.

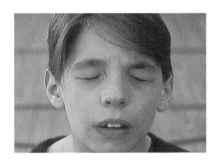

FIGURE 11.32
Close-up.

FIGURE 11.33
Single shot.

FIGURE 11.34
Wide shot.

FIGURE 11.35
Reaction shot direction.

FIGURE 11.36
Reaction shot.

FIGURE 11.37
Close-up.

FIGURE 11.38
Insert shot.

FIGURE 11.39
Wide-shot minimaster.

FIGURE 11.40 Vehicles should maintain a consistent direction. One way to change direction is to have the vehicle come toward the camera.

use what has been traditionally called a *second unit crew*. In video, it is called a *B-roll*. Second unit teams are small (usually doing exterior work), which means that they can move quickly and efficiently; they don't have to wait for

a truck to pass by for good sound conditions. The second unit can be used to photograph any action that doesn't require the principal actors.

The second unit may also be required to pick up shots that were not done during principal photography such as these:

- Establishing shots
- Transition shots
- Cutaways
- Insert shots
- Drive-bys

Keeping Score

The director risks losing the audience's attention if they are confused about technical points such as who is speaking to whom or where the characters are placed spatially in relation to one another. Both of these problems can easily occur, such as when a scene is shot exclusively in close-ups. Unless the director feels that disorientation suits the story, the audience needs reference points, such as a master shot that defines the space (see Figures 2.5 and 11.41 from *A Nick in Time*).

Specialty Shots

Confer with your DP to determine the best way to shoot special situations, such as variable speeds (slow motion, fast motion), manipulation of shutter speeds, shooting off the television, day for night, matte shots, miniatures, split screens, bluescreens, and underwater photography.

To get the high angle of the woman from *The Lunch Date* shown in Figure 11.42 required a ladder and a steady hand.

- **Multiple Cameras.** Some sequences (such as stunts or concerts) require that more than one camera be used at the same time.
- **Optical and Special Effects.** See Chapter 18.

FIGURE 11.41 Wide shot.

FIGURE 11.42 High-angle shot from *The Lunch Date*.

Greenscreen

To effectively composite a live action actor with a digital environment, the director of photography must shoot the actor against a uniform background that can easily be removed in the composite. These solid backgrounds are known as bluescreens or the more popular greenscreens (see Figures 11.43 and 11.44). The colors green and blue are used because they are at the other side of the color spectrum from most skin tones.

Setting up a greenscreen shot is not a simple task. The screen itself must have bright uniform lighting. The actor should be at least 10 to 15 feet from the screen and should be lit with separate, warmer toned lighting. The distance is necessary to prevent color bleed from the background on the actor. The bright, evenly lit background is essential to reduce the range of color to be keyed out. Most film schools will have some kind of greenscreen setup. Professional productions will most likely use greenscreen studios designed for this purpose. There are also small greenscreen field kits that can be purchased for a few hundred dollars, but they will limit the shot to a small, locked-down area. There is more information about greenscreen and CGI technology in Chapter 16 on postproduction. Prepping for greenscreen shots should be planned and scheduled separately, especially if these shots are to be filmed on a stage.

FIGURE 11.43 Green screen lighting control board.

FIGURE 11.44 Green screen studio and digital camera.

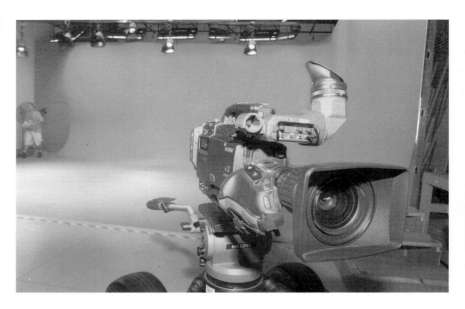

Lighting Style

The most significant addition to the composition of a frame is the use of light. Photographers have known this for years, which is why they describe their work as "painting with light." Light draws our attention to what is important in the frame. It defines the world of your film and how characters are revealed.

The script should dictate the mood and tone of your story. A chase sequence at night needs to be full of mystery—pools of light, areas of shadow. A comedy, on the other hand, is usually brightly lit. Based on the script, the director and the DP determine a look for the staging, photographic, and lighting style for the project. Following are the basic decisions that have to be made:

- What mood do you want to convey?
- Do you want high-key (Whistler, Degas) or low-key (Rembrandt, Caravaggio) lighting?
- Do you want high or low contrast?

This look can be naturalistic, stylized, or possibly a combination of both. Once a style has been determined, it should remain consistent throughout the shoot. The five case studies used in this book are good examples of a consistent look and style. *Truman*, a comedy, is evenly and brightly lit. *Mirror Mirror* has a glossy "studio" look. *The Lunch Date*, inspired by the black-and-white photography of Alfred Stieglitz, maintains a look that is consistent with that style (see Figure 11.1). Lighting is used to define the two time frames in *A Nick in Time*: the present is presented with dark shadows and contrast, and the past is bright and evenly lit.

Lighting Basics

There are two basic artificial lights: hard light and soft light. Hard light has a single, or point, source, such as a candle, a bulb, or the sun, whereas soft light has a broad, diffused source. Hard lights include incandescent, quartz, ellipsoidal, and Fresnel instruments. The sun is considered to be a hard light. Soft lighting instruments include scoops, strips, and banks. Hard lights have a longer throw than soft lights and create more contrast. Hard lights create hard shadows; soft lights fill in soft shadows.

Classic three-point lighting uses three lights: key, fill, and back. Key light provides the main source of light on the set or subject. Fill light provides detail within the shadows and softens the impact of the source light. Back light outlines the subject, separating it from the background. From this basic setup, both naturalistic and stylized lighting designs can be produced, depending on the angle, distance, and intensity of the light from these three positions.

Lighting should generally be motivated (i.e., we should know the source of the light). Sunlight or moonlight shining through a window can be the source, or key, light. Other lights can fill in the rest of the set to reduce contrast. Contrast should not be so pronounced that the part of an actor's face in the key light is well exposed but the other side of the face is dark.

Once the overall lighting approach has been established, the DP will need to consider the following questions:

- What is the intensity of the light?
- What is the quality of the light?
- What is the direction of the light?
- Is the scene intended to have natural or artificial light?
- What is the time of day?
- What is the source light?
- Do the shadows have hard or soft edges?
- Is the key light at a high angle, at eye level, or at a low angle?
- Is the lighting setup frontal, broad, narrow, or backlit?
- What are the practicals (real lamps) in the scene and how are they to be used?

- Must any practical lights be replaced?
- How can continuity of light quality be maintained from shot to shot?

> We kept the lighting very simple. We kept to very simple shots. Even the moves themselves were simple. Both the cinematographer and I felt the story itself was powerful enough that it didn't need any visual trickery. We wanted to keep the focus on the performances of the actors and let people fall into the story because it's basically a tale being told to you and the less movement that you give to the camera, the more you allow the audience to sink into the story, so that when the twist came you had totally gotten sold into the realty that you created for them.
>
> Be' Garrett

Lighting for Exteriors

Shooting outdoors can be tricky if the production relies only on the sun for illumination. The sun's arc in the sky causes the direction of the light, the shadows, and even the intensity of the light to change constantly. In addition, the sun is often obscured. Should you wait for the sun to come out from behind the clouds? A good trick is to look at the sky in the reflection of your sunglasses. The sun will appear as a bright ball behind the clouds, and you can estimate when it might emerge from behind them.

There are several methods for overcoming the powerful influence of the sun. One is to erect large translucent squares called *silks*, which can act as a filter for the sun. With silks, a soft constant light can be maintained all day. If the sun goes behind clouds, very large **HMI lights** (see Glossary) can be pumped into the silk to maintain a consistent stop (see the "Exposure" section later in this chapter). Silks work only for medium and close shots. In a wide shot, they might appear in the frame. Try to grab the wide shot when the light on the set is appropriate for the scene.

However, HMIs require a lot of power (and a generator) and never match the color temperature of the sun. On the other hand, bounce boards and reflectors do match the color temperature of the sun perfectly. Reflectors, or bounce cards, are commonly used in the field for fill light. When placed just off camera, these shiny or white surfaces reflect the sun's light (or any light source) onto the actors' faces. They produce additional light that separates the actor from the background.

When shooting outdoors, the company is at the mercy of the light and the weather. "Chasing the sun" is a common exterior location occupation. You cannot shoot until the sun has risen, and when it falls, the fading light will not be strong enough to light the scene.

Lighting for Interiors

Interior lighting comes with a different set of problems. Although day interiors can rely on the sun, you can't count on it. The sun moves during the course of the day. It is easier to maintain a consistent look with artificial lights placed outside the windows. Study your location. From where does the light come? What are the practicals doing?

The most important rule of lighting: turn off everything and see what the space naturally gives you. Is there a gorgeous skylight letting through sunlight that bounces off the white walls? Is there a time of day that sunlight passes through the stairwell, sending streams of light down the steps in an interesting way? Then go there and shoot at that time of day. Instead of spending money and lights and time to prelight, you can have nature sometimes do the work for you. If you are patient and observant, you can save a lot on lights. In most cases, using natural light is a matter of taking existing source light and enhancing it to obtain the desired f-stop.

The biggest hurdle to overcome with interior lighting is space. In a practical location, the combination of the lights, set pieces, crew, and actors allows little room to maneuver. It is recommended that you use **spreaders** (see Glossary) to create a grid from which to hang the lights.

> There were light problems: This gym was lit with fluorescent lights. I didn't have the time or money to gel all those fluorescent lights. There were over 120 of them, so we had to do all our lighting with the fluorescents, which meant we had to find an equipment house nearby that rented fluorescent fills.
>
> Howard McCain

Lighting for Documentaries

A documentary production company travels with little equipment. A few lighting instruments and a bounce card are usually sufficient to light a set for an interview. Outside, a sungun that runs off a battery belt will help fill in dark areas; there's no need to run the light to a power source. This gives the documentary crew freedom to be anywhere for filming. This is imperative when shooting cinema vérité style.

> As an aesthetic, I prefer exterior interviews. In documentaries I made about drive-in movie theaters and a traveling tent circus, it enabled me to use the exterior environment creatively in the interview setup. I like to avoid lights and usually just set up a flex-fill [bounce card] in an exterior location. I know that this is somewhat unorthodox because most documentarians put their subjects in offices or living rooms where they have complete control over the light. A major liability of exterior interviews is the sound. Documentary subjects always seem to live near a major airport!
>
> Jan Krawitz

Lighting for Video

In the past, heavy video cameras on pedestals in a three-camera setup required copious amounts of light. This is still true of any multiple-camera setup. If you want to capture an image from several positions at the same time, there must be a flood of light on any set. As the look of video steadily began to approach that of film, the lighting schemes also became similar.

Even today, the look of video is unlike that of film because the light sensitivities of film emulsion and digital video differ. This results in different depths of field and contrast ratios. Another major difference is the image size. Most video cameras have a CCD smaller than a 35mm print. Due to the law of optics, the depth of field is greater as the size of the captured image is smaller. So a small 1/4 or 1/3 CCD has a much greater depth of field than a 35mm between the depth of field, dynamic range (stops), frame rate (progressive versus interlaced), and handling of highlights. These are the criteria that the human eye perceives as being more "filmic" or not.

Film has 10 f-stops, or shades of gray, plus pure white and pure black. Video has 4 f-stops of gray plus white and black. This means that film has much more subtle detail and information than high definition (HD) as an acquisition format.

Another issue is the sensitivity of film verse HD. The finest HD camera has an ISO rating of 300 without gain boost. Gain boost is a form of making the video format more sensitive to light, but when you use gain boost, you add electronic noise that degrades the image. The fastest high-end quality film is 500 ISO, which amounts to almost 1 f-stop of light over HD. The net result is that HD stumbles at night in low situations, and you actually need more lighting work to get a quality image with HD versus film. However, a number of feature films have made use of HD at night. Michael Mann used it (to varying success) in *Miami Vice* and *Collateral*. These films were shot mostly with available light. But shooting in low-light interiors can result in an image that is "noisy" and "muddy."

Film can hold an average f-stop of 8 to 11 in a situation in which the light goes from an f-stop of 22 to 2.8, but video cannot. The contrast ratio of video is approximately 40:1, equivalent to 5 stops. Film has a contrast ratio of 128:1, or approximately 10 stops. Film has a range of nine grays, and video has only three. However, the gap may be closing because the Genesis and D21 cameras claim more than a 5-stop range.

The video image holds up well in close-ups, but the image begins to break apart in very wide shots. This issue is significant because one of the primary distinctions between these two media is projection. Video projection is limited, so most of what we see is geared for the television screen. This frame size also is good for close-ups, but it is difficult to hold wide shots because the elements in the frame are less distinct.

When shooting video, avoid white backdrops and red costumes. The white tends to "blow out" the frame, and red may bleed. Never shoot into the sun. A film camera can be adjusted to shoot at the sun, but direct sunlight can damage sensitive components in a video camera. Video is also very sensitive to colored gels; use them less than with film.

Most video cameras are programmed with an automatic iris. This means that if the camera is recording a scene in a room and then pans toward a window, the light from the sun in the window will force the aperture to adjust quickly. The adjustment, which is visible, is a dead giveaway that the image was produced by a video camera. To avoid this problem, use the manual iris override.

Ultimately, video production is tied to broadcast standards. Using a waveform monitor while recording allows the videographer to determine how much light is needed to create a signal on the monitor that conforms to broadcast standards. In some cases, lighting that is meant to set a mood will prove unacceptable. The solution is more light.

To illustrate this point, consider video distribution. Suppose that a film with many night scenes is scheduled to be released on video. It is transferred from its 35mm negative to an HDCam master for editing. Because of HD contrast compression or narrow contrast latitude, the night scenes can be so dark and muddy that it is difficult for the viewer to see what is happening. As a result of this problem, many buyers for the video market, especially the foreign market, do not want films with too many dark, moody, or night sequences.

Documentaries

For some documentaries, you might need cutaways and a reverse to the interviewer. These shots are usually mandatory so that the editor can keep the text flowing without a jump cut on the speaker. Besides learning from personal experience, the best way to learn coverage is to study great narrative and documentary film sequences. Count the number of shots and observe the variety of angles and how they cut together. On what line or movement is the edit made?

Equipment

As a director, you need not have a complete technical knowledge of the camera or other equipment, but you should be acquainted with its capabilities and uses. For example, if the director wants to move the camera, she should have an understanding of what her choices are, what they accomplish, and how they can enhance the story (see Figure 11.45). The lens is the tool the director must completely understand. Knowing how much of the world is revealed in each shot is integral to the ability to control how much information the audience sees at any given time. You should be completely familiar with the tools with which you will manipulate the content and ambience of the frame.

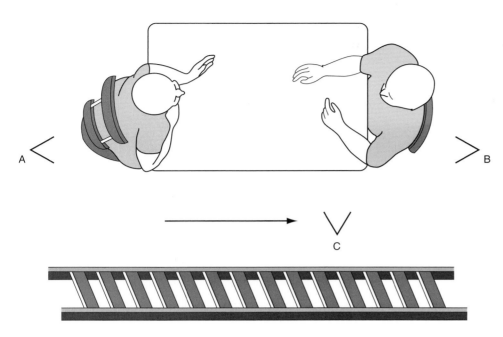

FIGURE 11.45 The camera angle on the left is a mirror of the angle on the right. A third position is added when camera angle C moves on the dolly from left to right. (Floor plan from *The Lunch Date*.)

Film Camera

A motion picture camera is a lightproof mechanical device through which the unexposed film travels. A film camera contains the following components:

- The *lens* focuses light from the world onto the film.
- The *lens mount* is an attachment to the camera body for lenses.
- The *viewfinder* allows the camera operator to see what image is being recorded on film.
- The *film chamber* is a lightproof compartment that holds the film before and after it is exposed to light. Many cameras use a detachable *magazine* to hold the film.
- The *motor* supplies the power to run the film through the gate.
- The *claw* pulls down each frame of film for exposure and holds it steady in the film gate during exposure.
- The *shutter* blocks light from the film as it moves between successive exposures.

Film Formats

Super8

In 1932, 8mm cameras were introduced that used a 16mm film slit down the middle. In 1965, Kodak brought out Super8 film that was 8mm wide, but with smaller, repositioned sprocket holes, it could record an image 50 percent larger than regular 8mm. Now 8mm film is almost obsolete.

Super8 film cameras are inexpensive, portable, and easy to use. Film is inserted in pocket-sized cartridges. Many Super8 cameras can record sound in camera, but magnetic-striped film stock capable of sound recording is hard to find. Super8 was once the format of choice for home movies, but small video cameras eliminated them from this market.

Super8 has recently undergone something of a revival because it is sometimes used in music videos, commercials, and even feature films (Oliver Stone and his DP Robert Richardson like to use it). It is being kept alive by companies such as Super8 Sound in Los Angeles (www.super8sound.com), which created the Pro8 Negative line of stocks by using a film-cutting machine to load Super8 cartridges with a wide range of color and black-and-white stocks. Rather than edit or distribute films in Super8, filmmakers are choosing to transfer the film to video or blow up (enlarge) to 16mm or 35mm.

Super8 can offer much of the flexibility of a small-format video camera, but with a superior image. The filmmaker may be looking for a rough, grainy image for stylistic reasons or may want to duplicate the look of an old movie. Instead of trying to degrade a 16mm or 35mm image, the filmmaker can shoot one of the grainier or more contrasty Super8 stocks.

16mm

Since it started out as an amateur format in the 1920s, 16mm film has gone through enormous changes. The portability of 16mm cameras made them the choice for news and documentaries. In the 1970s and 1980s, 16mm cameras and stocks improved greatly, and 16mm was used for TV documentaries, low-budget feature films, animation, and avant-garde films. By the mid-1990s, many productions that had been shot in 16mm were being done in video, and 16mm as a distribution format had almost disappeared.

FIGURE 11.46   A 35mm film camera.

Despite this trend, there are now newer, fine-grained 16mm (and super 16mm) film stocks that are capable of capturing rich images that rival 35mm, and 16mm is still being used for higher-budget documentaries, music videos, some TV shows, commercials, and many low-budget features.

Super 16mm

In the 1970s, Super16 was created by extending the image into the side of the 16mm film normally occupied by the soundtrack or the extra set of perforations on double-perf film. Super16 allows a 40 percent larger image to be recorded on each frame. It is not itself a release format but was designed for blowing up or enlarging to 35mm for theatrical distribution. Because Super16 records a larger and wider frame, less magnification and cropping are needed (than with regular 16mm) to create the 35mm widescreen image. Properly shot, Super16 films can look very good blown up to 35mm (*Leaving Las Vegas* is an example). Super16 is being used increasingly as an origination medium for programs that will be distributed in widescreen or high-definition TV formats.

Some cameras (such as most Aatons) can be switched between 16mm and Super16. To show a Super16 film, you have to transfer it to video, blow it up to 35mm, or make a special 16mm reduction print.

35mm

The standard format of feature films, television commercials, and TV movies not shot on video is 35mm. Traditional 35mm cameras are heavy and expensive to rent. The newer generation of lighter 35mm cameras can be handheld and, with stabilization devices such as the Steadicam, provide greater mobility and allow 16mm techniques to be used in feature films. (See Figure 11.45.)

Aspect Ratio

A film's format refers to the width of the film material itself, as well as the size and shape of the image that is recorded on it. The 16mm and Super16 formats use the same width of gauge (16mm), but the size of their frames is different. The *aspect ratio* refers to the ratio of width to height of the image both on film and on the screen (see Figure 11.47). The standard for several formats (8mm, Super8, and 16mm, as well as the traditional video/TV) is an aspect ratio of four to three, or 1.33:1. It is spoken as "one three three to one" or just "one three three."

In 35mm, the full frame for sound film has an aspect ratio of about 1.33:1 and is called *Academy aperture*, named for the Academy of Motion Picture Arts and Sciences that defined it. Though the Academy frame was once standard for theaters and is the traditional standard for television, it is considered too narrow for contemporary theater audiences.

Most movies viewed in American theaters are made to be shown at 1.85:1, which is a widescreen aspect ratio. European theatrical features are made for projection at

4:3 (1.33:1)
Academy Standard
Television, 35mm 16mm
and S-8mm film formats

(1.85:1)
American Widescreen
format

(2.25:1)
Vista Vision
format

(2.36:1)
70mm Full Aperture
format

FIGURE 11.47   Aspect ratio.

1.66:1, which, for the same height, is not as wide as the 1.85:1 image. Most widescreen systems work by cropping out the top and bottom of the Academy frame, making the image proportionally wider.

Some video cameras have 4:3 chip sizes to achieve the "widescreen" aspect ratio. They merely crop off the top and bottom of the chip information, which reduces the usable "real estate" of the chip. This technique is not ideal because it results in losing useful pixels. Newer cameras like the RED, F35, etc., use a larger "widescreen" chip, so depth-of-field characteristics and usable chip area are maximized. The effect is more filmic, and wide shots look better because you are not losing detail.

Camera Terms

Magazine

If the film stock comes on a very large roll (400 to 1,000 feet), it is placed in a *magazine*, which in turn is attached to the camera body for threading the film past the lens aperture. One side of the magazine is the supply reel. The film passes behind the lens for exposure and is spooled on the takeup side of the magazine.

Battery

Film cameras usually use separate rechargeable battery belts. Always check. Batteries put out much less power when they are cold.

Aperture

The plate between the lens and the film is the *aperture plate*. The aperture itself is a rectangle cut out of the plate through which light from the lens shines. The base of the film rests on the other half of the gate, which is called the *pressure plate*.

Shutter

Once the film claw has moved a frame through the film gate, the shutter opens to allow light to hit the film. The film comes to a complete halt before the shutter opens again for the next exposure.

Exposure

The amount of light that passes through the lens and the duration of time to create an image are called the *exposure*. Changes in the amount of light are measured in stops (f-stops and t-stops). On the lens is a ring that can open or close down the stops. Changes in exposure can also affect the depth of field. The filmmaker has the following means of controlling exposure: film speed, the lens, shutter speed, and the amount of ambient light.

Lenses

Lenses are interchangeable. The lens placed on the front of a camera is determined by the needs of the shot. One

shot might require a long lens (250mm), whereas the next shot might call for a wide-angle lens (5.7mm). Super-speed lenses (calibrated to be super-sensitive to light) can be helpful in low-light situations.

> Because it wasn't a thesis, I wasn't allowed to use a lot of equipment at Columbia. I basically got the dregs. I knew there were a couple of things we had to rent. I rented high-speed lenses for the stuff in Grand Central, which economically worked out better than renting the many lights it would have taken to get exposure.
>
> Adam Davidson

Although a wide variety of lenses is available in a camera package, most lenses fall into these basic categories for 16mm:

- **Wide-angle Lenses.** These lenses (5.9mm to 12mm) are used to capture a lot of information, or picture, in the frame. They take advantage of low-light situations, hold a large depth of field, absorb camera motion, and can be used to distort the image.
- **Normal Lenses.** Normal lenses (16mm to 75mm) are used to gain a "normal" perspective on a scene or character. They hold a considerable depth of field.
- **Telephoto, or Long, Lenses.** These lenses (75mm to 250mm) are used to shoot beyond unwanted foreground detail, to flatten and compress the perspective, or to create a dramatic visual statement.
- **Zoom Lens.** The preceding three types of lenses are fixed-focal length, or "prime," lenses. A lens with an assembly whose focal length can be continually adjusted to provide various degrees of magnification with any loss of focus, thus combining the features of wide-angle, telephoto and normal lenses, is a zoom lens. A popular lens (every camcorder comes with one), the zoom lens allows the director of photography to change frame sizes quickly merely by "racking" through the rings of the zoom lens. These lenses are not, however, as effective in low-light situations. Hard, or fixed, lenses, especially high-speed lenses, can expose film with less light than is needed for a zoom lens.

Filters

Filters, diopters, and gels can be placed directly in front of the lens to obtain a correct color balance or an interesting effect, to reduce light entering the camera, or as a **polarizer** (see Glossary).

Eyepiece

The camera eyepiece, which allows the director and the DP to see exactly what the lens sees, has a series of thin black frame lines that show what is inside the frame, on the edge of the frame, or outside the frame lines. This feature is especially helpful when determining how close the microphone can come to the actor without actually appearing in the frame.

These black lines also allow the camera operator to determine what will appear in the television frame if it differs from the aspect ratio chosen for the shoot. The television frame is smaller than the aspect ratio for film. If the action occurs within these lines, it is referred to as being "TV safe."

Light Meter

The light meter is a small calculator that accurately measures the light intensity values of a scene and then calculates a "proper" exposure in the form of *f-stops*. F-stops control the amount of light that is transmitted through the lens onto the film. The light meter allows the DP to see a scene the way your film stock is seeing it.

Light meters can give several different readings, depending on the specifications of the device. Some meters measure only the light falling on an object (incident meter), whereas others factor in the reflective value of the object into lighting calculations (reflective meter). For instance, if in a dim room there is a white wall and a black wall, the light falling on both may be equal. Because white is more reflective than black, a light meter that measures reflectively will adjust the reading for different surfaces, allowing the camera person to set the camera more accurately.

Video

Video Camera

Like film cameras, the video camera uses a lens to capture an image, but instead of focusing that image on a strip of film, the video camera focuses the picture on a light-sensitive computer chip called a charge-coupled device (CCD). The flat surface of the CCD is divided into a very fine grid of spots or sites called *pixels* (picture elements). Each pixel acts like a tiny light meter that reads the brightness of light at that spot. When the pixel is struck by light, it creates and stores an electric charge. A given CCD chip may have thousands or even millions of pixels in an area that is less than an inch across. The CCD measures the voltage of every pixel in the grid many times a second. It processes that information and sends it along as an electrical signal. The video signal can then be recorded or displayed on a monitor (TV screen).

Video cameras render color by separating the light coming into the camera lens into its red, green, and blue components. In single-chip color cameras, one method is to use tiny filters over the pixels that allow the CCD to measure the relative amounts of red, green, and blue light in a given area. In the generally superior three-chip color camera, a prism or mirror in the camera splits the light coming through the lens into separate red, green, and blue signals and then sends each signal to a separate CCD (much like

the original 35mm Technicolor film camera). The intensity of color in a video signal is called its *chrominance*.

Camcorder

The video camcorder combines a video camera and videotape recorder (VTR) into one unit. In studio settings, instead of camcorders, several independent cameras can be used with one or more separate VTRs. All camera/recorders share certain elements:

- The lens has controls for the focus of the image, the brightness of the image (using the iris diaphragm), and a zoom to change focal length.
- The CCD is the light-sensitive electronic chip that converts the light coming through the lens into an electronic signal.
- The camera processes the signal from the CCD before sending it on and adjusts the color of the image. It may also have the capability for adjusting the length of exposure using a shutter and changing the sensitivity of the CCD using the gain adjustment.
- The viewfinder is a small monitor that allows you to see the video signal.
- The VTR stores the signal on tape or flash cards. It includes a tape transport, which moves the tape past the heads, which transmits the signal to the tape. The signal may be recorded in analog or digital form, depending on the VTR.
- Most camcorders have built-in or attached microphones. All have provisions to plug in-external mics.
- The camera can be run on rechargeable batteries or by plugging into an AC power supply.
- Most cameras have the capability of generating timecode, which is important for postproduction.

Many camcorders, especially consumer products, are highly automated, allowing the user to "point and shoot." Some of these cameras do not even allow you to make adjustments. Because the ability to control focus, exposure, and color is part of the creative process of shooting, having these features automated is not normally useful. Professional camcorders are generally not so automated, or at least offer manual override for most features.

Monitor

Many monitors use a cathode ray tube (CRT) to convert the electrical video signal back into its visible image. Inside the monitor, a cathode ray gun fires a stream of electrons at the back of the video screen (the opposite side from which you watch). The inside of the screen is coated with a phosphor surface that glows when it is excited by the ray of electrons. The ray "paints" the image on the screen, line by line. The higher the current of the ray, the more brightly the screen glows. **The brightness of the video signal is called its *luminance*.**

The video system processes the image by dividing the picture into a series of horizontal scan lines. This pattern of lines is called the *raster*. The camera scans the image starting at the top, from left to right. It reads the brightness levels all the way across a scan line and then returns to the left side and moves down slightly as it scans across again. This process is much like the way your eye takes in a paragraph of written text. When the camera reaches the bottom of the screen, it returns to the top and starts over. The monitor's CRT makes the same scanning pattern, "painting" the image on as it goes. A sync signal makes sure the camera and monitor scan at the same time. Many monitors now employ progressive scanning. What is most important is that on a video shoot the monitor be calibrated accurately.

Interlaced Scanning

In the United States and 29 other countries, traditional broadcast video systems use a standard established by the National Television Standards Committee (NTSC) in the United States in 1954. *NTSC* video runs at 29.97fps and divides the picture into 525 horizontal lines (of which about 460 reach the home viewer), scanned in an *interlaced* pattern. In the United Kingdom, Western Europe, China, and Australia (59 countries in all), the video standard is called *phase alternating line*, or *PAL*. PAL was developed in Germany and the United Kingdom and first used in 1967. France, Eastern Europe, and Russia (23 countries in all) use the Sequential Couleûr à Mémoire (SECAM) standard. SECAM 625 was developed in France and first used in 1967. PAL and SECAM are also scanned in an interlaced pattern but run at 25fps and divide the picture into 625 horizontal scan lines, creating a sharper image (more resolution) than NTSC.

Interlacing the image allows the capture, broadcast, and display of two half-resolution images in such a way that they look like a single image on a TV set. Your brain doesn't notice that the images are half resolution as long as they are knit together accurately as a 1/30th of a second full-resolution image. In basic terms, video can be considered as being made up of numerous snapshots, called *frames*. The frame rate, or the number of frames displayed each second, is 29.97 in the United States and other NTSC-based countries. For the sake of simplicity, we can round this number to 30fps.

Television, however, does not deal with video in terms of frames as we know from film. Instead, it displays video using half-frames called **fields**. Each frame contains exactly two fields. One field is made up of the odd horizontal lines in a frame. This is called the **odd field** or the *top field* because it contains the top line of the image. The other field is made up of the even horizontal lines in a frame. This is called the **even field** or **bottom field**.

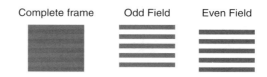

Television cameras actually shoot two separate exposures per frame, to capture the two video fields. The odd-numbered scan lines (lines 1, 3, 5, etc.) are shot first; then another field is shot to capture all the even-numbered scan lines (coming back to record lines 2, 4, 6, etc.). Thus, an image is captured in two separate passes. When the two fields are interlaced to fit together on TV, a frame is created from both fields to reproduce the full-resolution picture. Using the 480-line DVD standard as an example, the first 240 lines displayed are the odd-numbered lines (1, 3, and 5). The second 240 lines displayed are the even-numbered lines.

Because there are two fields in every frame, a television actually updates the display at 60 fields per second (or 50 fields per second for PAL/SECAM). Each field is displayed 1/60th of a second after the preceding field (or 1/50th of a second for PAL/SECAM video). Because two fields make up one complete frame, this results in video that runs at approximately 30fps (1/60th + 1/60th = 2/60th = 1/30).

A major benefit of displaying and broadcasting in an interlaced format is that it acts as a form of compression, reducing the overall bandwidth required for delivering signals. The disadvantage is a loss of vertical resolution, known as the *interlace factor*. As a comparison, images on a computer are drawn progressively. The computer captures the whole image one frame at a time. Because of this, both fields that make up a video frame are shown simultaneously. This is called a **progressive scan display**. Progressive video formats preserve the progressive nature of film but require more bandwidth for broadcast than interlaced video.

Television signals are interlaced because of the nature of early television sets and the nature of human vision. When a series of frames are presented, the frame rate (the time interval between frames) has to be high enough to achieve *persistence of vision*, a continuous image without noticeable flicker. The United States uses a 60Hz power cycle, but early television sets were able to display only at a 30fps frame rate. Interlacing two 30fps fields achieved an effective 60fps frame rate, which solved the problem of low bandwidth and was high enough to provide persistence of vision at lower bandwidths than progressive scanning. The European standards PAL and SECAM use interlacing at 25fps to achieve an effective 50fps frame rate because Europe uses a 50Hz power cycle.

Interlace Factor

If you are filming a stationary image, the interlaced images are excellent because both 1/60th of second images are identical. If there is motion, you may see the motion as jagged-edged or blurred advancements. Motion "artifacts" and horizontal "line twitter" are the most notorious NTSC artifacts. Jagged edges occur because the object is in a different location every 1/60th of a second. The even lines show the object in one position, whereas the odd lines show the image in a different position. When you knit the odd and even scan lines together, you see ragged edges around moving objects. Furthermore, thin horizontal lines in the original image that are the width of a single scan line (or smaller) will flicker on and off as the image is panned vertically or if the object with horizontal lines moves vertically when the camera is not moving. The closer you sit to your TV set, the easier it will be to see NTSC artifacts in images.

Component versus Composite Video

We have established that video cameras generate separate red, green, and blue (RGB) color signals. In **component video systems, the red, green, and blue signals, either in analog or digital format, are kept separate from one another.** The individual color components are sent in separate channels (using separate cables) from one piece of equipment to another. Component video offers the sharpest and cleanest colors. The pictures look good and suffer little generation loss with each dub. This type of video is expensive and requires special equipment that maintains the separateness of the colors.

In *composite* **video systems, the color signals are mixed (encoded) with the luminance into one signal that can travel on a single channel.** That channel composites them. Composite video makes recording and broadcasting easier, but results in marked loss of image quality. The real problem, however, is the generation loss when the signal is rerecorded many times.

The method by which the RGB signal is compressed and encoded is based on government-approved standards (such as NTSC, PAL, or SECAM). Composite video is inexpensive and simple. Composite originated when color television was first invented and engineers had to find a way to cram the additional information into the existing black-and-white television signal.

There is a third option using two cables of video, one for the luminance (brightness) and one for the chrominance (RGB). This is called *Y/C* or *S-video* (separate video). It combines the colors into one chrominance signal but keeps them separate from the luminance. The image is not as good as component, but it is better than composite. An S-video cable has wires for Y and C. This format is used in high-end consumer video in the form of Hi-8 and S-VHS. Following are the current digital formats and their relationship to component, composite, and S-video:

- **Component**: D1 (19mm digital), D5 (19mm digital), Betacam SP (½-inch analog), MII (½-inch analog), Betacam (½-inch analog), Digital Betacam (½-inch digital), DCT (19mm digital)

- **Composite**: D2 (19mm digital), D3 (19mm digital), 1-inch type C (1-inch analog), ¾-inch Umatic (¾-inch analog), ¾-inch SP (¾-inch analog), 8mm (8mm analog), VHS (½-inch analog)

- **Y/C (or pseudo-component)**: S-VHS (½-inch analog), Hi-8 (8mm analog)

Video Monitoring

Filmmakers have learned the value of a video tap on a film camera. It enables playback of footage shot on-site, an invaluable tool. It is understood that the playback is just to roughly monitor framing, performance, and other factors and is not a true rendition of the film's contrast or saturation. This understanding must carry over to monitoring of video.

The true measurement of a composite video signal is done with two oscilloscopes: a **waveform monitor** and a **vectorscope**. Originally, these were separate devices; however, it is now quite common for the waveform monitor and vectorscope to be combined into single unit that can switch between the two functions. Some units even allow for the two functions to be superimposed. The combined device is simply called a "waveform monitor."

The waveform monitor graphically displays and monitors the brightness, or luminance, level of a video signal regardless of its format (e.g., NTSC or PAL). It can be used to display the overall brightness of a television picture, or it can zoom in to show one or two individual lines of the video signal. It can also be used to visualize and observe special signals in the vertical blanking interval of a video signal, as well as the colorburst between each line of video (see Figure 11.48).

The waveform monitor is especially helpful in two phases of video production: shooting and online editing. Waveform monitors, together with light meters, are your primary tools for ensuring proper camera exposure and good video quality. If the average value of important information in the picture is more than 100 or less than 7.5 IEEE units, the exposure is off. This exposure can be adjusted by changing the camera's aperture or by adding more or less light to the scene. This capability is particularly important on multicamera shoots where many cameras are intercut together by a video switcher.

In an online edit session, the waveform monitor works the same way, only this time it measures the values of images from videotape or other online devices like character generators or special effects generators. It can monitor and maintain video quality and scene-to-scene consistency. It is also a valuable tool to assist in telecine (film-to-tape transfer), color correction, and other video production activities.

The vectorscope displays and measures the color, or chrominance, of the video signal. It is a reliable instrument to judge the accuracy of color and for setting up equipment to accurately reproduce colors. In a television signal, color is encoded into the main signal with a subcarrier. The vectorscope measures the color information in this subcarrier using a circular display, or graticule

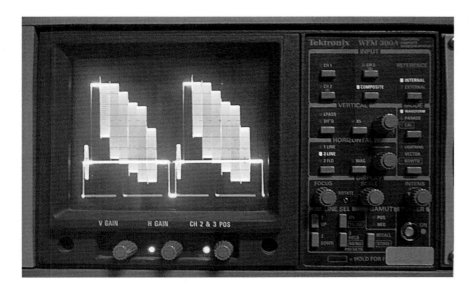

FIGURE 11.48 Image of a waveform monitor showing color bars (http://en.wikipedia.org/wiki/Image:Vectorscope_monitor.jpg).

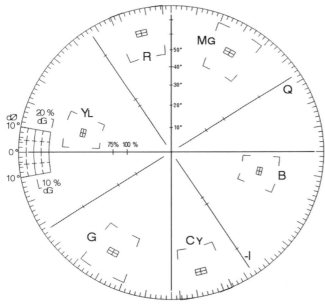

FIGURE 11.49 The graticule of an NTSC vectorscope (http://en.wikimedia.org/wiki/Image:Vectorscope_graticule.png).

(see Figure 11.49), for visualizing chrominance signals. The circle is overlaid with the color amplitude and phase relationship of the three primary colors (red, green, and blue). In the center of this circle graph is the luminance (black and white) value of the signal. Through this center point, three axes represent the primary colors.

In the online edit session, the vectorscope determines the proper colors through the use of color bars. The standard procedure is for the camera operator to record 60 seconds of color bars at the beginning of every tape. This technique ensures that, when edited, the colors will be the same from tape to tape and from any effect.

Because professional nonlinear editing systems (to be covered later) have both vectorscopes and waveform monitor screens that can be displayed, you can keep a constant eye on quality and make scene-to-scene adjustments as necessary. This is the only way that you will be able to consistently and unobtrusively cut a variety of scenes together during the editing phase.

Digital Impact

Originally, waveform monitors were entirely analog devices; the incoming (analog) video signal was filtered and amplified, and the resulting voltage was used to drive the vertical axis of a cathode ray tube. With the advent of digital television and digital signal processing, the waveform monitor acquired many new features and capabilities. Modern waveform monitors contain many additional modes of operation, including *picture mode* (where the video picture is simply presented on the screen, much like a television), various modes optimized for color gamut checking, support for the audio portion of a television program (either embedded with the video or on separate inputs), eye pattern and jitter displays for measuring the physical layer parameters of serial-digital television formats, modes for examining the serial digital protocol layer, support for ancillary data and television-related metadata such as timecode, closed captions, and the v-chip rating systems.

Modern waveform monitors have largely abandoned old-style CRT technology as well. All new waveform monitors are based on one of two display technologies: they either feature a flat-panel *liquid crystal display (LCD)* or else are sold without a display. The user is expected to connect a VGA monitor to the output. The latter type of device is commonly known as a *rasterizer*.

LCD is a type of display used in digital watches and many portable computers. It utilizes two sheets of polarizing material with a liquid crystal solution between them. An electric current passed through the liquid causes the crystals to align so that light cannot pass through them. Each crystal, therefore, is like a shutter, either allowing light to pass through or blocking the light. Although very expensive (check out the Sony LMD-9050 Portable HD LCD), as with all new technology, the prices become competitive as the market for a product grows.

Setting Up a Monitor

All these quality measures have to be displayed accurately on a TV monitor to be verified, so it's important to be able to trust your video monitor. For the shooter, you might wonder why you couldn't just look at a standard video monitor to see whether your picture looked all right. The problem is that the picture monitor is not a reliable guide to the picture you are recording or to how that picture will look in the finished videotape. A trip to a store that sells TVs will show how many different renditions of playback are possible for one signal.

However, a good HD monitor hooked up to a good HD camera that has been calibrated with a waveform monitor and color bars is a trustworthy video image provided your monitor is calibrated properly. The monitor becomes your light meter, and with a waveform monitor hooked up, you can actually see your exposure levels on a scale, not just judging by eye. Whereas on film, a video tap is merely a quick, dirty way to see the frame. It is not useful for color, focus, or resolution and has no relationship to the actual image you are capturing.

Video Formats

Unlike comparatively faithful film formats, video formats are continually being invented, changed, and dropped as new and better ones arrive on the scene (there will undoubtedly be a new one by the time this book comes out). Dealing with video formats is similar to buying a computer that could be outdated a few months after you bring it home. The positive side of this change is that the systems are getting smaller, cheaper, and more powerful. The downside is that equipment becomes obsolete.

With film formats, there is a rough correlation between the size of the format and the quality it is capable of. You cannot make that assumption with videotape formats. A VTR running ½-inch-wide tape may be much better quality than one running 1-inch tape.

Manufacturers generally identify the intended market for various pieces of equipment. The categories are not exact, but in descending order of quality there is broadcast, industrial, prosumer, and home/consumer.

Broadcasters have been traditionally exacting about the signal and image quality they will allow on the air, but small video cameras, especially, have clearly made substantial inroads.

Analog Formats

VHS

The video home system (VHS) is a composite, analog format using ½-inch wide tape. For many, the idea of home video is synonymous with VHS. It is inexpensive and convenient, and there are millions of VHS machines in the world. In terms of image quality, it is (other than Fisher-Price Pixelvision) the worst format at 210 lines of resolution. The VHS quality also degrades significantly with recording at slower speeds.

The VHS hi-fi format is an upgraded version of the home consumer model, except the VTR circuitry is more advanced, so the picture quality and audio are reproduced with greater precision.

Super VHS

Super VHS (S-VHS) was first introduced by JVC in 1987 in an effort to match the performance levels of ¾-inch U-VCR systems. S-VHS is an S-video system, which is higher in quality than composite but not up to component. The resolution of S-VHS is 400 lines as opposed to 250 for standard VHS. S-VHS uses special ½-inch videotape, made of specially formulated high-density ferric oxide, enclosed in a videocassette.

8mm and Hi-8

The 8mm video format is an improvement over standard VHS. The tape cassettes and camcorders tend to be smaller and the image quality is better. Hi-8 (highband 8mm) is an improved version of 8mm, and Hi-8 camcorders and tape are more expensive. Like S-VHS, Hi-8 can output S-video, and its resolution is about 400 lines. To get the most out of S-video, you need a monitor equipped with S-video inputs. Hi-8 is popular for home video use and became an effective news-gathering format where large cameras would be awkward, though digital video (DV) is now filling that role. Some Hi-8 systems have non-SMPTE timecode, and there are Hi-8 editing systems, but most often, 8mm, Hi-8, and S-VHS are bumped up to larger formats for editing.

1 Inch, 2 Inch, and ¾ Inch

Introduced in the 1950s, the Quadruplex VTR, or quad, is the original format of reel-to-reel VTRs using 2-inch wide magnetic video recording tape for broadcast. This system was replaced by improved 1-inch machines that became the standard throughout the 1980s and into the 1990s. As an analog, composite format, 1-inch was replaced by better-quality component and digital systems. Sony introduced the first U-Matic cassette recorder in 1971. Though inferior to 1-inch, ¾-inch systems were widely used for field recording, industrial, and broadcast applications. The ¾-inch decks are easy to use and the tape is rugged. At one time, ¾-inch was the chief offline editing format, though the image deteriorates with dubbing.

Betacam

Introduced in 1981, Sony's Betacam format was a response to the growing demand for smaller and lighter high-quality field equipment. Betacam was unique in that it created broadcast-quality images on a ½-inch videocassette using either a portable VCR or a camcorder unit that contained the camera and recorder in one lightweight package. Its high-quality recording is possible because it processes and records video in the component video format and provides outputs in both composite and component video. (Betacam, which is referred to as Beta, should not be confused with the little-used consumer Betamax format, which also runs ½-inch tape, but at a slower speed and with lower image quality.)

Sony later introduced Betacam SP (Superior Performance) production VTRs, which are compatible with the current Betacam format and offer four channels of high-quality audio. In addition to the two longitudinal amplitude modulated (AM) audio channels, Sony added two frequency modulated (FM) audio channels, which are simultaneously recorded with the video information.

By the 1990s, analog Betacam camcorders had become the standard tool for a wide variety of broadcast and industrial production. Beta editing suites ushered in an era of affordable component editing.

Digital Videotape Formats

Digital videotape, once the domain of the high-end, high-budget production, has now become the mainstream with more than 15 formats or versions of formats currently available. There is no simple decision on which format is best. Price considerations must be taken into account. But price goes to more than the cost of purchasing or renting a given deck. Tape must be factored in as well as maintenance of any new equipment. Some formats may shine in postproduction but may be too big (in equipment weight or tape size) to make it reasonable for fieldwork.

D-1, introduced by Sony in 1986, was the first industry-accepted format by SMPTE. It has become the universal component digital standard with approximately 460 lines of resolution. The signal is recorded on a 19mm oxide tape, offering the highest quality and the most flexible recording system. It is capable of recording compressed HD signals but does not compress standard signals. Although still considered a quality reference, D-1 is expensive to buy and use and has been mostly superseded by the more cost-effective later formats. It is still used for creating complex, layered graphics or as a mastering format for film-to-tape transfers and online video editing.

D-2, developed by Ampex around 1984, was the second SMPTE standardized digital system, but it is a composite system and thus doesn't provide the pristine video signal of component. The D-2 is accepted in many postproduction facilities because of its lower per-unit cost and because its composite video format is fully compatible with the existing composite analog equipment that the facilities already own. The videocassette casings used by the D-2 format are identical to the D-1 cassettes; however, the videotape itself is a metal particle tape chosen for its high packing density, which results in a higher signal-to-noise ratio. Neither D-1 nor D-2 is practical for use in a camcorder because of the physical size of the tape transport system.

D-3 and D-5, both developed by Panasonic, are compatible systems, despite D-3 being designed as a composite system and D-5 as a component system. Neither system compresses the video signal, and both use 12.5mm (½-inch) metal tape. While D-5 is still a studio format, D-3 camcorders are available from Panasonic. D-3 is used mainly in industrial and corporate communications, while D-5 is designed to record HD signals.

D-4 doesn't exist because number 4 is a major taboo in Asian cultures (pronounced the same as "death" in Japanese).

DCT (Digital Component Technology) is an Ampex format recording a compressed component signal on 19mm metal tape. DCT technology is targeted almost exclusively for postproduction and film transfer applications.

Digital S format was developed by JVC. It uses a VHS tape and is intended for field production. This offers the benefits of digital recording in a relatively low-cost package. However, Digital S tapes are incompatible with analog VHS.

HD D5, a high-definition version of D-5, has been introduced by Panasonic. It uses standard D5 videotape cassettes to record HD material, using an intraframe compression with a 4:1 ratio. HD D5 supports the 1,080 and the 1,035 interlaced line standards at both 60Hz and 59.94Hz field rates; all 720 progressive line standards; and the 1,080 progressive line standard at 24, 25, and 30 frame rates. Four uncompressed audio channels sampled at 40 kHz, 20 bits per sample, are also supported.

DV, DVCam, and DVCPRO

DV (digital video) records an excellent digital component image on a very small tape cassette. Aimed at the prosumer market, the mini-DV camera brings digital recording to an affordable level (see Figure 11.50). Within a few years of their introduction in the 1990s, mini-DV revolutionized independent and multimedia production the way Betacam once changed the broadcast world. For a few thousand dollars (probably lower by the time this book comes out), a videomaker can record video that rivals or surpasses that of an analog camcorder costing much more. DV has a resolution of 500 lines.

FIGURE 11.50 Panasonic Mini DV. (Courtesy of Panasonic Broadcast and Television Systems, Division of Matsushita Electric Corporation of America.)

FIGURE 11.51 Panasonic AG-DVX100. Courtesy of Panasonic.

For industrial, broadcast, and dramatic use, Sony introduced the *DVCam* and Panasonic makes the *DVCPRO* (see Figure 11.50). Both are fully professional systems that record the same signal as mini-DV, but the tape formats are different. (DVCPRO machines can play mini-DV and DVCam tapes with a cassette adapter. DVCam machines cannot play DVCPRO cassettes.) The professional systems are more costly but offer more features and better-quality camcorders than the mini-DV.

The *Digital Betacam* format (also called D-Beta or Digi-Beta) provides a very high quality component digital signal and is used for both production and postproduction. The cost and size of the D-Beta camcorder make it a tool for professionals only. The camera is easy to handhold and is the same size as the analog version. D-Beta sets a very high standard for quality and versatility.

One of the innovations of DV is the use of FireWire (IEEE 1394, also called iLINK) technology (discussed in Chapter 16). A FireWire cable allows a direct digital two-way connection between DV devices, for example, between a camera and an editing system or VTR. Digital information can be recorded directly onto a hard drive, a Zip disk, or DVD (most commonly used now).

HD

HD (high-definition television, also called HD and hi-def) represents a substantial leap in resolution over traditional, analog systems and results in an image that rivals 35mm film in clarity. It is a completely revised visual communication format for the production, postproduction, and transmission of television signals. HD provides the viewer with widescreen aspect ratio, vastly better image resolution, interference-free pictures, and CD-quality stereo sound.

Sometimes the term *digital television* (DTV) or *advanced television* (ATV) is used to refer to the new digital broadcast formats (see Figure 11.52). Of these, there are several high-definition formats (HD) and standard-definition formats (SDTV). One HD system uses 1,080 scan lines (more than twice NTSC's 525-line raster) with an aspect ratio of 16:9 or 1.78:1. The result is an extremely sharp, widescreen digital picture that is only slightly less wide than the U.S. standard 1:85 widescreen theatrical films (see Figure 11.53). Hard disk recorders now reach 4:4:4.

George Lucas and 24p

George Lucas wanted to work with HD but had one problem: it looked too much like video. He, along with others, suggested to Sony that the company should explore an HD signal that was similar to film. Sony responded and developed a complete line of 24 frame-capable HD gear. The company dubbed its new line "CineAlta," which has become a world standard for 24p HD. Panavision worked with Sony to provide the HDWF-900 HD camera with lenses for Lucas and *Star Wars Episode II*. Lucas went off to Australia to shoot and was incredibly happy with the results.

The camera's format is 1080i (vertical) by 1,920 (horizontal) and is capable of shooting 24p, 25p, 30p, 29.97p, 23.98p, or interlace formats (60i, 59.94i). HDCam, the tape format the camera records, is extremely versatile. The camera can deliver a signal that is ready for film transfer or down-conversion to standard definition (SDTV) in NTSC or PAL for broadcast. In addition, the camera is native 16:9, an aspect ratio that networks are increasingly demanding new content to be composed in for content.

FIGURE 11.52 Television aspect ratio 4:3 (http://en.wikipedia.org/wiki/Image:4_3_example.jpg).

FIGURE 11.53 HD aspect ratio 16:9 (http://en.wikipedia.org/wiki/Image:16_9_example.jpg).

What Is 24p?

Lucas wanted a video camera to capture the cinematic feel of film. Film yields a slight blur in moving objects. This is known as *motion blur*, and it results in a distinct fluidity of movement—a prime contributor to the "film look." Motion blur is caused by film's relatively low frame rate of 24 frames per second. A telltale sign of video is its extreme sharpness and lack of motion blur.

NTSC video runs at 30fps, so how can such a small difference account for the radical increase in sharpness? The reason is that there are two interlaced fields for every frame of video, so the effective rate is actually 60 images per second (30fps × 2 fields). This virtually eliminates motion blur, creating an image that is a bit too sharp and devoid of fluidity.

The answer to this problem is a technical breakthrough called *progressive scanning*, in which each frame is scanned once. In other words, the frame is scanned as a single field, with no interlacing. This process mimics a film camera's frame-by-frame image capture. The lower image rate reproduces motion blur comparable to film. These cameras generally use frame rates of 24fps to 30fps. The 24 frames progressive format, called *24p* (for progressive), simplifies combining video and film footage because there is a one-to-one frame relationship. The PAL version, *25p*, matches the European film speed of 25fps. Many state-of-the-art cameras have switchable frame rates and resolutions.

Another benefit of progressive scanning is a dramatic increase in resolution. This occurs because progressive scanning eliminates interlace artifacts (combed edges in movement) and interline flicker (noise in fine patterns). It has been shown that that perceived resolution in progressive scanning is 50 percent greater than interlace scanning.

Panasonic Enters the Arena

Eventually, Panasonic entered the field with its own HD camera, the AJ-HDC27F, commonly known as the Varicam. This DVC-PRO HD format camera distinguished itself as being able to shoot variable frame rates (4 to 60fps). The ability to undercrank or overcrank to create slow and fast motion was the next substantial step toward creating a video camera with the capability of a film camera. Before the Varicam, to achieve fast or slow motion effects on videotape, the tape speed had to be altered in postproduction.

In addition to variable frame rates, the film-like quality of the camera extends to its circuitry. The camera has two gamma files that closely mimic the tonal range (also known as the film's characteristic curve) of film as well as a gamma setting for video recording. The film settings extend the camera's ability to reproduce a wide array of colors in addition to gradations of light where other video cameras may not be capable.

24p Comes to DV

For a number of years, 24p was the sole domain of high-definition video. The next step was applying the 24p technology for standard-definition TV and mini-DV. Panasonic was in the vanguard in this evolutionary leap with the AG-DVX100, a 3 1/3-inch CCD mini-DV that can scan progressively or interlaced (24P, 24PA, 30P, 60i). It features one of the widest lenses (10 × 4.5) and has two XLR inputs for sound recording with professional-style microphones. The progressive formats are performed in-camera and 460 interlaced lines (traditional NTSC) are recorded on tape, so there is no extra equipment needed to post. Canon followed soon after with its line of XL1s. Even those filmmakers who are

not interested in transferring their video projects back to film may be transferring their shows to DVD, which is by nature a default 24p playback device.

HD + DV

The next logical step was to create an affordable HD camera. That's where *HDV* comes in. It is a way of getting HD on DV tape. The term *HDV* is a combination of "HD" and the very popular "DV" format. It's done by using **MPEG2 compression** (see Glossary), which is the same compression used for DVDs. MPEG2 is a much more complex **codex** (see Glossary) than DV, and this adds to the computer requirements. It allows a great amount of information to be compressed for recording and then decompressed for viewing. This is different than DV, which remains in its compressed state.

HDV is native 16:9 at a resolution of 1,280 pixels wide by 720 pixels tall. Supported frame rates are 60i (frames-per-second interlaced), 30p (progressive), 50i, and 25p. HDV is also an "open format," like DV, which means you do not have to stay with one brand to use the format. The HDV standard was established in 2003 by four companies: Canon Inc., Sharp Corporation, Sony Corporation, and the Victor Company of Japan, Limited.

Companies supported HDV because it is a based on the global DV standard, and the same DV mechanisms can be used for HDV. Moreover, since it employs the broadcast standard for image compression, MPEG-2, it is possible to connect HDV devices with TVs and personal computers. HDV can also be down-converted to standard definition so that the hundreds of thousands of SD TV sets and DVD players can view it today. Down converting the HDV footage can give you the best of all possible worlds.

By the time this edition is on the market, the future of HDV will be defined by how these cameras (and others) perform. Equally important will be how the format will be supported in postproduction.

FIGURE 11.54   Panasonic DVCPRO. (Courtesy of Panasonic Broadcast and Television Systems, Division of Matsushita Electric Corporation of America.)

The Cameras

JVC came out with the first HDV camera with the 2003 release of the single-chip GR-HD1 mini-DV and HD camcorder. In DV mode, the camera shoots at a standard 720 × 480 DV image at 30fps of 60 interlaced fields per second (60i) in a 4:3 aspect ratio. In SD mode, it shoots at the same vertical resolution (480 lines), but it shoots 60 progressive fps (60p) at a true 16:9 widescreen aspect ratio. Finally, the HD mode shoots 30p, 16:9 widescreen at 1,280 × 720. Unlike previous HD cameras, which were bulky, this camera is very small, about the same size as Sony's PD150.

JVC subsequently released a second-generation camera, the JY-HD10U, that added a color bar generator, XLR inputs, a higher-resolution view screen, and the ability to see audio levels on the screen. Since the first camera, Sony and Canon have entered the market, and JVC continues to upgrade its line.

Sony came out with the HVR-Z1U, a 3-CCD professional camcorder that delivers high-quality 1080i but does not have the 24p capability. It does, however, provide a "cinelook" effect that simulates the 24p film look. JVC then introduced the GY-HD100U, a professional high-definition (ProHD) progressive camcorder with true 24p capture that records to DV tape and provides a removable bayonet mount lens and the BR-HD5OU ProHD recorder player.

ProHD is an HDV-compatible video system with professional specifications, including four-channel audio, timecode, true 24p HD, and dual-media direct recording to HD cassettes and hard disks. JVC utilizes widely available nonproprietary technologies, such as MPEG-2 compression, DV recording media, and conventional hard disk drives to achieve an affordable HD solution.

HD

Finally, Panasonic is on the verge of introducing the AG-HVX2000 DVC PRO HD P2, which records in both 1080i and 720p formats and primarily to a memory card instead of videotape. Look for the new Sony PMW-EX1 HD camera with tapeless recording.

Ultra-high Definition

Ultra-high definition features an amazing 4,520 lines of horizontal resolution. Known as "4k" technology because the scan lines exceed 4,000, it will no doubt be the future industry standard. This is a comparison of the HD formats:

- 720 lines (HD; DV and DVM)
- 1080 lines of resolution (HD)
- 2048 lines of resolution (2k HD)
- 4520 lines of resolution (4k Ultra HD)

The first format represents the typical digital video frame (DV and DVCam). Notice how detail improves as the number of scan lines increases. The final format illustrates the huge leap in image detail 4k technology provides.

As a point of reference, the typical flat computer monitor has 2,000 lines of resolution. As perceived by the human eye, 35mm film falls in the mid HD range. The 4k technology is based on the proprietary 12-megapixel chip developed by the RED Digital Cinema Company. Its affordable RED One camera can shoot at all popular scan rates, including those shown in the preceding list.

The RED

Several years ago, Jim Jannard from Oakley decided to focus on producing a revolutionary video camera called The RED. It broke several barriers because it was an affordable camera rig (a computer with a lens) that records a 4K video image (not exactly) and mounts 35mm lenses using a traditional PL mount. Meanwhile, Sony and Panasonic and Arri were selling 2K cameras at three to four times that price. RED records in a raw format, meaning the video is "visually uncompressed," meaning some of the information captured is "compromised or squeezed" before being recorded on your media, but RED claims that this "squeezing" is not perceptible to the human eye. That way, in post, you have almost all the resolution, color space, and information to play with.

RED recently announced a new line-up of cameras: The Scarlet (filming at 2K) and the Epic. The Epic will have Super 35, full-frame 35, 645 (Medium format), and 617, equivalent to the Linhof Technorama Camera. Resolutions will range from 5K to 28K.

Tape Stock

Videotape, like audiotape, is composed of a Mylar backing and a thin magnetic layer that actually records the video signal. This magnetic layer was once made up of primarily ferric (iron) oxide. Now manufacturers make a variety of formulas for the magnetic layer, ranging from various oxides to higher-quality metal tapes that have no oxide. A higher-quality tape will have fewer defects and may allow you to record with less noise, clearer color, and better detail. But picking a tape stock is not like picking a film stock. Film stocks may vary in terms of basic color palette, contrast, and sensitivity to light. In video, the camera itself determines most of these things. The same video stock serves equally well for recording color or black-and-white, in daylight or indoors.

As video formats become smaller and attempt to record more information on narrower and shorter tapes, the quality of the tape stock becomes more important. Though tape stock is in theory reusable, each pass through the VTR adds to the likelihood of dropouts and other defects. Professionals usually use only fresh, virgin tapes for critical camera recording, as well as the best tape stock they can afford. Digital tape formats may have more leeway for reusing tapes. For editing purposes, used stock is fine for work tapes.

Finally, improperly stored videotape can deteriorate in various ways, including becoming brittle, stretching, or losing its magnetic charge. Keep tapes away from any magnetic fields. Store in places that are comfortable for humans (neither very dry nor very damp). No one knows how long newer tape formats will hold up over time. Because all tape formats eventually become obsolete, it's a good idea to transfer important masters to a new format every several years.

Tapeless Shooting

Flash memory is quickly gaining ground in both the video and computer worlds. It is a storage format that has no moving parts, unlike hard drives. Therefore, it is highly stable, fast, and reliable. As flash media cards are increasing in capacity, they are becoming a popular format for cameras to record to instead of tape. This format is also resistant to shock and movement, making it ideal for gorillas, or gorilla-filmmakers.

Another advantage of flash memory is in postproduction. In the past, tape had to be logged and captured in realtime by an editor. The new tapeless formats such as flash are merely computer files, binary code. So you just drag and drop the media onto your editing system as you would an MP3 or JPEG. No more logging!

P2 (P2 is a short form for "Professional Plug-in") is a professional digital video storage media format introduced by Panasonic in 2004, and especially tailored to ENG applications. It features tapeless (nonlinear) recording of DVCPRO, DVCPRO50, DVCPRO-HD, or AVC-Intra streams on a solid-state flash memory card. The P2 Card is essentially a RAID of SD memory cards with an LSI controller tightly packaged in a die-cast PC card (formerly PCMCIA) enclosure, so the data transfer rate increases as memory capacity increases. The system includes cameras, decks as drop-in replacement for VCRs, and a special 5.25-inch computer drive for random access integration with NLE systems. The cards can also be used directly where a PC card slot is available, as in most notebook computers, as a normal disk drive, although a custom software driver must first be loaded.

HD and Postproduction

HD has been supported by nonlinear editing systems like Avid and Apple's Final Cut Pro, among others. In addition, there is a growing movement toward a workflow known as Digital Intermediate (DI). In a DI workflow, the picture is acquired on film and then scanned at high-resolution HD (HDCam or HD-D5) or data files at 2K or 4K or higher.

Having 2k or 4k resolution means there are more dots on 4k. However, it seems as though the market is chasing after numbers, like megapixels, on your still cameras. More pixels is not always better. What we react to is not always how crisp the image is. In fact, many cinematographers use filters and other techniques to combat HD videos' "overcrispness and sharpness." Film isn't just sharp; it has a smooth, wet, organic quality that video has a hard time emulating. Often more important than resolution is the quality of the lens (using a Cooke lens provides a smoother image than a Zeiss DigiPrime), lighting, and depth of field. People don't react to pixels, unless it's the Super Bowl XLIV on ultra-HD or whatever is coming down the pipeline.

Then the images are color-corrected and manipulated before sending them back to film for projection. A reel of film at 24fps can be shown anywhere in the world because the playback equipment is everywhere (you can find more details about this process in Chapter 16).

Other Equipment

Grip Package

The grip package brought to the set includes all the elements needed to move the camera, including tripods, heads, a dolly, and track. Heavy rigging equipment, such as rope and clamps, rides with the grips. The grips are also responsible for the apple boxes, which are used to raise the height of set pieces, actors, or camera operators.

Head

To keep its movement fluid, the camera is placed on a head, which allows for smooth pans and tilts. The head can be placed on a dolly or crane so that the pans and tilts can be accompanied by the physical movement of the camera.

Tripod

For static shots, tilts, and pans, the head is placed on a tripod, or sticks. For low-angle shots or if the sticks are too tall, the head is placed on a plywood base, on a high-hat, or even directly onto sandbags.

Dolly

A dolly is a moving tripod system, usually with attached chairs for the camera operator and the director. If the surface on which you wish to dolly is smooth, you might not need to lay track. Track must be laid on rough surfaces, however. The dolly is placed on the rails, and it glides smoothly along the track. Different dolly types include the Western, Panther, Colortran, Crab, and Spyder. The more the wheels can pivot, the more versatile the dolly.

To extend the camera off the dolly, an additional piece of equipment, called a jib arm, is placed perpendicular to the post. The head is put on the end of the jib arm.

STUDENTS

A wheelchair makes a dandy dolly.

Crane

A crane is a dolly that has a movable extension arm. The camera is placed on this arm, which moves parallel to the ground and can lift the camera to great heights. Cranes are cumbersome, expensive, and unwieldy, but crane shots add a great deal of energy to a scene, especially one in which the director wants to move from a close shot to a very wide perspective, or vice versa.

Car, Helicopter, Boat

The ultimate in dynamic camera work is to shoot with your camera moving on a fast vehicle. Slow-moving cars are sometimes used as an alternative to a dolly. If you plan a shot from a car, it is useful to let some air out of the tires. This adds smoothness to the shot. Shooting into a car or from a car, helicopter, or boat requires special mounts. You can also rent a camera car, which is a truck equipped with camera mounts in several places for specific kinds of shots.

Steadicam

The Steadicam is used today to provide a steady, interesting movement shot in films and videos. In this system, a gyro-balanced camera is placed on a rig harnessed to an operator that enables the operator to go where a dolly cannot go and obtain a smooth tracking shot. For example, a Steadicam operator can go up a stairway, through a crowd, or from a walking position to a seated position on a crane.

Lighting Package

The lighting package consists of all the instruments and globes the DP requires, plus lengths of cable for moving the lighting instruments some distance from the power source. The film industry, especially in Hollywood, has become a super-specialized and sub-specialized megamarket. Simple items, such as wooden laundry clips, are renamed C-47S, and a specialty shop in Woodland Hills sells them for five times what you would pay for them in a Bodega in East LA.

The same goes for many lighting instruments. There are lovely low-cost alternatives. **Chinese lanterns**, available at IKEA or lighting shops, provide a gorgeous, wraparound, soft light that can make your actors look fantastic. They are often seen on professional film sets used as a key or fill light. Chimera makes one that costs hundreds of dollars, but you can make your own for under $25. You just need a lantern, a porcelain (not plastic) socket, a photoflood bulb (550w) or at least a 150–200 watt bulb with a small dimmer attached, and you are ready to go.

Another great way to go is to use practical lamps—lights that actually "live" in your scene, such as a floor lamp, a nice wall sconce, or a desk lamp (think the opening scene of *The Godfather*). These lamps not only serve as props, but actually light your actors. They should all be put on dimmers as well for quick adjustments.

Another useful "bang for the buck" is a **par can**. These relatively cheap theater lights give a big output and blast of light, useful for buildings and backgrounds and such in night exteriors.

The cheapest light of all: the sun. Its a billion-watt HMI waiting for you to use it. Renting four or five 4 × 4-feet mirror boards is much cheaper than a truck of HMIs, and a silent generator with Tony, the electrician, running it at $300 per hour. You can use the mirror boards to reflect the sun to wherever it needs to go, and can even pass it through 8 × 8 or 12 × 12-foot silks or diffusion to create soft light, all of this without using a single watt of electricity.

Tricks

Over the course of your career in the film business, you will be forced to devise unique solutions to problems, and these solutions will become part of your personal bag of tricks. Some common camera tricks you might someday need to employ are described in the following sections.

Poor Man's Process

To shoot a scene with characters in a vehicle at night can be expensive and time-consuming. At night, the rear window looks black. Shoot the vehicle in a stationary position, either inside or outside, and add these three elements:

- Have two crew members sit on the rear bumper and gently bounce the vehicle to simulate movement.
- Strafe the back window with a light at intermittent intervals. This technique simulates passing cars.
- In postproduction, add the sound of an engine.

Simple Mattes

Using a hard line in the frame, such as the horizon, black out the sky at the top of the frame and photograph the action in the bottom of the frame. Rewind the camera, black out the lower part of the frame, and reexpose the film with an image that will now be the "sky" part of the frame. This technique eliminates a costly painting and lab fee.

Night for Day

You will often run out of sunlight as you try to meet the day's schedule. For tight shots, HMI lights simulate the color temperature of the sun. Therefore, even when the sun has set, you can still shoot as if it were day, and the material should match. Use this technique in emergencies only. Do not attempt to shoot all day and then all night just because you can get the exposure.

Integrating Animation

The addition of live action actors creates a unique set of issues to be addressed when shooting animation. The easiest solution would be to carefully plan the shot so that the actor or puppet and the digital elements or set pieces are not on the same part of the screen. The composite can be achieved with relatively simple masking away from the primary focus. With live actors and digital elements in the same location shot, a good visual effects (visfx) supervisor will usually request the same shot without any actors so his CG artists and compositors have a clean plate as the basis for the final composite. The clean shot will also be a great help to the CG lighters later in the process.

Professional studios will often use a process known as high-dynamic range (HDR) imaging that more accurately calculates how the environment affects the lighting on the digital object.

In the case of puppet animation, all elements can be filmed together at the same time frame by frame.

> You have your soundtrack broken down to frames. You decide exactly how long each shot would be. I think when I came to shoot *Crazy Glue*, it was nearly edited in camera. I would just pick up the 16mm Bolex, put it down, animate the shot, move it to the next cut, and shoot from there.
>
> Tatia Rosenthal

PRODUCER

Support

The producer's goal is to keep the operation running smoothly with minimum personal involvement. The director runs the show during production, and the producer should not interfere unless he is needed. He should feel confident in his choice of director and allow her to complete her task.

The producer (and the director) needs to be well versed with the technology that is available to create a motion picture to be able to make the appropriate choices to creatively support the director within the confines of the budget.

Laboratory

The producer should establish a contact person at the laboratory who will serve as a liaison through production and postproduction. During the shoot, the liaison at the lab should report daily to the DP about the quality of the footage.

Equipment

The producer must make sure that the equipment package is kept up-to-date. Any equipment that is not being used should be returned.

> As far as equipment goes, develop a relationship with the vendors you are interested in renting from. If it is a student film, tell them! (Student filmmakers can get huge discounts on everything! Milk it for all it's worth.) **Never be afraid to negotiate or ask for a deal**. Make sure you get quotes from a few different places, so you have options and can see where you might be getting a bad deal. Take yourself seriously, and vendors will too.
>
> Jessalyn Haefele, Producer of *Citizen*

Rental House

It is the producer's job to negotiate with the film or video equipment rental house. This experience can be intimidating, but it is possible, even for the beginner, to work out a reasonable deal and to turn the process into a learning experience.

Treat rental houses as more than just a place to pick up equipment. Go there with all your equipment questions before you decide what you want. This is the first step in being a more informed consumer.

Negotiate with an equipment house for the best values just as you would deal with a car or stereo salesperson. The rental house has expensive equipment on the shelves, and the company would rather rent it for a fraction of the full cost than let it sit there. This means you can shop around to different equipment rental houses looking for the best value and use one bidder against another to get the best price.

The producer and the DP need to determine what lights, camera, and grip equipment actually are required. Visit the equipment house and ask to be shown around. Establishing an in-person relationship will make it easier for you to negotiate. A tour will also give you the opportunity to see if the rental house is an impressive establishment or a two-bit operation.

The most expensive way to rent a piece of equipment is by the day. If you need the equipment for a week, you can get up to half off the aggregate daily price. Ask what kind of discount you can get for a set period of time. Asking for a discount is easier, of course, if you have done business with the company in the past and have established your credibility.

The following are other well-known ways to get discounts:

- Weekends count as one day. If you pick up your equipment on a Friday and bring it back on Monday morning, you pay for only one day.
- Travel days and holidays often are not charged.
- Use cash as an incentive. After you have negotiated a deal, offer to pay cash up front. This might get you an additional 10 to 15 percent off the one-day price.

Equipment houses make money charging for accessories that you thought were included in the package. Get a complete list of what you need, and make sure the price you are quoted covers everything.

The rental house will need to see proof of insurance. The company won't let its equipment out without insurance. If you are not covered by a policy through your film or video program or are an independent that cannot afford private insurance, you will have to pay the rental house's rate. Most houses offer some kind of in-house coverage, which might cost up to 10 percent of the rental fee for the equipment.

> **STUDENTS AND INDEPENDENTS**
>
> Being a student or an independent on a low-budget project is not necessarily a liability. Tell those who are dealing with you that you must try to get the best price you can because you simply don't have the cash. This predicament might get you sympathy and a better deal.

Technical Considerations

Power

If a shoot needs more power or a different power source than that provided at the location, it is necessary to supply a generator to power the lights. Generators can be noisy, so be prepared to run extra cable to move the generator as far away from the set as possible.

Be prepared to change fuses on location if you are using the power from wall sockets. If you know how much power each instrument draws and you know how much amperage is available from each socket, you can plug in all your instruments without blowing a fuse. Ideally, the director of photography or the gaffer should gather this information during a preproduction location scout.

Lights

Lighting instruments are placed on heavy-duty legs called *light stands*. These supports can be lowered or raised to position the instrument at a specific height.

Sandbags are placed on the base of the stands for security. Flags, cookies, or tree branches are often placed directly in front of a lamp to create effects or to prevent the light from falling directly onto the camera lens, creating a flare.

> When you're in the field, you've got to trust the cinematographer because you don't want to interrupt the interview. I see the scene in a wide shot because of where I sit as a sound person. If you film in someone's living room and position your subject on a couch, I'm not sure they feel very comfortable because all of a sudden, their living room has been transformed into a film set. There are lights and cables running everywhere. I prefer the naturalness of exterior interviews for that reason and have used them quite extensively in all of my films prior to *Mirror Mirror*.
>
> Jan Krawitz

Camera Noise

Although 16 and 35mm sync cameras are designed to run quietly, often a camera leaks noise during a take. This is most noticeable when shooting interiors in a confined space. *Blimping*, or creating a soundproof housing for the camera, might reduce the noise that emanates from the lens mount, magazine, or body of the camera (this is the assistant camera operator's job). This muffling can be accomplished with a *blimp* or *barney*, which is a jacket that is specially designed for the camera. You can create your own blimp or barney with anything that will deaden the camera noise, such as a changing bag, foam rubber, or a coat or jacket.

Fans

Tight locations can quickly become warm under the lights. Be prepared to ventilate the room and turn on the lights only when necessary.

> It was very hot. The conditions were definitely not very pleasant because there were these lights, and the actors were wearing masks.
>
> Jan Krawitz

KEY POINTS

- Use camera language to shape the frame. This includes lights, camera positions, and lenses.
- What you shoot determines what can be edited, so shoot ample coverage.
- Plan your transitions from shot to shot and from scene to scene. Shoot overlaps.
- Blocking means that you can move the camera, the actors, or both.

Sound

DIRECTOR

Recording Clean Tracks

During the past 40 years, the processing and transmission of sound to film audiences have undergone a radical evolution. Today, projection sound systems such as THX, Dolby, DTS/SDDS, and surround sound have heightened the aural dynamic of the film experience. Digital sound reproduction has drastically changed the way audiences hear soundtracks in theaters. However, with everything that can now be done in postproduction to process and deliver a complex and exciting soundtrack, the most important step in this chain is still the first one: the recording of good, clean sounds, especially dialogue, during principal photography. These sounds will become the foundation on which the rest of the soundtrack is built.

Filmmakers have a range of options for recording audio. The industry was dominated for many years by the **Nagra** (meaning "will record" in Polish), a portable audio tape recorder that was developed by Stefan Kudelski in Poland in 1951 that changed the way production sound was recorded in the field. It was a high-quality magnetic recorder that was light, small, self-contained, and portable. This invention substantially impacted documentary production and fostered the development of the **cinema vérité** and **direct cinema** movements.

The Nagra has since evolved into the digital realm and is still considered the "Gold standard." However, a number of companies also manufacture digital recorders which record to either a hard drive or a flash card: Sound Devices, Tascam, Fostex, and Edirol all have competing products.

When you are shooting video, sound is recorded right on the videotape or P2 card. Different video formats have different audio capabilities. Some record digital audio, some analog, and some combine both technologies. Most professional video productions record sound "double

system" (separately from the picture), sending the production mix to the camera for a guide track at picture editing.

Although the tools have changed, the process of recording sound has remained basically the same. These new recording devices can't perform magic. If the microphone is not placed properly in a dialogue scene, no recorder will deliver a clear rendition of the actor's voice.

Why Getting Good Sound Is So Important

In general, audiences are more critical of what they hear than what they see. We receive approximately 90 percent of our information through our eyes. This creates a greater tolerance in the range of acceptability in visual images. People will watch poor-quality images if the audio is good. On the other hand, an audience will not put up with poor audio because it is more of a strain to make sense of the content. However, having a film or video image that is less than stellar is not nearly so distracting.

Production Sound

Production sound consists of dialogue, the natural sounds associated with each scene, and any other sounds that might be of value during the postproduction process. The person responsible for recording production sound on the set is the **production sound mixer** or **sound recordist**. Equally important is the **boom operator**, who positions the microphone for quality and purity of the sound. Although all sounds, including dialogue, can be re-created during the postproduction process, it is economically and aesthetically best to record as much of the dialogue and natural ambience as possible at the location during principal photography.

Audiences want to hear what the actors have to say, and dialogue recorded on the set is usually the best representation of each scene. However, considering how important sound is to the success of a screen story, it has been the longstanding lament of production sound mixers that the proper recording of sound on the set gets shortchanged. A crew may be willing to sacrifice all on behalf of photographing a good shot, but the sound team often needs to struggle to record one. This is especially true with beginners, students, and low-budget filmmakers.

Crew members may not spend the extra time on the set to get the sound right because they know that dialogue can be replaced later with a process called **automated dialogue replacement** or **ADR** (also known as **looping**). ADR requires that the actors report to a studio months after the shoot to duplicate their original performances line by line. ADR can be time consuming, costly, and problematic, especially for the beginner, but considerably less expensive than having to return to a location and assemble the entire cast and crew to duplicate a scene. (ADR is discussed in considerable length in Chapter 17.)

Bringing actors back months after principal photography to re-create the "magic" of the set in a sterile studio is a challenging endeavor. Martin Scorsese is known to hate ADR. For him, it is akin to directing the movie a second time. Of course, it is more of an aesthetic, not financial, concern for him.

However, there may be legitimate reasons to require ADR when unavoidable interference from traffic or airplanes prevents the recording of "clean" dialogue. If planes fly overhead during a take, the unit must either shut down periodically or record. Shutting down costs time (and money), but recording with the plane noises on the track (which can't be taken off) will cost the production unnecessary time (and money) in the ADR studio later.

Some of these "unavoidable" situations may have been avoided if the location had been scouted for sound, not just visual concerns. Hiring your sound mixer in advance to spend time in a location during the course of a day would have revealed that the location is not "sound friendly." A producer who is sensitive to sound issues might save himself considerable expenses in an ADR studio had he insisted that the production unit not shoot pivotal scenes under the flight plan of a local airport. It comes down to the familiar adage: you can pay now or pay later. It is certainly less expensive to hire a sound mixer for a day than to ADR an entire scene.

This concern is also valid for digital video projects. Films have traditionally been shot double system, the sound being recorded separately from the picture. Filmmakers who have only shot with digital video have not learned the basics of filming in this manner. Even though all digital video cameras have onboard microphones, the professional way to record sound is with a detached microphone feeding into a separate recorder. This approach allows for the most flexibility, control, and the appropriate placement of microphones.

Shooting in sound-friendly locations is especially important for documentaries. In unstaged documentary filming, you might be faced with only one chance to capture an important event or interview. Getting it right the first time is the only option.

In the long run, the production sound team can save the producer time and money by delivering an accurate rendition of the production dialogue. A little extra time setting up a microphone or stopping an annoying sound can save hundreds, even thousands, of dollars in postproduction.

This chapter identifies the sound team, their tools, and how they should optimally function on the production of a narrative or documentary project. With animation, dialogue is recorded before the pictures are animated.

> We scouted the gym and listened for noise. There weren't any classes because the school was closed, but the bell was still working on a timer and scheduled to go off every 45 minutes. We had the janitor dismantle the bell so it wouldn't go off in the middle of the shot.
>
> Howard McCain

The Sound Team

Production Sound Mixer

Production sound mixing is the complex craft of recording live dialogue, sound effects, and location ambience during principal photography of a film or video project. The production sound mixer (also called sound recordist) is the head of the production sound department. He is responsible for assembling the sound crew and choosing the appropriate equipment for the project. The production sound mixer should have a clear understanding of all the crafts that interact with him, such as camera, lighting, and grip. He needs to find a way to achieve the best sound possible within the limitations of each lens choice, camera move, and lighting setup.

Along with a mastery of his craft, the production sound mixer should have a thorough understanding of the postproduction process—that is, what happens to the sounds after they are recorded in production. Being aware of what can be accomplished in postproduction gives the production sound mixer a proper context for judging the work he must do and for properly evaluating the sounds he must sometimes fight for to be able to record clearly.

During preproduction the sound mixer consults with the producer and director on the best ways to approach the recording challenges of the particular show. Each project is different; each will dictate its particular needs. Following are some of the questions he would ask:

- Is the project to be shot on location, on a stage or a combination of both?
- If it is a location shoot, what kinds of weather conditions do they anticipate, such as cold, damp, hot, or humid?
- Are there multiple character scenes?

The production sound mixer is also responsible for supplying fleshed-out **sound reports** and sound notes (this topic will be covered later in the chapter) that help the picture editor and, later, the sound editors clearly understand what was recorded on set and where to find it. The mixer is also responsible for the following:

- Properly preparing for each project
- Knowing what is going to happen in each shot
- Making suggestions to the director (when appropriate)
- Working out a microphone strategy or approach for each scene (in conjunction with the boom operator)
- Approving the recorded take to the director as "okay for sound"
- Working with the script supervisor to make sure all wild lines and wild sound effects get recorded
- Recording room tone and location ambience

Boom Operator

The boom operator is one of the most underestimated positions on the entire crew. The layperson might think that the boom operator is just someone tall and strong enough to hold up a big stick with a microphone attached to the end. Novice producers often assume that a grip or PA can be assigned to work with the mixer. Student filmmakers usually find someone hanging around the set to hold the boom.

In truth, the boom operator is considered an equal partner with the production mixer. He must be strong, agile, attentive, and observant. It is no easy feat to hold a 15-foot long fishpole over his head at full extension, particularly with microphone, shock mount, and windscreen attached at the end, over the course of a 12-hour day for a five-day week for many weeks. Ultimately, a sound mixer is only as good as his boom operator. He can't record "clean dialogue" if the microphone is in the wrong position. The boom operator must

- Have thorough knowledge of microphone sensitivity and pickup patterns
- Be skilled on the operation of the Fisher Microphone Boom
- Keep the mic out of the frame line but still as close to the actor as possible
- Know how to rig lavalieres and radio mics
- Ideally be able to fill in for the sound mixer if necessary

To be most effective, the boom operator needs to learn the dialogue and the blocking of each scene so the microphone can be angled to face each actor just before the line is delivered. A fundamental rule of good microphone technique is that a sound source should be on-mic—at an optimal distance from the microphone and directly in its pickup pattern.

Finally, the boom operator must be totally in sync with the production mixer. With very little verbal or hand sign communication, they must be able to react like one person to situations on the set. Because the mixer/boom relationship is so important, the mixer should always demand the right to choose which boom operator to hire. For a producer to burden a mixer with an inept boom operator is a recipe for disaster. However professional the mixer, he is really only as good as his boom operator. If a microphone is badly placed in a scene, there is no magic solution to making the dialogue audible.

STUDENTS

As hard as finding a production sound mixer for a student shoot can be, finding a boom operator is equally difficult. The boom operator is usually some PA who is not doing something else or someone's best friend who is visiting the set. These are hardly the proper criteria for this important crew position. If a novice boom operator is recruited, it is recommended that the production sound mixer spend quality time before the shoot to rehearse proper boom techniques. Don't wait until the first real take!

Utility Sound Technician

If required, the **utility sound technician** is third person on the sound crew. In the old days, this position was known as the "cableman." Early Hollywood cameras were linked to sound recorders by thick cables that drove the sync motors. Microphone technology wasn't anything like today, so a few cablemen were needed to lug around these huge and heavy cables to support all the microphones they needed.

Today's technology (with crystal sync, portable recorders, radio and condenser mics) eliminates the need to run thick cables over great distances or even the need for that many mics. There can be, depending on the complexity and budget of the show, the need for a **utility sound person**. The word implies that this person should be able to do many things, a sort of "jack of all trades." The utility sound person can be used to

- Handle an extra boom
- Follow behind the boom operator with cable in hand
- Rig and test radio mics
- Be the playback operator
- Fill in for the mixer or primary boom operator if necessary
- Do second unit sound recording

Finally, there can be sequences on a shoot requiring extensive or complicated playback. (Music videos are all about playback.) To handle these situations, a specialist, called a **playback operator**, may be brought in.

Good playback operators should be able to understand and read music and communicate well with composers and choreographers.

The Equipment

The mixer should always assume responsibility for the selection and preparation of the equipment package. Along with the right personnel, good production sound requires the right tools. The sound package should be discussed with the director and DP during the location walk-throughs and final rehearsals so mic types and mic placement are anticipated.

It is quite common for the sound mixer to come with his own equipment. If he doesn't, he should personally oversee the choice of and thoroughly test equipment from a rental house. If the sound equipment package is left up to the production company, the staff will inevitably order what they believe is economically essential. There is a suggested equipment list near the end of this chapter.

Preproduction Planning

The sound mixer should prepare by analyzing the script from a sound perspective. The initial reading usually reveals many of the challenges. Often, a bit of business or a joke relies on the presence of a sound, or at least the cue of a sound, that will be added to the picture in postproduction, such as a gunshot, a doorbell, or the sound of screeching brakes. The script will also reveal

- Whether it is dialogue heavy
- How many characters appear in any given scene
- The nature of the locations (exteriors or interiors or both)
- Weather issues (cold, heat, or humidity)
- Any extra sounds that must be recorded
- Whether playback will be required

The answers to these questions will determine the size of the crew and the type of equipment required.

Site Visit

It is best that the mixer visit the set prior to filming. Walking through the actual spaces will reveal any inherent sound problems that he must deal with before the start of principal photography. The one location choice that has no inherent sound problems is a sound stage, which is a soundproof environment. The only noises you should hear there are the actors' voices. Following are some of the sound considerations that the sound mixer must to sensitive to:

- How large is the space? (Size will impact cables and microphones.)
- What are the acoustics of the space? (Hard surfaces reflect sound.)

- Will sound blankets solve the noise problems?
- Can a loud refrigerator or air conditioning system be shut down?
- Can neighbors be controlled?
- Are key windows right above traffic noise?

Knowing what challenges the mixer faces before the first day of production will enable him to come prepared with the proper equipment. The enemy of all sound mixers is locations with all hard surfaces. Sound bounces all over the place.

It's also possible (and usually the case) that the production sound mixer might walk onto the set for the first time on the first day of principal photography, whereas the director has visited it many times. In this case, the production sound mixer must play catch-up.

STUDENTS

Student productions are usually hard pressed to find one suitable location for their projects, let alone many. Because students may have to settle for the one that may not be so "sound friendly," they will spend the balance of the shoot struggling to make do with usually an inadequate sound crew. It is therefore critical that students spend quality time in every location with the intent of "sounding out" every location.

Responsibilities of the Sound Team

The following are the responsibilities of the film sound team. Some of these tasks are essential; some will depend on the demands of the script or the budget of the production.

- Record "clean" dialogue.
- Match the sound perspective with the camera angle.
- Record the scene so it will cut smoothly (sound consistency).
- Record room tone.
- Record sound effects to accompany the shot.
- Record additional sounds.
- Handle playback on the set.
- Communicate sound issues on the set.
- Keep accurate sound reports.

Dialogue

The production sound mixer's primary responsibility is to record all the dialogue spoken on the set "clean"—that is, unencumbered by any other ambient sounds connected with the shot. Just as the DP is responsible for focus and proper exposure, the production sound mixer strives to record dialogue at consistent levels that can be replayed clearly. A great effort is expended to create "magic" on the set, and it should be recorded properly. You can't duplicate a magical performance in a postproduction sound studio.

If it is impossible to record the dialogue clean, the sound team records it "dirty"—that is, cluttered with the sounds of airplanes, cars, or ocean surf in the background. Although unusable as the final product, this recording is used as a reference, or **guide track**, in the editing room for both cutting and ADR work.

Perspective

The dialogue should be recorded at as close a perspective as the framing allows with as little reverberation on the master track as possible.

Perspective is often added at the final mix stage. If the dialogue is recorded with perspective/reverberation/equalization (EQ) at the location, very little can be done at the mix to remove any inconsistencies. Ultimately, dialogue should be consistent with the point of view of the camera and from the perspective of the lens used for the shot. If the camera sees the action from across a room, the sound should approximate that visual perspective and should sound somewhat distant. In a close-up, the sound should have an intimate, almost overbearing presence. Ideally, viewers should hear the sound from the same point of view from which they see the visuals. Of course, there are times when it's necessary to sacrifice perspective, especially if proper perspective means that viewers will not hear the dialogue.

Sometimes the camera is so far away from the action that performers can be recorded only if their voices are transmitted to a receiver from microphones concealed in their clothing. An example is a scene of a couple walking along a beach shot with a long lens. The audience sees the couple from a distance but hears them as if they were right there. To help correct this "unnatural" perspective, sound effects of waves, seabirds, and wind can be added during postproduction.

Consistency in Sound Recording

The production sound mixer's goal is to record sound consistently from shot to shot. Audiences expect the sound quality of a motion picture to flow seamlessly and continuously. It does not matter to an audience that the final soundtrack was constructed out of numerous camera angles and takes, shot over a wide expanse of time. On-screen, it becomes one continuous mise-en-scène. The realistic consistency or continuity of the final soundtrack is the goal of the entire production and postproduction sound team. It all starts with the dialogue recorded on the set. The production sound mixer must be concerned with the following:

- Consistency within the shot
- Consistency within shots within the scene
- Consistency between scenes

Within the shot, levels should remain relatively constant between actors and also between background ambiences. Actors are not expected to match each other in terms of recording levels; variations are normal. But their levels should match themselves. As they speak, the actor's audio should appear somewhat constant. There should be no unwarranted sudden changes in volume, except when justified by dramatic intent.

In addition to the actors, the production sound mixer should be mindful of background noise. The side effect of continually adjusting the level of the microphones to balance the level of the actors may result in the background noise bouncing up and down. The problem can be avoided by taking advantage of the acoustic properties of the mics to control the relative levels of the dialogue by positioning and angling the microphones rather than by electronically adjusting the gain (volume) at the recorder or mixing panel. This is why the boom operator is such an important player and why he should be provided with a good headphone. The mixer and boom operator should also be present during rehearsals before the first take to familiarize themselves with blocking, dialogue levels, and possible overlapped dialogue.

When the camera changes angle, the mixer must be especially attentive that the levels of the new shot match the previous one as much as possible. This is done so the two angles can be edited together without drastic changes in audio levels.

Panning or cutting from one close-up to another of two people standing and talking does not constitute a major perspective change. Levels and background are expected to remain constant. However, when you move the microphone for a close-up, readjust the volume so that the actor's voice remains constant with the rest of the sequence.

A character's audio should be somewhat constant throughout the course of a scene, even as the shot changes from wide shot to medium to close-up. If you close your eyes, the changes in audio from shot to shot should not sound unnatural or unexpected. To minimize this bump in volumes at the editing stage, mixers often use shotgun or lavaliere mics that are more discrete in their sound-collecting properties. Matching ambience between the cuts in exterior locations that change often, like background traffic, requires skillful dialogue editors to smooth the transitions between cuts.

Not only does sound need to be consistent within a shot and from shot to shot, but also because this footage will be integrated during editing, the sound must match up when scenes are cut with other scenes. Throughout the duration of the production, try to establish and then maintain relative audio levels for all your characters. Of course, there are going to be some changes in the audio levels. The nature of production is such that we can't always control things as much as we like, such as mic placement and background ambience. The idea, though, is to try to keep the changes in levels minimal and as inconspicuous as we can when we record them and then to fix them during postproduction.

> The production sound mixer tried to record everything, which I think was a smart move on her part.
>
> Adam Davidson

Room Tone

The mixer will often be required to supply 30–60 seconds (although 10 seconds will due in a pinch) of sound presence, or "room tone," from each location. These 60 seconds of tone can then be copied and used in postproduction to fill in holes and smooth out the dialogue tracks when preparing for the mix. It is important that the tone be recorded with the lights on and the full cast and crew on the set, with the same microphone used to record the dialogue and at the same levels. It is recommended that the mixer arrange to do this before the camera rolls before the first take. Everyone will be in position, and the sound will be an exact match of the actual take. Waiting to ask everyone on a set to be still and quiet at the end of the last take will be a struggle for the mixer because cast and crew are ready and eager to wrap for the day.

It is also suggested that the mixer record the hum of a refrigerator, fluorescent lights, or other equipment separately. This gives the editor freedom to add that ambient sound during the editing process.

Sound Effects

Footsteps, cloth rustling, and prop movement should ideally be recorded on a **Foley** (see Glossary) stage with no ambience added. However, to avoid costly Foley work (it can be expensive), the production sound mixer can capture as many of the ambient sounds and live effects connected with the shot as possible. Examples of these are footsteps, hand props, slamming doors, ball bounces, and windows opening. These extra or "wild" sounds should be properly slated and labeled for future reference. They will be mixed in separately during postproduction.

For example, in a bar scene, after the principal photography is completed or before the extras are dismissed, the production sound mixer should ask the assistant director for a short recording session in which the crowd chats, drinks, sings, and cheers as though it were in a real bar. Two minutes of this sound will furnish the sound effects editor with ample material to create a full bar atmosphere. Because the main dialogue is recorded while the crowd is silent, the editor will have the dialogue and the background sounds on two different tracks, giving him complete control over volume levels.

The production mixer' primary responsibility is to record dialogue as clean and discrete as possible. If there is time and if any of the production effects are usable, recording them is an added bonus for postproduction.

Additional Sounds

Supplementary sound effects should be recorded and delivered to the editing room. If the crew is shooting in an interesting location, especially if it is distant, the sound team should record any particular sound that is unique to that area. Different parts of the country have their own aural "presence"—a combination of insects and birds that are characteristic to a particular environment. It saves time and money to record additional sounds during the shoot, rather than having to come back later.

During the shoot, for example, if the production sound mixer knows that a school is near the location, he might go to the schoolyard and record children at play. These sounds might be used for background ambiance, or they might not. Regardless, they give the sound editor a variety of choices and might even stimulate other sound ideas during postproduction.

> We sat down and made a list of wild sounds before the shoot, e.g., the sound of a squishing sole, a ball hitting the court, a hand on the rope....We had a list of sounds that took about an hour to get once the shoot was over.
>
> Howard McCain

Playback/Music Video

When examining the script, the production sound mixer looks for any situation that might require unusual equipment such as radio microphones or a playback machine. The latter is necessary when actors must sing, dance, or otherwise respond on the set to previously recorded music. Because this music will be used later in the film, it must be recorded with a reference pilot tone or **SMPTE timecode** (see Glossary) so it can be later synchronized with the picture. Unless the sound person is familiar with handling playback duties, he may need to bring in a specialist on days when playback is required.

If you are planning to shoot a music video, the music will come to you on tape, CD, or other format. During the shooting of the "video," the band will lip-sync with the song. The production sound mixer is responsible for playing back the song. Shooting a music video with video cameras is fairly straightforward. As long as the playback is on a stable, speed-controlled format, the singers' mouth movements captured on video should match up to the song in postproduction. Some video cameras may drift slightly in speed. A timecode or sync generator may be used to keep the audio playback and camera locked together. Even without it, if shots are kept short, they probably won't reveal noticeable sync drift.

Shooting with a film camera for release on **NTSC video** (see Glossary) is slightly more complicated. If the camera is run at the usual 24 frames per second (fps), the picture will not hold sync with the song during editing. The reason is that the picture will be pulled down in speed by 0.1 percent during the film-to-video transfer because of the frame rate difference between film and video (24fps versus 29.97fps). Compared to the master recording of the song, the singers on video will be moving their lips 0.1 percent too slow. The most common solution to this problem is to shoot at standard 24fps and pull up the music playback by 0.1 percent on the set. Several analog and digital recorders can be set to play exactly 0.1 percent faster. The lip-syncing is then done to the speeded-up song, but when the footage is transferred to video, it will drop down to the speed of the original song.

You should always consult with the laboratory or whoever will be transferring your footage before your shoot. In video, if the camera and recorder/playback are set at the same timecode rate, they will always stay in sync, even in double system mode. In film, the recorder or playback source should always be set at 30fps 60Hz. One second of sound is always equal to one second of film. If you are going to telecine, let the telecine house do the pull down to match the film/video transfer. Always note the sample rate, bit depth, and timecode rate on your sound logs.

Communication on the Set

The sound department is routinely asked to provide communication on the set. It is most common for you to be asked to supply an audio feed from your mixing panel or recorder for the director, producer, or script supervisor. The simplest way to do this is to rig a spare headphone feed, plug in a long extension cable, and give the headphones to the interested party. If more than one person needs to monitor the sound, the mixer will use some sort of headphone splitter box. The more effective way to accomplish this is a wireless connection. It is now standard in the industry to use a miniature transmitter on the sound cart. Anyone who needs to monitor the soundtrack is given a miniature receiver along with headphones. This allows the director complete freedom to wander around the set and still hear the dialogue.

Walkie-talkies are the other main form of communication on the set, the most popular being the Motorola. It is a professional-grade walkie-talkie, featuring 5-watt output and lots of channels. Depending on the size of the production, the sound department may be asked to furnish from four to six dozen for a project.

Sound Report

The production sound mixer should take clear and comprehensive notes of the dialogue recorded on the set and the "wild sounds" recorded on or off the set. He should confer with the script supervisor or assistant camera operator for the scene numbers and the director's comments. These notes, called a sound report (see Figure 12.1),

10639 Riverside Dr.   (Outside CA) (800)228-4429
North Hollywood , CA 91602   FAX (818)980-9911
(818)980-9891   Internet   www.locationsound.com

Title:		Date:
Production No.		Roll No.
Mixer:		Sheet No. ____ Of ____
Boom:		Location:

☐ SYNC: ____ Hz   ☐ WILD   Time Code: ____ FR/S ☐ Drop Frame

Head Tone ____ dBM   Sample Rate ____   Recorder ____

PRINT CIRCLED TAKES ONLY

Scene No.	Take	Roll	Notes	SMPTE Start
				: : :
				: : :
				: : :
				: : :
				: : :
				: : :
				: : :
				: : :
				: : :
				: : :
				: : :
				: : :
				: : :
				: : :
				: : :
				: : :
				: : :
				: : :
				: : :
				: : :
				: : :
				: : :
				: : :
				: : :
				: : :

IF LAST ROLL OF DAY—CHECK HERE ☐

FIGURE 12.1   Location sound report sheet. (Courtesy of Professional Sound Services, New York, NY, www.prosound.com.)

will later serve as a reference for the editor and eventually the sound effects editor. The sound mixer should be in close communication with the script supervisor and share all log information for the script notes. Sound reports have expanded over the years to a full-page-width report that allows the mixer more room for detailed notes.

The sound report is a record of all the hard work the sound team accomplishes on the set and, as such, is an invaluable guide to what has been recorded and where to find it. The more comprehensive and detailed, the more valuable it is. Sound editors need to know what is happening on the dialogue track and what kind of interference, such as airplane noise or off-screen chatter, may be marring the recording.

Keeping detailed notes of wild tracks is equally important as dialogue. These notes will determine what sounds the effects editor may need to refer to or authorize to have done when building tracks for the final film. It is also important to make note of a shot for which there is no sound recorded. Shots without sound are listed on the sound report as MOS. There are a number of apocryphal stories for this abbreviation ("Mit out sound" being one of them). The real origin may have been in the early sound days when sound was photographed "optically" on the film. If the director didn't require sync sound for a particular shot, the recording mixer listed the abbreviation MOS for "minus optical sound" on the sound report.

Additional information can include type of mic and coverage for each track recorded. This kind of information can be invaluable to telecine and the assistant editor.

> Every night during a location shoot, as exhausted as I am, I will listen to all the sound recorded that day and do my sound log. It keeps me familiar with what I have, and it enforces that discipline of keeping my material organized and not assuming that I have something on tape and finding out that I don't.
>
> Jan Krawitz

Video Shoots

For video shoots, someone may be assigned to keep logs of each take using a simple log form with columns indicating tape number, timecode start and stop, scene number or content, and any notes about whether the take was good or bad. There are electronic devices such as the Shot Logger, a handheld computer that allows information, including timecode start and stop, to be later uploaded to a nonlinear editing machine.

Approaches to Recording Sound

The recording of clear and crisp dialogue and sound effects is no easy task. The key is to start with some basic strategies and then work from there. However, the mixer needs to be prepared for as many contingencies as possible. For example, even though the shooting schedule calls for an interior shoot, directors have been known to move unexpectedly outdoors. The mixer must then be prepared with an exterior shotgun mic with a windscreen.

Following are the basic strategies of using microphones:

- Boom
- Plant
- Lavaliere
- Radio microphone

Boom

Using a boom is, in most cases, the best way to record dialogue. **Boom** is a generic term for any long pole with a microphone attached to the end of it that is used to record dialogue. It might be a complicated unit called a Fisher boom, which uses a pulley system to expand and contract, or a variable-length pole called a **fishpole**, with the microphone attached to a movable "shock mount" at the end. The latter is most common.

Fishpoles usually run from 12 to 18 feet in length and are rigid enough not to bend at full extension. (You don't want the microphone to dip into the shot.) The boom is used to position the microphone close to the scene to record dialogue between several actors simultaneously. The mount allows the boom operator to manipulate the microphone from one actor to another during the scene, depending on who is delivering lines. Because it is a mobile unit, the boom operator can follow moving action at a safe distance from the camera and still be close enough to pick up a clean signal from the actors.

Because fishpoles and microphones cause shadows, a skilled boom operator should be able to eyeball each lighting setup in relation to the actors in the scene to find the least conspicuous position to place the boom. He must also pay close attention to what his mic is picking up in relation to the other mics on the set. This is why the boom operator wears headphones and monitors the complete program mix, not just what his boom is picking up.

> The production sound mixer had done some documentary work, so he was used to both operating the Nagra and doing the boom at the same time. It was just luck. I don't remember thinking ahead, "Oh, we should get a guy from a documentary because I'm going to shoot this guerrilla style."
>
> Adam Davidson

FIGURE 12.2   The production sound mixer needs to be quick in a real location. Photo from the filming of *The Lunch Date*.

Overhead Boom

The optimum way to position the boom is overhead (see Figure 12.2). This position yields the most natural sounding dialogue with the least amount of mixing. Other reasons why overhead mic'ing is preferable are as follows:

- Two, three, or even a small group of people can be recorded from a single mic.
- An overhead boom will pick up sufficient sound effects, footsteps, and hand prop noise to give the soundtrack a rich texture.
- It allows for a fair amount of physical activity and movement by the actors.
- Audio perspective is easier to maintain.

If it is physically impossible to mic from overhead, the next best option is to boom from underneath. The mic can be positioned from knee, thigh, or waist level with good results. The sound will be more bassy than from overhead, but still quite acceptable. The increase in bass results from the microphone picking up more of the chest cavity.

During exterior shoots, a blimp-type windscreen is required to reduce the wind sounds the microphone picks up. Even when shooting interiors, always use a slip-on foam windscreen because some microphones (**condenser-shotgun**) are sensitive to even the most minute air movements.

The boom operator should use a set of headphones to monitor what is being recorded. The production sound mixer can give direction and speak to the boom operator through the headphones. This way, the production sound mixer doesn't have to shout to the boom operator.

A cable operator might be required if the shot calls for camera movement. This crew member keeps the microphone cables clear of the camera, grip, and electric equipment while the boom operator concentrates on following the action. The movement of the microphone cable might cause a rustling noise on the track, so it must be handled carefully.

Documentary sound crews usually do not have a separate boom operator. The production sound mixer acts as a self-contained sound recording unit. He does not have to be positioned far from the action and can easily handle the levels and position the microphone at the same time.

Plants/Stash

Plants or stash are microphones that are not mobile; they are "planted" or "stashed" in a fixed location for the duration of the scene. For example, they might be used to pick up the voice of an actor who is too far away from the boom. They need to be hidden from the view of the camera. They can be taped or mounted in doorways, on bed headboards, behind pictures, under chairs, in flowerpots, under car visors, and so on. A boom or directional mic can be used as a plant, but is usually an **omni** or **cardioid** mic with a wider pattern of sensitivity.

Lavaliere

A lavaliere is small, lightweight, **omnidirectional** microphone pinned under an actor's clothing or taped to the body. It must be carefully placed so as not to pick up the rustle of clothing as the actor moves, and it must be rechecked constantly in case it dislodges as a result of constant movement or moisture (if taped).

Lavalieres are effective microphones if the actor remains fairly stationary during a take, but if the actor is required to walk, dragging the microphone cable might be awkward. A radio microphone might be needed in this case. One could say that the handling and placement of lavalieres is almost an art form unto itself. There are sophisticated techniques and tricks of the trade that an experienced sound mixer/boom operator brings to these situations.

Perspective, however, is a problem with lavalieres that even an experienced sound mixer can't prevent. Dialogue recorded with lavalieres sounds as though it was recorded close to the camera even if the actors were in a long shot. Dialogue also sounds sterile and free of natural sound effects and ambiance. This is not a problem in interview situations for documentaries, which is why lavalieres are frequently used.

Radio Microphones

Radio microphones are lavalieres that are attached to a wireless radio transmitter which transmits a signal to a receiver. Radio microphones are used to cover hard-to-reach areas, such as a wide shot of a couple talking on a beach. If the actors are far from the reach of a boom, plant, or lavaliere, a radio microphone might be your only option. We recommend their use only if it is the option of last resort. There are many problems associated with wireless mics. The basic one is that they often pick up other frequencies, such as police cars, taxi transmissions, aircraft, walkie-talkies, and many more. Here are some of the other problems:

- They are expensive to rent.
- You must budget for batteries (they eat current).
- They are notorious for not working when you need them.
- They have the same inherent problems as lavalieres.
- Also, the range is never what you expect or what the company claims because you will never be working in a perfect environment.

The only problem that we had—and one that wasn't immediately obvious—was the noise. Most people, if they see a highway outside their window, understand they're going to get car noise in the background or they choose another location. But in this case, it was an unseen thing that got us.

Near the school, about 400 yards away, was a high-powered radio station antenna that broadcast country music. Surprisingly, the boom pole was acting as a receiver, and country music was being picked up at certain times and transmitted into the Nagra and recorded onto the tape. We discovered that on the first day of shooting and were horrified. We realized very quickly that the microphone had to be placed precisely and not moved. If you moved the boom slightly, it came back into frequency. So only after we had the microphone set up—and it took several tries—we could shoot.

Howard McCain

Variables for Placing Microphones

The placement and use of the different microphones depend on the many variables of a particular scene. The mixer and the boom operator must watch a rehearsal of the scene. Knowing where actors will be positioned and how they will move allows the production sound team to make informed decisions. They must be able to see what the camera is seeing to be able to keep mics safely away from the frame line. This is accomplished by looking through the camera's viewfinder. Evaluate the scene first, and then work with the following considerations.

The Director's Vision. Who and what does the director want to hear in the shot? Start with this as the basic premise of every decision.

Placement and Blocking of Actors. How much does an actor move in the shot? An actor pacing in the frame must be microphoned differently than one sitting still. A boom or two separate microphones might be necessary to record the sequence.

Placement of Camera. How far away is the camera from the action of the scene? This defines how close you can get with a microphone. If the most directional microphone is unrealistic, mics are then "stashed" within the frame of the master shot closer to the action.

Size and Composition of Shot. What is the lens seeing? This affects a number of issues. How close to the actor can the microphone on the boom be positioned without slipping into the frame line? The boom operator must be keenly aware of the frame line at all times. He should rehearse with the camera operator before the final rehearsal with the actors. Both the camera operator and the boom operator must be consistent in their moves. The size of the shot also affects the visibility of a lavaliere or radio microphone. A very tight shot of an actor will require that the microphone be more carefully disguised than in a long shot.

Lighting of Shot. The lighting plan can cause problems if the sound boom creates a shadow that can be seen in the frame. During the lighting setup, any boom shadows should be dealt with before the lights are fixed with the use of **flags** and **cutters** (see Glossary) on the lights. During the shoot, the elimination of boom shadows must be a coordinated effort between the boom and camera operators.

Movement of the Shot. If a dolly is used for a shot, the boom operator must rehearse his actions around those of the dolly. A production assistant or cable operator might be needed to keep the microphone cable free from the path of the dolly and clear of the electric cables. The mixer also needs to avoid picking up the sound created by the dolly.

Acoustics of Location. The production sound mixer might need to position the microphone away from disruptive sounds to minimize their presence on the track. Common troublemakers are refrigerators, air conditioners, fluorescent lights, traffic noise from the windows, and natural echoes in the location. **Sound blankets** might also be required to eliminate or at least lessen the problem.

Sound blankets can be used in a variety of ways to deaden the sound of "live" rooms by baffling the reflective sound echoes caused by hard floors, ceilings, walls, and windows. Sound blankets are heavy moving blankets, preferably with a white side and a dark gray or black side and grommets for hanging. They can be taped to walls, hung from C-stands and over windows, or even draped over refrigerators and air conditioning units to create a quieter environment.

Camera Noise. Although 16mm and 35mm sync cameras are designed to run quietly, often a camera leaks noise during a take. This noise is most noticeable when shooting interiors in a confined space. Blimping, or creating a soundproof housing for the camera, might reduce the noise that emanates from the lens mount, magazine, or body of the camera. (This is the AC's job.) This muffling can be accomplished with a blimp or **barney** (See Glossary), which is a jacket that is specially designed for the camera. You can create your own blimp with anything that will deaden the camera noise, such as a changing bag, foam rubber, or a coat or jacket.

One way of cutting down on camera noise is to position the camera as far away from the microphone as possible during the take. A small amount of camera noise can usually be camouflaged by the other sounds or music that will inevitably be mixed in during postproduction. This is a good example of why the production sound mixer must understand what happens during postproduction to be able to effectively evaluate the sounds recorded on the set.

Where to Place the Recorder. It is best placed on the edge of the set, close enough for the sound mixer to see and hear what is happening, but away from the traffic of lights and grip equipment. Careful attention must be paid to positioning the microphone cables. Electric AC current can induce hum into the signal in the microphone cable, making it impossible to record clean sound. A 60Hz notch filter will remove most AC hum.

The sound mixer and boom operator decide how many microphones to use, what specific kinds, and where to place them. Once the microphones are positioned, there should be a final rehearsal to enable the mixer to adjust for proper recording levels. Actors should speak at the level they will be projecting during the actual take. The mixer should do a test that can be erased when you start recording for real. Now the mixer is ready for the take.

Much of sound recording involves "riding levels," which means leveling out the extremes of performance and balancing multiple characters. For example, the production sound mixer might have to handle dialogue between one actor who speaks softly and another who bellows.

Balancing these two performances is part of the art of mixing. It also requires maintaining consistent sound among the different takes of the same scene. If you have already shot the master of a scene and the background ambience is clean but a plane flies over when you shoot the close-up, you should redo the close-up to match the background of the long shot. The sound mixer should always alert the director to these problems after the take is shot and note them in his sound logs. Logs should also contain any lines obscured by prop noise and signal dropouts.

Recording Concerns

One of the differences between how sound and film images are recorded is that you can immediately hear a sound take played back on the set. Video has this advantage as well, but film must be sent to a lab to be processed. With the sound, if there is any question of quality, the director can listen to a take with the headphones on to decide whether she wants to do the shot over for sound or performance.

The director will ask whether a take is good for camera and whether it is good for sound. Camera will be first on the list. Asking for another take because of sound problems is a judgment call the director makes after listening to the track. Many sound problems can be addressed in postproduction, whereas picture problems must always be handled during filming.

Pickups

If only a small section of a take is ruined because of extraneous sounds, it might not be necessary to do the complete take again. You might be able to "pick up" the section of the take that was spoiled. In a pinch, the sound can be also taken "wild" (audio recording only) and matched to the picture in postproduction.

If the day has been fraught with sound problems, holding a makeshift ADR session in a quiet room after the day's work can save a lot of money. If it is impossible to do it right after the scene is shot, have the actors come to the quiet area when they get out of makeup and costume. After the actors listen to their performance on headphones, they repeat the original dialogue for the production sound mixer. This material will most likely match well with the actors' lips in the editing room. If it does not, with some minor adjusting (stretching and shrinking), the new material can be made to fit. This method is most successful when used in wide shots when it is more difficult to see the actors' mouths.

Keeping It Clean

Be aware of actors who step on one another's lines. This is called **overlapping**. If two sounds are already blended on the track, they can never be controlled separately. They will be married forever. Record dialogue that can later be controlled in the editing room. In a single shot in which an off-camera actor has lines, he should make sure there is a pause between the on-camera actor's line and his own line. Recorded separately, or with a pause, lines can be manipulated in the editing room to create overlaps, but the editor will be able to control each voice.

If the director wants the lines overlapped for dramatic purpose, the off-camera dialogue should be microphoned as well. If the scene is a wide shot, overlapping lines may be an integral part of the drama.

Guide Tracks

The production sound mixer might not be able to achieve clean sound on a difficult set or location. Planes traveling overhead will destroy a sound take. Some locations, such as Grand Central Station, are too busy to control. If the company is on a flight path where waiting for good sound translates to little or no photography, the director will have to bite the bullet and plan for ADR work. However, it is still important to record production dialogue. It can be used as a guide track for editing purposes and as a reference track for the actors when they perform the lines during the ADR session. Clean ambience (background sound) should also be taken to mix or blend with the lines that will inevitably be recorded later.

Crowd Scenes

To record clean sound in a crowded bar sequence, the assistant director instructs the background extras to mime speech and the clinking of glasses. This means that during the take, the background actors move their lips, but utter no sound. They raise their glasses, but do not let the glasses touch. They dance to a predetermined rhythm, but there is no music playing. These sounds are added later.

This allows the dialogue recorded on the set to be "clean." It will not have any dirty crowd noise to fight the dialogue. To maintain the illusion, the speaking actors must project their voices as if they were fighting the din of the crowd and the music. (To help the actors with this, it is good to rehearse the scene with the full-blown background noise.) This way, when the three soundtracks—dialogue, music, and background noise—are married in the mix, the volume of each track can be controlled separately. The scene will sound natural, and the dialogue will come through so that the audience can understand it.

Video Sound

Most amateur video sound recording is done single system, with the sound recorded right on the videotape (there are situations when audio is recorded separately). Most camcorders have microphones built into the camera. These are simple and convenient but may result in inferior sound because the microphone is too far from the source for optimum recording. These on-board mics will pick up unwanted noises around the camera.

Different tape formats have different configurations of soundtracks, but most allow for stereo recording (two channels: left and right). Formats that allow you to record four separate tracks will give you flexibility in production, because you can assign different microphones to different channels. One of the virtues of video is that it is generally

easy to transfer the project from one video format to another. You could shoot with a Hi-8 camera, bump up (transfer) the tape during editing to a four-channel format, and then release in a six-channel DVD.

Professional-quality sound can be achieved only by using separate mics that are placed close to the subject. These may be fed to the camcorder or videotape recorder (VTR) through a cable or wireless transmitter. When a production sound mixer is on the crew, the mics are often fed to a mixer, which allows easy monitoring of sound levels and blending of multiple mics.

Most video productions record double system and send the production mix to the camera for a guide track at picture editing. There are several important reasons to separate sound and picture with video shoots:

Sound editors/designers prefer a separate production track. Often when working in postproduction, sound technicians will ask for a clone of the production track. Depending on the sound editing software they are using, they can use the production sound to redigitize the sound and cut it in an environment that has a higher bit rate and better audio code. In addition, they can pull takes from the tape that the editor chose not to use or replace small sections of takes with other takes. This allows the sound person more freedom to create the best work possible and also reduce needed ADR.

DV cameras can drift out of sync slightly when recording for long periods of time. It is a rare problem, but it happens. Sony has tried to rectify this problem with the introduction of its DVCam technology. The DVCam tapes and recorders use the larger tape width (6.35mm) to pack more audio information into the track. This feature is called **audio lock**. Friction increases between tape and recorder heads after repeated passes on the tape. DVCam tape has a significantly lower friction coefficient than DV. For the professional, this means greater recorded signal longevity, higher reliability, increased durability, and overall improved performance.

For numerous reasons, there have been digital audio glitches on videotape. Most of the time the problem is that the record head was dirty or possibly someone used the wrong kind of tape in the camera (depending on the camera, it is sometimes better to use lubricated tapes as opposed to nonlubricated tape; this is especially important with the Panasonic DVX100/a). Once there is an audio glitch, that take is unusable. If you have a separate digital recording as well, the chance that you will run into this problem is slim. And in the event that you have to replace the take, you have the backup tape.

It is always good to have a backup audio recording. The great thing about shooting with a video camera is that you can run a line-out from the digital recorder directly to the video camera. That way, you have sound on the videotape and a backup on the digital recorder.

Video sound crews vary according to the complexity of the production (how many characters have to be recorded in a sequence) and whether it is a location shoot or a studio shoot. A single-camera setup in the field might need only a one-person crew to operate the videotape recorder, mix the incoming microphone levels, and hold the boom. A scene with many characters requires a boom operator and a production sound mixer with a mixing unit that has anywhere from 2 to 12 inputs. A studio shoot with multiple cameras for one scene might use a mixing console of up to 18 tracks.

When you're shooting video, the choice of camcorder or VTR format is usually driven by picture needs, but these decisions will clearly have an impact on sound as well. In selecting a system, review these considerations:

- How many audio tracks do you need?
- Does the camcorder allow manual adjustments of audio levels?
- Can you use external mics?
- Are there professional mic connectors (such as XLR), or will you need adapters?
- If you are working with a production sound mixer, will you need a mixing console so he can control levels?

These are important questions for those shooting on small video formats such as Hi-8, S-VHS, and MiniDV. Most professional camcorders give you a choice between manual and automatic control of audio levels. Many consumer models have only automatic control, which is convenient but may result in inferior recordings. Always choose a camcorder that offers the option of manual level control. Also, the consumer shotgun microphone that comes with the camera will usually sound fine, but plugging in a professional mic may result in a lot of buzz, hum, and lower audio levels because the built-in mic preamp is not matched to the XLR/phantom-powered output professional mic. (Always use a separate mic preamp mixer.) Make sure to plan and test your video sound recording system well in advance. You want the advantages that video can offer without having to compromise when it comes to the quality of the audio.

Documentary

The recording of good, intelligible location sound is critical in documentary production. Unlike actors in a narrative project, the sound mixer can't ask for more takes from your subjects. He has to get it right the first time. Because documentary crews are usually small and mobile, the production sound mixer and boom operator is usually the same person. He must be adept at booming, mixing (if additional microphones are used), and

operating the recorder simultaneously. In narrative production, there is usually time to survey a location. In a documentary, the crew often arrives at the site for the first time on the day of the shoot.

An experienced sound mixer knows "the dance" that has to be done with the camera. He must follow the DP's lens while staying out of the shot but still get the best angles for recording. He must instinctively know what microphones are appropriate in any given situation. In unstaged documentary filming, it is important that the mixer be ready to roll at a moment's notice. If shooting is imminent, the recorder should be put on "standby" position, and the recording level should be set. If the scene looks interesting, the mixer should not hesitate to roll sound. Recording sound in any format is inexpensive. If the scene does not pan out, simply say, "No shot."

It is equally important to capture the ambient sounds or "room tone" of each environment. What may seem like routine background sound can bring shades and nuances to the visuals and play an important role in establishing the aural world of your characters.

> I always wear the headphones because I think you get in trouble if you simply trust the needle and assume that you are getting decent sound. I think the trade-off of looking a little odd is incidental. It does remind your subjects that they're being recorded, but so does all the other equipment. What's important to me as both the director and the sound person is to get the best sound, and the only way to assure that is to be monitoring what's coming off the tape, not what I'm hearing in the environment.
>
> Jan Krawitz

Web Site Information

- Microphones (sensitivity and pattern)
- Types of (dynamic, electret condenser, true condenser)
- Phantom Power
- Pickup patterns (Omni, Cardioid, directional, shotgun, eng)
- Shockmounts, windscreens

PRODUCER

Controlling the Environment

Because one of the producer's major concerns is managing the budget, anything that contributes to saving time and money will get his attention. In the area of sound recording, hiring a skilled production sound mixer and boom operator is the first step. Be sure the production sound mixer knows that his main concern is recording clean production dialogue.

The following are additional areas the producer must focus on:

- Ensuring that the equipment needs of the production are fulfilled (recording devices, microphones, etc.)
- Getting the best deals possible on the rental equipment
- Guaranteeing that all locations are "sound-friendly"
- Asking the production sound mixer to capture sufficient ambient and interesting sound effects from each location
- Ensuring proper care of the equipment

Equipment Needs for the Shoot

Once the production sound mixer understands the demands of the script and the locations, he can develop an accurate list of his equipment needs. These are appropriate for film and video shoots. They might include some of the following tools:

- Location sound cart
- Mini Disk, DAT, DVD Ram and/or Nagra
- Portable mixer panel
- Slate mic
- Wireless transmitter and receiver
- Shotgun (hyper-cardioid) mic
- Lavaliere mic, assorted clips
- Good condenser mics (selection of shotguns)
- Headphones (two or three sets)
- Microphone cables
- Cables for mic-to-mixer and camera-to-mixer connections (video)
- Tape stock (if appropriate)
- Shock mounts
- Slip-on windscreen
- Sound blankets
- Zeppelin windscreen
- Fishpole mic boom with shock mount
- Rechargeable batteries
- Mounting clips
- Extra batteries

How Big of a Sound Package and Crew Do You Need?

There are five different scenarios based on budget and crew size from low to high in ascending order. The tasks and the technical skills stay the same at each level, but the technical complexity multiplies from level to level. Recording sound is recording sound, but there is a base line below which accomplishing this task professionally cannot be done.

Low to High Budget:

- DV camera with an on-board shotgun (camera operator and sound are one person); real limitations with this setup regarding ability to record usable sound
- DV camera with separate recorder, mixing panel, boom microphones, lavalieres (two-person crew: mixer and boom)
- HD cam, stereo recorder, mixing panel, boom microphones, lavalieres, and wireless microphones (two-person crew: mixer and boom)
- HD/film camera–multitrack recorder, mixing panel, boom microphones, lavalieres, wireless microphones, set communication (three-person crew: mixer, boom, utility)
- All the above with a playback specialist

Digital recorders are the industry standard. They offer high quality in a small, light package and have had a huge impact on video and film production. There are many types of digital recorders used for field production. DAT machines, which were the standard when the previous edition of this book came out, have been replaced by machines that record on hard drives, flash cards, or computer tape data drives; chip-based systems such as the Nagra Ares C, which records on computer memory cards with no moving parts; and magneto-optical disc systems such as Sony's MiniDisk.

A notable example is Sound Devices' 702T Portable Digital Recorder with Time Code. The two-channel 702T is a powerful two-track file-based digital audio recorder with timecode. The super-compact device records and plays back to convenient, removable compact flash cards, making field recording simple and fast. It writes and reads uncompressed PCM audio at 16 or 24 bits with sample rates between 32kHz and 192kHz. Compressed (MP3) audio playback is also supported. The timecode implementation makes the 702T perfect for any dual-system video or film production application (see Figure 12.3).

These rugged machines have no moving parts and exhibit none of the problems of DAT machines. They are impervious to humidity and extreme temperature.

Microphones

Microphones are delicate instruments that convert sound waves into electric signals (refer to the web site for a detailed description of microphones). The production sound mixer must have a thorough knowledge of microphones and how they can be used effectively to capture sound under a wide variety of conditions. He must be able to identify the right microphone for each situation. Microphones (and speakers) are still analog, so sound is captured and reproduced using the same equipment regardless of the recorder format. The sound signal comes from the mic and goes to an analog-to-digital (A-D) converter. To play back the tape, the digital signals are then

FIGURE 12.3 Sound Devices' 702T Portable Digital Recorder. (Courtesy of Sound Devices, LLC.)

sent to a digital-to-analog (D-A) converter, which transforms the binary numbers back to an analog signal that can be heard through speakers or headphones.

KEY POINTS

- The production sound mixer should know what happens to sound in postproduction.
- Scout the location at the time of day or night for which the shoot is planned.

- During rehearsals, find the best places for the microphones and the boom. The boom operator should work out boom shadows and frame lines with the grips and the camera operator.
- Record room tone, wild sounds, and possibly even replacement dialogue at the end of the day.
- When shooting video, make sure that you plan your audio system well in advance. There are many video formats, and each has its own distinctive audio configuration.

Chapter 13

Art on Set

I think, as much as possible, it's important to visit your locations beforehand as many times as the budget and your schedule will allow.

Jan Krawitz

DIRECTOR

Guide

In the process of creating a motion picture, the art director, the set decorator, and the property master truly are magicians, often creating something out of nothing and making things appear from out of nowhere.

There is nothing like the feeling of walking on a dressed set for the first time: experiencing the culmination of weeks, maybe months, of preparation and planning by the director, producer, art department, and director of photography (DP). A great deal of imagination and hard work have transformed the words on the page into the world of the characters through the choice of sets, dressing, costumes, props, and furniture.

Final Walk-through

It is highly recommended that the director, the DP, and art director or set decorator walk through the set prior to the day of the shoot. This final walk-through allows the director to talk through her ideas and make sure the arrangement of furniture can accommodate what she has in mind. The one element that is constant in filmmaking is that everything changes. Ideas developed through the rehearsal process might have resulted in new approaches to blocking. Furniture may need to be rearranged. Other details may have to be altered. The DP needs to anticipate any changes (if they occur) so he can make adjustments to his lighting plan. Having an official walk-through before the camera rolls will give both departments time to make adjustments and prevent any unwarranted surprises on the day of the shoot.

Set Procedures

The day starts early for the art department. Finishing touches are applied to the set to allow the electrical department time to set up the lights. Other members of the art department are already working on the next set in anticipation of the company's next move. During the shooting day, the art department is constantly on standby to adjust the set, dressings, and props for the camera.

Let's look at an excerpt from *The Lunch Date* as an example of how the art department approaches a scene.

```
INT. LUNCHEONETTE—AFTERNOON
The woman walks into a station luncheon-
ette. It is a simple place—a grill, some
booths, and rows of refrigerated cabi-
nets filled with salads and sandwiches.
She reaches into a glass case and removes
a salad.
A COOK stands behind a white linoleum
counter. He fiddles with his white paper
hat and white apron.
                    WOMAN
            How much is this salad?
                    COOK
                Two dollars.
She puts the salad on the counter. She
rustles through her pocketbook.
                    WOMAN
Well, I'm not sure that I have that much.
The woman empties a dollar and some
change on the counter.
                    WOMAN
            One dollar...here's some.
The cook fingers through the change.
                    COOK
A dollar fifty...two dollars. Here ya go
lady. She grabs the salad plate and her
bundles.
                    WOMAN
                 Napkin.
The cook hands her a napkin. She walks
toward the booths.
```

The duties of the art department for the scene are as follows:

Location. The location is secured during preproduction. If a location falls through, the art department must be part of the plan to move to an alternate location.

doi: 10.1016/B978-0-240-81174-1.00020-8

Set Dressing. Sometime before shooting the scene, the set decorator, cleanup crew, and painters "dress" the set to match the description in the script and any drawings, paintings, or photos given to the dresser. During the shooting, the set dresser readjusts any set pieces that have been moved for camera framing continuity. If the shoot is going well, the set dresser can leave the shoot and move to the next location to begin preparing it.

Props. The props are gathered prior to the shoot. When the set is ready, the property master places the food in the glass case behind the counter. He prepares the woman's handbag with the appropriate change. When the performer is called to the set, he hands her the handbag and her packages. He places some napkins nearby for the cook.

Wardrobe. When the actors arrive on the location, they are sent to change clothes after a brief rehearsal. The costumer dresses both actors in the costumes defined by the script. She asks the cook to keep the apron and paper hat neat and clean so they will match for each take. At wrap, the costumer helps the actors undress. She puts the costumes away neatly to be used another day. If they need washing, she takes them with her to be cleaned after the wrap.

Makeup and Hair. After the actors are dressed, they move on to the makeup and hair department. Here, their makeup is applied and their hair coifed to match a previous scene or the art director's design. When this job is completed, the makeup and hair people stand by off set to make adjustments between takes. At the end of the day, they assist the actors in removing their makeup and any hairpieces.

Set Dressing

The set decorator decorates the set according to the art director's specific designs. This crew member is responsible for renting, buying, or making all the "dressing" that occupies the set—everything from the rugs on the floors to the magnets on the refrigerator. The set decorator should confer with the actor whose character "lives" in the location, and together they will create the character's environment.

The set decorator works in tandem with other departments, such as lighting. If the gaffer has lit the set brightly, a 100-watt bulb in a "practical" (see glossary) will not register on film or video stock. An electrician might need to replace the bulb with a special 500-watt lamp to balance light temperature correctly.

The set decorator is sometimes called on to assist other departments. The key grip might need help pulling up a rug during a take to get it out from under the dolly's wheels. Someone might be needed just off camera to jerk a curtain with monofilament wire (fishing line) to simulate the wind. These specialty positions often fall to the set dresser.

Not all set pieces are easy to find. If the director has a specific look in mind for a set piece, the art director and set dresser must make this item to the director's specifications if it cannot be found (see Figure 13.1).

My dad put up the rope. He was my PA. We found a rope in another school and took it down. We built a special iron clamp because there wasn't one on the particular ceiling. My dad had a friend who was a metallurgist; he designed a specific clamp so that we could fasten the rope to the ceiling and support a person.

One very difficult prop—so difficult that we didn't find it until two days before the shoot—was the fireman's net. They haven't been used since the 1930s. They're very dangerous and very heavy. The reason they're not being used was that people would hit them and bounce out. They really didn't save many lives. The one we used we found in some guy's barn under a bale

FIGURE 13.1 It's one thing to type the words *Fireman's Net* into the script and another to locate one for the shoot. Scene from *Truman*.

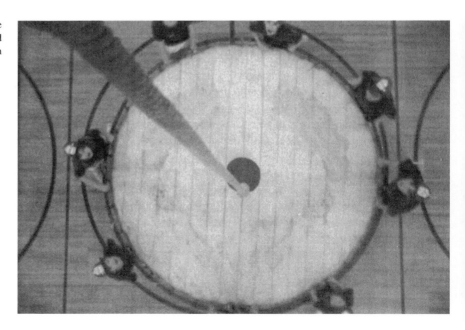

of hay. It was classic. The guy's father had been a fireman, and he let us take it out. It was very dirty and very, very heavy.

During the shot, the production manager was underneath the net, which weighed 400 pounds. The kids really couldn't lift it themselves, so he hid under it on his hands and knees, resting it on his back.

Howard McCain

Continuity

The set is maintained by the set dresser to match the uninterrupted succession of the script's scenes. If there is a fight scene, for example, the set is each take, and all the broken set pieces are replaced. The duplicated set is matched each time to the script supervisor's snapshots of the original set.

Duplicates

The set decorator should have duplicates of key items featured on the set in case they become damaged. Duplicates should also be provided for breakaway items. Breakaway chairs, for instance, are made of pieces of balsa wood that have been loosely glued together. A performer does not sit on this chair, but on the real chair. She is photographed as she stands up, and then the real chair is replaced with the breakaway chair. The character can then pick up the breakaway chair and heave it at another actor or stunt person. In the final product, this action will look real, but it is actually harmless. With the addition of sound effects, the audience viewing this footage will believe that the chair is hard.

Props

Weapons

The prop master is responsible for weapons before and after their use and must keep them in good shape. The prop master usually gives a weapon to an actor just prior to a scene. Props, especially weapons, should not be handled except during a rehearsal or a take. On an interior set, keep the prop secured until it is needed. On an exterior location, make sure everyone nearby, especially the police, is aware that a scene involving a weapon is about to be photographed. You never know when a passerby might misread the scene and return fire.

Because I had so few, I basically handled the props. It sounds kind of silly, but as a director you get very, very particular about certain props. I even went so far as to worry about what kind of kickball was used. It was important that it was one of those red, standard playground balls because that's what I grew up with. Gathering together those bows and arrows was also tough, as was getting permission to fire them in the gym.

Howard McCain

Continuity

The prop department is responsible for maintaining continuity of props from shot to shot. In a dining scene, the property master is responsible for all the food a character has to eat during the scene. If a scene requires the actor to eat a meal, for example, the level of the milk in the glass, the steam on the food, and the exact placement of the cutlery must be maintained.

Food that will be consumed on the set must also be provided in duplicate. If the script calls for a character to eat a salad (as in *The Lunch Date*), several complete salads should be standing by for each take. If it looks as though the production will run out of a food item, a production assistant is sent to the local store to purchase more. Make sure there is a system of disposing the half-eaten food and storing the fresh food properly between takes.

The salad—we were not prepared for that: how much salad we would need for the whole day. If you're going to do the take over, the salad has to look the same all day.

Adam Davidson

Duplicates

If a scene calls for a watch to be smashed, the watch might have to be destroyed many times in the course of covering the scene. The prop master must have enough watches standing by to allow the director to shoot the scene to her satisfaction. If it is decided in preproduction that the character will wear a special watch, duplicating it might prove difficult. The director should ask herself whether a more common watch, which can be easily and inexpensively duplicated, would compromise the story.

Personal Effects

The property master might be responsible for safeguarding the actor's personal belongings during the shoot. He might accept her valuables when he gives her the character's personal props, trading them back at the end of the day.

STUDENT

If any character is required to drink alcohol in a scene, IN NO CASE should real alcohol of any kind be allowed on the set. If a performer is required to be inebriated, he must "act drunk," not be drunk. The performer's job is to perform, and being literally drunk will hinder his ability to continue in a professional manner.

Improvisation

What if the production has run out of milk and the stores are closed? What if the location is in the middle of nowhere? The director might take the scene over and over to capture the best performance, and the props must be there each time. Even if the director tells the property master in preproduction how many takes she thinks she will need, the crew must be prepared with extra props.

The art department might have to improvise with the milk, keeping in mind that the actor actually has to consume the substitute on camera. Perhaps some creamer substitute mixed with water will match the color of the milk from previous takes. Tricks of the prop master's trade include using iced tea to simulate scotch, nontobacco cigarettes for nonsmokers, breakaway chairs for fights, sugar glass tumblers for breaking, and soup for vomit (see Figure 13.2).

> The makeup was another issue. We had to get a guy to make some fake vomit. When we were trying to get [Truman] to do the throw-up scene from on top of the scaffolding, he was really repulsed by the sight of the fake vomit and refused to get near the stuff. We wanted to put a little around his lips so after he had thrown up you could see the residue. Well, he refused to do it. At first, he laughed nervously, and then he actually started to cry. He went through a whole range of emotions. He just did not want to do this thing. I finally put some around my lips to show, "Hey, it's not bad. It's nothing but soup. Don't worry." That kind of calmed him down, and we made some jokes. About an hour and a half later—for something that was supposed to take only 15 minutes—we actually did it. That was the most difficult constraint, having to deal with the limitations of an eight-year-old boy. He did a great job. You have to remember, he was under a great deal of pressure, and I think he held up remarkably well.
>
> Howard McCain

Wardrobe

The company travels with all the costumes required for the show, including duplicate costumes for everyone and any sundry garb for the extras. It is important that the wardrobe be consistent with the setting.

In an exterior winter scene, for instance, everyone in the shot must wear a heavy coat to indicate the cold. This scene can be shot in hot weather, of course, because the audience knows the temperature only by what they see or hear.

Special Rigs

Special technical equipment is sometimes integrated into a costume, such as a radio microphone or a jerk harness. (When a character is shot with a big gun, he is jerked off the set by a wire attached to this harness.) The costumer works with the department responsible for the technical hardware to conceal it in the costume so that the audience will not be aware of the rigging device.

The costumer uses her bag of tricks during production. Quick changes and clothes that have to be removed during a take require special attachments. There is no question that the costumer's life became easier with the invention of Velcro.

Makeup
Continuity

After applying makeup to the cast, the makeup artist spends the remainder of the day on the set helping the actors maintain a consistent look. Under the hot lights,

FIGURE 13.2 Someone had to make the vomit. Photograph from the shooting of *Truman*.

actors perspire and must be powdered or tissued down to avoid a shiny complexion. With prosthetics work, touch-ups might require applying entirely new latex pieces, which could be just as time consuming as the original application that morning.

Positive Reinforcement

The makeup artist is usually the last person to work with the actors before they begin a scene. Actors might be in the makeup trailer for some time, so the individual who works with them there helps the director by doing whatever she can to sustain the actors in an agreeable frame of mind. A makeup artist with a pleasant personality can help actors maintain a positive mood.

Special Effects

Prosthetics work is very time consuming. It is not uncommon for an actor and the makeup artist to arrive on the set several hours before the crew call time to prepare and apply the makeup.

> The art director helped me with the puppets. In *Crazy Glue* the puppets were maybe ten inches tall, so the set was about six by six feet.
>
> Tatia Rosenthal

Hair

The hairdresser works in tandem with the makeup artist. The look of hair and makeup must be coordinated, as must their application.

Continuity

The maintenance of hairstyle continuity is very important. The hairdresser takes digital photographs of each hairstyle. These photographs serve as a reference, providing a convenient method for matching hair from scene to scene. This technique works well for all departments.

Hair gets mussed easily and therefore might not match a previous take, especially when shooting in a windy exterior location. Sustaining a consistent look can take a great deal of work. If an actress chooses not to have her hair touched up between takes because it disturbs her concentration, you might find in the editing room that the cuts do not match. The hairdresser has to be discreet in this situation. If the hair is passable, the hairdresser should not say a word, but if it will cause an obvious continuity error, the hairdresser should inform the script supervisor, the DP, or even the director. Ultimately, it is the director's decision to retake the shot or not.

Additional Crew

Depending on the nature of the shoot, the art department might also employ a standby painter, a special effects team, or a greens person (for on-set vegetation). In the production of a short film or video project, all these roles might be performed by only one or two talented people.

PRODUCER

Keeping Track

The art director or art department coordinator (on larger productions) oversees any set construction. One of the greatest skills a good art director must possess is the ability to estimate accurately (along with the construction coordinator) the material cost of building the set with as little waste (lumber and hardware and paint) as possible. She must also determine the appropriate number of crew (calculated in man-hours) needed to complete the task in time. For the art department, these steps must happen in this sequence:

- Allow the assistant art director sufficient time to complete and revise the construction documents, plans, and elevations to be approved by the art director (production designer), the director, the DP, and the producer
- Have the carpenters and construction grips build the set overseen by the art director or assistant art director to the drawn specs
- Allow scenic artists to plaster, paint, wallpaper, and age the set

The set dressers dress the set starting with flooring materials, like carpeting, tile, or linoleum unless wood graining or marbleizing the floor is required. Dress the furniture, lighting fixtures, paintings, draperies, and all the **smalls** (see Glossary) that really contribute to the set looking natural and realistic. The set dressers are also responsible for adding elements like outlet switches, phone wire, and radiators to help the set look more convincing.

The producer carefully monitors the schedule and the budget and how the art department is keeping to its part of the job. He is in charge of keeping track of how much is spent and on what (supplies, manpower, etc.). Sets take longer to build and things inevitably cost more than estimated. The types of set items that require more time to design and build are

- Removable, or *flying*, walls
- Well-braced doors (so that the set doesn't shake when a door is closed)
- Ceiling pieces
- Realistic painted scenes, or *backdrops*, outside windows

Having the extra time shouldn't be a problem if the art director has done her job properly and her department budget is "padded" enough to accommodate unexpected expenses. However, if this area begins to go over budget, creative compromises may have to be made, or the money must come either from another department or from post-production funds.

Items might be required in the heat of production that were not anticipated in the budget, such as extra supplies, incidentals, additional crew to complete construction on time, etc.

A producer well versed in the details of the art budget is best qualified to judge the validity of each request. This will lead to a more realistic discussion with the art director and director if creative compromises have to be made.

> I wanted to achieve the effect of a Greek chorus, so the natural corollary was to situate them in some kind of artificial set, which I had never done. It was completely unnatural for me, but it was a very conscious aesthetic choice that I thought would service the film. I came up with the idea of two different sets within a single studio (one for sitting, one for standing) and then had to define what they should look like.
>
> Jan Krawitz

Cover Sets

Weather can play a factor in any film shoot, unless, of course, the shoot is entirely indoors. The safest procedure is to schedule exterior scenes first. Then when you move inside to shoot the interiors, the weather will not affect production. If circumstances require that you shoot interiors first, you will be vulnerable to weather conditions when you move outdoors.

One way to protect the production is to maintain a **cover set**, as described in Chapter 4. This is an interior location the company can move to in case of inclement weather. Cover sets should be simple and require few actors. A true cover set is dressed and ready at all times during the production.

Wrapping Up

When the photography of a sequence is completed, it is customary for the art department to wait one day before disassembling the set. The art department waits to receive word from the editing room that the dailies are not damaged (if shooting film). If the footage is damaged and it becomes necessary to reshoot the scene, the set can be used again. Once the art director has been given the word that the dailies are good technically, the set is struck. It is taken apart if rented or destroyed if constructed.

Waiting to strike the set is done for mostly for financial reasons. Productions with large budgets will store the elements of the set throughout the postproduction process in the advent that pickups or additional scenes need to be shot. For low-budget and students projects, keeping the sets may not be realistic. In any event, hold on to as many of the key props and set dressings as possible in case you will need to reconstruct a scene weeks or maybe months later.

> There was no opportunity for reshoots, which was pretty scary. I had to strike that set the minute we finished, so I didn't even get the film back to find out if there was a scratched roll or any technical problems. To reconstruct the set would have been impossible. The mannequins had to be returned, and the cinematographer had to fly back to Boston.
>
> Jan Krawitz

KEY POINTS

- Have adequate duplicates to maintain continuity.
- Consult actors when choosing props, wardrobe, and even set dressing.
- Create a cover set, if possible, in case of weather problems.
- Allow time for predressing and striking. Do not strike a set until you have seen the dailies, unless it's unavoidable.

Part II

Production

The start of production is the moment when the score has been written, the musicians are assembled, and the conductor raises the baton. The ship has been constructed, the crew has been chosen, and the captain pulls up anchor and heads out to sea. By this time, the director will know intuitively how to influence the creative drive of the cast and crew.

During production, you can look back on the many hours of preparation, planning, and rehearsal and be thankful you took the time to refine the production schedule; looked for that unique location; established comfortable and productive working relationships; and explored all the possibilities the script, cast, and crew have to offer. If you are well prepared, the shooting period merely means shifting into a higher gear. If you are not prepared, you will experience problems that might be serious enough to force you to push back the start date.

Production is also called **principal photography**. This is the industry term for the period during which the first, or principal, unit completes photography. (Professional shoots sometimes employ a **second unit** to shoot action sequences that rarely involve sync sound or scenes that do not involve principal players.)

Principal photography can be an intense and trying period. Working with the same people for long hours many days in a row tests the mettle of the strongest personalities. During the shoot, you will discover firsthand how important crew selection and casting can be. You will recognize almost immediately whom you can rely on and whom you can't. If you have a problem with a crew member or an actor on the first day, you must decide whether you want to give this person time to improve or replace him.

There is ample time during pre- and postproduction to solve problems. During principal photography, however, time is more precious. The production unit must be flexible but be prepared to make expeditious decisions. Even though compromise is inevitable during a shoot, there is no reason to sacrifice quality and integrity.

The best way to be flexible is to maintain the flow of communication among all parties, creating a Gestalt mentality. If, during preproduction, you anticipate all possible variables of what could go wrong on any given day, these problems can be addressed or a satisfactory compromise can be found with relative ease during the shoot.

To reach this level of communication, learn everything there is to know about the production process (see Figure II.1). This part of the book is organized to familiarize you with what happens during principal photography, when hard work and creative fervor transform the words on the page into the images and sounds that will become your final product.

A film is put together with some degree of magic and chance. Listen to the project as if it had a voice of its own. The finest films are greater than the sum of their parts.

THE PRODUCER

The producer's responsibility is to ensure that from the beginning of the shoot, all the people involved have a precise idea of what they are supposed to be doing, when and where they are supposed to be doing it, and most importantly, that they have the necessary the resources to accomplish their goals.

Being able to accomplish this task requires the following:

- Clear chain of command
- Realistic budget
- Day-out-of-day schedule

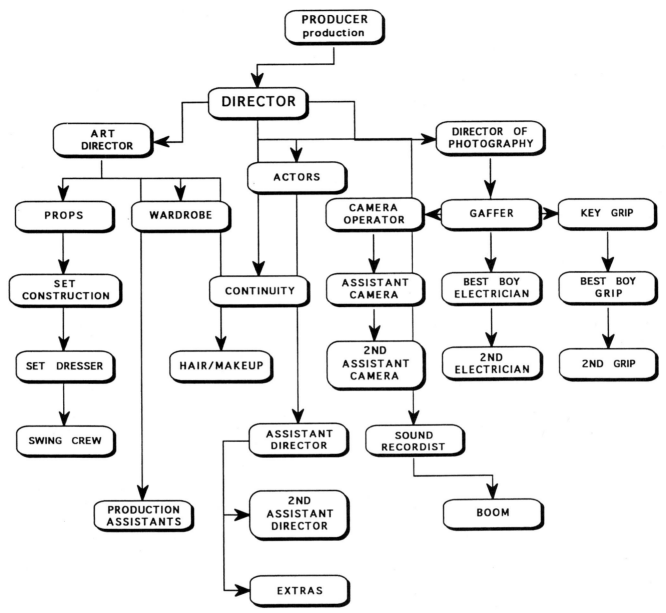

FIGURE II.1   Production flow chart.

- Call sheets
- Enough crew to carry out the director's visual plan
- Secure and safe locations
- Meals and craft service
- Transportation schedule

SAFETY ON THE SET

The producer must also ensure that when shooting on a location, interior and exterior, all production operations are conducted in a safe and secure environment. Many personal injuries, thefts of personal property,

damage to equipment and locations, and other costly incidents come as a result of insufficient safety and security measures. (Equipment and personal items on the set are covered by the company's umbrella insurance policy, but these policies come with large deductibles.)

These are a few of the many safety concerns that must be followed to prevent loss or injury:

- Proper attire such as work gloves and insulated work boots must be worn on set.
- Equipment or valuables must not be left on the set or in a vehicle unattended.

- Lighting instruments must not be placed near pictures, drapes, or other items that are sensitive to heat. Lights can heat up certain types of heat-sensitive sprinklers and have disastrous results.
- Lighting units must be secured and properly weighted down with sandbags.
- Electric cables must be kept away from sound cables and water.

Appendix E contains a comprehensive list of safety concerns listed under these categories: general safety guidelines on the set, proper attire, special effects (smoke machines), chemical and flammable materials, set construction, lighting and electricity, grips and rigging, ladders and scaffolds, dollies, grip trucks.

SAFETY OFFICER

To ensure that all safety precautions are adhered to on set, the producer can appoint a **safety officer** and ensure that, if necessary, safety specialists such as stunt coordinators, fire marshals, and weapon masters have been hired. The most likely candidate for safety officer is the assistant director. He would have the authority to intervene when appropriate. In this capacity, he can start his day by making sure that all crew members are properly attired for their job.

BASIC PRINCIPLES

- **Clarify the Chain of Command to the Crew.** Make sure everyone knows who's in charge. If there is a problem on the set, every crew member must know where to turn for an answer.

- **Delegate Responsibility.** Don't take on more than you can handle. Spreading yourself too thin usually means that nothing gets done properly.
- **Avoid Duplication of Energies.** It is not efficient to have two production assistants running around looking for the same prop.
- **Double the Time Allotted for Anything Out of the Ordinary.** Stunts; special effects; fire effects; car mounts; visual effects (green screen); anything shot on water, with kids, or with animals; and even special effects lighting always take longer than you anticipate. The phrase "hurry up and wait" was created for the picture business.
- **Do Not Assume Anything.** Check and double-check all arrangements for cast, crew, transportation, and meals.
- **Avoid Passing the Buck.** If someone makes a mistake, don't waste time and energy placing blame. Doing so is counterproductive. Put your energy into correcting the mistake. At one time or another, everyone will make a mistake, even professionals.
- **Be Sensitive to the Needs of the Actors.** Actors should always be in a positive frame of mind. If there is tension on the set, relax the actors while you deal with the problem.
- **Keep Murphy's Law in Mind.** Be prepared for the worst, but accept the best. Don't keep waiting for the other shoe to drop because it just might not.
- **Stay Healthy.** You are no good to anyone if you are sick, especially during the shoot when there is no downtime to rest.
- **Keep the Cast and Crew Healthy.** Good wholesome food for meals and a large container of vitamins on the craft service table are must-haves! Crew members run on their stomach!
- **Remember to Have Fun!**

Chapter 14

Set Procedures

They told me, "Don't worry. Everything's fine. He's all set; he knows what he's doing." So the actors took their places, and we started, rolled sound, rolled camera. I called action, did the shot, called cut. It was great. Then, I suddenly notice there's a commotion going on next to me. I look over, and there's yards of magnetic tape spewing out of the Nagra, and the homeless guy, who was trying to help, now has his hands over his face. We quickly went back to the original way of the sound man operating the recorder by himself.

Adam Davidson

DIRECTOR

Inspires

The hierarchy of the crew is a pyramid, with the director on top. Creating a motion picture may be a team effort, but on set the director has the final word. A confident and prepared director creates a tone, attitude, and pace that allow the team to respond to whatever problems and challenges arise. An insecure and inadequately prepared director, on the other hand, brings down morale and slows the natural pace of a well-oiled and capable crew. The most appropriate analogy is director as captain of a ship. She commands and the crew follows; she falters and chaos ensues.

Her goal is to shoot the script within the schedule and to walk away with enough shots to tell the story adequately. A prepared director is able to make choices and swift decisions because she's spent hours upon hours formulating and interpreting the script in her mind and developing her ideas with key creative people.

A director often seems to function by intuition. Her decisions might be right or they might be wrong, but they are for her to make. She is free to consult whomever she chooses, and she can always change her plan for a scene. Ultimately, the vision of the piece is in her head, and it is her job to impart that vision succinctly and successfully to the cast and crew through her words and performance. A director is, however, only as good as her crew. The best laid plans can fall apart if the crew is not able to fulfill the technical requirements of the director's visual plan in the number of days scheduled.

Organized Chaos

When cast and crew descend on a set, bodies and equipment are moving in all directions (especially in small spaces). It can appear chaotic even on the most professional productions. To accomplish the day's work, the set must be run like a military operation. In a platoon, every member has a specific job to perform. A film crew works in the same way. The director defines the mission; the DP, art director, and sound mixer take their orders to their respective crew, and the AD keeps track of it all so the director can concentrate on telling the story with the actors.

Each crew member must follow the orders of his team leader and execute his part of the director's mission in an orderly and professional manner. This means that everyone must know what he is responsible for. Otherwise, everyone does everything and is responsible for nothing. Achieving this goal becomes more complicated with a crew that is working short handed. The 3–30 rule requires that crew members combine duties. These duties should be carefully thought out and communicated to everyone so there is no duplication of labor. For example, the duties must be clearly laid out for camera, grip, and electric. If they aren't, three people will be grabbing the same light stand, the same table, prop, etc.

Set Etiquette

The success of a shoot depends on everyone treating each other with respect and civility. When you walk on the set, you leave your ego at the door. Every member of the crew is equally important to the success of the shoot, no matter what the position. If the film magazine isn't loaded properly, this failure could ruin a whole day's work. In addition,

- Crew members should not give advice to those outside their area unless asked.
- No one gives direction to the actors except the director.
- Everyone should be on time! When you are late, you waste other people's time and will lose respect.

doi: 10.1016/B978-0-240-81174-1.00021-X

STUDENTS

Chapter 6 presented the 3–30 rule for smaller shoots, which assists the director and producer with their staffing needs. Often in a short piece the director has raised all the funds with which to make the picture although this is normally the producer's function.

The fact that the director has raised the funds should by no means force her to feel compelled to also "produce." The more the director can delegate authority to the producer, the more time she will have to actually direct the film. The producer, in turn, besides taking on the responsibility of assuring the funds are allocated in a professional and reasonable manner, often takes on the role of production manager to oversee the day-to-day operations.

By coming to terms and agreeing on their roles prior to the shoot, the director and producer will function as a better team. Having this arrangement in the form of a written agreement forces both people to deal with issues up front.

A Typical Day

Following is the course of events that happen on a typical day during production.

The director often arrives at the location before the cast or crew begins to arrive. It is a good idea to walk around the set to get a feel for the location. It might be the first time you have been on the fully dressed set. (It is highly recommended that the director, DP, art director, AD, and sound mixer conduct a walk-through before shooting begins).

The producer or production manager will have notified the crew of the staging areas (the area where the dramatic action will occur) so that every piece of equipment (cameras, lighting, sound, props, makeup, costumes, etc.) can be stored in a secure place for the duration of the shoot.

The cast and crew arrive on the set. The call time, indicated on the call sheet, tells each cast and crew member when to arrive (see Figure 14.1). **The assistant director makes these arrangements.** If a particular department needs lead time, the call times can be staggered. For example, if an actor has to undergo a lengthy makeup application, the location manager, makeup artist, and actor will be called before the rest of the crew. Call times should be arranged so that when the actor is ready, the crew is in place and he need not wait to begin rehearsal.

The director should greet the actors before they go to hair and makeup. They may have questions or concerns about the scene that will be performed that day, and it's best to handle these issues before walking on set in front of the crew. Even if they don't, the director has made a positive connection and focused the actors in the direction of the day's work.

The shot is blocked for the camera. As soon as the actors arrive on set, it is customary for the director to conduct a run-through rehearsal of the first scene scheduled for that day for the DP, sound mixer, boom operator, 1st assistant director, and script supervisor. An art department representative should also be present (props, set dresser) in case adjustments have to be made to the set, furniture, or props (see Chapter 13 for more details on the art department on set). As the actors move around, the camera and sound crews note their positions on the set. On the basis of the rehearsal, the director might decide to shoot the scene differently than originally planned. Seeing the completed set or dressed location might inspire her to reveal the environment or characters in another way. This is the time to discuss any changes.

If the director is pleased with how the scene is blocked, she and the DP will review the shot list, storyboards, or floor plans as well as information gleaned from the rehearsal. They will then decide on the first setup, where the camera will be placed, and what size lens will be used for the shot. (Lenses are discussed thoroughly in Chapter 11). If a dolly move had been planned, they will discuss the logistics of where the shot begins and ends with the dolly grip present.

This discussion will inform the DP and gaffer about the first lighting setup. For the sound team, knowing where the actors will be positioned and how they will move is a critical first step in devising the most effective strategy to record the production dialogue. This entails, among other considerations, where to position the sound recorder and how to best to mic the scene. (Considerations for proper mic placement are covered in Chapter 12). The set dressers will know which furniture will need to be moved to accommodate the lights and dolly.

The actors are dressed and made up. The actors are then released to be made up and fitted in their wardrobe. If necessary, this is also an opportunity to rehearse off set.

The game plan is set for the morning scene. Once everyone is clear about what has to be accomplished for the morning shoot, the AD consults with the DP and gaffer, the sound mixer, and the art department as to how much time they will require to prepare for the first setup. If it is an interior location, the DP and gaffer will supply the AD with a time frame for lighting the set and, if camera moves are called for, for prepping the dolly.

It is the assistant director's job to keep track of each department's progress. Meeting the day's schedule, or "making the day," is based on getting the first shot off at a certain time. The estimate of the number of scenes or shots for a day is based on the DP's projected setup time at each location. The DP bases his setup time on the complexity of the shot, the location scouts, and the final walk-throughs. If the DP has done his homework properly, his estimate should closely match what had been scheduled. If it appears that the lighting team will fall behind on its projected schedule, adjustments to the shot list might be required. The sooner this situation can be addressed, the better.

A Nick In Time

CREW CALL

8:00AM

PRODUCTION CALL - 7:30 AM

Production Office:
10th of November Films, Inc.
372 Fifth Avenue, #3C
Brooklyn, NY 11215
917-549-3820 O

Production Office:
EyePatch Productions
309 W 49 Street FL7
NY, NY 10019

Production: 917-549-3820 - Greg Vena

Production Fax: 801-217-7653

SCRIPT: Version 4 - Blue

SUNRISE: 7:14am
SUNSET: 5:01pm
WEATHER: 30%, scattered showers

WINDS: WNW 9 mph

HI: 49° LO: 33°

Crew Call: 8:00 AM
Shooting Call: 10:30 AM
Lunch: 2:00 PM

NO FORCED CALLS WITHOUT PRIOR APPROVAL OF UPM	NO VISITORS ON SET WITHOUT PRIOR UPM APPROVAL	ALL CALL SUBJECT TO CHANGE BY AD'S

DATE: Sun., JAN. 22, 2006	DAY 1 OF 2	HOTEL LOCATIONS	
Director: Be Garrett	NEAREST HOSPITAL:	N/A	
Producer / UPM: Gregory Vena	**Brooklyn Medical Center**		
1ST AD: Barbie Painter	**121 De Kalb Ave**		
	718-250-8000		

SET/SCENE DESCRIPTION	SCENES - SET UP - SHOT			CAST #	D/N	PGS.	LOCATIONS/NOTES
INT - BARBERSHOP							**HeadHunters Barbershop**
	1,3,11	2	A-H	1,2,3	D for N		**1092 Bedford Ave**
INT - BARBERSHOP							**Bed Stuy, Brooklyn 11216**
	1,9	3	A-D	1,2,3	D for N		**btw. Lexington & Green**
INT - BARBERSHOP							
	11	7	A	1,2,3	D for N		Parking :
LUNCH							TBD
INT - BARBERSHOP							
	5,7,9 & 11	6	A-E	1,2,3	D for N		Holding:
INT - BARBERSHOP							M.W. Enoch Grand Masonic Lodge
	7,11 & 9	5	A-D	1,2,3	N		423 Norstrand Ave at corner of Jefferson
INT - BARBERSHOP							718.622.6996
	1 & 5	4	A-E	1,2,3	N		Nearest Subway:
EXT - BARBERSHOP							G train to Bedford Classon
	1	1	A-B	1,2,3	N		A,C train to Franklin & Nostrand
				Total Page Count:		11	

CAST MEMBER	CHARACTER	SWF	PU	CALL	WARD	M/U	HAIR	SET	REMARKS
Isiah Whitlock	1. BOB DELAGARD	SWF	N/A	8:00a	8:15a	8:30a		9:45a	SELF REPORT
Jas Anderson	3. EVAN WILEY	SWF	N/A	8:00a	8:45a	8:15a		9:45a	SELF REPORT
Keith Bullard	2. TED DUPREE	SWF	N/A	8:00a	8:30a	9:00a		9:45a	SELF REPORT
Teen Boy	9. TBD	SWF	N/A	TBA					TBD

ATMOSPHERE
Sc.3 - (1) TEEN lingers outside store- time TBD

SPECIAL INSTRUCTIONS	
PROPS:	**SET DRESSING:**
Sc. 1, 3, 5, 7, 9, 11 - Present day barber tools	**Sc. 1, 3, 5, 7, 9, 11** - Posters of MLK Jr, Malcom X, Muhammed Ali
Sc. 1, 3, 5, 7, 9, 11 - Chessboard	
Sc. 11 - Ted's prop gun, badge & police uniform	

ADVANCED SHOOTING SCHEDULE
MONDAY, JANUARY 23, 2006

SET/SCENE DESCRIPTION	SCENE	CAST	D/N	PGS	LOCATIONS/NOTES
INT - BARBERSHOP (FLASHBACK)					**Barbershop**
Judge Rivers & Bessie enter. Young Bob cuts hair.	2	4, 5, 6, 7, 8, 10-14	D	3 5/8	
INT - BARBERSHOP (FLASHBACK)					**1092 Bedford Ave**
Bessie watches Young Bob cut Judge's hair.	4	4, 5, 6, 7, 8, 10-14	D	4/8	**Bed Stuy, Brooklyn 11216**
INT - BARBERSHOP (FLASHBACK)					**btw. Lexington & Green**
Young Bob makes mistake.	6	4, 5, 6, 7, 8, 10-14	D	4/8	
INT - BARBERSHOP (FLASHBACK)					
Young Bob fixes mistake w/Bessie watching.	8	4, 5, 6, 7, 8, 10-14	D	3/8	
INT - BARBERSHOP (FLASHBACK)					
Young Bob finishes Judge's hair. Judge and Bessie exit.	10	4, 5, 6, 7, 8, 10-14	D	1 1/8	
		Total Page Count:		5 3/8	

UPM: Greg Vena	1st AD:	Barbie Painter	Key 2nd AD: Bruce Hall

FIGURE 14.1 Call sheet for *A Nick in Time*.

Continued

CAST & CREW CA 8am

Item	Name	Call	Remarks	Item	Name	Call	Remarks
PRODUCTION				**HAIR & MAKE-UP**			
Director/Writer	Be Garrett	8am- Drive	917-825-3241	Make-Up Artist	Ingrid Okola	8am- WB Van	917.770.1960
Producer / UPM	Gregory Vena	7:30 am - Cab	917-549-3820	Barber/ Consultant	Ty Devour	8am - Drive	267.738.0775
Production Coordinator	Casse Casogrove	8AM- WB Van	917-459-2271				
ProductionCoordinator	Cristina Sanchez-Amyot	7:30 AM - TBD	646-479-6882	**WARDROBE**			
PA- Truck	James Foreman	7:30 AM- CUBE	937-532-3161	Wardrobe	Mary Casey	8am- Drive	917-705-0778
PA- Truck	Raul Ravello	7:30 - A Traiin	917.361.7342	Wardrobe Assistant	Lincoln Cochran	8am - TBD	918.808.2795
PA- Shuttle	Brad Saville	7:30- A -Train	646.642.0273				
Business Manager	Marta Infante	N/A	212-237-5054				
ASSISTANT DIRECTORS				**CATERING / CRAFT**			
1st AD	Barbie Painter	7:30am TBD	917.681.0867	Craft / Catering	Afi Ekulona	7:30am - Cab	917-701-5335
2nd AD	Bruce Hall	7:30am - cab	347.678.9591	**PROPERTY**			
				Art Director - Prop Master	Brian Urbina	8 AM- ART VAN	917-439-2239
				Art Assistant/ Props	Kenny Urbina	8 AM- ART VAN	718-751-5419
CONTINUITY				**MUSIC**			
Script Supervisor	Shakima Landsmark	8 am - Drive	917.627.5865	Music Supervisor			
CAMERA				Composer			
Dir. Of Photography	Barry Markowitz	8AM- Drive	917-364-4392	**EDITORIAL**			
1st AC	Rosanna Rizzo	8am- WB VAN	917-648-0900	Lost Planet	TBD		
2nd AC/ Loader	Chris Aran	8am - A Train	201.927.1757	**GRIP & ELECTRIC**			
				Gaffer	Al Rivera	8AM- Drive	917-627-6833
Stills Photography	N/A			Key Grip	Travis Pitt	8AM - WB Van	214.240.6778
CASTING							
Casting	Stacy Gallo	N/A	212-625-5634				
Casting	Paul Davis	N/A	646-509-1945				
SAG Rep	Leo Sanchez	N/A	212-827-1478				
ADDITIONAL LABOR							
	n/a	N/A					
	n/a	N/A					
LOCATIONS				**SOUND**			
LocationScout	Lucien Charles	N/A	718-974-8136	Sound Mixer	Fred Helm	8AM- Drive	917-455-3673
Location Manager	Cassie Cosgrove	8AM- WB Van	917-459-2271	Boom Operator	Web Wilcoxen	8AM- - Drive	917.225.2670
Asst. Location Mgr.	n/a			**VIDEOGRAPHER**			
Parking Coordinator	Vernon Rodriguez	7:30 AM	347-524-4331	Videographer	n/a	n/a	
				GRAPHICS			
				Designer	n/a	n/a	

SPECAIL INSTRUCTIONS/TRANSPORTATION					
VEHICLE	**DRIVER**	**CAST/CREW**		**PICK-UP LOCATION**	**PU Time**
15 pass Van	Cassie Cosgrove	Ingrid, Rosanna, Travis,		195 Grand Street btw. Bedford & Drigg	7:30 AM
Art Van	Brian Urbina	Kenny Urbina		66-22 108th Street, Forest Hills	7:30 AM
Cube Truck	James Foreman	N/A		Wooster parking	7:00 AM

PLEASE REPORT ANY NAME CHANGES/ADDITIONS/DELETIONS TO GREGORY VENA

FIGURE 14.1—cont'd

> The scenes in the cafeteria I diagrammed from an overhead floor plan—the camera here, her walking this way and that. And the scenes in Grand Central I designed with storyboards. But you've got to get to the camera; you've got to look through the camera; you've got to see.
>
> Adam Davidson

The set is lit. The DP directs the gaffer to set the lights and the grip crew to set the camera. As the lights are being positioned, turned on, and aimed, the DP moves around with his light meter, checking light readings from each unit. Once the lights are in place, a stand-in sits or stands where the actor will eventually be placed so the camera team can reestablish focus, lens size, and lighting. During these technical rehearsals, the gaffer tries to keep the lighting instruments out of the shot and tries to block, or flag, any glare from hitting the camera lens.

The set is prepped for sound. The sound mixer and boom operator position the sound cart and prepare the appropriate microphones for the scene. As they watch the lighting setup, they are conscious of where boom shadows may occur. If a camera rehearsal is taking place, the boom operator will coordinate the placement of the mic with the frame line of the shot.

A run-through is held for the actors, camera, and sound. Once the technical aspects of the shot have been finalized, the actors are brought back to the set for a final dress rehearsal. During this time, the director should observe through the camera, video monitor, or video tap to review her choice of lenses, the framing and composition of the shot, and the staging of the action.

The focus marks are set. The assistant camera operator sets the focus for the actors' movements. Each time the camera or an actor moves, the operator adjusts the footage ring on the lens to maintain focus.

Marks are placed on the floor for the actors and camera. If the blocking of the actors or camera is complicated, the key grip will put tape on the floor to mark the actors' and camera's positions. Any camera move, such as a dolly, is rehearsed for smoothness.

> The camera was on a dolly, so we could put tape on the floor to mark the exact position of the camera for both setups. The positions had to be precise from one interview to the next in order to ensure a jump-cut aesthetic. We were a little off on some of them. If you look closely, you can see the composition shift just a tad, but it's not something anyone really notices.
>
> Jan Krawitz

Adjustments are made for the actors and camera and sound. Between the rehearsal and the lighting period, technical adjustments or new creative ideas might require altered or additional blocking for the actors and camera. The director may have requested framing adjustments, etc. The sound team may have to reposition the microphones and adjust the recording levels.

Rehearsal. If additional work needs to be done that does not require the actors on set, the director has an opportunity to rehearse the scene further (stand-ins can be used at this point). She can then take the actors away from the set to another room.

The scene is shot. When the director is ready, she positions herself close to the camera lens (not behind the video monitor) and turns the set over to the AD. The AD confirms that the crew is ready for a take and signals for sound and camera to roll (slating is covered later in the chapter). The director calls "Action!" and shooting begins.

Each time the scene is shot from a particular angle with a specific lens, it is referred to as a **take**. At the end of each take, the director's first responsibility is to connect with the actors. Don't leave them hanging to discuss a technical problem with the DP or sound mixer. If the performances were wonderful but the take must be repeated for a technical problem, make sure they know right away.

The director shoots as many takes of each shot as she feels are necessary to tell the story. If she is happy with a particular take from a performance point of view, she needs to get affirmation from the DP that the take is "good for picture" and from the production sound mixer that it is "good for sound." She will also check with the script supervisor, and if there are no continuity issues, she can move on to the next scene.

The director might request a retake for any number of reasons. Filming a scene requires that many technical and creative activities be executed precisely. It is hard enough to achieve this even with seasoned veterans manning each position. Following are a few of the common reasons why the director may require additional takes of a scene:

- The director or an actor wants an adjustment in the performance.
- Technical problems occurred with the camera or lights.
- An actor flubbed or misread a line.
- An actor didn't hit his or her focus mark.
- The dolly didn't hit its mark.
- A microphone dipped into the frame.
- The boom shadow entered the frame.
- A light bulb popped during a take, or an airplane or loud noise buried the sound.

Even if the director is satisfied with the first take, it is wise to take each shot at least twice, with one of the takes acting as a safety. Unforeseen mishaps often necessitate a safety shot being used in the editing room to get around a problem. The benefit of shooting video or having a video tap and a digital assistant is that the director can view a particular "problem take" on the spot and decide if it needs to be repeated.

If any or all of these occurrences happen during the course of shooting a scene, the crew may be thrown off its planned shooting schedule. The production unit may then have to make adjustments to how many shots it will realistically be able to accomplish before moving on to the next scene. A crisis like this tests the mettle of any crew. The director, DP, AD, and producer should confer as how to proceed. (See the "Be a Troubleshooter" heading in "Producer" section of this chapter). In this kind of situation, make sure the cast is given a break and sent away from the set. You do not want your talent to sense any tension with the crews.

The two-day shoot did not go without a hitch. Day one was smoother than day two. The only problem we had was when we were getting to the end of the first twelve-hour day, we hadn't gotten the shots outside the barbershop looking in. I have to give credit to my line producer who said we should jump outside the shop and look inside for a couple moments. So, when the night came to an end we were rushing to try to get that shot and I had to start thinking about overtime. This wasn't a union crew, but you don't want to take advantage of folks. So, we rushed as much as we could to get those exterior shots.

Be' Garrett

Pickups. There are situations when one section of a take has either a technical problem (bad sound), there are performance issues, or maybe an actor flubbed one or two lines. Instead of filming the entire take again, the director will often shoot a **pickup** of that part of the scene that has to be redone. Shooting a pickup conserves film and the energy of the actors.

The camera is moved for the next setup or sequence. When the director is satisfied that all the required takes from a particular camera angle have been shot, she requests that the camera be moved to the next camera position. This may require a relight. In this case, the actors are released until the DP is ready for the next setup.

In this way, the director works her way through the script. The most important information coming from the day's shoot is whether the director has enough coverage to be able to edit each scene properly. (Advice on this matter comes from the script supervisor and, if you have one, a digital assistant who can assemble a rough edit of the scene right on the set.)

I didn't think I had everything by the end of the production. I thought, "Oh, my God, there are shots that I don't have." By the time I put the rough cut together, it occurred to me I could go back and get those shots, but the cost would have been too great.

Adam Davidson

Camera Moves

Camera moves often slow down the progress of the production unit. Every time you decide to use a moving camera, even for a small pan or tilt, you'll need time to rehearse the camera, the actors, and the sound team. Each crew member has a particular function that must be performed properly and consistently on each take.

In a dolly, crane, Steadicam, or even a handheld shot, the DP must light the entire area the actors and camera travel along and must make sure that everything is in focus. These moving shots often require that precision moves by the dolly grip or Steadicam operator and the boom operator be repeated exactly for each take. The camera operator needs to coordinate with the boom operator to ensure that the microphone is out of the shot and no shadows are being thrown. Actors may have to hit precise marks on specific lines of dialogue. All this increases the chance of something going wrong.

- The shot is blocked for camera and sound.
- Marks are placed on the floor for actors.
- Marks are placed on the floor for the camera.
- The camera sets focus marks,
- A run-through is done for the actors, camera, and sound.
- Adjustments are made for the actors, camera, and sound.
- Another run-through is performed.
- Take.

If the shot must be terminated because of a technical error from the cast or crew, the script supervisor marks the shot as a false start. Out of 10 takes, there might be only 2 complete takes.

On the other hand, static shots, in which the camera does not move, are generally easier to set up and less risky to shoot than dolly or Steadicam shots. They also require less rehearsal time. It is highly recommended to always have a plan B to photograph the scene with traditional coverage in case the best laid plans fall apart.

We did the long dolly shot with [our actor] walking down the hall in the middle of the day. It was being set up while we were shooting the doctor scene. Ryan was filming the examination in that room while our extras were all arriving gradually. As soon as the dolly shot was set up, we switched gears and shot it so we could release the extras as soon as we could.

James Darling

Video Tap

Many directors use a *video assist* (also called a *video tap*). The video tap diverts some light from the film camera to a small attached video camera that allows the director and others to watch the take as it happens on a monitor. The video tap can be recorded to a laptop and a hard drive, enabling the take to be studied immediately afterward (see the following section, "Digital Assistant"). This tool can be helpful for reviewing takes for framing and performance, logging, or even editing footage before processing. It is especially useful for continuity when staging a complicated camera move. A video assist is crucial for Steadicam, crane, or car shots in which the camera operator cannot look through the viewfinder.

Video tap is also extremely helpful when the director is acting in the project. Being objective while acting is difficult. After the take, the director can watch the playback on the video monitor and judge for herself whether to move on or shoot another take.

There are, however, potential problems. Having the director or others look at each take can slow down the production process. The image quality is usually poor and can misrepresent what the film will eventually look like. And because you are not seeing the actual film, the tap can't inform you about other problems such as scratches or even a run-out.

Finally, those who are watching often become instant critics. As mentioned earlier, the only audience during principal photography should be the director.

> I personally don't like video tap. It's a good way for producers to look at your dailies while you're on the set.
> Adam Davidson

Digital Assistant

When working with tapeless formats like P2 or RED, the digital assistant is essentially handling the equivalent of your master tapes or film negative, so you need to hire someone who will take great care with this job! However, digital assistants can also be a valuable addition to any crew, regardless of shooting format. When working with film or tape, a DA can still capture a digital dub of all the footage from the director's monitor and sound mixer, allowing rapid nonlinear video playback and on-set editing. When used effectively, the digital assistant can be an invaluable aid to the director, DP, script supervisor, and art departments, helping to ensure continuity and coverage of scenes.

The ability to literally assemble your footage into sequences as it is being shot opens up a whole new window of creative exploration on the film set, but it can be double-edged sword. Having all the footage at your fingertips can easily become a distraction for cast and crew, and it is important to establish a clear set etiquette around the digital assistant. For example, some actors may insist upon reviewing their footage, which can sometimes be a hindrance to performance. The digital assistant is not to be confused with a **digital imaging technician**, or **DIT** (see Glossary), a very technical position required now on upper-end HD cameras.

Slates

In film, it is necessary to identify each take with a clapboard. This is also referred to as a slate, claps sticks, or simply sticks. Even shots filmed without sound (MOS) must be slated. Written on the clapboard, or slate, is pertinent information about the take for the editing process (see Figure 14.2). Information on the slate can include the name of the film, director, DP, scene and take numbers, sound take number (if any), camera and sound roll numbers, and date. If you are shooting film, a small **gray card** (see Glossary) should also be included to assist in color correcting the work print or video transfer.

FIGURE 14.2 A slate contains information for the editor.

When the sound and the developed film arrive in the editing room, the assistant editor matches the clap of the slate on the soundtrack to its corresponding film image. This is called *syncing up the footage*. This ensures that all the sound will be perfectly in sync with the picture. The editor must be able to read the material on the slate so she can relate her log books to the script supervisor's notes.

Slating Procedure

The sequence if you are using traditional clapboard is as follows. On the set, when the assistant director or camera operator calls for the slate, the assistant camera operator holds up the slate in front of the lens with the clapper open. The AD then calls for the sound person to "roll sound." The production sound mixer turns on the digital recorder and calls out loudly, "Speed!" The AD then calls out, "Roll camera!" at which point the camera operator turns on the camera and calls out, "Rolling!"

At this cue, the assistant camera operator, or whoever is holding the slate, reads the information off the clapboard: "Scene 49 apple, take 2." ("Scene 49 apple" refers to scene 49A; using "apple" eliminates any confusion. "Baker" would then be used for *B*, "Charlie" for *C*, etc.) Scene 49 refers to that particular scene in the shooting script.

After the assistant camera operator has called out the slate information, he slaps down the upper bar onto the slate, which makes a sharp "clap" sound (see Figure 14.3). The assistant camera operator hustles behind the camera position, crouches, and waits patiently and is very still until the take is completed.

When shooting the slate, the goal is to be able to read all the information clearly in the editing room. The slate must have ample light on it, be held steady when it claps,

and be close enough to the camera to enable the editor to read the small print. In a low-light situation, the AC may shine a flashlight on the slate. Try to avoid panning or zooming to accommodate the slate. This will only waste film (not an issue for video). Also, if the camera misses the slate, and you have to do it another time, announce "Second sticks" to alert the editor.

Smart Slates

Timecode offers many benefits for film production when editing will be completed on nonlinear or other video equipment. It can automate the syncing process as well as identify and locate audio material by timecode number (see Chapter 16 for more details on the basics of timecode). It does this with the help of a timecode slate called a smart slate. With this system, a timecode generator feeds code to the audio recorder as well as to the smart slate. This slate looks much like a standard clapboard with timecode display embedded on its face. Slates are handled in the usual way. When the clap sticks are lowered on the slate, the timecode at that instant is held for a few frames on display. Any sync sound camera can be used. After the film is processed, the sound is synced up either during the film-to-video transfer or after. The frame with the slate is stopped on the screen. The timecode is read visually and then entered into the computer. The system then locates the same timecode in the audio, and then the shot can be placed in sync with the sound.

When using timecode with film equipment, you have several options in terms of frame rates and timecode settings for camera and audio recorder. Before shooting, be sure to contact the laboratory or post facility that will be doing your transfer to find out its preferences. It is advisable to shoot a test before beginning a production to make sure all systems are working.

FIGURE 14.3 Assistant director David Hamlin holds a slate to mark the beginning of a take on the set of *Truman*.

Action! Cut!

After the slate has been clapped and only when the director feels that everything is ready, she calls, "Action!" The scene plays as long as the director deems necessary, and then she calls, "Cut!" The director will ask for as many takes as needed or as time allows to get the best material "in the can." The cast and crew make adjustments after each take. Hair, makeup, and continuity must be maintained from take to take.

No one on the set can call "cut" except the director and no one stops his job until the director calls "cut." The director may want to linger a beat longer after a scene ends, but if the camera operator turns off the camera because he thought the scene was over, the moment is lost. In fact, the director should always make a habit of waiting a few moments at the end of a shot before calling "cut." These extra beats could serve as good cutting points for your editor.

Calling the Shot

- **Quiet on the set!** (AD) This signifies the calm before the storm.
- **Roll sound!** (AD) The sound recorder is activated. The slate is called off.
- **Roll camera!** (AD) The camera is turned on and is recording.
- **Mark It!** (Camera operator) An electronic clapboard is placed in front of the lens to identify the shot. The clappers are snapped shut to mark the beginning of the scene and to create a digital timecode to match sound and picture.
- **Action!** The director signals for the actors to begin or for the camera to move.
- **Cut!** The director signals for the actors or camera to stop.
- **Check the gate!** (Director or DP) This call is to make sure the take was clean and that no dust or hairs were caught in the film camera pressure plate (if shooting film).
- **Back to one!** (AD) This signals a repeat of the shot.
- **Camera moves!** (AD) When the shot is satisfactorily "in the can," the camera moves to the next position or setup.
- **Martini shot!** (AD) The last shot of the day.
- **That's a wrap!** (Director or AD) Principal photography for the day ends.

Slate Lights

Another slating device is called a *slate light*. This device is a trigger connected to the recorder that, when pushed, flashes a small light and produces an audible beep. This system often is used in documentary filmmaking.

In-Camera Slates

There is a more sophisticated method of recording timecode using a camera with "in-camera" timecode capability. Timecode is recorded on the edges of the film while filming. With this system, both the camera and the audio deck are recording essentially identical timecode with their respective media. In postproduction, properly equipped telecines can read the film timecode and automatically sync it to the audio code. Auto syncing can also be done later on an editing machine.

Informal Slates

If you do not have a slate, you will still need some distinct event that can be clearly seen in the picture and heard on the track. You can make do by holding up fingers to indicate the take number and then clap your hands together sharply. Another informal slate is called a *mic slate*. Hold up the microphone to the camera lens and tap it. The number of taps is the number of the take. This makes a sharp "bump" sound on the track by which the editor can sync up the material.

> I would start the Nagra, then slate the shot with a clapper, and then return to my seat and start the interview. Normally, when we're on location shooting observational footage, because there's not a third person, we use a bloop slate or a mic tap rather than a clapper.
>
> Jan Krawitz

Tail Slates

When an opening slate would be impractical or inconvenient, a tail slate can be used. For example, the opening shot might have a very tight frame and then pull out to a wide one. In this case, slating the scene at the head of the take might prove difficult. It would be easier to start the scene without a slate, and when the director calls "Cut," keep the camera, Nagra, or DAT rolling and slate the take at the end, or tail, of the shot. Other appropriate uses for tail slates would be emotionally acted scenes or unstaged documentary filming because they don't disrupt the beginning of a take. When tail slating, the clapboard is usually held upside down, and the person announcing the slate calls "Tail slate" or "End sticks."

Video Slates

Slating is used in video for identification purposes only (unless a separate audio track is being recorded—the sound will then have to be synced up, just like film). There is no need to create a "clap" because the sound is recorded directly onto the tape stock. It is wise to log each shot into a notebook to keep track of what you have photographed. (Refer to Chapter 12 for more information on recording sound for video.)

Script Supervision

The script supervisor keeps track of the slates, maintains the continuity within each scene and from scene to scene, and makes notes in her script about each shot. Besides taking notes about each shot, the script supervisor is responsible for ensuring that the material delivered to the editing room can be cut together. She bears the responsibility of making sure that the action is matched or duplicated from one shot to the next. For example, an actor crosses to a chair, sits down, and crosses his legs. Did he put the left leg over the right, or vice versa? So as not to confuse the audience, the same actions need to be repeated exactly from each camera angle.

The script supervisor's tools include a digital camera (to record continuity) and a stopwatch (to time the shots). The script supervisor's book contains shooting notes and a lined script for the show like the one in Figure 14.4. Her notes include the following:

- Brief description of what happened during the take
- At what point in a scene an actor does what

- Length of each shot (timed with a stopwatch)
- Lens used
- Director's comments
- DP's comments

After photography has been completed on a scene, the script supervisor transfers her notes onto a "lined" or "continuity" script. This copy of the shooting script has a series of vertical lines on it that indicate from which angle and in which take each part of the script was shot. If, at the end of production, a part of a scene does not have a line through it, it probably was not photographed. A precise record of what was shot is an important guide for the editor. Once in the editing room, the assistant editor can identify material to be used by first referencing the lined script. This saves time sifting through material from the digitized (or undigitized) takes.

In working with a small crew, often the duties of the script supervisor fall to the entire crew. The director, actor, DP, or anyone who is a witness can identify continuity mistakes. But in the heat of shooting, some continuity issues can be missed. This problem is exacerbated by the fact that most scripts are filmed out of continuity. The pressure is usually so great on a director that she will opt to move on with the day's photography rather than spend time laboring over whether a shot may or may not match in the editing room. This happens to all directors, but as a director becomes seasoned, she begins to value the role of the script supervisor for the time saved in the editing room solving shooting problems and for helping avoid expensive pickups or reshoots.

When a director finally comes out the other end of the shooting period and settles down to work with the editor, problems that arose or were neglected on set become glaringly difficult to fix. Even with a script supervisor, editorial problems can arise, which is why directors are encouraged to shoot cutaways and inserts, as these small pieces of film or tape can be used to good effect solving editing or continuity problems.

An actor sits down on a chair, takes a glass of water with his right hand, and crosses his left leg over his right leg. Later in the day, a tighter shot is done, but this time the actor uses his left hand to drink the water and crosses his legs right over left. To cut from a wide shot to a tight shot with two different leg crosses may look like a jump and could distract the audience from the flow of the story. Often an audience won't notice this continuity error. But, if the director has an insert shot of the hand reaching for the glass and lifting it out of frame, there is less chance the audience will notice the left hand/right hand, left leg/ right leg continuity jumps.

If at any point in the film the audience takes a moment to ask themselves, "Did he pick up the glass with his right or left hand?" you have lost them for that moment and possibly for the duration of the show. A director's job

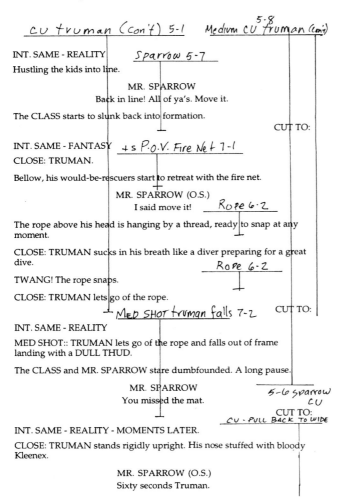

FIGURE 14.4 A lined script from *Truman*.

is to create such a dynamic story that continuity errors will not break the suspension of disbelief, which is part of the contract between the audience and the screen. This is what editors mean when they say they try to achieve a "seamless picture."

On some occasions continuity errors are acceptable. Sometimes it is more important to make a cut for performance, pace, or emotional kick than it is to attempt to correct a continuity error. The director and editor make the judgment call in the editing room as to the gravity of a continuity error. If a script supervisor can work with the director, DP, and actors during the shoot to guarantee seamlessness, the effort to make a good cut will be less of a struggle.

Script supervision may seem like a luxury, but besides fulfilling her duties on set, which are numerous and take great skill of observation, there is one other aspect to the position that is of great help to the director and DP. At the beginning of the shooting day, after a run-through for blocking and lighting, the director will conference with the DP and script supervisor on the coverage they will shoot to record and develop the scene. The script supervisor not only makes notes and suggestions but may often assist in organizing the coverage to reflect editing style and schedule as well as continuity. It is the script supervisor to whom the director turns after every shot and asks, "What are we going to cut to, and what are we cutting from?"

Here are some examples of script supervision editing reminders:

- **Overlap the Action**. When a character walks to a chair and sits down, always overlap the action. This means that in a wide shot, the character walks to the chair and sits. In the tighter shot of the character sitting, he must sit into the shot or, in other words, start with a clean frame and let the actor make an entrance and then sit down. Shooting the scene in this manner makes a very smooth cut.
- **Exit and Leave the Frame Empty**. When an actor or action exits the frame, let the frame be empty for a few beats. This gives the editor options in making the next cut.
- **Inserts Should Be Lower and Slower**. When shooting an insert, such as reaching for a glass on a table, shoot the insert at a slightly lower angle and ask that the actor to reach slowly. The reason is that the action in the wider shot seems to take more time, so the low angle and slower motion make a better match on the insert of the hand reaching for and clutching the glass. Overlap the action by letting the hand enter the frame, and let the hand with the glass exit the frame before the director says, "Cut."
- **Match Frame Size for Obligatory Reverse Shots**. When shooting matching close-ups, over-the-shoulder shots, reaction shots, or POV shots, be sure the frame size and composition are similar.

Dailies

Video dailies are instantly available for viewing and discussion. At wrap, the editor takes this material to the screening room. There, she meets the producer, director, DP, and department heads, and they screen the footage. During the screening, important decisions can be made about the progress of the project. Should an actor's hair be changed? Does the lighting match? Should a costume be more distressed?

If you originate on film and are unsure whether the dailies are giving you accurate image information, the DP may request the lab to make a print of one section of the footage to ensure the intended quality is on the negative. Laboratories may take over a week to develop your film, in which case the DP must rely on a lab report and view all the footage after principal photography.

During dailies screening, the director makes comments to the editor about the different shots. For example, she might instruct the editor to use the head of one take and the tail of another, to start it tight and reveal the master shot further into the scene, or to use a specific take because of performance.

PRODUCER

Coordinate

During production, the producer keeps a daily watch on both the budget and the material that is shot. This requires that he oversee all aspects of the production. During the shoot, the producer does the following:

- Keeps on top of daily cash flow
- Finalizes location arrangements, transportation plans, and meal plans
- Deals with schedule changes
- Completes daily production reports

However, unless the producer is also serving on the crew as the assistant director, there is no traditional position for him on the set. (Even the production manager is usually off.) The AD runs the set and keeps the production unit moving in accordance with the agreed-upon schedule. This allows the producer the freedom to deal with the problems that inevitably arise during the course of any shoot. (Murphy's Law applies to every aspect of the picture-making process.) The producer becomes involved with set operations only in special situations, such as these:

- He is needed as a troubleshooter. (See the following sections for details.)
- The production unit starts to go over schedule.
- He has to alleviate tension between the director and the DP.
- He has to reassure an actor.

Guidelines

Each shoot presents unique challenges and obstacles. The producer must be ready to deal with each as it arises. The following guidelines should help the novice understand the producer's basic priorities, which can be applied to any production.

Act as Coordinator

During principal photography, you must see to it that arrangements for locations, transportation, and food are confirmed and reconfirmed. (Never assume anything.) This task includes establishing a regular system of getting the exposed film stock to the lab. (This is not an issue with video.) You must always keep ahead of the production unit to ensure that each day will go as planned. During this time, you should also be confirming the postproduction arrangements, such as editing space.

If exteriors are planned for the week, keep on top of the weather forecast. If the forecast is for rain, either have a cover set ready or assemble proper gear for shooting in the rain, such as umbrellas and parkas. The actors will need a dry and comfortable place close to the set.

Support the Director and the Creative Team

Support the director and the crew by creating a comfortable work environment that includes good food to eat. Production is stressful and physically demanding work. If the crew performs well, show your appreciation. Don't take the crew for granted; the success of your project rests on their shoulders. If you treat crew members well, they will be more likely to go that extra mile for you.

Watch the Budget

The budget dictates what the director can do. You must know from day to day if the production is on, over, or under budget. To do this, you must approve of and account for all expenditures and keep track of the daily cash flow—that is, the money being paid to vendors for food, supplies, or expendables. Keep a complete itemization of every expenditure and a thorough collection of receipts and bills.

Keep Morale Up

As the producer, you are the head cheerleader and support person. You should remain positive and unflappable even under the most trying circumstances. Keep a "happy face," no matter what you are thinking or feeling.

Be a Troubleshooter

You will need to find creative ways to solve problems if you don't have the money to do so. There is often a great deal of satisfaction in "saving the day" and allowing the creative team to complete photography by solving a difficult problem with your head rather than with cash. Some of the potential problem areas are described next.

Department Heads. There needs to be a creative bond between all the department heads (camera, sound, art department) and the director. If there is tension, it can affect the entire crew. The director sets the tone and the pace of the production, and if she is unhappy, dissatisfied, or angry, it will have a ripple effect on everyone around her. Working on the set is difficult enough under the most ideal circumstances. Stress and tension between the key players can drain the energy and enthusiasm from the best of crews.

If there is a problem with the director's relationship with any of the department heads, the producer serves as the mediator (if the director and producer have words, they should take their discussions off set). Some personality conflicts you must live with; others you must confront. For example, a strong, experienced DP might take over the set and override an inexperienced director's designs. If the DP is slow, you may need to replace him, even if the material looks terrific. If you have a suitable replacement, you might decide to fire the DP. Use your best judgment to resolve the situation quickly.

Crew. During the first days, it will become clear whether you have hired the correct number of crew members. The effective people will stand out; the slackers will be revealed. It is good to cut the deadwood from the crew quickly so as not to slow down shooting. Finding replacements should not be too difficult if you kept a list of available crew people. (Always have backups.)

Schedule. The key to making the daily schedule is to get the first shot by a specific time. The department heads agree to this time beforehand. If the crew does not complete the shot per this plan, it not only pushes them back for that day, but inevitably pushes them back for the entire shoot. The crew must either make up the lost time that day or squeeze it into another day. If the crew is pushed to make up the time, it infringes on proper turnaround, pushes the next day back, and so forth.

There are several ways to get the crew back on schedule so that one bad day doesn't throw off the whole shoot:

- Cut scenes or pages.
- Cut shots.
- Collapse several shots into one.

All these options must be considered and agreed to in a timely and calm manner with the producer, AD, director, and DP, and all discussions should be off set and away from the actors. It is the producer's job to serve as a stabilizing influence on what could be tough decisions for the director and DP. Compromise is an unfortunate but necessary part of the process. Having to make changes in the original plan doesn't necessarily mean that the original idea is compromised. Sometimes, the best ideas emerge from economic necessity.

On the basis of your experience with the crew's pace during the first few days, you might have to adjust the schedule. If the crew picks up speed along the way, so much the better.

Location. Losing a location can throw a monkey wrench into the best-laid plans. If you are prepared with backups, the loss will be only momentarily disruptive. However, it will require that the DP, art director, AD, and sound mixer visit the new location after wrap so they can adjust their plans to the new space.

Transportation. You must carefully monitor and coordinate key moves from set to set. Travel, even if across the street, eats some precious time from your shooting schedule. Company moves must be executed quickly and efficiently.

Keep the Production Moving Ahead

Always keep the production unit focused on moving ahead. Don't let problems interfere with the momentum on the set or with the schedule. Keep problems away from the cast and crew if possible.

Proper Wrap Out

Make sure you leave each location in as good or better shape than when you arrived. This is proper professional behavior. One way to alleviate a major cleanup is to lay down plastic or butcher paper where the crew will be working. If objects, furniture, lights, pictures, or knickknacks have to be moved or put away before the crew can shoot, someone (usually a set dresser) should make careful notes of where these items were, arrange to have them stored properly, and then return them to the correct place when wrapping out of the location. It is helpful to record the original layout by taking digital photos before starting.

Keep in mind that you might need to come back to the location for additional work or reshoots. Even if you will never see the owners again, think of each location as if it were your home. Someone should be assigned to keep an eye on what is happening to the location during the shoot. Here are a few things to watch out for:

- **Placement of Gaffer's Tape**. This tape has a tendency to peel paint off walls. Remove it carefully.
- **Hot Lights Near Delicate Objects**. These include paintings, fabrics, curtains, etc. Having hot lights near these objects can also be a fire hazard.

- **Scratches to Floors, Upholstery, and Furniture**. Avoid putting film equipment on the furniture or flooring, unless it is covered by plastic tarps, sound blankets, or cardboard. You will be amazed at how easily these things become scratched by the slightest contact with camera cases and other gear. Protective materials such as these can be purchased anywhere film supplies are sold.
- **Garbage Disposal**. A crew can generate a lot of garbage. Make sure it is packed up and disposed of regularly.
- **Major Cleanup**. On leaving a location, arrange to have the area cleaned and, if need be, repainted.

Also, have someone do what is affectionately called and **idiot check**. This is a final check of the area to confirm that order has been restored and no pieces of equipment have been left behind once the location has been swept clean of crew clutter.

When you are on a student film, where most of your crew is probably working for free, there is nothing holding these people to you. They are not indebted to you. But they are all there, every single one of them, because they love what they do, and more than anything else, they want to make movies.

Always remember that. And always, thank your crew. Thank your cast. Thank your vendors and your locations and every single person who helped you out. When a film I produced wraps, I always try to write everyone (no matter how big or small their job) a personal thank-you note. Gratitude goes a long way, and making a movie would be absolutely impossible without a group of dedicated people behind you. So let them know how much you appreciate them.

Jessalyn Haefele, Producer of *Citizen*

KEY POINTS

- The director has the final say on the set.
- Put safety first.
- Move the camera to the next setup position only after you are confident that you will not have to return to that position.
- Give the art department ample lead time to dress and strike the set.
- Wrap out carefully.

Chapter 15

The Actor

It helps the actors when the director is prepared. Oftentimes actors are looking to be reassured, to help them get where they need to be. It's like being a parent. They want to please. They want to be stroked and told, "Yeah, you've done it." So, I think by you being calm and understanding you can help take the actors where they need to be.

Be' Garrett

DIRECTOR

Direct

Actors are the director's primary storytelling vehicles. A good actor can breathe life into a character and a script. Being able to aid and guide the actors through the production is the director's job.

The relationship between a director and an actor is an important one. The director should know what the actor is capable of in any given situation. Casting and rehearsals will give the director a strong indication of the actor's talent and range, but the critical point comes when the cameras roll. Many intangible elements must come together in front of the camera when the director calls, "Action!" These elements include emotional tone, pace, projection, and the arc of the characters. Some actors behave quit differently when they have to perform "for real" and it is up to the director to find ways to ease this anxiety.

A primary goal for the director is to create a supportive and creative environment that is conducive to good work. The actors will be able to focus on their work if the atmosphere created by the director and her crew is relaxed and cooperative. If bickering and general chaos occur on the set, it will be difficult for the actors to concentrate.

The well-known British director Joseph Losey (*The Servant, The Go-Between*) said this about directing actors:

Security is I think essential. If an actor doesn't feel secure, two things can happen. He starts to fail. Or else he sets up a psychological barrier to protect himself. Actors do their best for me when they feel free to make fools of themselves... when you have a good actor who knows what you want and is continually looking for things inside of himself, and knows that you are not going to make a fool of him either on the set or on the screen, then you can see extraordinary things happen.

Joseph Losey

The Process

There is a set order to the process of shooting a short film. The director needs to follow that order so that everyone on set knows what is happening at each moment. Within that process, each director will develop her own approach or style to working with the actor. The goal is to capture true behavior on-screen and have each line spoken as if for the first time. To this end, it is essential that the director know what she wants from the actor and how to get it.

When you are the director, your energy is one of the greatest directorial tools you have. If you are down or feeling negative, the actors will pick up that feeling. If you are up and cheerful, they will have a tendency to become lighter as well. A positive attitude will infect not only the cast, but the entire crew.

Call Time

The actor arrives on the set at his appointed call time and checks in with the assistant director. If the assistant director has scheduled the actor's arrival correctly, he will have very little time to wait before he is called to the set for his scene. Do not call the actor to the set until the set is ready. On the other hand, make sure the actor doesn't keep the entire crew waiting.

The first order of business is to conduct a brief run-through of the scene. This is an opportunity for the director and the actors to discuss any blocking issues or questions about the scene. Once the scene has been loosely blocked to the director's and director of photography's liking, the actor is sent to makeup. After makeup, the actor goes to wardrobe to put on his costume. After another stop at makeup and hair for touchups, he is ready for the camera.

If the actors are meeting for the first time on the day their scene is to be shot, the director should conduct off-set rehearsals and discussions to allow them to warm up.

doi: 10.1016/B978-0-240-81174-1.00022-1

They will then require some time on the set to explore and get comfortable with the physical environment they will be performing in. Conduct the first run-through with more relaxed blocking.

Makeup and Hair

The director should be keenly aware of the personalities of the makeup and hair team. These crew members see the actor just prior to his arrival on the set. It is important that they do their jobs effectively without disturbing the actor's concentration. Talented makeup and hair people who are friendly and supportive are priceless, but they must be sensitive to each actor's need for personal space as they prepare for the day's shoot.

Stand-ins

To free the actor from the set until his work begins, it is advisable to employ a stand-in. When you are preparing a scene, many time-consuming camera functions require that a live body be standing or moving in the actor's blocked positions. When you need to flag and focus the lights and to practice camera movements, any body of roughly the same size will do as a stand-in for the actor.

On Call

An important consideration for the production unit is how the actor is treated while he is on call. Although this is primarily the responsibility of the assistant director, all principal parties must be aware of the actor's schedule and working environment.

For the actor, the emotional rhythm of a typical day is like a roller coaster ride. The actor might have to wait for long periods while the crew prepares and lights the sequence. Once the camera begins to roll, he must be able to find his peak energy level. To ensure that he has the opportunity to perform at his best, the production must provide food, a comfortable place to rest (the green room), and a call time that does not abuse his energies.

Consider the alternative: you are shooting in a freezing exterior location. The actor waits outdoors for the set to be dressed and lit. He is tired, hungry, and irritable. When you ask him to get in front of the camera, even the most disciplined actor might have difficulty "getting up" for his part. His poor performance will be reflected in the dailies and ultimately in the final product.

Final Staging

After the crew completes the time-consuming work of preparing for a scene, the director will conduct a final staging rehearsal, during which last-minute technical adjustments are made. Actors should make a point of noting their positions and movements in the scene because they will need to repeat them for the camera.

While performing on set, actors might discover moments, or "business," that were not part of the rehearsal process. Props, set pieces, or a painting on the wall might inspire the actor and be just the thing to make a scene work better. If the technical adjustments are major (a total relighting of the set, for example), the actors should be excused and encouraged to return to the green room, makeup room, or rest area.

Gaffers and set decorators will make subtle adjustments, or "tweak" a set, until they are told to stop. As soon as the director feels that the set is ready, she should get to work shooting the scene. The assistant director is helpful here in determining the preparedness of the set and being aware of the director's schedule.

> I didn't have my two actors, Scotty and Clebert, together until the first day of shooting. In fact, the whole interaction with the salad, the orchestration of her sitting down and what she would say, him sitting at the table, getting up and getting the pepper, and putting that on the table—that took five minutes in between setting up the shots. I sat down with them, and we quickly figured out a little routine to do.
>
> Adam Davidson

Technical Requirements for the Actor

The technical requirements for the actor are a large part of film acting. An actor must not only expose his emotions, but must do so with his head tilted just right to catch the light. His raised hand must be placed so as not to block another actor who is framed in the background, and his eyes must be directed at what the character is supposed to see. Stage and nonprofessional actors who are unfamiliar with technical aspects of film might cause the director problems. It might be exciting to find someone who is a "natural" for the part, but if he can't be "natural" and adhere to the technical requirements at the same time, the director's schedule might fly out the window.

Lenses

Generally, actors should be conscious of what lens is being used and how many cameras are rolling. The general rule is that the tighter the shot, the less the actor has to "perform" to create an emotion. Inform your actor if you plan a tight close-up, for example, so he will be aware of the frame size and won't exaggerate his movement or bob in and out of the frame. In a wider shot, if the actor shakes his head violently, he should be instructed to compromise the movement to match the lens size. Conversely, if the camera angle is very wide, the actor should know that subtle actions on his part will not be seen.

FIGURE 15.1   Controlling the people in Grand Central Station was next to impossible. Scene from *The Lunch Date*.

Eye-line is another technical area in which the actor must be concerned about his relationship to the lens. An actor might have to look just to the right or left of the lens to give the illusion that he is speaking to another character. If the actor to whom he is speaking cannot put his face in the correct position for the eye-line, the camera operator might put a piece of tape on the camera in the correct position, challenging the performer to act to a piece of tape.

The director should be aware of any obstacles in the way of the actor's eye-line. If in the distance, just off set, people are watching the shoot within the actor's line of vision, he might not be able to concentrate. In this case, have the assistant director clear the actor's eye-line (see Figure 15.1).

When we were doing the shot where she loses her wallet, we covered it from a few angles. One of the angles I wanted was a dolly shot through Grand Central, right through the main hall. No tracks, but we had a dolly with wheels. It would cover Scotty after she looks at the boards and starts walking, and suddenly Bernard Johnson would enter the frame as she's walking, as we're dollying, bump into her, and then we'd cover it.

Because I wanted to leave it ambiguous as to where she actually lost the wallet, I had to have her lose the wallet somewhere in the shot without giving it away how she lost it. We start off in a tight shot, Scotty takes out the wallet, she looks up, we start dollying and she starts moving. As she was walking, she was going to drop the wallet so you wouldn't notice it.

People say New Yorkers don't care. Well, every time we did this shot, somebody inevitably would yell out, "Hey, lady, you dropped your wallet." And one woman even was so bold as to see the wallet being dropped, not pick it up, but turn and

yell to Scotty that she had dropped her wallet, and when Scotty didn't respond, she ran over to her and hit her on the shoulder while the camera was rolling!

So that shot eventually was preceded by my assistant director yelling out, "This is a movie. This lady is going to drop her wallet. Please don't pick it up!"

Adam Davidson

The most important point we can make about eye-line is that the camera must see the actor's eyes. This small part of the frame (bigger in XCU) is a shining star that attracts the audience's attention. Cheat if necessary to ensure the camera can see the actor's eyes. If an actor is standing under an overhead light, or if he has a deep eye socket under a protruding brow, make sure to alert the DP so he can shine light directly into the actor's eyes to make sure they are exposed.

Hitting Marks

It is often awkward for an actor to move in such a way as to play to the camera. Besides performing, the actor might be required to walk and stop at a particular point, called a **mark.** If the actor overshoots his mark, he might go out of the frame or out of focus. Grips sometimes place sandbags at the actor's final stopping position. This enables the actor to walk to his mark, feel the bag with his feet, and not have to look down.

We were on a tight schedule with the fence location in Westchester, and could only have one take of the character running up to that wall. The actor knew that it was a wide shot so he needed to play the action a little broader so it would read on film. He also knew that as he approached the camera that it was a closer shot and therefore had to adjust his performance for the size of the lens.

We got really lucky. He missed his mark on the way up but my DP, who knew I wanted to get the scene in one continuous take, made a judgement call and reframed in mid shot. That became my cutting point. In the final film, I started the scene in wide and as he overshot the frame, I cut to my DP's reframed shot.

James Darling

Apple Boxes

A common actor-to-lens adjustment is for height. An actor who is much shorter than his partner might need to be raised slightly in a two-shot or over-the-shoulder shot. Apple boxes, which are wooden boxes of various heights, enable the DP to put an actor at the required level so he can be in the same frame as the other performers (see Figure 15.2).

FIGURE 15.2 Apple boxes have many uses, including adding height to actors.

Locations

The art department works its miracles to make a set look the way the script says it should. However, the art department takes care only of the area that the camera will see. An actor working on a complete set or in a location needs to know where he is and how his character would use the space. Give all the actors time to explore each environment, even allowing them to bring in small props of their own to place around the set.

> Our last shooting day was in the restaurant. The first thing in the morning, we were setting up the equipment, and Scotty comes in. She looks around and sees the pushcarts and the things hanging from the ceiling. She sees the whole messy room. She comes over and says, "Adam, I have to talk to you." She has a very concerned look on her face. I say, "Scotty, what's wrong?" She says, "I've been trying, but I just don't see how my character would eat in a place like this!" I said, "Don't worry, you're only going to see the clean part in the shot."
>
> Adam Davidson

The Director's Tools

The director can use camera, lights, and editing to help shape a performance. The camera can magnify a performance in a close-up, or it can distance the audience with an extreme long shot. Unlike the theater, film and video acting requires little or no projection, and the camera is very unkind to overacting. If the director is dissatisfied with an actor's interpretation of his character, she might opt to shoot the actor from a distance and avoid close-ups in difficult acting scenes, even if she had planned close-ups in her storyboards.

If the director is dissatisfied with an actor's interpretation of his character, she can make sure she has enough shots from different angles (coverage) to give her more choices in the editing room. Performances can be shaped in the editing room as long as the director has options.

Lighting can also be employed to disguise a weak performance. Imagine a scene where the actor is in a shadow. The audience's imagination will fill in a great deal of information that the actor does not provide. The director can control the performance even more by having the character to whom the actor is speaking well lit so that the audience concentrates on that character's reaction to the dialogue.

> The one non-actor I was working with was the doctor. I didn't have to give him any direction because he was just doing what he would do. He automatically had this coldness about him because he knew it was supposed to be a military physical. I didn't have to tell him to be indifferent. He just was. He was just kind of indifferent to the whole process of everything going around.
>
> James Darling

Types of Characters

The three types of script characters with which the director must be concerned are primary, secondary, and background characters.

Primary Characters

The director's main job is to work with the primary characters who motivate and act out the plot. The audience should care about their lives. There are many different acting styles, and it behooves the director to blend them all into a convincing whole.

If the project is well cast and rehearsed, the director might expect the cast to perform with a minimum of direction. If working with less-talented or less-experienced actors, the director might have to rehearse the actors both off and on the set until the dramatic points of the scene are clear and solid. She might have to shoot many takes and work with the actors to improve each take before moving on to the next setup.

I could do things on the set, like say, "This is just after you lost your wallet, and this is going to happen." And Scotty (who played the well-to-do woman) would know where she was in terms of the character's emotions, but she'd also be able to divert from things and stay open. It was interesting. One time I was going over that shot where she is crying, after losing her wallet, and I said, "How did you find that? What were you going through?" And she said, "It was easy for me because the location gave me everything." She didn't have to draw something out of a bad childhood experience. She just was in the moment there. She's a great actress, so I was very lucky.

Adam Davidson

Secondary Characters

Secondary characters are those characters who have several scenes, one scene, one line, or even only an interaction with the main characters. Unlike the background players, who are usually instructed by the assistant director merely to stop and go on cue, the secondary players need specific instruction from the director.

> INT. BAR—NIGHT
> Joe enters the bar. He sees the love of his life, Amy, sitting at a table across the room. The bar is smoky and crowded. Joe winds his way through the crowd toward Amy's table.
> Joe passes by a coworker who shakes his hand and whispers something that makes Joe laugh. Another person at the table, Sam, pulls Joe aside.
> **SAM**
> Watch out for Amy. She's pretty angry.

In this scene, the coworker and Sam are not extras, but secondary characters. In the luncheonette scene in *The Lunch Date*, the cook is also a secondary character (see Figure 15.3).

Background Characters

Background characters, also referred to as **extras** or **atmosphere**, are the characters that fill out and populate the frame but have no direct relationship to the main players. Background characters "people" the sequence and represent the world of the story. (There are casting agencies that specialize in supplying extras for film and television).

The presence or absence of background players contributes to the story. Imagine *The Lunch Date* without Grand Central Station teeming with people from all walks of life. What would the luncheonette scene in *The Lunch Date* be like with customers at every table?

FIGURE 15.3 In this scene from *The Lunch Date*, the cook is a secondary character.

Imagine, for example, that a scene takes place in a crowded bar:

> INT. BAR—NIGHT
> Joe enters the bar. He sees the love of his life, Amy, sitting at a table across the room. The bar is smoky and crowded. Joe winds his way through the crowd toward Amy's table.

It would be difficult to stage this scene as written without people to fill the barroom. If staged with only the main characters, the scene would project a surreal quality and say something very different from what the scriptwriter intended.

The types of people in the background will tell the audience a lot about the specific bar. Is it in a large urban setting or in a small Midwestern town? Does it cater to an upscale, middle-class, or lower-class clientele? Are the patrons working people or retirees? Is this a rowdy or sedate group? These decisions are important and will be reflected in the types of characters that are chosen, their age range, clothes, and behavior.

The AD is in charge of directing the background activity. To create this illusion, he must choreograph a "mini story." This is done by giving specific objectives such as "a waiter comes by to take an order"; "someone gets up to go to the restroom"; "two people are shown to a table," etc. Each extra must know what she should be doing and maintain continuity from shot to shot. If, when Amy rises from her stool to greet Joe in the bar, a dancing couple stops to return to their table, they must do so in every take from every angle. The assistant director often calls, "Roll sound. . .roll camera. . .background action." Then, when the director is ready, she calls, "Action!" The assistant director and the script supervisor watch the extras closely to ensure that they perform consistently throughout the sequence.

Most importantly, they must "act" in silence. Extras mime their noisy actions. They clap without clapping, clink glasses in a toast without allowing the glasses to touch, and throw their heads back in a laugh without making any noise. Nothing should interfere with the dialogue of the foreground action. Later, in postproduction, the sound editor will add the sound of clapping, glasses clinking, and belly laughs.

If the scene requires the extras to dance, the sound mixer can play some appropriate music before the take and then shut it off before the director calls for action. This way, the extras share the same rhythm and appear to be dancing to the same beat.

> In terms of extras that was our biggest day. We had about 20 people on that line. Feels like more, because we spaced them out effectively. I wanted more, but it was the day of the blizzard and I was grateful for whoever did show up. Half of those on that line are my closest friends who knew they were going to be in their boxers. The rest were underwear models my producer found. So it was like schlubby guys and then beefcake guys. They were all really tall too, compared to my lead actor, which was sort of effective. My producer told me she was very grateful to me that day, working with all these half-naked men. She said it was one of the highlights of her film career.
>
> James Darling

Special Situations

Children and Animals

If your script calls for a child or a pet or wild animal, you may face unique challenges. Animals are unpredictable A professional animal trainer, wrangler, or other guardian for the animal should be on set at all times Allow a grace period in your schedule for these tricky performers and be prepared to simplify or cut a shot. An uncooperative dog can be filmed so that it is out of the frame. The actors' reaction and the sound of a barking, panting dog will give the illusion that the dog is in the scene. With an animal, it is highly recommended to shoot the rehearsal.

With a young child (see Figure 15.4), your approach will depend on whether you are directing one with little or no experience or directing a professional. Some children who have been acting since they were very young understand how to relate to the camera and can take direction. Those who are not as experienced will require a different approach. If you have cast a child who is confident and motivated, the rehearsal period would have revealed if the child can take direction, repeat a performance, and is not distracted by a camera.

However, there are stricter time limits for how long children can work in a day. A baby, for instance, is allowed to work only 10 minutes at a time, which is why so many twin babies are cast, allowing a director to have the "same" baby for 20 minutes each hour. Consider the child labor laws in the state in which you are working. The Screen Actors Guild can be helpful in determining proper work hours. Actors under 18 years of age may have to be tutored or have a social worker/teacher on set.

> Our single most difficult problem—besides the kids' stamina and interest—was the boy who played Truman. It wasn't an ego problem; it was an age and maturity problem. He was an eight-year-old boy, kind of hyperactive, who didn't want to be an actor. He got shanghaied into this because it sounded like fun. He looked right, and I convinced his parents.
>
> He had never been away from home. His first night on location, he cried for an hour on the phone to his mom; he was frightened. He was also embarrassed to have to stand in front

FIGURE 15.4 Working with children can be quite challenging. A child actor receiving direction during the filming of *Truman*.

of all these people and pretend to be something he really wasn't. His natural reaction in dealing with pressure and insecurity was to giggle or to smile. Even though he had been to rehearsals, this was different. It was no longer just him and me, but a group of people with the camera rolling, everybody staring. He would smile or giggle or lose his composure halfway through the take. We were burning up so much film we had to buy extra.

Howard McCain

Stunts and Nudity

Actors will do almost anything you ask of them with the exception of stunts and nudity. If nudity is required for your project, this issue should have been clearly stated in the casting notice and brought up during the auditions. On set, make sure to be sensitive to the actor who must either perform in the nude or play a love scene. You may have to clear the set of anyone who is not essential to the shot.

Although some actors can perform their own stunts, it is imperative to employ a stunt double for dangerous sequences (and have a stunt coordinator on set). If an actor is injured while performing a stunt, you might have to shut down production. Besides performing stunts, stunt people often can inform the DP about the best angles for recording the stunts.

Continuity

An extremely important aspect of the shoot is maintaining continuity. Continuity is the uninterrupted succession of events. On the screen, a character appears to be moving from scene A to scene B to scene C, and so on. However, the norm is to shoot out of continuity: first B, then A, then C.

I tried to stick close to continuity, but where things like locations became important, we would go away from continuity. For example, as I mentioned before, we were only allowed to shoot on the platforms [at Grand Central Station] when the supervisor came down. So suddenly in the middle of the day, we would have to stop and do that.

Adam Davidson

In scene A, the actress has on a blue shirt. In scene B, she changes clothes and puts on a yellow dress. Scene C finds her in the same yellow dress. This is the progression in the script. The progression of the shoot requires you to shoot scene B first, with the actress in the yellow dress. If the next scene is A, to sustain script continuity, the actress must change to the blue shirt. The wardrobe designer or dresser maintains the continuity of the costumes the actors wear. This is accomplished with the aid of script notes, breakdown sheets, and digital photos of the actors in their various outfits.

Continuity was the AD's department (because we were short on crew). I felt the film was so well scheduled that the production manager, the AD, and the DP all understood what was supposed to happen each moment. It was fixed in our minds that each of us could have caught the other in a major continuity mistake. Thus, the AD, besides running the set, was handling the continuity. It would have been nice to have a continuity person, but it wasn't necessary. Except for the fantasy costumes, the kids were always in the same dumpy gym clothes, including the same socks with their names on them, so we knew they were getting the same costumes.

Howard McCain

Here is another example of continuity: the shooting schedule calls for a shot in which the actor crosses his legs when he sits in a chair. Later that day, the director shoots a wide shot in which the actor walks into the room, sits down on the chair, and crosses his legs. Which leg did he cross in the previous shot? Will the two actions match in the editing room?

Script supervisors watch constantly for the matching of liquid in glasses, hand movements, lengths of cigarettes, eye-line, and any action. Actors need constant reminders of how to repeat the actions of a preceding take and at what point in the scene these actions happen. If there is no continuity person on the set, it becomes the duty of all parties to watch for this critical aspect of the shoot.

Overlapping Action

Whenever possible, the director should watch for places to overlap action. Action makes for a very smooth cut because the audience is concentrating on the character's movement in the frame. A cut from movement to movement is less obvious than a cut from a static frame to a static frame. For example, suppose that an actor sits down in a medium shot. When the director calls cut and moves the camera in for the close-up shot, she should have the actor "sit into" the shot in case she or her editor wants to make a cut on the action.

Directing Actors

The process of directing actors on the set started with casting the right actors, rehearsing and building their characters and connection to the material, developing their personas through wardrobe and props, and creating a world of the film for them to inhabit. The challenges on the set have a lot to do with overcoming your insecurity and that of the actors as well. You both want each take to be the best it can be.

Many things happen during the course of a shooting day: general nervousness, the forgetting of lines, tension among actors, technical problems that can interfere with the flow of a scene, etc. It is unforgivable for actors to not know their lines, but it happens. What if actors want to try something very different in their performance than what you had in mind? (Let them do it as long as you have what you want and there is time.)

Novice directors often give actors too much direction. There is also a tendency to give the actors a "result" direction, such as asking an actor to be angry or compassionate or ironic. This is how their performance might be interpreted by the audience in the story, but not an effective way to get that result on the set. If an actor is having difficulty creating a particular emotion, try speaking in terms of *what the actor wants* rather than how he is supposed to feel. Actors usually respond more effectively when given positive actions in a scene rather than results like "being angry" or "being sad." In the Chapter 3, we broke down the scene from *The Lunch Date* into specific actions that created such responses as anger, frustration, and even sadness. The actions you come up with will create the circumstances for the feelings you would like to arise.

The Director as Audience

In the theater, the rapport between the audience and the performers has a profound effect on the energy level and direction of the performance. In a film, the actors play for the director. She alone knows how all the little bits and pieces will come together in the editing room, and she evaluates the performance. In this relationship, it is important to keep in mind that actors need feedback. Make sure they hear from you after each take. The director's attention is always divided between cast and crew. Make sure that the actors feels that they are your priority.

STUDENTS

Make sure to talk to the actors as soon as possible after each take, giving them encouragement before asking for changes. Too many student directors get into long discussions with the DP while the actors wait around.

Tips for Directing

- Novice directors sometimes feel uncomfortable working with actors for the first time. Their language and work methods can be intimidating. Be honest and upfront with your talent. Do not try to sound as if you know what you are doing if you do not. Keep your direction simple and to the point. The actors will most likely help you.
- Make all the actors feel they are important, no matter how small or large their part. Regardless of their screen time, each character is integral to the whole. After you call "Cut" at the end of a shot, do not ignore the actors or seem dissatisfied with their work.
- Resist the temptation to make each take perfect. A film is a series of moments. Part of one take may flow

better with the part of another rather than using all the material from a single take. Watching each take either on set or on the video monitor tends to identify the take as a whole, rather than as a part.

- Shoot a scene as many times as you feel is necessary. If the scene is not working, shake things up: shoot from another angle, change the blocking, shoot reactions, or break for lunch and come back to the scene later.
- Some actors need several takes to warm up; others get it on the first take. Seek a take that allows all the actors in the scene to be at their best.
- If an actor looks as though he is "acting" too much, give him an activity that makes sense in the context of the scene, such as a shoe that won't stay tied.
- Shoot the rehearsal. Often the best take is the first because it is fresh and spontaneous.
- Half your battle will be won if you cast well.

Interviewing for Documentaries

In a documentary, the performance comes from either the subject's actions in life or from her responses to the director's questions. Interviewing is an art form. Here are some suggestions for obtaining the best and most informative responses from a subject:

- Create a mood or setting that makes the subject feel at ease.
- Get the subject talking. Start with an open question. The words will be edited at a later stage.
- Ask questions about the subject's personal experience rather than questions of a general nature.
- Ask questions in an order that will lead the subject to reveal herself.
- Don't put words in the subject's mouth.
- Be patient.

If you have researched your subject thoroughly, you should be able to adjust your questions during the interview to ensure stimulating responses.

I let the women informally talk during the preliminary group meetings. I took notes after each session so that I could elicit those same responses again. You figure out the questions you need to ask to catalyze the stories and sentiments you may have heard in a preinterview. In *Little People*, we met people a year before the shoot. In the interview, we could say, "When we were here last year, I remember you saying things about how you felt your parents felt guilty that you were born a dwarf. Could you talk about that?" And generally, they would discuss the same things we heard a year earlier. We all have our repertoire. It's reassuring to know that you can get a story again by asking the right question, but it's also important to be open to new and unheard responses.

Jan Krawitz

Interview Questions

Thirteen women were interviewed in *Mirror Mirror*. Filmmaker Jan Krawitz asked four questions of each woman, using a different camera setup for each question. Two sets were built in a single studio. In one set, each subject was seated in a row of theater chairs, surrounded by naked mannequins. Jan asked two questions in this location, one filmed in a medium close-up and the second filmed in a wider shot. The second set required the subject to stand in front of a mural that depicted the "Ideal Proportion, Female." Jan asked the following questions:

1. Seated mannequin set, wide shot: "At what point in your life did you first become aware of your 'body image'? Was this awareness catalyzed by a particular incident?"

2. Seated mannequin set, medium close-up: "How do you feel people respond to you or make assumptions about you based solely on your physicality?"

3. Standing mural set, wide shot: "Describe your body from head to toe, commenting on specific body parts—which parts please you and which displease you?"

4. Standing mural set, medium shot: "If you could redesign your body, what would it look like?"

Questions 1 and 2 resulted in distinct answers as predicted, so the responses to these questions were cut into two distinct sequences, using the jump-cut aesthetic in which the composition and background remain constant while the subject changes in the foreground.

In the editing stage, Jan realized that there was often considerable overlap between the responses to questions 3 and 4. She ultimately constructed a single mural sequence in which the shots cut back and forth between the two compositions, dictated solely by the text of the interview.

It was different with *Mirror Mirror* because here I had the four set questions, which is different from the way I usually interview. I generally allow the conversation to flow in directions that might not be preordained. I think it's important not to get too locked into your agenda. You want to remain open to a digression that could be fruitful for the project.

You have to really listen to the person and gently guide the direction of the interview. You can't be sitting there worrying about your next question or how much film is running through the camera and how long they're taking to answer each question. You really have to listen because it's in those moments that you might hear something that causes you to ask something completely different from what you thought your next question would be.

Jan Krawitz

PRODUCER

Accommodating

As long as the work is going well and the actors are comfortable, the producer is not involved in directing the actors. However, he may become involved as a mediator if a problem arises.

Socializing

The director and crew are busy all day long, but the producer has the opportunity to socialize with the cast and make them feel comfortable. He can lift their morale if they are feeling low and cue them on their lines. The time spent with the actors between scenes can be productive if their spirits are buoyed by the interaction.

Contracts and Deal Memos

Even if the talent is working for no pay, a simple contract or deal memo between the production company and the artist is standard operating procedure. The following information should be included in this document:

- The amount or rate you will pay or any alternate compensation such as deferred money or a copy of the film or tape
- The "on or about" dates to lock the actor into your schedule
- Any unusual requests such as nudity or stunts

On or about is a legal term that allows the production company a grace period of two or three days on either side of the start date. If you are scheduled to start shooting on May 10 but for some reason do not start until May 13, the contract with the actor is still valid. If you postpone until June 15, though, the contact is void and will have to be renegotiated.

A release is required of everyone who performs in your project. The deal memo or letter acts as your release. It gives you permission to use the actor's picture and voice in your project. The release is a very important document. If not handled properly, it might adversely affect your ability to secure distribution for the picture. (See Chapter 19 for more information regarding distribution.)

The longest day you can employ an actor is 12 hours. Violating the 12-hour day or the 12-hour turnaround can result in penalties to your production. It is also common sense to make sure actors are not too tired to perform. Often the temptation for a director is to shoot until the scene is completed, no matter what the consequences (please refer to the tragic story of Brent Hershman in Chapter 4). A responsible producer can help a director find a reasonable solution.

As long as you honor the terms outlined in the deal memo, the actor should be content. If you try to violate the conditions detailed in the memo or exploit the artist, you may incur problems. For example, if you ask an actor to play a scene in the nude without having discussed the scene with him or written the request into the deal memo, the actor has every right to balk.

Consider the following questions when preparing a deal memo:

- Are there any production dates that conflict with the actor's personal schedule?
- Should you ask the actor to provide his own wardrobe? Will you dry-clean the garments after production?
- If you will supply meals, does the actor have special dietary requirements?
- Are you obligated to provide the actor with a DVD on completion?

Wrap Out

Once a production has been completed, the producer ties up any loose ends with the talent. The SAG account must be closed, the actor's own wardrobe cleaned and returned, and time sheets handed in.

Firing Talent

After you have hired and rehearsed the actors, it might seem strange to consider firing them, and, in fact, actors are rarely fired once shooting has begun. Everyone behind the camera can be replaced at a moment's notice, but to fire an actor means reshooting all the shots in which he appears. Firing someone has catastrophic implications on the budget and on morale. Still, if a casting mistake has been made, it is better to face the situation and replace the actor as soon as possible. Actors cannot be changed in the editing room.

KEY POINTS

- Respect the actors.
- Do not call them to the set until you are ready for them.
- If a scene or shot is not working, rehearse until it is right.
- After each take, acknowledge the actors' efforts in a positive way.

Part III

Postproduction

This part of the book takes a traditional approach to the editing process. The book is predicated on the director-producer relationship. This part is no different. We have also introduced the editor into the mix. We will call this a professional model, one that mirrors the history of motion pictures. We will follow the more professional path, but we recognize that many of you will be doing it alone and we acknowledge the pitfalls of doing so. In fact, the beginner/student reading this book may be functioning as the writer, director, producer, and editor.

Your film is now shot, or "in the can." The task of assembling and polishing the final product can now begin. During postproduction, the pictures and sounds that have been recorded are shaped to tell your story. It is time to create the "final draft" of the script, the draft that is pieced together with film or tape.

PRODUCER

Much of what an audience perceives on the screen is created during the postproduction process, when the raw material accumulated during the shoot is transformed into a product. This final phase involves thousands of details, a multitude of decisions, and many complex technical steps. Fortunately, it doesn't involve nearly as many people as production, so the overhead is manageable. However, it does demand a detailed plan and schedule.

The producer must always be aware of the big picture. He should understand the financial repercussions of every creative decision, keep track of all the expenses, and even be looking ahead for fundraising opportunities. Time is still money, and though the daily rates are lower now, postproduction might seem to take forever. If the production phase is akin to a sprint, postproduction is more like a marathon. Each project has many variables, so it is difficult to estimate how long a project will take to edit. The producer's goal is to surround the director with the right creative team to complete the project. This team includes not only the right editor, but the entire postproduction crew, the sound effects team, and if appropriate, the composer.

The importance of sound and music to a picture should not be ignored. Having been brought up in a predominantly visual environment, novice filmmakers can distinguish a wonderful camera move or visual effect more readily than they can identify an effective sound or piece of music. Easily seduced by illusion, many novices do not spend enough time deconstructing all the elements of a film, and the contribution of aural elements eludes them. After the pictures and dialogue are cut, however, sound and music communicate a tremendous amount of information. Pictures can be only half the story; sound and music flesh out the experience.

DIRECTOR

During preproduction, the director translates the screenplay into floor plans, storyboards, and finally into a shot list. During principal photography, she transforms the shot list into dailies. This material is now ready to be delivered to the editing room for assembly.

Postproduction is an exciting period but without the time pressure of principal photography. Shaping the material one on one with an editor is an intense and exhilarating adventure for the director. She comes to the editing room filled with the enthusiasm and experiences of the shoot.

The final picture will be only as good as the dailies with which the editor works. A finished project can be made only from in-focus, well-exposed shots; it is not created from ideas, wishes, cut lines, or the big shot that got away (unless you are able to reshoot). Guided by the director's vision of the story, the editor is responsible for manipulating the images so that the picture flows from one shot to the next. The goal is to produce the best picture possible.

If there is one rule of thumb for the director at this stage, it is to become as ruthlessly objective with the footage as quickly as possible. It is natural to fall in love with what you've shot, making it difficult to cut out anything. However, to give the film a pace, the raw material must be shaped and trimmed. It is all right to hold onto footage for a while, but there comes a time when the editor must eliminate anything that does not propel the story forward.

Film director Alexander Mackendrick (*The Man in the White Suit*, *The Ladykillers*, *The Sweet Smell of Success*) had this to say about how the director's role changes when editing begins:

Between the period of the shooting and the editing stage some fascinating changes are likely to occur. Once principal photography has been completed, your role as director changes quite abruptly. It can be an odd switch in your way of thinking. You become another person, now standing outside the material you directed, exploring from an entirely new point of view. What you may have remembered may now present itself to you as having not only many problems, difficulties and shortcomings, but also new and unexpected values.

Alexander Mackendrick

IMPACT OF HOME SYSTEMS

Technology has compressed the process and condensed the systems that are able to perform the production tasks that used to take place in editing rooms. Students and independents have access to technology to complete the picture and sound editing in a small apartment, especially picture editing. Nursed on basic editing software like IMovie, they transition easily to Avid Media Composer (Soft) and Apple's Final Cut, both software-based systems that have taken the place of $100,000 systems only a few short years ago. Film editor Walter Murch (*The Godfather*, *Apocalypse Now*) cut *Cold Mountain* on Final Cut Pro and several off-the-shelf G-4s. He sifted through 600,000 feet of film to create a 2½-hour film on a system that any student can buy for less than $1,000 (including the cost of a computer). As this edition was being written, the student price for Avid Media Composer is $299.

From a producing standpoint, editing at home gives the director/editor unlimited time (without the cost of renting a facility) to experiment with the structure of the film.

The downside is that beginners can get lost. Someone who writes, directs, and edits may quickly lose any objectivity to whether or not the piece works. A person who spends hours in a small room staring at screens making sense out of hundreds or maybe thousands of images can only succeed by enlarging the scope of the process to include those who will view various cuts and versions of the material. It is the producer's responsibility to see that this happens.

THE POSTPRODUCTION PROCESS

For over 85 years, thousands of films were edited without the aid of a computer. It is important to acknowledge this fact. Everyone shot film, edited film, and finished on film. For those originating on video: they edited video in a linear fashion (see web site for information on this process). The technology that has been adopted by the professional world has been around for only a relatively short time. This is the history:

Film editing, c. 1900
Talking pictures arrive, 1928 (cutting synchronous sound and picture)
Analog audiotape editing, c. 1945
Videotape editing, 1956
Videotape editing with timecode, 1970
Digital disk-based audio editing, 1985
Digital disk-based picture editing, c. 1989

We are not going to argue about which is better. The fact is that the film and television industries have converted to the new technology. University film and television programs have been training their students with the nonlinear editing machines for years. Those who have worked primarily in video have easily adapted. It is those who come from a film background who were challenged to make the transition. It is for this reason that most of the computer-based nonlinear systems that were developed were designed to be "film friendly" in their interface. Many of the terms were borrowed from film editing (editing bins).

The merging of these two media has opened up a realm of possibilities for the beginning filmmaker. These are some of the options:

- Shoot film, edit digital, finish on film (see Figure III.1)
- Shoot video, edit digital, finish on film
- Shoot video, edit digital, finish on video
- Shoot video, edit video, finish on DVD
- Shoot film, edit digital, finish on video
- Shoot film/video, edit digital, finish digital (YouTube/DVD/New Media)
- Shoot HD/Card based, edit digital, finish digital (YouTube/DVD/New media; see Figure III.2)

SHOOT FILM – EDIT DIGITAL – FINISH FILM

FIGURE III.1   Shoot film, edit digital, finish film

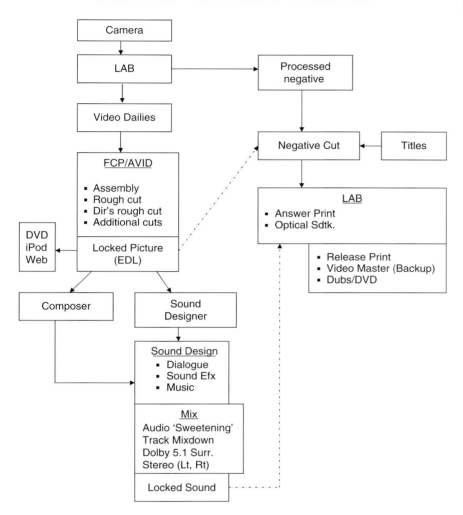

The choices seem overwhelming and confusing. The traditional "filmmaker" must not only adapt to a completely new editing machine, she must also have basic understanding of video. Part of this is an understanding of the glue that holds film, sound, and video together: timecode. Timecode was developed in the 1970s to facilitate accurate video editing (this is mentioned in Chapter 16). It is also the key ingredient that enables the filmmaker to shoot on film, edit digitally, and match back to film. This process can be complicated because of the different frame rates of film and video (24 frames per second versus 29.97 frames per second, respectively).

The positive side is that there are now many more choices, and some are cost effective for the beginner. The low cost of shooting video and the speed and flexibility of computer nonlinear systems are attractive. And if you still want the "look" of film, the line between film and video has narrowed. Cameras have filters that produce the "film look"; 24p video cameras can duplicate the frame rate of film; and NLE systems have

filters to simulate the film look as well. HD systems with card-based storage are now affordable.

There are also tape-to-film transfers (the expensive part of this equation). The decision to follow a particular path has to do with aesthetics, money, availability, your distribution plan, and time.

What hasn't changed are the steps. Technology has aided the process, but certain creative and technical steps still must be adhered to. In previous editions, we started this part with a comprehensive review of traditional postproduction steps for film and linear video editing. For some beginners, it may be important to have an understanding of the first two because nonlinear digital editing is based on the foundation of traditional film and video editing. Interested readers will find this discussion on the companion website for this book at www.booksite.focalpress.com/companion.

Technology is a tool; it is not a magic wand. Students and beginners have to learn how to take advantage of its power and understand that some parts of the process will never change.

HD P2 WORKFLOW

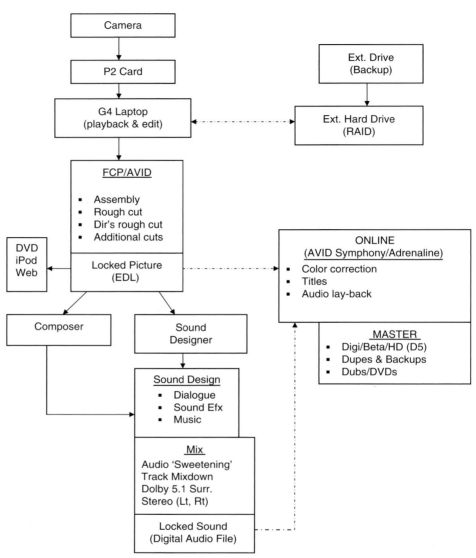

FIGURE III.2   HD P2 workflow

Chapter 16

Pix Postproduction

The initial script itself from the time it was done was always a fifteen-page script. The final film was about ten minutes. So, we lost about five pages in the editorial process, which I think is part of the reason why when I initially saw the first cut I was kind of jolted. Your words are precious and what you are seeing is a fifteen-minute short film and there are certain things in it that you think are telling a story but when you get into [the] editing process you realize you don't necessarily need everything you wrote. We began to economize and kept asking ourselves, is it telling a story? If it doesn't tell a story, get rid of it. That was our mantra throughout the entire editing process. Tell the story. Tell the story.

Be' Garrett

DIRECTOR

The "Final Draft"

Whether the director edits the film herself or collaborates with an editor, her vision for the material must now extend itself to the editing room. Much of the editing process is trial and error. Success is usually attributed to 10 percent inspiration and 90 percent perspiration. It is only through perseverance and patience that the project will come together.

> There were two moments that I felt some satisfaction, which both had to do with the salad sequence. When I started shooting the salad sequence, and then when I started editing it together, I felt, "There's something here; I don't know what it is, but something is working here."
>
> Adam Davidson

The Director as Editor

Most beginning directors cut their own projects. They feel attached to the footage and want to shape the final product themselves. In physically joining the shots herself, the director can learn whether her visual plan was adequate to tell the story. Does she have enough shots? Do these shots cut together? By reflecting on how each scene was approached visually, the director can learn what worked, what didn't, and why. She can apply these lessons in storytelling to her next project.

Equally valuable to the writer–director is how the structure of the script holds up as the first cut comes together. She might discover that certain moments were overstated and that others were not stated at all. Seeing ideas realized on film is an important part of learning dramatic and visual writing. Even if the director discovers she doesn't like editing, it is an important learning experience for her to edit at least one project herself.

However, the director as editor does present some inherent problems. Many first-time directors get bogged down by the mechanics of editing and organization. This process inhibits their creative drive and may have a negative impact on the outcome of the project. The director needs to step away from the material to gain some objectivity before she begins to edit. If the director does decide to edit, she should try to delay editing for several weeks while she winds down from production mode and is fully able to concentrate on the task at hand. The director is usually exhausted after the film is wrapped. The last thing she wants to do is run into an editing room to start logging the footage. There is no reason to slow things down while the director recuperates.

Most importantly, directors can exhibit a possessiveness that can hinder their ability to be objective about the raw material. This condition is exacerbated if they have also written the piece. Being emotionally attached to the project can impair a director's ability to "see the forest for the trees" and make tough editing decisions.

The fact is, the director need not personally edit her own film to put her creative stamp on the material. The editor is the technical guide who implements the director's ideas. Her skills and creative input can bring objectivity to the process and free the director to concentrate on aesthetic concerns. We discuss the value of having an editor on the project in the producer part of this chapter.

For the director to succeed as editor, she must be able to let go of the script; what happened on the set; and what she should have, could have, but didn't get "in the can." The editing process can be an exciting journey. She will get the most out of her footage by listening to what the images are telling her. It can and should be an exciting journey of discovery.

doi: 10.1016/B978-0-240-81174-1.00023-3

The advantage to editing the film myself was that I was learning the process. The disadvantage was that I found myself losing myself, my perspective on the film... because I started concentrating on each specific cut rather than on the whole picture. You start fiddling around with a frame here, a frame there, which becomes insignificant compared to whether the sequence is moving.

Adam Davidson

The Editor

The editor is a craftsperson, technician, and artist who has the patience and facility to create order out of thousands of images. Beginning directors can learn much about the craft of editing and storytelling from an experienced editor. The editor's manipulation of sounds and images is often needed to realize the creative potential of the material. The script might be recorded on the set, but the film is built in the cutting room.

For many directors, the craft of editing has been an effective stepping stone. Robert Wise edited *Citizen Kane* before he went on to direct *The Set-Up, West Side Story,* and *The Sound of Music.* David Lean, director of *Lawrence of Arabia* and *A Passage to India,* was one of England's premier editors before being hired to codirect *In Which We Serve* with Noel Coward. Hal Ashby was one of Hollywood's better known editors before being given the chance to direct a small picture called *The Landlord.* He went on to direct *Harold and Maude, Coming Home,* and *Being There.* Roger Spottiswoode edited *Hard Times* for Walter Hill and *Pat Garrett & Billy the Kid* and *Straw Dogs* for Sam Peckinpah before directing such films as *The 6th Day, Under Fire,* and *Shoot to Kill.* George Lucas, a talented director, preferred for many years to work solely in postproduction. These outstanding filmmakers spent years practicing the art and craft of storytelling while fixing the mistakes of the directors with whom they worked. They learned about rhythm and pacing and how to control it—all the tools a director must master.

The Editor Speaks

In the producer section of this chapter, a professional film editor, Camilla Toniolo, will give the 21 steps to how she approaches the editing process from an editor's perspective. A former film student, she has cut 19 feature films such as *Living in Oblivion, Buffy the Vampire Slayer, Infamous,* and *Game 6.*

The Documentary Editor

The editor's job on a documentary functions more like a second director. She must be capable of intelligently interpreting the materials and contributing creative judgments on her own. Crafting a documentary occurs in the editing room. Because the editor lacks a narrative script as a guide, the process of shaping the hours of interviews, archival footage, etc., takes considerable skill, patience and perseverance.

The steps outlined in this chapter also apply to the journey that must be taken to discover the story that lies beneath the hours of raw footage, interviews, images, or whatever makes up the raw material with which you are fashioning your film.

Don't force the film into preconceived notions. Let the film find itself. Sometimes the script doesn't work.

Jan Krawitz

The Editing Process
The Creative Steps to Editing

One of the major differences between production and post is the lack of a defined structure. The production period is structured by the script, the budget, and the shooting schedule. There is, however, no equivalent to the shooting schedule in postproduction. Certain things must happen but not always in a set order. The film is finished when you say it is. It may take a week, a month, or even a year. Money may define the boundaries of how long you have to edit. In this case, you have as long as you can afford unless the producer can raise more money. For beginners who are editing on a system at home or at a film school, time or money may not be an issue.

Either way, we want to offer an approach that has developed over the years from traditional film and video editing. This is not a paint-by-numbers solution. Each film is tailor-made, and each has its own creative challenges. This is a road map with specific benchmarks and certain tried-and-true techniques that we hope will help you navigate your way through the postproduction process so you can make the best project possible from your footage. These are the basic steps:

- Sync Dailies
- Loose Cut
- Rough Cut
- Fine Cut
- Lock Picture

What Is Editing?

There is an analogy to the editing process in scriptwriting. The axiom "Writing is rewriting" can be applied to editing as well. You are, in fact, writing your film with real images and sounds. Remember how many drafts were required before you created the final draft of your screenplay? Just as many if not more might be required before realizing your project. This time you are creating the final draft of the script, the draft that will be the film that audiences will see.

There are a few basic concepts that we believe can help this process along. Many believe that editing is just about cutting out the bad parts. This is a common misconception. Think of editing as fashioning a beautiful building out of the raw materials from the set. You are not just eliminating what is unnecessary; you are constructing a work of art.

Screening the Dailies (Working with an Editor)

At the end of the second day of principal photography, traditional film directors screen the first day's dailies with the editor to choose selected takes. It usually takes a day to process and print the film. More time might be required if the laboratory is far away or if it develops your type of stock only when there is ample material to justify filling a bath. (Film is developed by placing the negative in a bath of photographic chemicals.) Video dailies, on the other hand, can be screened immediately because they do not require chemical development.

This initial session allows the director to offer immediate feedback about how she would like to approach the first cut of the film, which moments to use, and which to avoid. The director's notes will be the editor's guide, and he assembles the first cut of the film. Here are some suggestions that will ultimately help the editing process.

Take notes on all your first impressions. This is the only time you'll see the footage as the audience will ultimately see it. Record all the good moments of performance, camera moves, and shots. Also record how these moments made you feel. These moments and the emotions attached to them will become the ultimate building blocks of each scene. Beyond the script, these moments will become your ultimate guide, the structure of your story.

Also take notes on any technical problems in the frame, such as dirt, scratches, exposure, and focus problems. Let production know if they have to reshoot something before they tear down that set.

> I didn't give my editor too much direction. He did his cut and I did mine. I wanted to see what kind of original ideas he would bring to the table and I wanted to do my own uncompromised version. We then brought them together, watched each other's version and joined forces. He had a lot of good ideas but there were certain things that I definitely wanted to keep from my version.
>
> James Darling

Shaping the Story

The Loose Cut—The Assembly

First, the story is put together in the order indicated by the script. This loose cut sometimes includes only the master shots pieced together one after the other. It allows the editor, director, and producer to experience the flow of the story and gain a sense of the direction the film is taking. Some editors like to string together the coverage of key performance moments to get a quick feel of what works best. Many directors opt to skip this step and move right to a rough cut.

The Rough Cut

The **rough cut** is an attempt to view the picture as a whole with traditional editorial techniques. The rough cut includes shots to establish location, close-ups to provide emphasis, insert shots to orchestrate the story, and if appropriate, dissolves to show the passage of time. This cut can be difficult to view because it shows the story yet lacks music, sound effects, and overlapping dialogue. In short, the entire sound design will not be present to assist the viewer in appreciating the full impact and flow of the film. (There are no hard and fast rules. Some editors include some sound effects and temp music at this stage.)

The rough cut should also follow the continuity of the script exactly. This is an important rule to follow. There should be no deviations, even though obvious changes might be required. One of the primary goals of this first cut is to evaluate whether the structure of the original script works. It isn't until you decide on the structure of your scenes that the true editing begins. Revelations that affect the rest of the editing process will come from viewing this cut.

> I did a shot where I thought I needed to build up more to the character's anxiety about being in this unfamiliar world. So I shot a quick little scene where Scotty, the actress, goes into the women's bathroom at Grand Central. I don't know if you've ever seen what that's like, but it's horrible. I did a shot where she walks in and then backs out two seconds later. But by the time I got to putting together the film, the scene was unnecessary.
>
> Adam Davidson

Guidelines for Editing the Rough Cut

Speed in Editing. Editing a scene means using sounds and images to create a rhythm that tells the story of the scene properly. Each scene forms a unit that, when joined with the other scenes, creates the rhythm of the entire film. The process of editing demands that the editor get into a rhythm of cutting. There is a direct relationship between the speed with which you cut and your ability to get in touch with and properly interpret the appropriate rhythm of any scene. It is a visceral experience as much as an intellectual one. You can't really know if a cut will work until you make it.

When in doubt, make the cut and move on. The more quickly you make one cut, the sooner you can move on to the next one. There is no point agonizing over each cut.

Excessive thought about it is counterproductive; it only slows you down. You can do over the edits if the cut doesn't work (and save each version if you want as well). Work quickly and trust your judgment. This is especially important at this stage, when subtlety is secondary to seeing a first cut of the film.

STUDENTS

It is common for students or beginners who are editing their own projects to get bogged down with the editing process because with each shot, they are reliving the details (good and bad) of the shoot. Ridding oneself of the emotional baggage from the set is an important step to evaluating the footage in the context of the film. This is an experience an editor will not have. An editor is not involved with the shoot and doesn't care how long it took to execute a shot that may not be appropriate to tell the story properly. The director needs to think and act more like an editor and less like the director.

Rough Cut Editing Tips

- Take out any extraneous sounds on the track that will be distracting, such as the director saying "Action" or "Cut."
- Use straight edits when cutting dialogue. Do not begin to overlap dialogue yet. It is not necessary.
- Do not insert sound from other takes.
- Do not waste time fine-tuning scenes until they are seen in the context of the whole. You must have a sense of the rhythm and tempo of the complete piece before adjusting each scene.

Each stage is about discovering the story because you have what you think is the film on paper, in your script, and suddenly, as soon as you start casting it, as soon as you pick a location, suddenly what's on the paper gets more specific, so it starts changing. Then you start editing the film, and it starts changing once again. What I originally thought would be the film was nothing like what it turned out to be. Yet, I think you accept that. You don't accept necessarily the end result, but you accept the process. I think it's an interesting process. If you keep yourself open to it, you can make interesting discoveries.

Adam Davidson

Analyzing the Rough Cut

You and the producer have just seen the rough cut, the first complete cut, of your film. Many feelings are evident in the room. You might feel depressed or exhilarated or something in between. You might even be in shock and ready to give up. Why? In this premier screening, you might make many discoveries:

- Do you have a story? Does it work?
- If you have a story, does the current structure work?
- If the story doesn't work, what can you do about it?
- Do you need to shoot more footage (if you can) to make the story work?
- Does the existing structure need to be severely edited?
- Do you need to come up with a new structure?

If the basic structure of the film works, you are off to the races. You can truly begin to edit the project. If not, you must focus on coming up with a new structure. Either way, you can put away the script. It has served its purpose. The film has now taken on a life of its own. Unless you can do more shooting, you must deal with the footage at hand.

We developed the film to get one light dailies. We edited on an Avid. I got back the film, looked at the rushes and I thought it was horrible. I thought it looked horrible. No sound, no anything and you just look at it and say, "Oh my God this is a horrible film. I can't believe I directed it." So I turned it over to the editor and said call me when you've got a cut that you want me to see. That took a couple of days. I took a copy of the cut home and looked at it once more and then I put that copy away and never looked at it again. Then we just began editing in earnest.

Be' Garrett

Screening for Story

If you are unclear about how to proceed, it is extremely valuable to preview different cuts of the film in a screening room or small theater. Invite a combination of those who are familiar with the project and those who have never seen it. It may also be valuable to invite key experienced people to serve as consultants. (If you are just learning, you will require assistance.) The fresh eyes may discover something that has eluded you. A key bit of exposition that you take for granted may be missing. A character's motivation may be unclear. You live with a project for months and what typically happens is that the more you look at it, the less you see, especially if you have been involved with the project from script stage.

Listen to what new viewers have to say and take notes. Suggestions can come from anywhere. Their ideas might not be on the money, but their perspective should stimulate your thinking about the story. Pay particular attention to the problems mentioned by viewers, especially if several have the same issue, but be less concerned about specific changes they suggest. That is, audiences reveal problems with your movie, but you're the only authority on how to fix them.

> The most critical thing was screening it for as many people as possible, making sure people understood what was happening by the end, and that they were coming out of it with a certain experience and a certain feeling. I wanted to tell the audience as much as possible with as little as possible. There are still some people that it does not play for, but for those that do get it, it seems to be a much more satisfying experience than had it been spelled out in the front with some sort of voice-over or title card.
>
> James Darling

Screening for Pacing

Screening your film in a large room will help you evaluate its true rhythm and pacing. There is a clear and distinct difference between how a film plays on the monitor of an NLE system and how it plays on the big screen. This is due to the difference in how we perceive images and how that change in perception impacts the flow of the story. Having worked with thousands of student filmmakers over the years, we have never failed to hear the students' reaction to the first time they see their project projected on a big screen. The common reaction: "It drags." Certainly, if you intend to enter your film in festivals, you should always make an effort to preview cuts on as big a screen as you have access to.

Electronic Feedback

Circulating your work in progress for feedback can be accomplished efficiently and economically by electronic means. If you have already set up a web site for the project, you can create a link to a QuickTime file for selected people. You can email those interested parties with a QuickTime link as well. Finally, you can post your film on YouTube in a private location, as James Darling did.

> We also received a lot of feedback from exporting a rough cut and putting it online. This is a big way the Internet helped in the editorial process. We did not put it on YouTube; we put it in a private location and were able to send the link around to people. In this way, we were able to reach out to anyone in the world.
>
> James Darling

Restructuring the Picture

An efficient way to preview what a different scene order might look like is to try it out on paper first. Reduce each scene to one line of description (similar to the one-liner in the scheduling process), and write down the order in which the scenes now appear in this version. You can also perform this paper cut with index cards taped to a wall. With this written overview, the creative team can discuss possible variations before actually making another cut.

Paper edits can be used effectively any time you have a structural problem during the editing process. This efficient and time-saving device enables you to previsualize different structures without having to cut the film or tape.

> I did a paper edit. I cut up the transcriptions and highlighted what I thought were the important phrases, so I had pages and pages with highlighted lines. Then I xeroxed it, so I had a master, and then I cut out the lines that looked good. I started doing a flow chart with them. I hung them on the wall and I would move them around, and I would read them out loud. If I cut from so and so saying, "I really hate my hips," to "My hips are the greatest thing since sliced bread," I could read them out loud and see what it would sound like before I actually made the cut.
>
> Jan Krawitz

Screening the Second Cut

Screen a cut of the new structure. If the new version still doesn't work, the restructuring should have given you a clearer sense of what you need to try next. From this point, how long it will take to achieve a fine cut and picture lock will depend on a number of variables:

- How much productive time the editor can spend on the project
- Whether there are restrictions on money and the editor's availability
- How quickly the changes can be made after you've had a major screening and discussion

As in the first cut, prepare to be brutal with your cutting decisions. Avoid attachment to your footage. Don't worry about minor continuity problems. If you keep the story moving, no one will notice them. So what if there is a slight boom shadow? Only film professionals notice them, not the general audience—as long as they are engrossed in the story. Always cut for the performance.

Walter Murch is an editor, sound designer, and rerecording mixer of such films as *American Graffiti, The Godfather, Apocalypse Now*, and *The English Patient*. In his informative and inspiring book *In the Blink of an Eye*, he lays out his principles of what makes a good cut in order of importance, with the top three outweighing the bottom technical factors:

- Emotion
- Story
- Rhythm
- Eye-trace (concern with the audience's focus of interest within the frame)
- Two-dimensional plane of screen
- Three-dimensional space of action

He goes on to say:

For many years, particularly in the early years of sound film, you struggled to preserve continuity of three-dimensional space, and it was seen as a failure of rigor or skill to violate it. Jumping people around in space was just not done, except, perhaps, in extreme circumstances—fights or earthquakes—where there was a lot of violent action going on.

I actually place this three-dimensional continuity at the bottom of a list of six criteria for what makes a good cut. At the top of the list is Emotion, the thing you come to last, if at all, at film school largely because it's the hardest thing to define and deal with. How do you want the audience to feel? If they are feeling what you want them to feel all the way through the film, you've done as much as you can ever do. What they finally remember is not the editing, not the camerawork, not the performances, not even the story—it's how they felt.

An ideal cut (for me) is the one that satisfies all the six criteria at once. . . . Emotion, at the top of the list, is the thing you should preserve at all costs.

Walter Murch

Refining the Story

Editing Techniques

There are editing techniques you can use to smooth over rough spots, make transitions flow, and even perform miracles with a scene that refuses to work. These tricks range from standard editing techniques to less conventional solutions for editing problems. The film experience is an illusion. You might need to use a little smoke and mirrors once in a while to make the illusion complete.

In the end, all that matters is telling the story as best you can. Do not force the footage into what you would like it to be. Create the best from what you have and build on that. The more you edit, the more confident you will become and the more you will trust your instincts. There can be great joy and satisfaction in solving a problem and in seeing your film come together, moment by moment and scene by scene, through hard work and perseverance.

At this point, logging notes made at the front end of the project can quickly become obsolete when the structure of the picture changes. Sometimes a shot that was cataloged for one context might now work for another. Keep all possibilities open when editing. You never know.

Following are some editing and transition principles to keep in mind and experiment with as you refine your story:

Dialogue Overlaps. A common device, when attempting to duplicate the normal speech patterns of people talking to one another, is to overlap dialogue and picture. This requires the use of the reaction shot—that is, showing the person whom the speaker is addressing, rather than the speaker. This way, we hear the dialogue while witnessing (and sharing) a reaction with the non-speaking character.

Cutting on Movement. Cuts work well when they are made on a movement of some kind. For example, a cut made as a character sits down makes for a very smooth transition between shots. Even shots that have no logical connection with one another (and no continuity of space and time) can be cut smoothly with some movement in each shot to "mask" the cut—for example, the match cut of a cloud passing by the moon to a razor slicing a human eyeball.

Kinds of Cuts. A *cutaway* or *reaction* shot is a shot away from the action that can be used to cover discontinuities or to condense the action. An insert shot serves the same purpose. Figures 16.1 and 16.2 are two examples from *The Lunch Date.*

Continuity. Do not be a slave to continuity. If you can't find the right reaction shot for a key dramatic moment in a sequence, look to another part of the scene for a shot you can "steal." It might be out of continuity, but as long as it works, why not use it? You might even be able to steal a shot from an entirely different scene, as long as it was filmed in a similar location with matching light. If you are looking for a quiet reaction shot, try stealing a close-up of an actor the moment after the slate is pulled and the director calls "Action."

Dissolves. A *dissolve* is a cross-fading of two scenes to overlap images for dramatic or emotional effect. Dissolves can be short (8 to 16 frames) and called *soft cuts,* or long (24, 32, 48, 64, or 96 frames) and called *lap dissolves.* Lap dissolves create the feeling of time passage.

Fades. A *fade* is a gradual picture transition from or to blackness. Fades can smooth out the transition from one scene to another and create the illusion that time has passed. They have the effect of closing "one chapter" and beginning another.

FIGURE 16.1   Reaction shot from *The Lunch Date.*

FIGURE 16.2 Another reaction shot from *The Lunch Date*.

Sound Takes. For off-camera dialogue, look for the best line readings. It might be possible to combine parts of different readings of the same line as long as they are from the same aural perspective. That is, the background sounds should be the same. Moving bits of sound around can solve many editing problems.

New Lines. The addition of a line or phrase often adds a piece of exposition that wasn't clear in the script. A line can be added to the beginning or end of a speech while the actor is either turned away from or completely off-camera. For example, suppose the character says, "In my life, I have made no mistakes." The director can add to the line "...except when I fell in love with you." If this tag line is recorded by the same actor and added to a shot where his back is toward the camera, the director can significantly change the meaning of the scene.

Voice-overs. Any voice-over indicated in the script or created during the editing process should be recorded (even if it is a scratch track) and refined during picture editing to ensure proper timing before manufacturing the final soundtrack.

As you edit, keep these points in mind:

- Ask yourself, does this cut work? This is the only criterion for leaving a shot in the picture. It doesn't matter if it is a cheat (trick).
- Just make the cut! A cut won't happen by itself. You can't know if it will work or not until you try it.
- Cut as tight as you can. There is no reason to keep scenes loose. You can always put back what you've taken out. The sooner you see the potential of the piece, the better.

> It's so hard to cut a scene that you spent days working on, but if it doesn't work or it's not necessary, you've got to lose it. That does not devalue the work done on that scene, because it is still part of the story whether it is on-screen or not.
>
> James Darling

Temporary Music

To ensure that the story has a flow and pace that will satisfy an audience, include a temporary music track, even in the rough-cut screenings. Always have temporary music added when screening important cuts in front of an audience. Even a seasoned filmmaker might have difficulty watching a silent sequence that normally requires music or sound. Previewing different kinds of "temp" music will shape the director's ideas about what she eventually will want for the soundtrack.

Temp music offers a wonderful opportunity to experiment with different kinds of themes and tempos for your picture. If you are going to be working with a composer, previewing a variety of pieces helps illustrate the kind of music you want. If you use preexisting music, be careful not to fall in love with a popular piece that might be out of your financial reach. If your goal is to distribute the project commercially, you must secure the rights to your music selections in advance. The rights to a small portion of a well-known tune might cost thousands of dollars. Even if you are only planning to screen your piece noncommercially at festivals and exhibitions, limited or "festival rights" must be secured.

Cutting with Sound in Mind

With the many tracks that are available on most NLE systems, the editor can preview and experiment with a wide assortment of sounds that will eventually represent the aural world of your film. Each environment has its own unique sound or sounds. The off-screen world of your story can be equally important as what is happening on-screen. If a particular sound effect will be used as an important tension-building device in a scene, transfer the sound and use it while you cut your picture.

For example, two people are having a tense conversation. Right in the middle of that conversation, the phone rings. The original scene, however, was not designed to have the phone ring. Now, in the editing room, you get the idea of adding this sound effect, even though the characters do not answer or even acknowledge it. A sound effect like this might shift the meaning of the scene and even the entire story. The addition of the phone ring, if it works, would then require the editor to lengthen the shot to allow viewers to ask themselves why the character doesn't answer the phone.

Adding Reshoots and Stock Footage

Many things change during the editing process. Shots that you thought you needed during principal photography but couldn't get may not be needed anymore. Before spending money on new material such as reshoots or stock footage (these items are expensive), wait until your film has found its proper structure before you evaluate your needs.

FIGURE 16.3 Stock footage can evoke the past, a telling moment from *Mirror Mirror*.

Other than inserting stock footage, editing might reveal the need for additional footage to tell the story properly. Putting in a single shot can sometimes make the difference between a scene working or not. "Connectors" that are often needed at this point include the following:

- Transitions between scenes
- An important close-up of a character to punctuate a moment
- An insert shot of an object to make a story point clear

Once your film has found its proper structure, any new material, such as reshoots and stock footage, can be assembled and cut into the project.

> It is difficult to obtain footage from the Library of Congress because they're more there for research than for reprinting, but the National Archives is a completely separate building. It's in a different place. It's where Nixon's tapes are. They have a motion picture and record administration, and they have all the government footage that is public domain, and some protected material as well, such as NASA footage.
>
> Jan Krawitz

There are many companies that supply filmmakers with stock footage. This footage covers a wide variety of events taken over many years, including news, sports, nature, history, personalities, and distant locations. Images of almost any person, place, or thing can be found and used in your film. Most of the available footage was photographed in 16mm or 35mm film and is sold by the foot. *Mirror Mirror* incorporated stock

footage very effectively from newsreels of a beauty contest during the 1920s and shots of women on antiquated exercise machines from the 1930s (see Figure 16.3).

> Everyone should screen their film for non-film people. Everyone watches movies, but film students watch movies in a very different way than regular audiences. I think it's important to get that unfiltered perspective. Did you enjoy this as a movie?
>
> James Darling

Evolution of the Edit

An actor slips on a line, stutters, or fumbles, but finally gets back on track with the dialogue. In the editing room, the director might decide that this human foible is perfect behavior to help the audience understand the character. After all, the actor was "in character," so it might very well have been a slip on the part of the character rather than the actor. Furthermore, the director might decide at dailies that the stutter should be maintained throughout the production to distinguish the character's actions.

A director must be open to all elements that come into play during production that might affect the project, including mistakes and accidents. Never forget that accidents (both good and bad) that happened during principal photography—tones, moods, emphases that shifted, and new ideas—all become part of this editorial phase.

In *The Lunch Date*, homeless people are integral to the story line. However, it was difficult to keep the real homeless people who congregate in Grand Central Station from looking into the lens, breaking the fourth wall, and therefore spoiling shots.

I worked on food lines at Grand Central every night before filming, and I asked some of the homeless men to show up when we were shooting. I saw Willie the night before, and he had this harmonica and a great face, so I asked him to show up too. I didn't even think he heard me. But we had a shooting schedule, so at about the time we needed to shoot this shot of Scotty reentering the station, we started looking around for Willie. We did a couple of takes with her just looking around for somebody. Then we did a couple of takes of her entering the station and being upset just by herself.

Then I looked over, and I saw Willie! I approached him and said, "Willie, I want you to play the harmonica when I tell you." And he said, "Ah, okay, okay." I told Scotty that I didn't know what was going to happen, but just to go with it, to stick to her basic motivation, which was to be upset, and we'll see what happens. We rolled the camera, I cued Scotty, I cued Willie, and he entered. He did that number with the harmonica, looking almost straight at the camera, and then he walked off. I yelled "Cut," and my crew looked at me like I was crazy. I thought that it probably was a mistake. Willie walked off somewhere, so I couldn't get him back. I decided to go with a couple of different takes of Scotty by herself.

But when I got into the editing room, there was something I liked about the shot. I knew it was a little dangerous because he looked in the camera, but it didn't bother me enough not to use it because there was something that was real about it that I liked.

Adam Davidson

The director of *The Lunch Date* chose to use several of these shots in the final cut of the film because they give viewers a documentary feeling, the sensation that they are there with the character at the station (see Figure 16.4).

At one point the editor said he thought about cutting it out of order, different from the way the script was written, which was quite linear. While I was shooting, I also had the idea that the story could be told in a nonlinear fashion. Once he started working the film with flashbacks, I knew that was the story.

Be' Garrett

FIGURE 16.4 What seemed like a problem on the set turned into a bit of gold in the editing room, a moment from *The Lunch Date*.

Shifts in Tone

When a shipbuilder puts a plan down on paper, like the script, it is not written in stone. As the ship is being built, as the film is being made, the work becomes three-dimensional. This growth is the creative process. It should be nurtured. This process can constantly change the shape and even the very nature of the work. Filmmakers must be responsive to the material and not be afraid to try radical ideas along the way. Solutions can only come sometimes if you shake up the order of scenes almost arbitrarily.

Both *Citizen* and *A Nick in Time* altered the narrative structure of the script. To compare the script with the film, you can find the script of *Citizen* in Appendix 3 and the script of *A Nick in Time* on our web site. As an added feature, the screenplay for *Citizen* is marked to indicate which moments from the script had been taken out for the final cut of the film. This will give you an idea of what was written and what James Darling and his editor felt was not necessary to tell the story.

The script for *Citizen*, which had initially been titled *The Compatriot*, started with the young man driving toward the Canadian border. The narrative follows his path to the border, under the border wall, only to be captured by Canadian border guards and returned to the United States. These scenes were intercut with flashbacks to the young man receiving his physical for the army.

In the editing process, we discovered that there was an ambiguity that we could play with in terms of the order of events. I think this is much more true to life. Life is not so much cause and effect, as we think of traditional stories, it is much more contemplative. The decisions we make are based both on our experience and our speculation. I feel like we live our lives in a much more nonlinear way than we even acknowledge.

James Darling

During the editing process, James and his editor mixed up the order of scenes. The film now starts with several quick POV shot of the woods, an over-the-shoulder shot of the young man with the guard standing in the background, and then a cut to a frontal shot of the young man raising his arms. Fade to black and title. Fade up on young man in the doctor's office. The film now begins with the end, so to speak. James wanted a hook, something to throw the audience into the film and, at the same time, pose the question that is answered during the course of the film.

In the *The Lunch Date*, Adam Davidson describes in the following quote some changes he made in the final cut:

> After the woman discovers that she sat at the wrong place, she goes and gets her bag and comes back into the station. I saw the film ending with her getting back on the train. I wanted to make a statement that people don't change. She certainly didn't change. When I shot it, I had a man begging for money. All my takes, I had her saying something to him. Basically, it was harsh—"Get a job" or "Get lost" or "Don't bother me"—because I thought this is true, this is what would happen. But while editing the film, I discovered that it was too harsh because something was working in the sequence with the salad. It just felt like a different movie, to have this sequence of her telling the guy to get a job. I like to believe that that was the film speaking to me.
>
> Adam Davidson

Adam saw that to force the line into the film, just because it was in the script, would have been a mistake. The director must "listen" to the film. When screening various cuts of the film, the director must become as objective as the audience members who view the film for the first time.

A good example of shifting tone is the approach the director takes with a documentary. The final script for a documentary is made during the editorial phase, not during preproduction. The director initially does her research and approaches her subject with an idea of what she would like to accomplish.

Along the way, however, the idea for the documentary might change. The chosen subject sometimes turns out to be less interesting than some other aspect of the narrative that begins to unfold to the director.

> I think the editing is half of making the film in documentary. Much of the creation of structure and themes occurs at the editorial stage.
>
> Jan Krawitz

Speed Is Not Everything

Speed is great, and NLE systems work as fast as the click of a mouse. Editing, however, is not just about speed. Sometimes it requires distance and perspective. There may come a time when you can't solve an editing problem, when you can't see the trees from the forest. This is the time to take a small vacation from your film. Films need to percolate. Finding the right balance of all the dramatic elements may require a different kind of energy that is the opposite of speed.

Although NLE systems can quickly and efficiently execute the ideas when you get them, they can't edit the project for you. The good news is that you have many options to play with and can save every single version. But for beginners, too many choices can be overwhelming.

> I had done the digital, nonlinear thing; that is how I got into filmmaking but having that exposure to the physical act of cutting film was one of the seminal experiences of my career. Just being able to hold 24 frames in your hand and knowing: that is a second. I did go to a negative cutter with my first film and having that vocabulary was very helpful. It also taught discipline. With digital, you can do a million cuts but you are going to waste so much time. At a certain point, you have to trust your instincts. I feel that is one of the great problems with the digital age. Rather than doing the right thing, you do everything.
>
> James Darling

Locking the Picture

Finally, the picture is screened, cut, trimmed, and shaped to the liking of everyone on the creative team. The picture is now considered to be **locked**, and the product is known as the **fine cut**. Locking the picture means that the timing of each scene is fixed, and no more picture changes should be made. At this point, sound work can begin. Sound is either handled by the editor or farmed out to a specialist known as a **sound designer** or **sound effects editor**. A composer must now be selected if the choice hasn't already been made.

> It's hard to give it up, to know when you're done. I think the same thing probably happens in every process. Certainly with writing, you always feel like you can redo one scene, get a better line here, or whatever. Certainly, when you're shooting, there were more things you felt like you wanted to get. But with editing, you can tinker and tinker and tinker and tinker.
>
> Adam Davidson

Technical Considerations When Editing Film on Video

Unless you are planning to finish your project on film, there are no real differences when editing film digitally. For those who have shot on film, cut digitally, and want to finish on film, there are some issues to keep in mind while editing. Video and film are different creatures, and some things you might do in a video edit do not easily translate back to film. These are some of the important considerations if you plan to strike a film print.

When you are editing video, you can repeat a shot as many times as you want. In film, every shot is based on one piece of negative, which normally can be put in only one place in the movie. If you want to use the same shot twice, that footage will have to be **duped**, or copied, from the original negative.

At the head and tail of every shot, the negative cutter needs at least a half frame to cement splice the negative. If you take a shot and cut it into two pieces, you need to leave at least one cutting frame unused between the pieces. Some nonlinear systems have a feature like Avid's "dupe detection" that warns you if you have reused any part of a shot or left insufficient cutting frames between shots.

When making fades and dissolves, video editors can choose virtually any length effect. Film contact printing machines offer only a standard set of fade and dissolve lengths. Standards usually include 16, 24, 32, 48, 64, or 96, which at 24fps translates to 0.67, 1, 1.33, 2, 2.67, or 4 seconds. Fades and dissolves may look different in film than they do in video.

Digital Basics

Key Terms

Before beginning this part, we present the basic terminology that is the foundation on which nonlinear digital computer-driven editing systems are based. This book can't get into all the dense, complex layers of technical information. We do, however, hope to give beginners an overview. Many excellent technical books are available (some are listed in the Bibliography). Also, the Internet has become an excellent resource (we give you the URLs of some key sites in the bibliography).

SMPTE Timecode

In the early 1970s, videotape editing adopted the use of timecode. This had a tremendous impact on video editing. Before timecode, there was no standardized way to repeat the edits of an editing session or to automatically reedit old work. In the United States and other parts of the world where the National Television Standards Committee (NTSC) is standard, video runs at about 30 frames per second. The idea of timecode is to assign a number to every frame of picture or sound to easily identify those frames and work with them.

Timecode is a running 24-hour clock that counts hours, minutes, seconds, and frames (01:00:00:00) and goes as high as 23:59:59:29. One frame later it returns to 00:00:00:00. Note that because there are 30 frames per second, the frame counter only goes up to :29. This timecode system is called *SMPTE nondrop timecode* (pronounced *simpty*).

The use of timecode sped up the editing process and was considerably more frame accurate than the earlier and cruder control track editing. Timecode is similar to the edge numbers found on film. It is an arbitrary number assigned to each frame of video, similar to street addresses assigned to pieces of property, enabling the computer to quickly locate the frame. Timecode is the way professionals make sure they are "reading off the same page."

Drop and Nondrop Frame Timecode

There are two kinds of timecode: *drop frame* and *nondrop frame*. *Drop frame timecode* (DF) is more time accurate, meaning that one hour of timecode is equal to one hour of videotape. *Nondrop frame timecode* (ND) is not time accurate. An hour of nondrop frame timecode is equal to one hour and 3.6 seconds of videotape. In other words,

- One hour of realtime is one hour.
- One hour of drop frame timecode is one hour.
- One hour of nondrop frame timecode is one hour and 3.6 seconds.

The difference between the two types of timecode came about because the NTSC determined that color television signals would run at 29.97 frames per second rather than 30fps (black-and-white TV signals ran at 30fps). You can't see the difference, but this 0.1 percent reduction in speed affects the way timecode keeps time. Over one hour, the 0.03 frame per second discrepancy adds up to 3.6 seconds. The reason is that your videotape is actually playing more slowly. This is not a problem if your project is not meant for broadcast.

However, because broadcasters need to know the exact length of a program, *drop frame timecode* was developed. A system was devised to drop certain numbers from the counting. The numbers that are dropped are the :00 and :01 frames at every new minute, except at the 10-minute marks (10 minutes, 20 minutes, 30 minutes, etc.). This amounts to 108 dropped numbers, or 3.6 seconds, and allows drop frame timecode to keep accurate time. It also gave DF its name.

With drop frame timecode, no actual frames of video are dropped, and the frame rate doesn't change. It is how the frames are counted that is affected. Switching a camera from ND to DF has no effect on the picture or on the number of frames that are recorded every second. The only thing that changes is the way the digits in the timecode counter advance over time.

Programs created for broadcast television are completed with DF timecode. Many editing systems work with either drop or nondrop, and shooting with nondrop doesn't prevent you from finishing with drop. Nondrop is often used for production. Mixing the two formats in the same project can, however, cause problems. DF is sometimes indicated with semicolons instead of colons between the numbers (01;13;26;15). (In Europe and other parts of the world where PAL is standard, video runs at exactly 25fps. **EBU** [see Glossary] timecode uses a similar 24-hour clock, except the frame counter runs up to :24 instead of :29. EBU code keeps realtime, so there is no need to drop frames.)

Analog versus Digital

Until the 1980s, virtually all video and audio production was done using analog tape recorders. In the analog system, video and audio signals are represented by constantly changing electrical waves that correspond to picture or sound information. If you record someone with a microphone and a tape recorder, and the person speaks louder, the voltage of the signal sent from the mic to the recorder increases. The level of the electrical signal is **analogous** to the loudness of the sound.

There are many high-quality analog video and audio recording devices, but analog has a few key drawbacks. The electronics of any recording device and the tape stock on which you record are never perfect and may be susceptible to a certain amount of background noise. This may be noticeable as a low hiss during quiet passages on a sound recording. It may show up as grain or snow in a video image. When you make a copy or dub of an analog tape, noise builds up and other distortions are introduced into the signal. After several generations, this can be a serious problem.

The idea of digital recording is to measure the level of the electrical signal from moment to moment and record those measurements as discrete numbers. The original signal can be created later by referring to those numbers. Digital recording works by **sampling** the video or audio signal at regular intervals. Each sample is a measurement of the voltage at that moment in time. The rate at which the fixed intervals sample the original each second is called the *sampling rate*. That voltage measurement is then converted to a number that can be recorded on tape or on disk. In digital systems, the numbers are in a binary code, which uses a series of ones and zeros. Each digit in a binary code is a *bit* (101 is a three-bit number). Eight bits make a *byte*. Converting the original voltage into a number is called *quantization* or *quantizing*. The more bits you use per sample, the finer the gradations you can represent in color or brightness.

Sampling can be understood by thinking of a film camera that takes 24 still pictures per second. A sampling rate of 1/24 second is perfectly adequate to record most visual activities. Although the camera door closes after each 1/24 of a second and nothing is recorded, not enough information is lost to affect the perception of the event. For example, a running man does not run far enough in the split second the shutter is closed to alter the naturalness of the movement. If the sampling rates were slowed to 1 frame a second, the running rate would be quick and abrupt; if it were slowed to 1 frame per minute, the running would be hard to follow.

The entire process of converting a video or audio signal to digital form is called *digitizing* and is done by an *analog-to-digital (A-D) converter*. The converter may be a part of the camera, or it may be part of the audio or video recorder. To view or hear the signal, it can be reconstructed in its analog form using a *digital-to-analog (D-A) converter*.

Sampling Rate

How often a video or audio signal is sampled affects how accurately it can be re-created. It is the difference between sampling the rate of a turtle walking across a path and that of a hare.

In audio and video recording, the speed with which the signal changes is related to its frequency. The higher the frequency, the faster it is changing. Frequency is measured in **hertz** (see Glossary). To make high-quality recordings, high frequencies need to be captured. If a sound recording lacks high frequency, it may sound dull or muddy. If a video signal lacks high frequencies, fine detail in the image may be lost, making it not appear to be sharp. It was determined several years ago that the sampling rate has to be at least *twice* the maximum frequency that one wants to capture. Humans can hear sounds up to about 20,000 Hz (20kHz), so a digital recorder needs to sample at least 40,000 times a second to capture the full range of sound. Generally, 44.100 equals CD quality and 48.000 equals digital video (DV) quality.

Digitizing video is a more complex process than for audio. Sound is measured in amplitude (loudness) and frequency (pitch) that change in time. A moving picture must be sampled in both time *and* space. Sampling in time is what a film camera does when it captures still images at 24 frames per second. Sampling in space is the process of capturing each single image. For film, the chemistry of the film emulsion responds uniquely to light. For video, it is a screen of dots. A digitized image looks a lot like a TV image. The picture must be broken down into tiny pieces, small enough that the viewer sees only the big picture and not the discrete pieces. The smallest piece of the video image is called a *pixel* (picture element). If you look closely at your TV, you can see them.

There are two kinds of information per pixel: *chrominance* and *luminance*. Chrominance refers to the color part of the signal relating to hue and saturation, and luminance is the brightness of the signal measure from black to white. The smaller the pixels, the sharper the image will look.

Advantages of Digital

For years, audiophiles and engineers have debated the merits of digital audio versus high-end analog systems, and to this day, there are audiophiles who swear by their analog systems. Digital audio has emerged as the winner by most accounts, but it's still useful to understand the advantages of digital versus analog audio because many audio systems contain a mix of digital and analog components.

The advantages of digital audio can be summed up as follows: it has wider dynamic range and increased resistance to noise, it is easier to copy, and it offers filmmakers the ability to use error correction to compensate for wear and tear. Digital audio can be copied from one digital device to another without any loss of information, unlike analog recording, where information is lost and noise introduced with every copy. Even the best analog systems lose about 3dB of signal-to-noise ratio when a copy is recorded. After several generations of analog copies, the sound quality will deteriorate noticeably. With digital audio, unlimited generations of perfect copies can be made. Perceptible noise will occur only if recordings are made with dirty heads.

Digital equipment will eventually be used for the entire video chain from shooting to recording to editing to broadcast and finally for display. Until then, it will be used for various parts of the process. Digital images can be fed directly into a CPU via a *FireWire* (IEEE) without the need for a capture card or digitizing process.

FireWire, also known as IEEE (Institute of Electrical and Electronics Engineers) 1394, was developed by Apple Computer and is a standardized method for high-speed connections among a wide variety of professional and "prosumer" equipment. A project shot on a small DV camcorder with up to 500 lines of resolution can be input directly to a desktop computer. Different consumer machines can be interconnected and controlled by a FireWire-capable computer. At the writing of this edition, there are now FireWire 400 and 800 ports. Filmmaker should make sure they are working with a FireWire-compatible drive for digital video and audio editing. The speed of the drive is important too; it has to revolve at 7200 rpm, not 5400 rpm. There are many small USB drives that run at 5400 rpm and are ideal to use for backup purposes or transporting media, but they should not be used as an editing drive.

Broadcast Quality

Broadcasters have numerous requirements referring to the aspects of the video signal. For years, the Society of Motion Picture and Television Engineers (SMPTE) set rules, adopted by the Federal Communications Commission, that defined what you could or could not broadcast. However, the relationship of image quality to broadcast quality is incidental. Although broadcasters were concerned with getting tapes with broadcast-quality video signals on them, the networks and stations were most concerned about the actual quality of the image. Each network came up with its own image quality criteria, but in time, limitations on image quality were dropped (hence the broadcast of favorite home movies). Therefore, the term *broadcast quality* comes from requirements for the *video signal*, not the way the image *looks*. This is important for the end user of a nonlinear system: "broadcast-quality video" is an objective description of a video signal. As far as image quality goes, there is no such thing as required broadcast quality.

Resolution

Resolution refers to a system's ability to capture fine detail. It plays a part in how sharp the image can look. When fine detail is rendered clearly, an image will usually look sharp to the eye. There are, however, many factors that come into play in determining sharpness. They include the measurable fine detail of the image (resolution), the contrast of the picture, and the distance from which we view it. In general, high-resolution images look better, sharper than low-resolution images. Sometimes filmmakers deliberately soften a high-resolution image with filters for a particular look.

The term **resolution** also applies to the concept of how much information is stored in each film or video image or each second of an audio recording. There are various ways to measure how much information or data are used to capture and record an image or sound. With digital video recordings, we can count exactly how many digital bits of data are used for each frame. As a general rule of thumb, the higher the resolution, the finer the detail in the image and the more information or *storage space* is needed to record it. For example, 35mm film is a higher resolution format than 16mm, the 35mm image being more than four times bigger. We will address the storage issue in the next section because it is important when it comes to editing.

Digital Compression

Digital cameras and recording devices are being developed that are capable of capturing images and sound with greater clarity and fidelity. It takes a lot of information to record a full-resolution video image. (On the other hand, digital audio requires far less information and doesn't need to be digitally compressed for production work.) To make the cost-effective and efficient use of digital video recordings, we have to find ways to minimize the amount of storage, processing, and transmission equipment needed to deal with them. Some of the ways to do this are to make the picture smaller, to decrease the color quality and the frame rate (an unattractive alternative for editing), and to use some form of video compression.

Video compression takes the digitized information about an image and encodes it in such a way as to take up less space while maintaining the best possible picture and sound quality. Video and audio are compressed for storage and transmission and then decompressed in order to view and hear the signals. Compression schemes are sometimes called *codecs* (which stands for compression/decompression). The amount of compression to use is determined by the amount of storage capacity, the amount of source material, and its image complexity. After images and sound have been compressed, they take up less storage space on tape or computer disk. This allows us to use smaller and cheaper camcorders (production), load more footage into an editing system (postproduction), or fit a longer movie onto a disk for playback at home.

Compression is also useful because systems are often limited in how much data they can process per second. After a video signal has been compressed, it can be sent through a narrower pipeline or smaller *bus* of a computer. For example, images sent through the Internet may be compressed so they can be sent through telephone lines. Many homes still use old-style copper phone wires that pass much less data per second than a typical video cable, which is to say their *bandwidth* is less.

Types of Compression

Compression can be done in many different ways, and because technology is constantly changing, we will focus on some basic concepts and the two systems that have been used most widely. Compression involves compacting the digitized video information (a computer file) into a smaller space. For viewing, the data must be expanded or decompressed. **Lossless** compression means that after the file is decompressed, nothing is lost and it can be restored to its original condition. **Lossy** compression throws away information that can never be restored.

One approach to video compression is to delete information from individual frames, known as *intraframe* coding. Only one frame is compressed at a time, with no reference to other frames. This technique is used in several digital cameras. For example, Digital Betacam reduces the data by half (2:1 ratio), whereas the DV format compresses at 5:1. Compressing in the camcorder reduces the amount of information recorded per second, allowing for longer recording times on a tape, and it produces a very clean low-noise signal. With intraframe coding, every frame of the original signal is stored on tape or disk, so we can easily isolate frames when needed to edit the material. This form of compression is called **JPEG or motion-JPEG (pronounced jay-peg)**. It was created in the late 1980s by the Joint Photographic Experts Group as a method of compressing still color images. Most nonlinear editing systems use JPEG.

Another method of compression, developed by the Moving Picture Experts Group in the early 1990s, is called **MPEG (pronounced empeg)** and was specifically tailored for moving pictures. MPEG doesn't just look at a single frame and compress it; it looks at adjacent frames to see which pixels are changing and which are mostly the same. This is called *interframe* encoding. For example, if your face is on the screen and you are just talking, probably the only part of the screen that is changing significantly is your mouth; the rest of you remains pretty much the same. By just concentrating on the interframe changes, MPEG greatly reduces digital video data, significantly more than JPEG. Another feature specific to MPEG is that it is designed to handle sync audio; the JPEG techniques deal only with pictures.

JPEG and MPEG are not products, only standardized techniques. Before they were standardized, companies developed their own way to compress video. With standardization, editing system and computer chip manufacturers utilize these methods in their designs. JPEG is considered the compression scheme of choice for applications that are concerned with still images, such as desktop publishing, electronic photo processing, digital scanners, and color laser printers. It is also an inexpensive and simple method; the same JPEG chips that compress can be used in reverse to decompress. This is called a *symmetrical* technique.

MPEG is an *asymmetrical* technique. Compression and decompression are handled differently, by different sets of chips (or software). This makes MPEG suited to different kinds of applications: playback of precompressed video from digital videodisks or CD-ROM, multimedia applications, and so on. It is designed for moving images and sync sound but has some trouble (presently) handling edits.

There are currently three versions of MPEG compression. MPEG-1 was designed for VHS-quality pictures (352×240 at 30fps). MPEG-2 was designed for full-screen, higher-quality images (however, MPEG-1 looks better than MPEG-2 at certain compression rates). MPEG-2 offers resolutions of 720×480 and $1,280 \times 720$ at 60fps, with full CD-quality audio. This is sufficient for all the major TV standards, including NTSC, and even HDTV. MPEG-2 is also used by DVD-ROMs.

MPEG-3 was designed to handle HDTV signals at 1080p in the range of 20 to 40 megabits per second. MPEG-3 was launched as an effort to address the need of an HDTV standard while work on MPEG-2 was underway, but it was soon discovered that MPEG-2, at high data rates, would accommodate HDTV. Thus, in 1992, HDTV was included as a separate profile in the MPEG-2 standard and MPEG-3 was rolled into MPEG-2.

MPEG-4 is a graphics and video compression algorithm standard based on MPEG-1, MPEG-2, and Apple QuickTime technology that was standardized in 1998. MPEG-4 files are smaller than JPEG or QuickTime files, so they are designed to transmit video and images over a narrower bandwidth and can mix video with text, graphics, and 2D and 3D animation layers. MPEG-4 provides the standardized technological elements enabling the integration of the production, distribution, and content access paradigms of digital television, interactive graphics applications (synthetic content), and interactive multimedia (World Wide Web, distribution of and access to content)

When digitizing video or audio material into an editing system, you can usually select how much compression you want to do. The more you compress, the more footage you can store on the disks and the lower the image quality. For example, Avid uses several AVR ratios to indicate different degrees of compression.

All the companies manufacturing nonlinear editing systems that utilize digitized source material must deal with all these parameters in designing their systems. The remaining factors—image size, resolution, color range, compression—must be dealt with in terms of the limitations of the system's memory storage and computer processing power. Ultimately, the question that always must be answered is, how good does an image have to be for offline editing? The answers seem to vary according to whom you ask, from D-1 quality to something better than recognizable.

Basic Workflow of a Nonlinear Editing System

This section provides the basic simplified flow chart for creating a project in a nonlinear editing system. Each system, such as Avid or Final Cut, will have its own variation on how these steps function.

- Shoot video (Mini DV, DVCam, HDV, HD) or transfer developed film to tape.
- Clone your original source material to end up with two tapes with identical timecode.
- Input (log and digitize) the source footage from clone to storage disk.
- Organize the footage. The editor organizes the footage in "bins."
- Edit the project (using your system of choice).
- Output the completed material to DV, QuickTime, DVD, and so on.

An important step that most students and beginners forget is to clone (copy) their original material. The original tapes should be cloned and stored away in a safe place. This step is similar to what occurs with the original film negative, which is kept in the laboratory. However, when you are shooting with the new tapeless formats, holding onto the "original" can be elusive. If you shoot on a P2 card, download the media into a computer on set, dump the media, and load the P2 card back on the camera so that the original is now on a hard drive. The on-site editor or digital assistant must now back up the data on two separate drives.

Basic Nonlinear Interface

A nonlinear editing system is basically software loaded in a computer with various devices attached or installed internally. The processing speed of the computer affects how quickly the system can create (render) video transitions and other effects.

Basic Terms

Project. In some systems, the project folder contains all files of your project (in Final Cut Pro and Avid, the project file just points to the media files on the disk). The project window is the place where your work is organized. It contains all the information about your current job, including a listing of all the bins and folders in the current project.

Bin. The "bin" is the storage container for the clips and sequences (edited programs) in your project. Depending on your system, you might also be able to store bins within folders for one extra level of organization. A bin is the digital equivalent of the physical bin in which film is stored from retrieval during editing. Shots are logged and digitized into a bin and stored there for the editor.

Clip. A clip is a pointer (reference) to actual video or audio media. It does not contain the actual picture and sound data, just references to them. Think of the media file as your actual footage and the clip as an electronic pointer to the media file. When you play a clip, the system looks for media files that contain the video and audio.

Sequence. The sequence is your edited program, or "master tape." It is a "virtual master," easily created and modified. You create a sequence by editing clips together and storing them in a bin. When you play the sequence, the editing system accesses the clips.

Storage

Having enough storage makes all the difference with nonlinear editing. Digitized video and audio clips are stored on computer disks. Hard drives are generally used because they provide fast access time to quickly find material on the disk, and they can move large amounts of data per second (have a high data transfer rate). Sometimes drives are grouped together in sets to increase performance, such as redundant array of inexpensive disks (RAID).

Currently, Fire Wire drives are affordable ways to handle the storage issue. You will need a fast (7200 rpm) drive with adequate disk storage. The storage capacity of computer drives is measured in megabytes (MB) or gigabytes (GB), commonly called *gigs*; 1GB equals 1,000MB. The buzzword, up to now, has been that *resolution costs money*, but disk storage is relatively cheap now. A student should start with a terrabyte drive (1,024 gigabytes = 1 terabyte).

Monitors

The editing system's monitor allows you to view the picture and the graphical interface used to control the system. Most systems will include a source monitor to view the footage and a record monitor to play the sequence. It is important to have a TV monitor connected to the system. The reason is that the RGB computer monitor doesn't display the image the way it will look after it has been converted back to composite or component video.

Capturing and Organizing Clips

Before editing can begin, video and audio must be loaded into the system. Some systems allow you to digitize video and audio material at various quality levels or resolutions (Avid Media Composer Soft gives you only one option). The higher the resolution, the better the picture looks, but the more space the material will occupy on the hard drives. It will also slow down the time needed to render an effect. If you have sufficient storage capacity on your hard drives, digitize at the highest resolution. If you have more footage than can be stored on disk at full resolution, you have the following options:

- You can digitize at a lower resolution. This approach uses more compression to reduce the amount of data needed for each second of video and will reduce picture quality.
- You can digitize only enough material to work on a portion of the project at a time.
- You can start by digitizing the project in low-quality draft mode. When you're done with your rough cut, you can delete the unused material or outtakes and redigitize the movie.
- You can delete media files you no longer need.
- You can render only when necessary. If you render frequently, you end up rerendering effects multiple times, which consumes disk space. Any time you render an effect, the system creates a media file that takes up drive space.
- You may want to look for the best balance between image quality and conservation of space.

The compression you choose for your edit will be lower than the compression needed for the final product (if you're finishing on video).

Digitizing

When you digitize or capture a section of video or audio material into the system, it becomes a computer file (digital data) that is written (recorded) into the system's hard drives. This file is called a **media file** (or a **source media file** or **source file**). Say you digitized a shot of a man mowing the lawn and then digitized a shot of him relaxing in a hammock. Each shot would become a separate media file (actually, each shot would have one media file for the video portion and one for the audio).

When you edit your project and decide to put the mowing shot before the hammock, you are not moving the media files around. Instead, you move or arrange *clips*, which act as "pointers" that tell the computer to go to a certain media file and play a portion of it. For any media file, you could have many different clips. For example, you could use a short clip of the man starting the mower at the beginning of the project and then use a longer clip showing him mowing the backyard later. Different clips can reuse the same source media data as often as needed (unless this project was shot and will be finished in film). Clips are stored on the computer's internal drive and don't take up much space. Media files require substantial storage space and thus are stored on separate, large-capacity external hard disks.

Digitizing or capturing a continuous section of video onto the computer drives is referred to as **digitizing a clip**. The captured material becomes a media file. The clip that points to all the media files is the *master clip*. Any portions of the master clip used in the edited project may be called **subclips**.

The editing system allows you to give each clip a name and type in comments or other information about the clip. Clips may be digitized on the fly, which means that they are defined and labeled as they are loaded into the system. Some people prefer to preview the material before actually digitizing, when they can view the footage and log which clips they want and give them labels. This can be done using the editing system or, if the system is not available, using a VTR and a personal computer with a logging program such as MediaLog. To log the footage, go through the camera tapes, specifying by timecode address where clips are to start and stop, giving each clip a name, and indicating which footage not to digitize. The log can be entered into the editing system, which then proceeds to batch digitize or batch capture, automatically recording the selected footage onto the computer drives while labeling the clips.

A large amount of work can be done on logging software, saving time (and money) on your editing system. You can even pick your preferred takes and their mark-ins and mark-outs, essentially creating a rough assembly before you even digitize. The more complete and detailed your logging is at this stage, the more smoothly the editing will go later.

Setting Color and Audio

When the video and audio material is loaded into the editing system, various settings need to be adjusted or checked. Audio levels should also be set properly before and monitored during digitizing. Many editing systems give you the choice of sampling rate for digitizing audio: 44.1kHz at 16 bits per sample is the equivalent of CD quality; 48kHz is DAR quality, which is higher. If your audio is coming from a digital source, you want to use the same sampling rate as your source. If you are editing a project originally shot on film, audio material may need to be slowed down (pulled down) when it is digitized into the system because of the 24fps/30fps differential. Some audio decks and editing systems have an audio pulldown setting to accomplish this. Some systems run at exactly 24fps. This permits you to bring audio recorded in sync with film (synced up at the lab) in and out of the system without changing speed.

It is important to note that digitizing takes place in *realtime*: while the tape deck plays the source material, the nonlinear editing system digitizes the footage into the computer. A 20-minute tape takes 20 minutes to digitize (new DV and Betacam SX systems might soon increase this rate of transfer to four times realtime). As the editor is doing the digitizing, she can use the time to get familiar with the footage. The time it takes to digitize will be more than saved when doing the first cut, which can be done in a fraction of the time it would have taken in a linear environment.

Finally, before digitizing, you will need to decide on the image quality of the digitized footage, which, as we have stated, is determined by the resolution or the level of compression at which you digitize the source material.

Organizing Clips

Logging and organization are important when using any film or editing system. As clips are captured, they can be grouped for convenience. Just as film editors use various bins to hang pieces of film or sound, nonlinear editing systems have *folders* or *bins* in which certain clips or edited *sequences* can be kept separate from the rest of the material. Clips can be viewed in the form of a text and a single-image frame from the scene.

The list will have different fields of information about each clip, including the name of the clip, the starting and ending timecode, and the tape from which the clip came. For projects originating on film, you may need to keep track of keycode numbers, in camera or audio timecode, as well as camera roll, sound roll, and telecine reel numbers. Many editing systems have sophisticated database management programs that allow you to quickly sift through lists of clips.

Your editor may organize bins to make the clips easy to access and conform to her working methods. The time the editor spends organizing the footage at the front end will save you time and money during the edit by making it easy to locate needed footage.

Editing Sequences

Editing Interface and Time Line

Like word processing software, nonlinear editing systems differ in their particulars but have certain fundamental concepts in common. The **editing interface** is the method by which you control the system; it is where the actual editing takes place. This interface is displayed on one or more computer screens divided into several areas or *windows* on the *desktop*. Usually, two windows display video; one of them is the equivalent of a source monitor in linear tape editing. This window is used to view unedited clips and mark the portions you want to use (see Figure 16.5 below). The second window is the record or program monitor. This window displays the edited sequence you are creating. There may be other open windows on the desktop, such as titling or effects tools. The bin monitor displays the available clips in a bin.

Most systems also utilize a **time line** that graphically illustrates how the clips are edited together (See Figure 16.5). Colored rectangles are used to represent video and audio clips. Time lines move from left to right, with markings showing time (timecode) advancing as

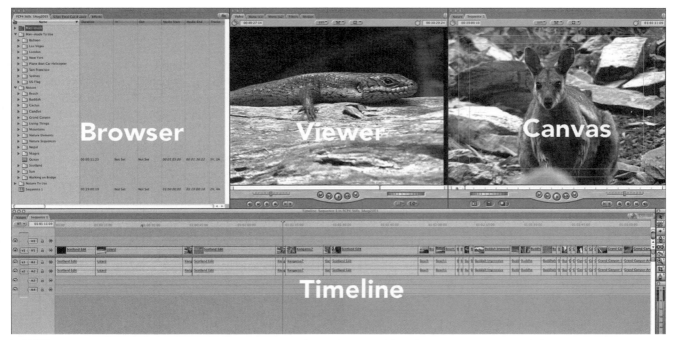

FIGURE 16.5 Sample Final Cut Pro interface showing Browser, Viewer, Canvas, and Timeline. Screenshot courtesy of Rick Young, *The Focal Easy Guide to Final Cut Pro 7.*

you move to the right. The length of a clip on the time line generally corresponds to the length of time the clip will play on the screen.

Audio clips are represented by another set of tracks. These tracks can be edited independently of the picture or locked together with the video to preserve the sync relationship. Most systems use a long vertical bar that crosses all the tracks and indicates the point at which the system is in *play mode* or in *edit mode*.

It's Only Virtual

It is important to realize that clips arranged on the time line are nothing more than pointers to the media files that are stored elsewhere on the hard drives. You are able to move, delete, change, or copy clips without affecting the original media they refer to. And like most word processing programs, they have *undo commands* in case you make a mistake.

However, as anyone who has used a computer knows, strange and mysterious things can happen. Files can be corrupted or lost, or your system can come crashing down unexpectedly. Make sure to *back up* your sequences and other files at least at the end of the day (and ideally more often than that). Media files are usually not backed up because they are too big.

Marking and Assembling Clips

To begin editing, start by identifying the clips you want to use. On most systems, you simply move the mouse to a clip in the bin and double-click to play it in the source monitor. If you use only a portion of it, mark an IN point (start mark) and OUT point (end mark). You have just marked the clip. It is ready to be put in the film or video.

On some systems, you can place a clip on the time line simply by using the mouse to drag a clip from the source window to the time line *(dragging and dropping)*. As in linear tape editing, most edits can be defined with three points, and you can string shots together without having to define the OUT points right away (leaving them open-ended). Most systems allow you to do a given task several different ways. You can use the mouse, the keyboard, or a combination of both. You will find the style that works best for you.

Adding Clips

As you edit, you build up a sequence of shots. When you want to add a new clip to an existing sequence, you indicate *where* on the time line to insert the new shot. In nonlinear editing, you have two options about how the new clip will affect the clips that are already in the sequence: *splicing* and *overwriting*. Splicing has the same function in nonlinear editing as splicing in film. When you splice, material you select in the source monitor is inserted into

the sequence at a specified point. Any shots in the sequence after the edit point move down (or *ripple down*), lengthening the sequence.

Overwriting is the digital equivalent of a videotape insert edit. Using the Overwrite button, the editor replaces (writes over) existing sections of the sequence with new material. Overwriting does not change the sequence's length. You might use overwriting to add a cutaway over an existing interview in a documentary.

Removing Clips from a Sequence

There are two options to removing a shot. You can extract a shot from a sequence, which removes material and closes the gap left by its removal. Extracting, like splicing, changes the duration of the sequence. It is comparable to removing frames from a film.

The second choice is to lift footage from a sequence, which removes material and leaves black or silence, a gap that will be filled later. Lifting, like overwriting, does not change the duration of the sequence.

Trimming Clips

After clips have been added to the time line, you need to be able to adjust their length. Trimming and editing in the time line might be the most powerful operations of the nonlinear editing system, the fundamental part of editing. Most systems have a **trim mode**.

In video terms, "trimming" means adjusting an edit point to either extend or shorten a shot. The trim editor may allow you to preview the edit with a **looping** feature, which plays the transition repeatedly while you preview it. There are many types of trimming methods, and different systems call them by different names, such as single roller trim, ripple edit, trim tail, dual-roller trim, rolling edit, trim joint, and slim trim. Compared to film or linear videotape editing, trimming shots with a nonlinear system is a breeze.

Basic Sound Editing

Editing audio on a nonlinear system is fast: sounds can be cut, pasted, copied, and manipulated at will. Most editing systems give you a choice of editing individual tracks independently or locking them to the video or audio tracks. When tracks are locked together, you can change them simultaneously with a single edit. When sound and picture are brought into the system in sync, as they are in digitizing a typical camera tape, many systems will tell you whether the audio and video tracks remain in sync. If, during editing, you slip sync or move the audio relative to the video, a display will show you how many frames have displaced the audio.

Audio clips may appear on the time line as colored blocks. Many systems can also display **waveforms** that show a tracing of the actual audio signal. Waveforms make it easier to determine exactly where words or other sounds begin and end. An audio *scrubbing* feature helps you find individual sounds by playing only short bursts of audio or by slowing down the speed of the playback.

All systems allow you to set the volume level of each clip individually; some will allow what is called **rubberbanding**, a way of continuously altering sound levels throughout the clip. Depending on your system, you may have up to 99 audio tracks (with Final Cut Pro) and be able to listen to 2, 4, 8, or more tracks at a time. If you want to monitor more tracks than you are allowed, some systems enable you to combine multiple tracks and mix them down to a single track. You can then hear all your sound and still monitor new material on additional audio tracks. The mix down is performed digitally and is of high quality. Even though the tracks are mixed down, they remain separate tracks.

It is important to note that if the picture editor alters the sound for screening (i.e., applies a plug-in effect), she always makes sure that the original unprocessed clip is available in the time line. It can be muted and placed on an adjacent track.

Delivering to the Sound Designer/Sound Effects Editor

The convenience of experimenting with sound effects and music ideas during the evolution of the picture cut is undeniable. However, unless your picture editor is also cutting your sound, he should not make final decisions on such effects as EQ (equalization) and reverb. If the sound work is going to be exported to a sound editor, the original unprocessed sound clips should remain available on the time line (muted and placed on an adjacent track).

The picture editor needs to ask the sound editor what he requires. It will most likely be

- A digital file of the locked picture with guide track (usually a QuickTime movie file).
- A working Open Media Framework Interchange (OMF; see Chapter 17) of the exported audio files as they are edited into the time line. This can be exported as a file that links to a folder full of audio files or as a self-contained embedded file.
- A folder of all the audio dailies.

Special Digital Video Effects

Nonlinear editing systems differ in their effects capabilities. High-end systems can do complex effects in real-time. With lower-end systems, the machine may need to first *render* (create) the effect before you can watch it with the rest of the project. Depending on your system, you might be able to create 2D effects, digital video effects (DVEs), or 3D effects, each with variations in real-time capabilities and rendering times.

Types of Effects

Most systems offer a wide range of effects. Some are applied to a sequence or clip (shot), and others are applied to the transitions between sequences.

Transitions

Transition effects are used as transitions between two shots. You can simply apply them to your sequence or customize them by reversing them, repositioning them, adding a border, and so forth. Examples of transition effects are dissolves, wipes, spins, peels, and fades.

Segment Effects

Segment effects are applied to an entire shot or segment. Once an effect is applied, you can customize it, much like the transition effects. These are some examples. A *mask* masks out an area of the image and displays it over any background color. A *color effect* applies a color to the entire image. You can adjust parameters such as luminance, hue, saturation, contrast, and brightness. This effect can be used for color correction, as well as for special effects such as making an image black-and-white or sepia tone, solarizing, and even controlling the color grain. A *flop* reverses the camera angle, a *flip* places the image upside down, and a *resize* resizes the image and places it over the background color.

Multilayer (Layered or Composited) Effects

Multilayering allows you to combine and play two or more video layers simultaneously. You can create picture-in-picture (PIP) in a fraction of the time possible with a linear system. Two types are split screen and superimposition.

Keys

Keying is a way to superimpose two layers of video; one layer forms a sort of keyhole through which the other can be seen. In a *chroma key*, the keyhole is made up of every part of the image that is a certain color. A familiar example is a televised weather report, where the TV meteorologist performs in front of a blue wall. The chroma key "keys out" everything that is blue and replaces it with the weather map.

The *luma key* (for luminance key) carves out the keyhole based on brightness levels. Luminance keys are useful when the keyed graphic does not have a wide range of tones or brightness values. Examples include simple titles, graphic objects, and "spotlights" over an image.

The *matte key* applies a stencil to the sequence, creating a hole in the background shot that is filled with a foreground image. Matte keys are often used to create unusual blends between images and custom transitions.

Motion Effects

Motion effects allow you to create freeze frames, speed up or slow down a shot, or create a strobe motion effect. You can use motion effects to give your video a film look.

Creating Titles

Your editing system may have a Title tool that creates text and graphics that can be saved over a color background or keyed over video (See Figure 16.6). You may be able to control font size and style, kerning and leading, color and color blend, transparency, outlines, shadows, and rolling/scrolling or crawling text.

Performing Real-Time versus Rendered Effects

Real-time effects can be performed immediately after they are applied. Rendered effects need to be calculated ahead of time by the computer and stored on the hard disk as a separate media file. As a result, with rendered effects, you need to be concerned with rendering time and disk storage. Two factors affect whether the effect is realtime or rendered:

- **System Configuration**. If your system has a board with real-time effects capability, it can play many effects in realtime, without rendering them.
- **Nature of the Effect**. Dissolves and superimpositions might be real-time effects, whereas *nested effects* (multiple effects added to a single segment of video) need to be rendered.

Working with Third-Party Graphics Applications

Software packages such as Adobe Photoshop and After Effects enable you to manipulate images in ways that previously were the exclusive domain of specialized graphic illustrators and designers. The software is relatively easy to learn and use, is (relatively) inexpensive, and can be run on just about any system.

There is an infinite number of ways you can take advantage of the integration of nonlinear editing systems and third-party graphics programs. Graphics software can be used to perform a range of functions, from fixing a problem to enhancing an existing image to creating a completely new graphic element.

FIGURE 16.6 Avid Media Composer sample trim view courtesy of Avid.

Film Match-back Issues

If you have shot film and will be matching back for a final print, be careful with all the special video effects. Do your research, understand what the film lab or optical house is realistically able to duplicate, and, if so, how much it will cost.

Ending a Session

At the end of each session, you should back up the project file twice to a CD-ROM or even another FireWire drive. If your drive crashes, you will have lost media, which can be redigitized, but not the project file that contains all the logging data as well as your creative choices.

Animation

Animation has become a very large and significant segment of filmmaking. With the advent of digital media, the definition of animation has expanded to include large portions of the visual effects and commercial production industries.

Computer-Generated Images (CGI)

CGI, or just CG, has become the most popular form of animation and visual effects in film and video production. Usually, the term *CG* refers to 3D computer animation and modeling. It is called *3D* because three-dimensional virtual models of all the characters and models are constructed within the computer. CGI has proven to be an effective method of producing almost anything a filmmaker can imagine. Hollywood films from *The Incredibles* to *The Matrix* trilogy have relied on CG to astound audiences with effects and believable animation that were not achievable without the computer. As the costs have dropped dramatically, independent filmmakers have been drawn toward CG for relatively low-budget films. For a CG effect to be effective in a live-action film, it must be photorealistic with believable lighting, texture, proportions, and scale. A CG character must be equally convincing with lifelike movement and behavior to blend seamlessly with shot footage. Photoreal effects and animation require a great deal of skill, knowledge, planning, and long, hard hours to achieve, so a filmmaker should use them only when necessary and with the proper resources.

Tools of the Trade

As recently as the mid-1990s, the software and hardware necessary to produce CGI was prohibitively expensive. It was therefore rare to find independent artists working as CGI animators. The cost of powerful computers and their components has dropped dramatically. The software has become more feature rich, inexpensive, and user-friendly, leading to the rise of many small one- and two-person shops. With that said, there is still a steep learning curve and price tag for a CGI studio.

The most common professional animation software is Maya. Many other excellent packages are available. For instance, 3D Studio Max, Soft Image XSI, Lightwave, and Cinema 4D all have their followings as well. Digital compositing and editing packages have also become more ubiquitous and inexpensive. The most popular are Apple's Shake, Adobe After Effects, the Avid line of composing products, Apple Final Cut Pro, and Combustion (and the higher-end versions Flame and Inferno). The list goes on. You will find that each software package tends to have its own niche market and loyal following. For example, 3D Studio Max (or just Max, as it is known in the trade) is favored by game artists because of its extensive modeling capabilities, plug-ins, and software development kit. Many broadcast designers use Cinema 4D with After Effects because they are straightforward on the Mac platform. Maya and Shake are favored by feature filmmakers because of the extensive features and node-based compositing. The popularity and capabilities change with each software upgrade. So the preceding combinations of tools will vary a bit from year to year.

Digital Sets and Set Extensions

Perhaps the most cost-effective and straightforward use of CG would be the digital set or set extensions. The complexity of a digital set will vary depending on the length of the shot, the available assets, and, of course, the complexity of the set.

In its simplest form, CG can be used to enhance a still or stock image. The CG artist must match the virtual camera lens, distance, and position to the actual camera and then build CG objects and buildings with matched lighting and perspective. The process is relatively simple technically because the artist can easily touch up the final with image editing software such as Photoshop to assure a seamless composite. If the shot is held for even a short while, it is always better to make it live by adding some looping animation. An animation loop is a bit of action that seamlessly repeats so that the first frame can serve as the last. An animation loop can consist of smoke coming out of a chimney, a flickering light, rain, rippling water, waving leaves, or any other subtle motion that tells viewers they are not looking at a static image.

Adding digital set extensions to a live action shot with a moving camera becomes a more elaborate process. Depending on the complexity of the move, and especially if there are multiple shots of the same digital set, the CG artist will most probably opt to use match-moving software. Match-moving software works by identifying certain points in an image and then determining the position of the camera at a given frame by calculating the difference of those points on-screen over time. The software then generates a virtual camera that closely matches the movement of the original real camera. The accuracy of the match is greatly enhanced with the addition of real data such as lens type, as well as the height and position of certain objects.

Keyframe

When most people think of computer animation, they are most probably envisioning keyframe character animation. In this process, the animator sets the character in a series of poses over time. The computer software then interpolates the movement of the character between each pose. The set poses are known as *keyframes*. Of course, the process is more complex than just that. A technical director (or TD) can spend months preparing a model to be animated. Seemingly simple things like hair, clothing, eye movement, and even breathing need to be accounted for to create a convincing character. It is therefore cheaper and more advisable for a short film to use CG characters sparingly. Having the character on-screen for only a short time, seen in the distance, or with limited movement will help speed up the process.

Film to Video

The sequence of film to video presents the most technical challenges. Filmmakers who want to shoot on film, cut digital, and match back to film must pay attention.

Telecine

The **telecine** is a device for converting film to video. It has a transport to move the film footage across a scanner that reads each frame and converts it to a video signal. Broadcast-quality telecine can handle a variety of film formats (35mm, 16mm, Super 16, Super 8). The telecine's precision film transport can accommodate either positive or negative film at several different speeds with no danger of scratching. One of the widely used telecines is the Cintel (formerly the Rank Cintel) *flying spot scanner*. CCD scanners and film chains are also used to transfer film to tape. Commonly, the word *telecine* is used to mean any film-to-tape conversion. The telecine works with a color corrector and various audiotape decks for transferring production sound.

In Europe and countries where PAL or SECAM video is standard, transferring from film to video is fairly straightforward because film footage is shot at 25fps and video runs at 25fps. Each frame of film is transferred to one frame of video in a simple one-to-one (1:1) relationship. The process becomes more complicated in North America and other places where NTSC video runs faster, at 30fps (actually 29.97). If we simply transfer each frame of film to one frame of video, when we later play back the video, the action will run too fast. Something that took a minute on film will last only 48 seconds on video. Motion will look speeded up, and the soundtrack will quickly go out of sync. There needs to be a way to stretch out the film as it goes to video.

To keep the footage at the correct speed, some frames of film are transferred to more than one frame of video. A standard sequence called a *3/2 pulldown* (three-two) or *2/3 pulldown* distributes every group of four film frames to five frames of video (see Figure 16.7). This creates six additional frames every second, bringing the total from 24 to 30fps. The term *pulldown* in this sense refers to the idea of the intermittent film shutter mechanism that pulls down a frame.

Audio, on the other hand, does not have "frames" and thus does not move at 24fps. It just keeps moving constantly all the time.

The 29.97 Complication

There is a complication that adds a wrinkle to this formula. As was mentioned before, NTSC actually runs at 29.97fps (the color signal addition), which is 0.1 percent slower. The 3/2 pulldown creates a successful relationship between 24fps film and 30fps video. However, because the video is in fact running 0.1 percent slower, at 29.97fps, we must also slow down the film in the telecine by 0.1 percent, to 23.976fps. The eye cannot detect this slowdown, but it means that realtime is disrupted. The importance of this wrinkle is that if you record sync sound while filming, *you must also slow the sound* by 0.1 percent during the transfer to keep it in sync with the picture.

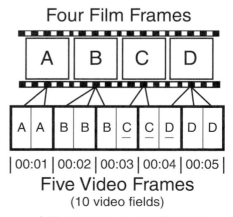

Four Film Frames

Five Video Frames
(10 video fields)

= fields captured in an Avid 24fps project.

FIGURE 16.7   3/2 pulldown.

The pulldown sequence can be one of the most confusing concepts in filmmaking. It doesn't concern someone originating in video, only when using nonlinear or videotape editing systems to generate film cut lists or EDLs.

Video Dailies

For video dailies, the lab prepares the footage for the transfer and may need to check it over. The transfer technician must be instructed how the lab wants the transfer done. This is a very critical part of the process. Your negative cutter is your guide in this matter.

Film/Video Dailies

The first decision to make is the format of your dailies. Film dailies allow you to view the film as *film*, projected, large, on-screen. This is the only way to really see what you have, and it is most advantageous to see your dailies this way. However, often your budget may not allow you to get both film and video dailies made. If you forgo film dailies, you must remember that you are not really seeing all your material. You must keep in mind that the material you are cutting and viewing is video and it will inherently look and feel quite different from your final film print. You will have to make decisions thinking ahead to what that might look like on projected film. Also, the smaller screen can affect the level of detail you are seeing, and sometimes what may be a small, unnoticed detail on video can become a large and obvious mistake (grip stand, lights, an actor looking into the camera, etc.).

Synced Dailies

For an extra cost, the lab can give you your video dailies synced. There is a great advantage in having one tape as your master, containing your synced audio and video with one timecode. If the lab is syncing your dailies, make sure that the slates are shot correctly. You do not want the lab technician to take extra time trying to read them. The slates need to be clear, large in frame, in focus, in light, and so on. You will also want to give the lab clear camera and sound reports. "Smart slates" are commonly used now in production. This, along with a recording on a timecode flash card, should make the syncing process go smoothly. If you choose to forgo getting synced dailies, you will receive video-only dailies from the lab, and your sound will remain your flash card. You will have to sync your material later on videotape or on a nonlinear system. You will have two distinct source tapes (video and sound) with two distinct timecodes.

Windowboxed Dailies

The video frame and the film frame are not the same aspect ratio. Therefore, it becomes necessary to have the lab "windowbox" your film frame within the video frame so you do not lose any information from the edges of the frame. The film frame is scaled down and fitted within black borders inside your video frame. If you do not do this, you will not see the image area around the edges of the film frame and could miss light stands, booms, and so on.

Burn-Ins—Visual Timecode (VTC)

Important information can be burned in (superimposed) to your video image. The most common burn-ins are timecode and keycode. This information gives you a visual connection to every frame's corresponding timecode and keycode. Other information can also be burned in, such as audio timecode and camera roll. You should check with your negative cutter and make sure you are giving her what she wants burned in.

Telecine Logs (Flex Files)

Telecine logs (also known as *flex files*) are files on disks that contain the relationship between your video dailies' timecode and your original film's keycode. They are given to you in a format that can be imported into your logs. By importing them, you have a reference in your logs back to your original film. Later, when you output a cut list for the negative cutter, all the cutting you did on the nonlinear system, which was timecode based, can then be converted back to keycode.

Color Correction

Generally, video dailies are made from the camera original. Color correction may be minimal ("one lite" transfer) or may be carefully done if no further transfer is planned. The colorist can adjust the image either for each scene or once for the entire roll (which is less expensive).

Video Format

Most transfer houses offer a variety of video recorder formats to choose from. For video dailies on projects that will be finished on film or when another transfer is planned after editing, you might use a low-cost format that is compatible with your editing system. If the audio will be synced up in the telecine, consider transforming to a format that has high-quality audio capabilities, such as DVCam, Digibeta, or HDcam.

Logging

Video dailies, either picture-only or synced, must now be logged. If your sound is on a separate source, to be synced later, this information must also be logged. Logging used to be done with special software and then imported into the system you were going to use to cut your project. It is now possible to log through most NLE systems.

Bring in all your source tapes to the system. The station should be equipped with source decks (DVCam, Digibeta, HDcam, flashcards) and a monitor. You can now create your bins and log all your clips with as much detail as you want. If your dailies are not synced, remember that you will be logging both video and audio separately. As you control the deck with the interface, you log beginning and ending timecodes, duration, tracks selected, tape name, and any other comments that can help you identify the footage. When logging is completed, save the project to a disk.

The P2 Workflow

The workflow chart (see Figure III.2 in the introduction to Part III) gives an overview of the HD P2 workflow. There are many variables and details to be factored into the equation, and for these, you will need to contact technical people who know the ins and outs of shooting with tapeless storage. The important part of the equation is, as we have stated several times, you need to know where you want to end up before beginning.

PRODUCER

Advise

One of the producer's major responsibilities is to be one step ahead of what is happening. During preproduction, he assembles a well-run production unit, which allows the members of the creative team to function at their optimum ability. Once production is in full swing and, it is hoped, on schedule, the producer's next job is to prepare for postproduction. This is the time for the transition from producer as production manager to producer as postproduction supervisor.

Think of postproduction as a separate period with its own unique set of challenges and problems. Unfortunately, many novice filmmakers tend to resist beginning this part of the process. Much of their hesitation is due to their disappointment with the rushes. What was captured on film or tape might not have lived up to their expectations of the script. Each viewing during postproduction might revive some of the nightmare of production. This negativity must be replaced with the excitement and anticipation of being able to sit down and solve all the problems.

The producer can play an invaluable role in helping the director get over this psychological hurdle and get back on track. Even though editing can be downright frustrating, it should be an exciting experience. There might not be troublesome weather or temperamental actors to deal with, but there are still many creative challenges to face.

What You Want from a System?

Nonlinear editing systems vary in their capabilities. Some systems are capable of very high picture quality, whereas others work at lower quality. Some have the software and hardware to do complex sound editing, and others have only basic sound capability. There is the question of what other kinds of software you want to interface with and the matter of graphics and effects capability. For example, Adobe Premiere Suite offers Premiere Pro, Photo Shop, After Effects, and Sound Booth. All these applications work into the same time line. It is a complete integrated software package.

As with other aspects of film and video, to be able to choose the right system for you and to work with the one you have, you will need to trace back from the end product. What level of video do you need? If the project is for broadcast, the standards for video are higher than if you are making a multimedia project for a web site. If you are interested in distributing the project, contact the distributor. Do you require film match-back capability?

How complex are your sound needs? Do you need just one track of sync sound and a little narration, or will you need to be able to build a multilayered soundtrack with music and effects? Do you hope to do the sound work on one machine, or will you be outputting to a digital workstation?

Although every editing system may seem to be unique, they all share certain commonalities that, once understood, need only be translated when switching from one system to another. Once you know one editing system, learning others becomes considerably easier. These are not a special set of features, but rather defining characteristics of professional nonlinear editing systems.

What Is Available?

Many systems are available out there, and more come on the market all the time. Following are just some of the better-known ones:

- Avid Media Composer
- Final Cut Pro
- Adobe Premiere Suite
- Sony Vegas Movie Studio
- Pinnacle Studio 12 Plus
- Roxie Creator 2010

If you are doing your homework, you can find reviews of these systems online.

Avid versus Final Cut

Avid and Final Cut are the two heavyweights (as of now). Avid has been the professional standard for years, but Final Cut has made a sizable dent into Avid's profile. The following is a general overview of the basic differences between these two giants courtesy of Steve Elliot, filmmaker, film editor, and editing instructor.

Avid is a well-designed editing system that allows you to edit, title, and do effects within a closed architecture. Clips are captured or converted to their own proprietary format. Media must be stored in a folder that is designated by the program, and to my knowledge cannot be transferred from one project to another. Organization of the material can happen only within the confines of the program.

Final Cut Pro is a well-designed system as well; it allows you to edit, title, and do effects, but it is an open architecture that allows you to organize a project to your own specs or employ the default system that FCP provides. Media is converted into QuickTime movies from a variety of formats. You can exchange clips from one project to another or import them into new projects. Organization or the material can be manipulated both within the program or without. [This means the editor has to be very careful when moving material around, or it will get lost or confused.]

Avid's evolution from a hardware/software inclusive package gave it a mindset to keep its system as proprietary as possible for as long as possible, resulting in an inflexible attitude toward consumers and educators, and a number of various programs that are variations on their original software, Media Composer. That has been rectified lately by making Media Composer available as a standalone.

Final Cut Pro took the opposite tact. Although it is made exclusively for the Macintosh computer by Apple, the concentration was on making software as sophisticated as it could while keeping it affordable. Its ability to be adaptable and more powerful over time means it is used for everything from home movies to feature films. The interface has grown over time, but the original layout has stayed constant for users of all levels.

Avid appeals to editors who feel most comfortable working on a system that is a bit more technical and disciplined or who first learned on it, whereas the Final Cut system appeals to those who like to structure a project to their own preferences.

The rest is how one feels about the tools. Someone might like the trim tool on the Avid over the trim tool on FCP. One might find the movement of segments on the time line easier on Final Cut, or vice versa. It becomes a matter of taste as to which system one ends up using. For example, an NBC graphic artist remarked to me as I marveled at a Paintbox: "Yes, it's a wonderful tool, but you still have to know art." In the final analysis, it's the end result, and either product will take you there. It's really the skill, experience and taste of the editor.

Steve Elliot

Editing Room

It is the producer's job to see that the editing room is properly equipped and that enough money is budgeted to last the entire postproduction period. The producer negotiates the deal with the editing facility or vendor that supplies the editing suite. He must also arrange for screening facilities (which is not usually an issue if the filmmaker is a student).

Postproduction Schedule

With the mix date as your goal, create a schedule, relying on the steps outlined in this chapter. This schedule will undoubtedly go through changes. How long it takes to arrive at the fine cut of your project depends not only on the structural challenges of the picture, but also on how much time it takes to complete the changes for each cut. For students and independents, the availability of editing facilities will have an impact on postproduction progress. Fine-cutting a 10-minute project might take a professional several weeks, but for a beginner, it might take several months.

These various steps serve as benchmarks of your progress through the postproduction period. A convenient aid for staying on schedule is a large calendar board. This larger-than-life visual representation of your postproduction schedule will help the creative team stay focused on its goals as each level is achieved.

Finding an Editor

Good material is the most effective selling tool for attracting creative people. Make an interesting film or video, and people will want to be associated with it. How much you have to pay for their services (if anything at all) depends on what you can negotiate. It is a given that you do not have much to spend. However, any compensation will create a business relationship and give you some leverage when asking for a 100 percent commitment.

INDEPENDENTS

Advertise through the local media organizations and the editors' guild. You might be able to find a professional assistant editor who works on features, documentaries, or industrials and is looking for projects to expand his reel and gain experience as an editor. It takes awhile for an assistant editor to work his way up the union ladder to become a full editor. Short projects offer assistant editors an opportunity to express themselves creatively, and they provide valuable credits. Alternatively, you might find a commercial editor who is looking for narrative or documentary work or a video editor who is looking for film work.

STUDENTS

Ask around and advertise. Put together and post a professional-looking flier for your project. Search for talented students who are interested in pursuing editing as a career. They will be looking for projects like yours to gain valuable experience and expand their professional reels.

Evaluating Prospective Editors

Evaluating an editor's contribution to another film requires more than just judging the work. You will need to talk to the director and producer and anyone else involved in the editorial process to find out exactly what the editor's contribution was to the postproduction process. To what extent was the editor responsible for creating the rhythm and pace of the piece? How active a role did the director play in the editing process? Did she stand next to the editor and suggest cuts, or did she stay away from the editing room? Here are some other questions to ask: Was another editor involved? Did the director have to take over? Who was ultimately responsible for the final product?

- **Speed.** How fast did the editor put together a first cut, and how closely did that first cut resemble the final product? How long did the editing process take? Were their other editors involved with the project?
- **Footage.** What kind of footage did the editor have to work with? Was the coverage terrific? Did it "cut like butter," or did the editor have to perform miracles in the editing room to salvage a piece that was not coming together easily?
- **Range of Talent.** Can the editor serve as a sound editor as well? An editor with this flexibility can save you money and time.

- **Formats and Equipment.** Does the editor have extensive experience in the format and gauge in which you are working (film: 35mm, 16mm; video: DV, HDV, HD, RED) or the different nonlinear editing systems?
- **Organization.** Media management is the key to success in the editing room.
- **Response to the Material.** The director does not want to work with someone who sees the project as just a job. An editor should be inspired by the material and want to spend weeks or months shaping it into a final product.
- **Temperament.** In the editing room, all the mistakes of production are played over again and again. The editor must be sensitive to the director's ego.
- **Support Crew.** Budget permitting, it is helpful for the editor to have an assistant with whom to work. The editor will know an assistant to bring on board.
- **Compatibility with the Director.** The editor–director relationship is important because the two of them will probably have to spend hours together in a small dark room, debating the progress of the project. If the director develops a good working relationship with an editor, she will probably want to continue working with him. They will develop a shorthand communication. The editor develops a feeling for how the director works and vice versa.

---

21 Key Issues for Editing
by Camilla Toniolo, Film Editor

1. Read the script a few times, trying to understand what the tone of the film is. Scripts are very dry; that's why they need a few passes. Since lots of things go wrong between the written page and what is finally committed to film, reading the script thoroughly will give you a sense of what the director's vision is. Although editing is mostly an intuitive craft and a lot of problem solving, it does not mean that you can be ignorant of the intentions and the hopes of the filmmaker.

2. If you can, participate with the life of the set at least one day or even a few hours. Observe the director at work and the actors as well. Mostly, editors stay away from the set to preserve their objectivity, but to be aware of the geography of a scene and the mood on the set can be helpful. Either way, when you are ready to start editing, do the following:

3. Screen your footage in a calm, quiet environment, with no interruptions. Take it all in and make mental notes of what you like. Do not stop and start; just screen. You should do this on a scene-by-scene basis. The second time you screen a scene's footage, take notes (written or on the computer) of the following: the takes you like the most, basing your comments on performance for now, and it could be the first part of take three and the second of take one and so on; the shot you are planning to use to open the scene, to close it; and any other note you can

think of. Remember that editing is very intuitive and that screening the footage for the first time happens only once and those first-gut reactions to how you want to put it together are precious.

4. Start putting your scene together, following a plan based on your notes. Unless you designed shots specifically for an opening, start with your master and stay on it until you can't stand it anymore. When it peaks, cut.

5. Cut into the coverage; approach the film from a slightly conventional point of view. This will allow you to have a strong base from which you can take off on less conventional tangents if you want. Use the shots that you have tagged; don't delete any lines; and don't overanalyze or get stuck at this precious stage of near objectivity of the material. Keep to the script and don't worry about mismatches for now. Try to keep in mind the following:

6. Always cut for a reason, not to show you can do it. The cut has to serve the story, and the best cuts are the ones that happen when the audience wants them to happen, therefore appearing seamless.

7. Avoid confusion and avoid giving the audience a "claustrophobic" feeling. Establish your geography well with your masters and fall back onto them any time you don't have to give a character an emotional punch by using a close-up or when someone is entering or leaving a scene.

Continued

---

21 Key Issues for Editing—cont'd

8. Avoid boring the audience by keeping to a minimum entrances and exits. Do set up the geography of a place, but don't waste too much time doing it or you'll lose your audience.

9. Try not to show an actor waiting to act, waiting to turn or enter. Cut in motion whenever possible, as the film seems less staged that way.

10. Cut longer rather than shorter for the first time around. It's much easier to trim than to add.

11. If you get stuck on a scene and nothing that you try to do helps, but on the contrary you fall deeper and deeper into despair, stop. Put it away. Come back the next day, screen your dailies for that scene again, and give it another try. Most of the insurmountable issues you were facing will be easier to solve with some objectivity.

12. Be open to try everything. Never apply too much rational thinking to a cut, as there are so many happy accidents. The famous saying "the only rule is that there are no rules" really applies to film editing. I am not advocating total anarchy, but you should be open and remember that everything is undoable. Having said this, here are a couple of rules:

13. Don't cut from a moving shot to a still one, and vice versa.

14. Don't cut between a shot of a certain size, say a medium, and another shot of the same character where the angle has changed very little, say 20 degrees. This will be confusing, as the backgrounds will change, but not quite enough, giving the impression of a jump.

15. When you are done assembling your scene or sequence, screen it without stopping and be aware of the impact it has on you. Jot a few notes down if it helps you, and start working at your changes right away. Different editors' styles differ on this point, but I like to work on a scene until I am completely happy with it; otherwise, if I "put it on the shelf" without liking it, when I assemble all the scenes together to watch them continuously, I will have too many things I am unhappy about and it will be distracting. I still adhere to the script and use every line, but in general I am happy with all the individual cuts and the energy of the scene.

16. Once all your sequences are edited and strung together, screen the completed film.

17. At this point your notes and changes should be based on the rule: Movie first, scene second, moment third. You have to preserve what serves the entire story and its characters, and forget about those gems that may be working wonderfully in a vacuum but bog the movie down or even hurt it.

18. At this stage, you should get your dialogue track in pretty good shape, replacing off-camera lines with audible ones, cutting in easy-to-find sound effects such as bells, doors, traffic, etc., and adding some music, which, even if temporary, will help you and anyone else you might "screen" for look at your work without being distracted or confused.

19. Work at finessing your cut until you are happy with it, dedicating time to the parts that are troubling you. This is a very delicate process, because the balance of the story can be tipped one way or the other, and a change or deletion made in the first five minutes will affect the entire film, so you will have to review it very carefully each time. Same with the middle or last five minutes. The most important thing to remember is that it is the way in which editing uses trickery and slight of hand to make the story work, to create a world, to give rhythm and a heartbeat to a flat screen that is what engages an audience visually and emotionally, and not a series of perfect cuts. Analyzed one by one, more than a few of the cuts of wonderful classic movies are mismatched, but they still became classics.

20. The next is a very critical step of the editing process because you are ready to commit to the final version of your picture cutting and to get other people involved in the completion of your film. They are unaware of what it took you to get to this version, that scene 83 may be in place of scene 1 and scene 1 is in the end crawl, so you better seek their involvement when you are finished and happy about your cut because it is expensive and very time-consuming to undo the version that your dialogue, music, and effects editor are working on.

21. So, when you are ready, sit down with your collaborators and screen the film for them, with the objective to add more layers and make your story that much more powerful.

Stepping Back and Looking Ahead

The person who is most responsible for spearheading the editorial process is the director. At this point in time, the producer steps aside and lets the director concentrate on shaping her vision of the film. The director might not want the producer anywhere near the editing room during this period. This gives the producer an objective point of view for the screening of the director's first cut.

While the editing is proceeding, the producer looks ahead and begins setting up the final leg of the postproduction process. An organized producer has already made a deal with a laboratory for all work on the film, from dailies through release prints. Now he must begin looking around for the best deals for the postproduction facilities and personnel who are going to be intricately involved with transforming the work print into a finished film. The postproduction personnel will be responsible for the following:

- Sound design
- ADR/Foley
- Music score

- Mix
- Optical track (if film)
- Titles/opticals
- Negative cutting (if matching back to film)
- Timing/color correction
- Answer print (if matching to film)
- Online editing for video

Finding the right people and the right facilities for this last leg of the production involves research, phone calls, and bids. The more you know, the better prepared you will be to secure the best deals without jeopardizing the creative integrity of the project.

STUDENTS

Many schools have their own mixing, ADR, and Foley stages and transfer rooms. Major metropolitan areas such as New York, Los Angeles, Chicago, and San Francisco have postproduction houses that are willing to give excellent deals to students and independent filmmakers on tight budgets. In New York City, for example, postproduction facilities allow students to mix at night for reduced rates with mixers in training. However, students are advised to take advantage of whatever facility their program offers. It will save them money and enable them to take their time.

KEY POINTS

- Follow the steps described in this chapter in the proper order.
- Be ruthlessly objective in the editing room.
- Cut a film together based only on the material in the editing room. The final product might be different from what you intended. Listen to the material.
- Don't think that technology is a substitute for hard work. Films need time and patience.

Chapter 17

Sound Postproduction

A sound designer may cut dialogue, record music, perform Foley, edit the film, direct the film or perform any one of a hundred other jobs. But anybody who shapes sound, edits sound, or even considers sound when making a creative decision in another craft, is designing sound for the movie, and designing the movie for sound.

Randy Thom, Sound Designer

DIRECTOR

Sound Design

Sound on film came late to motion pictures (circa 1928), although many tried unsuccessfully to marry sound with pictures since the first film was projected in a Paris studio by the Lumiere brothers in 1895. Those who pioneered the medium never thought that watching a film without hearing what was on the screen was natural or creatively fulfilling. It was only half the story.

Many motion pictures in the 1930s and 1940s relied on production sound—that is, all the dialogue and extra sounds recorded live on the set. Soundstages were quiet, controllable environments for recording not only "clean" dialogue, but also footsteps, door slams, or other sounds necessary for the scene. However, there were particular sounds that couldn't be created live. War movies, westerns, gangster films, horror films, or boxing films required their share of gunshots, explosions, face punches, and thunderclaps to authenticate the visual experience.

To supply these films with these kinds of sounds and more, each Hollywood film studio developed its own sound library. For example, whenever a studio recorded sound for a western or a war movie for the first time, it would put a lot of creativity into the process and then store these sounds for reuse. RKO's sound library was bolstered by the animal sounds recorded live for the landmark sound effects film *King Kong*. Warner Brothers recorded many kinds of exterior gunshots and bullet ricochets for its big battle movie, *The Charge of the Light Brigade* (1936). The studio sound department used these same ricochets for decades. Two or three are familiar to modern audiences because they were used when the cartoon character, the *Road Runner*, zips away.

Throughout the 1950s and 1960s, sound effects editors created what today we would call "sound design" on such science fiction films as *War of the Worlds* (1950), *The Time Machine* (1960), *Forbidden Planet* (1956), and *The Day the Earth Stood Still* (1951) without the digital technology available today. When one marvels at the power and realism of the epic chariot race in *Ben Hur* (1959), consider that every single sound, from the grunts of the horses to the chariots crashing, was designed, placed, and ultimately mixed to create a seamless integration of sound and picture. Not one of those sounds was recorded live on the set. How much of that power would be there without the sound to draw us in? (Check out the silent version of *Ben Hur* to compare.) Not coincidentally, the sound effects editor, Van Allen James, worked on both *The Time Machine* and *Ben Hur*.

In the 1970's, George Lucas brought a level of appreciation and importance to the value of sound in films. Sound editors, such as Walter Murch and Ben Burtt, elevated the craft of sound design to new levels. With the advent of digital technology, audiences today have greater expectations of what they will hear as well as see when experiencing a film.

For the beginner, the process of creating the final soundtrack can seem overwhelming. When the picture is cut, it feels finished. In truth, your film is only halfway there. You and your team have yet to manufacture what will become the entire aural experience of the film.

Work must still be done to create the sounds related to the world of your picture. Separate sound effects and music tracks must be designed and eventually mixed together to form your soundtrack. Think of this stage as the final opportunity to polish and refine your picture by adding an exciting dimension of sound to complement and enhance the visual story.

What Is Sound Design?

Think of sound design as the aural equivalent of the visual mise-en-scène. As every detail in each frame is carefully thought out and planned, so should every sound. In the best of all worlds, there should be nothing on the soundtrack that is accidental or arbitrary. The sounds in your film contribute to telling the story as much as a good shot or an outstanding performance. Among other effects, sound defines the aural world of your story. Audiences not only want to see where the movie is taking place, they want to hear what those places sound like.

For those with experience in shooting only video, when sound is immediately "married" to picture, it is commonly taken for granted. For those with experience shooting film, when sound is recorded separately, it is easier to grasp that sound and picture have their separate but equal journeys. Each sound in your film should be selected with as much loving care as any other creative aspect of your film.

Sound Equals Space

The sounds you choose will complete the film experience because they bring reality to the illusion of the image. We need to hear sounds that match the images on the screen: traffic on the street corner, birds chirping in a garden, or waves breaking on the shore. These natural elements bring us closer to the drama because they make us believe that what we are seeing is real. The bottom line is that we do not believe something unless we hear it. If we see an actor knocking on a door with no sound, it is not really a knock.

Sound can connect objects in space that have no inherent relationship to one another. Different shots of city streets can be unified with the addition of a bell tower chiming. If we hear the chimes while seeing the different city shots, we will believe that these streets are all part of the same town. The cafeteria in *The Lunch Date* seems to be a part of Grand Central Station, though shot blocks away, because of the simple train announcements in the background.

A sound can subtly affect how we respond to a scene emotionally. Imagine a scene with a couple in the woods at night, with the sound of crickets and an owl in the background. If, after a while, you add the sound of a howling wolf, it will give the scene a very different feeling. The wolf signals fear; the owl, comfort.

Sounds can indicate a world outside the frame—a world the audience need not see to believe. Imagine: A couple is trying to have a quiet dinner at home when a rock band begins to practice next door or a couple is having a fight, or kids are playing kickball. We need only hear these sounds to believe they are happening. The rule of thumb for this approach is **off-screen sound expands on-screen space**.

An excellent film to study for its effective use of off-screen sound is Robert Bresson's *A Man Escaped* (France, 1956). The film is set in a prison during the Second World War in France. Most of the film takes place in small cells. The film's claustrophobic visual approach is counterbalanced with its effective use of sound outside the frame and the prison walls. The sounds of birds chirping, trolley cars, kids playing, and trains passing remind the prisoners daily of how close they are to a freedom they can only hear, but probably will never see again.

> The whole element of sound—both music and sound effects—was a rediscovery for me of what the story was. My first idea behind making the film was to tell a story visually, silently. So in the beginning I cut the film together without sound. I wanted to see if it worked. By first doing the images, then doing the sound—suddenly I could think of the story as being a whole set of sounds as well: the train station, the track boards flipping, salad crunching.
>
> Adam Davidson

Sound Equals Production Value

Building the soundtrack for your project not only is creative and exciting, but it can be cost-effective, too. A well-placed sound or noise brings much to a picture for relatively little expense. You do not have to shoot a rock band to include them in your project. The audience need only hear them. Police cars, fire trucks, or a parade can pass by your character's window without ever being seen.

How We Perceive Sound versus Picture

It is understandable that most beginners (and many professionals) have trouble understanding how a soundtrack is developed. It is partly due to fundamental difference between how we experience sound and images in films. Images require continual redirection of attention; we can really "see" only one shot at a time (even when the screen is split into pieces).

We register sounds differently. Unlike the eye, the ear is sensitive to sounds reaching it from any direction, all at the same time. When a new sound comes within our audible range, it does not displace the others (as a shot would), but becomes part of the "total sound" we hear; it is *omnipresent and layered*.

Imagine a film that begins at a farm on a warm summer day. The first scene starts with a few establishing shots of the barn and the fields. The soundtrack, however, might contain several layers of different sounds: various kinds of birds, crickets, bees, a flowing stream, wind through the trees and fields, animal noises, a creaking barn, all blended together to create the aural feel of the environment.

Respect for Sound

Most of the information we derive from the world around us comes to us visually. In every environment there exists a rich and densely varied world of sound. However, we do not consciously hear it. If you wish to gain an appreciation for the inherent sounds of any space, try this simple but effective experiment. All you need is a blindfold and a partner you trust. Put on the blindfold and have your partner lead you around the streets of your town or city. As your brain shifts from processing information from the eyes to processing information from the ears, you will begin to hear every sound around you. You will also begin to see things because of what they sound like rather than what they look like. Cars will pass by, and you will be able to track their physical relationship to you solely from their sound perspective. A supposedly quiet afternoon will be transformed into a cacophony of sounds. This exercise should be an aural awakening for you: You will realize how selective your hearing is. If you try this experiment at home, you will discover the many subtle sounds that fill your apparently quiet room.

Your soundtrack need not include all the sounds that exist in a space at any given time. A soundtrack can easily become indistinguishable with too many simultaneous sounds. You should select sounds for inclusion on your track, basing your decisions on the criteria discussed in this chapter. Your choices will have a profound impact on the audience's response to the world your characters inhabit.

When I try to explain what a movie sound designer does it's always difficult. The idea that a sound designer is somebody who fabricates sci-fi sound effects is probably the most widely held notion on the subject. But it doesn't describe very accurately what Ben Burtt and Walter Murch, who originated the term, did on *Star Wars* and *Apocalypse Now*. On those films they found themselves working with directors who were not just looking for neat sound effects to attach to a structure that was already in place. By experimenting with sound, playing with sound (and not just sound effects, but music and dialogue as well) all through production and postproduction what they found is that sound began to shape the picture sometimes as much as the picture shaped the sound. The result was very different from anything we had heard before. The films are legends, and their soundtracks changed forever they way we think about film sound.

Randy Thom, Sound Designer

What Is a Soundtrack?

A film soundtrack is composed of dialogue (which includes voice-over), music, and sound effects. Your completed track is a complex blend of these elements. Dialogue usually takes prominence (unless there isn't any, of course). Then it becomes how sound effects and music are used to surround the dialogue and/or voice-over to enhance the dramatic value of each moment of the film. There shouldn't be a struggle for dominance. Each element should be integrated harmoniously to support the visual story. This is what sound design is all about.

This chapter presents a model for how a soundtrack is professionally created—the basic steps of how dialogue, music, and sound effects are designed, manufactured, and mixed. Because many of these jobs may performed by only a few people on smaller productions, it is important to know what has to done to create a professional soundtrack.

The process of creating a soundtrack is an evolution. Thinking of how your film should "sound" could start at the script stage. For example, a piece of music or a song may serve as an inspiration for a story, scene, or sequence. As the picture editing evolves, ideas for music and sound effects can be explored and layered into the many tracks available in most NLE software. Much can happen from the first cut to the last. As the film takes shape, your outlook on the role of sound in your film may change. You may have had a particular song or type of musical style in mind early in the script stage, but now that the film has taken on its own life, it may not fit any more. Structural changes may require a different aural approach such as the addition of some kind of voice-over or written narration. The lesson is: be responsive to the material. Following are the basic paths to creating a soundtrack for your film.

Post Flow Options

How your soundtrack is edited and finished will depend on your resources, your budget, and where the film is intended to be seen. For example, is it a project intended for the Internet versus one that will be screened in festivals?

Projects Shot on Video

Basic Nonlinear Sound Edit. Picture and sound editing is completed on the nonlinear editing system. This method is best for simple or low-budget projects, especially those headed for the Internet.

Basic Nonlinear Sound, Mix in Studio. Sound editing is completed on the nonlinear editing system. Audio tracks are outputted as *Open Media Framework Interchange*, or *OMF*, files so the engineer can import them into a Pro Tools session as separate tracks, in sync. You should only expect a basic leveling of your tracks with this mix.

Nonlinear Edit, Sound Design on a DAW, Mix in Studio. Picture editing and basic sound work are done on the nonlinear editing system. After the picture is locked, the sound files are exported to a digital workstation as OMF files. AAF interchange is used with MXF formats (go to the Avid web site for more complete information). Sound editing is done on Pro Tools. Your completed sound materials are brought to the mix in a Pro Tools session. Mixing is done in a studio with good speakers and an optimum environment to judge the mixed soundtrack.

Projects Shot on Film

Film-to-Tape Transfer, Edit Nonlinear. Film is transferred digitally for editing. Production audio is transferred with it (already synced up) or synced up on the system. Basic sound work can be done on the system. After this point, the project can follow any of the three video options.

However, if you are finishing with a film print, make sure the project is prepped for an optical transfer.

Whether you are editing and completing the soundtrack on Avid or Final Cut Pro, or working with a sound designer and planning to mix, these are some of the important sound issues to consider as you edit your film:

- How are you going to "hear" the story? (What role does sound play in your story?)
- How much music (if any) will you require?
- What kind of music? Preexisting or score?
- What kinds of sound effects? Realistic? Surreal?
- What is the balance between sound effects and music?
- What are the opportunities for the subjective use of sound?

Do You Need a Sound Designer?

Whether you are creating a 3- or 30-minute project, your sound needs are determined by the complexity of your ideas. A short picture, 5 to 10 minutes in length, might end up with 5 to 10 tracks of dialogue, music, and effects or many more. Having 5 to 10 tracks may be manageable for a novice editor or director-editor. With projects demanding more ambitious sound work, many beginners and students decide to work with a sound designer. Having just learned picture editing, they tend to be overwhelmed by the prospect of sound work. They know it is necessary but are intimidated by this completely new technical challenge. If they can afford it, they bring in someone who will take them through the process, providing a valuable learning experience at the same time.

Working with a sound designer has obvious benefits. Ask to be involved in all the sound design steps for your picture. Take advantage of the learning experience. Share your ideas, express your concept of sound, but give the sound designer the creative space to explore other interesting sound possibilities. A sound person who has been in the business for even a short time not only will have access to sound libraries, but will have built up his own "library." Give the sound editor accurate sound reports and continuity notes because he will need to get to the original production material recorded on the set.

Working on a short film offers novice sound editors the opportunity to gain experience and build their sample reels. They might be drawn to your project because it offers a particular challenge or an opportunity to work with interesting material. If a salary is involved, it is probably below the norm for seasoned professionals.

Following are some of the tools for the digital sound designer:

- Digital audio workstation (DAW)
- ADR/Foley stage
- Cue sheets
- SFX library

> The film came together because of the sound editor. He was the one who came in and said, "Listen, you've got to define this opening. Here's how we're going to use music and sound effects to do it, and what you're going to do is intersperse the titles," which really gave the opening a sense of focus. If you had the titles before the montage, it would seem very repetitive: titles, montage, and then Truman. By breaking up the montage with the titles, which was the sound editor's idea, and using the music the way we did, it gave an unexpected energy and a drive to that moment when we come down the rope and see Truman and the film officially starts.
>
> Howard McCain

The Design of Sound

Following is a partial list of the many people who are involved in creating a soundtrack:

- Sound designer
- Supervising sound editor
- Dialogue editor
- Foley artist
- Foley mixer/editor
- Effects editor
- Automated dialogue replacement (ADR) supervisor
- ADR recordist
- Rerecording mixer

For low-budget projects, one or two people handle the duties of many of these positions (think the 3–30 rule in post). If your editor will cut the sound on your project, she might also serve as the dialogue, effects, ADR, and Foley editor and might perform many of the Foleys herself. (See the discussion of Foley effects in the section "Sound Effects Tracks" later in this chapter.)

Let's look at the responsibilities of each position in more detail.

Sound Designer. This term was first used as a professional craft designation in theatrical film in 1979, when an Academy Award for sound design was given to Walter Murch for *Apocalypse Now*. The sound designer is responsible for the development and design of all soundtrack materials. He oversees the entire production and might fulfill his duties by supervising the sound editor.

This relatively new position arose out of the need for an overall style for many projects. It is, however, more of a designated title than an actual job description like the supervising sound editor. Make sure anyone who advertises himself as such has the technical know-how to actually cut sound.

> I owe a lot to the sound designer because one thing was that he got me to stop fiddling around with cutting the picture. The other was that we started discovering the story again. I basically became his assistant. I went to Grand Central again, getting more ambience, getting more sound. I went with a Nagra from school. I went to Penn Station and got train announcements. I did all the Foleys: the salad crunching and things like that. Then we started working on putting the tracks together, and it was a very interesting process.
>
> Adam Davidson

Supervising Sound Editor. This person handles the creation of the dialogue and effects tracks, either working alone or supervising others.

Effects Editor. The effects editor provides all the required sound effects for the picture—everything from birds chirping to cars screeching to doors slamming. These sounds come from sound effects libraries or live recordings on the set or are created by the effects editor. He is responsible for editing all sound effects and for their placement in the soundtrack to facilitate the final mix.

Dialogue Editor. The dialogue editor is responsible for all technically good dialogue tracks. She prepares the tracks to be mixed properly.

Foley Editor. This individual spots (identifies) and records all the studio-made Foley effects. The Foley editor cues all the effects needed and supervises the Foley artist for correct sound of effect and sync. He often does the engineering if it is a small project. For a feature film, there would be both an editor and an engineer.

Foley Artist. The Foley artist creates sounds for a picture in a studio using his body and a variety of gadgets, hand props, and tools. These sounds must sync up precisely with the action on the screen.

Foley Engineer. This person supervises the Foley sessions and records the Foley artist.

ADR Supervisor. This individual programs (spots) each line that must be replaced by ADR and supervises the recording sessions.

ADR Recordist. This sound person operates the ADR recording machine. He is responsible for microphone placement for perspective and matching of original dialogue.

Rerecording Mixer. Formerly known as a **dubbing mixer**, the rerecording mixer is responsible for the final soundtrack of your film.

> We wanted the film to sound like the outside world; ambiences, luscious footfalls were pretty key. Because my sound recordist was also my sound designer, he was able to spend time in the field building his library. When certain scenes were wrapped, he was able to go with the actor and record the crunching sound his boots made in the snow. Another big thing was the hunter scene. The gun firing was all sound design, so it was critical that that be pulled off entirely in the aural spectrum. The chase did not have as many shots as I wanted it to be. We knew that in the editing room. That was somewhere where we were really reliant upon what we could create in the sound realm. If people find that exciting, I think it is entirely because of the sound and music.
>
> James Darling

The Digital Audio Workstation

The digital audio workstation, or DAW, has become an integral part of the audio postproduction process. Today, most film sound is done digitally on digital workstations. Using digital storage techniques, combined with computer hardware and software such as Pro Tools by Digidesign, audio professionals have the capacity to perform most of the audio postproduction process right in the DAW system. For example, musicians can record directly onto the hard drive, create up to 48 virtual tracks, edit the tracks, create music effects, mix unlimited versions of the music piece, and then output the finished piece at master quality, even surround sound.

The DAW is used to record the edited master audio track, instantly recall and precisely edit sound effects and music cues from libraries stored on hard drives, record and edit voice-overs and narration, and record and edit ADR and Foley effects. Then it is used to mix the finished product in mono, stereo, or versions of both.

Digital audio workstations can provide instant access to all stored media, design and texture original sounds, and work with almost unlimited numbers of virtual tracks and interface with digital picture playback. DAWs can be integrated with and networked to a collection of devices, such as other audio, video, and MIDI sources.

Spotting

Once a picture is locked, the job of sound design begins in earnest. The director sits down with the sound team and decides what is needed to flesh out the soundtrack of her film. This process is called **spotting** the picture. The director, sound designer, and editor look at the picture in a precise and deliberate way, scene by scene, and indicate which sounds are appropriate at any given moment.

Most sound effects editors approach each project as if there will be no music and give the director enough sounds to create a full and rich track. Sound effects can stir audiences' emotions in a way similar to the impact of music. However, the director should keep in mind how she plans to blend effects and music in a scene. Too many sound effects might interfere with the dialogue, the mood of the scene, or the music the director is planning to use. (The use of music is discussed later in this chapter.) During the spotting session, the director and sound team discuss the following:

- **On-screen Sounds.** These are the "hard sounds" you can see being made in the frame, such as footsteps and door slams.
- **Ambient Sounds.** These sounds are associated with the natural ambience of a space—for example, birds chirping, wind blowing, and traffic.
- **Off-screen Sounds.** Off-screen sounds occur outside the frame. Examples are neighbors arguing in the hallway and a television blaring in the next room.
- **Unusual Sounds.** These sounds are not associated with the scene either on- or off-screen. If the director is planning a stylistic approach to sound, she might use surreal or manufactured sounds (the electronic buzz of the light sabers in *Star Wars*, for example) or ordinary sounds used out of context. An example is the climactic fight sequence of Martin Scorsese's *Raging Bull*, which features sounds that are not normally found in a boxing ring, such as wind blowing and animal growls.
- **Enhanced Sounds.** For example, a lion roar could be used to emphasize the power of a wave.
- **Production Dialogue.** The spotting session is an opportunity to review the quality of the production dialogue. The film editor should be able to point out the tracks that are good and those that might have to be replaced with new lines recorded with ADR.

Only when the picture length has been finalized can the sound editor know the exact timing required for dialogue or effects tracks. All picture changes after the lock must be announced to the sound designer so that he can adjust the timing to keep the soundtrack frame-accurate. This is important to remember. Most filmmakers, and especially beginners, don't understand the ramifications of changing even one frame.

Constantly making changes is labor intensive, time consuming, and costly, however small they are. The sound editor must sift through and find the little frames that have been cut out of the picture and make adjustments to the tracks and the cue sheets.

Dialogue Tracks

Unless a piece has no dialogue, your first responsibility is to make sure the audience can clearly hear what the actors are saying. This includes words spoken by actors on-screen, off-screen, and in voice-overs. Analyze the production tracks and decide which ones are acceptable and which ones might have to be replaced with ADR. Replacements can be confirmed during the spotting session. The "clean" tracks and the "dirty" tracks should be obvious. Ask for advice with the questionable ones.

Much can be done in the mixing stage to clean up a line of dialogue. Inappropriate sounds such as camera noise or floor squeaks can often be removed. The question is how much background noise can be tolerated. You don't want the audience to strain to hear the words. Background noise will become even more of an issue when the mixed track is transferred to the final digital master or optical track (for a film print). Because some parts of the sound spectrum can be eliminated on the track, you might need to have a professional sound editor or a mixer analyze certain tracks. You might be forced to replace some or all of the "dirty" lines using ADR.

The editor now separates or splits the lines of dialogue onto enough tracks to enable the mixer to easily blend and equalize the dialogue (see Figure 17.1). Following are some situations that require separate dialogue tracks:

- **Control Levels.** A piece of dialogue must be separated if it requires its own sound level in a scene. It is difficult for a mixer to make radical adjustments between different lines of dialogue on the same track. If character A, meant to be played softly, is immediately followed by character B, whose delivery is meant to be loud, the mixer will not have time to set a new level for the incoming sound if it is on the same track. With separate tracks, the mixer can preset the appropriate levels.
- **Background Changes.** Different camera setups sometimes involve different background ambiences. For example, a scene with two people talking on a street corner might have one background on the traffic side (loud traffic noises) and one on the sidewalk side (people walking). These two setups require two different levels.
- **Camera Perspectives.** Different camera angles (wide, medium, and close) of the same scene have different sound perspectives. The lines for these camera angles might have to be put on different tracks to enable the mixer to set the appropriate levels. Sound perspectives ideally should match camera perspectives. Cutting between the different perspectives in the same scene will require separate sound adjustments so that the cutting seems more natural.

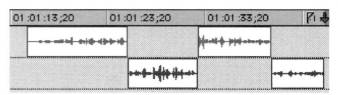

FIGURE 17.1 Split audio tracks.

- **Overlapping Dialogue.** If an on-camera character speaks and is interrupted by an off-camera character, the editor can overlap the two pieces of dialogue. Speech is overlapped in real life. Splitting tracks allows the editor to simulate this reality and allows the mixer to control properly the blending of the two voices on the final track.

- **Telephone Conversations.** Tracks are also split to enable cutting between two characters who are having a phone conversation. The editor will cut between a clean sound and one with "futz" (the sound of a voice filtered through a phone line). Even though most of the conversation will be heard this way, it should be recorded clean on the set. Any sound that is to be deliberately distorted through bad speakers or behind doors should always be recorded clean on the set to give the dialogue editor and mixer complete freedom to control the nature of the sound.

- **Mixing Different Conversations.** Imagine a character walking through a busy party. She hears snippets of different conversations as she passes from one group to another. Each conversation must be separated on a different track to enable the mixer to control the tone as well as the changing perspective of each voice as the main character approaches and moves farther away.

Cutting Dialogue

Much of what the dialogue editor contributes to the soundtrack is unheralded because when she does her job well, no one notices. You can appreciate how much work went into this step only if you hear original production tracks cut together.

A great deal of dialogue editing consists of evening out background ambience or room tone of each scene and replacing the holes, or empty spots, in a track. The editor blends together different shots with different backgrounds by creating what are called **dialogue extensions**. This requires adding extra room tone (preferably from the existing take) to the head of one dialogue track and the tail of another so the mixer can do a quick sound dissolve fade, or segue, between the two. The result is a softening of the "sound bump" that might be heard when cutting between two different sound backgrounds.

Dialogue editors are also adept at substituting lines of dialogue from a clean take (of a scene) to replace one that needed to be rerecorded (see the following section). This shift retains the original performance and, by eliminating the need for ADR, saves the production money.

Automatic Dialogue Replacement (ADR)

What happens if the sound was not recorded well? What if there was a helicopter buzzing overhead during the take you want to use in the scene? What if you shot a scene by the ocean, and the rhythmic pounding of the surf does not match from cut to cut?

Mixers are miracle workers. They can sometimes dial out a low hum or even an airplane in the background, but dirty tracks are dirty tracks. The only way to fix a badly recorded track is to replace the dialogue. **Looping** (see Glossary) a line with ADR does this. In this electronic process, the actor stands in a soundproof studio in front of a screen and wears headphones. The scene is projected on the screen. The actor sees and hears the way the line was spoken and practices matching its cadence.

When ready for a take, the actor waits for a visual or aural cue and repeats the line into a microphone (see Figure 17.2.). He might get it right on the first try, or he might have to repeat the line a number of times before achieving proper sync and performance. In cases of lengthy lines or even speeches, he might have to pick the speech apart line by line or even word by word.

Pg. 1

CHARACTER/LINE #	TIME CODE	LINE BEING REPLACED / ADDED	TAKES (SELECTS 0/ALTS △)
JOE 101	01:01:56:22	"How did you make it?" REASON: Prod. Noise	1 2 /3\ 4 (5)
JOE 102	01:02:35:14	"I really like it. It's great." REASON: Added line	1 /2\ (3)
JOE 103	01:02:46:03	"Would you like to go—[for a walk?]" REASON: Overlap during interruption	1 2 3 4/5\6 (7)

Pg. 2

CHARACTER/LINE #	TIME CODE	LINE BEING REPLACED / ADDED	TAKES (SELECTS 0/ALTS △)
STACY 101	01:01:59:27	"I just glued it onto the wood…" REASON: Prod. Noise	1 2 3 (4) 5 /6\
STACY 102	01:02:39:03	"Thanks. I'm glad you do." REASON: Added line	1 2 /3\ (4)
STACY 103	01:02:47:19	"Hey! I have an idea —" REASON: Overlap during interruption	/1\ (2) 3

FIGURE 17.2 Sample ADR cue sheet. Courtesy of Alex Raspa.

Some actors are adept at this process, and some are not. Some are intimidated by having to duplicate in a dark and sterile room what was created naturally during the shooting of the film.

The editor then cuts the rerecorded line into a new dialogue track. If the actor has made a good match, the editor can simply drop in the new material. More often, the editor has to play with the line, cutting a frame here, adding a frame there, until the dialogue is in sync with the performance.

The ADR editor has many functions, including these:

- Programming ADR lines
- Selecting the exact footage and the exact line to be rerecorded
- Creating ADR cue sheets
- Helping actors with sync
- Cutting lines into the show

Some directors use ADR not because of the quality of the sound, but because they want to improve or change the nature of a performance. Having the budget to accomplish this is a luxury for most beginners, who usually can't afford ADR at all.

Proper preparation for the ADR session plays an important role in its success. Paying for a studio and the engineer's labor is expensive. You do not want to waste any time in confusion over what needs to be recorded.

There are ways of creating effective ADR lines without going into a studio. You can create your own soundproof environment at home or in the editing room and perform many of these tasks there. With looping techniques and a portable recording device it is possible to have the actor listen to a line reading a number of times and repeat that line in a clean environment. It is not necessary to repeat long speeches. They can be broken up one line at a time or between breaths.

DIRECTORS

If you are shooting a scene that will obviously need to be looped, take the actors and the production sound mixer off to a quiet room immediately upon completion of the scene. Have the actors listen to their lines on headphones and repeat them into a microphone and another tape recorder. This new dialogue might save you a trip to the ADR room. The actors are fresh from the scene and might be able to duplicate their tone and cadence perfectly. The lines might not be exactly in sync, but a good ADR editor should be able to shift them into place easily.

ADR Spotting

It is sometimes easier to replace an entire scene with ADR than to replace a few lines. It is certainly easier to redo a whole line rather than try to replace a word. Trying to match a line spoken on the set with one recorded in the soundproof environment of a studio requires some finesse. The sound editor must "dirty" the words with background ambience and other sounds. The mixer also has ways to help match the two. However, there always remains a perceptible difference between the tone and ambience of ADR and production dialogue, no matter what magic is performed to blend them together.

On the other hand, rerecording an entire scene allows the editor to create a consistent background ambience throughout the scene. Viewers accept the ADR and the background as natural because they are not comparing it to dialogue that was recorded on the set.

Adding and Altering Lines with ADR

During picture cutting, the director might realize that she needs to add off-camera lines that were not in the script. ADR offers an opportunity to add characters to a scene without visuals. They can exist outside the frame through sound as long as there is some logic behind their presence. In *The Lunch Date*, the audience could have heard the voices of a couple arguing in another booth. While the woman wandered through Grand Central Station, she could have heard bits and pieces of the conversations around her.

It is also possible to alter dialogue spoken on-screen. For example, if a character turns his head in the middle of a line and the director decides that she wants him to say something else, the new line can be dubbed in. The head turn distracts viewers from noticing that the mouth and the lines do not exactly match. It is possible to change a line without a physical distraction, although it is a little harder. The farther away the lips are from the camera, the easier it is to fudge the dialogue. Suppose the director wants the character to say, "I want to go to Miami" instead of the recorded line, "I need to get a new pair of shoes." Here are three ways to make this change:

- Dub in the new line as the character turns away.
- Match the new line to a reaction shot of the character to whom the line is addressed.
- Dub in the new line over a long shot in which the character's lips are not visible.

These simple manipulations can have a profound effect on the outcome of your story. The alteration of one line can change the dramatic content of an entire scene. The possibilities of postproduction ADR give the director other storytelling devices that can enhance and complement what she achieved on the set. These manipulations might seem like tricks, but remember that making a film or video involves illusion. It is best to make these decisions before locking the picture because these types of alterations affect picture as well as sound.

Walla

Walla is a specialized form of dialogue: the sound of generic voices that were not recorded on the set. These sounds flesh out the background, providing verbal atmosphere for a busy bar or restaurant, a party, or any space with people talking or murmuring.

If the production sound mixer was unable to record wild atmosphere on the set, the sound effects editor can program a Walla recording session. Some experts in the industry have a special talent for looking at a scene and improvising general noise and whatever specific comments the scene requires.

The special voice-over groups, or "loop groups," that perform Walla can also duplicate major characters who are not available for ADR postproduction work. If an actor is busy when you schedule the ADR sessions, rather than wait for her schedule to free up, you might employ a "voice-alike" to impersonate her.

Voice-overs and Narration

A *voice-over* is a separate or nondiagetic voice (or voices) placed over the images in your film. The voice-over may be spoken by someone who appears on-screen or as an unseen narrator. This voice could represent, among other things, the main character commenting on or narrating the story or reflecting on his inner thoughts or feelings.

Some stories start off with a voice-over integrated in the structure of the script. Even films without this script device can end up with some sort of voice-over in the final product. In the course of editing, the director might discover the need to bind the audience more closely to the main character or narrative. Key exposition might be missing, the story might lack focus, or it might not engage the audience sufficiently. The use of voice-over as a device can help unify the narrative into a cohesive story.

Voice-over narration has existed since the beginnings of cinema and has been an integral part of some of the masterworks of narrative film, from *The Magnificent Ambersons* to *Double Indemnity* to *Jules and Jim* to *Taxi Driver* to *The Royal Tenenbaums*. It spans all genres and national cinemas, utilized in a myriad of distinct styles to complement, clarify, or complicate the filmed story. It has been a standard device used in documentaries since the 1930s.

European directors like Robert Bresson, François Truffaut, Alain Resnais, Jean-Luc Godard, and Ingmar Bergman used voice-over extensively. Stanley Kubrick relied heavily on voice-over in *Lolita*, *Dr. Strangelove*, *A Clockwork Orange*, and *Barry Lyndon*; Martin Scorsese in *Taxi Driver*, *Goodfellas*, and *The Age of Innocence*; Arthur Penn in *Little Big Man*; Terrence Malick in his classics *Badlands*, *Days of Heaven*, and *The Thin Red Line*; and Woody Allen in films too numerous to list.

In the past few decades, independent filmmakers and studio productions alike have used voice-over narration to convey a personal tone and a postmodern sensibility, notably in *Clueless*, *American Beauty*, *Fight Club*, and *Amélie*.

There are three basic approaches to employing a narration:

- First person (the main character is telling the story, in his voice, as used in *Taxi Driver*, *Fight Club*, *A Clockwork Orange*, and *American Beauty*)
- Third person (a secondary character is telling the story, as used in *Badlands* and *Days of Heaven*)
- Omniscient (a voice of someone not in the film is telling the story, as used in *Barry Lyndon*, *The Age of Innocence*, and *The Royal Tenenbaums*)

Impact

If a story needs a unifying point of view, voice-over can do this very simply. It allows the audience to enter the world of the story through a particular perspective. Voice-over can also do the following:

- Strengthen the main character's point of view and thus the audience's emotional connection to that character by personalizing what viewers see
- Communicate important exposition that is not clear in the narrative
- Present the audience with a different point of view with which to experience the action of the story

Voice-overs can also be fragmentary streams of consciousness as well as poetic in nature. Michael Herr's phrasing in Francis Ford Coppola's *Apocalypse Now* and Martin Sheen's soft, bitter delivery make memorable and evocative such lines as "Everyone gets everything he wants. I wanted a mission, and for my sins, they gave me one."

If there is one rule with narration, it is this: do not use voice-over to tell viewers what they are seeing. Doing this would be redundant (unless you intend it to be for comic or ironic purposes). Think of voice-over as a device to broaden understanding of the story, characters, or conflict.

Be' Garrett used voice over in *A Nick in Time* to personalize the audience's connection to the action. We hear the barber's voice supply the subtext to the haircut that changed his life and woman who gave him that opportunity.

Refining the Narration

To properly integrate the voice-over into the structure of the film, you need to work with a temporary track while editing the picture. A rough recording by the director or editor will do, just to get an idea. Even if the voice-over was in the original script, it may be completely rewritten during the fine-cut stage. A polished recording with the actor will be made in a studio at the same time as ADR. It can either be done wild or to picture, if that enhances the performance and saves editing time.

> To me sound is as important as picture. So, we got into the sounds and the nuances and the ambient sounds and the stuff that you cannot even hear. We attempted to get the sound to enhance the picture, like when you would see the young character Edwin Wiley talking and then all of a sudden you hear shots in the background; this was sort of symbolic of what was to happen. Or you hear the dogs. He was like the ravenous dog that was out as the predator.
>
> We made sure that the clippers felt authentic because the actor had never barbered in his life. I had to have a technician teach him how to barber so that when he did it on film it looked authentic. Even then sound had to sound right when he clicked it on and clicked it off. So we did those kinds of things as well. We spent time getting those things right over and over again until we felt like it was perfect. Those are the things that I was trying to infuse in the movie as subtext.
>
> Be' Garrett

Sound Effects Tracks

Sound effects add a whole new dimension to a picture. The first step is to isolate the sounds viewers can visually identify, such as footsteps or someone knocking on a door. The next step is to choose the sounds that are identified with a particular environment. In *The Lunch Date*, these are the sounds of Grand Central Station. From this point, the editor begins to assemble sounds that will enlarge the world of your project and add a level of information that doesn't exist in the picture.

Once the picture is spotted, the sound designer begins to accumulate the sounds needed to flesh out the director's ideas. These sounds come from many places:

- Wild sounds recorded on the set
- Sounds manufactured live on location
- Wild sounds recorded after principal photography
- Prerecorded effects from sound effects libraries
- Online sound effects libraries
- Electronically manufactured sound effects
- Effects manufactured in a studio (Foley effects)

All these sounds must be dubbed from their original format to digital sound for video. Let's look at each of these sources in more detail.

Wild Sounds Recorded on the Set. *Wild sound* refers to any recorded sound that is not in sync with the picture. In addition to recording dialogue and room tone, during principal photography the production sound mixer should capture any wild sounds that might be used in the editing room. These sounds include the pounding surf, frogs, wind in the trees, and any distinctive ambient sounds that are unique to a specific location.

Sounds Manufactured Live on Location. The production sound mixer sometimes records live sounds that accompany a shot—that is, sounds that happen within the frame, such as footsteps or door slams. The editor cuts them in later.

Wild Sounds Recorded After Principal Photography. The sound effects editor must sometimes record certain effects that are not available in a library and were not recorded on the set. This task involves going out into the field with a flash recorder and picking up or creating unique sounds and aural effects. For example, the sound effects editor might need the sound of a broken lawnmower on a hot summer's day or the rumble of an old pickup truck.

Prerecorded Effects from Sound Effects Libraries. Many sound effects are available on CD. They offer a wide range of backgrounds and specific sounds such as birds, crickets, traffic, gunshots, tire squeals, or car noises.

Electronically Manufactured Sound Effects. Some sound effects can be manufactured on a synthesizer. Various live sounds can be recorded and then layered electronically one on top of another to create interesting and unique effects.

Online Sound Libraries. There are many web sites dedicated to sound effects and music. Many offer royalty-free effects and music. Sounddogs.com and sonomic.com are two of the largest online sound effects libraries on the Internet. Soundsonline.com is a source for professional copyright-cleared, royalty-free sounds in the industry offering more than 1,000 virtual instruments and sound libraries to choose from. Soundrangers.com was created to fulfill the sonic needs of a new technological generation. It specializes in generating state-of-the-art, royalty-free sound effects and music for such high-tech platforms as virtual user interfaces, games, online and CD-ROM entertainment, web sites, and communication devices. SoundFX.com distributes the Sound Effects Libraries, Music Libraries, and Pro-Audio Software worldwide.

Effects Manufactured in a Studio (Foley Effects). Sounds that must sync up precisely with the picture can be created on a Foley stage. This includes all types of body movement, such as footsteps, or eating sounds. The specialists who perform these sounds are called Foley artists. The term comes from Jack Foley, the sound editor who pioneered this process.

> I didn't go into the ADR studio at all. I didn't rerecord any of the dialogue. It was all there. The only material I had to add was some of the smaller sounds, which I Foleyed myself.
>
> Adam Davidson

A Foley stage has many different kinds of floor surfaces that characters might walk on in the course of a scene, such as cement, hardwood, sand, and earth. It also includes an oddball selection of hand props and tools that can be used to create a wide range of noises. On a Foley stage, you might find wind machines, buzzers, door latches, various kinds of bells, drinking glasses, nuts and bolts, mallets, and so forth.

	01:00:00:00	01:00:30:00	01:01:00:00	01:01:30:00	01:02:00:00
FOOTSTEPS 1	FS Concrete Boots Joe	FS Grass Boots Joe	FS Hard Wood Floor High Heels Stacy		
FOOTSTEPS 2	FS Concrete Shoes Fred	FS Grass Shoes Fred			
FOOTSTEPS 3	FS Concrete Shoes Pat	FS Grass Shoes Pat			
SPECIFIC FX 1	Backpack handling Joe		Sit down Wood Chair Stacy		
SPECIFIC FX 2	Flashlight out & handling Joe		Book down wood table Stacy		
SPECIFIC FX 3	Tree branch hit on metal Fred		Wine glass grab off table Stacy		
SPECIFIC FX 4				Wine bottle grab & down	
RUSTLE	←-- Rustle ---→				

FIGURE 17.3   Sample Foley cue sheet.

The key to this process is that the sounds themselves do not have to be created with the exact objects or movements seen on the screen. All that matters is that the sounds appear to match the visuals. A Foley artist chomping on an apple can imitate the effect of a branch breaking. When shaken, a belt buckle will sound like a horse's bridle (see Figure 17.3 for a sample Foley cue sheet).

Before starting sound work, the student or beginner is urged to visit a Foley stage and watch the process in action. Foley artists are talented mimics. They can watch a person on the screen walk down a hall once and, upon playback, can duplicate perfectly the rhythm and cadence of the actor's unique walk.

However, Foley rooms and Foley artists can be expensive. You can achieve usable results from taping sessions at home while screening a video copy of the project. If the recording is not in perfect sync, some effort in the editing room moving the sounds back and forth should make the material effective.

We knew we were going to have to buy two hours of Foley time. We booked two hours, and that's all we used. We were very specific about what we were going to get. We didn't go after everything. We were going to go after footsteps and that was it, footsteps in the gym. The other Foley effects I did myself—the ones that didn't have to be in sync but could be slugged in. We could slug them into the track and get them into sync ourselves.

A Foley artist, which student films don't normally use, did the actual Foley sounds. In the gym where we filmed, the sound of real footsteps was nonexistent. I wanted all the sneaker squeaks, how they resounded and how they echoed. We didn't hear them at all because of the way the floor was waxed. I thought the footsteps in the gym said something about this place, and I knew I had to re-create them, and a student really can't do that. You can't really cut several thousand footsteps into sync; you don't have time to do that. Those

things had to be done by a Foley artist; they had to be put on 35 full coat and had to stay in sync.

I also had some other ideas. I wanted Truman to have his own specific set of footsteps. I wanted them to have their own character and their own sound. So we got a very old pair of sneakers, put a sponge in them, and filled them with water. The Foley artists walked with wet sloppy sneakers on, and then we modified it so it had these squishy sounds.... All of his footsteps sounded like that.

We spent the last two weeks of our five-week postproduction schedule putting effect sounds into place—adding the arrow sounds, adding the rope breaking (which was really the sound of a whip slowed way, way down), doing the Foley, bringing in my own Foley effects, taking sound effects off the CDs, and putting it all together.

Howard McCain

Unique or Enhanced Sounds

For some reason, you might need to create an unusual sound for your picture. You might need to manufacture or invent something new. This is what sound designers are paid to do. If you are doing the sound on your own, look for ways to fabricate strange and interesting sounds from simple ideas. Natural sounds can be altered to resemble something completely different. The amplified and distorted sound of a person breathing can be terrifying, for example. Sounds can also be layered to create effects that are more interesting than any individual sound.

The editor might also need to go out into the field to record a specialized sound with a digital recording machine. If you are looking for the sound of a revving 1967 Volkswagen Beetle, you might have to find the car and record it yourself. Creating and previewing many of the sounds before locking the picture will ease the crunch during the final postproduction phase.

One takes the storyboards and makes a story real with the sound-track. So you record both actors, animating later the soundtrack frame by frame, so you know exactly which syllable, which letter is sitting on which point in time, frame by frame.

Tatia Rosenthal

Music Tracks

The final major creative element attached to the picture is music. Music has been part of the motion picture experience since the days of silent films, when a piano, organ, or small instrumental group accompanied the actions on the screen. The reason for the music at first may have been pragmatic, to cover up the noise of the projector, but it was discovered that music added considerably to the emotional mood of the film. It also supplied an audible continuity that helped hold together the separate images on the screen.

In the early days of sound on film, music was used only sporadically or not at all because it had to be recorded as part of the scene or played offstage separately (which was why musicals became popular). It was not until 1932 that a sound mixing process was developed that permitted music to be recorded separately from the dialogue, thus allowing it to be edited and added at a later time.

From 1932 to the present, there exists a rich and varied history of film music to explore when looking for musical ideas for your short film. However, we advise that you concentrate your research of the role of music in the short film. If you have been carried away with Maurice Jarre's richly powerful score for *Lawrence of Arabia*, understand that the scope and depth of that score matches that of the film. Your 10- to 20-minute epic will get blown away with anything close to the majesty and power of that music. Listen to music from our short films and to any others.

Source

Music for films can come from a number of sources:

- Preexisting music (you will need the rights)
- Preexisting songs (you will need the rights)
- Rerecording of preexisting music or songs (you will need the rights)
- Original score written for the film (you will own)

Appendix F covers in depth the steps to securing the right to use preexisting songs or music.

Function

There are two basic approaches to using music to support the story in a film: **score** or **source**. Score (or **nondiagetic**) music plays under the action but with no visible or implied source within the frame. It is music that is performed by an unseen orchestra, jazz band, rock group, singers, or even a single player with no logical source in the drama itself.

Source (**diagetic**) or background music emanates from a visible or implied source within the frame, such as a radio, live band, or CD player. Source music is a kind of sound effect, and as with sound effects, the audience doesn't necessarily have to see the source to accept its presence; a radio might be turned on in another room, or a band might be playing in the next apartment. Put simply, source music is music that the people on-screen can hear, whereas underscoring or a score is the music they can't hear but the audience can.

Source music can be chosen from preexisting songs or music or composed specifically for the project. Often, the concept of using source music begins with the screenwriter. The script may indicate that a character is listening to a specific piece or kind of music that may reveal a particular state of mind. If the song is identifiable, the producer needs to license the music rights. The earlier this issue is addressed, the better (see Chapter 1 on scripting with sound in mind).

Although this kind of music comes from a "source" on-screen, it can be used in a variety of subtle and sophisticated ways. Walter Murch expresses the impact of source music in this quote from *The Conversations: Walter Murch and the Art of Editing Film* by Michael Ondaatje:

That is the great power of source music—music that comes within the scene, either because an orchestra is playing and you see the orchestra or because somebody has a radio or record player on. It has a musical effect on the audience, but they are insulated from feeling overtly manipulated musically because the sounds are explained by the scene. It seems almost accidental: Oh! This music just happened to be playing while they were filming the scene; it isn't read as having anything to do with the subtext of the film. Of course, it does. But your conscious impression is that it doesn't. Sound effects work very much the same way.

Walter Murch

In Alfred Hitchcock's film, *Rear Window* (1954) there is no traditional underscore. All the music we hear under the action comes from the individual apartments in Jimmy Stewart's character's courtyard; especially prominent is music from a composer who lives directly across from him. The impact of this "source" music (although written specifically for the film) is stronger than a traditional score because it feels organic, not imposed in the way that an underscore does. Yet it still affects us emotionally because each music "cue" was chosen deliberately to serve the story.

Impact

The impact of music on your project cannot be underestimated. Music comments on, defines, or suggests the way you want your audience to feel about your characters and your story. Music has the power to guide the audience emotionally and intellectually through the narrative. The reason is that music can work on both the intellect and the heart. Emotionally, nothing sets the mood more efficiently. It touches the audience on a gut, immediate level. We hear a sad song, and it makes us sad and reflective. We hear an upbeat tune and our mood changes immediately. Intellectually, it works in subtle and not so subtle ways as it alters and enhances our perception of visuals. Music can be used to play against the action on the screen. The use of Samuel Barber's "Adagio for Strings" in the Oliver Stone film *Platoon* is an example of this.

A well-chosen and well-placed melody can take your piece to a higher emotional level. On the other hand, inappropriate or excessive music can overwhelm the delicate fabric of your story.

Music has the ability to

- Trigger emotional responses from the audience.
- Serve as the connective tissue of the film by smoothing over otherwise abrupt changes between shots and scenes.
- Drive a sequence, instilling it with energy and purpose.
- Complement or underscore the drama on the screen, either by enhancement or counterpoint.
- Strengthen a character's presence through theme. If viewers can identify a character's theme, music can place the character in a scene without his presence.
- Transport the audience to another time and place. A single instrument can be associated with an entire culture. When we hear bagpipes, we think of Scotland. The music of any time period has the power to carry us back in time immediately.
- Create an emotional expectation of what the story is all about. Wistful music denotes a sad or melancholy piece. A light and bubbly melody over the same footage sets up the audience for an entirely different story.

To get an understanding of this power, try this experiment. Screen a montage sequence from a well-known film that already has music on it. Then find a piece of music with a very different mood or feel. If the original piece of music is light and airy, choose a piece that is suspenseful or dark. Play the sequence again, substituting the new piece of music for the original soundtrack. You will discover that music has the power to alter completely how we perceive a series of images. Respect the power of music when choosing a selection for your short piece.

> Despite music's strong influence on the film and video experience, the composer is one of the last creative voices to become involved in a picture. It is very unusual for the composer to be called in at the script stage. I often go to see films that use really bombastic film music, and I'm completely distracted by it. I'm offended as a viewer when the music tells me what to feel. It usually indicates a failure of the footage to do its job. I frankly think fiction film is more guilty of this than documentary, although every once in a while you see it happening in a documentary, where music will underscore an interviewer's words. I'm much more into a minimalist approach.
>
> Jan Krawitz

The Music Team

A complete music team consists of the following individuals:

- **Composer.** The composer is responsible for writing the original score. He might also arrange, orchestrate, and conduct the music as well as perform it on a synthesizer.
- **Arranger/Orchestrator.** The arranger adapts a piece of previously written music or the composer's basic musical ideas for the score and arranges it for the orchestrator, who creates parts and assigns them to various instruments.
- **Copyist.** The copyist extracts the parts for the individual instruments from the score for use by the musicians and the conductor.
- **Music Supervisor/Producer.** This person, a representative of the studio or production company, is responsible for overseeing the business, practical, and creative aspects of scoring the film or video.
- **Music Editor.** The music editor handles all the details regarding synchronization of the score with the picture.
- **Music Contractor.** The music contractor hires musicians, books the studio, and coordinates all business and financial activities for the recording sessions.
- **Musicians.** Musicians perform their parts during the recording of the score. The number of players required depends on the nature of the arrangement.
- **Conductor.** The conductor interprets the score and directs the orchestra to play on cue. It is not unusual for the composer to also conduct, especially on indie and student films.
- **Mixing Engineer.** The mixing engineer is responsible for mixing the various musical sounds into the recorded composite version.

The Original Score

Music for a picture can come from two sources. It might be either an original score written and orchestrated specifically for your project or prerecorded existing music. It is just as common (arguably more) to rerecord existing music.

Finding the right composer for your project is important. Your goal is to find someone who is sensitive to your story. Not all composers are right for all pictures. Some directors work with young composers who are interested in building their reels and gaining valuable experience. They need you as much as you need them. When working with a composer, you should provide him with a DVD of your fine cut. Increasingly, composers are getting cuts of the film by logging onto secured web sites. The composer will use the cuts to develop musical ideas.

Finding a Composer

Finding a composer for a short project is much easier than you may imagine. Composers who want to make the move into the film and video market are eager for experience and are willing to work either free or for very little. As for all crew positions, you must advertise and ask around. If you see a short film with an impressive musical score, get in touch with the producer and director. Ask about their experience working with the composer. Then contact the composer and ask to hear more of his work. (At the end of this chapter, film composer Gavin Keese talks about working on student films.)

You might want to let the composer hear the temp music you have cut to the picture. The risk of this method is that the composer might try to duplicate the temp music rather than come up with new musical ideas. The other method is to let the composer come up with his own ideas in response to the material. Give the composer the space to be inspired by the material.

There are several advantages in using a temp score when developing a relationship with a composer. It can give the composer insight into the director's musical ideas and serve as a point of departure from which the two can discuss musical ideas for the film or video. The danger of a temp score is that the director might fall in love with music the composer cannot top and that is unavailable because it is too expensive.

> We did use temp music primarily to figure out what moments could be sustained with score, but I did not want to show my composer the temp music, because I did not want him to do sound-alike cues.
>
> James Darling

Music Spotting

Once you have settled on a composer, you can begin spotting the picture in earnest. With the composer, review the entire picture, scene by scene, to discuss the *music cues*— that is, the moments that are appropriate for music.

Speaking the language of music can be frustrating if you aren't musically literate. In the absence of a temp track, you can give the composer an idea of what you are striving for by playing themes, instrumental pieces, and tempos you think are appropriate and talking about different genres of music.

The composer can help bridge this potential communication gap by bringing in selected music cues to play against the picture. This will help the composer get a clearer understanding of what the director wants. Yet what might be right for the composer might be wrong for the director or producer.

When you spot the picture with the composer, make sure to point out any possible conflicts. The addition of music will greatly enhance the film experience, but so will the sound effects. If there is dialogue or a specific effect you want the audience to hear, don't let it fight with the score. Have the composer keep the music gentle or use no music at all during that section of the film.

One way to approach the spotting session is to let the composer go off with a video copy of your piece and spot it without your feedback. Allow the composer the freedom to respond to the material alone.

The Music Editor

After the director and composer agree on where music should be placed and on a musical style that is appropriate for the piece, the composer has two challenges:

- To write music that enhances "story" effectively
- To make the music fit precisely into exact music cues

It has traditionally been the music editor's role to break down each music cue into a series of beats by employing "click tracks." A click track is a synchronous metronome that is locked to the picture. It allows the composer to write a melody or musical riff that will stay in sync with the picture. The beats can be altered to satisfy any rhythmic changes, from slow and easy to fast and frantic. The important thing is for the composer to create a piece of music that can later be laid perfectly against the picture. (On low-budget and student films, the composer will also serve as the music editor.)

Computer programs calculate absolute times, allowing the composer to work at home. It is now customary for film and video composers to work with the **Musical Instrument Digital Interface (MIDI)** standard. With a MIDI-compatible synthesizer, contemporary composers can create an entire score in the privacy of their home or studio.

In the traditional method of composing for film, the composer writes the score, an orchestrator arranges the score for instruments, the copyist copies the different parts, and the composer-conductor scores the picture in a large scoring stage with the picture running.

This method is still sometimes used, but more and more composers prefer to work on a score in a layered fashion with synthesizers and a video copy of the picture. The video has SMPTE timecode burned in, showing the exact footage and times. When the composer works with a synthesizer, the director can preview the composer's work in progress in a more complete form than with the traditional method, in which the composer could only play themes on a piano.

Working with a Composer

A good working relationship with the composer is an important part of getting the best score for your project. It might be necessary to preview musical ideas from time to time to see whether the composer is on the right track. Do not let the composer complete an entire score without having heard at least his general approach. Scoring a picture can be an emotionally draining experience for both the director and the composer because so much is expected of music and so much depends on how it works. Allow the composer the time and space to work at his own pace.

Finding a language to communicate with the composer is imperative. Even musically inclined people must find some way of expressing their ideas about the score to the composer. Here are several methods to help you steer the composer in the right direction:

- Tell the composer how you want the audience to feel. It is possible to work through the film, scene by scene, talking in emotional terms.
- Communicate with the composer in terms of drama. What is the film about? What is the overriding theme, the message the director wants to communicate, and how does that play out scene by scene?
- Play existing music that appeals to you. The temp music you played with the picture for screening purposes will give the composer an idea of your musical designs.
- Explain to the composer the emotional values you are interested in expressing through the music. Is it a sad scene requiring sad music, or would you prefer the counterpoint of a calliope or banjo?
- Identify specific instruments and themes for characters. Listen to *Peter and the Wolf*, which was designed with a different instrument for each character. In many scores, the main character is identified by a theme played on a specific instrument.
- Study the work of the great film composers. Watch how they work their musical themes against the picture.
- Look for places where music can also be an effect. If a glass falls and breaks on camera, do you want the sound of a breaking glass or perhaps a cymbal crash?

After the score has been completed and the music cues are ready to be cut into the film, there is a time of fine adjustment. A cue might have to be edited slightly or shifted to fit the exact requirements of the film. The only other change that can be made is to drop cues from the film during the mix. This is often done because directors usually ask in the spotting session for more music than required. The extra music allows some flexibility in the mix. It is better to have too much than too little. By the time you are involved in the mix, it is too late to ask for new music.

My composer was actually a former roommate who had done the score to my last film. His name is Eric Desedario. By the time we were doing this film, he had actually moved to L.A. The Internet was an invaluable tool to facilitate our collaboration. I could send him a cut and he could send me back an MP3 that I could sync it up. The *Full Metal Jacket* score was a big influence. We shared albums and movie scores and talked about them, but I did not want him to be thinking about any specific beat or melody.

We tried to approach the score in a similar way to the film, the militaristic drumbeat. The big dramatic moment was when he is walking down the hallway at the end. Everything is kind of building towards that cue, hopefully when the audience is putting the pieces together. That was the first thing that was written, and then the rest of the score was elements of the final theme played earlier in ways even more subtle than I could detect. That final score, the melody and the percussive elements are playing quietly throughout the rest of the movie. It was military marches but also cues that reflect the internal life of the character, because he is not saying a lot.

James Darling

Preexisting Music

Preexisting music has some advantages. The audience knows the music or is familiar with it. Popular songs and music can make your piece accessible. To say that using preexisting music is less expensive than working with a composer is not always true. Of course, a piece of music that is in the public domain costs you nothing.

However, don't fall in love with a Sinatra ballad or a Beatles tune, because the price tag for popular and current music is probably out of your price range. If you must use preexisting music, try to obtain music from a group that is not very well known and might relish the opportunity to have its work showcased in your project. (See Appendix F for more information on music rights.)

A special type of preexisting music is *canned music*, which is created to be sold and used in bits and pieces. This generic music can be purchased from a music stock house or from sound effects records. At a stock house, you buy a piece of music by dropping the needle onto the record (or beginning the tape or CD) and then lifting the needle when you have the amount of music you need. This is referred to as a *needle-drop* (now called *laser-drop*) purchase.

Playback is another form of source music; it is prerecorded music, with or without lyrics, played back on the set during principal photography. The music is used to give dancers a tempo or for singers to lip-sync a song.

The material is played back on the set on a recording device and recorded on a second recording device as a *scratch track*. In the editing room, the original music is used, and the sequence is cut to that track.

STUDENTS

The temptation to flood the screen with music often stems from an insecurity with the material. Some stories require music from end to end ("wall to wall"), whereas others need none at all. You must have the courage to do the right thing for your project.

The Mix

It is during the mix that the total aural experience of your picture is created. The elements of dialogue, sound, and music are recorded and blended together to become a seamless unit. During the mixing procedure, the director and other members of the creative team can make significant artistic decisions about the relative balance between tracks, equalization, the amount of echo, the use of this track or the other, the amount of music to use, and so on.

The success of the mix depends as much on the preparation of the tracks as on the ability of the mixer to blend them together into an organic whole. The prepared tracks represent your major creative decisions. You should have determined the specific sound effects, music, and dialogue you want to use before you walk into the mixing studio. These tracks should not only properly reflect your creative choices, but also meet the highest technical standards to maximize your time with the mixer.

The tracks are divided into narration, dialogue, music, and effects. If any of these elements must be changed later, such as substituting a foreign language track for the English dialogue, it can be done without affecting the other tracks

The director's job during the mix is to inform the mixer about the levels at which the sounds should be recorded in relation to each other. You might have specific ideas about how each scene should sound and how the entire piece should resonate. Communicate these ideas to the mixer, but also listen to her creative input. Don't relegate the mixer to the role of technician. You want to get her best work from her. Listen to what she has to say. At the same time, if you are not happy with what you hear, don't be afraid to ask her to do it again, even if you have to go over one moment many times.

The balance between sound effects and music is an aesthetic choice the director should make in the editing room to avoid too much trial and error during the mix. Most mixers will offer advice about levels, based on their experience.

Many mixing facilities provide written material that gives beginners a thorough explanation regarding how to prepare properly for the mix (see Figure 17.4). This can save embarrassing, time-consuming, and costly delays in what is already an expensive part of the postproduction process.

Beginners should sit in on as many mixes as possible before their session to get a feel for the rhythm and pace. Mixing sessions involve a lot of waiting around. You will, of course, be anxious to start because every minute costs money. However, you must give the mixer time to become familiar with both the picture and the tracks. Remember that you have spent months with your show and know it inside-out. The mixer sees it for the first time that day. She must slowly feel her way through the film, scene by scene.

It's important to note that a well-equipped digital audio workstation can do everything a regular mixing studio can do—but it also holds the potential to create conflict in terms of job assignments. Because the sound editor does not usually perform the task of the mixer, how much processing and volume control (essentially premixing) should be expected of the sound editor? The question of how extensively she should prepare the soundtracks prior to the mix should be discussed in advance with the sound mixer (see Figure 17.5). Ultimately, the decision whether to mix within a workstation or in a traditional film-mixing studio is most likely determined by budgetary concerns. Either way will probably achieve the desired effect, with the skill and talent of the mixer being the main variable.

The producer's main criterion then should be to select a mixing studio that best represents the ideal screening environment for the final product. If it is slated for a home video or television release, mixing in a small studio is fine. If, however, the production is to be theatrically released, it is desirable to mix in a large studio to more closely represent what the production will sound like in a large theater.

When we went into finishing mode during the final mix we used Pro Tools for the soundtracks. At that point we began to then nuance all the sounds even more. Build them up, bring them in, layer them, and bring certain things down, change the levels. I had a dynamite mixer and we just sat there with the board and we just played with everything. Eventually we got to the point where we loved the sound.

Be' Garrett

Different Formats

Today, most films are shown through more than one form of distribution. A project may be shown in theaters, on television, through home video, and possibly in different languages. Distribution technologies include DVD, television (broadcast, satellite, or cable), the Internet, and film prints. The various routes may call for different adjustments during the mix or for different mixes altogether. Make sure you communicate clearly with the mixer in advance.

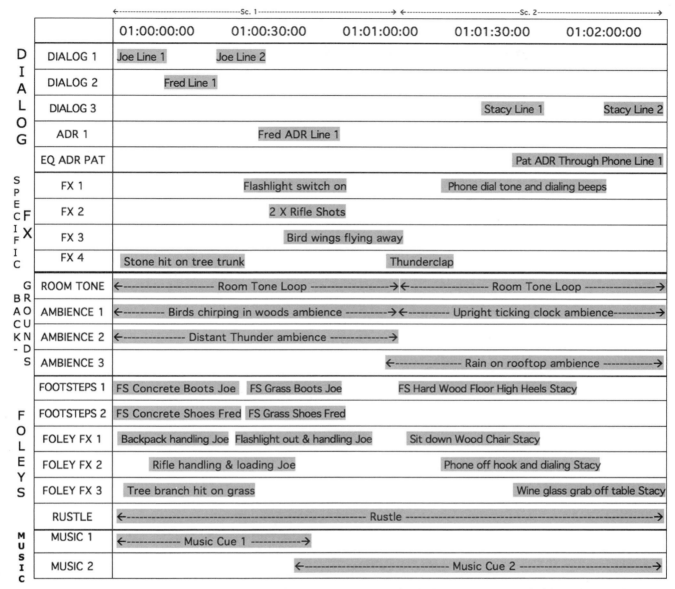

FIGURE 17.4 Sample cue sheet. This mix consists of three dialogue tracks, two ADR, four background sound EFX, six foley and two music tracks. Courtesy of Alex Raspa.

Music Tips for Students and Beginners

In this section, student film composer Gavin Keese describes how to work with a composer to acquire an original score for your student film. Gavin graduated from the USC Film Scoring program, as well as the NYU Music Composition program, where he was the winner of the Composition Award and the Presser Scholarship for Excellence in Music. His credits include the award-winning orchestral score to *Captain Valedor*, a Middle Eastern score for the film *Nasser*, and music for *Giant Steps*, a documentary on Cambodian arts. In 2008, he was awarded the ASCAP Fellowship for Film Scoring and Composition. He has worked with numerous directors on shorts and student films.

An original score can greatly enhance a student film, and if you know where to look, it's easier to find a good composer than you might expect. Many student directors find it difficult because they limit their search to recommendations from friends and colleagues. This can help you ensure your composer is dependable, but if you want a great-sounding score, it's a good idea to cast your net a bit wider.

Continued

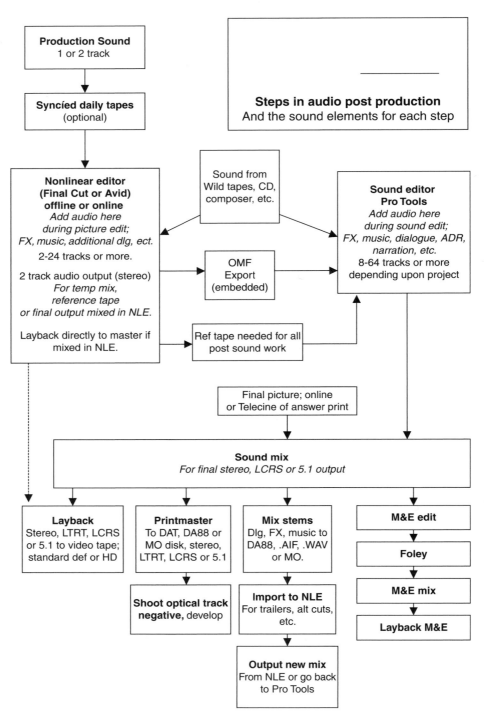

FIGURE 17.5 Sound post flow chart.

One of the best resources for finding composers is the composition departments at music schools, which are usually teeming with people interested in scoring student films. Simply contact the administrative faculty, and they'll often be able to forward your request to their entire composition program. You can also turn up quite a few applicants by posting ads on the music schools' bulletin boards and listservs.

Another great way to meet composers is to attend events related to film music. For example, the major performing rights organizations, ASCAP and BMI, often host film music

Continued

panels and presentations, and typically, most of the attendees are composers interested in scoring student films. It's also quite easy to find composers at film festivals. If you hear a score that impresses you, write down the composer's name, and if possible, get their contact info from the director. Most film composers have web sites, and with a simple web search you can quickly find their demos and get in touch.

You can also advertise for composers on web sites such as www.mandy.com and www.craigslist.org. These kinds of ads can draw a large number of responses very easily, but be prepared to weed through a few less-than-serious applicants.

When choosing a composer, consider not only his skills at writing music, but also his sense of drama. A good film composer should have a great understanding of the relationship between music and film, and he should be skilled at choosing what to write for a given scene. To get an idea of your applicant's dramatic abilities, take a look at his previous scores, and ask him what kind of approaches he could bring to your film.

You should also consider your composer's attitude. Does he show enthusiasm for the project? Does he arrive early to meetings and listen carefully to your ideas? A composer with a great attitude can be much more rewarding to work with than someone who writes great music but doesn't take your film seriously.

Composers writing music for student films will seldom have an extensive list of credits, so don't worry too much about finding a composer that has previously scored in the exact style you want for your film. It often pays to take a small leap of faith and collaborate with a good composer who is scoring in that style for the first time. Film composers tend to be more versatile than people realize.

CONTRACTS

Many filmmakers don't bother with contracts on student films, but they are actually quite useful, even when working with friends. Contracts ensure that everyone is on the same page, and they can be enormously helpful in keeping the project on schedule. A simple one to two page agreement will suffice. Here are the main items to include:

- Services of the composer
- Budget and composer's compensation
- Timetable for the scoring process, including deadlines for:
  1) Delivery of the final cut to the composer
  2) Recording date (if live musicians are used)
  3) Completion of the score
- Composer's Screen Credit
- Ownership of the music

People typically find the last item the most confusing, because the ownership of the music is often treated differently in student productions than in major feature films. On projects with low-to-no budgets, composers will rarely do "work-for-hire". Instead, short scores are usually "licensed", meaning the composer retains ownership of the music. The filmmakers pay for the specific use of the music in their film,

and typically only in non-profit settings, such as film festivals and nonprofit Internet exhibition.

Since most short films are low budget and are not distributed commercially, the license agreement is usually advantageous; composers will customarily charge far more for work-for-hire. However, if you anticipate possible commercial distribution for your film, it is advisable to include a provision for this in the composer's contract. This could be either a percentage of revenue or a flat fee, allowing for the continued license of the music in the event of commercial distribution. Alternatively, if you have the budget for it, you could negotiate a work-for-hire arrangement from the beginning. This would give you ownership of the music, and you could distribute the score however you wanted, with or without the film.

There is one common variation on the usual guidelines. In some film programs, a student project belongs to the school. These programs will have a standard agreement for original scores, which will typically allow the school to use the score in any setting, profit or non-profit. This essentially gives the school the flexibility of a work-for-hire arrangement, while the composer retains ownership of the music.

Budgets and Spotting

The budgets for student film scores can range from thousands of dollars to zero dollars, depending on the music you're looking for. With today's technology, most composers can create a passable score that will often suffice for a no-budget film. However, when it comes to music production, you get what you pay for. If you are spending money on the production of your film, you should budget for music so that your soundtrack will match the quality of your visuals.

However, the two main components are still the same as in feature films: the production costs and the composer's fee. The primary factor that determines production costs is the number of live musicians. A recording with live players will usually sound far superior to one created entirely from synthesizers and sampled instruments. The expenses for using live musicians quickly add up, though.

In addition to the payments for the musicians themselves, there are the expenses of studio time and recording engineers. Thus, the production costs for a short film score with a few live musicians will often be several hundred dollars, and a score for a large ensemble, like orchestra, can easily cost several thousand. An entirely electronic score, on the other hand, might have no production expenses at all, as it could be produced entirely in a composer's home studio.

This is why temp tracks should be handled with particular care in student projects. Just like in feature films, temp tracks can be very helpful in figuring out what music works with the picture, but student films don't have the million-dollar music budgets of studio features. And if you're temping your film with *Spiderman* and *Star Wars*, but you've only given your composer $300 to produce your score, you will probably be disappointed with the result.

To ensure you can afford the music you're imagining, talk to composers as early as possible, preferably in preproduction. Even if you wait until postproduction to select your

Continued

composer, it is important to find out what kind of music you can afford with various budgets. Every composer's situation is unique, and the production costs will vary depending on the resources he has available. A composer at a top music school could have access to talented student musicians, whereas another might work at a recording studio where he could record the score for free. If you get estimates from composers early on, you can budget accordingly.

It is also a good idea to collaborate with your composer on the temp track. That way, he can help you select music that he is sure could be produced on your budget. Just as important, he will likely have ideas for musical approaches that you may not have considered.

The second part of the music budget is the composer's fee, the actual payment to the composer for creating the score. For a smaller project, you probably will not have to pay anything. Composers primarily score student films to hone their skills and build up a solid demo reel, so their compensation consists of a credit and a copy of the film. And if your film offers an opportunity for a particularly impressive demo piece, even an experienced composer may be willing to work for no fee.

Composers with substantial demo reels, however, have less incentive to work for a credit alone, so they will often charge for their services. A composer's fee for a student film will typically equal 20–40% of the music production costs. . A Composer's Fee for a student film will typically equal 20–40% of the Music Production Costs, though these numbers do vary drastically from one to another.

Even if your composer is willing to work at no cost, it's a good idea to pay something on a larger project, if only $100. It demonstrates that you appreciate your composer's hard work, and it will help keep him engaged and on task. Another great motivator is to offer a percentage of any awards won at festivals. Even if this is unlikely, it is a nice gesture, and your composer will work harder for you if he has a real share in the project. Along the same lines, be sure to promptly send out the DVD and QuickTime of the finished film. This is the true "payment" for the score, and it means a lot to a composer to get it on time.

Composing and Recording

Student filmmakers are often apprehensive about the composing phase, because they feel they are no longer in control of their own work. The film is not out of the director's hands, though. In fact, you will usually get a much better score if you stay engaged throughout the process.

The most important thing a director can do to help create the score is to communicate. The more clearly you can tell the composer what you want to accomplish with each scene, the better chance he will be able to get the music right on the first try. You don't necessarily need to know what you want musically, but it's important to know what you want dramatically. For example, what aspects of the story do you want to emphasize? Do you want the film to be theatrical or naturalistic? How do you want the audience to feel?

Remember that student films are learning experiences. If you're not sure what a scene needs dramatically, don't be afraid to say "I don't know." This kind of honesty is extremely helpful to the composer, because he can then approach the scene with the attitude that it will take more experimentation to find something that works.

Almost every student film score will require some kind of rewrite. On average, about 20% of a score will require a trip back to the drawing board, and about half of the cues will need a minor tweak or two. However, if more than a third of the score is being significantly rewritten, or if a cue still isn't right on the third try, communication between the director and composer has likely broken down somewhere. If this happens, look for a different approach to getting your ideas across.

It's also important to keep your composer up-to-date on the progress of the film. If you fall behind in the editing phase, let your composer know immediately, and at least try to give him a rough cut. There is often a substantial amount of the composing that can be initiated with only rough footage. If your composer is getting started while you are finishing your final cut, the scoring process will not be delayed as significantly.

It generally takes a composer between three to four weeks to completely produce 10 minutes of score for a student film. Larger projects involving many live musicians might take twice as long, whereas very simple scores with no live musicians can often be finished in as little as two weeks. Keep in mind that it is the amount of music that determines the size of the project, not the size of the film. A 10-minute film with wall-to-wall score is a much larger project than a 20-minute film with only a couple minutes' worth of cues.

Because composers of student film scores typically do much more than simply write the score, the actual amount of time spent composing is often less than half of the entire scoring schedule. The rest of the time is spent recording, editing, and mixing. If live musicians are used, a substantial portion of time will be spent preparing mockup cues, recruiting the players, and creating the printed parts for the musicians to read at the session.

Most of today's student film composers assemble and mix their scores on computers, so the most common method of delivering your film to the composer is to convert it to a QuickTime file, or a similar format. The composer records the score, and then delivers the mix to the director as a stereo audio file, typically WAV. The quality of the music files should be at least 16 bit and 48kHz, in case the film airs on TV. It is also important that the director, composer, and sound designer all use the same frame rate, to avoid synchronization problems. (For American film, this is typically 29.97 nondrop.)

Mixing

Mixing is probably the most overlooked aspect of student film soundtracks. Your composer might write the best score since *Braveheart*, but it won't count for much if either the music mix or the final mix is done improperly. Imagine if

Continued

an artist spent months on a painting, then went to the exhibition with a cheap photograph of his work. This is very similar to a filmmaker taking his film to festivals with a poor mix.

If you plan on exhibiting your work, you should hire a qualified mixing engineer to handle your final mix. Many film composers are also experienced with sound design and mixing, so they can sometimes handle not only the music mix, but the final mix as well. If not, there are many talented recording and mixing engineers who are willing to work for very reasonable rates in order to get their foot in the door. They travel in the same circles as film composers, so if your composer doesn't already have regular collaborators, they can probably turn someone up for you.

Even as a student director, your possibilities for original music are vast. Take the time to get your score done right, and your film will sound nothing less than professional.

PRODUCER

Supervising Postproduction

The producer keeps on top of all expenses incurred during the postproduction period. He sees that everyone adheres to the budget and that all additional expenses can be covered with the money that is left. However, films do go over budget, and what usually suffers is postproduction. Sometimes, all work on a project is suspended until further money is raised. This is not an uncommon situation for students and beginners.

There is a general rule to keep in mind when striving to keep your project on budget: it is the "Good," "Fast," or "Cheap" scenario. You can have only two out of the three.

● The work performed can be good and cheap, but it won't be fast.
● It can be good and fast, but it certainly won't be cheap.

For example, mixers will cut deals with beginners or student projects, but the work will mostly be done at night and over time. It will be good, inexpensive, but not quick. Projects go over budget for several reasons:

Unexpected Production Expenses. This predicament is common but unavoidable, even for professional productions. Expenses that arise in the "heat" of principal photography must be covered if production is to be completed. You shoot more stock than anticipated or spend more on art direction, food, or transportation. With beginners especially, the original budget might not have been realistic. It is easy to say that you can "take it out of post" because postproduction seems to be a long way off when you are in a distant location and your van has broken down. With the entire cast and crew on payroll, spending the extra money to get a scene right seems justified.

Unexpected Reshoot Expenses. Additional filming might be needed if the production unit did not shoot all the planned coverage or if it becomes evident after extensive editing that there must be more shots to tell the story properly. This expense usually comes out of the budget contingency unless, along with other overages, the contingency has already been exhausted.

Hidden Postproduction Costs. Beware of the hidden costs that surface during postproduction. These costs often cannot be predicted because so much of postproduction is trial and error. For example, different pieces of music might be tested against the picture during cutting. The original music is transferred each time the director wants to preview the music or cut it to the picture. This requires labor hours and transfer time, which costs money.

Extended Postproduction Period. It is not uncommon for the student or beginner to run beyond the planned postproduction schedule. There is no way to know definitively how long it will take, and many variables can influence the creative process. (Some of these issues are discussed in Chapter 16.) Students might have limited access to their program's facilities, and independents on a limited budget might be able to edit only during the evenings because of job conflicts.

The following situations are equally difficult to predict:

● The editor needs to use the same shot twice during the film and thus has to make a new negative (if finishing on film).
● The director decides she wants some unusual CGI effects.

Or not even "unusual":

● The mix goes over the schedule.
● The lab has problems printing an acceptable answer print of the film, and there are a number of passes before the lab gets it right.

These are just some of the situations that will cost money that might occur in the course of postproduction. However, all these extra expenses spring from the desire to make the best film or video possible.

Howard McCain designed the end of *Truman* around an optical effect called an *iris* (look ahead to Figure 18.3). As Truman is suspended over the class holding onto the rope, the image closes in on him, or irises, until all we see is Truman before fading completely to black. This effect isolates Truman at the end of the film. It is an effective use of the optical but was more expensive than a simple fade to black.

The following is a partial list of postproduction items to look out for (many are not very costly by themselves but will add up over the long run):

- Screenings
- Scratch or temp mixes
- CGI effects
- Online color correction
- Academy leader
- Elaborate title sequences
- Transfer time
- Reprints
- Transfer to video

All these additional expenses can hold up the postproduction process. Once the budget has been depleted, you might have to stop work at whatever stage you have reached. Perhaps you were ready to mix, cut negative, or online your show. You must now look for more financing to complete the picture. When raising money at this juncture, you have an advantage that you lacked in the early fundraising stage. You now have a picture. Having something concrete to show will help you attract potential investors who perhaps were not interested in your project at the idea stage.

...And Distributors

You can now organize fundraising screenings of the work in progress. Keep in mind that for these screenings, the film should sound as polished as possible. Most audiences are not used to hearing an incomplete soundtrack. You might need to add a few effects and music and make a temp, or scratch, mix. This rough mix does not reflect what the piece will eventually sound like, but at least it gives the picture a professional feel and covers up the obvious sound gaps. The goal is to have your project in the best possible condition for the screening.

You might find other opportunities for additional funds, such as postproduction grants or finishing funds, now that you have something tangible to show. Look into local, national, and university grants. Many film and television programs make funds available on a competitive basis for students with projects in the postproduction stage.

The Moral

When the process is all over, make sure that you benefit from the lessons you've learned about the real costs of postproduction so you can be better prepared the next time. Your subsequent postproduction budgets should reflect the insight and experience of your previous project. Keep extensive records and receipts to document what happened on the entire shoot, and keep an accurate time log of the postproduction period so you will have a clearer idea of what has to happen, and when, the next time around.

KEY POINTS

- Sound design involves dialogue, effects, and music, with dialogue being the most important element.
- Effects can be in sync, ambient, or "Foleyed."
- Once the picture is locked, spot it for effects and music cues. The footage marks for these cues should never change.
- Take the time to develop a communication link with the composer. Consider how you can best express your ideas to the composer.

Chapter 18

Finishing/Online/Laboratory

I don't think people should overlook the credit sequence. From the time the film starts I wanted to get you "locked in." If you are making a certain kind of film like a thriller, make sure your titles have some sort of feel or something that gets you set. It could be subtle, but it gets you set for what you are about to do. A director is responsible for everything from the opening to the close. You are telling a story so I want to control your experience from the time you watch it to the time you finish.

Be' Garrett

DIRECTOR

The Finished Look

The picture is locked, the soundtrack has been mixed, and your film is ready to be finished. What remains to be done is to create a professional and individualized look to your film. This involves **color correction**. Color correction is the process of fine-tuning the tonalities and exposures in each scene for balance and consistency and to polish the final visual impression of the film. This process ensures that color and brightness values are consistent from shot to shot and scene to scene and that color temperature and exposure problems are smoothed over. A unified color scheme provides your film with a visual mood that complements and enhances your vision for the material.

In the traditional film postproduction workflow, color correction is called *timing* the film, and it is performed in a film laboratory by the **timer** (described later in chapter). All the visual effects or "opticals" are also either designed or created in the lab or in a separate optical house. All these functions can now be handled by one person on a computer editing with Avid, Final Cut, or any number of software programs.

The Choices

If you are shooting and finishing on video, the lab plays no part in your workflow. If you are shooting on film and finishing digitally, your involvement with the lab extends to developing your negative and providing you with video dailies. However, if you are shooting on film and want to match back to film, you must establish a relationship with the lab early in the process.

The path you choose will be dictated by decisions made in preproduction (acquisition format) and where your film is destined to end up (distribution). Is your film headed straight for the Internet or the festival route? Have you explored distribution possibilities? Are you looking to sell your film online?

This first part of this chapter will cover the traditional film and video workflow and innovations in that area. Many feature films are still shot on film and released on film. However, there has been a technological revolution in the mastering process. Spectacular visual effects can now be incorporated into the final print as a result of a relatively new method of mastering, the Digital Intermediate. In simplest terms, the Digital Intermediate process, or DI, is the conversion of film to digital bits and then back to film again. This new process bypasses the traditional step of cutting the negative. To appreciate and understand what it is and does, we will describe the traditional steps before DI and then after DI.

This chapter is organized to describe

- Film workflow
- The role of the film lab
- Traditional online video
- Tape-to-film transfer
- The Digital Intermediate (DI)
- NLE finishing

Film Workflow

You have shot on film, edited digitally, and will either finish with a film or digital copy. The success of your film depends in part on the lab work. The lab is responsible for taking care of your original negative and creating a final product that represents the best your film can be. A laboratory representative should be assigned to your project from the beginning to establish a timeline and workflow schedule. It is proper and professional to meet the lab representative in person to become acquainted.

During the production and postproduction process, direct any questions, problems, or concerns to this individual. Visit the lab and ask to be taken around to see the facilities. Remember that representatives talk to hundreds of people a day on the phone. By being more than just another voice, you will be certain to get better results.

doi: 10.1016/B978-0-240-81174-1.00025-7

Treat the relationship you develop with the lab as the beginning of a long, fruitful partnership that will carry you through many films. If you are a student or beginner and plan to continue making films, the lab will hope to keep you as a customer, especially with so many filmmakers turning to digital video.

> Since I shot *Crazy Glue* pretty much on a one to one, editing was somewhat easy. Once I got the film out of the camera, I took it to Duart and got a one light work print. The lab was helpful every step of the process.
>
> Tatia Rosenthal

The laboratory is involved in the following steps in the filmmaking process:

- During principal photography, the laboratory develops and processes your film. The lab provides you with a digital video dailies (which can be posted online), which is what the editor digitizes for cutting. The negative is kept for you in a vault at the laboratory.
- While the sound is being designed, the laboratory develops your titles and opticals.
- After the soundtrack has been mixed, the laboratory can arrange for your negative to be cut (including the titles and opticals) and matched to your edit decision list (EDL).
- During the sound mix, the director, director of photography (DP), or both color-correct, or *time*, the film with the timer at the lab.
- Once the mix is completed, the mix is shot onto an optical track, and the laboratory marries the printed film to the soundtrack.
- During the printing of the A and B rolls of 16mm negative, the laboratory can perform simple fades and dissolves if you request.
- Cutting a 35mm negative follows a different path (see below).
- The lab then strikes your first answer print.

Opticals

Optical effects, which include everything from simple transitions like fades and dissolves to elaborate CGI sequences, are created either at an effects house (in film or video) or on the computer in your edit suite. Computer-generated images can easily be married to your digital output if the final destination is digital video projection, television, or the Internet. If you plan to output back to film, opticals and effects can be shot on film or generated by computer and then transferred to film. Labs offer digital video-to-film transfers.

The process of creating opticals for 16mm is different than for 35mm. All 35mm optical effects must be designed and shot beforehand at a special effects house and developed at the lab. This process involves making a new negative. The nature of 16mm negative cutting allows the laboratory to create dissolves and fades during the printing process itself. (See the next section for information on A and B rolls.)

An important technical consideration is having enough film on either side of the dissolve so that the two shots can cross-fade with each other. Spend some time talking with the negative cutter before designing any film opticals.

Any opticals other than simple fades and dissolves must be shot by a company that specializes in visual optical effects. (The lab you are using might have its own optical division.) This is a time-consuming and costly process that sometimes requires trial and error. The optical house might not achieve the results you want the first time around. For example, the image that you want "blown up" is shot, and the new negative is sent to the lab to be developed and printed. You preview a work print of the new optical to be used in the film, but it doesn't work. It must then be shot and developed again, costing yet more money.

> I wanted a crawl at the end and I wanted an iris effect, so I knew there was going to be an optical in both cases. To get those, you have to shop around, just like for a caterer or for anything else. Again, by looking at other students' work, you can tell which work you like and which work you don't.
>
> Howard McCain

Following are some of the opticals that require a **wedge test** and must be run separately from the final printing: this is a test in which the elements of the optical (lap dissolves, superimposition, mattes) are photographed with one frame of each f-stop. When the test film is developed, the laboratory can identify the exact exposure reading that will produce the best effect:

Superimposition. Superimposition is placing two or more images over one another.

Lap Dissolve. Especially long dissolves, usually more than 96 frames, are referred to as lap (as in overlap) dissolves.

Step Printing. The film can be slowed down or sped up by printing more or fewer frames than exist on the negative.

Blowup. An image can be enlarged to eliminate a boom pole or other unwanted element in the frame. Blowups are a last resort for solving an image problem because when you reprint a shot, the grain on the film gets larger and thus creates a mismatch to the grain size of the shots before and after the blowup.

Titles. You might want to superimpose your main or end titles over images from the picture or create some special visual effect with your main title.

End Credits. You might want the credits to scroll up or "crawl" continuously over black or over images for the end credits. Often, preceding the head credits is an FBI disclaimer like the one put on *Truman* (see Figure 18.1). Figure 18.2 shows a title card for the tag to *The Lunch Date*. Note the fancy font that accents the timeless, storybook quality of the story.

Reprints. If you need to duplicate a scene several times in the picture but have only one take of it, you will need a duplicate negative, or *dupe*, created from the original negative of the scene.

Special Visual Transitions. Wipes and irises are examples of special visual transitions (see Figure 18.3). Optical work is expensive. If you have your heart set on a special visual effect, it is best to find out what it will cost before editing a sequence around it. This applies also to fancy title sequences. Laboratories execute opticals either on film or as computer effects to be transferred to film.

Some of the other visual effects handled by the lab are image stabilization, film restoration, freeze frames, repositioning, image removal, motion tracking, rotoscoping, scratch and dirt removal, slow motion/fast motion, reversing angle, reversing action, blowups to 35mm from 16mm and Super 16mm.

Cutting the Negative

After the mix, when the filmmaker is positive there will be no more changes in the picture, the editor sends an EDL to the negative cutter to have it cut, spliced, and prepared for

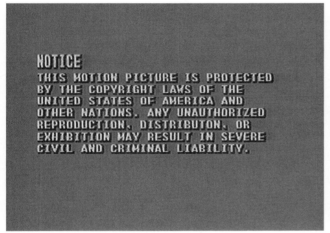

FIGURE 18.1 Disclaimer from *Truman*.

FIGURE 18.2 End credit from *The Lunch Date*.

FIGURE 18.3 *Truman* ends with an optical: an iris-out.

printing. Negative cutting, also known as **negative matching** or **negative conforming**, is the process of cutting a motion picture negative to match precisely the final cut of the film. The director or editor can set up a clean room in which to cut the negative, but this is a somewhat tedious and critical part of the postproduction process. A mistake here could lead to disaster. A negative that is not cut or spliced properly could break apart in the printing process, permanently damaging part of your film.

The processes for cutting 16mm and 35mm negatives are fundamentally different. Cutting the original negative in 16mm and 35mm requires that a part of the emulsion of one frame be scraped off and laid on top of the next frame. These are glued together and sealed with a heated splicer, creating a *hot splice*. The heat enables the splice to seal properly. Scraping off a frame of 16mm film exposes part of the frame line, which will then print through as a white line. Because of the density of 35mm film, frame lines are not a problem.

To avoid having this visible splice, you never cut the original 16mm negative with another piece of original negative. Instead, you cut a shot to a piece of black leader (the A roll) and attach the next shot to a second roll (the B roll). The use of two separate rolls creates a checkerboard pattern called *A and B rolls*. This prevents one piece of original negative from being cut with another and makes it possible for the lab to print fades and dissolves (see Figure 18.4).

If you plan to shoot film, edit digitally, and match back to film, make sure that your material is prepared for the particular lab and negative cutter you are using. Knowing that you will be matching back to film will impact how the lab will set up your material for video transfer for digitizing. This process is complex, and there are different approaches to executing the match back. The frame discrepancy between film and video needs to be addressed, as well as how the video dailies are prepared. You need to be absolutely clear about your options.

FIGURE 18.4 A and B rolls. (Used with permission from the American Society of Cinematographers.)

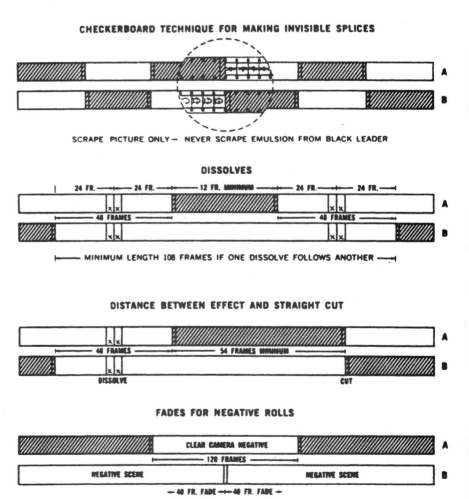

Some labs and negative cutters offer pamphlets with a list of recommended procedures. World Cinevision Film Services, Inc. (New York City; Contact: Stan Sztaba, Phone: 212-265-4587) and Northeast Negative Matchers (800-370-CUTS; www.nenm.com) are specialists in working with Avid Media Composers and offer their own proprietary "Video Matchback Checklist."

> You've got to be very, very careful when cutting the negative; most students aren't that careful, not even with their own material. Everybody I know hired a negative cutter. To find a negative cutter, you call other students, see who they use, and find a good price. Prices do vary greatly, anywhere from $4 a cut to $1.50 a cut; it makes a big difference. There were 198 edits in Truman. That's a lot of cuts for a 10-minute film.
>
> Howard McCain

Film Matchback

When you first transfer your film dailies to video, the telecine generates video timecode that gets recorded on the telecine tapes. The tapes are edited on either a traditional videotape editing system or a nonlinear editing system. You will generate an EDL that lists all your editing decisions according to video timecode. Through the process of *film matchback*, a negative cutter can take that EDL and create a *film cut list*, which tells the cutter how to cut the film negative to match your video edit. The matchback process converts a 30 frames per second video edit to a 24fps negative cut list.

The process is as follows. Prior to the original telecine session, a punch mark is made on each roll of negative as a starting reference (you can find more information on video dailies in Chapter 16). In the telecine session, the film key number and the video timecode at that reference punch are logged. After editing, to find any point on a roll, we relate it back to the reference punch.

To help automate this process, the keycode system was devised. Using keycode, a nonlinear editing system can perform the matchback itself and generate a film cut list. Keycode is a machine-readable version of the key numbers that are exposed along the edge of the film negative. During the initial film-to-video transfer, the telecine machine reads the keycode and can burn in the key numbers on the screen so a human can read them during editing. The telecine can also create a database or log that correlates the key numbers to the video timecode that can be loaded into the nonlinear system. When you are done with your offline edit, the nonlinear editing system crunches these numbers and generates a film cut list, which saves the negative cutter from having to create her own list. Not all nonlinear systems can do matchback.

There are several types of film cut lists. A *pull list* tells the negative cutter which shots to take or pull from each camera roll. A *scene pull list* indicates all shots taken in their entirety from flash frame to flash frame. An *assemble list* shows all the shots in the movie in their final order. A dupe list shows which material needs to be duplicated. An *optical list* is a way to re-create on film those effects created and previewed on video. Many systems will locate effects in an edited sequence and generate a count sheet for an optical house to build the identical effect using film elements. This tool is useful for translating the film.

24/30 Frame Issues

The 24/30 frame discrepancy between film and video is not an issue if you shoot on video, or if you shoot on film and are finishing on video and not matching back to film. It is an issue if you are shooting on 24p. If you are working on a 30fps system and want to match back, be aware that during the matchback process (whether calculated by the nonlinear editing system or by the negative cutter), there will often be discrepancies between the video and the film. Most matchback programs are designed to drop or add a frame at the end of certain shots to keep the overall length and sync relationship between the film video and audio within a frame, plus or minus. Usually you won't notice the error.

To avoid these complications, films shot at 24fps are often edited on a nonlinear system that runs at 24fps, such as the Avid Media Composer. This solution offers a simple one-to-one relationship between the original film frames and the frames displayed on the nonlinear system. It allows you to edit at 24fps and create frame-accurate film cut lists that correlate exactly with the original film negative, with none of the matchback discrepancies caused by converting from 30fps to 24fps.

Timing

At the laboratory, a technician called a **timer** consults with the DP to create visual continuity for the film. This means giving each scene a consistent color and tone as well as giving the whole film a specific look, whether it be cool (tending toward the blues), normal, or warm (tending toward the oranges).

> We took the film to the lab for color correcting and we took the warm lights out, which looked horrible, and then we did a transfer on HD. Se we finished our film in HD sixteen for sixteen nine. Also for four three center cut as well. Understanding that if I ever needed to broadcast in HD I would already have it set for that. In the color correct, I was able to bring out those blues that we shot for the night. It looked like night, but it had crushed blacks and it kind of created the ominous sort of threatening feel to it. Then in the daytime I wanted to create more of a homey kind of engaging feeling where people come together and gather to talk and shoot the breeze.
>
> Be' Garrett

It is not unusual for shots within a scene to be warmer or colder in color or lighter or darker in tone. They might have been shot at a different time of day or with a different batch of film stock. The timer tries to smooth out these inconsistencies in color film. She does this with a Hazeltine machine, which tells the printer how many points the valves should open on each light. There are 50 lights, each representing 1/12th of an f-stop. To complement the film color (cyan, magenta, and yellow), light bulbs—"lights" of green, red, or blue—are required in the final printing of each sequence. Color film is broken down into these three dyes. The balance of these three colors creates accurate skin tones. The timer sets the number of lights per color to make the flesh tones match the character.

The director and DP sit with the timer and make special requests if they want something other than "normal" printing. Suppose, for example, that a sequence was shot so that the dailies are bright and well saturated with color, but the director wants a dark and moody feel to the scene. The timer can instruct the printer to bleed some of the color from the scene and to make it less bright. If the timer has a lot of latitude, she can make some adjustments to the look of a scene. This requires that the negative be well exposed, or dense. There is not much a timer can do with a "thin" negative. The Hazeltine is not a magical instrument.

It is important to note that the timer cannot alter the color balance or flesh tones of only a part of the frame. Every adjustment, however minor, affects the entire image. The director can change the color scheme but must live with how it affects the characters' flesh tones.

Black-and-white film goes through a similar timing process, although the visual concerns are different. The timer works with a grayscale and black-and-white contrast ratios. She strives to smooth out the inconsistencies of lighting, to enrich the blacks, and to create a consistent tone for each scene and for the entire picture.

> I went to get the answer print, and I called up the cinematographer, and we watched it together. I brought him there specifically to make sure they were printing it with enough richness and stuff. We went for a second printing and darkened it a little bit, just in some areas.
>
> Adam Davidson

Color timing can be done when transferring film dailies to digital or tape for use in a nonlinear editing system.

Types of Prints

The first print struck from the negative is a work print (or video, if you choose video dailies). The material is either timed scene by scene to correct for proper flesh tones or developed by one-light, which is an overall timing of one setting for the entire roll. When the negative is cut, you will begin to strike prints for screening purposes. The following sections describe the types of prints the laboratory can provide.

Mute Print

Before the mix is married to the optical track, the laboratory sometimes prepares a mute print. This is a picture-only print from the negative, which the director, editor, and DP can examine for color corrections or optical errors before an answer print is made.

> The timer looked at the work print to get a sense of the film. It was really an odd film to time because the backgrounds had to look completely consistent, so the flesh tones become subordinate to the backgrounds. I'm sure if he had timed every shot according to flesh tones, he would have come up with quite a different timing. But you know, you can't have the gradation of the black-and-white floor changing or the mannequins' flesh tone jumping around from shot to shot.
>
> Jan Krawitz

First Trial

When the optical track is married to the print, the laboratory screens this print, called the *first trial*, for the production team to review for final corrections.

Answer Print

When all the corrections have been made, the next print the laboratory strikes is called the *answer print*. Once the answer print has been approved, additional prints can be struck.

Release Print

The next step depends on the number of prints you will eventually need (a distribution issue). The general rule is that the less you run your original negative (A and B rolls) through the printing process, the better. Too much wear and tear could damage the film or break the splices. Therefore, if you are planning to make more than a couple of release prints, it is best to strike an interpositive (IP) and then an internegative (IN). An *internegative* is a single strand of negative that can be run through the printer many times with no risk (it has no splices).

Digital Copy

You will want DVD copies of your picture for cast and crew members, festivals, promotions, distributors, and so on. The print should be transferred to a master that will serve as your original, and dubs will be made from it. Today, Digibeta is the format of choice for the master. Make sure the sound used in the transfer is from the original mix. The sound quality is superior to the optical track on your print.

Traditional Linear Video Online

The online edit session is the time to rerecord the program at the highest possible quality. Some houses still employ linear or tape-to-tape online suites. These houses like the quality of the larger tape formats and distribute exclusively to television.

After a show is built, the original materials are taken to an online edit room to be completed. Here, all picture and sound elements are conformed to the cut made on the offline master. A new online master is made, and it becomes the final product.

The goal of online editing is to complete the offline decisions with effects, color correction, titles, and audio sweetening. Online rooms, although expensive, provide the director with opportunities for elaborate and exciting opticals and titles.

The edit decision list, made from the offline edit, can be fed into the online computer to tell it where what images and what sounds should be placed on the master tape. Copies can be struck from the master tapes for distribution.

Video-to-Film Transfer

Video-to-film transfers are used to make film negatives or prints from video material. The big-budget features use this technique to convert special effects created in computer graphics workstations back to film. The lower end of this market are the makers of independent or television movies who cannot afford to shoot film (or choose to originate in video for other reasons) but need to make film prints to show in festivals or for theatrical release. Projects originating in film and edited in video can be transferred directly back to film (without returning to the negative) to save time and costs.

For video-to-film transfers, new technologies are developing, the quality is improving, and demand for these transfers is increasing, mostly for the longer projects but for shorts as well. At the same time, video projection is improving rapidly. Many theaters now offer digital projection that bypasses the need for a print.

Systems

Several different systems are available for converting video to film, and they range widely in complexity and cost. At the highest current level are film recorders. These systems use either a cathode ray tube or a laser to record very high resolution images onto 35mm film. Film recorders are very slow, taking several seconds per frame. They are also very expensive; each frame costs several dollars.

The *electron beam recorder (ERB)* uses an electron beam to transfer to three successive film frames, the red, green, and blue information from each video frame. The three film frames are then optically printed with colored filters to create a normal film negative. ERB tape-to-film transfers are done by Four Media Company (4MC) in Burbank, California. The Sony Pictures High Definition Center (SPHDC) uses ERBs with high-definition video technology. Standard-definition videotapes are up-converted to HDTV and put through a line doubler to increase resolution. ERB transfers cost from a few hundred dollars for the complete transfer up to several hundred dollars a minute.

Du Art Lab in New York City uses a video to 35mm process that involves digitizing your video or digital tapes to computer files. For NTSC source material, the lab converts to 24fps with a proprietary algorithmic process that removes frames in a way that limits motion artifacts. Then it "uprezzes" the images to 2K resolution (2048 × 1556 pixels) with interpolation. This algorithmic process analyzes the original pixels and creates new information (other methods just duplicate original pixels.) The lab then records to 35mm Kodak Intermediate Stocks on Arrilaser Film Recorders.

The original video-to-film conversion method is the kinescope. This system uses a high-quality color monitor with a special film camera running at 23.976fps (for NTSC) with a 144° shutter to create a flicker-free image from the video. A kinescope is the most economical transfer method and produces good results.

Most systems cannot transfer to both 16mm and 35mm. You may need to do a blowup or reduction to get the final format you want. A comprehensive list of places that transfer either from NTSC or PAL to film is given on our web site. The DigiEffects web page (digieffect.com/frames/main/html) offers excellent technical advice. Newer systems coming online laser-write the tape to film (see Digital Intermediate in next section).

Because of the variability in the lighting conditions under which your tape was shot and the format you used, it is impossible to predict what will be created from a video-to-film transfer. Tests are crucial to find out what works. Keep these considerations in mind:

- Get the framing right for your release medium. Are you going to 1:66, 1:78, 1:85, or some other aspect ratio? You need to know before you shoot.
- Know that pans and other camera moves may not look the same on film.
- Remember that visual effects that look smooth on a monitor at 29.97fps may not look as good (or may look different) at 24fps.

- Pay attention to audio specifications. It is best to record the audio apart from the video with a flash recorder and then sync it up in postproduction.
- Be sure you know how much the services will cost and what you are paying for. Some facilities will not give you the negative for the quoted prices, only one print.

> Post has changed immensely. It's desktop now, which is fantastic and easy. I think it's good if you're a short filmmaker to have some knowledge of computers and what you can do with them—to have more options.
>
> Tatia Rosenthal

Digital Intermediate

The digital intermediate process is rapidly becoming the standard in the film industry and also an option for student productions wanting to finish on film (see Figure 18.5). The film is transferred to digital video through telecine. A timecode file is made as well as a record of the corresponding keycode on the actual negative (flex file). The show is edited on a nonlinear system, and an EDL is generated.

At this point, instead of going to an online session (if you were finishing on tape, this is what you would do), the negative is scanned again at a high resolution (2k or 4k at 10 bits per color channel) on a machine such as a Spirit DataCine, DaVinci, or Thomson Spirit Data Cine. Only the footage that was used in the edit is scanned, usually with handles of 150 frames on either side of each cut. Some facilities will color grade the film on the scanner before converting it to bits, and some will scan the negative and then color grade.

The director of photography will spend about two weeks with a colorist grading the film and setting the overall final look for the project. From scene-to-scene color consistency to advanced skip bleach looks, in the digital lab a great colorist has the ability to create almost any look imaginable. In most facilities the colorist will use a Pandora Megadef or a Da Vinci 2k color correction console with a film color-calibrated CRT or projector. These advanced consoles give the operator the ability to manipulate everything from basic RGB color control to advanced secondary color correction in specific regions of a frame.

Once completed, the color corrected data are moved onto a powerful workstation for conformation. On the workstation, usually a Discreet Logic Inferno or other real-time 2k workstations, the data are conformed to the edit decision list and compared to the locked offline output for editorial consistency. During this process, things like dust busting, scratch removal, speed changes, transitions, title graphics, and end credits are added. Additionally,

simple effects, wire removal, and boom removal can be performed. If the film includes visual effects or other digital elements, they will be imported into the project while on the workstation. On most projects the conforming and cleanup process takes only a few days.

At this point digital masters are output to tape, and a high-resolution/uncompressed frame sequence is output to a hard drive. This is nicknamed the **digital answer print**.

The movie is then finally laser-recorded to a film print negative stock, with all the effects and color changes intact. It also has the same generational quality of the original camera negative (if not better). Some filmmakers choose to then optically time the film to make sure that the translation of the colors and levels are consistent from the HD environment to the film print. From this negative, prints can be struck and optical or digital sound added. Although expensive, this method allows the director to create more effects and transitions without having to think about optical printing or generation loss.

After conforming and cleanup, the Digital Intermediate process allows for a digital answer print to be created. The digital answer print can be played back in a digital cinema and approved before committing the project to film out. While not yet perfected, the latest digital projectors can give you a very good idea of what the film will look like at the cinema. In addition to the advanced color control advantages of Digital Intermediate, the process also avoids many of the conventional optical printing steps in the film delivery process. Because the original camera negative is scanned and all subsequent processing is done digitally, it is possible to eliminate the interpositive to internegative process altogether. During the film-out process, you can directly create an internegative or interpositive on polyester or acetate base to allow release prints to be reproduced. In the case of mass duplication, several polyester internegatives can be digitally recoded, thus totally eliminating the interpositive step.

Once the digital answer print has been approved, it will be filmed out to meet the requirements for film distribution. The film recording process gives you the ability to select different film stocks with different grain and look characteristics. The output from the film recorder will create a distribution master that will require only one light printing with no further color or printer light changes, greatly simplifying the printing process. The end result is higher quality print in the cinema and a digital master ready to be delivered to any tape or other distribution medium without remastering.

Nonlinear Online Edit

Digital technology and NLE systems have made it possible for student and beginning filmmakers to create a

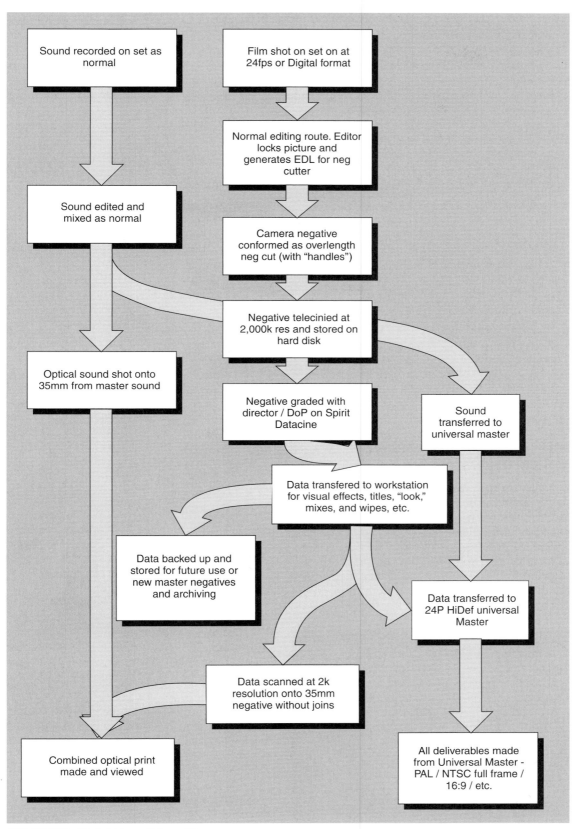

FIGURE 18.5 Digital intermediate workflow.

polished and professional-looking product on one piece of software. You can design and master the title, create a wide assortment of visual effects, and color-correct on Final Cut, Avid, Premiere Suite, as well as other high-quality programs.

These systems can also enable filmmakers to execute complex *digital video effects (DVEs), motion effects,* and hundreds of various *filter* effects. Titles and graphics can be created on the nonlinear system or imported from other software applications and plug-ins (added, standardized software). The use of software such as AfterEffects and Photoshop from Adobe Systems, Inc. (www.adobe.com) has brought about a convergence of TV and computer graphics. Higher-end systems include Combustion, Flame, and Smoke. Complex two- and three-dimensional animation as well as multilayered (composited) images can be created and merged with video. Many types of file formats can be used to import graphics into the nonlinear system, including QuickTime, JPEG, TIFF, and BMP.

For example, Final Cut Pro includes a comprehensive set of real-time color correction tools, including primary and secondary color correctors; image control filters; broadcast-safe filters; tools for matte and key operations, as well as luma and chroma range checking; real-time scopes and monitors; and a frame viewer for comparing your shots.

Animation and CGI: Rendering and Compositing

The final step in CG animation is rendering and compositing. When 3D software renders, it calculates the effects of light, shadow, color, reflectivity, transparency, diffusion, and hundreds of other properties on the surface of the CG geometry. A final render can take anywhere from a few seconds to days per frame. To quickly view the progress of the piece, a CG animator will create test renders and a playblast (see Figures 18.6 through 18.8).

FIGURE 18.7   Tree filled in.

FIGURE 18.8   Cartoon sketch giant squatter tree.

FIGURE 18.6   Tree wire armature.

A playblast is a crude (usually low-resolution) render of the scene intended to show movement and timing. The playblast will show the models as they appear within the program without complex calculations of light and color. The test renders will be sample frames from different parts of the scene that will show the final look of the piece. Around one third of the computing resources of every major CG studio is dedicated to the task of rendering. It often requires what is known as a "Render Farm" to accomplish timely results.

There are usually more technical directors overseeing the lighting and rendering of a film than character animators, so do not underestimate the importance of this phase of production.

Many studios will render out the final frames in passes or plates. In a pass, the CG artist will take a portion of a scene, such as the foreground characters or shadows or even highlights, and render them out as a separate, silhouetted image. Unlike with live-action greenscreens, the elements are all generated in the computer. The masks are therefore perfectly registered and accurate to the pixel. The CG artist has a great deal more control when working with separate passes. For example, the shadow pass can be easily modified in a compositing program to have soft edges and darker areas toward the middle. If there is a change to one part of the scene, like a character's movement or a background color, the entire scene does not need to be rerendered.

PRODUCER

Keeping Track and Looking Ahead (and Back If Necessary)

The producer plays a pivotal role during this final stretch of the postproduction process. He serves as creative partner, negotiator, deal maker, troubleshooter, independent eye, and promoter.

There is one certain fact: postproduction can be a quagmire if you don't know the terrain and have not done your homework. It can also drain whatever funds are left in your budget. There are many hidden expenses. The rule is to always give yourself a financial cushion in the post budget, but some of this might have been already eaten up by unanticipated cost overruns during the shoot.

For this process to go smoothly, the producer needed to have carefully planned the workflow of the film in ADVANCE. The workflow is the formal path your project will take from origination to exhibition. As we stated in the early chapters, work backward, know where you are going, and know what you need to get there. Postproduction must be fully integrated into the production timeline from the beginning.

If you are not quite sure, know the technical and financial repercussions of each option: festivals, distributors, YouTube, iPod, Internet, etc. If the DP and director wanted to use a new camera (like the RED, for example), take the time to research the impact of using that or any camera on the entire workflow of your project. If you are targeting your film for the Internet, do you need all that 4K resolution for that tiny screen?
Remember:

- Acquisition (film, DV, HDV, HD)
- Edit format (Final Cut, Avid, Premiere, etc.)

- Master Format (Digibeta, MPEG4 file, HDcam)
- Deliverable (DVD, HD, DV)
- Distribution (?)

The producer must also do the following:

- Create a postproduction timeline: what has to happen, by whom, and the anticipated costs (estimate). The time it takes for each will most likely change, but at least you have a starting point.
- Negotiate the overall deal with the lab (if shooting film). This should be done in preproduction.
- Negotiate a deal with a postproduction facility (sound effects, ADR, Foley, mix).
- Serve as an independent eye for the director throughout the timing process. Review color-corrected prints for quality control.
- Review the bills for all postproduction expenses (lab, ADR, Foley, mix, online) to check that they are consistent with the work done and create an actualized budget.
- Collate and organize the film's chain of title (e.g., IP contracts, underlying rights, music, etc.).
- Help organize the names and the design for the end credit sequence. Thanking the appropriate people and organizing the names in order of priority and contractual obligations can be a big job.
- Troubleshoot if there are problems with the lab or the postproduction facilities. This process might go smoothly, or it might be a struggle. There might be a variety of technical problems that invariably cost money. Remember that these jobs are done by humans who sometimes make mistakes. Unfortunately, they are not always willing to acknowledge them. Your work might be just a small project to the lab, but it is *your* film. Be prepared to fight for what you want.

STUDENTS
Act like a professional, and you will be treated like one.

Looking Ahead/Key Points

It is now time to begin planning what must be done once the film is finished. Here is a list of tasks the producer must handle as the physical process of creating the project winds down:

- Set up screenings for the cast, crew, and investors.
- Prepare a marketing plan.
- Prepare a list of potential distributors to contact.
- Put together the press kit for festivals and distributors.
- Know what festivals and distributors require in the form of deliverables (Sundance requests films be submitted on a single DVD-R or DVD+R disc. They will also screen Blu-Ray and HD-DVD formats.)

- Budget for and check the deadlines for key festivals. (The Sundance fee is $35.)
- Decide how many DVDs are required and who needs them. This issue should have been spelled out in the deal memos for crew members.

- Write thank-you letters to vendors, volunteers, and the key people who helped to make it all happen. Thanking people for their hard work is easy to do and can go a long way in creating goodwill and support for your next project.

Chapter 19

Distribution/Exhibition

When I made this film it was Sundance or nothing. As I told people at Sundance, my Mom had called me about two years prior to making the film and said she had a dream that we were at Sundance. For me that is the biggest film festival you can be in. Prior to screening it for my family, which was a nerve-wracking event, I had already submitted to Sundance, but I did not know whether I was in or not. It was the only festival that I had submitted to at that point. For me it was all about Sundance.

Be' Garrett

PRODUCER

Launching the Film

There is nothing like the feeling of having produced a creative work. What might have begun as a simple notion or image is now a completed film. You should congratulate yourself and all those who helped in the realization of this project.

The question now is, what are you going to do with it? Let's go back to the beginning for a moment to examine the reasons why you took on this project in the first place. It might have been to create a "calling card" to advance your career as a producer or director. Perhaps you sought a learning experience, or maybe the picture is rooted in your fascination with the subject matter or your desire to say something profound with the visual medium. A sponsor motivated by the desire to serve a specific corporate or educational purpose of the organization might have financed the project. In any case, you have done your job and are ready for the next project.

Truman got me some professional recognition, which is what I originally wanted. Besides being entertaining, I wanted Truman to be something I could put on a résumé reel. I wanted it to say, "I can make a movie, I can direct, I can put the camera in the right place, and I can do something fun." It did well for me. I got a manager and an agent out of the blue, so I was thrilled. In terms of its goal and its aspirations, I think Truman more than fulfilled them. It also got distributed. It put me on a professional path. It's making a little money now, and all of this for 10 minutes.

Howard McCain

You might have thought that there was a predetermined audience, or market, for your project that would eventually lead to financial remuneration. This might not have been the sole reason for your effort, but you probably want people to see your work, and it would be nice if they paid for the privilege. A project that an audience never sees is like a tree that falls in the woods: does it make a sound?

Looking for financial gain does not taint or undermine your serious or "artistic" intentions. If people pay to see your project, that is a tribute to its power.

In addition, having a paying audience will make it easier for you to raise money to make more projects. Remember that there are now investors with whom you have a business relationship. They might not have expected a return from your first project, but repayment of the debt will foster goodwill and perhaps lead to future investments.

All filmmakers want their vision and ideas to be experienced by as many people as possible. All artists want their work to be displayed, but there is a different relationship between the work and the audience in film. Most art is experienced on a one-to-one basis. Our relationship to a book, poem, or painting is a private one. Although many viewers might have similar reactions to a painting and appreciate its artistic merit, they do so as a result of an individual, not a group, experience.

A unique aspect of film is that much of its power stems from the dynamic of being experienced by a group. The impact of a piece resonates with an audience. A film viewed by a large audience offers a group catharsis. This is most evident while watching a comedy. Laughter is contagious. The consensus of the group grants the audience permission to express not only laughter, but also the myriad emotions that play throughout the piece.

The exhibition of motion pictures in front of an audience is a vital component of their existence. If your goal is to expose the piece to the audience it deserves, you will need a calculated way to reach that audience—in other words, a coordinated marketing and distribution plan.

Certainly, the emergence of YouTube, Facebook, and MySpace has forever altered the ways films are able to reach an audience. Traditional models created an opportunity for filmmakers to have their work shared with thousands. The Internet has changed these models and given beginning filmmakers opportunities to expose their

doi: 10.1016/B978-0-240-81174-1.00026-9

work in ways not even imaginable to filmmakers previously. Along with this change comes a responsibility to be smart.

There are several things to keep in mind as you consider seeking formal distribution. These are the items that will be a turnoff to potential buyers: a lot of nudity or perfunctory nudity, drug use, and excessive bad language, even if it fits the character.

Start Early: Have A Plan from the Beginning

If you are interested in exploring distribution options for your short project, we recommend starting your research in preproduction.

Set aside money for distribution, festivals, and promotion materials. If you decide not to pursue the distribution route, these funds can be used to prepare for the festival circuit, especially for making extra prints (film) or dubs of your project for festivals (students are usually surprised to discover how much it costs to enter festivals). You will need money for press kits, postcards, travel, etc.

Talk to as many distributors as possible (a partial listing is given on our web site). Contacting distributors early in the project's life will, to begin with, make the task of finding a distributor that much easier. It may also give you a realistic sense of the market potential for your proposed project. For example, if you are planning to do a documentary on deforestation in the Northwest, distributors can tell you if the market is saturated with this kind of project, and if it is, whether your project offers a fresh viewpoint that hasn't been explored before.

Make sure you have someone taking professional looking stills (B&W and color) from the actual scenes during production. Digital photos can be from your film. These photos are for your web site, your press kit, news stories, to post on the Internet, or for your DVD cover.

Think about promoting your project in the local press. There may be something newsworthy or controversial about your subject matter; a documentary about pollution in the local river could garner some press attention. Many of our students who come from small towns have been able to exploit themselves as human-interest stories: "Local media heroes take first steps toward Hollywood." These articles will form the foundation of your press kit (described later in the chapter). Preproduction can also be the time to prepare a brief synopsis of the story, biographies of the cast and crew, and background information about the project. Some sort of graphic image to identify your project would be helpful, but it's not absolutely necessary.

Start selling before you begin to shoot. The preparation work done in preproduction will jump-start your efforts to find an audience for your project. Whether or not you decide to go this route, these efforts will help you promote your film to festivals. Your web site can be used as your hub.

> I think the short is as healthy as ever. I think we are seeing a proliferation of film and video festivals that welcome the short form, whether fiction or documentary.
>
> Jan Krawitz

The Markets

Following are the markets for short films:

- Exhibition (festivals, etc.)
- Internet
- YouTube
- iTunes
- Internet sites
- Cell phones
- DVD
- Television (U.S. and Foreign)
- Theatrical markets
- Nontheatrical markets

The first part of this chapter is devoted only to the United States and Canada, which is known as the *domestic market*. Foreign distribution is discussed briefly later in this chapter.

Exhibition

Exhibition is a broad term that represents the many opportunities filmmakers have to screen their work in front of an audience. These are some of the venues that fit under this category:

- Festivals (domestic and foreign)
- Museum showings
- Cultural societies
- Film school festivals
- School and community groups

Exhibition opportunities serve a number of purposes. They give the filmmaker an audience response to the picture, public acknowledgment for excellent work, the potential for financial reward, and valuable exposure.

National Festivals

Festivals provide a wonderful opportunity to share your work with an audience. They give the general public an opportunity to see new films. For distributors, festivals provide an opportunity to look for new products. For the filmmaker, they can provide valuable contacts and the experience of reaching a broader and more critical audience than friends and family. There can be much to learn (and grow from as a creative person) from a variety of opinions and public responses to your work. Different venues will lead to different reactions. That is why it is important to enter more than one festival.

Many festivals are competitive or have competitive sections in which prizes or cash are awarded. The valuable exposure you receive after winning awards at various festivals can elevate your status in the industry, not only for the purpose of finding work as a producer or director, but also for building an impressive portfolio. (Receiving awards is also very useful if you are interested in attracting a distributor.) This portfolio will come in handy when you are raising money or applying for grants for future productions. It seems as though new festivals sprout up every year.

The largest festivals are the Sundance Film Festival, Tribeca, Slamdance, Telluride Indiefest, New York Film Festival, San Francisco International Film Festival, Montreal World Film Festival, Toronto International Film Festival, Berlin International Film Festival, Cannes International Film Festival, and Oberhausen International Short Film Festival. Other noteworthy ones are The Hamptons International Film Festival, Nantucket Film Festival, and The Los Angeles Independent Film Festival.

For documentaries, the Hot Springs Documentary Film Festival, The Margaret Mead Film and Video Festival, and the Yamagata International Documentary Film Festival (Japan) are just a few of the well-known ones. The Independent Documentary Association (IDA), an excellent organization that supports the documentary field, holds its own Documentary Awards Competition and the David L. Wolper Student Award Competition.

> To see your film up at Sundance and you see the Sundance logo it is beyond the beyond. It is everything that you think it would be and more. Just the idea that you are there. That you had come from where you had come and you are here and accepted as a filmmaker—to me was validation.
>
> Be' Garrett

Genre Festivals. If your project falls into a specific category or genre, there may be one or several festivals that are more appropriate. You will find festivals that focus on particular areas of interest such as Latino, Native American, gay and lesbian, Jewish, Asian American, underground/experimental, and digital art, to name just a few. If you have made a short comedy, the Just for Laughs Festival in Montreal is for you.

> I think film festivals are springing up all over the place. We have a new one in San Jose. I recently went to the Rocky Mountain Women's Film Festival in Colorado Springs, which was in its fifth year. I'm going to Louisville in a couple of months to judge their festival. I think there's a lot of people with initiative who are starting film festivals in small communities and providing a forum for this work to be shown, and I think that will continue.
>
> Jan Krawitz

Withoutabox.com

Withoutabox.com has become the one-stop clearinghouse for festivals and online distribution for short films. It offers filmmakers unprecedented access to major channels for promoting and distributing their work, including screening at international film festivals, streaming on the Internet via IMDb video, and selling DVDs and Video On Demand downloads on Amazon.com and other channels via CreateSpace.

Withoutabox helps festival staffs streamline their festival management and boost their submission numbers. Festivals can request submissions via the web and manage incoming submissions electronically, in the past a very manual and paper-based process. In addition, festivals can market their events to over 200,000 active filmmakers already on the Withoutabox platform, accept submission fees from them electronically, and automatically notify filmmakers for acceptance into their event.

When filmmakers submit to festivals using Withoutabox, they receive instructions as specified by the festival where to send a screener and in what format (e.g., DVD, VHS, 16mm, 35mm, etc). The ability to upload films in electronic formats (QuickTime, Flash, WMP, etc.) to Withoutabox for festival staff

online screening is not yet supported. Filmmakers find festivals using the Withoutabox search engine or through weekly festival update emails, or they get referred from festivals' own web sites.

The service is entirely free to filmmakers, except for any entry fees the festival may charge. Filmmakers apply via an online entry form, completing all required application information and paying electronically. Using Withoutabox online management tools, festival staff track incoming submission materials and fees via the Withoutabox Festival dashboard. All data can be exported as needed for use in festivals' own custom applications and databases. Listings in the Withoutabox Deep search engine are entirely free. Filmmakers can set up their own new listings in less than an hour. Having a listing allows over 200,000 Withoutabox filmmakers to find your festival and apply though your normal channels.

Be sure to use Withoutabox sensibly. Over 125,000 people are members, and 2,000 festivals partner with it. That is a lot of festivals to consider. Do your research. Go to the web sites of different festivals. You might want to enter around 30 festivals. How do you start?

Shorts Only. Shorts only festivals have an obvious appeal: they feature only short films. You are not competing with full-length films that usually get all the attention. Also, with any luck, you will be spotted by the many short film acquisition executives in attendance. These are the top five:

- Clermont-Ferrand Short Film Festival. It is considered the "Cannes of short film." By having your film screened, it is automatically placed in the festival's market, where buyers from all over the world come to look for products.
- Aspen Shortsfest
- Canadian Film Centre's Worldwide Short Film Festival in Toronto
- Palm Springs Shortsfest
- L.A. Shorts Fest.

One way to quality for an Oscar nomination is to win the appropriate prize at a festival the Academy of Motion Pictures Arts and Sciences recognizes. The list can change from year to year, so check the Academy's web site for updates.

Applications. Most of these festivals can be located through the Internet. Some applications can be printed right off the web. Most have entrance fees between $20 and $50. Ultimately, you need to compare the benefits of a particular festival to the costs of submitting your work. The entrance fees, although not expensive individually, can add up. Other usual requirements are an advance video copy, a composite print (if a film), a synopsis of your project, a cast and crew list, a time framework for completion (for example, must have been completed no later than...), and a time limit (short films can be as long as 40 minutes). Some festivals will even require a press kit.

> The "festival game" is expensive. You've got to be selective, and the way to be selective is to look in the magazine *The Independent*, which lists all festivals throughout the world and what kinds of films these festivals are looking for, what they're interested in.
>
> Howard McCain

Museum Screenings

Museums regularly screen the work of emerging film and video artists. This type of screening is highly prestigious and an excellent opportunity to have your work seen by a potential distributor or buyer.

Cultural Societies

If your film or video deals with ethnic issues or concerns, research organizations that are seeking a visual device as a springboard for discussions.

Film School Festivals

All film and media programs hold an annual screening of their students' work. These festivals provide an opportunity to be recognized by your institution and to be seen by the industry. If your film or television program is located in a major urban area, it is likely that distributors, agents, and industry professionals will attend to become familiar with the new talent.

> In Israel the Sam Spiegel School was turning out amazing, amazing short work. I would go to year-end screenings, and there would be five fabulous pieces. All the graduating films were absolutely amazing. So there were many years in Israel where short films was where you could see the talent of filmmakers because there was no money in the industry so the features were not as good. But whatever was done in film school was remarkable.
>
> Tatia Rosenthal

School and Community Groups

The final exhibition category includes church groups, union organizations, local institutes, corporations, and youth programs.

> What's most satisfying out of all the things that have happened with *The Lunch Date* is the requests I get from schools and other instructional institutions and groups like the Girl Scouts, asking for the film because they're using it to discuss race relations. That, for me, is what I had set out to say with the picture. So that's been very rewarding for me: that the film is being used for instructional purposes.
>
> Adam Davidson

The Internet

The Internet has clearly become the "next mass medium," but with economic models vastly different from those of other mass media such as television or radio. On the one hand, the Internet's ability to **narrowcast** (see Glossary) and reach niche audiences has opened up tremendous opportunities for individuals and organizations to spread their messages or content. However, the noise of millions of web sites trying to attract an audience means that it is not clear how these sites will find a large enough audience to justify the cost involved in producing and "webcasting" content, especially video.

To a degree, this is true today. The Internet is currently capable of sending audio and video, and it is available at the click of a mouse, or in other words, "on demand." However, quality problems exist, as good-quality video cannot be transmitted over a normal phone line. With faster connections, which are growing in use, decent video is available.

Even with a high-bandwidth connection, the problem remains today that most users are accessing the Internet via a personal computer. This is not an ideal environment to watch a longer video program because viewers tend to be in an active mode in front of the PC as opposed to the more passive mode of sitting on a couch watching television.

So what will an Internet user watch today? If we want to overcome the hurdles mentioned, the content needs to be unique (unavailable in any other medium) and short. Short films and animation ("shorts") fit this category perfectly and are indeed growing in popularity on the Internet via sites such as AtomFilms.com. In addition to their technical and sociological (the active environment of the PC mentioned earlier) advantages of being short, they have traditionally been too "niche" to be broadcast or played in movie theaters, but have a strong consumer following. The economics of Internet webcasting are still forming, but it is clear that there is room for innovative programming, and shorts fit this need perfectly.

At this juncture, it is difficult to generate profit from the Internet. It behooves the filmmaker to be aware that selling Internet rights may negate sales to other venues. The Internet has the potential to overexpose work, so a traditional short film outlet, such as the educational or television market, would prefer a product that has retained Internet rights. Putting your film or video on the Internet may prohibit you from selling your film to a distributor.

In most cases, the Internet is not really a market because there is no payment involved. The Internet is a place to showcase your work. If you have a short that plays at a number of festivals, web sites may contact you to allow them to stream your work on their sites. Getting your work online may be a great way to promote yourself to get attention for future work (see the Bibliography for web distributors).

YouTube

With over 150,000+ videos uploaded daily, there is no doubt about YouTube's popularity. It is currently the number one destination site for online video watching (although *Hulu* is catching up). Whether or not you made your film originally for the web, your film, an excerpt, or your trailer will most likely end up there. However, one of the biggest mistakes beginning filmmakers make is posting their entire film online before they have exploited other markets. Following are the pros and cons of posting on YouTube.

The Pros

- You can reach anyone in the world at any time.
- You can receive direct, unfiltered feedback from viewers.
- Viewers can contact you and you can contact them.

- Your film can be linked to and embedded in other web sites.
- You can potentially earn money with advertiser revenue sharing.

The Cons

- Once your film goes online, you lose control of it. Anyone can put it on other sites without your permission.
- Festivals and television stations may not want to program your film if it is already exposed on the web.
- People may not want to pay for your film in other formats (iTunes downloads, DVD purchases, etc.) if they can watch it online free.
- The Academy of Motion Picture Arts and Sciences considers a short playing on the Internet as broadcast. As a result, your short will be ineligible for academy consideration unless you qualified before it was broadcast.

iTunes

iTunes delivers thousands of downloads a day. There are no statistics to how many short films make up that total, but this is clearly a great opportunity for filmmakers. Unfortunately, iTunes doesn't like to deal with individual filmmakers partly due to the amount of work needed to legally check and collect assets for each individual film. The best way to get in is through a distribution company that already has a deal with iTunes. However, iTunes isn't the only way to offer digital downloads for sale; Amazon, Movielink, Jaman, GreenCine, and CinemaNow also offer these services.

> During Sundance one of the things they ask you is if you want to distribute your film via iTunes. So, for me, I felt like it was a chance to get a lot of exposure. More so to expose the film so people could go see it. Short film festivals usually play it at the festival and they don't really have a wide circulation. I felt like if I can put it in a place where people could conveniently go get it for $2.00 or whatever, people would see it. So, as a result of that I have gotten emails at various times over the last year and a half from people who have seen the film and asked for copies of it or downloaded it and watched it and shared comments. It just continues to validate the fact that the film itself hit its mark, told a story and that it tells me to keep shooting, keep going. No matter how hard it gets, no matter what, keep making films.
>
> Be' Garrett

Internet Sites

Internet sites are usually looking for movies for free. Only a few right now are paying well. Most have not worked out a model for revenue sharing with the individual filmmakers or distributors. If you want to make money on YouTube, you need to get into its *Partners Program*. Once your film is vetted (determined that you own all the rights to everything) and accepted to be a part of the program, advertising will be added to your film's YouTube page. It could be in the form of a text ad, a banner ad, or an in-video. The better the short does, the more money the filmmaker can make.

Cell Phones

Cell phones represent the largest distribution platform on earth. Unfortunately, the content applications are still primitive, and the competition is very intense. The question will become: how does a short film compete with episodes of *The Simpsons*? A film may be able to compete *because* it is short. Mobile companies have their own constraints, and one of them is running time. These companies presently don't want anything that is over three minutes in length. They are also leery of bad language, violence, and anything edgy.

In 2008, the Sundance Institute invited six influential independent filmmakers to craft original short films specifically for mobile phone delivery. With the two-inch screen and international audiences front-of-mind, they created a collection of shorts that premiered at the 3GSM Congress in Barcelona that year. A year later, the films made their way to every continent, popping up everywhere from Hong Kong to Helsinki.

DVD

Because DVD is the perfect format for short film compilations, new DVD series are constantly being launched. *Wholphin* and *Cinema 16* are two great examples. *Cinema 16* offers wide selections of both U.S. and European shorts. For documentary projects, The Full Frame Documentary Film Festival annually releases a collection of the best short documentaries of that year. DVD companies are generally interested in dealing with individual filmmakers, but these commercial compilations do not generate any real money for the filmmakers. What they do offer is exposure.

If you want to make and sell your own DVDs commercially, you may want to investigate Amazon's CreateSpace service. Similar to those services that offer individual book publishing on demand, CreateSpace makes it possible to sell the DVD of your short on Amazon.com, Amazon Video On Demand, and other channels. Filmmakers still control their own rights and earn a percentage of the retail price of each sale. Because CreateSpace is part of the Amazon family, your title becomes eligible for listing on IMDb.com.

Television

Television might seem to be a natural conduit for the short subject, but this market is in transition. Licensing to television has the most potential for profit, but the opportunities have shrunk. It is the long-established foreign television channels, such as France's Canal+, which pay the biggest licensing fees (paying by the minute). In the United States, independent film-orientated cable channels like IFC and PBS still buy short films. In Canada, Movieola shows shorts 24 hours a day. However, fewer and fewer channels are buying shorts. There was a time when cable networks such as HBO, Showtime, A&E, Bravo, and MTV offered the short film airtime. This has stopped.

> The other myth is, "I'll sell my film to cable television. There's a lot of money in cable television." Well, it's become increasingly harder to sell films to HBO, Showtime, or A&E. They've all dropped their short tapes programs. If they do buy, they pay very, very little. There is no market for a short film in television—what are you going to do with a 10-minute piece? It's not long enough to program any commercials around; it doesn't draw any names. It's not worth anything in terms of advertising time, so stations will basically use it as fill. The market has definitely decreased all the way around for short films.
>
> Howard McCain

Theatrical Markets

There are few possibilities for short films to be released in theaters. Festivals are the places where short films get theatrical distribution, but the filmmakers don't get any money from that. Rarely is an individual theater or chain willing to pay to show a short before a feature. (At one time, an animated cartoon and newsreels in addition to previews for coming attractions preceded feature films.)

Usually, the packaged touring shows have been successful theatrically. They include a collection of Academy Award–winning short films distributed by Magnolia Pictures that are also available for rental and purchase on DVD.

The Animation Show, launched in 2003, was started as an annual feature-length theatrical compilation of short films from around the world. Annually curated by Mike Judge (*Office Space*, *Beavis and Butt-Head*, *King of the Hill*), a sister series of high-quality Animation Show DVDs now supplement the theatrical tour with additional insights and brand new lineups of films. Animated short films for a variety of programs are licensed from theatrical and DVD collections, to iTunes, web, and for television (via MTV).

There have also been several occasions when feature-length films have been deliberately constructed from three or four short pieces (*New York Stories*, *Akira Kurosawa's Dreams*, *ARIA*); these are referred to as *anthology films*.

Nontheatrical Markets

The most substantial domestic market and potentially the most lucrative one available to the short film or video is nontheatrical. Nontheatrical customers are institutional buyers who integrate video into their training and educational programs. For example, a ninth-grade biology teacher will buy videos to supplement her classroom lecture. Nontheatrical distributors supply fictional and nonfictional films and videos: narrative, documentary, animated, and experimental. The basic criterion for a successful film in this market is subject matter that can serve some kind of educational or instructional need.

This market covers a broad spectrum of interests. The best way to discover whether your project fits into this market is to submit it for consideration to one or all of the nontheatrical distributors that interest you (see the Bibliography). Educate yourself about what products have traditionally performed well in these markets. Keep in mind that documentaries form a large part of the nontheatrical market. They have obvious educational appeal because they are factual explorations of real events; they serve as both historical and behavioral models.

Fiction work, whether narrative, animated, or experimental, doesn't fall automatically into any educational niche, although adaptations of children's books can do well in the K–3 language arts curriculum.

There must be something in the subject matter that can be used in an educational context. The story must provoke a moral or ethical discussion. Narrative stories, whether they are live action or animated, can offer strong metaphors for human behavior. If your story explores the nature of human relationships in a poignant way that could serve as an educational model, it might have a continued life in the nontheatrical marketplace.

The nontheatrical market is truly content driven. If you want your film to be distributed, you must have something libraries or schools would want to buy because they are the major purchasers of short films in this country. The short film market is about education. Can you sell your project to a library or school? If your film is a wonderful art film, in all likelihood it just isn't going to be distributed. There are distributors who will pick it up, but it will probably sit there. Sometimes, the overseas market is a little different because the short film life is longer, foreign audiences have a wider appreciation for it, and this market can sell the film to foreign television.

> Now I'm making money off of *Truman*. Someday, I might make all the money back—maybe 20 years down the road. But I'm starting to see $500 here, $500 there, which is great. I did not expect it. Schools and libraries have limited budgets. If they can go out and buy *The Wizard of Oz*, with Judy Garland, at $19 a copy, what would possibly motivate them to pay $75 for a 10-minute copy of *Truman*? That's what the educational market is running into; there are very limited resources, and Hollywood is dumping tremendous amounts of videotape on the market at very, very cheap prices.
> Howard McCain

Within the nontheatrical family, there are four basic markets: education, institutional, corporate training, and health care. The education market can itself be subdivided into a number of categories: kindergarten through 12th grade (K–12) and colleges, universities, and graduate schools (higher education).

Educational Market

K–12. The K–12 market represents a potential audience of more than 100,000 schools and approximately 55 million students. Teachers use videos to supplement lectures and lesson plans and have specific criteria about program format and content. Video is widely used in the classroom; in fact, more than 90 percent of the country's classrooms contain at least one VCR. Teachers, librarians, media buyers, or principals make buying decisions. When producing or adapting a film or video for this market, consider the following.

The Curriculum. The project must directly support the teacher's classroom activities and ideally support the curriculum. Many states publish curriculum guidelines. You can get copies by calling the state departments of education. (Much of this information is now on the states' web pages. Also, try an Internet search with the word "curriculum.")

Funding for Education. Each year the federal government appropriates funding to youth education and assistance programs. These funds support a variety of programs, some of which involve media acquisitions. There has been, in the past, an emphasis on substance abuse prevention, AIDS education, violence intervention, self-esteem, and multiculturalism. For more information, you can contact the U.S. Department of Education.

Length of the Program. The standard class period is 45–50 minutes. The ideal project length for K–4 should run about 12 minutes, and then increase in length as the grade level rises.

Appropriateness. Schools are very conservative. It is important that projects used in the classroom reflect cultural and ethnic diversity and gender equity. Media material must not have excessive profanity, nudity, sexually suggestive situations, or violence, or promote negative ethnic stereotypes. It is also suggested that you present a balanced political perspective.

Teacher's Guides. A teacher's guide must accompany every project for the school market. Discussion or activity guides help teachers integrate the project into their teaching plans. They can provide a brief overview of the project and also feature a list of suggested activities and discussion topics for the classroom. Your distributor will assist you in putting together this kind of guide.

Marketing to schools is largely the domain of 15–20 educational distributors who reach buyers through a combination of direct mail, telemarketing, print advertising, sales representatives, exhibits at conferences, and now also with a substantial presence on the Internet. The major trade journals for this market include *School Library Journal, Media and Methods, Curriculum Administrator, T.H.E. Journal*, and *Science Books & Films*. These journals all have their own web sites on the Internet.

Higher Education. This market of more than 7,000 institutions, most of which are two- and four-year colleges and universities, doesn't offer the same potential as the school market. As with schools, funding cuts have hurt colleges and universities. The college market is more decentralized than the school market. Professors and department chairs have more discretion than grade school teachers about how they will teach a subject and are the primary decision makers about the purchase of textbooks and other media. In general, videos are used to supplement a lecture rather than to teach a core concept.

Videos that have potential in the high school market often have crossover potential in the higher education market and vice versa. This market is reached in much the same way as the school market.

Institutional Market

Libraries. There are approximately 16,000 public libraries in this country. About three quarters of these have video collections. Their buying decisions reflect consumer interest because they buy on behalf of their patrons. State and local budget cutting has hurt libraries, however. Without a mandate to build video collections, many have stopped buying videos. Most traditional nontheatrical distributors no longer find direct marketing to libraries cost effective and instead rely on wholesalers such as Baker & Taylor and Ingram (both accessible on the Internet).

The head librarian makes the purchase decisions. Most library collections represent a mix of feature films and how-to titles, with a small selection of higher-quality documentaries and educational programs. The key to library sales is favorable reviews in a handful of trade journals: *Library Journal, Video Librarian*, and the *Video Rating Guide for Libraries* (all available on the Internet).

Community and Religious Groups. Community and religious groups such as churches and local PTA chapters also buy videos for Sunday schools, after-school activities, guidance and counseling programs, and discussion groups. These groups buy general-interest programs, with a special emphasis on guidance subjects such as substance abuse and personal ethics. Some distributors market to religious and community groups through direct mail and telemarketing. However, most of the purchasing takes place through retail outlets and wholesalers.

Prisons. Prisons buy videos as well. Many inmates work toward high school and college equivalency degrees through correspondence courses. Videos are also used in counseling and therapy sessions.

The Corporate Training Market. Corporations spend billions of dollars on staff training and development and close to $2 billion on off-the-shelf materials such as books, videos, computer courseware, and other prepackaged training products. Video has been the most popular information delivery system. Companies use videos to motivate staff and to improve skills. In contrast to the school market, tough financial times have not hurt businesses. In the corporate arena, a well-trained and informed workforce is a valuable commodity, and video and other forms of media are cost effective.

In a larger company, the people responsible for staff development (human resources or training departments) make purchasing decisions. In the smaller companies, it is often the president or a high-level manager who makes these decisions. Companies buy directly from distributors and from wholesalers such as Baker & Taylor. Some of the leading distributors in this field are CRM Learning, Blanchard Training and Development, and Video Arts. The two best sources of information on the corporate arena are the American Society for Training and Development (www.astd.org) and *Training Magazine*.

The Health Care Market. Hospitals, health care centers, and emergency service providers such as emergency medical services and police forces are considered part of the larger corporate training market, but they require very specialized kinds of programming. The ever-changing health care landscape calls for a continuing stream of up-to-date information for patients and staff training in OSHA regulations, health care procedures, and issues. Heath care information is one of the growth areas in the nontheatrical market.

There are more than 6,500 hospitals and 500 HMOs in this country purchasing off-the-shelf material for training. Psychiatric and mental health care facilities also purchase videos. Health care video distributors can de divided into two general categories. Distributors such as the *American Journal of Nursing* and Medcom-Trainex market products that are highly technical. Distributors such as AIMS Media, Pyramid, and Fanlight market a broader array of products that range from technical to general-interest treatments of health care issues (autism, disabilities, physical challenges, psychological issues, etc.). These companies also distribute to the educational and institutional markets.

Foreign Markets

The short film is considered more of an art form in Europe and around the world than it is in the United States. For films made in the United States or Canada to have an appeal in the foreign or European market, the film's basic narrative must come through in the visuals. It must be driven by image, not dialogue. Comedies do not necessarily travel well because humor sometimes reflects national sensibilities.

What is clear about foreign markets is that they are generally much more creative from a programming perspective. The BBC programs short dramatic pieces in the afternoon so that a school class can turn them on and watch. After the piece is finished, the class uses the short film as a tool to deal with language skills, social studies, group dynamics, or whatever the strength of the piece is. The BBC puts together study guides to go along with the short pieces so they can be used within a proper educational context. This approach has been so successful that the BBC has programmed these short films during the evening prime-time slot as well.

Foreign distribution plans must also consider issues related to subtitles. Some distributors arrange for subtitles to be shot locally. Others put into your contract a requirement that you must deliver a print with subtitles already burned in. In either case, the producer is required to supply a complete transcript of the project. You may also need to clear rights for foreign distribution and pay for the PAL conversion.

The market is currently growing as new regional cable and satellite stations are coming on the scene in the Middle East, Asia, and Latin America as well as in Europe. Talk to as many foreign distributors as you can.

Distribution Options

Self-Distribution

One option is to distribute your film or video yourself. The primary advantage is that no one is going to care about your film or video as much as you do. Self-distribution is, however, a full-time job. It requires a realistic evaluation of the film's or video's market, money, a professional approach, strategic thinking, busywork, and, most important, a sincere commitment to the process. It also requires a great deal of self-promotion and the ability to "think outside the box." In many ways, it is a natural outgrowth of production work. Distribution completes the circle. One of its rewarding aspects is the opportunity to interact with the groups and individuals whom you hoped would see your work when you decided to start this project.

If you are successful at self-distribution, you will save yourself the considerable distribution fee. Distributors often retain as much as 75 percent of net sales to cover their costs and profit and pay the producers the remaining 25 percent. The figures of a distributor's percentage of sales are

Television Market = 20%–30% of gross
Education Market = 60%–70% of gross
Home Video Market = 70%–80% of net

> I approached SAG because the film was going to be commercial, and you have to do this. I paid the actors their wages. Then I purchased the music rights, and so I own it now. I distribute the film myself. I like knowing where it's going. I like to give the film away free to hear feedback because I get a lot of requests from institutions. There wasn't a distributor that really interested me.
>
> Adam Davidson

Self-distribution can be an excellent way to raise your profile and build networks with the people who are interested in seeing and promoting independent media. Following are the basic steps of self-distributing your projects.

Evaluation

- Evaluate the market for your production.
- Evaluate your costs.
- Get quotable reviews.
- Do well in festivals.

Production

- Get photographs.
- Make a video master and strike 50 DVDs.
- Create a DVD cover.
- Set a realistic price for your work.

Marketing

- Obtain suitable mailing lists.
- Have a brochure made up.
- Have a system in place to receive and place orders.
- Be professional!

Distributor

On the other hand, you can place your project with a distributor. Most filmmakers would rather spend their time producing and let the distributor, who is presumably more expert at marketing, do this important job.

> Because *Mirror Mirror* focused on women's issues, I contacted Women Make Movies as a possible distributor. I sent them a tape, and they were very interested, as was a second distributor. I decided to go with Women Make Movies because I felt that the subject matter fit their catalog and that it might find a larger audience through their mailing list.
>
> I negotiated for a one-sheet flier for *Mirror Mirror* that they would send out as a special mailing at their expense. I signed with them in the fall of 1990 and gave them nontheatrical rights. In the winter of 1992, I placed the film with Jane Balfour Films in London for international nontheatrical and foreign TV.
>
> Since I retained domestic television rights, I entered *Mirror Mirror* in the PBS series *POV*, which showcases

independent documentaries. It was accepted and was broadcast in the summer of 1991. It was clustered with four other short films into a 90-minute program. The license agreement with POV was the standard PBS exclusive: four broadcasts in three years. Unfortunately, after the initial broadcast, it will not be aired again, but I am prevented from marketing it further until the license agreement expires later this year.

I think it has done well in nontheatrical distribution. I'm not ready to retire off of the royalties, but they have probably sold about 80 video copies in three years, and the rentals are four times that amount. It has an active rental life in both film and video, which I like.

Jan Krawitz

Approaching a Distributor

Many distributors specialize in the short form in both the domestic and foreign markets. Ask for catalogs from the distributors that interest you, and study them thoroughly before approaching anyone.

Rather than run out and find a distributor first thing, I did what I always do, which is to show it at a couple of festivals and see how people respond. It's easier to get a distributor if you have a product that other people have conferred recognition on. It becomes more marketable.

Jan Krawitz

One way to find out whether a particular distributor is right for you is to set up a meeting and ask the following questions.

General Distribution

1. What kinds of markets does your company target?
   - Nontheatrical
   - Theatrical
   - Video
   - Television
   - Foreign or domestic
2. With which markets have you had the most success?
3. How has current technology affected the marketplace?
4. What are some examples of successful shorts from your catalog?
5. Do you work with a publicist? Do producers have approval or input over marketing and distribution plans?
6. What kind of subject matter is easiest to market and sell? Is there any type of picture you are specifically looking for now?
   - Narrative
   - Documentary
   - Animation
   - How-to
   - Sports
   - Fine arts
   - Business and industry
   - Health sciences
   - General interest
7. What lengths or running times have been most successful for you? Is there a relationship between the length of a project and its success in the marketplace? Is there an ideal length for any particular market?
8. What rights do you handle (i.e., nontheatrical, television, etc.)?
9. Is there much potential revenue in the television market?
10. Do you use film festivals to promote your new products? Which festivals in particular do you feel are the most important?
11. How do you use preview copies?
12. Do filmmakers ever approach you with an idea for a new project? How do you respond? Do you offer advice about the chances of that particular idea for distribution?
13. What do you offer to a film- or videomaker that your competitors do not?
14. Do you cover the costs of duplication?
15. Do you use a tiered royalty scale based on the market of a film? Is this a gross or net point? Is it based on the cost of the film rental and sales?
16. Do you give advances?
17. What is the average contract length and is it automatically renewable?
18. Does it matter if a product is on film or video? Which formats do you prefer?
19. What materials do you require from a film- or videomaker?

Foreign Distribution

1. Do you handle foreign rights for any of your films or videos?
2. How familiar are you with the foreign markets: theatrical, nontheatrical, television, video?
3. On which markets do you focus?
4. Which film festivals are most important overseas?
5. Which film markets do you attend (Cannes, Berlin, Clermont-Ferrand, or Oberhausen)?
6. Does your company use sales agents or subdistributors abroad?
7. What are the strongest foreign markets for the short today?

The responses to these questions will help you decide which distributor to employ. When all is said and done, most distribution contracts are similar. Your decision will most likely be based on the people who run the company, their track record with works of a similar nature, and your gut response.

Show the contract the distributor offers you to an entertainment attorney. You will need to understand the difference between gross and net points, deferments, and the various positions for recoupment. A lawyer can help you understand the difference between a profit and a non-profit company. However, because the filmmaker is in no position to verify the accounting, it makes sense to ask for a small percentage of the gross, paid from the first dollar, than a larger percentage of the net, which hardly ever pays anything. The Bibliography lists several books to assist you with contracts.

Contracts

To own the copyright, the filmmaker must have releases or contracts for everything related to the picture. This list may include the following:

- Story rights for adaptations
- Rights for clips and stock footage
- Actors and extras
- Music rights (see rights sections)
- Locations: any private or public property
- Décor: any and everything on the walls or furniture or exteriors of buildings and other people's copyrighted material (posters, book covers, paintings, etc.)

Marketing Your Short Film

It is up to your distributor to sell your film project, so ask prospective distributors about how they would market it. *Marketing* means promoting what is best about your work, giving buyers a reason to want to own or rent it. Any ideas you have about how and what to promote will help the distributor devise a successful marketing campaign. You'll need a good marketing plan to make your venture into the marketplace a fruitful one.

Deliverables

Distributors of short films will require most of the same items required by a feature film distributor at your own expense:

- One Beta SP (Stereo) videotape master of the picture in NTSC format (PAL if requested for foreign sales)
- Five VHS NTSC videotape copies
- Five DVD copies
- One dub from the digital video master
- Current list of festivals and awards
- Stills (usually color) in JPEG format
- Postproduction script (lined script)
- Key artwork
- Music cue sheet
- Copyright registration for the film and other chain of title and insurance information
- Release print(s) in available format if requested for theatrical rental
- An authorization to the laboratories and suppliers of preprint materials and foreign tracks
- Copies of all release forms and contracts

The Press Kit

You can promote yourself and your product by creating a press kit. A press kit presents your project to the public and to prospective distributors and entices them to screen it (see Figure 19.1). All the information developed for a

FIGURE 19.1   Publicity still from *Truman*.

press kit can be posted on your web site. The kit should contain at least the following:

Cover

- Title
- Length and type of film or video (comedy, drama)
- Your name
- Contact number and address

Inside

- Black-and-white production still
- Still from the show
- Your résumé and telephone number
- Details about the production
- Reviews and clippings
- Credit list
- Transcript for foreign markets

Make a Postcard

Some filmmakers print up posters for their shorts. They tend to get lost among the feature film posters, however. Postcards are a better investment. They become the thing you are mailing and handing off as your business card. The postcard's design should convey the feel of the film. It is important to use a strong single image that captures the essence of what the film is all about. With crucial information on the back, the postcard becomes your calling card and the calling card of the film.

DIRECTOR

Publicity

There is no better person than the director to publicize the short picture or to build an audience for it. The best sales tool is the picture itself. Favorable word of mouth, festival prizes, and ultimately distribution are based on the quality and salability of the final product.

We end this chapter with the extraordinary festival and distribution stories of *A Nick in Time* (Be' Garrett), *Citizen* (James Darling, writer, director; and Jessalyn Haefele, producer), *The Lunch Date* (Adam Davidson), *Crazy Glue* (Tatia Rosenthal), *Truman* (Howard McCain), and *Mirror Mirror* (Jan Krawitz), as told by the filmmakers themselves.

A Nick in Time

I ended up getting into Sundance. They sent me an email but I was in New Zealand, of all places. I was on the telephone with my girlfriend browsing through my emails. I had just arrived and I saw an email that read "Welcome to Sundance." When you see "Welcome to Sundance," you know you're in. I think at that point I was just trying to process it, and I could not believe I had gotten in. So, she and I were just talking on the phone screaming back and forth, "We're in Sundance." That was really refreshing and really great.

I tried to get posters made because Sundance asks you to make movie posters. I was scrambling around trying to get someone in New York City that makes movie size posters at a reasonable rate. I needed business cards made. It was a mad scramble to be ready and prepared to go out to Utah. That is what I basically spent the Christmas holidays doing, getting ready. The most rewarding thing of making Sundance was about my Mom. My Mom has been my biggest supporter since I was young and I said I wanted to do the whole film thing. Most parents would have been like "What are you going to do with film? Why don't you get a job?" but they never discouraged me. So, the idea of going to Sundance for me was like one of the most rewarding things I could do was to call my Mom and say hey, we made it.

I say we because it was a family effort. It was us putting our money together, believing in the dream that I had and fulfilling it. That was the best. What we ended up doing was we ended up pulling our resources and renting a condo. I think about ten or twelve of us stayed in this condo and we all just piled in. It was a family affair. We were all just bunked in together and we just had a blast.

The screening at Sundance was great. It was one of the biggest theaters in front of a movie called *Weapons* which had a lot of heat prior to coming. So, there was a lot of hoopla. So preceding him we came in and Robert Redford came up and spoke a few words. I saw him prior to the actual screening and he came up and said, "Very nice work. Welcome to Sundance." That was really awesome, the director of Sundance, a gentlemen, opening up the festival on day one, comes in and says that to you. Then I went up and said something about my film in front of this massive audience and then the film came on. To see your film up at Sundance and you see the Sundance logo it is beyond the beyond. It is everything that you think it would be and more. Just the idea that you are there. That you had come from where you had come and you are here and accepted as a filmmaker—to me was validation.

While you are at Sundance you are approached by a lot of folks, bombarded by a lot of people all looking for the next ingénue, the next sensation. You take a lot of meetings, a lot of talk and things like that. Coming out of Sundance, the thing that I wanted was to get an invitation to the Writer's Lab, the Sundance. That was really what I wanted. It ended up happening on the flight back. On the layover my girlfriend ended up getting a call from one of the people at Sundance who would like me to submit a script for the Lab. That meant I had broken through. Your name definitely registered. People know who you are. That made me go home and prepare a script.

Tribeca

After Sundance it was preparation for a couple of the smaller festivals and then it was Tribeca. Tribeca in and of itself was different than Sundance because it is all of New York City, so it doesn't have the compact feel that Sundance has. Nonetheless just as dynamite. A lot of fun. I met a lot of really great people. Really good screenings. I enjoyed myself. I really enjoyed

A Nick in Time—cont'd

being back home in front of a New York crowd and showing myself.

Cannes

After Tribeca *Moving Pictures Magazine* had a short film contest and as the winner of the short film contest they then flew you to Cannes and screened your film at Cannes. We ended up winning that contest and we screened our film in Cannes. And so I, my girlfriend and one of my actors all went to Cannes. We had never been and we just got to experience another film festival that is like Sundance times twenty because the whole world shows up. That experience in and of itself kind of just broadened my horizons and allowed me to see how big this could be and where you want to be in a few years with a feature film.

Distribution

During Sundance one of the things they ask you is if you want to distribute your film via iTunes. So, for me I felt like it was a chance to get a lot of exposure. More so to expose the film so people could go see it. Short film festivals usually play it at the festival and they don't really have a wide circulation. I felt like if I can put it in a place where people could conveniently go get it for $2.00 or whatever, people would see it. So, as a result of that I have gotten emails at various times over the last year and a half from people who have seen the film and asked for copies of it or downloaded it and watched it and shared comments. It just continues to validate the fact that the film itself hit its mark, told a story and that it tells me to keep shooting, keep going. No matter how hard it gets, no matter what, keep making films.

Be' Garrett

Citizen

I submitted all the big ones, Sundance, Slamdance, Toronto, Tribeca, Cannes—did not get into any of those. I did not screen at any of the top 10 festivals, but I had success at the First Run Film Festival at NYU. I also screened at a couple of student film festivals; one in Denver called The First Look Student Film Festival. Then I just started sending it off to more of the genre film festivals, which I kind of resisted. I was like, no, I am making a serious, political commentary piece. It took me awhile to accept the sci-fi aspect of the film. When I started sending it off to those festivals, it started doing well, one at Comic-Con and one at Screen Fest in L.A. this past October. There are basically three more film festivals I am waiting to hear back from. I am holding off on its online premier until I hear back or it screens at the Fantastic Fest in Austin, Fantasia in Montreal and the Toronto after Dark Film Festival, which is sort or horror and genre festivals. I guess I ended up screening around a dozen film festivals. I really wanted to go to the Tel Aviv University International Student Film Festival in Israel; when was the next time I was going to get a chance to go to Israel? They were not able to pay for travel, but they were able to put us up, which was pretty nice. The Crossroads Film Festival in Mississippi was really nice; also Riverside, California.

You reach a point with the festivals where you are spending all this money on entry fees and travel costs to go to the festivals, and some of them are admittedly kind of disappointing. The people watching your movie are you, and if you are lucky, three other people. Another big thing for me was that I had somehow managed, after the first run and with all the grants, I actually managed to break even on my film. What I had spent on the movie I got all back through grants and prizes. I kept submitting to the big festivals, but the lack of love was certainly discouraging. I always wanted to plan for an online movie at some point, and I feel some online promotion will be sufficient for me. Being able to say "winner" here and "best this and best

that." I could use those festival laurels. I think it is important to try to find some attention and recognition. Also a big thing for me was to be able to have something you could just give to people who you met. What have you done? Anything I could see? That was another reason I wanted to keep my film to 10 minutes. Once you start getting into the 15-, 20-minute area it becomes expdientially harder to get someone to actually sit down and watch your film. It is a lot easier to plan to watch something for 10 minutes than say half an hour long.

James Darling

While we were in the process of getting the final print of the film made, James and I began to think about film festivals. There are thousands and thousands of film festivals all around the world, and the trick is to know which ones to apply to. It's kind of like applying to colleges, in a way. I suggest you first understand the market for your film. Who is your ideal audience? Is your film a romance, a comedy, etc.? Once you have figured out what demographic of viewer you are marketing to, you should then begin to look at film festivals designed for that niche. Entry fees can be quite expensive, so I recommend making two rounds. The first set of entries should be for your top choice film festivals, the ones you would absolutely die to have your film in (examples usually include Sundance, Tribeca, Cannes, Toronto). These are also usually the most selective. Then, pick a few more niche-specific or regional festivals that you think your film would succeed in, and enter those as well. Also remember, it's not the size or prestige of the festival, but how the film is received. You might have a wonderful film that gets rejected for Sundance, but does exceptionally well at some smaller festivals.

When you go to festivals, it is very important to network. Having a press kit and a web site for your film is a great idea. Having business cards available is another great idea. People

Continued

Citizen—cont'd

may come up to you and ask you what else you are working on—this is a great time to potentially pitch your next film. So have answers ready! Also make sure you explore other options for your film's longevity. There are tons of TV channels that now broadcast short films, short films are available to watch in-flight on some airlines, and there is a wealth of exposure possible from the web.

One thing I learned from *Citizen* is that a short film could have global interest—we did not get into any of the "big" festivals with this film, but it did win some awards at NYU's First Run Film Festival, which helped put it on the map in a big way. The film played at some niche-specific festivals around the U.S., including Comic-Con, where it won an awesome trophy for "Best Action Short Film." Before the film played at Comic-Con, James was contacted by Tel Aviv University. They

had seen the film on a DVD of award-winning student shorts that NYU had distributed, and were interested in screening it at their bi-annual film festival. If we came to Israel for the festival, we would get to participate in a 24-hour film festival, and the university would put us up in housing. How could we say no? And what an experience it was! Some of the students helped us translate posters for *Citizen* into Hebrew, and we got to meet young filmmakers from all over the world: from Australia to Italy to Japan. It was also extremely interesting to see how the film, with its commentary on an enforced military draft, would fare in a country where joining the military is mandatory. I feel very fortunate to have shared such an experience with James. It not only helped me make new friends, but also reminded me of the power of film to globally connect people.

Jessalyn Haefele, Producer of *Citizen*

The Lunch Date

The first three festivals I sent *The Lunch Date* to didn't accept the film. I found this very discouraging. I think the first festival to accept it was San Francisco, and then suddenly every festival I applied to, it got into. I believe the film took on a life of its own. Once you're done with a film, it's out of your hands. There's nothing you can do. It has its own life, and who knows what that's going to be. I got very lucky: first in Atlanta and Houston—it won prizes there—and then AFI, which was non-competitive. The only one I went to out of all of those was the AFI because it was an excuse to go home. For all those who I'm sure are wondering how the hell it got into Cannes, I can tell you it was just a fluke of luck.

Cannes

Around the time I finished the film, I screened it for my professor, Vojtech Jasny. After showing it to him, he told me two things. One was that I should submit the film to Cannes, which I thought was completely crazy. He said, "Submit it; the festival is coming soon." I didn't act on that right away. I delayed. Eventually, I sent the film to Cannes.

The other thing Vojtech told me was that he had a friend who was a casting director, Diane Crittenden, who was in New York casting a film, and she was looking for an intern, an unpaid intern, to run a video camera during the casting of her next movie, and would I be interested? And I said, "Sure." I always like to work, and casting was part of the process I had not gotten to see. I was working part time doing the same kind of thing at a commercial house, but I was interested to see how different it was for a movie. So I spoke to Diane, and she said she had heard from Vojtech that my movie was good, and would I send her a tape? She was going to Los Angeles, but she would call when she got back.

I sent her the tape, and a few weeks went by. We eventually got in touch again, and she said that she didn't need anybody anymore, but that she had seen my film and she liked it. We

had a little talk on the phone, and she suggested I come down to meet with her, just to talk. We set up a date.

I ran all the way over from Fifth Avenue to Eleventh Avenue where her office was, and for some reason it didn't connect with me what she might be doing. I went up in the office, and there were all these signs for Green Card, and I thought that was her casting company or something. I got upstairs and saw it was a film production, and I realized, "Oh, this is *Green Card*, Peter Weir's film." So I went into the office, and I asked someone if they could show me to Diane Crittenden, my name is Adam Davidson. The receptionist said, "Oh, you're the person who made that short film, the one that takes place in Grand Central?" And I said, "Yeah, yeah." Then she said, "Diane's been showing everyone that film, and we all love it." I said, "Really?!"

I went down into her office and met Diane, and she said yes, she had been showing it to everyone. In fact, she had shown it to Peter Weir, who loved it and had taken the tape home to show Gerard Depardieu. Then she said, "Do you mind that I gave the tape out?" I was flabbergasted.

Then I got a call at work which I thought was a joke: "Hi, my name's Andy. I'm Peter Weir's assistant. I just wanted to tell you that Gerard Depardieu has recommended your film to Cannes, and he has given me this number that he wants you to call to contact Cannes." And I thought, "What! This is unbelievable." I called this number, and it was a French film office in New York. They said, "We got a call from Gerard Depardieu, and we would like to see your film." And I said, "Well, I submitted it about three months ago on my own. You have it. It's in France." "We have it?" "Yes, yes." "OK, we'll get back to you."

About a week later, the French woman from the Cannes office called, saying, "Your film has just been accepted at Cannes." It was amazing, absolutely amazing. I went over to Cannes. It was interesting.

The Lunch Date—cont'd

First of all, I went there with these very naive film-school fantasies of what Cannes would be like. I figured, it's the oldest film festival, it's France, the last bastion of where film is considered an art. I could walk down the street and see Akira Kurosawa and say, "Hey, Akira, let's go get a cup of coffee and talk about film and talk about cinema." Of course, it's nothing like that. It's a market. Now there's the festival there, and there's also the Cannes film market. There are these beautiful châteaus there, and these beautiful hotels, covered with giant Schwarzenegger posters and giant Stallone posters. It's a zoo, and I hated getting in a tux.

It was incredible because when I was going there, they were showing the new films of my heroes. Kurosawa was there with *Dreams*. Godard was there with *Nouvelle Vague*. Fellini was there with his film *La voce della Luna*. So I was happy to have a chance to see these movies.

Supposedly, I could get into any film, but I had to report to this one office every day. It was always the same story. I'd go in, and I'd have this list, and I'd say, "I'd like to see this at this time, and this at this time." I tried to only see the films during the day because going at night meant getting in a tux. There was only one way to enter the theater. You have to enter down the red carpet where people have gathered the whole day to get a glimpse of whoever was in the movie. So there I would be—alone—walking down, just feeling like the biggest loser in the world. I tried to go during the day when the press was going.

But every time when I went to get tickets, it was always the same answer. "Non, monsieur, c'est complet. Je suis désolée. I'm very sorry, but we're all filled." And then I'd sit there. I don't know why it is, it seems with the French, their first answer is no. Because then you sit there and ask, "Don't you have one, just any ticket?" And they say, "Oh, let me check." Then she'd open the door beside her, and she'd say, "Oh, I do have one." So I'd get my one ticket. So the screening of films came about.

There are all these shorts. In Cannes, the short category can be anything as long as it's short—under 15 minutes. So there were, in my category, a few animated films and something that resembled a documentary. Most of them were 35mm. Most of them were color. After seeing that screening, I was convinced that I didn't have a chance. It didn't matter. I was glad to just be there.

I was convinced the film wasn't going to win, and the day of the awards ... I hadn't received anything about if I should

go, where I should go. And I went down to the office to speak to the same woman and said, "What am I supposed to do?" And she said, "You're supposed to get a ticket." "Well, do you have one?" "Non, monsieur, je suis désolée. C'est complet." I said, "Are you sure?" She opens up the drawer, and there is one.

So I go to the awards thing, and they seat me. It was in the front row! And I'm sitting between two guys who are in the short film category. One guy turns to me and says, "Is my hair okay?" And I say, "Yeah, it looks fine." And he says, "Good. This is my third time here." I said, "Great. Congratulations."

The show starts, and it's strange. It's like a mixture of *The Dating Game* and something else. It goes by very fast. It's not like the Academy Awards, where they stop to do numbers and things like that. The host came out, the back door opened up, and—like *The Dating Game*—the eight jurors come out on this sliding platform, sitting on stools. Bernardo Bertolucci was the head of the jury that year. They're going through the different categories, and with my French, I'm picking up some of it. And then they get to the short film. They announce the award for the short film, and the two guys sitting next to me both get up at the same time and go up. And I thought, "Whoa, what a relief. It's over. The anxiety is over. I don't have to worry anymore." And these guys go off. Then Bertolucci starts speaking again because he gives the award as the head of the jury. He starts talking about short film again. And he says, "the Palme d'Or," which is the grand prize in Cannes "... goes to Adam Davidson." I went up on stage. He handed me what looked like a diploma thing, and I didn't know what the hell to do.

The next thing I know, I'm standing before this microphone, and I just wanted to make sure that I had thanked people. Well, as I'm speaking—and I was very nervous—I hear the emcee, who is a Johnny Carson type guy, start speaking too. And I was convinced (because I wasn't really listening) that this guy was saying, "What the hell is the stupid American doing? We don't want to hear it. It's just a short film. Get on with it." What I didn't know was that he was trying to translate. I just looked over at him and just kind of said, "That's it."

The whole thing with Cannes was a fluke. If it wasn't for the chance that Depardieu had seen it accidentally, I don't think it would have gotten in, even though I had sent it out there.

Adam Davidson

Crazy Glue

I was just hoping to make a good film that would take care of itself and that's what happened. One festival brought another festival and I got some purchase requests from various television stations. It was distributed by Atom Films for a while. It was never a money-making venture, but it did get some

awards and some additional sales. Since it's so short—short films are sold by the minute—it was never a huge amount, but it was nice. The market definitely paid back the $2,000 it cost me to make the film.

Tatia Rosenthal

Truman

Truman did well in the festivals, but the "festival game" is expensive. It's $25 to $50 a shot, and you have to put out for the tapes, which you don't think of. This is one of the nice things about distribution: once a distributor makes you a one-inch video master, and they have it, they can make dubs for you very cheaply, and they just charge it back to whatever profits you make. So it's a nice way to get dubs and a nice cover for your video copies.

The magazine *The Independent* lists all festivals throughout the world and what kinds of films these festivals are looking for, what they're interested in. You have to be careful, but even if you're careful, you can still pick 25 festivals for the year. The festivals I submitted to were recommended to me by my distributor, Direct Cinema, and they said it would help enhance the market for the film in terms of the educational market. The film won the Princess Grace Fellowship, a Warner Bros. Film Fellowship, was a Regional Finalist—Student Academy Awards; it screened at the Sundance Film Festival, was voted one of the top 10 best children's films of 1992 [American Library Association], and is one of the highest-grossing children's films of 1992.

It was really a learning process, going through this negotiation process for a short film, because a short film is not like another kind of contract. The whole means of supply and return is different; the market is different. The first thing that came as quite a shock is that when you get your film distributed, they have to make it an interpositive so they're not striking prints from your original negative. Well, guess who pays for the interpositive? You do, because it's yours; you own it. This is a huge expense, even for a 10-minute film. It was around $3,000 for the interpositive. So whatever money you make for the first year or so goes into paying off this interpositive you bought and/or whatever video, whatever dubs, you get struck for yourself.

It's been several years now, and I've only started to make money, even though the film has drawn astronomically well for [the distributor]. For a 10-minute film, it has done very well. In fact, a year ago, I think it was one of the top 10 children's films in the USA—short films. But, again, now I'm just starting to see money. I never expect to make all my money back.... The only film market that really exists for short films is the educational market. Now, I never imagined my film would be considered educational, but [middle schools] often buy it as a way to entertain kids on a rainy day, which is always how I imagined it, so it's turned out well.

It's only 10 minutes long, so it's really a diversion for kids at school, and because it's what's called an evergreen film, that's part of what's attractive about it. Evergreen means that it is always in season. There is nothing about this film that will date it. It is what it is: kids in a gym with sneakers. I mean, the themes in it, what it's about, will never get old. So it's attractive to schools even though it's not directly educational. If they have this film in their library, they can always pull it out for another 20 years to show the students, and it will always be of interest. That's really what a film distributor looks for because the short film market is about education. Can I sell this to a library or school?

I heard a story about my film that tickled me a little bit and surprised me because I didn't know what had happened. Apparently, when the film was done and it did well at the NYU screenings, it began to circulate. Copies get out that even you don't know about. People make dubs of dubs, and they start circulating the picture. I met this friend two years later who had another friend who was a West Coast junior agent for a while. He was talking to his friend, and his friend said, "There's this film that's the hot thing in Hollywood right now. Everybody's trying to get it, and there are very few copies available. Everybody wants to see this film, and I can't get a copy of it. I think it's an NYU student. Have you heard about it? It's about this kid climbing this rope."

This all went on unbeknownst to me. All of a sudden, without my knowing it, my film was a hot thing in Hollywood, and everybody wanted to get their hands on it, and there weren't enough copies to go around. That was two years ago, and I found out about it a year later. So if your film finds a certain niche, people will start talking about it, people will hear about it, and it will get around. Which is how I guess my agent found me. He must have been one of those people who had seen the tape, and he just called me out of the blue.

Howard McCain

Mirror Mirror

The first real public screening of *Mirror Mirror* was at the Margaret Mead Film Festival, which I had entered the previous spring with a videotape because the film wasn't completed at the time I entered it. People liked the film at Margaret Mead, and they started asking questions about this statement versus cross-cultural perceptions of body type. The kinds of questions you get at festivals are like that, which was fine. And then the film started doing very well. The next good thing that happened was it won the best documentary at the New York Film Expo. It won the director's choice at Black Maria Film Festival, and a Jury Award at the Big Muddy Film Festival. It won best documentary at the Humbolt International Festival and was the Judge's Choice winner at the Louisville Film and Video Festival. It was shown in London at the London International Film Festival. It didn't get into Sundance, although the director wrote me a note and said it came very close. So it wasn't a total flat-out rejection.

For distribution, I contacted Women Make Movies. I sent them a tape, and they were very interested. I felt comfortable about putting the film with them because if people don't

Mirror Mirror—cont'd

know about this film but they're teaching a "Media and Women" course at Podunk U. and trying to find a film, it seemed to me that they would look up the Women Make Movies catalog first. If they called around and asked if there is a distributor who distributes films about women, that's where they would end up.

I did negotiate for them to do a one-sheet flier just on this film, which to me meant a lot because it meant they would target this film—and direct it to a mailing list that was appropriate and so on—at their expense. So I signed with them in the fall of 1990. I only gave them nontheatrical; I retained domestic TV rights for myself, and I retained international, which eventually went to Jane Balfour Films in the winter of '92.

In terms of domestic TV, because I had retained it for myself, I entered it in *POV*, and it got in. It was broadcast in the summer of '91. I received all the revenue since I was the one who had made the deal. Now they have an exclusive.

I can't do anything with it, cable or PBS, for three years. That's their deal. Because it is a PBS contract, it has been on two other PBS series. First was the *Territory* series that comes out of Houston, so it's been shown down on Texas public television independently of *POV*, on this other series in Houston, Corpus Christi, and Austin. So I got some more money for that. And then it's also been on the *Through the Lens* series, which I think is on WYBE. It's a public station in Philadelphia. They put together a program of independents, unbeknownst to me—they actually went through Women Make Movies to get it—so it was on there. And now actually it's showing this month in the "What's Happening" series at MOMA. I think it's done well. I'm not getting rich off it, but when I look at the statements—I don't know how it's done compared to the distributor's other films—but I think it's really getting out there.

Jan Krawitz

The Academy Awards

The Academy Award is the highest honor a film artist can achieve. It is a massive career jolt, often a box office boost, and most definitely an emotional high. The award is a ticket to an elite club that, once given, can never be taken away. What one makes of the opportunity is, of course, always up to the winner.

Some are stymied by the attention; others brush it off as merely a career milestone. But whatever the reaction, receiving an Academy Award is a good thing.

The Academy Award is focused on feature-length films, but both short narrative and short documentary films (less than 30 minutes) have received Academy Awards over the years, and their impact on the filmmaker and the film community is no less profound.

But there is trouble in paradise. The Academy of Motion Picture Arts and Sciences has been shaking the awards tree of late, hoping to shed excess fruit. As anyone who watches the Academy Awards show knows, it is long. Between the dance numbers, the singing of all the Academy-nominated songs, and the passionate speeches where leaving someone off a thank-you list might prove politically devastating, the television producers are always looking for ways to trim the length of the show. In 1996 and in 1998, the short format came under fire and would have been excluded if not for the efforts of all the filmmakers who value the nature of the format and the learning curve associated with short work.

The Academy's argument is simple. The Academy Award is for theatrical motion picture work. Whereas in the past shorts had a life on the big screen, this is no longer the case. For a film to qualify for Academy consideration, it must play for at least one week before January 1

on at least one screen in Los Angeles. Because most short narrative and documentary films are not destined for big screens, the filmmakers must negotiate with theater owners for screen time around Christmas to be eligible for the award.

So, in 1996, the Academy said that short narrative films do not screen theatrically, and therefore the category should be eliminated. The same statement was made two years later referring to short documentary work. The outcry from the creative film community was overwhelming. Many filmmakers got their start experimenting with the short form before graduating to longer work. Letters and protests caused the Academy to back off and allow these two categories to remain—for now.

I submitted the film on my own to the Student Academy Awards. It won in the category there. I was informed that since my film won there, it qualified for submission to the Academy Awards. I'd had enough of awards and things, so I said, "No thanks." After the urgings of a few people, family, and agents and at the insistence of Rich Miller, the head of the Student Academy Awards, I said I would submit it. It was nominated. So I went to Los Angeles for the awards ceremony.

I decided to bring Scotty [the lead actress in the film] as my guest, but she doesn't fly, so like her character, she took a train all the way out to Los Angeles. She telephoned me the day of the ceremony and said, "What time is the limo coming by to pick us up?" I said, "Well, the Volkswagen will be by at such and such a time." We went together. We were seated in the middle of the row. You know how a mind works: I figured, "Obviously, this whole show is rigged, and they seat the people who they know are going to win by

Continued

the aisles so they can get out easily. So at least I don't have to worry about that."

And then I saw my mother, and she came and sat down behind me. It was pretty quiet in that theater, in that space, and she leans over and not too quietly says, "Adam, do you have enough room so you can get out?" And everybody— all the other nominees—just turns to look at me scornfully.

The category came up, and the film was announced. It didn't hit me. The name was said, and I heard this primal yell. It was my father, who was touching the roof of the theater. I got up—and I was just hoping I wouldn't trip—and got up on stage. It's pretty terrifying. You suddenly face 6,000 people, and the cameras are on, and they have this huge television monitor that they wheel in front of you, which basically flashes "30, 29, 28, 27 . . ."—how long you're allowed to speak. I think I thanked everybody. It was funny. I had gotten a seat for Garth Stein, my friend and the film's co-producer, and he was seated up in the balcony. When I thanked Garth, I said something like, "I'd also like to thank Garth Stein." And I looked up and said, "Who's somewhere up there." I think a lot of people imagined Garth had passed away or something.

The moral of this story about the film is that it does take on a life of its own. I would say to any student out there: Don't be discouraged if you don't get into your first couple of festivals. It is important to try to give the film a chance.

Adam Davidson

A Short History of the Short Film

The short film played an important part in the development of the modern cinema. From Thomas Edison to George Lucas, filmmakers have depended on the short format to exhibit new technology, advance artistic ideals, or simply catch the eye of the ever-important audience.

It was the audience that first motivated Thomas Alva Edison to commission his assistant, William K. L. Dickson, to begin research in 1889 on a device that would enhance his earlier invention, the phonograph. Photography had become increasingly popular since its inception in the 1860s, and with the invention of rolled celluloid film by George Eastman, the time was right. In 1891, Dickson projected the first motion picture images for his boss. Edison was granted a patent in 1893 for his Kinetoscope, an odd cabinet with a peephole viewer, and cinema was born.

Edison's first films were necessarily short. The Kinetoscope's compact design limited the length of the first films to 50 feet. The limitation was a commercial one. Edison knew that to make motion pictures financially viable, he needed to distribute not only films, but also miniature theaters.

These early Edison films were simple: one shot of a simple action. The photographic record of a sneeze, gloriously titled *Fred Ott's Sneeze*, is thought to be the oldest remaining motion picture film. The Kinetograph, Edison's camera, was a clunky contraption that could not be moved beyond the walls of its dark studio, the Black Maria. This was not a problem for Edison. His films were novelties, short glimpses of a new technology for a price.

The creative constraints of Edison's distribution and production were soon resolved by two brothers on the other side of the Atlantic. Auguste M. L. N. and Louis Jean Lumière developed a motion picture camera that could also develop and project film. The Cinématographe was portable and depended on a hand crank, rather than electricity, for power. In 1895, the brothers produced their first film, *Workers Leaving the Lumière Factory*, a short static exterior shot of workers leaving their factory. The Lumière brothers opened their first public theater on December 28, 1895, in the basement of the Grand Café in Paris, France. At the showing of *L'Arrivée d'un Train en Gare*, the audience screamed and ran from the theater as a train barreled toward them on the screen.

Early filmmakers continued to use the convenient and economical short film format. Improvements in cinematography and a growing sophistication of content led to multishot narratives. An excellent example is George Méliès's *A Trip to the Moon* (1902), which involved several static shots at different locations edited together. Edwin S. Porter's short film, *The Great Train Robbery* (1903), innovated continuity editing to build the narrative.

Motion pictures were by this time big business. Edison's company and others, including American Mutoscope and Biograph, began to compete for a piece of it. Nickelodeons, large store theaters, began spreading across the country after the first opened in Pittsburgh in 1905. The nickelodeons created an additional demand for films and kept the short film alive until great directors such as D.W. Griffith insisted on creating feature-length films. By 1914, the feature film (four or more reels) had become the dominant form, and the studios began to relegate the shorts to the role of filler in a feature program. There were few exceptions.

The demand for product was a catalyst for the creation of serials. These short episodic films were centered around a few key characters, and they were exhibited in installments. In 1912, Edison's Kinetoscope Company began the first serial, *What Happened to Mary*. With a unique publicity campaign involving the *Ladies Home Journal*, which printed the new story each week, the format became highly successful. The clichés of the cliff-hanger soon appeared. Studios such as Selig Polyscope Company and later Metro-Goldwyn-Mayer capitalized on the format to become major contenders in the business.

A young director named Mack Sennett, unable to produce comic films under Edison or Biograph, formed the independent film company Keystone Pictures. The Sennett shorts were characterized by their sight gags and slapstick humor. In 1913, British actor Charlie Chaplin joined Sennett. Chaplin later created several great shorts, including *The Tramp* (1915), *One A.M.* (1916), *Easy Street* (1917), and *A Dog's Life* (1918). The Chaplin comedy shorts were unique in that they presented social commentary under the guise of silliness. Later, the short film became a vehicle for other comic giants, including Buster Keaton (*The Goat*, 1921) and Laurel and Hardy (*Putting Pants on Philip*, 1927).

All was not comical in the early years of the twentieth century, however. Artistic movements triggered by World War I and the Russian Revolution influenced all media, including film. Directors became proponents of German

Expressionism (Erich von Stroheim, Ernst Lubitsch, and Fritz Lang) or Soviet Montage (Sergei Eisenstein and Vsevlod I. Pudovkin). The short film became an experimental form for these new cinematic ideas.

Documentary, which had been reduced to travelogues and novelty films, gained momentum as a genre with Robert Flaherty's *Nanook of the North* (1922). Flaherty's work gave legitimacy to the documentary form and began an important artistic tradition.

Sound was the next major technical hurdle. There had been several attempts to synchronize sound and film during the early years of motion pictures. By 1919, a workable system had been devised. Lee de Forest, inventor of the vacuum tube used for amplification, began showing the first sound films, which he called *Phonofilms*. These were short demonstrations by famous personalities speaking or singing on screen. Vitaphone (the first commercial sound film company) and later William Fox's Movietone both began to distribute short sound films.

An example of one of these early sound shorts is Movietone's *Shaw Talks for Movietone News* (1928). In 1927, Fox-Movietone premiered the first newsreels.

At the end of the 1920s, Disney introduced its first *Silly Symphony*, titled *Skeleton Dance*. These animated shorts coupled recent advances in film sound with Disney's unique artistic vision to create fantastic musical revues.

While Disney was busy with his favorite mouse in *Steamboat Willie* (1928), the avant garde movement was awakening, led by such filmmakers as Jean Renoir, Man Ray, and Luis Buñuel. Classic short films such as *Ballet Mecanique* (Fernard Leger, 1924), *Un Chien Andalou* (Luis Buñuel and Salvador Dali, 1929), and *Entr'Acte* (René Clair, 1924) revealed the strong intellectual influence on film from painting, psychology, and other areas.

Television changed films in general, but especially short films. With the inception of television, the 30-minute and 60-minute format became popular. In 1951, Columbia formed Screen Gems to produce product for television, marking a new area for studio dominance.

During the 1950s, several independent animators experimented with techniques such as pixillation and drawing on film. With his experimental shorts *A Chairy Tale, Neighbors,* and *Pas de Deux*, Canadian director Norman McLaren is the best known of this group. Animation techniques further influenced directors such as Albert Lamorisse (*The Red Balloon*, 1956).

In the wake of World War II, a new wave of filmmakers emerged in France. A strong documentary tradition pushed these new filmmakers toward fresh artistic expression in documentary shorts. The stylistic devices of the documentary—location shooting, direct sound, and handheld camera work—further influenced their narrative work. Leaders in this movement included Alain Resnais (*Night and Fog*, 1955), Chris Marker (*La Jetée*, 1962), Jean-Luc Godard (*All the Boys Are Called Patrick*, 1959), and François Truffaut (*Antoine and Colette*, 1962).

The 1960s, a time of social and cultural change, saw the growth of the underground independent short filmmaker. Many classic short films were produced during this era, including Roman Polanski and Jean-Pierre Rensseau's *The Fat and the Lean* (1961) and Robert Enrico's *An Occurrence at Owl Creek Bridge* (1962). The introduction of the 8 mm and 16 mm formats made film more accessible and affordable to more people. Andy Warhol, the famed pop artist, was one of those who crossed over into film as an alternative medium.

The accessibility of film to the public allowed younger and younger people to dabble in filmmaking. Film schools began to appear throughout the United States and the world. George Lucas's student film, *THX 1138*, inspired his later science-fiction feature with Robert Duvall. Francis Ford Coppola, Steven Spielberg, Oliver Stone, and others began as student short filmmakers in the late 1960s and early 1970s.

Today, the short narrative and documentary film survives in film schools and festivals throughout the United States and in the booming European film community. Other forms, including music videos and television/film commercials, have given new filmmakers applications for their cinematic ideas. With the continued growth of film schools and the proliferation of video technology, the short format probably will continue into the future.

Genres and Animation

ANIMATION

Animation has become a very large and significant segment of filmmaking. With the advent of digital media, the definition of animation has expanded to include large portions of the visual effects and commercial production industries.

Animation is not a separate genre. You will find animation utilized in many genres: commercials, children's programs, feature films, short narratives, experimental films, video art, TV sitcoms, and animated features.

Animation has been a part of our visual and popular culture since the turn of the century, mostly in the form of cartoons. Hanna-Barbera, Disney, Fleischer, and Chuck Jones are names that represent a rich and dense body of creative work.

Most animation projects are short. The production principles are similar to those for live-action film and video, except that instead of actors, an animator employs characters and/or designs that are created from scratch. Drawing on paper, molding clay, or generating images on a computer are among the numerous techniques that bring animated characters, graphics, and special effects to the screen. The work of creating an animated film is time-consuming and requires great patience.

Creating an animated film involves creating an entire world from scratch. Anything that can be manipulated in space can be animated. Animation characters range from stick figures and paper cutouts to three-dimensional clay figures and elaborate Disney-style cel animation.

The styles of individual artists can be as varied as their imaginations. The animators Norman McLaren, John and Faith Hubley, and Frank and Caroline Mouris developed their unique non-Disney styles with great success. Clay animation, perfected by Will Vinton and others, has been incorporated into mainstream entertainment. Year after year, animated features, a popular form of entertainment that is accessible to all ages, are traditionally the highest-grossing films. Some of the most original and visually dynamic films of all time were animated.

We are now experiencing technological revolutions in this field. Computer techniques and the enhancement of existing images are creating a branch of animation that will be available to everyone. The use of home computers for applications such as morphing and image manipulation will allow more of us to storyboard, animate, and tell stories in a visual manner unlike anything we know today.

EXPERIMENTAL, ALTERNATIVE, AVANT GARDE

The short film or video has been an ideal form for experimentation. Filmmakers have been experimenting with the possibilities of what film can do since the time of George Méliès'. Many major European directors who became famous in the 1930s and 1940s began their careers in the 1920s with short films: Jean Renoir, René Clair, Luis Buñuel, and Julien Duvivier are among them. The artists Man Ray and Marcel Duchamp both explored the possibilities of film's pure visual form. Many early experimental pieces relied on seemingly random images, with no apparent story or narrative expectations to engage the audience. These filmmakers played visual tricks with the medium, dealing with surrealistic film fantasies. They later incorporated into their features many of the filmic ideas explored in these short experimental films.

The independent avant garde, or underground, movement in the United States began as a protest against Hollywood's conventions and standard narrative expectations. Many of the early short films in the 1920s focused on pure images and had little form or content. It was Maya Deren in the early 1940s who realized that noncommercial, personal short films could do more than just photograph a series of shapes and forms. She created a series of surreal films that played with the perception of space and time as well as the line between dream and reality. Her films greatly influenced the underground movement in the United States in the 1950s and 1960s. Aided by the increased availability of 16mm and 8mm film equipment, new filmmakers such as Stan Brakhage, Robert Breer, Shirley Clarke, Bruce Conner, Kenneth Anger, Bruce Baille, George Kuchar, Jonas Mekas, Ed Emshwiller, and Andy Warhol emerged as explorers in "personal filmmaking."

The availability of portable video in the 1970s and 1980s allowed a new generation of artists to emerge, aided by the technological ease with which images could be created and the endless possibilities for electronic manipulation. No longer were images relegated to one screen. Installations became an intricate part of experimental presentations, embodied in what are referred to as *video walls*.

Multimedia, which mixes live performances with video installations, became an effective tool for musicians and dancers such as Meredith Monk, Joan Jonas, and Bob Flanagan to use in expanding the reach of their art. Media organizations and artist support groups have sprouted up across the country to support new generations of visual artists who are expressing themselves in radical new ways. In the 1990s, the lines between film and video blurred with the impact of digital technology. Compact digital cameras and home desktop editing systems are empowering those who wish to express themselves in alternative ways. Visual artists are looking to the Internet as a viable distribution outlet for their short works.

CORPORATE

Businesses and other types of organizations (including educational and nonprofit institutions and government agencies) use short films and videos (usually 10 minutes or less in length) for a variety of purposes: to help launch new products or services, to explain new ideas or strategies, and to educate and train employees. Such media are known collectively as *corporate* or *sponsored* media.

With the rise of the Web, video has become a communication commodity—ubiquitous, but not as hot as it was in the 1980s and early 1990s. Often, video (and sometimes film) pieces are incorporated into other formats, particularly web sites and CDs, as well as trade show presentations and mixed media installations in museums or other exhibits. Currently, the lack of Internet bandwidth and slow connection speeds put severe limits on the length of web-based motion segments.

The objective of most corporate media is to communicate messages and information to specific, targeted audiences in such a way as to move them to some desired action or change their attitudes about an issue. Most corporate work is produced in video, rather than film, and uses a variety of creative approaches, including computer graphics, animation, documentary, and dramatic narrative.

Despite the general decline of the influence of video, high-quality pieces are still produced when an important message needs to be delivered and distributed widely and requires a running time of several minutes. The best corporate work can transcend its business objectives and achieve the status of art. *Powers of Ten* (1978), by Charles and Ray Eames, was sponsored by IBM to help audiences understand the scale and power of large computers. *Knowledge Navigator* (1987) was produced by Apple Computer to provoke audiences into thinking about the future of interactive computing; it was aired on network television, shown at conferences, and analyzed in major publications such as *Scientific American* and *Fortune*.

In today's constantly changing, culturally and geographically diverse organizations, these media have become important means of communication. Many businesses maintain extensive production facilities for both traditional and new media; others contract with agencies, producers, and design firms that specialize in corporate work. Many writers, producers, directors, shooters, designers, programmers, and others find corporate work interesting, creatively demanding, and financially rewarding—but not the best way to fulfill personal artistic ambitions.

COMMERCIALS

A commercial is a short. It has a beginning, a middle, and an end. It sets up conflict at the beginning and tries to persuade us that the only way to resolve that conflict is to buy a particular product—and it does this in as few as 15 seconds. Commercials are small, succinct stories that carry a great deal of weight. For many young people, the television commercial is their only opportunity to experience an idea expressed in less than a half-hour.

The one thing that can be said about any commercial, whether "good" or "bad," is that it has tremendous power. Commercials disrupt our regular viewing, creating a hostile relationship, but then are able to sway us emotionally and sell us something. The power of a television commercial is in its manipulation of the medium for one purpose. There are different kinds of commercials, including political commercials, which are designed to sell a candidate, and public service announcements (PSAs), which are designed to communicate an important issue. Whether they are designed to tell us whom to vote for, about the dangers of AIDS, or what detergent to use, commercials are about the power to persuade.

Since television commercials were first introduced in the early 1950s (when they were broadcast live), they have managed to manipulate contemporary technology and current social and economic trends to successfully sell their wares. They exploit popular icons and ideology in an effort to access our personal psyches—all this to promote toothpaste or beer. Millions of dollars are spent on 30 seconds of screen time. During the 1960s, there was a renaissance in commercial activity, and commercials were almost considered the best thing on television. This soon stopped. People were so entertained by the commercial that the product went almost unnoticed.

In the 1990s, there was a return to more entertaining commercials with dazzling displays of technological wizardry. Advertising agencies with huge expense accounts utilize high-end computer-driven systems to create sophisticated

3D graphics. Some campaigns have steered away from the old-fashioned "hard sell" to subtler, almost abstract approaches aimed at the modern consumer. Comedy has even resurfaced as a selling tool.

MUSIC VIDEOS

Although they are called music "videos," these short pieces have been traditionally shot on film. They emerged in the 1980s as vehicles to revive the music industry. The idea of showcasing musical talent and songs was born, however, many years before. There is a long tradition of performing songs on film and television; musicals were a Hollywood staple from the introduction of sound up until the 1960s. Many of these were based on Broadway revues, themselves vehicles to showcase songs and talented performers with a bare thread of a plot to tie them together.

First radio and then television used the variety show format to showcase popular music and its performers. The *Ed Sullivan Show* was one of the earliest and certainly one of the most popular in television. It featured singers or groups such as Elvis Presley, the Beatles, and the Rolling Stones. Later, popular recording stars such as Sonny and Cher and the Smothers Brothers would have their own variety shows. The 1960s spawned music/dance shows such as *American Bandstand* (1957–1989), *Shindig*, and *Hullabaloo* (1964–1966), and in the 1970s, *Soul Train*. Groups such as the Beatles, the Beach Boys, the Righteous

Brothers, Chuck Berry, Sam Cooke, Neil Sedaka, and the Everly Brothers appeared on these shows, giving audiences a chance to see their favorite entertainers performing their hit songs (although they were usually lip-syncing). Music documentaries such as *Don't Look Back, Monterey Pop*, and *Woodstock* made an indelible mark with young audiences by featuring live performances in concert.

The music video liberated the performers from the context of a show or concert and gave each song—and performer—its own self-contained presentation. Earlier music videos tried to adhere to some narrative that was loosely based on the lyrics of the song, but this format has largely disappeared. Narrative expectations have vanished. Many display random images and visual non sequiturs strung together by the persona of the artist, hip visual effects, and, of course, a song. From the record company perspective, their primary purpose is to create an image for the group rather than to sell a particular song.

The music video owes its stylistic debt to the Beatles' first feature, *A Hard Day's Night* (1964). Directed by Richard Lester, this highly successful film dazzled audiences with its frantic pace, zany antics, jump cuts, and, of course, the endearing personalities of the Fab Four. Music videos have been a successful training ground for many directors and a wonderful opportunity for beginning film- and videomakers to get valuable experience and create a body of work.

Script Sample

In this appendix you'll find a sample of a properly formatted script. For additional scripts please visit the companion site at http://booksite.focalpress.com/companion/IrvingRea/.

The Compatriot
(aka *Citizen*)
by James Darling

FADE IN:

INT. MINIVAN - CONTINUOUS

JONATHAN EVERMAN (18) sits alone in the center of the middle seat staring straight ahead blankly. He is bundled up with a jacket, cap, scarf and gloves. The leafless trees of the expansive forest fly by in the vehicle's windows.

JONATHAN'S POV: The lines of the highway stream forward from the horizon. His MOTHER (45) sits in the passenger seat and his GRANDPA (67) drives.

The radio plays the start of a news cycle: "The warmest December on record.... Twenty-seven troops killed abroad... Holiday terrorism feared... Illegal immigration continues to be hot topic in Congress-" Grandpa turns off the radio.

                         GRANDPA
               We're nearly there.

The empty expression on Jonathan's face breaks. Anxiety and sadness begin to surface, and he looks out the window at the tall grass that streams by.

INT. DOCTOR'S OFFICE - DAY (FLASHBACK)

The door is closed by a Male DOCTOR (40) who walks past Jonathan, who is sitting in his boxers and socks in a chair. The Doctor takes a seat at his desk and pulls out a clipboard.

                         DOCTOR (O.S.)
               Are you Jonathan?

                         JONATHAN
               Yeah.

                         DOCTOR
               Date of birth?

                         JONATHAN
               February 26, 1993.

EXT. FOREST ROAD - DAY

The Minivan is parked by the side of the road. A handicapped tag hangs in the dashboard. Jonathan hugs his Mother at the edge of the tall grass, while his Grandpa looks around anxiously.

Continued

                              MOTHER
                    Oh, my poor baby. I love you.

Jonathan takes the hug graciously, but releases himself quickly.

                              MOTHER (CONT'D)
                    Please be safe.

                              GRANDPA
                    He'll be a lot safer soon.

Jonathan slips a BACKPACK over his shoulders.

                              GRANDPA (CONT'D)
                    Just follow the instructions.

                              JONATHAN
                    I will.

His Mother hands him a sandwich wrapped in tin foil.

                              MOTHER
                    It's peanut butter and jelly.

Jonathan nods and slips the sandwich into his coat pocket. He stands awkwardly for a
moment.

                              JONATHAN
                    Well... bye.

Jonathan extends his hand to his Grandpa, who shakes it vigorously. Jonathan heads
toward the tall grass, but his mother catches him with another hug. This time Jonathan
squirms with annoyance.

                              JONATHAN (CONT'D)
                    Bye!
He releases himself and continues forward towards the grass.

Grandpa and Mother turn back towards the car. Seen clearly for the first time, Grandpa is
MISSING HIS LEFT ARM. The sleeve is pinned up to the shoulder.

As Jonathan reaches the edge of the tall grass, he looks back briefly at his family members as they drive off and then continues marching forward into the brush.

INT. DOCTOR'S OFFICE - DAY (FLASHBACK)

The Doctor still remains focused on the computer and not Jonathan.

                              DOCTOR
                    Any allergies?

                              JONATHAN
                    Penicillin and cats.

The doctor types.

                              DOCTOR
                    Have you ever been sexually active?
Jonathan hesitates for a moment.

                              JONATHAN
                         (mildly ashamed)
                    No.

EXT. FOREST - DAY

Jonathan emerges from the tall grass to a clearing in the forest. He walks slowly through
the thick underbrush. The ground CRUNCHES and CRACKS noisily beneath his boots.

Continued

After several steps, Jonathan stops and looks around, clearly disoriented.

He reaches into his pocket and pulls out a small CELLPHONE. He presses a few buttons and a GPS readout comes on the display. He holds it like a compass as it beeps quietly.

Upon the Cellphone's instruction, he looks off just to his right. Something SHIMMERS against the horizon.

Jonathan quickly closes the cellphone, pockets it, and accelerates to a sprint.

INT. DOCTOR'S OFFICE - DAY (FLASHBACK)

                              DOCTOR
                    Do you exercise regularly?

                              JONATHAN
                    Track and field at school.

EXT. FOREST - DAY

Jonathan's feet kick up leaves and dirt from the ground. His arms swing vigorously at his sides. His face fills with anticipation.

CRUNCH! CRUNCH! CRUNCH! CRUNCH! CRUNCH! CRUNCH!

Jonathan stops. His eyes look upward.

He is standing a few yards from an enormous METAL WALL that is nearly twelve feet tall and seems to stretch endlessly through the forest. It is made of horizontal aluminum strips that ripple every few inches, which are reinforced with vertical steel poles that drive into the ground.

INT. DOCTOR'S OFFICE - DAY (FLASHBACK)

                              DOCTOR
                    Any history of mental illness?

                              JONATHAN
                    I was treated for mild A.D.H.D. as a kid.

                              DOCTOR
                    Hmph. Some say that can actually
                    be an asset. Multitasking.

Jonathan nods ambivalently.

EXT. FOREST WALL - DAY

Jonathan walks along the edge of the Wall with his left hand extended so his fingers ride along the ridges of the metal.

He spots a discolored area at the bottom of the Wall just ahead and pauses momentarily.

Jonathan reaches inside his jacket and pulls out the cellphone.

He presses a few buttons and photos of the discolored portion of the wall appear on the display. He presses another button on the phone and a photo of a distinct BUSH appears.

Jonathan looks around and sees the Bush down at the base of the hill leading up to the fence.

He runs down toward it, kneels down and clears some shrubbery.

EXT. FOREST WALL - DAY

There is a SMALL HOLE visible in the concrete that leads underneath the Metal Wall. The opening is barely a foot-and-a-half wide and leads into darkness.

Continued

Jonathan looks at his entrance uncertainly. It's a tight squeeze, even for a thin guy like himself. He stands up slowly and looks at his bulky winter clothes.

INT. DOCTOR'S OFFICE - DAY (FLASHBACK)

                                    DOCTOR
                        I'll need you fully undressed.

Jonathan stands up and complies with little enthusiasm.

EXT. FOREST WALL - DAY

The backpack flies over the wall.

Jonathan is now wearing only his boxers, socks and a T-shirt in the freezing cold weather.

He has tied the rest of his clothes into a big BUNDLE using his scarf. He holds the bundle from a jacket sleeve like a ball and chain made of fleece and starts to SWING.

After getting enough momentum going back and forth, Jonathan vigorously THROWS the second bundle skyward and over the fence.

BUMPH! It has landed *somewhere* on the other side.

Jonathan walks down to the hole and gets down on his hands and knees. He approaches the opening head first.

INT. UNDERGROUND TUNNEL - CONTINUOUS

Loose dirt on all sides. Jonathan cannot even look straight forward with his head as he wriggles his way inside.

It is slow going. He pulls with his fingers, which are up by his chin, and he pushes with his toes, which are still just outside the tunnel.

His right knee SCRAPES against something. Jonathan winces and bares his teeth in pain.

He keeps inching forward, a little more cautiously now.

The crown of his head eventually touches the far end of the dirt tunnel.

The ceiling of this end blankets his head in a soft diffused light. He arches his head upward and feels a soft surface.

Jonathan pushes his head up firmly against the surface and it gradually gives way.

Light pours into the tunnel as Jonathan's head emerges into:

NOTE: Cross cut Doctor writing furiously, not talking to Jonathan.

EXT. FOREST WALL - CONTINUOUS

Jonathan's eager eyes peek out onto the other side of the Metal Wall. The soft surface is a WOODEN HATCH, which is two feet long and leans on Jonathan's partially emerged head.

JONATHAN'S POV: Just more forest, but he happily spies his bundle of clothes and backback a few yards away.

Jonathan wiggles his way out more, enough to free his arms. He grabs the hatch and pushes it aside.

He is overcome with joy and rapidly grabs the edge of the hole's mouth, pushing his body upward and outward.

EXT. FOREST WALL - CONTINUOUS

Continued

Suddenly, as his legs move towards the light, one of them is CAUGHT by a JAGGED EDGE of concrete!

EXT. FORREST - CONTINUOUS

The sudden stop KICKS Jonathan's whole upper body backwards and his head FLIES into the Metal Wall behind him.

BANG! The sound reverberates across the metal strips and echoes throughout the forest.

Jonathan is on his knees. He rubs the back of his head and contorts his face: a minor ache, but not bad.

He is clearly more concerned about the sound he has made. His eyes look around furiously into the deep recesses of the forest. Thankfully there seems to have been no one around.

Stepping out from the hole, he sits back down with his knees pointed upwards. Jonathan looks himself over.

His right knee has a small scrape. Jonathan nods with relief, but then looks to his left leg: Blood is dripping down the back of his left foot from a deep gash in his calf.

Jonathan SIGHS in frustration.

INT. DOCTOR'S OFFICE - DAY (FLASHBACK)

The Doctor lifts up a needle that is filled with fresh blood. Jonathan's arm has been BANDAGED with cotton balls. The Doctor removes the bottle and starts writing on the label.

                    JONATHAN
          Need any other "samples"?

The Doctor looks back at him quizically.

                    DOCTOR
          Just one...

He lifts up a plastic URINE SAMPLE CONTAINER.

EXT. FOREST WALL - DAY

Jonathan pees on the wall on an area that has already been discolored. He is fully bundled up again and has made an amateur BANDAGE out of a ripped t-shirt, which is tied around his left calf.

He puts one last handful of leaves over the Wooden Hatch, which he has put back across the opening.

Jonathan rises to his feet. He begins walking away from the Wall and into the forest.

INT. DOCTOR'S OFFICE - DAY (FLASHBACK)

                    DOCTOR
          Just relax.

EXT. FOREST - DAY

Jonathan walks leisurely through the endless woods. He pauses his advance momentarily and reaches into his jacket pocket. He pulls out the tinfoil package and unwraps the flattened but appetizing SANDWICH. The peanut butter and jelly is on white bread with the crusts cut off.

He smiles momentarilty and then devours it in a few bites.

INT. DOCTOR'S OFFICE - DAY (FLASHBACK, CROSS-CUT)

Continued

The pressure cuff of a BLOOD PRESSURE MONITOR squeezes around Jonathan's bare arm.

In the forest, Jonathan hears a sound from behind his back. He turns around suddenly.

The heart rate display on the Pressure Monitor rises from 55 bpm to 58 bpm.

Jonathan sees a YOUNG HUNTER (25) a quarter of a mile back with a RIFLE in his hands. The Figure gazes down at the ground.

The heart rate monitor rises from 61 bpm to 69 bpm.
Jonathan's chest heaving up and down.

The Hunter looks up in Jonathan's direction and Jonathan turns to run.

73 bpm to 82 bpm. Eyes widening.

Jonathan sprints at full speed through the woods. Leaves and dirt fly in every direction.

85 to 95. Hands clenching.

Jonathan trips on some branches, but gets right up again.
99 to 104. Beep.

BANG! A gunshot rings through the forest!

Jonathan stops dead in his tracks and looks to the shot tree on his right.

He looks back at an OLDER HUNTER, who is about 80 feet off to his right. The hunter has a full beard, wool cap, knit gloves, rustic jeans and a white winter vest over a flannel jacket. His rifle is aimed skyward.

> HUNTER
> Don't be stupid.

The Hunter lowers the rifle to aim squarely at Jonathan.

> DOCTOR
> You're blood pressure is a little
> high for your age. Probably just
> stress. Otherwise you're perfectly
> healthy. Fit for duty.

Jonathan looks disturbed.

EXT. FOREST - DAY

The HUNTER walks slowly forward, rifle still fixed on Jonathan. He is now fifty feet away.

> HUNTER
> CITIZENSHIP!?

The Hunter's feet stepping lightly on the ground. There is now forty-five feet between them.

> JONATHAN
> (hesitantly)
> I'm Canadian!

Forty feet.

> HUNTER
> I've heard that before.

Jonathan looks on anxiously. Thirty-five feet.

Continued

                              HUNTER (CONT'D)
                          Hmm... Who's our President?
Thirty feet.

                              JONATHAN
                                Uhh...
Twenty-five. The Hunter looks at him skeptically.

Jonathan's face fills with realization.

                              JONATHAN (CONT'D)
                          You don't have one!
The Hunter stops advancing at twenty feet <u>and lowers his rifle</u>.

Jonathan visibly relaxes.

                              HUNTER
                      Don't you mean, **WE** don't have one?
Jonathan's face fills with horror.

Jonathan turns to run!

He takes only two steps before being SMACKED in the face by the butt of another rifle.

Jonathan FALLS to the ground, unconscious.

<u>The Younger Hunter</u> was right behind him.

The two Hunters come together. "CIVILIAN BORDER PATROL OF CANADA" is printed on the back of their vests.

INT. PUBLIC SCHOOL HALLWAY - DAY (FLASHBACK)

A DOOR with a temporary "Selective Service - Physical Examinations" sign posted. The Doctor opens the door for Jonathan, who slips his arms into his sleeves as he exits.

                              DOCTOR
                          Next, please.
As Jonathan steps out, (MORE) another TEENAGE BOY (<u>18</u>) steps into the office and begins to disrobe.

Jonathan turns down the hallway of this dilapidated public school, passing a seemingly endless line of MALE TEENAGERS.

As Jonathan walks, he gazes at their young and distinct faces, many of whom respond with a friendly nod and a look of fearful understanding.

<u>EXT. BRICK WALL - DUSK</u>

<u>Jonathan stands in handcuffs beside a resolute and armed BLACK SOLDIER (22). The Soldier</u>
<u>watches Jonathan out of the corner of his eye, while Jonathan looks off.</u>

<u>Jonathan turns to the soldier hesitantly.</u>

                              JONATHAN
                      <u>You believe in what you're doing?</u>
<u>The Soldier ignores him.</u>

                              JONATHAN (CONT'D)
                      <u>You think this war is justified?</u>
                      <u>You think this is all worth it?</u>

                                                              Continued

> BLACK SOLDIER

That's not what this is about.

> JONATHAN
> What is about then? Honor? Duty?
> Patriotism?

The Soldier does not respond.

> JONATHAN (CONT'D)
> Why should I have to fight your war!?

The Soldier turns and stares straight into the eyes of the Draft Dodger.

> BLACK SOLDIER
> If you don't fight it, my friends
> over there will never come home!
> Just because you don't show up, it
> doesn't mean we have an empty
> uniform lying around! Someone
> still has to fill these boots!

A door opens behind the soldier.

> WHITE SOLDIER (O.S.)
> Come on!

EXT. BORDER STATION - CONTINUOUS

A WHITE SOLDIER steps out of a small office with some paperwork he stuffs into his pocket.

> WHITE SOLDIER (CONT'D)
> Let's get him in with the other cowards.

The Hunters are visible in the distance watching with pride, as the White Soldier takes Jonathan by the arm towards a waiting PRISONER VAN.

It is parked in the second lane of a line of three TOLL BOOTHS. A Border Guard with American insignia examines the passport of a couple in a car in the furthest booth. Canadian and American flags fly on a tall flag pole.

The White Soldier opens the door and shoves Jonathan inside.

INT. PRISONER TRANSPORT - DUSK

The side doors fly open and Jonathan is SHOVED inside by two U.S. ARMY SOLDIERS.

Jonathan looks at his fellow prisoners: Half-a-dozen YOUNG MEN (late teens and early 20s) who sit on benches attached to either side of the vehicle. They each gaze at Jonathan with the same look of fearful understanding.

Jonathan turns around as the side doors are SLAMMED SHUT.

The Soldiers open up their respective doors in the front of the vehicle and get inside.

The Prisoner Transport grumbles to life, pulls away from the booth and accelerates down the road, quickly passing a "Welcome to America" sign.

                                                                    FADE OUT.

Screening List

The following is a partial list of recommended short films. Many can be found on DVD collections, iTunes, or YouTube.

SHORT FILMS

The Lunch Date. Written and directed by Adam Davidson, 12 minutes, B&W, Academy Award—Best Live Action Film, 1990, USA. A chance encounter between a wealthy suburban woman and a homeless man at a lunch counter in Grand Central Station.

Truman. Written and directed by Howard McCain, 12 minutes, color, 1992, USA. An 11-year-old boy confronts his imaginary fears about climbing a rope in gym class.

Crazy Glue. Adapted and directed by Tatia Rosenthal, 5 minutes, color, 1997, USA. Tatia Rosenthal, Tel: 917-613-2667, rosenthal@yahoo.com. An animated clay puppet short adapted from a story by Israeli author Etgar Keret. This claymation (see Glossary) film tells the story of one innovative attempt to patch up a disintegrating marriage—through the use of Crazy Glue!

Mirror Mirror. Directed by Jan Krawitz, 17 minutes, color, 1990, USA. Women Make Movies, 462 Broadway, Suite 500, New York, NY 10013, Tel: 212-925-0606, Fax: 212-925-2052. A documentary exploring women's feelings about their bodies; 13 masked women speak about their bodies, intercut with historical footage.

Citizen. Written and directed by James Darling, 10 minutes, color, 2007, USA. In an eerie not-too-distant future, a young man tries to escape from his homeland in the dead of winter. As this teenage boy is chased by hunters through the harsh wilderness approaching the border, he recalls the perilous steps of his journey and the fateful doctor's visit that motivated his departure.

A Nick in Time. Written by Be' Garrett and Shakima Landsmark, directed by Be' Garrett, 10 minutes, color, 2006. An old-school barber recounts an incident from his past to a troubled young man who is on the verge of making a major life-altering decision. But can the barber get through to him before things spiral out of control?

COLLECTIONS

Akira Kurosawa's Dreams. Directed by Akira Kurosawa. 119 minutes, color, 1990, Japan/USA. (Home Warner Video). A collection of tales based on the actual dreams of Akira Kurosawa. Very personal short films with breathtaking imagery.

Cinema 16 Collections. Internet collection of award-winning international and U.S. short films.

Full Frame documentary shorts. DVD collections of short documentary films from the Full Frame Documentary Film Festival

Pascal Aubier (27 short films). DVD collection of one of the greatest French short filmmakers.

EARLY SHORTS BY WELL-KNOWN FILMMAKERS

All the Boys Are Called Patrick. Directed by Jean-Luc Godard, 21 minutes, B&W, 1959, France. Two roommates both meet boys named Patrick; they begin to suspect and later realize that their two Patricks are actually the same boy.

Amblin'. Directed by Steven Spielberg, color, 24 minutes, 1968, USA. Two wanderers meet and hitchhike together, but when they reach their destination, the beach, the girl discovers that the boy is not what he seemed to be.

THX 1138. Directed by George Lucas, color, 1969, USA. A future where love is the ultimate crime.

The Big Shave. Directed by Martin Scorsese, 6 minutes, color, 1968, USA. (Available on DVD *Three by Scorsese*). As he shaves, a young man cuts himself until he is covered in blood; a statement on the Vietnam War.

What's a Nice Girl Doing in a Place Like This? Directed by Martin Scorsese, 9 minutes, B&W, 1963, USA. A writer becomes obsessed with a picture of a boat on a lake. He attempts to regain a normal life but eventually succumbs to his strange anxiety. An experimental satire by one of today's most influential directors.

Les Mistons. Directed by François Truffaut, 18 minutes, B&W, in French with English subtitles, 1957, France. Truffaut's first film is about a group of boys who fall in love with a charming girl and how they come closer to understanding their own feelings.

Un Chien Andalou. Directed by Luis Buñuel, 20 minutes, B&W, silent, 18 fps, 1929, France. The classic surrealist film made up of abstract and bizarre images.

Entr'acte. Directed by René Clair, 20 minutes, B&W, silent, 18fps, 1924, France. Infused with the Dada spirit of mockery, a surrealist classic in which inanimate objects have a will of their own; "delightfully preposterous."

A Girl's Own Story. Directed by Jane Campion, 27 minutes, B&W, Best Direction—Australian Film Awards, 1984, Australia. A look at three teenage girls in the Beatles era.

Peel. Directed by Jane Campion, 9 minutes, color, winner of the Palme d'Or at Cannes Film Festival, 1982, Australia. A father, his son, and the father's sister on a drive back home. The boy continuously throws orange peels out the window, and the situation soon gets a little intense.

Passionless Moments. Directed by Jane Campion, 13 minutes, B&W, Best Short Film—Sidney Film Festival, 1983, Australia. A film about everyday moments in the lives of 10 characters, each with an uneasy familiarity.

La jetée. Written and directed by Chris Marker, 29 minutes, B&W, 1962, France. Utilizing a series of still images, this futuristic film explores apocalyptic post-World War III Earth, in which survivors live underground and perform experiments in time travel.

The Fat and the Lean. Written and directed by Roman Polanski and Jean-Pierre Rousseau, 15 minutes, B&W, 1961, France. An allegory about the tyrant-slave relationship, employing a combination of mime and surrealism.

Two Men and a Wardrobe. Directed by Roman Polanski, 15 minutes, B&W, 1958, Poland. Two men emerge from the sea carrying a large wardrobe; an allegory on isolationism and man's tendency to shun strangers, the film considers the costs of private lives in the modern world.

DOCUMENTARIES

The Battle of San Pietro. Directed by John Huston, 32 minutes, B&W, war documentary, 1945, USA. A documentary about the Battle of San Pietro, in which more than 1,100 U.S. soldiers were killed while trying to take this small Italian village from the Germans.

Dream of the Wild Horses. Directed by Denys Colomb de Daunant, 9 minutes, color, 1960, France.. A breathtaking slow-motion film of wild horses in the Camargue region of France.

City of Gold. Directed by Wolf Koenig, Colin Low, 21 minutes, B&W, produced by the Canadian Film Board, 1956, Toronto, Canada. (National Film Board of Canada) This film tells the fascinating history of Dawson City during the Klondike Gold Rush.

Night and Fog (Nuit et Brouillard). Directed by Alain Resnais, 30 minutes, color, subtitled documentary, 1955, France.. Filmed at the postwar site of Auschwitz, this film is one of the most vivid depictions of the horrors of Nazi concentration camps. It tells the story of the Holocaust and of the horror of man's brutal inhumanity.

Number Our Days. Directed by Lynne Littman, 29 minutes, color, Academy Award—Best Documentary Short, 1976, USA. (Direct Cinema). A documentary about a group of elderly Jews in Venice, California.

Sweet Sal. Directed by Tony Buba, 25 minutes, B&W, documentary, 1979, USA. (Chicago Filmmakers). A documentary about a small-time hustler in a dying steel town, the depth of insight and range of emotion he conveys make this a standout portrait.

À propos s de Nice. Directed by Jean Vigo, 23 minutes, B&W, silent, 1929, France. . A landmark film in cinema history, this silent documentary is an ironic satire on the French Riviera.

EXPERIMENTAL/AVANT GARDE/POETIC

Meshes of the Afternoon. Directed by Maya Deren, 20 minutes, B&W, 1943, USA. One of the major American experimental films of all time. Deren plays a woman driven to suicide by her obsessions and hallucinations.

Rain. Directed by Joris Ivens and Mannus Franken, 12 minutes, B&W, documentary with music track, 1929, Holland.. Impressionistic study of a rain shower in Amsterdam, using no titles or narration.

An American Time Capsule. Written and directed by Charles Braverman, 3 minutes, color, 1968, USA. Two centuries of American history condensed into 3 minutes. It uses 1,300 still images flashed before the eyes.

The Life and Death of 9413, A Hollywood Extra. Directed by Salavko Vorkapich and Robert Florey, 12 minutes, B&W, experimental, 1928, USA.. The story of the Extra and a successful movie star named Mr. Blank was the first American experimental film influenced by German Expressionism. Greg Toland *(Citizen Kane)* shot it.

L'étoile de mer. Directed by Man Ray, 15 minutes, silent, 18fps, B&W, 1928, France. An attempt to visually create the mood and images of the surrealist poem by Robert Desnos.

Moods of the Sea. Directed by Salavko Vorkapich and John Hoffman, 10 minutes, B&W, 1942, USA. A visual experience of light and motion that juxtaposes images of breaking waves with music.

Pas de deux. Directed by Norman McLaren, 14 minutes, B&W, experiment with dance, 1969, Canada. Blending sound and motion into visual poetry, McLaren has fragmented, overprinted, and utilized frame repetition to create an innovative classic.

ANIMATION

Bambi Meets Godzilla. Directed by Marv Newland, 2 minutes, animated, B&W, 1969, USA. Movie credit titles run over the animated image of Bambi, until Godzilla comes into view to squash Bambi.

Betty for President. Directed by Max Fleischer, 7 minutes, color, 1932, Betty Boop cartoon, USA. Betty Boop's campaign against Mr. Nobody tries to appeal to everyone. It is a parody of real candidates, and the House of Representatives is portrayed by elephants and asses.

A Chairy Tale. Directed by Norman McLaren, 10 minutes, B&W, 1957, USA. Pixillation is used to tell the story of a young man and a chair that refuses to be sat upon.

The Man Who Planted Trees (L'Homme qui plantait des arbres). Directed by Frederic Back, 30 minutes, color, animated, Academy Award—Best Animated Short, 1987, Canada. (Direct Cinema). The story of a shepherd who repairs the ruined ecosystem of a secluded valley by single-handedly cultivating a forest over a 30-year period.

Moonbird. Directed by John and Faith Hubley, 10 minutes, color, Academy Award—Best Animated Short, 1960, USA. A delightful adventure of two small boys who go out one night to catch a "moonbird"; captures the wonder and mystery of childhood.

Frank Film. Directed by Frank Mouris, 9 minutes, color, Academy Award—Best Animated Short, 1973, USA. (Direct Cinema). A continuous flow of thousands of overlapping images/incredible collages recounts the events of Mouris's life.

Sundae in New York. Directed by Jimmy Picker, 4 minutes, clay animation, Academy Award—Best Animated Short, 1983, USA. (Direct Cinema). In this clay-animated film, a character resembling Ed Koch (one-time mayor of New York City) sings a variation on *New York, New York.*

CLASSIC SILENT SHORTS

Big Business. Directed by James Wesley Horne, 20 minutes, B&W, music track, 1929, USA. Cast members: Stan Laurel, Oliver Hardy. Laurel and Hardy are in the business of selling Christmas trees.

The Critic. Written and directed by Ernest Pintoff, color, 1963, USA. A comedy that pokes fun at the meaningless symbolism of avant garde cinema, employing ever-changing abstract patterns.

The Cure. Directed by Charlie Chaplin, 19 minutes, B&W, music track, 1917, USA. Charlie Chaplin wreaks havoc at a health spa.

The Dove (De Duva). Directed by George Coe and Tony Lover, 15 minutes, B&W, 1968, USA. A hilarious satire on Bergman films.

Dr. Ded Bug. Directed by Ethan Cohen-Sitt, 10 minutes, B&W, 1989, USA. A comedy about a mad chef who goes insane trying to kill a cockroach in a restaurant kitchen.

A Day in the Country (Une Partie de Campagne). Directed by Jean Renoir, B&W, 37 minutes, 1949, France. A Parisian shop-owner's family spends a day in the country, where the daughter falls in love with a man at the inn.

Fetch. Directed by Lynn-Maree Danzey, 7 minutes, color, Best Short Comedy—Just For Laughs Comedy Festival, Montreal, 1998, Australia. A man arrives at a woman's apartment to take her out on a first date, but events conspire against him. An amusing and dark look at the bad luck that can plague even the most innocent circumstances.

A Game of Catch. Directed by Steven John Ross, adapted from short story by Richard Wilber, 15 minutes, color, 1990, USA. (Pyramid Film & Video). A 12-year-old boy tries unsuccessfully to play catch with two other boys with almost disastrous results. The film conveys the heartrending feeling of being an outsider and explores the tension between imagination and reality.

The Great Train Robbery. Directed by Edwin S. Porter, 10 minutes, tinted, music track at silent speed, 1903, USA. The first American film with a complete story line; pioneered parallel editing and double exposure, among a number of other early innovations.

Hardware Wars. Directed by Ernie Fosselius and Michael Wiese, 13 minutes, color, 1978, USA. A parody of *Star Wars*; special effects are made using household appliances found in any hardware store.

Leon's Case. Directed by Daniel Attias, 25 minutes, color, 1982, USA. The story of a 1960s activist who has been living as a fugitive for 12 years and decides to surrender.

Minors. Directed by Alan Kingsberg, 36 minutes, color, USA. Winner Student Academy Award, 1st Prize FOCUS Awards, 1984. (ADK Films, 212-529-2440). The story of a teenage girl who needs a subject for her science project and a minor league pitcher struggling to make it to the majors.

No Lies. Directed by Mitchell Block, color, 16 minutes, 1972, USA. (Direct Cinema). In conversation, an interviewer's questions strip away a young woman's defenses, revealing the trauma of sexual assault. *No Lies* is not a documentary, but the film is produced in the style of "direct cinema," creating a provocative tension between fact and fiction.

NY, NY. Directed by Francis Thomson, 16 minutes, color, Academy Award—Best Short Film, 1957, USA. New York City is bent, stretched, fractured, and shattered; a classic experimental film creates a beautiful variation on the reality of a great city.

An Occurrence at Owl Creek Bridge. Directed by Robert Enrico, 27 minutes, B&W, 1962, France. A Civil War soldier is about to be executed by hanging, but escapes to find his way home, with an ironic ending. Film utilizes compelling distortions of time and sound.

One Week. Directed by Buster Keaton and Eddie Cline, 20 minutes, B&W, 1920, USA. A newlywed couple receives a build-it-yourself house kit and a plot of land—but the numbers on the boxes have all been altered, and Keaton builds a completely crazy house.

La Poulet (The Chicken). Written and directed by Claude Berri, 15 minutes, B&W, subtitled, Academy Award—Best Short Film, 1963, France. A young boy becomes so fond of a rooster bought by his parents for Sunday dinner that he decides to trick them into thinking it's a hen to keep it alive. His ploy works until the rooster one day wakes them up with its crow.

The Red Balloon. Written and directed by Albert Lamorisse, 34 minutes, color, nonverbal, 1956, France. A parable about a lonely boy who rescues a red balloon that then follows him. A charming and witty film.

The Rink. Written and directed by Charles Chaplin, 19 minutes, B&W, music track, 1916, USA. The girl of his dreams invites Chaplin to the roller skating rink. He starts a riot, the cops show up, and then he escapes by hooking his cane onto an automobile and skating away.

Screen Test. Directed by Frank and Caroline Mouris, 20 minutes, color, 1975, USA. Nine of Mouris's friends dress up and ad lib every situation imaginable; bizarre, funny, campy, sad, and unpredictable.

A Shocking Accident. Directed by James Scott, 25 minutes, color, Academy Award—Best Short Film, 1982. (Direct Cinema). Adapted from a Graham Greene story. An English schoolboy learns from his boarding school headmaster that his father has been killed in a bizarre accident. The death haunts him for years until a girl he meets helps him shake the terrible memory.

Some Folks Call It a Sling Blade. Written by Billy Bob Thorton. Directed by George Hickenlooper, 1994.

Sticky My Fingers, Fleet My Feet. Directed by John Hancock, 23 minutes, color, 1973, USA. Norman and his friends are a group of huffing, puffing middle-aged men addicted to Sunday touch football in the park. When they patronizingly let a boy join their game, his performance leaves them dazed.

String Bean (Le Haricot). Directed by Edmond Sechan, 17 minutes, color, 1964, France. A simple and beautiful tale of an old lady who cultivates a potted plant with tender devotion.

A Trip to the Moon. Directed by Georges Méliès, 10 minutes, B&W, 1902, France. This science fiction film contains a great number of the earliest special effects and is the most popular of Méliès's films.

Safety Issues

1) GENERAL SAFETY GUIDELINES

When you are shooting on location, whether interior or exterior, safety and security should be at the forefront of concerns for production. Many reported personal injuries, thefts of personal property, damage to equipment and locations, and other costly incidents often come as a result of insufficient safety and security measures.

- Assign a member of your crew to act as a "safety officer" on all shoots.
- Bring a basic first-aid kit to every production or, where applicable, inquire as to where the first-aid kit is located.
- The director and crew must correct any safety issues brought to their attention immediately.
- Verbalize whenever possible so that others can be warned or updated as to your intentions or movements. For example, call "Striking" when turning on a light; call "Hot Points" when moving objects that could poke or gouge somebody; call "Behind you" or "On your left," etc., so that people know you are moving; call "Camera moves" when picking up a camera and moving it; call "Got it" when someone hands you something, and so on.
- Pranks and other types of horseplay are unacceptable. Distracting crew members could result in accidents and injuries.
- Alcohol should never be consumed on set or during scenes, regardless of age. Use prop liquids instead and make sure to store in a box labeled "Props" when not in use and labeled "Hot Set" when in use but left unattended.
- Obey all "No Smoking" signs.
- Familiarize yourself with emergency procedures for each location.
- Maintain good housekeeping at all times. Walkways and work areas are to be kept clear of materials, trash, equipment, and debris.
- Do not leave property unattended, and be watchful of your surroundings to avoid accidents, loss, or theft.
- Do not block hallways or other access areas with equipment, cast, or crew.
- Check for fire exits, smoke alarms, and fire extinguishers and plan escape routes for any location. Communicate this information to your crew. Fire equipment (hydrants, extinguishers, hoses, sprinklers, etc.) must be accessible at all times.
- All decorative set materials should be flame retardant or made of noncombustible materials, if such materials will be exposed to hot lamps, fire effects, and other such flammable environments.
- It is imperative that crews keep their sets and staging areas tidy and organized to avoid accidents.
- All cables should be neatly routed and secured, and other "trip hazards" should be labeled. Cables in walkways and traffic areas should be covered with mats.

Attire

- Wear proper protective clothing when working with tools or equipment (safety glasses, gloves, respirator or dust mask, etc.).
- Work gloves are strongly recommended for both lighting/grip and set building.
- Wear closed-toe shoes when working on set. Sandals do not protect your feet.
- Consider wearing long pants and avoiding loose-fitting clothing when working on set.

Special Effects

- If you are working somewhere that allows smoke/fog machines, be sure to check that smoke detectors will not be triggered, notify others in the building and thereabouts in person and with signs so that the fog is not mistaken for a real fire, properly ventilate the room, and do not over fog. Allow fog to dissipate between takes.
- Any scenes involving ignited items of any kind (matches, candles, etc.) should be planned thoroughly and discussed with appropriate building and safety representatives.

Chemicals and Flammable Materials

- Be careful when working with oil paint, spray paint, and wood stains. Be sure the area is properly ventilated and that you wear a respirator and eye protection if necessary.

- Be very careful of fine particulates, solvents, and any hazardous airborne substances. Wear respirators and keep safe distance from lights or other heat/spark sources.
- Do not throw aerosol cans or other paints or stains into the trash.
- Do not pour paint or other potentially hazardous waste down sinks or place into regular garbage. You should know and follow proper handling and storage procedures for all combustible or flammable materials. Disposing of these materials this way is unsafe and could be illegal.
- Store any possibly hazardous materials in a proper container. Properly label all containers to indicate their actual contents if the container is not labeled. Paint, chemicals, and other materials should not accumulate on stage floors, under platforms, or in other work areas.

Set Construction

- Remove nails, screws, and staples from debris when breaking down your set.
- Get a tetanus shot if you haven't had one in the past seven years.
- Watch for nails, screws, and staples when cutting wood.
- Use the proper tools for any job. Do not use improvised tools.
- Ensure that all equipment is in proper working order and that all protective guards are in place and used.
- Do not attempt to alter, modify, displace, or remove any existing safety equipment.
- Do not stand on chairs or other "improvised" items. Use a proper ladder or scaffold.
- Separate any dangerous items (glass, sharp objects) from general trash, wrap them appropriately, and label them to avoid accidents.

Lighting and Electric

- Lights become extremely hot. Use gloves and always allow lights to cool before removing from stands or grids. Placing hot lights directly on a floor could damage the floor and the light.
- Do not unplug lights by pulling on the cable itself. Always pull at the socket or connector.
- Keep lights a safe distance from anything potentially flammable, such as cloth, wood, paper, or even gels.
- Never overload circuits. If cables or extension cords get warm or hot, try a heavier gauge cable.
- Keep lights at a safe distance from any flammable items (walls, flats, plastic or paper light fixtures, curtains, etc.).

- Before patching lights into wall or grid outlets, be sure light is turned off, and in the case of lighting boards, be sure that the dimmer is in the off position.
- Regularly check all cables and connectors for frays or possible damage.
- Be careful when using lights or other electrical equipment near water. Be sure you are properly grounded and that lights and cords do not come into contact with water.
- Do not use metal ladders when working with electricity. Use ladders made of wood, plastic, or fiberglass.
- Do not place lights directly on the floor or against flats, walls, curtains, or props.
- For small lights at floor level, use pigeon stands on apple boxes.
- For larger lights, use turtle stands. Do not place lights on sandbags because parts can melt.
- Many HMI and fluorescent lights (kinos, fluotechs) are nondimmable. Damage may occur if these lights are dimmed. Unless an HMI or fluorescent light is specifically identified as dimmable or has ballast with dimmer controls, do not dim these lights.
- If you see or smell smoke, burning plastic, or the like, stop shooting immediately and address the problem.
- Lights and barn doors may sometimes smoke or smell when they are new; this is a normal occurrence as the paint is heated. In such cases, allow the lights to warm up in a well-ventilated space until they are broken in. Watch them carefully to be sure there is not a real problem.
- The smell of burning plastic is usually the first sign of trouble. Always locate problems early and avoid letting them worsen over time. No shot is worth an accident.
- NEVER try to repair equipment yourself! Attempting to repair it yourself puts you at risk of injury and affects warranties.
- Do not touch bulbs with your bare hands; always use gloves. Oil from your fingers will damage bulbs and could result in fire hazard or broken glass.

Grip/Rigging

- Avoid placing or rigging any items at or near eye level. If you must do so, use a tennis ball, Styrofoam cup, or light-colored tape on the end of any items that could cause trip or gouging hazards so people see them.
- Secure all hanging lights and other items. Use safety cables, safety chains, rope, or other designated and safe securing apparatus. For example, all barn doors must have safety chains in place, lights and clamps should be attached to a grid with safety cables, etc.
- Use adequate braces and sandbags to support sets, stands, or rigging.

- Cover C-stands for proper etiquette (i.e., place so that as weight pulls down, the knuckle tightens; where to place long leg and sandbag, etc.).
- Keep all C-stands, stirrups, and other retractable items in a tightened position to prevent the flailing out of pipe when being moved around.
- Learn and use appropriate knots for the job when using rope for rigging. Always tie an extra "safety" knot.
- Tape down cables and identify any trip or safety hazards with signs or other "flags."
- Remember that duct tape and gaffers tape tend to damage painted surfaces.

Lifting and Moving Heavy Objects

- When working on any potentially hazardous job, pay attention and do not get distracted.
- Lifting loads improperly can cause back injuries. Lift with your legs and not your back.
- Request assistance with any heavy or awkward items.
- Avoid lifting heavy objects whenever possible by using carts, dollies, and other mechanical devices.
- Before lifting any load, check for jagged edges, nails, and other sharp protruding objects.
- Often when a heavy item falls, it is best to get out of the way and let gravity do its thing. If you can't safely stop it, warn others and get out of the way.

Ladders and Scaffolds

- Secure anything hanging from the ceiling grid (studio).
- Tighten all clamps securely, but do not overtighten.
- Use ample safety cables and chains for barn doors, lights, and clamps.
- Leave absolutely nothing above head level on the scaffold, ladders, flats, and so on.
- Inspect all ladders before each use.
- Never place ladders in doorways unless protected by barricades or guards.
- Never stand on the top two rungs of a ladder.
- Do not stand on top of a ladder.
- Never modify or remove any part of scaffolds or ladders.

Dollies

- When booming on a dolly, make sure nobody is standing or leaning over the boom because it could swing up quickly and cause injury if hydraulics malfunction or proper finesse is not used. Watch hands, feet, and cables when working on or around a dolly.
- Always use breaks and/or sandbag wheels to avoid rolling.
- Do not overcharge the hydraulics. Watch the gauges.

Grip Trucks

- When using lift gates on trucks, assign one person to operate the lift and vocalize all movements ("Coming down," "Coming up"). Watch hands and feet and work slowly to avoid accidents.
- When packing trucks, place heavier items lower and lighter items above. Be sure to balance the load and use tie-downs, etc., to secure the load.
- Never leave equipment unattended even if locked up.

2) STUNTS, PROP WEAPONS, AND PYROTECHNICS

Fire and Pyrotechnics

Pyrotechnic and other explosive devices must be operated only by trained personnel. A licensed fire safety official may be required. Fire extinguishers must be made readily available. When filming, make sure that you secure the proper equipment needed to protect the camera and other film equipment, or make sure you are operating at a safe distance. Filming these scenes requires careful consideration and control; filming without these precautions is not recommended.

Guns, Knives, and Other Prop Weapons

Treat all weapons as though they are loaded and/or ready to use. Do not play with weapons and never point one at anyone, including yourself. The use of weapons, especially in public areas, will require special permits and/or supervision by qualified personnel. All cast and crew must be informed of safety precautions and the safe handling of prop weapons.

   Please Note: Real firearms of any kind should not be used in a student film.

Physical Stunts

In film and television production, any physical action requiring an actor to fight, fall, jump, run, and/or perform in an athletic manner and any other potentially hazardous situation are considered stunts. Depending on the type of stunt being performed, a trained stunt coordinator may be required to supervise.

Filming Stunts in Public

For any stunt work, use of prop weapons, pyrotechnics, and any other potentially hazardous scenes conducted on public property, or within view of the public (e.g., a storefront) must also be cleared by the local mayor's office and police department.

Special Effects

Some special effects will require the supervision of a professional special effects coordinator. Do not use any special effects machinery without proper training. Even the use of smoke machines must be carefully regulated.

Motor Vehicles

Shooting on any public street, thoroughfare, road, or highway is strictly prohibited by local, state, and federal laws, unless you have secured proper permits and other paperwork. Car mounts should be rigged by a professional or someone with experience in the safe handling of this equipment. The use of aircraft, watercraft, cars, or any other vehicles in production requires special permits and/or operator certifications.

Water Scenes

All cast and crew members working on or near bodies of water should wear life vests or other water safety gear when appropriate. When using watercraft, be aware of load capacities. Only required cast and crew should be on watercraft. Safety lines, nets, and/or safety personnel should be used when filming in rivers or other bodies of water.

Additional Safety Considerations

- Obey all federal, state, and local laws.
- Before filming a stunt or special effect, the involved cast and crew should perform an on-set dry run or walk-through.
- Always post emergency information on set, including the address and directions to the nearest hospital. This and other important information regarding stunt work must be posted on call sheets and distributed to cast and crew in advance.
- Wear appropriate clothing, such as rubber shoes, work gloves, safety goggles, and/or a face mask when necessary.
- Use professional earplugs when working around loud sounds for a scene.
- Have a first-aid kit and working fire extinguisher(s) on set at all times.
- It is recommended that someone on the crew know basic first aid and CPR.

3) LIGHT SAFELY

Grip Kit: Here is a list of supplies that come in handy for lighting during a shoot:

- Durable work gloves
- Extra fuses

- Clothespins (wooden)
- Gaffers tape
- Flashlight
- Leatherman, Swiss Army, or other utility knife
- Sash cord (#8 or #10)
- Pliers
- Set of screwdrivers
- Tape measure
- Ground Fault Circuit Interrupter (GFCI)

Do You Know What to Look Out For?

If you need to determine the electrical needs for lighting a set, a general approximation is 1000 W per 10 amps. On average, a room will run on one 15–20 amp circuit (i.e., 15A =1500W, 20A= 2000). This information should be labeled on the circuit breaker or fuse box for the room. It is also recommended that you use a testing device to check proper grounding of ordinary household outlets. When you are lighting a room, a safe estimation to keep in mind is not to exceed a maximum of 2000W per room or approximately two lights per circuit. Never overload a circuit.

Electrical Tie-Ins

Under no circumstances should a student or other untrained crew member be "tieing-into" electrical mains. Electrical tie-ins and any other special electrical wiring must be performed by a licensed electrician.

Location Scout

Do a thorough location scout before using the location so you can check the amperage and locate the circuit breaker/fuse box. Remember to notice the other appliances that are plugged into a circuit: refrigerators, computers, stereos, TVs. Kitchens generally have their own circuit. When you're working with a location that has a fuse box, a good idea is to take note of the types of fuses that are used in case you need to buy replacements.

Blowing a Fuse

If you blow a fuse, be prepared to turn the breakers back on or replace the glass fuse if it's an older fuse box. Circuit breakers are a set of switches that reset fuses. A fuse box contains a set of actual glass fuses, which must physically be replaced.

Using Gels

When rigging gels, always use wooden clothespins. To keep the gels from melting, keep the lamps set on "flood." This is especially important when using open-faced lights, as opposed to fresnels (with the "lighthouse" style cover), which contain lenses that are used to adjust the throw of the light.

Set Etiquette

Call out "Striking" whenever turning lights on. This lets everyone around you know that you will be turning on a very bright light. Turn the lights toward a wall so as not to blind anybody. Also, these lights give off a lot of heat and can melt things.

Changing Bulbs

Never touch the bulb itself. If you do, the oils from your hand will boil on the glass and cause it to crack and/or explode. If you do blow a bulb, unplug the light immediately and allow it to cool off. Use a glove or cloth to unscrew and replace the bulb.

Additional Concerns

- Always examine electrical cables for breaks or cuts in the insulation. Never use cables that are damaged.
- Stage your lighting at a safe distance from walls and the ceiling, as well as anything else that can burn or melt. Turn off the lights when you aren't using them, and be careful to let them cool down before touching them or packing them back in the case. Always wear gloves when handling the lights. Complying with all these tips will limit your risk of suffering third-degree burns!
- Use tape to secure cables along flooring and secure cable with mats in walkways and other high-traffic areas.
- Be particularly careful around water, especially when filming in the rain.
- Make sure that lights are placed far enough away from props, sets, and other materials that pose a fire risk.
- Be particularly careful around water and when shooting in rainy conditions. Lights should never be turned on, plugged in, or left out in the rain.

4) SAFETY IN THE STUDIO

Working on a soundstage or any type of studio environment brings up a number of safety concerns for filmmakers. Most stages come equipped with lighting grids that allow you to rig lights, scaffolds, and other equipment from up above. Naturally, equipment that is not secured properly runs the risk of coming loose and potentially falling or collapsing. Following are a few points to keep in mind for in-studio safety.

Lighting Grid

When you're rigging equipment to the grid, only one person at a time should use the ladder set, and all other crew should keep clear of the set until rigging has completed. Safety cables should always be used to secure lights to the lighting grid. Before you work with lights on the grid, all lights should be faded down or turned off completely. When applying gels, use only wooden clothespins to attach to hot lamps.

Sets and Flats

Keep in mind that flats, props, and other set pieces are fragile. Flats are not built to be leaned on or climbed on. Close prop doors gently. Put back all props and furniture safely and in their proper place so that they do not fall on people.

Two crew members should work together setting up a flat. One holds the flat and A-frame while a second person tightens the C-clamp on the bottom first. When attaching C-clamps, no one should be working below. Once a second C-clamp is attached to the top flat and A-frame, secure with a sandbag onto the bottom of the A-frame going across. There is always a chance that a wall may come loose during production because it was not properly anchored down. For more information, refer to the General Guidelines section.

5) SHOOTING IN EXTREME WEATHER CONDITIONS

Extreme Cold

When shooting in extremely cold weather, wear proper clothing that insulates from the cold and provides protection from wind, rain, and snow. Cover your neck and head, and protect your hands and feet to prevent frostbite. Provide adequate heated shelters for cast and crew. It is also a good idea to get a portable heating unit, which can be rented at most grip and expendables houses.

Extreme Heat

When shooting in extremely warm weather, make sure that you keep your cast and crew hydrated! Stocking up on fresh drinking water and Gatorade-type drinks is highly recommended. Avoid caffeinated drinks. Provide adequate sunblock or sunscreen on set, and provide overhead sun protection, such as an EZ-up tent or pop-up. When shooting in interior locations with poor air circulation, provide electric fans and portable air-conditioning units to keep everyone cool and comfortable. These items can also be rented from most grip and expendables houses.

Inclement Weather

Shooting outdoors in bad weather, such as rain, snow, sleet, or high winds, is not recommended. Doing so will lead to damaged equipment and can be potentially harmful to your cast and crew. If it starts to rain, use precaution when powering down lights and other electrical equipment. Always keep adequate rain gear in your equipment inventory, to protect sensitive camera and sound equipment from rain, humidity, and other damp environments.

6) LENGTH OF A SHOOT DAY

On the Road: What You Can Do When You're Tired

- Don't just roll down the window and turn up the radio. These "fixes" work only for seconds or minutes.
- Use caffeine wisely. Two cups of coffee may increase alertness for two to three hours. For a long trip, skip coffee or soda for most of the day before. Your brain will get more of a boost from the caffeine.
- Nap. If you can't keep your eyes open, find a safe area to nap. A 20-minute nap can refresh you for one to three hours. Allow time to recover from grogginess.
- Share the driving. Always make sure someone else in the car is awake to keep the driver engaged.

All in a Day's Work: The Length of a Shoot Day

Although tight shooting schedules and tight budgets may add stress to a production, it is imperative that student film shoots comply with the recommended maximum 12-hour shoot day, which should begin at crew call time and end at wrap time. Subsequently, crew must also be given proper turnaround time before reporting to set the following shoot day. When working with SAG actors or any union performers and minors, please abide by all union rules regarding maximum work-day requirements.

The following is a true story about the dangers involved when cast and crew are subjected to extremely long shoot days (excerpt taken from the IA Local 600 web site at http://www.cameraguild.com):

On March 5th, 1997, Brent Hershman, the second assistant camera person on the movie *Pleasantville* drove an hour from home to work in Long Beach for a 6:30 AM call. He worked for nineteen hours. After helping to wrap three cameras and a Power Pod, he reminded his co-workers on the camera truck to drive carefully and left for home. Midway through his trip, the exhaustion overcame him. He drove his car off the road and was killed. He leaves behind a daughter, Hannah, who is three and a half, and his wife, Deborah.

This incident sparked an industry-wide campaign for more humane working conditions, which generated a petition with the names of over 10,000 industry professionals, calling for a limit on the number of hours worked in a single shoot day. As a result, all local labor unions and performers' guilds have joined forces to promote the limiting of hours worked on motion picture sets.

Under no circumstances should cast or crew operate any vehicles without adequate rest. If necessary, the production must provide accommodations for cast and crew that live far from home. For local shoots that wrap late at night, consider the safety of cast and crew. No one should travel home alone. Provide cab fare if necessary.

Finally, we cannot overemphasize the importance of adequate rest. Film production is hard work that requires plenty of energy to be able to operate successfully. You need energy to be able to focus and to be able to think strategically and creatively. Lack of sleep will affect not only your health, but also the quality of your film.

7) USING ANIMALS IN FILM

The American Humane Association publishes a series of safety regulations called *Guidelines for the Safe Use of Animals in Filmed Media*, which is designed to ensure the comfort and well-being of all animal actors. The guidelines are periodically updated to address new issues. You can download a copy of the guidelines from the AHA web site at http://www.americanhumane.org/protecting-animals/programs/no-animals-were-harmed/.

Following are some additional tips on working with animals:

- Animals are unpredictable. Always have an animal handler on set.
- The owner or other guardian for the animal should be on set at all times.
- Do not feed, pet, or play with any animal without the permission and direct supervision of its trainer or owner.
- When you are working with exotic animals, the set should be closed and notices posted to that effect, including a note on the call sheet.

Music Clearance and Insurance

MUSIC RIGHTS

All music is subject to copyright protection unless it is in the public domain (see the next section). It is very important that before deciding on using a particular piece of music or a song in your film or video, you secure its clearance.

Clearance means determining who owns the copyright to a piece of music and negotiating a license to use that material for exhibition and distribution in specific territories and media in exchange for the payment of a fee to the copyright owner. If the clearance process is begun ahead of time, the producer can determine whether the budget can accommodate the price of a particular song or musical selection.

If you want to use a preexisting recording, you will need to obtain permission to use the musical *composition*, as well as permission to use the particular *recording* of it. Generally, songwriters assign or sell the copyright to their work to a publisher, who pays the writer a share of the royalties if the song is used in a film or video. The record company that paid for the recording session or that had the recording artist under contract usually owns the recordings.

To secure rights to a composition, start by approaching the author; the author's estate, lawyer, publisher, or agent; or the organization that represents the publisher and licenses those rights on its behalf. One such organization is the Harry Fox Agency (with offices in New York and Los Angeles and online at www.harryfox.com). It represents thousands of publishing companies. If this agency doesn't handle the composition you want, contact one of the performing rights societies: American Society of Composers and Publishers (ASCAP), Broadcast Music, Inc. (BMI), or Society of European Stage Authors (SESAC). All have offices in New York; BMI and ASCAP are also located in Los Angeles; and all have web sites.

To include a musical composition in your project, you need *synchronization* or *sync rights,* so named because the music is synchronized to the picture. To perform the music in public, you need *public performance rights.* In the United States, public performance rights are generally included in the deal you make for sync rights; you don't have to pay for them separately. For projects that are broadcast on TV, the broadcaster usually pays for the performance rights.

If you want to use a preexisting *recording* of the song, contact the owner of the recording, usually the record company (look on the sleeve of the CD for the address). You will need a *master use license* to use the actual recording (performance) in your project. So for the classic situation of trying to clear a recording by an artist you like, you will be requesting two licenses: a sync license with public performance from the publisher and a master use license from the record company.

If you use a song that has not been cleared, you carry the risk of being caught. Failure to clear the music might result in an injunction and large legal fees. You may have to pay an out-of-court settlement or have to make extensive changes to your show to remove the musical selection. Some public broadcasting entities, such as PBS, have blanket agreements and compulsory licenses that may allow you to use music without clearing it with rights holders. This only applies to television broadcast. You may still need other rights if the project is shown elsewhere.

Festival rights might not require any payment at all; however, festival rights are negotiated in the same manner as if you were seeking commercial rights.

There are music clearance houses that handle all the details of locating the rights holder, negotiating a deal, and sending out or requesting the contract. Because they handle a volume of business, professional clearance people can accomplish these tasks in a fraction of the time and many times negotiate a better deal. As a result, the cost of their services is reasonable. These are a few of them:

David Powell (Los Angeles)
The Music Bridge, LLC
www.themusicbridge.com
thabridge@aol.com
310-398-9650

The Copyright Clearing House, Ltd. (Los Angeles)
www.musicreports.com
818-558-1400

B.Z. Rights (New York)
www.bzrights.com
info@bzrights.com
212-924-3000

Diamond Time, Ltd. (New York)
www.diamondtime.net
jen@diamondtime.net
212-274-1006

Public Domain

Music created after January 1, 1978, is protected by copyright for 70 years after the death of the last surviving writer. Works that were made for hire, such as an original film score, are protected for 75 years from publication or 100 years from creation, whichever is less.

You might have heard that you can use a few bars from a song for free. This is false. "Fair use" is another questionable area. This is an exception to the exclusive rights of copyright owners. Fair use permits limited use of a copyrighted material in a number of circumstances. In theory, the public interest is served when the material is used for purposes of criticism, comment, news reporting, scholarship, teaching, and so on. Parodies using the material for humor or social commentary are also allowed, but this area of law is constantly changing and should be reviewed carefully.

For help in this area, get some legal assistance. If you cannot afford an entertainment attorney, you'll find free legal aid groups in major metropolitan areas that can answer many of your basic questions. One example is Volunteer Lawyers for the Arts. You may also check an excellent web site at www.pdinfo.com (for public domain information).

INSURANCE

Insurance plays an important role in motion picture and video production. Having insurance is as essential as having film stock or the right camera. In the course of normal life, calamities can happen and life goes on. In the course of a production, a car accident, sickness, a robbery, or a fire can bring the production to a screeching halt.

A budget, even with a contingency of 10 percent, is not flexible enough to cover keeping a crew standing for days, even weeks, while the lead actor recovers from an accident. This is why you need some type of protection for the unexpected occurrences that could happen in the course of the finely orchestrated movement of material, equipment, and people. Think of it as insurance for the possibility that Murphy's Law will prevail and everything will go wrong.

Some insurance companies specialize in entertainment insurance packages. They will evaluate the needs of the production and provide a price for appropriate coverage. You might not be able to afford everything the company recommends, but it is highly recommended that you carry at least equipment and comprehensive liability coverage. You don't want to be personally responsible for property damage or injury on the set. Equipment houses will not rent to you without equipment insurance. Some offer their own insurance, but many don't.

What follows is a brief description of the many types of coverage available to film and video producers. The most common types of insurance are covered here. There are also special types of coverage that reflect unique demands.

Comprehensive Liability

Comprehensive liability coverage protects the production company against claims for bodily injury or property damage liability that arise from filming a picture. Coverage includes use of all nonowned vehicles (both on and off camera). This coverage is required before filming on any city or state roadways or at any location site.

Comprehensive liability policies do not cover accidents arising from the use of aircraft or watercraft. This coverage must be purchased separately.

Miscellaneous Equipment

The miscellaneous equipment policy covers you against risk of direct physical loss, damage, or destruction to cameras; camera equipment; and sound, lighting, and grip equipment owned or rented by the production company. Coverage can be extended to cover mobile equipment vans, studio location units, and similar units upon payment of an additional premium.

Third-Party Property Damage Liability

Third-party property damage liability coverage pays for the damage or destruction of the property of others (including loss of use of property) while the property is in the care, custody, or control of the production company and is used or is to be used in an insured production.

This coverage does not apply to the following: liability for destruction of property caused by operation of any motor vehicle, aircraft, or watercraft, including damage to the foregoing; liability for damage to any property rented or leased that may be covered under props, sets, or wardrobe, or miscellaneous equipment insurance (although loss of use of any such equipment is covered).

This protection is not included under the comprehensive liability policy. Property damage coverage written as part of the comprehensive general liability policy excludes damage to any property in the production company's care, custody, or control.

Errors and Omissions

Distributors usually require errors and omissions coverage before the release of any production. It covers legal liability and defense against lawsuits alleging copyright infringement; unauthorized use of titles format, ideas, characters, or plots; plagiarism; unfair competition; and invasion of privacy. It also protects against alleged libel, slander, defamation of character, and invasion of privacy suits.

Cast Insurance

Cast insurance reimburses the production company for any extra expense necessary to complete principal photography due to the death, injury, or sickness of any insured performer or director. Insured performers or directors must take a physical examination before they can be covered. Coverage usually begins three weeks before the beginning of principal photography.

Negative Film and Videotape

Negative film and videotape coverage insures against all risks of direct physical loss, damage, or destruction of raw film or tape stock, exposed film (developed or undeveloped), recorded videotape, soundtracks, and tapes, up to the amount of insured production cost.

This coverage does not include loss caused by fogging; faulty camera or sound equipment; faulty developing, editing, processing, or manipulation by the camera operator; exposure to light, dampness, or temperature changes; errors in judgment in exposure, lighting, or sound recording; or from the incorrect use of raw film stock or tape.

Faulty Stock, Camera, and Processing

The faulty stock, camera, and processing policy covers loss, damage, or destruction of raw film or tape stock, exposed film (developed or undeveloped), recorded videotape, soundtracks, and tapes caused by or resulting from fogging or the use of faulty equipment (including cameras and videotape recorders); faulty sound equipment; faulty developing, editing, and processing; and accidental erasure of videotape recording.

Props, Sets, and Wardrobe

Props, sets, and wardrobe insurance provides coverage for props, sets, scenery, costumes, wardrobe, miscellaneous rented equipment, and office contents against all risk of direct physical loss, damage, or destruction during the production.

Extra Expense

Extra expense coverage reimburses the production company for any extra expense necessary to complete principal photography due to damage or destruction of property or facilities (props, sets, or equipment) used in connection with the production. It protects against loss that delays production.

Workers' Compensation

State laws mandate that workers' compensation coverage be carried. It applies to all temporary or permanent cast or production crew members. Coverage provides medical, disability, or death benefits to any cast or crew members who become injured in the course of their employment. Coverage applies on a 24-hour basis whenever employees are on location away from their homes. Individuals who call themselves *independent contractors* are usually held to be employees as far as workers' compensation is concerned. The failure to carry this insurance can result in having to pay any benefits required under the law plus penalty awards.

Hired, Loaned, or Donated Auto Liability

Hired, loaned, or donated auto liability insurance covers all company-owned, hired, or leased vehicles used in connection with the production. Only vehicles that are being rented under the company's name and are issued certificates of insurance are covered under this policy.

Hired, Loaned, or Donated Auto Physical Damage

Hired, loaned, or donated auto physical damage coverage insures company-owned, hired, or leased vehicles against the risks of loss, theft, or damage (including collision) for all vehicles used in company-related activities. It covers vehicles rented from crew or staff members when the production company has assumed responsibility for the vehicles.

Guild/Union Travel Accident

Guild/union travel accident coverage provides Motion Picture/Television Guild or union contract requirements for aircraft accidental death insurance to all production company cast or crew members. Coverage is blanket, and the limit of liability meets all signatory requirements.

Office Contents

Office contents insurance is "all-risk" coverage (subject to policy exclusions) on office contents, subject to a low deductible.

Animal Mortality

When animals are used in the production, consideration should be given to special animal mortality coverage.

This policy insures against the death or destruction of any animal covered. A veterinarian's certificate is usually required for this coverage. If the animal is a principal character, the cost to be paid to finish principal photography might be covered under cast insurance.

State Film Commissions

Alabama Film Office
401 Adams Ave.
Montgomery, AL 36130
800-633-5898
334-242-2077 (fax)
http://www.alabamafilm.org/

Alaska Film Office
3601 C St., Ste. 700
Anchorage, AK 99503
907-269-8137
907-269-8136 (fax)
http://www.film.alaska.gov/

Arizona Film Commission
3800 N. Central Ave., Bldg. D
Phoenix, AZ 85102
602-280-1380
800-523-6695
602-280-1384 (fax)
http://www.film.alaska.gov/

Arkansas Motion Picture Office
1 State Capital Mall
Room 2C-200
Little Rock, AR 72201
501-682-7676
501-682-FILM (fax)

California Film Commission
7080 Hollywood Blvd.
Ste. 900
Hollywood, CA 90028
323-860-2960
800-858-4749
323-860-2972 (fax)
http://www.film.ca.gov/

Santa Cruz County Film Commission
701 Front St.
Santa Cruz, CA 95060
408-425-1234
408-425-1260 (fax)

Colorado Motion Picture & TV Commission
1625 Broadway

Ste. 1700
Denver, Co 80202
303-620-4500
800-726-8887
303-620-4545 (fax)
http://www.coloradofilm.org/

Connecticut Film, Video & Media Office
865 Brook St., Bldg. 4
Rocky Hill, CT 06067
800-392-2122
860-571-7130
860-721-7088 (fax)
http://www.cultureandtourism.org/cct/cwp/view.asp?
        a=2126&q=302556&CCTNAV_GID=1637

Delaware Film Office
99 Kings Highway
P.O. Box 1401
Dover, DE 19903
302-739-4271
800-441-8846
302-736-5747 (fax)

District of Columbia Mayor's Office of Motion
Picture & TV
717 14th St., NW 12th Floor
Washington, D.C. 20005
207-727-6600
202-727-3787 (fax)
District of Columbia Mayor's Office of Motion Picture & TV

Florida Entertainment Commission
505 17th St.
Miami Beach, FL 33139
305-673-7468
305-673-7168 (fax)
http://www.filminflorida.com/

Georgia Film & Video Office
285 Peachtree Center Ave.
Ste. 1000
Atlanta, GA 30303
404-656-3591
404-651-9063 (fax)

http://www.georgia.org/GeorgiaIndustries/Entertainment/
    Pages/default.aspx

Hawaii Film Office
P.O. Box 2359
Honolulu, HI 96804
808-586-2570
808-586-2572 (fax)
http://www.hawaiifilm.com/

Illinois Film Office
100 West Randolph
Ste. 3–400
Chicago, IL 60601
312-814-3600
312-814-8874 (fax)
http://www.filmillinois.state.il.us/

Chicago Film Office
North LaSalle, Ste. 2165
Chicago, IL 60602
312-744-6415
312-744-1378 (fax)

Indiana Film Commission
1 North Capitol, #700
Indianapolis, IN 46204
317-232-8829
317-233-6887 (fax)
http://www.in.gov/film/

Iowa Film Office
200 East Grand Ave.
Des Moines, IA 50309
515-242-4726
515-242-4859 (fax)
http://www.iowalifechanging.com/film/

Kansas Film Commission
700 SW Harrison St., Ste. 1300
Topeka, KS 66603
785-296-4927
785-296-6988 (fax)
http://kdoch.state.ks.us/kdfilm/index.jsp

Kentucky Film Commission
500 Mero St., 2200
Capitol Plaza Tower
Frankfort, KY 40601
502-564-3456
800-345-6591
502-564-7588 (fax)
http://www.kyfilmoffice.com/

Louisiana Film Commission
P.O. Box 44320
Baton Rouge, LA 70804

225-342-8150
888-655-0447
http://www.louisianaentertainment.gov/film/default.cfm

Maine Film Office
State House Station 59
Augusta, ME 04333-0059
207-287-5703
207-287-8070 (fax)
http://www.filminmaine.com/

Maryland Film Office
217 E. Redwood St., 9th Floor
Baltimore, MD 21202
410-767-6340
800-333-6632
410-767-0067 (fax)
http://www.mdfilm.state.md.us/

Massachusetts Film Office
10 Park Plaza, Ste. 2310
Boston, MA 02116
617-973-8800
617-973-8810 (fax)
http://www.mafilm.org/

Michigan Film Office
201 N. Washington Square
Victor Centre, 5th Floor
Lansing, MI 48913
517-373-0638
517-241-0593 (fax)
http://www.michigan.gov/filmoffice

Minnesota Film and TV Board
401 North 3rd St.
Ste. 460
Minneapolis, MN 55401
612-332-6493
612-332-3735 (fax)
http://www.mnfilmtv.org/

Minneapolis Office of Film, Video & Recording
323 M City Hall
350 W. 5th St.
Minneapolis, MN 55415
612-673-2947
612-673-2011 (fax)
http://www.ci.minneapolis.mn.us/oca/

Mississippi Film Office
Box 849
Jackson, MS 39205
601-359-3297
601-359-5757 (fax)
http://www.visitmississippi.org/film/

Missouri Film Office
301 West High, Rm. 770
P.O. Box 118
Jefferson City, MO
65102
573-751-9050
573-751-7385 (fax)
http://www.missouribusiness.net/film/

Montana Film Office
1424 9th Ave.
Helena, MT 59620
406-444-3762
800-553-4563
406-444-4191 (fax)
http://www.montanafilm.com/

Nebraska Film Office
700 South 16th
P.O. Box 94666
Lincoln, NE 68509-4666
402-471-3680
800-228-4307
402-471-3026 (fax)
http://www.neded.org/content/view/515/1254/

Nevada Film Office
555 East Washington
Ste. 5400
Las Vegas, NV 89101
702-486-2711
702-486-2712 (fax)
http://www.nevadafilm.com/

New Hampshire Film & TV Bureau
172 Pembroke Road
P.O. Box 1856
Concord, NH 03302-1856
603-271-2598
603-271-2629 (fax)
http://www.nh.gov/film/

New Jersey Motion Picture/TV Commission
153 Halsey St.
P.O. Box 47023
Newark, NJ 07101
973-648-6279
973-648-7350 (fax)
http://www.njfilm.org/

New Mexico Film Office
1100 South St. Francis Drive
P.O. Box 20003
Santa Fe, NM 87504-5003
505-827-9810
800-545-9871

505-827-9799 (fax)
http://www.nmfilm.com/

New York State Governor's Office for Motion Picture
& TV
633 Third Ave, 33rd Floor
New York, NY 10017
212-803-2330
212-803-2339 (fax)
http://www.nylovesfilm.com/index.asp

North Carolina Film Office
430 North Salisbury St.
Raleigh, NC 27611
919-733-9900
800-232-9227
919-715-0151 (fax)
http://www.ncfilm.com/

North Dakota Film Commission
604 East Boulevard
2nd Floor
Bismarck, ND 58505
701-328-2874
800-328-2871
701-328-4878 (fax)

Ohio Film Commission
77 S. High St., 29th Floor
P.O. Box 1001
Columbus, OH 43216-1001
614-466-2284
800-230-3523
614-466-6744 (fax)
http://www.clevelandfilm.com/

Oklahoma Film Office
440 South Houston, Ste. 304
Tulsa, OK 74127-8945
918-581-2660
800-766-3456
918-581-2244 (fax)
http://www.oklahomafilm.org/DesktopDefault.aspx

Oregon Film & Video Office
121 SW Salmon St.
Ste. 300A
Portland, OR 97204
503-229-5832
503-229-6869 (fax)
http://www.oklahomafilm.org/DesktopDefault.aspx

Pennsylvania Film Office
200 N. 3rd St.. Ste. 901
Harrisburg, PA 17101
717-783-3456
717-772-3581 (fax)

Philadelphia Film Office
100 S. Broad St.
Ste. 600
Philadelphia, PA 19110
215-686-2668
215-686-3659 (fax)
http://www.film.org/film/index.cfm

Puerto Rico Film Commission
355 F.D. Roosevelt Ave.
Formento Building, #106
San Juan, PR 00918
809-758-4747
809-754-7110
809-756-5706 (fax)
http://www.puertoricofilm.com/

Rhode Island Film Commission
150 Benefit St.
Providence, RI 02903
401-277-3456
401-277-6046 (fax)
http://www.film.ri.gov/

South Carolina Film Office
P.O. Box 7367
Columbia, SC 29202
803-737-0490
803-737-3104 (fax)
http://www.scfilmoffice.com/

South Dakota Film Commission
711 East Wells Ave.
Pierre, SD 57501-3369 605)
773-3301
800-952-3625
605-773-3256 (fax)
http://www.filmsd.com/

Tennessee Film, Entertainment & Music Commission
320 6th Ave. North
7th Floor
Nashville, TN 37243-0790
615-741-3456
800-251-8594
615-741-5829 (fax)
http://www.tennessee.gov/film/

Texas Film Commission
P.O. Box 13246
Austin, TX 78711
512-463-9200
512-463-4114 (fax)
http://www.governor.state.tx.us/film

U.S. Virgin Islands Film Promotion Office
P.O. Box 6400
St. Thomas, VI 00804
809-775-1444
809-774-8784
809-774-4390 (fax)

Utah Film Commission
324 South State, Ste. 500
Salt Lake City, UT 84114 801)
538-8740
800-453-8824
801-538-8886 (fax)
http://film.utah.gov/

Vermont Film Bureau
134 State St.
Montpelier, VT 05602
802-828-3384
802-828-3233 (fax)
http://www.vermontfilm.com/

Virginia Film Office
901 East Byrd St., 19th Floor
P.O. Box 798
Richmond, VA 23206
804-371-8204
800-854-6233
804-371-8177
http://www.film.virginia.org/

Washington State Film Office
2001 6th Ave., Ste. 2600
Seattle, WA 98121
206-956-3200
206-956-3205
http://www.washingtonfilmworks.org/

West Virginia Film Office
State Capital, Bldg. 6
Room 525
Charleston, WV 25305
304-558-2234
800-982-3386
304-558-1189 (fax)
http://www.wvfilm.com/

Wisconsin Film Office
123 West Washington Ave.
6th Floor
Madison, WI 53702-0001
608-267-3456
800-345-6947
608-266-3403 (fax)

Film and Media Programs

The latter part of the twentieth century saw the emergence and proliferation of film and television schools. Whereas in the middle part of the last century it was the goal of many young artists to express themselves by writing "the great American novel," in this new century it is now their goal to make "the great American film."

> I am from a low-income household in Toronto and never had a camera growing up, but I always had a computer. That was something my mother always made sure I had access to. It was through the evolving technology that I got into film. I got exposed to the more traditional stuff when I went to film school. That was the main reason I thought film school would be valuable. I felt pretty well versed in the emerging software and technology, but I wanted to know the traditional techniques and rules. I knew I was not an expert with that, or even well educated. I was not someone who went to see every movie. I was not a student of cinema. I did not even take the History of Cinema class at my high school. It all came from a very practical and production sort of mindset. Let's keep making things.
>
> James Darling

And no wonder. Film and television are the two potent communication tools in the world today. More than 500 universities in the United States and Canada now have programs involving communications or media arts studies or film, television, or radio production. The magnetism, influence, and responsibility of the film and video communications artist are not to be taken lightly.

> I'm a supporter of film schools because I think it's a quick and dirty way to get a lot of experience under your belt. If the school is run right, it teaches you to work under the kinds of constraints that will exist in the outside world, in terms of budget, deadlines, and peer review.
>
> Jan Krawitz

Film and television programs offer the fledgling communications artist many educational opportunities not afforded in the past. At the core of the experience is a chance to experiment, to fail, to work out ideas, and to make contacts and liaisons that could last a lifetime.

The film and television industry is a tough nut to crack. We believe that a film school education not only can qualify a student for a career in film or television, but also can provide skills in communications, writing, and interpersonal conflict management that are useful for any of a number of fields in the communication and media arts: politics, advertising, education, radio, social work, and so on.

PROGRAMS

Film and television programs offer a variety of graduate and undergraduate degrees that concentrate on the study or writing and production of film, television, and radio. Also, many programs offer degrees in such areas as mass communications, telecommunications, media arts, broadcast journalism, communications arts, and other specialties.

> I decided to go to film school because I realized after going to high school and seeing that my hobbies were painting, photography, and acting that film would be the one discipline in which I can combine all my hobbies. I think also through the years film has been my favorite pastime along with reading. I went to film school expecting that I will adapt books by Israeli writers eventually as my career into films and bring them to a more international audience. Surprisingly, it sort of went in that direction. I wound up adapting short stories by my favorite Israeli writer who became my partner in quite a few projects. Film school was in itself wonderful. I don't think I had in mind how fragmented an experience it could be as far as the different crafts. You can learn each of the crafts, but you're still not a filmmaker. That was something I had to struggle with—how to combine every tool I got in film school into voice. By the end of it I felt very, very happy and satisfied.
>
> Tatia Rosenthal

The undergraduate degrees offered are bachelor of arts, bachelor of science, and bachelor of fine arts. B.A. and B.S. degrees usually involve only two years of production or media study, whereas B.F.A. programs involve four years of training or study in a major. There also are junior colleges that offer film, television, and communications-related programs.

Graduate programs offer a master of arts, master of fine arts, and doctorates. The highest degree for programs concentrating on production is an M.F.A. Generally, a Ph. D. is offered for cinema studies and mass communications studies, among others.

Among this list are art schools, where the emphasis is on film, graphic arts, photography, or video. Certain programs focus on different disciplines within their curriculum, such as documentary, experimental, narrative, or animation. Video production has taken the place of film in many programs; students wishing to make "films" should check out schools carefully.

> Everyone who received their acceptance letter and came to the first day of class thought that the guy next to them was the next Scorsese. After a few days you realize everyone is in about the same boat. That was a big relief to me.
>
> Howard McCain

Pick a program that is in line with your overall goals. There are obvious advantages to schools located in major urban areas like New York, Los Angeles, Chicago, or Boston, but there are plenty of excellent programs in smaller communities around the country. Look at the size of the program as well. Big is not always better when it comes to the kind of individual nurturing and guidance needed for film and video courses. (A complete list of prominent schools here and abroad follows.)

> Film schools can really choose, as I see it, between two things. One is to be a stepping stone into the industry. Now that the apprentice system isn't really in place anymore in Hollywood, there isn't any building up of one's craft. Film schools can say, "We're out here to be your stepping stone into the film industry. Come here, we'll make films that Hollywood will like. We'll teach you how to make them, and we'll show them off to Hollywood." Or it says the opposite, "We don't care what Hollywood is doing. We want you to come here to learn things and to try things and to fail. You're safe here."
>
> I think that if a school chooses to do the latter, they will eventually get Hollywood's attention. Because Hollywood is always looking for material, and if there's a school where suddenly things are coming out of it that are interesting and different, and some of it's bad, but some of it's really wonderful. Hollywood will take notice.
>
> Adam Davidson

REFERENCES

Individuals interested in applying to a film and television program can begin by reviewing the following two reference guides. Don't assume, however, that all the information in these guides is up-to-date. Check out the information for yourself.

Princeton Review. *Television, Film, and Digital Media Programs: 556 Outstanding Programs at Top Colleges and Universities Across the Nation* (College Admissions Guides). Princeton Review, Random House, Inc, New York, 2006.

Pintoff, Ernest. *Complete Guide to American Film Schools and Cinema and Television Courses.* New York: Penguin, 1994.

A list of some of the film programs in the United States and abroad follows.

UNITED STATES AND CANADA

American Film Institute
Center for Advanced Film and Television Study
2021 N. Western Avenue
Los Angeles, CA 90027-1657
323-856-7721
Degree offered: M.F.A.

Boston University College of Communication
Department of Film and Television
640 Commonwealth Avenue
Boston, MA 02215
617-353-3483
Degrees offered: BS in Film or TV, MS in TV, MFA in Film

California Institute of the Arts
School of Film and Video
24700 McBean Parkway
Valencia, CA 91355-2397
661-255-1050
Degrees offered: B.F.A., M.F.A.

Canadian Film Centre
Windfields
2849 Bayview Avenue
Toronto, Ontario
Canada, M2L1A8
416-445-9481

Chapman University
Dodge College of Film & Media Art
1 University Drive
Orange, CA 92866
714-997-6715
B.F.A., B.A, M.F.A.

Columbia College Chicago
School of Media Arts
600 S. Michigan Avenue
Chicago, IL 60605
312-344-8220
Degrees offered: B.A., M.F.A.

Columbia University
School of the Arts, Film Division
513 Dodge Hall
2960 Broadway

New York, NY 10027
212-854-2815
Degree offered: M.F.A

Emerson College
Department of Visual Media Arts
120 Boylston Street
Boston, MA 02116
617-824-8500
Degrees offered: B.F.A, B.A., B.S., M.A. (video only)

Florida State University Film School
Undergraduate Film Program
A3100 University Center
Tallahassee, FL 32306-2350
850-644-0453
Degree offered: B.F.A.

Florida State University Film School
Graduate Film Program
University Center 3100A
Tallahassee, FL 32306-2350
850-644-7728
Degree offered: M.F.A.

Ithaca College
Roy Park School of Communications
350 Park Hall
Ithaca, NY 14850
607-274-3242
Degrees offered: B.S., B.F.A.

Loyola Marymount University
School of Film & Television
One LMU Drive
MC8320
Los Angeles, CA 90045-8347
310-338-3033
Degrees offered: B.A., M.A.

New York University
Tisch School of the Arts
Kanbar Institute of Film and Television
Undergraduate Division
721 Broadway, 11th Floor
New York, NY 10003
212-998-1700
Degree offered: B.F.A.

New York University
Tisch School of the Arts
Department of Film and Television
Graduate Division
721 Broadway, 10th Floor
New York, NY 10003
212-998-1780
Degree offered: M.F.A.

Northwestern University
Radio/TV/Film
1920 Campus Drive
Evanston, IL 60208
847-491-7315
Degrees offered: B.S., M.A., Ph.D., M.F.A.

Ohio University
School of Film
Lindley Hall 378
Athens, OH 45701
740-593-1323
Degrees offered: B.F.A., M.F.A., M.A.

San Francisco Art Institute
Filmmaking Department
800 Chestnut Street
San Francisco, CA 94133
415-771-7020
Degrees offered: B.A., M.A.

Stanford University
Documentary Film and Video Program
Department of Art and History
450 Serra Mall
Stanford, CA 94305-2050
650-723-1941
Degrees offered: B.A., M.F.A., Ph.D.

Temple University
Department of Film and Media Arts
School of Communications and Theater
Annenberg Hall
Philadelphia, PA 19122
B.A. Program: 215204-3859
Degrees offered: B.A., M.F.A., Ph.D.

UCLA
School of Theater, Film, and Television
102 East Melnitz Hall
Box 951622
Los Angeles, CA 90095-1602
310-825-5761
Degrees offered: B.A., M.F.A.

University of North Texas
Division of Radio/Television/Film
P.O. Box 310589
Denton, TX 76203-0589
940-565-2537
Degrees offered: B.A., M.A.

University of Southern California
School of Cinema/Television
Office of Admissions & Student Affairs
University Park, CTV-G130
Los Angeles, CA 90089-2211

213-740-8358
Degrees offered: B.A., B.F.A., M.A., M.F.A.

University of Texas–Austin
Radio-Television-Film
1 University Station A0800
Austin, TX 78712-0108
512-471-4071
Degrees offered: B.S., M.F.A., M.A., Ph.D.

York University
Department of Film
224 Centre for Film and Theater
Toronto, Ontario
Canada, M3J 1P3
416-736-5149
Degrees offered: B.F.A, B.A., M.F.A., M.A.

INTERNATIONAL

Australian Film and Television School
Box 126, North Ryde
N.S.W. 2113
Australia

Deutsche Film- und Fernsehakademie Berlin GmbH
Pommernalle 1
1 Berlin 19
Germany

Dramatiska Intitutet (The Swedish Media School)
Filmhuset
Borgvagen
Box 27090, S-102
51 Stockholm
Sweden

Film and Television Institute of Tamil Nadu
Department of Information and Public Relations
Government of Tamil Nadu, Madras
Adya, Madras 600 020
India

Film and Television School of India
Law College Road
Poona 411 004
India

Hochschule für Fernsehen und Film
Ohmstrasse 11
8000 München 40
Germany

L'Institut des Hautes Études Cinématographiques
  (IDHEC)
4 Avenue de L'Europe
94360 Bry-sur-Marne
France

London International Film School
24 Shelton Street
London WC2H 9HP
England
Tel.: 01-240-0168

National Film and Television School
Beaconsfield Film Studios
Station Road
Beaconsfield, Bucks HP9 1LG
England
Tel.: 04946 71234

Panswowa Wyzsza Szkola Filmowa, Telwizyjnai
Teatraina im Leona Schillera, U1
Targowa 61/63
90 323 Lodz
Poland

Vsesoyuzni Gosudarstvenni Institut
Kinematografi Ulitsa Vilgelma Pika 3
Moscow 129226
Russia

A and B cutting A method of assembling original 16mm film material in two separate rolls, allowing optical effects to be made by double printing (A and B printing).

A/B editing (video) An editing system that can control more than one playback machine and perform dissolves.

A- and B-wind When a roll of 16mm film, perforated along one edge, is held so that the outside end of the film leaves the roll at the top and toward the right, A-wind has perforations on the edge of the film toward the observer, and B-wind has perforations on the edge away from the observer. In both cases, the base surface faces outward on the roll.

above-the-line The part of a production budget earmarked for the creative aspects of production, including the salaries of the producer, director, writer, and talent.

abrasion mark A scratch on film caused by grit, dust, improper handling, emulsion buildup, and certain types of film damage such as broken perforations.

Academy leader A film leader, placed at the head end of a projection reel, that contains identification and timing countdown information for the projectionist and is designed to meet the specifications of the American Academy of Motion Picture Arts and Sciences.

acetate A commonly used base for film stock, which is coated with light-sensitive emulsion.

AD See **assistant director**.

A-D (analog to digital) Electronic circuitry for converting analog audio or video signals to digital.

address A precise frame location on a videotape identified by timecode number; also, the location of specific data in a computer memory.

ADR See **automatic dialogue replacement**.

aerial shot Shot taken from the air.

AES/EBU American Engineering Society/European Broadcasting Union.

AGC See **automatic gain control**.

agent/talent agent An individual or company licensed by the state to represent a particular talent in the entertainment field and to seek employment and negotiate contracts on his or her behalf. The standard fee is 10 percent of the client's salary. Agents can represent above-the-line talent (actors, writers, directors, producers) or below-the-line talent (art directors, directors of photography, editors).

aliasing Erroneous frequencies occurring in digital recordings when frequencies greater than half the sampling frequency are sampled.

ambient noise (1) Background noise. (2) Sounds that occur naturally in a location or in a studio, without dialogue or other production-created sound.

amplitude The scientific measure of the comparative intensity of a signal. Most commonly used to measure the loudness of sound.

analog A recording system that creates modulations analogous to the modulations of sound or video waves.

anamorphic A term used to denote a difference in magnification along mutually perpendicular meridians. Anamorphic systems are basically image-distorting systems. A wide formatted image will be compressed horizontally, creating a "squished" looking picture to fit into a narrow medium (film or video). For proper viewing, the image must be expanded back to its original wide format.

angle With reference to the subject, the direction from which a picture is taken—that is, the camera-subject relationship.

animation The act of making inanimate objects appear to move. This can be done by exposing one or two frames of film, moving the objects slightly, exposing one or two more frames, and so on.

answer print The first print of a completed film project in composite form (audio is married to the print), which the laboratory offers for approval. It is usually studied carefully by the director, producer, and DP to determine whether changes in color or density are required before the lab makes any additional prints.

aperture (1) In a lens, the orifice, usually an adjustable iris, that limits the amount of light passing through the lens. The width of a lens aperture is expressed in f-stops. (2) In a motion picture camera, the mask opening that defines the area of each frame exposed. (3) In a motion picture projector, the mask opening that defines the area of each frame projected.

aperture plate A metal plate, containing an aperture, that is inserted into a projector or camera.

Arriflex Brand name of a high-quality 16mm and 35mm film camera.

ASA The exposure index, or speed rating, that denotes the film's sensitivity to light, as defined by the American National Standards Institution. (It is actually defined only for black-and-white films, but it is also used in the trade for color films.) The stock used in videotape does not determine the light levels required for image recording. It is the camera's pickup tube or its charge-coupled device (CCD) that determines the sensitivity to light.

ASC American Society of Cinematographers, www.theasc.com.

ASCII American Standard Code for Information Interchange; the standard that governs the sequence of binary digits on a computerized timecode or video editing system.

aspect ratio Screen size as expressed by the ratio of the width to height, such as 1.33:1 (16mm), 1.85:1 (35mm), or 2.35:1 (70mm).

assemble edit In film, the assemble edit includes all the shots with their slates, assembled in proper viewing order. In video, the assemble edit is the product of an offline editing session.

assistant director (AD) In video production, the person who relays the director's commands from the control booth to the studio floor and who keeps an accurate account of time. In film production, the person who helps the production manager break down the script during preproduction and keeps the director on schedule during production. The AD also hires, controls, and directs background action, including extras and camera vehicles.

asymmetric compression Compression techniques that require a greater amount of processing power to compress a signal than is required to decompress a signal.

atmospheric effect An environmental special effect such as fog, mist, rain, or wind.

attack (sound) The beginning segment of an audio cue.

audio sweetening Enhancing the sound of a recording with equalization and various other signal-processing techniques during the postproduction process.

automatic dialogue replacement (ADR) Also referred to as automated dialogue replacement, this is a process during postproduction in which an actor replaces any of his lines in the film or video because of disruptive sounds on the set or the need of the director to change the performance. Also called *looping*, it is accomplished by replaying the scene over and over in the studio while the player lip-syncs to the picture.

automatic gain control (AGC) A device that maintains a constant audio or video signal level on a videotape or audiotape recorder.

B roll In film, the incoming shot of an AA/B roll. In video, it is the copy of an original tape (a dub) or background or extra material shot for cutaways.

baby legs A small, miniature tripod for low-angle shots.

back lighting Lighting from behind the subject.

back story The events stated or implied to have happened before the period covered in the film or video.

bandwidth The number of bits per second of material. The computer is tasked with processing a number of bits per second when digitizing; that number becomes a limiting factor. The computer can process only a certain number of frames and a certain amount of information for each frame every second.

barn door A frame with adjustable flaps that is attached to a lighting instrument to control unwanted spill light or the spread of the beam of light.

barney A lightweight padded covering that reduces the sound emanating from within the camera, such as noisy gears or takeup reels. Heated barneys are sometimes used to facilitate shooting under extremely cold outdoor conditions.

bars Standard color bars that are generated in video systems, usually by the camera.

base makeup Makeup that hides blemishes and creates a consistent overall texture and color on the performer's face, arms, and hands.

battery belt A belt containing a rechargeable camera battery.

battery pack A battery power source for a camera or other location equipment.

baud Unit for measuring the rate of digital data transmission. Usually, one baud equals one bit per second.

beat (1) The point in a scene where a character's tempo, meaning, or intention shifts. (2) A musical tempo used for timing motion picture action.

below-the-line The part of a production budget allocated to the technical aspects of production, including the salaries of the crew and equipment and material costs.

binary code A series of ons and offs (or ones and zeros) that digitally represent a wide range of values in coded form.

bins In film editing, the large metal storage tubs with thin metal hooks used to hang trims. In nonlinear editing systems, the "bin" is the storage container for the clips and sequences (edited programs) in your project.

blanking Portion of the composite video signal between the active picture segments for making the horizontal and vertical retrace scan lines invisible.

blimp A soundproof enclosure that completely covers a camera to prevent camera-operating noise from being recorded on the soundtrack. A blimp is similar to a barney but is made from a solid material.

blocking How the director positions the actors and the camera on the stage or set.

blow up To enlarge a portion of the original image to full frame size in the copy by means of an optical printer. Running the entire film through an optical printer can enlarge 16mm film to 35mm size.

blue screen An effect (in film) in which a character or object is photographed in front of a blue backing or screen. Later, in an optical printer, that object or character is combined with a background image by eliminating the blue area of the foreground. The process in video is electronically controlled and called a *chroma key effect*.

boom A support pole, held by a boom operator, used to hang the microphone close to the performers but just out of the shot.

bounce light Light that is reflected off white cards, ceilings, or walls to illuminate a subject indirectly.

breakdown sheet A list made from a script that includes all elements needed to produce a sequence.

breakup Disturbance in the picture or sound signal caused by loss of sync or by videotape damage.

broad light A soft, floodlight-type lamp that cannot be focused.

business Activity invented by actors to identify their characters' behavior. Business is a physical action that arises from dialogue, silences or pauses, or audio cues (such as a doorbell or ringing phone). It might involve movement from one part of the set to another (crosses) or the use of props and set dressing. Examples: lighting a cigarette at a key moment in a scene or jiggling a set of keys to break a tense silence.

byte Computer term for a group of binary digits operated upon as a single unit. In most editing system computers, one byte equals eight bits.

cable television A means of distributing television signals to receivers via a coaxial cable.

call back To ask actors to audition for a second or third time.

call sheet A daily production schedule indicating where and when the production takes place and who is to be where and at what time.

camera axis A hypothetical line running through the optic center of the camera lens.

camera car A specially equipped truck that can tow a picture vehicle and offers several shooting positions from the truck. This enables the actors to act and not drive.

camera operator The person who operates the camera. This person might also be the director of photography.

canted angle See **Dutch angle**.

cardioid microphone A microphone whose responsiveness to sound forms can be described by a heart-shaped pickup pattern.

catharsis (1) A purifying or figurative cleansing of the emotions, especially pity and fear, described by Aristotle as an effect of tragic drama on its audience. (2) A release of emotional tension, such as after an overwhelming experience, that restores or refreshes the spirit.

cathode ray tube The electronic device, a type of vacuum tube, that creates the picture in a television set by sending a directed stream of electrons at a phosphorus material that covers the inner viewing surface of the tube. Cathode ray tubes are also the picture-making elements found in computer monitors, vectorscopes, and oscilloscopes.

CCD (charge-coupled device) An electronic chip that converts light into electrical impulses used by most modern video cameras.

CD-ROM Compact disc, read-only memory.

CG See **character generator**.

CGI Computer-generated images.

changing bag A black light-tight cloth or plastic bag used to load and unload camera magazines with film stock.

character (1) A person portrayed in an artistic piece, such as a drama or novel. (2) Single letter, number, or symbol used to represent information in a computer or video program.

character generator (CG) An electronic device that creates letters on a television screen for titles and other purposes.

chroma Pure color in video, without gray or black.

chroma key A method of electronically inserting an image from one video source into the picture from another video source by selectively replacing the "key color" with another image.

chrominance Saturation and hue characteristics of the color television signal: the portion of the TV signal that contains color information.

cinema vérité A documentary film technique in which the camera is subservient to real events.

clapsticks Two boards hinged at one end that are slapped together to indicate the start of a filming session (take). Editors use clapsticks in conjunction with a slate, which provides the corresponding visual cue, to synchronize sound and image.

claymation See **pixillation**.

clear To obtain written permission from the proper individual or entity to use a certain item, music as an example, in your film.

clicktrack An audio track with rhythmic clicks used as cues for music or rerecording sessions.

clone Digital video process of duping in which there is no generational loss.

close-up (CU) A tight shot of an object or an actor's face and shoulders.

C-mount A screw mount for 16mm film and video lenses.

coding Edge numbers that are placed on the film and mag stock so that a number of picture and sound rolls will have the same sequence. This gives the editor a visual reference to maintain accurate sync.

color bars The standard video test signal, which involves a series of vertical bars of fully saturated color: white, yellow, cyan, green, magenta, red, blue, and black.

color correction The process of altering the color of a scene or scenes. In video, it is done either with a time base corrector or color corrector. In film, color correction is called *timing*. It is performed in the laboratory where the timer determines the best density printing values of each color and the overall balance of the entire film.

color internegative A negative-image color duplicate made from a positive color original. It is typically used for making release prints.

color negative A negative (opposite) image. The colors in the negative are the opposite of the colors in the scene: Light areas are dark, and dark areas are light.

color reversal film Like photographic slides, reversal film uses a different development process from negative and yields a positive image that can be directly projected without the need of a print.

color saturation The degree of absence of white in a color. The more saturated a color (the less white), the more intense the color appears.

color temperature The color quality of the light source, expressed in degrees Kelvin (K). The higher the color temperature, the bluer the light; the lower the color temperature, the redder the light.

colorist An individual who understands color. Interfaces between a production's need for color treatment of images and the equipment necessary to accomplish that treatment. Colorists have traditionally worked with telecine film output and now also work in tape-to-tape applications in SD and HD.

component video A video signal in which the luminance (the black-and-white levels) is recorded separately from the chrominance (color information).

composite print A film print that contains both picture and optical soundtrack.

composite video A video signal that transmits or records luminance and chrominance as a combined signal.

composition (1) The arrangement of artistic parts to form a unified whole. (2) The balance and general relationship of objects and light in the frame.

compound lens See **lens**.

compression (audio) In analog audio, term for the process of reducing the dynamic range of the audio signal.

compression (video) In analog video, term for the lack of detail in either the black or the white areas of the video picture, due to improper separation of the signal level. In digital, term for leaving out amounts of video information in order to store more video data on a storage device.

computer-enhanced graphics Images (drawings, photos, graphs, graphics) that are photographed by a camera and then manipulated by a computer and an operator.

concept A general idea derived or inferred from specific instances or occurrences in a film. This idea drives the story.

conflict Opposition between characters or forces in a work of drama or fiction, especially opposition that motivates or shapes the action of the plot.

conforming In film, it is the matching of original material to an edited work print. In video, an online editing session at which camera original footage is conformed to an offline work print.

contingency fund A sum of money, approximately 10 percent of the budget, which is added to the overall production budget in case of cost overruns and production problems.

continuity The smooth flow of action or events from one shot or sequence to the next.

continuity script A script made for postproduction by the script supervisor. A continuity script contains a shot-by-shot account of the contents of the film.

contrast A comparison of the brightest portion of the picture to the darkest. Film has a higher contrast ratio than video.

control track Portion of the video recording used to control the longitudinal motion of the tape during playback.

cookie A thin panel with regular or irregular shapes cut out, permitting light directed through it to form a particular arrangement on a part of the set. Also known as a *kukaloris*.

costume designer The person who designs and supervises the making of garments for the actors.

cover set A predressed location available in case inclement weather forces the company to move indoors.

coverage The different angles from which a particular scene is shot.

craft services The person or persons responsible for feeding the crew.

crane A boom that supports the camera and can be raised or lowered during the shot.

crawl Graphic information moving either vertically or horizontally through the picture.

cross fade A transition in which one sound source is faded out while another is faded in over it.

crystal sync A synchronization system in which separate crystal oscillators in the film camera and in the synchronous sound recorder drive the camera and the sound recorder extremely accurately, enabling double-system synchronous sound to be obtained without a cable connection.

CS Close shot. See also **close-up**.

C-stand (century stand) A tripod-based stand for holding lighting instruments, flags, gobos, and sound blankets.

CU See **close-up**.

cue To instruct the computerized editing system to shuttle a videotape reel to a predetermined location.

cutaway A shot of an object or a view that takes viewers away from the main action.

cuts only An offline or work print editing system that does not have a switcher installed in the system. Without a switcher, the only transition that can be made is a cut.

D-1 A component digital videotape format, 19mm wide, that records its information using three separate encoded signals rather than one, which makes for more precise reproduction of the original signal. It is preferred for effects and graphic work.

D-2 A composite digital videotape format, 19mm wide, that stores its color information in one encoded signal. D-2 is the preferred editing and show format and is fully compatible with other standard video editing house equipment.

D-3 A component digital videotape format (half-inch wide) that was developed by Panasonic as a cost-effective alternative to D-1 and D-2, and possibly one-inch.

D-5 A component digital tape format (half-inch wide) that employs 10 bits per pixel sampling. As a result, D-5 provides superior performance to D-1, especially with regard to keying operations for multilayering.

D-A (digital–to-analog) Electronic circuitry for converting digital audio or video signals to analog signals.

dailies Picture and sound work prints of a day's shooting; usually, an untimed one-light print, made without regard to color balance.

DAT See **digital audio tape**.

data transfer rate The amount of information a computer storage drive can write and read in a given amount of time.

DAW Digital audio workstation. The DAW, such as Pro Tools by digidesign®, is the audio equivalent of the nonlinear editor, an electronic device that uses digital audio rather than audiotape to combine sound sources.

day out of days A detailed schedule of the days the actors will work on a film or video production.

D-Cinema Digital Cinema. Digital distribution and projection of cinematic material. Advances in digital video technology, digital video projectors, and new methods of duplication and distribution are coming together to offer a new distribution model that doesn't involve film prints.

deal memo A letter between two parties that defines the basic payment and responsibility clauses and the spirit of what will later become a contract.

decay The gradual diminishing of a concluding sound.

decibel (dB) A unit of sound measurement.

degauss To erase recorded material on videotape or audiotape.

depth of field The range of object-to-camera distance within which objects are in sufficiently sharp focus.

deus ex machina An improbable event imported into a story to make it turn out right.

dialogue The portion of the soundtrack that is spoken by the actors.

diffuse light See **soft light**.

digital An electrical signal encoding audio, video, or both into a series of assigned numbers or binary code rather than analog voltage.

digital audio tape (DAT) A superior recording system achieved through the conversion of sound into a binary stream of ones and zeros that are computer stored for later signal conversion and amplification without the risk of distortion. See also **binary code**.

digital Betacam The digital Betacam format (also called *D-Beta* or *Digi-Beta*) provides a very high-quality component digital signal and is used for both production and postproduction. The cost and size of the D-Beta camcorder make it a tool for professionals only. The camera is easy to hand hold and is the same size as the analog version. D-Beta sets a very high standard for quality and versatility.

Digital Intermediate (DI) A Digital Intermediate is the result of the process of shooting in high definition, or shooting on film followed by scanning to film-quality data files, editing the project in high definition, and applying the creative process of color correction and color treatment to the completed master. This Digital Intermediate then becomes the master for video, DVD, or for theatrical output by transferring this data master back to film. The big advantage over the conventional method is in the creative process. Once you have scanned your feature to a data master, you have the same creative ability and freedom that is available when mastering a television movie or high-end television commercial. Creative decisions on effects like speed ramps, freeze frames, dissolves, dips to color, wipes, multilayers, and reuse of material are all very simple. Most "optical" effects are part of the automatic conforming process in online editing. Trailers can be cut from actual film footage because the original film now exists in an HD digital format.

digital S JVC has the digital S format, which uses a VHS tape and is intended for field production. This offers the benefits of digital recording in a relatively low-cost package. Digital S tapes are incompatible with analog VHS.

digital video A video signal encoded in electronic units of ones and zeros. Rather than representing a video signal through continuously varying voltages (analog), digital processes divide a signal into extremely minute units of time, measure the signal strength within each time unit, and then represent that strength in numeric code.

digital video effects (DVE) A generic word that indicates the manipulation of the information composing a frame of video through the use of a special electronic processor. Also a generic term for the electronic devices that that perform digital video effects.

digitize The process of measuring the video waveforms at regular intervals and converting the voltage information into a binary code.

directional microphone A microphone that picks up sound only from the direction in which it points. A commonly used directional mic is a *shotgun microphone*.

director The person who interprets the written book or script and oversees all aspects of a film or video production.

director of photography (DP) In production, the person who directs the cinematography (the lighting and camera setup and framing).

dirty dupe A splice-free print of the work print, also called a *slop print*. Used in the mix to avoid breaking splices. Using the dupe frees the work print to be sent to the negative cutter.

disc Generally refers to devices containing video or audio information, such as video discs, lasers discs, or compact discs.

disk Generally refers to devices containing computer data, such as floppy disk, hard disk, or magneto-optical disk.

dissolve An optical or camera effect in which one scene gradually fades out as a second scene fades in. There is an apparent double exposure in the middle of a dissolve sequence where the two scenes overlap.

distributor A company that sells, leases, and rents films.

DIT A digital imaging technician. A designation of Local 600, IATSE, the cinematographer's guild. Advanced coloring (controller duties); setup, operation, troubleshooting, and maintenance of digital cameras (oversight of camera utilities), waveform monitors, downconverters (high definition to other formats), monitors, cables, digital recording devices, terminal equipment, driver software, and other related equipment. Complete understanding of digital audio acquisition and timecode process and how they are integrated into digital acquisition format and postproduction environments. Also responsible for in-camera recording. Supervisory responsibility for technical acceptability of the image.

Dolby™ A trademarked audio noise reduction system, developed by one of the original inventors of videotape, Ray Dolby. The concept behind the Dolby system is to push the audio levels higher during recording and then to lower them during playback plus notch a portion of the high spectrum where tape hiss is found.

dolly (1) A truck built to carry a camera and camera operator to facilitate movement of the camera during the shooting of scenes. (2) To move the camera toward or away from the subject while shooting a scene.

double (multiple) exposure The photographic recording of two or more images on a single strip of film.

double printing Optically slowing down film action by printing each frame a multiple of times.

downconversion The process of converting high-resolution video to lower-resolution video.

DP See **director of photography**.

dress rehearsal The final rehearsal or technical drill for a production before actual filming. A dress rehearsal involves costumes, props, and dressed sets.

drop frame timecode SMPTE timecode format that skips (drops) two frames per minute except on the tenth minute, so the timecode stays coincident with realtime. Compare to **nondrop frame timecode**.

dropout An area on videotape that is missing oxide and thus can have no picture or audio information recorded there. Dropouts may be the simple result of defects in tape stock or produced by mishandling or malfunctioning equipment.

dub To copy from one electronic medium to another. Both sound and video picture can be dubbed.

dubber A long vertical machine with supply and takeup reel that is capable of reading the audio on the film mag. A dubber is used in the audio mixing (dubbing) process of film postproduction.

dubbing The process of melding several sound components into a single recording.

dump To copy stored computer information onto an external medium, such as hard copy, paper, paper tape, or floppy disk.

dupe/dupe negative A duplicate negative, which is made from a master positive by printing and development or from an original negative by printing followed by reversal development.

Dutch angle A shot made with the camera deliberately tilted. Also known as a *canted angle*.

DV Digital video.

DVC Digital videocassette.

DVCAM Component digital video format introduced by Sony.

DVCPRO Component digital video format made by Panasonic.

DVD Digital versatile disk, disk of the size of a CD, but with a storage capacity of up to 17 gigabytes. The single layer one side DVD stores up to 4.7 gigabytes, more than eight times as much as on a CD. It is an ideal media for video and multichannel audio applications. The term *DVD* has become synonymous with DVD-Video, which holds MPEG-2 compressed video, multichannel audio, subtitles, menus, and other features onto a DVD disk for playback in industry standard players.

EBU European Broadcast Union.

edge numbers Numbers on the edges of film that identify the film. They are used to help match original film and sound to the edited work prints. Latent-image edge numbers are put on by the manufacturer and appear during development. Also known as *key numbers*.

edit controller An electronic device used to switch among various video inputs to record on a videotape recorder. It controls the edit by preroll cueing, edit auditioning, and performing the edit by punching in and punching out.

edit decision list (EDL) A list of edits performed during offline editing in video. The EDL is stored in hard copy, floppy disk, or punch-tape form and is used to direct the final online editing assembly or negative cut.

edited master The final edited version of a tape program.

editing The process of selecting the shots and sequences that will be included in the final product, their length, and the order in which they will appear.

editor The person who decides which scenes and takes are to be used, how, where, in what sequence, and at what length they will appear.

EDL See **edit decision list**.

effects track An audio track with sound effects only, without music or dialogue.

electrician A technical crew member who moves and places lights and electrical connections. The electrician works under the direction of the gaffer.

emulsion The chemically active portion of film that preserves the photographic image. The emulsion side of the film is the dull side; the shiny side is the base or celluloid backing.

encoding Adding technical information such as a timecode, cues, or closed caption information to a video recording.

end crawl The names of the cast and crew who worked on a production that rolls up, or "crawls" vertically, at the end of a film or video.

equalization (EQ) Altering the frequency/amplitude response of a sound source or system to improve the sound quality. Treble and bass are adjusted, as is the relationship of various frequencies.

establishing shot A shot that establishes a scene's geographical and human contents.

exposure The amount of light that acts on a photographic material. Exposure is the product of illumination intensity (controlled by the lens opening) and duration (controlled by the shutter opening and the frame rate).

exposure index A number assigned to a film stock indicating that film's sensitivity to light.

exposure latitude The range between the lowest and highest exposures that will ensure a readable image on the screen.

exposure meter, incident A meter calibrated to read and integrate all the light aimed at and falling on a subject within a large area. The scale might be calibrated in footcandles or in photographic exposure settings.

exposure meter, reflectance A meter calibrated to read the amount of light, within a restricted area, reflecting from the surface of a subject or an overall scene. The scale might be calibrated in footcandles or in photographic exposure settings.

eye-line The line from an actor's eye to the direction in which the actor is looking. If the actor looks at coperformers and behind them is an audience, the actor might become distracted. It is important to keep crew members out of an actor's eye-line during auditions and principal photography.

f-stop The ratio of the focal length of a lens to the diameter of the lens opening and, thus, a unit of measure for the lens opening, or aperture. This formula allows you to know exactly how much light is falling onto the film or photosensitive mechanism. Each successive f-stop is a doubling or halving of the amount of light admitted to the film through the aperture. The 10 standard f-stops are f1, f1.4, f2, f2.8, f4, f5.6, f8, f11, f16, and f22.

fade-in A gradual visual transition from black to picture.

fade-out A gradual visual transition from image to black.

fast lens A lens that admits large amounts of light to pass through it. Also called *super-speed lens.*

feed The part of a recording device that supplies tape or film.

fiber optics A small cable through which information, carried by light, travels through a telephone line. Also used for lighting.

field One-half of a television frame consisting of every other scanline of video information (in NTSC video, 262.5 horizontal lines at 59.94Hz; in PAL, 312.5 horizontal lines at 50 Hz). Two fields make a frame.

fill Old, unneeded film used to temporarily replace audio tracks to maintain sync with picture in areas where soundtrack is missing.

fill light Light used to fill in shadows, either on a set or on a face.

film chain See **telecine system.**

film cut list The film counterpart of an edit decision list, important for matchback purposes.

film gate The components that make up the pressure and aperture plates in a camera, printer, or projector.

film perforation Holes punched at regular intervals in the entire length of film. The perforation is engaged by pins, pegs, and sprockets as the film is transported through the camera, projector, or other equipment.

film rights A film industry term for a collection of different rights. Those rights include the right to make a film for initial exhibition in theaters or in television, the right to make sequels and remakes of that film, the right to distribute the film on videocassettes and other media, even those that are not invented yet.

film speed The sensitivity of a film's emulsion to light.

film-to-video transfer The process of copying a film on videotape through a telecine or flying spot scanner.

final cut The last editing of a work print before conforming is done and before sound work prints are mixed.

Final Cut Pro Apple's Final Cut Pro (www.apple.com/finalcutpro) editing software.

fine grain Emulsion in which the silver particles are very small.

Fire Wire FireWire, also known as *IEEE* (Institute of Electrical and Electronics Engineers) *1394,* was developed by Apple Computer and is a standardized method for high-speed connections among a wide variety of professional and "prosumer" equipment. A project shot on a small DV camcorder with up to 500 lines of resolution can be inputted directly to a desktop computer.

fishpole A handheld microphone boom.

flag An opaque sheet that is separate from a lighting instrument but is used to shape the light and prevent light from falling on certain areas.

flare A streak of light that is recorded on the film or video stock when the light of the sun or an artificial instrument shines directly into the camera lens.

flashing A technique for lowering contrast by giving a slight uniform exposure to the film before processing.

flats Relatively lightweight, flat, rectangular boards that can be lashed together to create a temporary wall in a studio.

flip A revolving effect. In film, the optical printer is used to squeeze one image into the center of the frame and then reveal a new scene. In video, this process is accomplished through the use of a digital video effects device.

floodlight A lighting instrument without a lens that uses reflectors and diffusers to spread and soften the light it emits.

floor plan A scale drawing of a location that is used to plan lighting, camera, and actor blocking.

floppy disk Flat, flexible magnetic medium used to store data in computer-readable form. In video editing, floppy disks are used to store edit decisions lists (EDLs).

flying spot scanner System for transferring film to videotape in which the electron beam inside a cathode ray tube continuously scans the moving film.

f-number A symbol that expresses the relative aperture of the lens. For example, a lens with a relative aperture of 1.7 would be marked f1.7. The smaller the f-number, the more light the lens transmits. Also known as *f-stop.*

focal distance The length between a camera's lens and the point of focus of the subject.

focus To adjust a lens so that it produces the sharpest visual image on a screen, on a camera film plane, and so on.

Foley Named for sound effects editor George Foley, who created the process. The producing of sound effects in a studio in synchronization to the picture.

footage (1) The length of a scene measured in feet. (2) All the visual production material of an individual program or scene.

footcandle (fc) A unit of light intensity that equals the power of one standard candle at a distance of one foot. Footcandles are measured with incident light meters.

forced development A use of increased time or temperature in the development process of film to adjust for underexposure of the original film during production. Also called *pushing* the film.

foreground The part of the scene in front of the camera that is occupied by the object nearest the camera.

format The size or aspect ratio of a motion picture frame.

fps Frames per second.

frame rate The number of frames per second that are being displayed. The standard frame rate of film sound is 24 frames per second, NTSC video is 30fps (actually 29.97), and PAL video is 25fps.

freeze frame An optical printing effect in which a single frame image is repeated so as to appear stationary when projected.

full coat A film stock used for audio recording whose width is completely coated with oxide. Full coat is usually delivered at the end of a dubbing session. On the full coat would be four mixed tracks: music, narration, dialogue, and effects.

gaffer The head lighting technician for a film or television program. The gaffer is responsible for carrying out the plans of the director of photography.

gain Amplitude (strength) of the video or audio signal.

gate The aperture assembly through which the film is exposed in a camera, printer, or projector.

gel (gelatin) Translucent material in a variety of colors that is placed in front of lighting instruments to alter the color of the light. Gels are held in place by barn doors.

generation The number of duplications away from the camera original. First generation would be one copy away from the original camera image.

genre A category of film categorized by a particular style, form, or content, such as horror, sitcom, western, or domestic drama.

glitch Any short interruption of a video signal that can be caused by bad tape stock, a poor edit, or a broadcast transmission problem.

gobo A panel of opaque material on a footed stand with an adjustable arm. Gobos are used to confine the area that a light illuminates or to keep light from shining directly into the camera lens.

golden time A rate of pay equal to triple the base hourly wage.

grain Fine photosensitive crystals of silver halides suspended in the gelatin of a film emulsion that become exposed to light and developed into an image.

gray card A commercially prepared card that reflects 18 percent of the light hitting it. Visually, it appears as a neutral, or middle, gray halfway between black and white.

green room A comfortable holding area for the actors.

grid A system of ceiling pipes for hanging lighting instruments over a stage. See also **spreaders**.

grip A crew member responsible for moving camera support equipment, such as the tripod, dolly, and any other items, in and around the camera.

guide track (1) A temporary audio track for the purpose of presentation. (2) An audio track recorded during production used for lip syncing (ADR) in postproduction.

guillotine splicer A device used for butt-splicing film with splicing tape.

hard disk Rigid disks, coated with magnetic oxide, for storage and fast retrieval of computer data; these are available as fixed, removable, or disk packs.

hard light Illumination made up of directional rays of light that create strong, hard, well-defined shadows. Also known as *specular light*.

hardware Mechanical, electrical, or magnetic equipment used in video recording or editing.

Hazeltine Manufacturer's name for a film electronic timing device and color analyzer. The Hazeltine analyzes the film negative and sets the timing lights.

HDTV See **high-definition television**.

head Magnetic pickup device in a VTR used to record, erase, or reproduce video or audio signals.

headroom Compositional space in a shot above the actor's head.

hertz (Hz) The number of vibrations or successive waves of sound that pass a specific point each second.

Hi-8™ (High Band 8mm) A Sony Corporation trademarked name for its 8mm-wide video format that is an improved version of 8mm. Like S-VHS, Hi-8 can output S-video and its resolution is about 400 lines.

high-definition television (HDTV) High-resolution (approximately 1,000 lines) television signals, which can produce wide-screen images that are roughly comparable to film images in terms of overall sharpness and detail (lines of resolution).

high-hat A tripod head mounted onto a flat board. This allows the camera operator to place the camera on the ground or on a table for a low-angle shot.

high-key A lighting style that produces an overall and even brightness with few shadows. The low contrast is created by a low lighting ratio of key to fill light.

highlights The brightest areas of a subject. In a negative image, highlights are the areas of greatest density; in a positive image, they are the areas of least density.

HMI light The high-intensity, daylight-balanced light produced by energy-efficient, portable, lightweight HMI lamps.

hook A dramatic device that grabs viewers' attention and secures their involvement in a story.

hue The sensation of a color itself, measured by the color's dominant wavelength.

Hz See **hertz**.

image lag An afterimage left on a video monitor, usually resulting from bright objects.

IN See **internegative**.

in-camera timecode Timecode data exposed onto the film negative between perforations.

in-point Starting point of an edit.

insert A close shot of detail.

insert edit Electronic edit in which the control track is not replaced during the editing process. A new segment is inserted into program material already recorded on the videotape.

intensity (light) The total visible radiation produced by a light source. The term refers to the power (strength) of the light source.

interface Device used to connect two pieces of equipment.

interframe coding A method for compression in which certain film or video frames are dependent on previous or successive frames. Used with MPEG compression.

interlace scanning NTSC scanning process in which two fields of video are interlaced to create one full frame of video. This is done by first scanning the odd-numbered lines and then the even-numbered lines. The two scans, each a field, constitute a single video frame.

interlock A system that electronically links a projector with a sound recorder and is used during postproduction to review the edited film with the soundtrack to check timing, pacing, synchronization, and so on.

internegative (dupe negative) A negative film created from the interpositive (IP). Internegatives are used for making positive prints for distribution.

interpositive (IP) A positive film created from the original camera negative. The IP is used as protection for the cut negative or as an intermediate step in the process of making a print for protection. The IP produces a timed internegative.

iris (1) An adjustable opening that controls the amount of light passing through a lens. (2) An optical effect that starts with a small dot of an image and "irises out" with an expanding circle to fill the entire frame with the next shot. This iris effect can also be used in reverse.

jam sync Process of locking a timecode generator to a videotape and then recording that generator's code back onto that original tape or onto another tape.

jib arm A miniature unmanned camera crane that is remotely or manually operated. A video tap is often used because of the difficulty in seeing through the eyepiece while a jib arm is in use.

jogging Process of moving the videotape forward or backward one frame at a time.

JPEG (Joint Photographic Experts Group) A group set up to standardize techniques for digitally storing still images.

jump cut The seeming jump of aspects of a picture when two similar angles are cut together.

key Electronic method of inserting graphics over a scene (luminance key) or of placing one video image into another (chroma key).

KeyKode™ Eastman Kodak's machine-readable bar code, created to enable computerized identification and tracking of film segments.

key light The main illumination of the subject.

key numbers See **edge numbers**.

key-to-fill ratio See **lighting ratio**.

kicker A separation light placed directly opposite the key light to create side and back light.

kinescoping A film image made by photographing a television monitor.

kukaloris See **cookie**.

laboratory A facility that processes and prints film and sometimes offers additional services, such as coding, negative cutting, editing, and film storage.

lavaliere microphone Small lightweight, usually omnidirectional microphones that are pinned under an actor's clothing or taped to the body.

layback Transferring the finished audio track back to the edited videotape master.

leader Blank film, either black or white, used to maintain sync in A/B editing or to slug small amounts of the program where the trim (footage) is missing, or placed at the front or tail of a reel.

lens (1) A ground or molded piece of glass, plastic, or other transparent material with opposite surfaces, either or both of which are curved, by means of which light rays are refracted so that they converge or diverge to form an image. (2) A combination of two or more such pieces, sometimes with other optical devices such as prisms, used to form an image for viewing or photographing. Also called *compound lens*.

letterboxing Film transfers that preserve the aspect ratio of the film as originally shot.

lighting director In video production, the person who designs and supervises the lighting setup.

lighting ratio The ratio of the intensity of key and fill lights to fill light alone.

light meter An electrical exposure meter for measuring light intensity.

limiter Electronic circuitry used for preventing the audio signal from exceeding a preset limit.

linear A term used to describe editing systems that are locked into a straightforward, or "linear," approach to putting scenes together, as in traditional video editing systems.

lined script A script marked by the script supervisor to show the editor which take number was used to record each part of all scenes.

line item A budget entry.

lip-sync The simultaneous, precise recording of image and sound so that the sound appears to be superimposed accurately on the image, especially if a person is speaking toward the camera.

liquid gate A printing system in which the original is immersed in a suitable liquid at the moment of exposure to reduce the effect of surface scratches and abrasions.

list management On computer editing systems, a feature that allows the editor to change, trim, or shift editing decisions stored in the editing computer's memory.

load To transfer data to or from a storage device.

locked picture A picture whose editing is finished.

longitudinal timecode (LTC) Type of SMPTE timecode that is recorded on the audio track of a videotape. It is a digitally encoded audio signal and can be read only when the tape is in motion.

long shot (LS) The photographing of a scene or action from a distance or with a wide angle of view so that a large area of the setting appears on the film and the scene or objects appear quite small.

looping The process of lip-sync dubbing. See also **automatic dialogue replacement**.

lossless compression The process of compressing information without irretrievably losing any of the data that represents that information. To be lossless, a great deal of analyzing must be done.

lossy compression The process of compressing information that results in a loss of some portion of the data in the original message.

low-key A lighting style that uses intermittent pools of light and darkness with few highlights and many shadows. The contrast is created by a high ratio of key light alone to key and fill lights.

LS See **long shot**.

luminance The amount of pure white in a video image.

MII™ Panasonic's half-inch broadcast video format whose major competitor is Sony's half-inch Betacam format.

magazine A removable container that holds fresh or exposed film.

magic hour The time between sundown and darkness when the quality of light has an especially "magic" or warm quality—twilight.

magnetic film (mag) Audiotape with sprocket holes and the same size as production film. It is used in the editing process to cut audio.

magnetic sound Sound derived from an electrical audio signal recorded on a magnetic oxide stripe or on full-coated magnetic tape.

master license License to use a specific recording. This name refers to the fact that you are licensing the master recording of a song.

master shot Usually a long shot in which all action in a scene takes place. Action is repeated for the medium shot and close-up, which may be cut into the same scene.

master tape The tape to which other material will be added during videotape editing.

match cut A cut made between two different angles of the same action using the subject's movement as the transition.

matte An opaque outline that limits the exposed area of a picture, either as a cutout object in front of the camera or as a silhouette on another strip of film. In video, it is a form of key.

meal penalties A fine levied against the production to pay additional money to actors who were not allowed to eat at the prescribed break time.

medium shot A scene that is photographed from a medium distance so that the full figure of the subject fills an entire frame.

MIDI Musical Instrument Digital Interface; the interface responsible for the translation of musical information into digital terms.

mise-en-scène The totality of lighting, blocking, camera use, and composition that produces the dramatic image on film.

mix To combine the various soundtracks—dialogue, music, and sound effects—into a single track.

mix cue sheet A list of all dialogue, effects, and music cues for a sound mix. Mix cue sheets are organized sequentially for each soundtrack.

mixer (1) Circuitry capable of mixing two or more sound inputs to one output. (2) The audio console at which mixing is done. (3) The person who does the mixing.

moire In video, a beating pattern produced by harmonic distortion of the FM signal.

MOS Short for "Mit out sound," which is what German directors in Hollywood called for when they intended to shoot silent.

motion control A computer-assisted camera and rig with multiple moving axes, enabling high-precision, repeatable camera moves.

MPEG (Moving Picture Experts Group) A group set up to standardize compression techniques for digitally storing moving images, digital audio, and audio/video synchronization. It is a lossy compression method.

multitrack An audiotape with multiple tracks or an audiotape recorder/player capable of accessing multiple audio tracks.

Murphy's Law The observation that "anything that can go wrong will go wrong."

music clearance Obtaining the permissions necessary to use specific preexisting pieces of music in a film.

music cue sheet A list of all music cues and timings for the picture to be used for royalties and publishing.

music publisher An entity that manages a song and collects money for the writer from the royalties derived from its exploitation.

Mylar™ A polyester film used as the base for magnetic tape. Mylar is the base of magnetic film (mag), quarter-inch audiotape, and videotape.

Nagra Brand name of a quarter-inch audiotape recorder/player used in film production audio recording.

narration The off-screen commentary for a film. Also known as *voice-over (VO)*.

narrowcast To transmit data to selected individuals.

needle-drop fees One means by which royalty payments for music library selections are made. A fixed fee is charged each time a phonographic needle is dropped on a particular recording—that is, each time it is played.

negative cost The amount of money required to complete the film or video.

negative cutting The process of conforming camera original negative to the editor's fine-cut work print.

neutral-density filter A filter that is gray in color and affects all colors equally. It is used to reduce the amount of light passing through the lens without affecting color.

NLE Nonlinear editing.

noise Distortions in a signal, such as "snow" in video and "hiss" in audio, which are created by multiple-generation duplication.

nondrop frame timecode SMPTE timecode format that continuously counts a full 30 frames per second. Since video runs at 29.97fps, nondrop frame is not coincident with realtime.

nonlinear A term used to describe editing systems that are capable of working out of sequence or in a random manner, as in film editing.

NTSC (National Television Standards Committee) The American color television standard system, which defines video as having 525 interlaced scan lines per frame, a frame rate of approximately 30 frames per second (30fps at nondrop frame and 29.97 at drop-frame), and a 60Hz transmission standard.

offline edit Preliminary postproduction session, used to establish editing points and to prepare an edit decision list. Compare to online edit.

OMF (Open Media Framework) It is a format for file compatibility to fully describe all relationships between source material and effects.

omnidirectional Responsive to sound from all directions.

180°-axis-of-action rule A means of camera placement that ensures continuity and consistency in the placement and movement of objects from shot to shot.

online edit Final editing session, the stage of postproduction in which an edited master tape is assembled from the original production footage, usually under the direction of the edit decision list. See also **offline edit**.

on-screen sound A sound emanating from a source that is visible within the frame.

optical Any visual device, such as a fade, dissolve, wipe, iris wipe, ripple dissolve, matte, or superimposition, prepared with an optical printer in a laboratory or online for video.

optical printer A printer that is used when the image size of the print film is different from the image size of the preprint film or when effects such as skip frames, blowups, zooms, and mattes are included.

optical sound A system in which the photographic (optical) soundtrack on a film is scanned by a horizontal slit beam of light that modulates a photoelectric cell. The voltages generated by the cell produce audio signals that are amplified to operate screen speakers.

optical track Soundtrack in which the sound recorded takes the form of density variations (variable-density track) or width variations (variable-area track) in a photographic image.

option The exclusive right to purchase something in the future, on fixed terms and conditions.

original negative The film negative that was exposed in the camera. Also called *camera original*.

out-point End point of an edit.

outtake A take of a scene that is not used for printing or final assembly in editing.

overexposure The result of a purposeful or accidental allowance of excess light onto each frame of film giving the image a pale, washed-out look.

over-the-shoulder shot A shot in which a camera is placed behind and to the side of an actor, so that the actor's shoulder appears in the foreground and the face or body of another appears in the background. This type of shot tends to establish a specific subject's physical point of view on the action.

overtime Additional salary that is paid if someone is asked to work longer than his contracted hours.

oxide Metallic coating on videotape that is magnetized during the recording process.

PA See **production assistant**.

pace A subjective impression of the speed of the sounds or visuals.

painting Adjusting the color controls on a video camera or a telecine system.

PAL (phase alternating line) A color TV standard used in many countries consisting of 625 lines scanned at a rate of 25 frames per second. Compare to NTSC color video standard.

pan A camera move in which the camera on a fluid head appears to move horizontally or vertically, usually to follow the action or to scan a scene. In animation, the effect is achieved by moving the artwork under the camera.

paper edit Preparing a rough edit decision list made by screening original material, but without actually performing cuts.

performing rights society (BMI and ASCAP) An organization that monitors the performance of music and collects royalties due the songwriter from performance on film, radio and television, in restaurants, lounges, bars, hotels, and so on.

perspective The technique of representing three-dimensional objects and depth relationships on a two-dimensional surface.

pistol grip A handheld camera mount.

pixel The smallest unit of a reproduced image. Short for *picture element*.

pixillation The frame-by-frame movement of an object in a live action setting.

playback Previously recorded music or vocals to be used on the set for the actors to perform to or mime. Playback is used when filming songs (music videos), instrumental performances, or dance.

playback head A magnetic device that is capable of transforming magnetic changes on a prerecorded tape into electrical signals.

plot (1) The plan of events or the main story in a narrative or drama. (2) The arrangement of incidents and logic of causality in a story. The plot should act as a vehicle for the thematic intention of the piece.

point-of-view (POV) shot A shot in which the camera is placed in the approximate position of a specific character. It is often preceded by a shot of a character looking in a particular direction and is followed by a shot of the character's reaction to what she has seen. The last shot is sometimes called a *reaction shot*.

pot A dial that can be rotated to increase or decrease the sound level. The term is short for *potentiometer*.

POV shot See **point-of-view shot.**

practical light A source lighting instrument on the set, such as a floor or table lamp, that appears in the frame.

prerig To set up the lighting instruments based on a lighting plan devised by the director of photography a day or two before the shoot date. Prerigging can be done by a "swing crew" the night before the shoot.

preroll Process of rewinding videotapes to a predetermined cue point, so the tapes are stabilized and up to speed when they reach the edit point.

presence A recorded soundtrack from the location used to fill sound gaps in editing.

prime lens A fixed focal length lens, as opposed to a zoom lens, which has a variable focal length.

production assistant An inexperienced crew member who floats from department to department, depending on which area needs help the most. Duties can range from running for coffee or holding parking spaces to setting up lights and slating.

production supervisor An assistant to the producer. The production supervisor is in charge of routine administrative duties.

prosthetic makeup Makeup and latex pieces designed to transform the appearance of a performer's face or body. Examples include a long nose for Cyrano or stitches and a big head for Frankenstein's creature.

protection copy Duplicate of the edited master reel, kept as a backup in case the master is damaged.

proximity effect A poor-quality audio transmission caused by having the microphone too close to the sound source.

public domain Literally, "owned by the public." A property to which no individual or corporation owns the copyright.

pull-down claw The metallic finger that advances the film one frame between exposure cycles.

punch tape A paper punch record of videotape edit decisions for a computer or for printing commands in film printing.

quantization In digital recording, the amplitude value of the analog signal at the instant of sampling, rated in binary bits per sample. For example, 8 bits/sample = 2^8 = 256 increments of measurements per sample period.

QuickTime[TM] A set of operating extensions to the Macintosh Computer platform that allows Macintosh computers to display time-dependent media such as video, audio, and animation and to combine these media with time-independent media such as text and graphics.

rack focus A focus that shifts between foreground and background during a shot to prompt or accommodate an attention shift (a figure enters a door at the back of the room, for instance).

random access memory (RAM) Computer memory system that allows users to store and retrieve information rapidly.

raster Area of the TV picture tube that is scanned by the electron beam. Also, the visual display present on a TV picture screen.

raw stock Unexposed and unprocessed motion picture film, including camera original, laboratory intermediate, duplicating, and release-print stocks.

reaction shot A close-up of a character's reaction to events.

reference white A white card or large white object in the frame that can be used for white balance or the proper color adjustment in video.

reflected light Light that has been bounced or reflected from objects, as opposed to direct or incident light.

reflected reading A light meter reading of the intensity of light reflected by the subject or background.

reflector Any surface that reflects light.

registration The steadiness of a film image in the gate or aperture.

release A statement giving permission to use an actor's face or likeness. It also releases a producer from future legal action, such as for slander or libel. It is signed by people appearing in a video program or film who are not professional performers.

release print In a motion picture processing laboratory, any of numerous duplicate prints of a subject made for distribution.

rendering When an effect is desired that cannot be accomplished in realtime, the entire effect, or a portion of it, must be recorded to disk or RAM in order to see the effect play in realtime.

research (1) To study something thoroughly so as to present it in a detailed, accurate manner. (2) The process of uncovering sources of information about a prospective video or film topic or audience.

residuals A payment made to a performer, writer, or director for each repeat showing of a recorded television show or commercial.

resolution The amount and degree of detail in a film or video image.

reticle A grid or pattern placed in the camera viewfinder used to establish scale or position. See also **TV safe.**

reversal film Film that is processed to a positive image after exposure in a camera or in a printer to produce another positive film. See also **color reversal film.**

RGB The primary colors: red, green, and blue.

room tone The natural acoustical ambience of the area around which a scene is shot. Room tone can later be mixed with dialogue to smooth cuts and create a more realistic presence of a space.

rough cut A preliminary stage in film editing in which shots, scenes, and sequences are laid out in the correct approximate order, without detailed attention to the individual cutting points.

royalty fees Money paid to composers, authors, performers, and so on for the use of copyrighted materials.

rushes Unedited raw footage as it appears after shooting. Also called *dailies*.

S-video The S-video signal is one in which the luminance channel is separated from the chrominance signals, but unlike component analog, the chrominance signals are not separate.

SAG The acronym for the Screen Actors Guild. The SAG contract also covers members of Equity (stage actors), AGVA (Variety members), and AFTRA (television actors).

sampling frequency In digital recording, the number of times per second that an analog signal is examined. For example, 13.5MHz = 13.5 million times per second.

saturation Amount of color in the television picture.

scale The base union wage.

scanning The process by which a video signal is converted into an image that is displayed on the inner surface of a cathode ray gun. A stream of electrons emitted by an electron gun within a tube precisely traces this inner surface in a pattern of horizontal lines, illuminating phosphors coating the inner surface and creating the image.

score Music composed for a specific film or videotape.

scratch mix A preliminary or trial mixing of sounds against picture.

scrim A translucent material that reduces, like a screen, the intensity of the light without changing its character.

script supervisor The person who maintains the continuity in performer actions and prop placements from shot to shot and who ensures that every scene in the script has been recorded.

SCSI Small computer systems interface. Common hardware and software method for connecting computers and peripheral devices. (Pronounced "scuzzy.")

SDTV Standard-definition television.

SECAM (Sequential Couleur à Mémoire) A TV standard developed by the French and used primarily in France, Russia, and Eastern Europe. Like PAL, SECAM has a normal playback of 25fps with a similar scan rate.

setup The combination of lens, camera placement, and composition to produce a particular shot.

SFX See **sound effects**.

shading Adjusting the brightness level, light sensitivity, and color of a video camera.

shock-mounted microphone A microphone that is designed to minimize all vibrations and noise except those inherent in sound waves.

shooting ratio The ratio of the material recorded during production to that which is actually used in the final edited version.

shooting script The approved final version of the script with scene numbers, camera setups, and other instructions by the director.

shot An unbroken filmed segment; the basic component of a scene.

shotgun microphone See **ultracardioid microphone**.

shutter An opaque device in a film camera that rapidly opens and closes to expose the film to light.

sides Part of a scene given to actors to read during an audition.

signal-to-noise ratio The ratio of desired to undesired sound, the latter of which usually comes from equipment or tape noise.

silhouette An outline that appears dark against a light background.

slating The process of placing, at the beginning or end of a shot, a common reference point for separate but synchronous film images and sounds as well as an identification of the recorded material. See also **tail slate**.

slaved timecode Timecode that is taken from a source videotape and fed into a timecode generator, which replaces the source code.

slop print See **dirty dupe**.

slow motion The process of photographing a subject at a faster frame rate than used in projection to expand the time element.

smart slate An electronic slate used in film production that displays an LED readout of the sound reel timecode. This allows the film to be quickly synchronized with the sound reel during the telecine transfer.

SMPTE Society of Motion Picture and Television Engineers, the organization responsible for defining standards and specifications for the motion picture and broadcast industry including SMPTE timecode, NTSC, HDTV, and so on; www.smpte.org.

SMPTE timecode A binary timecode denoting hours, minutes, seconds, and frames that was standardized by the Society of Motion Picture and Television Engineers.

snip book A notebook used to store trims without identifiable edge code numbers.

soft cut A very short dissolve.

soft light Light made up of soft, scattered rays resulting in soft, less clearly defined shadows. Also known as *diffuse light*.

sound effects (SFX) Any sound from any source other than the tracks bearing synchronized dialogue, narration, or music. The sound effects track is commonly introduced into a master track during rerecording, usually with the idea of enhancing the illusion of reality in the finished presentation.

sound gain An adjustment to control the sound recording level.

sound speed The reference to running film or tape at standard speed for any format: film is run at 24fps, NTSC at approximately 30fps (29.97), PAL at 25fps.

specular light See **hard light**.

split diopter A special filter placed on a camera lens that allows portions of the frame to remain in focus, even though they are beyond the lens's depth of field.

splits A shooting period that consists of half a day and half a night of principal photography.

spotlight A lighting unit, usually with a lens and a shiny metal reflector, that is capable of being focused and produces hard light.

spot reading A light-meter reading of the intensity of the light reflected by the subject in a very narrow area, as determined by the angle of acceptance of the spot meter.

spotting The process of viewing a film or video in order to accurately locate the start and stop points for music, sound effects, ADR, and narration.

spreaders A bracket system for placing pipe or two-by-four lumber to act as a lighting instrument grid.

sprocket A toothed wheel used to move the perforated motion picture film.

spun glass A flexible light diffuser made out of fiberglass.

staging The process of planning how the action of a scene will take place.

stand-in Someone who takes the place of an actor during setup or for shots that involve special skills, such as horse riding or fight scenes.

Steadicam® A registered trademark for a servostabilizer camera mount attached to the operator's body to minimize camera vibrations when the operator moves with the camera.

Steinbeck™ Brand name of a flatbed film editing machine.

sting A musical accent to heighten a dramatic moment.

stock The physical recording medium on which an image or sound is recorded.

storyboard Semidetailed drawings of what each shot will look like; similar to a multipanel cartoon.

streaming A technique for transferring data (audio and video) such that it can be processed as a steady and continuous "stream."

stripboard A scheduling device. Each shot is represented by a strip of cardboard on which is encoded all the pertinent breakdown information. The strips are put in the desired order of shooting and are affixed to a multipanel stripboard. This board can then be carried to the set in the event that adjustments need to be made in the schedule.

subjective point of view A story told from the perspective of a specific character or participant in the action.

subjective shot A presentation of images supposedly dreamed, imagined, recollected, or perceived in an abnormal state of mind by a character or participant in a videotape or film.

subtext The underlying personality of a dramatic character as implied or indicated by a script or text and as interpreted by an actor in performance.

sun gun A high-intensity, portable, battery-powered light. It is usually used for news or documentary work.

supercardioid microphone A microphone with a highly directional pickup pattern.

superimposition Two images occupying the entire frame at the same time. Normally, one image is dominant and the other subordinate during a superimposition to avoid visual confusion. The more detailed the images, the less clear and visually pleasing the superimposition is likely to be.

super objective The overarching thematic purpose of the director's dramatic interpretation.

S-VHS A technical improvement over VHS home video format. An S-video half-inch format that is comparable with Hi-8.

sweetening process Process of mixing sound effects, music, and narration with the edited master's audio track. Also called *audio postproduction for video.*

swing crew A team of gaffers or grips that sets the stage, lights, or both for a big or complicated sequence before the main production unit arrives.

swish pan A rapid turning of the camera on the tripod axis, causing blurring of the image. A swish pan can be used as a transition device between scenes.

switcher A video editing device that controls which picture and sound sources are transmitted or recorded. It can be used during multiple-camera production or during postproduction.

symmetrical compression A compression technique that requires an equal amount of processing power to compress and decompress an image. This is important because, in applications designed for editing, the compression of a frame must occur in realtime. Decompression of that same frame must also occur in realtime.

sync Maintaining the corresponding relationship between soundtrack and picture. In video, the coordination of the vertical and horizontal blanking pulses with the electron beam of a television or camera so that the picture remains stable both horizontally and vertically.

synch rights The rights to record music to be heard as a part of a film.

synchronizer A film editing device that maintains several picture tracks and soundtracks in sync during the editing process.

T-grain™ A trademarked film and development process of the Eastman Kodak company. The T-grain is a grain of silver halide that is rectangular rather than globular, presenting a wider, flatter surface that provides thinner emulsion and more sensitivity.

t-stop A calibrating system for determining how much light a lens transmits to a film. Unlike f-stop calibration, which measures transmitted light only as a factor of the lens aperture, the t-stop system uses both aperture dimensions and factors of lens absorption and reflection to determine the actual amount of light that will fall on the film. T-stops offer a more accurate number.

tail slate A sync mark used when a scene begins in action or from an extreme close-up, making it difficult to slate from the beginning. After the director has called "Cut," the slate is clapped, upside down, to give the editor a sync mark.

take A photographic record of each repetition of a scene. A particular scene might be photographed more than once in an effort to get a perfect recording of some special action.

TBC See **time-base corrector**.

telecine system An optical/electronic system for transferring film to videotape. Also known as a *film chain*.

telephoto lens A long focal-length lens that foreshortens the apparent distance between foreground and background objects.

telescope story A script or editing device used to make a leap in time.

tent (1) A tent of heavy black velour drapery that can be rigged around a window to allow a sequence shot during the day to simulate night. (2) A box built outside a window that is draped but allows enough room to place a light outside the window, permitting a constant light source to appear through the window.

theme (1) A central concept, idea, or symbolic meaning in a story. (2) A repeated melody in a symphony or long musical composition.

three- or four-point lighting A basic lighting technique that helps create an illusion of three-dimensionality by separating the subject from the background, using key, fill, and separation lights.

three stripe The magnetic 35mm film on which the sound is mixed together. This full-coat mag has three tracks: one for dialogue, one for sound effects, and one for music. Should a track need to be replaced—to make a foreign dub, for example—the remaining two tracks will be undisturbed.

3:2 pull-down (2:3) Telecine method of converting 24fps film to 30fps video by transferring each film frame at an alternating rate of two video fields and then three video fields.

tilt The process of swiveling the camera in a vertical arc, such as tilting it up and down to show the height of a flagpole.

time-base corrector (TBC) Electronic device used to correct signal instability during the playback of videotape material.

timecode A frame monitoring system that provides an exact numerical reference for each frame of film or videotape. Timecode is divided into hours, minutes, seconds, and frames.

timing A laboratory process that involves balancing the color of a film to achieve consistency from scene to scene.

title search A legal process whereby it is determined whether a show title is available for use.

tracking Speed and angle at which the tape passes the video heads.

trims The unused pieces of film cut out of a scene. They are labeled and stored throughout postproduction until the final prints are struck. In video, trimming means subtracting or adding frames from an edit point.

trompe l'oeil A style of painting, sometimes used in interior decorating, in which objects are depicted with photographically realistic detail.

turnaround The time between ending one day's work and beginning the next day's.

turret A pivoted plate that allows a choice of lenses to be swung rapidly into position.

TV safe The innermost frame outline in the viewfinder is called *TV safe*, or the area that will be seen when screened on a television monitor. Elements outside this frame line may be missed. See also **reticle**.

Tyler mount A helicopter or airplane camera mount that reduces vibrations.

ultracardioid microphone A microphone with the most directional (narrowest) pickup pattern available. Also known as a *shotgun microphone*.

underlying rights The foundational rights that you must control to have the right to make and distribute a film based on a script that is based on an underlying property (such as a novel, short story, play, or true story).

upconversion The process of converting lower resolution video to higher resolution video.

variable-speed motor An electric drive motor for a film camera whose speed can be varied and controlled.

VCR (videocassette recorder) Usually referring to a tape machine that accepts only cassettes. An open reel machine is often referred to as a VTR.

vectorscope A special oscilloscope used to monitor hue and color saturation in video signals.

vertical interval timecode (VITC) Timecode that is inserted in the vertical blanking interval of a video signal. The vertical blanking interval is the period during which the TV picture goes blank as the electron beam returns (retraces) from scanning one field of video to begin scanning the next.

video assist A video camera attached to a film camera for instant dailies, allowing the shot to be immediately judged on playback. Also known as *video tap*.

video gain An adjustment to control the picture recording level.

video tap See **video assist**.

video-to-film transfer Copying a videotape on film. Also known as *kinescoping*.

viewfinder An eyepiece or screen through which a camera operator sees the image being recorded. See also **reticle**.

visualization The creative process of transforming a script into a sequence of visual images and sounds.

visual timeline Computer display of the edit decision list as a series of stacked bars representing video and separate audio channels running horizontally across the screen.

VO Voice-over. See **narration**.

VT Videotape. Oxide-coated, plastic-based magnetic tape used for recording video and audio signals.

VTC Visual timecode burned into the lower part of the frame for a visual frame accurate reference.

VTR Videotape recorder.

VU meter A device that measures audio levels.

waveform monitor A type of test equipment used to display and analyze video signal information.

wedge test When an optical is made, a test is done in which the elements of the optical (lap dissolves, superimposition, mattes) are photographed with one frame of each f-stop. When the test film is developed, the laboratory can identify the exact exposure reading that will produce the best effect.

whip pan A very fast panning movement. Also called a *swish pan*.

white balance Electronic adjustments to render a white object as white on-screen.

wide-angle lens A lens with a wide angle of acceptance. Its effect is to increase the apparent distance between foreground and background objects.

wild (1) Picture shot without a synchronous relationship to sound. (2) Sound shot without a synchronous relationship to picture.

wild sound Sound that does not have a synchronous picture or recordings of sound effects that are available on the location and may be hard to either obtain or create at a later time.

windowdupe Copy of an original master recording that features character-generated timecode numbers inserted in the picture.

windscreen A porous cover that protects a microphone's diaphragm from air currents.

wipe Special effect transition in which a margin or border moves across the screen, wiping out the image of one scene and replacing it with another.

wireless/radio microphone A cordless microphone that transmits its output to a recorder via a receiver.

work print A print derived from the original negative to be used in the editing process to establish, through a series of trial cuttings, the finished version of the film. The negative is later conformed to the work print when a final cut is achieved.

wrangler An animal trainer and supervisor.

wrap The period at the end of a day of shooting during which the crew must store the equipment.

Y/C (or pseudo-component) Symbol for luminance separated from chroma (color) information; a type of recording used in S-VHS and Hi-8. Also called *S-video*.

zoetrope An optical toy with a series of pictures on the inner surface of a cylinder. When the pictures are rotated and viewed through a slit, the toy gives the impression that the pictures are moving. This device, a precursor to film projection, was a popular form of entertainment in the nineteenth century.

zoom lens A lens whose focal length varies between wide and telephoto.

ACTING

Hagan, U., & Frankel, H. (1973). *Respect for Acting*. New York: Macmillan.

Meisner, S., & Longwell, D. (1987). *Sandford Meisner on Acting*. New York: Vantage Books.

Moore, S. (1965). *The Stanislavski System*. New York: Viking Press.

Stanislavski, C. (1948). *An Actor Prepares*. New York: Theater Arts.

Stanislavski, C. (1981). *Building a Character*. New York: Theater Arts.

Young, J. (1999). *The Master Director Discusses His Films*. (Interviews with Elia Kazan by Jeff Young). New York: Newmarket Press.

ANIMATION

Blair, P. (1989). *Animation and How to Animate Film Cartoons*. New York: Walter Foster.

Canemaker, J. (1987). *Felix: The Twisted Tale of the World's Most Famous Cat*. New York: Abbeville Press.

Canemaker, J. (1999). *Paper Dreams: The Art & Artists of Disney Storyboards*. New York: Hyperion.

Layborne, K. (1998). *The Animation Book*. New York: Three Rivers Press.

Solomon, C. (1983). *The Complete Kodak Animation Book*. Rochester, NY: Eastman Kodak Co.

White, T. (1986). *The Animator's Workbook*. New York: Phaidow Press.

ART DIRECTION

Ettedgui, P. *Production Design and Art Direction* (Screen Craft Series). Focal Press.

LoBrutto, V. (1992). *By Design*. Westport, CT: Praeger.

Olson, R. (1993). *Art Direction for Film and Television*. London: Focal Press.

Preston, W. *What an Art Director Does*. Silman James Press, 1994.

Rizzo, M. *The Art Direction Handbook for Film*. Focal Press.

CAMERA

Almendros, N. (1985). *Man with a Camera*. New York: Simon & Schuster.

Carlson, V., & Carlson, S. (1985). *Professional Lighting Handbook*. Boston: Focal Press.

C.G. Clarke (Ed.). (1993). *American Cinematographer's Handbook*. Hollywood: American Society of Cinematographers.

Brown, B. *Motion Picture and Video Lighting*. Focal Press.

F. Detmers (Ed.). (1986). *American Cinematographer Manual*. Hollywood: ASC Press.

Elkins, D. (2000). *The Camera Assistant's Manual*. Boston: Focal Press.

Fielding, R. (1985). *The Technique of Special Effects Cinematography*. New York: Hastings House.

Malkiewicz, K. J. (1989). *Cinematography: A Guide for Filmmakers and Film Teachers*. New York: Prentice-Hall.

Millerson, G. (1982). *The Technique of Lighting for Television and Motion Pictures*. Boston: Focal Press.

Samuelson, D. (1979). *Motion Picture Camera Data*. London: Focal Press.

Schaffer, D., & Ritsko, A. (1984). *Masters of Light*. Berkeley and Los Angeles: University of California Press.

CRAFTS

Baker, P. (1992). *Wigs and Make-up for Theatre, TV and Film*. Boston: Focal Press.

Kehoe, V. J- R. (1991). *Special Make-up Effects*. Boston: Focal Press.

Hanke, J., & Yamazaki, M. *Green Screen Made Easy: Keying and Compositing Techniques for Indie Filmmakers*. Studio City, CA: Michael Wiese Productions.

La Motte, R. *Costume Design 101: The Business and Art of Creating Costumes for Film and Television*. Studio City, CA: Michael Wiese Productions.

Maier, R. (1994). *Location Scouting and Management Handbook: Television, Film, and Still Photography*. Boston: Focal Press.

Miller, P. P. (1990). *Script Supervision and Film Continuity*. Boston: Focal Press.

DIRECTING

Caine, M. (1990). *Acting in Film: An Actor's Take on Moviemaking* (Videocassette). New York: Applause Theater Book Publishers.

DeKoven, L. (2006). *Changing Direction, A Practical Approach to Directing Actors in Film and Theater*. New York: Focal Press.

Kingdom, T. (2004). *Total Directing: Integrating Camera and Performance in Film and Television*. Silman - James Press.

Mackendrick, A. *On Filmmaking: An Introduction to the Craft of the Director*. Faber and Faber, Inc., 2004.

Mamet, D. (1991). *On Directing*. New York: Viking Press.

Proferes, N. T. (2008). *Film Directing Fundamentals*. Focal Press.

Rabiger, M. (1997). *Directing, Film Techniques and Aesthetics.* Boston: Focal Press.

Travis, M. W. (1997). *The Director's Journey.* Studio City, CA: Michael Wiese Productions.

Weston, J. (2001). *Crafting Memorable Performances for Film and Television.* Studio City, CA: Michael Wiese Productions.

DISTRIBUTION/EXHIBITION

Bowser, K. (1992). *The AIVF Guide to International Film and Video Festivals.* New York: Foundation for Independent Video and Film.

Council on International Nontheatrical Events (1993–1994). *The Worldwide Directory of Film and Video Festivals and Events.* New York: Council on International Nontheatrical Events.

Franco, D. (1990). *Alternative Visions: Distributing Independent Media in a Home Video World.* Los Angeles, Washington, DC, and New York: American Institute Press.

Gore, C. (1999). *The Ultimate Film Festival Survival Guide.* Los Angeles: Lone Eagle Publishing.

Warshawski, M. (1995). *The Next Step: Distributing Independent Films and Videos.* New York: Foundation for Independent Video and Film.

Wiese, M. (1989). *Film and Video Marketing.* Studio City, CA: Michael Wiese Productions.

DOCUMENTARIES

Baddeley, W. (1975). *Hugh. The Technique of Documentary Film Production* (4th ed.). New York: Hastings House.

Hewitt, J., & Vazquez, G. (2010). *Documentary Filmmaking: A Contemporary Field Guide.* New York: Oxford University Press.

Ivens, J. (1969). *The Camera and I.* Cambridge, MA: MIT Press.

Rabiger, M. (1987). *Directing the Documentary.* Boston: Focal Press.

Rosenthal, A. (1990). *Writing, Directing, and Producing Documentary Films.* Carbondale and Edwardsville: Southern Illinois University Press.

EDITING

Dmytryk, E. (1984). *On Film Editing.* Boston: Focal Press.

Hollyn, N. (1990). *The Film Editing Room Handbook.* Los Angeles: Lone Eagle.

Hollyn, N. (2009). *The Lean Forward Moment: Create Compelling Stories for Film, TV and the Web.* New Riders.

LoBrutto, V. (1991). *Selected Takes. Film Editors on Editing.* New York: Praeger.

Murch, W. (1995). *In the Blink of an Eye.* Los Angeles: Silman James Press.

Ohanian, T. (1992). *Digital Nonlinear Editing.* Boston: Focal Press.

Oldam, G. (1995). *First Cut: Conversations with Film Editors.* Los Angeles: University of California Press.

O'Steen, S. *Cut to the Chase: Forty-Five Years of Editing America's Favorite Movies.* Studio City, CA: Michael Weise Productions.

Reisz, K., & Millar, G. (1968). *The Technique of Film Editing.* Boston: Focal Press.

Rosenblum, R., & Karen, R. (1979). *When the Shooting Stops...the Cutting Begins.* New York: Da Capo Press.

Rubin, M. (1991). *Nonlinear: A Guide to Electronic Film and Video Editing.* Gainesville, FL: Triad.

FILM AND VIDEO BASICS

Adams, W. B. (1977). *The Handbook of Motion Picture Production.* New York: John Wiley & Sons.

Hurbis-Cherrier, M. *Voice & Vision: A Creative Approach to Narrative Film and DV Production.* Focal Press.

Pincus, E., & Ascher, S. (1999). *The Filmmaker's Handbook.* New York: New American Library, Plume.

Weise, M., & Weynard, D. *How Video Works: From Analogue to High Definition.* Focal Press.

Wiese, M. (1990). *The Independent Film and Videomaker's Guide.* Boston: Focal Press.

GRANTS

The Foundation Center (site for grants) fdcenter.org.

L. Gibbs (Ed.). (1992). *National Alliance for Media Arts and Culture Member Directory.* Beverly Hills: NAMAC.

Niemeyer, S. (1991). *Money for Film and Video Artists.* New York: American Council for the Arts/Allworth Press.

Renz, L. (1987). *The Foundation Directory.* New York: Foundation Center.

Warshawski, M. (1994). *Shaking the Money Tree: How to Get Grants and Donations for Film and Video.* Hollywood: Michael Wiese Productions.

THE INDUSTRY

Eaker, S. (1991). *The Back Stage Handbook for Performing Artists, revised and enlarged ed.* New York: Watson-Guptill, Back Stage Books.

Kindem, G. (1982). *The American Movie Industry: The Business of Motion Pictures.* Carbondale and Edwardsville: Southern Illinois University Press.

Litwak, M. (1986). *Reel Power.* New York: William Morrow.

Mayer, M. F. (1978). *The Film Industries: Practical Business/Legal Problems in Production, Distribution and Exhibition.* New York: Hastings House.

Squires, J. (1983). *The Movie Business Book.* New York: Simon & Schuster, Touchstone.

MUSIC FOR FILM

Bell, D. (1994). *Getting the Best Score for Your Film.* Silman James Press.

Carlin, D., Sr. (1991). *Music in Film and Video Production.* Boston: Focal Press.

Karlin, F., & Wright, R. (1990). *On the Track: A Guide to Contemporary Film Scoring.* New York: Schirmer Books.

Pendergast, R. M. (1992). *Film Music: A Neglected Art.* New York: W. W. Norton.

Thomas, T. (1973). *Music for the Movies.* South Brunswick, NJ: A. S. Barnes.

ON FILMMAKERS

Behlmer, R. (1972). *Memo from David O. Selznick.* New York: The Viking Press.

Bogdanovich, P. (1997). *Who the Devil Made It: Conversations with Legendary Directors.* Alfred A. Knopf.

Buñuel, L. (1986). *My Last Breath.* London: Flamingo Press.

Capra, F. (1971). *The Name Above the Title.* New York: The Macmillan Company.

Kurosawa, A. (1983). *Something Like an Autobiography.* New York: Vintage Books.

Lumet, S. (1995). *Making Movies.* New York: Alfred E. Knopf.

Tirard, L. *Moviemakers' Master Class: Private Lessons from the World's Foremost Directors.* Faber and Faber.

Truffaut, F. (1967). *Hitchcock.* New York: Simon & Schuster.

PRE-VISUALIZATION

Block, B. *The Visual Story: Seeing the Structure of Film, TV and New Media.* Focal Press.

Dunn, L. G. (1983). *The ASC Treasury of Visual Effects.* Hollywood: American Society of Cinematographers.

Katz, S. D. (1991). *Film Directing: Shot by Shot.* Studio City, CA: Michael Wiese Productions.

Nilsen, V. (1985). *The Cinema as Graphic Art.* New York: Hill & Wang Foreword by S. M. Eisenstein.

Simon, M. *Storyboards: Motion in Art.* Focal Press.

PRODUCING

Baumgarten, P., Farber, D., & Fleisher, M. (1992). *Producing, Financing and Distributing Film,* revised and updated ed. New York: Limelight.

Chamness, D. (1988). *The Hollywood Guide to Film Budgeting and Script Breakdown for Low Budget Features.* Hollywood: Stanley J. Brooks.

Curran, T. (1985). *Financing Your Film: A Guide for Independent Film Producers.* Westport, CT: Praeger.

Davies, S. (1986). *The Independent Producer: Film and Television.* London: Hourcourt, Howlett, Davies, Moskovic, Faber & Faber.

Goodell, G. (1982). *Independent Feature Film Production: A Complete Guide from Concept through Distribution.* New York: St. Martin's.

Gregory, M. (1979). *Making Films Your Business.* New York: Schocken Books.

Litvak, M. *Contracts for the Film and Television Industry.* Silman—James Press.

Simon, D., & Wiese, M. (2006). *Film and Video Budgets.* Boston: Michael Wiese Productions/Focal Press.

Singleton, R. S. (1991). *Film Scheduling: Or, How Long Will It Take to Shoot Your Movie?* Los Angeles: Lone Eagle.

Singleton, R. S. (1984). *The Film Scheduling/Film Budgeting Workbook.* Los Angeles: Lone Eagle.

Wiese, M. (1991). *Film and Video Financing.* Boston: Michael Wiese Productions/Focal Press.

REFERENCES

Brook's Standard Rate Book. (1994). Los Angeles: Stanley J. Brooks [Union rates and rules.] 310-470–2849.

Donaldson, M. C. (1991). *Clearance & Copyright, Everything the Independent Filmmaker Needs to Know.* Los Angeles: Silman-James Press.

Konigsberg, I. (1997). *The Complete Film Dictionary.* London: Meridian.

The New York Production Manual. (1997). New York: Producer's Masterguide.

Singleton, R. (1986). *Filmmaker's Dictionary.* Los Angeles: Lone Eagle.

SOUND

Alten, S. R. (1981). *Audio in Media.* Belmont, CA: Wadsworth.

Anderson, C. (1986). *MIDI for Musicians.* New York: Amsco Publications.

Holman, T. (2005). *Sound for Digital Video.* Focal Press.

LoBrutto, V. (1994). *Sound-on-Film. Interviews with Creators of Film Sound.* Praeger.

Mott, R. L. (1990). *Sound Effects: Radio, TV and Film.* Boston: Focal Press.

Nisbett, A. (1990). *The Use of Microphones.* Boston: Focal Press.

Sonnenschein, D. (2001). *The Expressive Power of Music, Voice and Sound Effects in Cinema.* Boston: Michael Wiese Productions.

E. Weis, & J. Belton, (Eds.). (1985). *Film Sound: Theory and Practice.* New York: Columbia University Press.

Viers, R. *The Sound Effects Bible. How to Create and Record Hollywood Style Sound Effects.*

Yewdall, D. L. (1999). *Practical Art of Motion Picture Sound.* Boston: Focal Press.

ONLINE SOUND LIBRARIES

Many web sites are dedicated to sound effects and music. Many offer royalty-free effects and music.

Sounddogs.com and **sonomic.com** are two of the largest online sound effects libraries on the Internet.

SoundFX.com distributes the Sound Effects Libraries, Music Libraries, and Pro-Audio Software worldwide.

Soundrangers.com was created to fulfill the sonic needs of a new technological generation. It specializes in generating state-of-the-art, royalty-free sound effects and music for such high-tech platforms as virtual user interfaces, games, online and CD-ROM entertainment, web sites, and communication devices.

Soundsonline.com is a source for professional, copyright-cleared, royalty-free sounds in the industry offering more than 1,000 virtual instruments and sound libraries to choose from.

VIDEO

Beacham, F. (1994). *American Cinematographer Video Manual.* Hollywood: American Society of Cinematographers Press.

Huber, D. M. (1987). *Audio Production Techniques for Video.* White Plains, NY: Knowledge Industry Publishing.

Mathias, H., & Patterson, R. (1985). *Electronic Cinematography: Achieving Photographic Control over the Video Image.* Belmont, CA: Wadsworth.

Millerson, G. (1992). *Video Production Handbook.* Boston: Focal Press.

Ratcliff, J. (1999). *Timecode, A User's Guide.* Oxford: Focal Press.

Watkinson, J. (1994). *The Art of Digital Video.* Boston: Focal Press.

Wiese, M. (1986). *Home Video: Producing for the Home Market.* Westport, CT: Michael Wiese Film/Video.

WRITING

Armer, A. (1985). *Writing the Screenplay for Film and Television.* Belmont, CA: Wadsworth.

Cowgill, L. J. (1997). *Writing Short Films.* Los Angeles: Lone Eagle.

Eisenstein, S. M. (1988). *The Short Fiction Scenario.* Methuen: Calcutta, Seagull Books.

Goldman, W. (1984). *Adventures in the Screen Trade.* New York: Warner Books.

Howard, D., & Mabley, E. (1995). *The Tools of Screenwriting.* New York: St. Martin's Press.

McKee, R. (1997). *Story: Substance, Structure, Style and the Principals of Screenwriting.* New York: Harper Collins.

Phillips, W. H. (1991). *Writing Short Scripts.* Syracuse: Syracuse University Press.

Seger, L. (1987). *Making a Good Script Great.* Hollywood: Samuel French.

PERIODICALS/NEWSLETTERS

American Cinematographer
Backstage
Film Comment
Millimeter
Variety (daily or weekly)
Videomaker www.videomaker.com
Video Magazine

SCREENWRITING SOFTWARE

Final Draft (http://finaldraft.com)
HollyWord® & SidebySide® Simon Skill Systems (http://simon1.com)
Movie Magic Screenwriter, Screenplay Systems (www.screenplay.com)

Scriptware, Cinovation, Inc. (http://scriptware.com)
Script Wizard™ (www.warrenassoc.com)

INTERNET

Databases

www.lib.berkeley.edu/mrc/africanamvid.html. African-American Video Media Resource Center.
www.film.com
www.frameline.org. Exhibition, distribution, promotion, and funding of lesbian and gay film and video.
www.indiewire.com/onthescene/festivals. indieWIRE's festival page.
www.imdb.com. Internet Movie Database. Utterly comprehensive.
www.lcweb.loc.gov Library of Congress: Links to copyright and film preservation board.
www.netspace.net.au/~haze/index.html. RML Movie Page: Comprehensive; tons of links on films, schools, resources, and so on, based in Australia.
www.Screenwriter.com. Comprehensive screenwriters' resource center with links to top script sites.

Casting Resources

http://aftra.org
www.backstage.com
http://breakdownservices.com
http://nowcasting.com
http://reelact.com
www.Sagindie.org Screen actors' guide to low-budget agreements

Festivals

www.creativeplanet.com
www.filmfestivals.com
www.variety.com/filmfest
www.withoutabox.com

Industry

The Hollywood Reporter online: www.hollywoodreporter.com.
Variety online. www.variety.com

Production

Film Underground.com: Resource for low-budget film- and videomakers www.filmunderground.com
Mandy's International Film and TV Production Directory: Listings of jobs, services, and free homepage service for film/TV professionals, arranged by state www.mandy.com

New York City Mayor's Office of Film, Theatre, and Broadcasting www.ci.nyc.ny.us/html/filmcom/home.html

New York Production Guide Online: www.nypg.com

Producer's Masterguide Online: www.producers.masterguide. com

Producer's Source: Excellent film resources, www.producerssource.com

Resource site created by Kevin Spacey www.triggerstreet.com

Web Distribution

www.AtomFilms.com

www.Hollywood.com

www.ifilm.com

www.inetfilm.com

www.indiefilmpage.com/short.html

www.shockwave.com

www.zeroland.co.nz/film_short.html

Note: Page numbers followed by *f* indicate figures; *b* indicate boxes.